The Foundations and Future of Public Law

The Foundations and Future of Public Law

Edited by

ELIZABETH FISHER
JEFF KING
ALISON L YOUNG

OXFORD
UNIVERSITY PRESS

OXFORD
UNIVERSITY PRESS

Great Clarendon Street, Oxford, OX2 6DP,
United Kingdom

Oxford University Press is a department of the University of Oxford. It furthers the University's objective of excellence in research, scholarship, and education by publishing worldwide. Oxford is a registered trade mark of Oxford University Press in the UK and in certain other countries

First Edition published in 2020

Published in the United States of America by Oxford University Press
198 Madison Avenue, New York, NY 10016, United States of America

British Library Cataloguing in Publication Data
Data available

Library of Congress Control Number: 2019952911

ISBN 978–0–19–884524–9

For Paul Craig,
in honour of his scholarship, mentorship, and friendship.

Contents

List of Contributors xv

1. Foundations and Futures: A Brief Introduction 1
   Elizabeth Fisher, Jeff King, and Alison L Young

PART I: THEORY

2. The Diverse Objects of Public Law: Taking Theory to the Next Level 19
   Neil Walker
3. The Authority of the Administration 45
   Janet McLean
4. Law and the Point of the State 67
   NW Barber

PART II: CASE LAW

5. Public Law Cases and the Common Law: A Unique Relationship? 83
   Alison L Young
6. The Mutual Judicial Influence of National Courts and the European Court of Justice through the Preliminary Rulings Mechanism: Evidence from the United Kingdom 107
   Gráinne de Búrca
7. How Judges Make Law 127
   Timothy Endicott

PART III: LEGISLATION

8. The Province of Delegated Legislation 145
   Jeff King
9. Legislating and Adjudicating: Where and How to Strike the Balance 173
   Eleanor Sharpston
10. Law, Democracy, and the Absent Legislator 193
    Philip Sales

PART IV: INSTITUTIONS

11. The Open Road? Navigating Public Administration and the Failed Promise of Administrative Law 209
Elizabeth Fisher

12. The EU Automated State Disassembled 233
Deirdre Curtin

13. The Administrative State and the Fundamentals of Public Law 257
ACL Davies

PART V: PROCESS AND PROCEDURE

14. Proceduralism and Automation: Challenges to the Values of Administrative Law 275
Carol Harlow and Richard Rawlings

15. The Foundations of the Duty to Give Reasons and a Normative Reconstruction 299
Joana Mendes

16. Process and Procedure in a Disordered State 323
Mark Freedland

PART VI: CONSTITUTIONS

17. Challenges of Multilevel Constitutionalism 339
Cheryl Saunders

18. A Hard Law Approach to States Systemic Violations of Article 2 of the Treaty of the European Union: Reasons and Means 363
Miguel Poiares Maduro and Benedita Menezes Queiroz

19. Brexit and the Challenges of a 'Post-Sovereign' Legal Landscape 381
Sionaidh Douglas Scott

PART VII: CONCLUSION

20. Six Dimensions of Public Law: Pressure-Testing the UK and EU Systems 399
Paul Craig

Index 431

Detailed Contents

List of Contributors xv

1. Foundations and Futures: A Brief Introduction 1
   Elizabeth Fisher, Jeff King, and Alison L Young
   I. An Overview of the Project 2
   II. Foundations 5
   III. Future 10
   IV. Conclusion 14

PART I: THEORY

2. The Diverse Objects of Public Law: Taking Theory to the Next Level 19
   Neil Walker
   I. Beyond the State 19
   II. The Consummate All-Rounder 22
   III. Candidate Conceptions of (Public) Law 25
   IV. The State and the European Union: Structural Variation 29
   V. The Special Place of Public Law in the European Union 35
   VI. Conclusion 42

3. The Authority of the Administration 45
   Janet McLean
   I. Introduction 45
   II. Office in the High and Low Politics of the Seventeenth Century 47
   III. Propriety and the Official 51
      A. Reinforcing civic virtue 53
      B. Upholding independence 56
      C. Restoring independence in property 57
   IV. Democracy 61
   V. Conclusion 64

4. Law and the Point of the State 67
   NW Barber
   I. The Point of the State 67
   II. The Point of the State and the Point of Public Law 74

PART II: CASE LAW

5. Public Law Cases and the Common Law: A Unique Relationship? 83
   Alison L Young
   I. Why Common Law Reasoning May Not Suit Public Law 85

II. Evaluating Common Law Reasoning 91
III. Is Public Law More Suited to Inductive Reasoning? 97
IV. Conclusion 102

6. The Mutual Judicial Influence of National Courts and the European Court of Justice through the Preliminary Rulings Mechanism: Evidence from the United Kingdom 107
Gráinne de Búrca
I. Introduction 107
II. The Influence of UK Membership on the European Court of Justice: A Summary 108
III. Mutual Influence of the UK Courts and the Court of Justice via the Preliminary Reference Procedure? 111
A. The influence of the CJEU on UK courts through preliminary rulings 112
B. The influence of UK courts on the CJEU through preliminary references 115
(i) Encouragement from the CJEU to national courts to adopt provisional views 117
(ii) Influence of the provisional views of the UK courts? 120
IV. Conclusion 122

7. How Judges Make Law 127
Timothy Endicott
I. Case Law is Source-Based 127
II. The Primary Role of a Court is to Give Judgment 128
III. Giving Judgment is Making a Particular Norm 129
IV. The Two Aspects of the Legal Effect of a Judgment: Ostensive and Explanatory 131
A. The value of the ostensive aspect of case law: coordination 132
B. The value of the explanatory aspect of case law: expertise 132
V. Equity 133
VI. The Paradox of Judicial Law-Making, and the Incidental Jurisdiction to Change the Law 134
VII. Judicial Law-Making: The Standard Case and the Heroic Case 136
VIII. The Open-Endedness of the Common Law 137
IX. Conclusion 141

PART III: LEGISLATION

8. The Province of Delegated Legislation 145
Jeff King
I. The Origins and Rationale for Delegated Powers 146
A. The problems of wide delegation 149
B. A question of safeguards 150

II. The Current Practice 152
A. The structure of parliamentary oversight 152
B. The steady expansion of delegated powers 154
C. Reasons for seeking delegated powers 156
D. Criteria for deciding between primary and secondary legislation 157
III. Parliamentary Accountability and the 2018 Withdrawal Act 161
A. The inadequacy of parliamentary scrutiny 161
B. The European Union (Withdrawal) Act 2018: a case in point 163
(i) Remit 164
(ii) Reaction 165
(iii) Reassurances 167
(iv) Realisation 168
IV. Conclusion 169

9. Legislating and Adjudicating: Where and How to Strike the Balance 173
Eleanor Sharpston
I. Introduction 173
II. The Court Deciding Not to Take Steps that Might Be Construed as 'Legislating' 181
III. The Court Going to the Limit of 'Constructive Re-Interpretation' of a Text 183
IV. How Far Should the Court '*Bend*' a Text? 186
V. Conclusion 189

10. Law, Democracy, and the Absent Legislator 193
Philip Sales
I. Courts' Response to the Absent Legislator 195
II. The Absent Legislator and Brexit 199
III. Conclusion 205

PART IV: INSTITUTIONS

11. The Open Road? Navigating Public Administration and the Failed Promise of Administrative Law 209
Elizabeth Fisher
I. Public Administration and Factual Evaluation 212
II. Emerging Legal Discourses 216
III. Attempts at Navigation 222
IV. Learning from History 226
V. Conclusion 230

12. The EU Automated State Disassembled 233
Deirdre Curtin
I. Introduction 233
II. A Web of (In)formal Institutions and Officials 236

III. The Deputisation of Private Actors 239
A. Data assemblages and private actors 239
B. Legality challenges 240
IV. Interoperable Public Platforms in Europe 243
A. Regulating interoperability 243
B. Policing by hits 247
V. Disassembled Accountability 250
A. Information disconnect 250
B. Secrecy road-blocks 251
C. Decisional opacity 253
VI. Conclusion 254

13. The Administrative State and the Fundamentals of Public Law 257
ACL Davies
I. Context 258
II. A Changing Agenda 262
A. The *Hutchinson* and *Shepherd* cases 264
B. The fundamentals of administrative law 267
III. Conclusion 271

PART V: PROCESS AND PROCEDURE

14. Proceduralism and Automation: Challenges to the Values of Administrative Law 275
Carol Harlow and Richard Rawlings
I. Scene-setting 275
II. Values and Tenets 278
III. From Bureaucratic Rule-Making to the Age of Managerialism 282
IV. Judicial Engagement: Waves of Development 286
V. Technological Revolution 291
VI. Conclusion 296

15. The Foundations of the Duty to Give Reasons and a Normative Reconstruction 299
Joana Mendes
I. Introduction 299
II. The Constitutive Function of Executive Actors and its Procedural Implications 301
III. The Duty to Give Reasons: Constitutional Function, Norm of Control, and Norm of Conduct 304
IV. The Origins of the Duty to Give Reasons in EU Law 308
A. Giving meaning to a novel duty 308
B. The constitutional foundations of the duty to give reasons 309

C. Making the common market a 'glass house': political significance and legal implications 311
D. Public understanding in the shade of judicial review 313
V. From Constitutional Foundations to Reconstruction 315
VI. Conclusion 320

16. Process and Procedure in a Disordered State 323
Mark Freedland
I. The Processes and Procedures of the Administrative State in Normal Times 323
II. Constitutional Process in Times of Crisis 328
III. Conclusion 331

PART VI: CONSTITUTIONS

17. Challenges of Multilevel Constitutionalism 339
Cheryl Saunders
I. Introduction 339
II. Multilevel Government and Constitutionalism 341
A. Multilevel government 341
B. Constitutionalism 345
III. Multilevel Constitutionalism 349
IV. Politics 353
V. Law 356
VI. Conclusion 359

18. A Hard Law Approach to States Systemic Violations of Article 2 of the Treaty of the European Union: Reasons and Means 363
Miguel Poiares Maduro and Benedita Menezes Queiroz
I. Introduction 363
II. EU Protection of Fundamental Rights in its Member States: Reasons and Instruments 365
III. Reasons for the EU Role in Enforcing the Rule of Law at National Level 370
IV. Correcting and Preventing Member States Systemic Rule of Law Problems Through Judicial Enforcement at EU Level 371

19. Brexit and the Challenges of a 'Post-Sovereign' Legal Landscape 381
Sionaidh Douglas Scott
I. The Westphalian World, 'Post Sovereignty', and Legal Pluralism 381
A. EU law 383
B. Legal pluralism 385
II. Brexit: The Challenge to 'Post Sovereignty' 387
A. Three different conceptions of sovereignty 389
B. Britain as 'unsettled state' 390
III. Conclusion 394

PART VII: CONCLUSION

20. Six Dimensions of Public Law: Pressure-Testing the UK and EU Systems 399
Paul Craig
I. Theory 400
A. UK: parliamentary and popular sovereignty 400
B. EU: intergovernmentalism and supranationalism 403
II. Institutions and Accountability 405
A. UK: Prime ministerial government, parliament, and the devolved regions 405
B. EU: two presidents, institutional decision-making, and liaison with Member States 408
III. Constitutions and Rights 410
A. UK and EU: constitutions 410
B. UK and EU: rights 414
IV. Process and Procedure 416
A. UK: two dimensions of process 416
B. EU: two dimensions of process 419
V. Legislation 420
A. UK: two dimensions of legislative complexity 421
B. EU: two dimensions of legislative complexity 423
VI. Case Law and Doctrine 424
A. UK: framing the political discourse through structural constitutional review 424
B. EU: framing the political discourse through structural constitutional review 426
VII. Conclusion 429

Index 431

List of Contributors

Professor **NW Barber**, Professor of Constitutional Law and Theory, Faculty of Law, University of Oxford

Professor **Gráinne de Búrca**, Florence Ellinwood Allen Professor of Law, New York University School of Law

Professor **Paul Craig**, Emeritus Professor of English Law, Faculty of Law, University of Oxford

Professor **Deirdre Curtin**, Professor of European Union Law, Department of Law, European University Institute

Professor **ACL Davies**, Professor of Law and Public Policy, Faculty of Law, University of Oxford

Professor **Sionaidh Douglas-Scott**, Anniversary Chair in Law, School of law, Queen Mary, University of London

Professor **Timothy Endicott**, Professor of Legal Philosophy, Faculty of Law, University of Oxford

Professor **Elizabeth Fisher**, Professor of Environmental Law, Faculty of Law, University of Oxford

Professor **Mark Freedland**, Emeritus Professor of Employment Law, Faculty of Law, University of Oxford

Professor **Carol Harlow**, Emeritus Professor of Law, Department of Law, London School of Economics and Political Science

Professor **Jeff King**, Professor of Law, Faculty of Laws, University College London.

Professor **Miguel Poiares Maduro**, Director, School of Transnational Governance, European University Institute

Professor **Joana Mendes**, Professor of Comparative Administrative Law, University of Luxembourg

Dr **Benedita Menezes Queiroz**, Assistant Professor at Universidade Católica Portuguesa, Faculdade de Direito, Escola do Porto, Portugal

Professor **Richard Rawlings**, Professor of Public Law, UCL Faculty of Laws

Lord Sales, Justice of the UK Supreme Court

Laureate Professor Emeritus **Cheryl Saunders AO**, Melbourne Law School, University of Melbourne

Eleanor Sharpston, Advocate General, Court of Justice of the European Union

Professor **Neil Walker**, Regius Professor of Public Law and the Law of Nature and Nations, Edinburgh Law School, University of Edinburgh

Professor **Alison L Young**, Sir David Williams Professor of Public Law, Faculty of Law, University of Cambridge

1

Foundations and Futures

A Brief Introduction

Elizabeth Fisher, Jeff King, and Alison L Young

Public law in the United Kingdom and European Union has undergone significant change over the last fifty years. Some of these changes have been the product of explicit events and reforms. For example, the passing of the Human Rights Act 1998, devolution, EU treaty revision, and the UK Referendum on leaving the European Union. Other changes have been incremental—a steady shift in practices, laws, and institutions. Public law has become globalised. Administrative law has been consolidated in both the United Kingdom and the European Union. Legal doctrines have evolved. Overall, the public law of 2019 looks very different from the public law of 1979. It is also certain to be the case that the public law of 2059 will be different again.

Or will it be? One of the most important virtues of law is its stability. While it is hoped and desired that science in 2059 is a world away from that of 1979, the expectation is that law has a more 'homeostatic' quality.[1] And in the case of public law, particularly so. Its principles and foundations, while evolving, are expected to endure. Its architecture is perceived to reflect carefully accrued balances over good government. None of this is to say that public law is frozen in time. Rather, the point is that in any process of change, the foundations of public law matter for understanding both the past and the future of the field.

In this collection, leading figures in UK and EU public law address this complex and nuanced interrelationship between the foundations and futures of the field in both regions. They chart and explore this interrelationship in many different ways. In some chapters, authors delve deep into legal detail. Others trace historical narratives. Some chapters plot new paths over well-trodden routes. Others reflect on how laws have evolved. There are chapters that explore theory whilst other chapters confront the current challenges of public law. Others remind us of the enduring nature of many themes. Like all acts of charting, these chapters are the product of 'reflexive' and 'tactile' engagement with the materials of public law.[2] They are

[1] Bruno Latour, *The Making of Law: An Ethnography of the Conseil D'État* (trans Marina Brilman and Alain Pottage, Polity Press 2010) 242–443.

[2] Rob Kitchin, Martin Dodge, and Chris Perkins, 'Introductory Essay: Conceptualising Mapping' in Rob Kitchin, Martin Dodge, and Chris Perkins (eds), *The Map Reader* (Wiley-Blackwell 2011) 6.

Elizabeth Fisher, Jeff King, and Alison L Young, *Foundations and Futures* In: *The Foundations and Future of Public Law*. Edited by: Elizabeth Fisher, Jeff King, Alison L Young, Oxford University Press (2020).
DOI: 10.1093/oso/9780198845249.003.0001

examples of scholarly and legal craft in action.[3] Overall, these chapters make clear that the interrelationship between foundations and futures is a profoundly important one. As scholars and lawyers, we ignore this at our peril.

The inspiration for this book is the work of Professor Paul Craig, Professor of English Law at St John's College at the University of Oxford between 1998 and 2019, now Emeritus Professor of English Law at the University of Oxford. We say inspiration because this book is not so much a *Festschrift* but rather an occasion for a group of scholars to rise to the intellectual challenge that Craig has set for us. Our hope was that Craig would be honoured on the occasion not by personal tribute but by the production of deep and original scholarship reflecting on the foundations and future of public law. Our hope was not so much met but surpassed in the result.

For the last forty years, Craig has been one of the most important scholars of EU and UK public law. This can be seen most obviously in the many editions of pioneering texts such as *Administrative Law*,[4] his collaboration with de Búrca, *EU Law: Text Cases and Materials*,[5] and numerous editions of his landmark book, *EU Administrative Law*.[6] In each of these texts, Craig has given intellectual depth and structure to the amorphous. In doing so he has set the intellectual and legal agendas in these subjects, but he has done more than this. He has also confronted change in public law head on and his countless other pieces of scholarship are prime examples of this. In his various works, Craig has erased the distinction between finding structure in, and giving structure to, the legal doctrine of each legal order, much to the enlightenment of jurists in both.

I. An Overview of the Project

Public law is primarily the law of government. It plays an important role in constituting, limiting, and holding government to account, and imposing duties upon it to carry out public functions. However, these activities are not the sole province of law. As Craig wrote in 2015, the foundations of administrative law are 'broad' and include 'conceptual, judicial, theoretical, administrative and regulatory foundations'.[7] He also went on to note that while they are often discussed, there is also much about them that is imperfectly understood.[8]

[3] Elizabeth Fisher, 'Back to Basics: Thinking About the Craft of Environmental Law Scholarship' in Ole Pedersen (ed), *Perspectives on Environmental Law Scholarship: Essays on Purpose, Shape and Discretion* (CUP 2018).

[4] Sweet & Maxwell. 1st edn (1983); 2nd edn (1989); 3rd edn (1994); 4th edn (1999); 5th edn (2003); 6th edn (2008); 7th edn (2012); and 8th edn (2016).

[5] OUP. 1st edn (1995); 2nd edn (1998); 3rd edn (2002); 4th edn (2008); 5th edn (2011); 6th edn (2015).

[6] OUP. 1st edn (2006); 2nd edn (2012).

[7] Paul Craig, *UK, EU and Global Administrative Law: Foundations and Challenges* (CUP 2015) 3.

[8] Ibid 4.

There are many different ways of thinking about 'foundations'. The approach taken in this book was developed in collaboration with Craig. To that end, the chapters are structured around what we have identified as six thematic building blocks of public law: theory, case law, legislation, institutions, process, and constitutions. We do not pretend that this list is exhaustive. We also recognize that these themes capture the different materials involved in any public law system. The key thing, as Craig notes, is that 'the six-part divide captures the principal dimensions of public law, irrespective of the particular polity in question'.[9] In doing so, it allows an open and wide-ranging exploration of public law.

These features of public law are not new to public lawyers; they are so obviously part of the public law landscape as to be unremarkable features of it. As public lawyers, we know our subject is normative. We are constantly handling case law and legislation. We need to think about public institutions and the procedures they engage in. We continuously keep the constitutional architecture in mind. But at the same time, we rarely have the opportunity to explore these constituent elements of the subject unencumbered by the urgency of a specific question or concern. More significantly, it is difficult to examine these different features side by side or explore them across a range of legal systems.

In this collection, each foundation is explored through three chapters: two chapters which use UK and EU law as a starting point, and a chapter providing a more reflective essay on the topic, prompted by the two earlier chapters. The book concludes with a closing chapter from Craig that examines how Brexit is 'pressure testing' all six of these public law foundations right now. The chapter is an important reminder that at the time in which we find ourselves, understanding foundations and futures is more important than ever.

As we noted earlier, in identifying these six foundations, the remit we provided to those involved in the project was to explore them in an open-ended way. The first foundation that is examined is theory, with contributions from Janet McLean, Neil Walker, and Nick Barber (Chapters 2, 3, and 4). As Craig stated in 1990: 'the nature and content of constitutional and administrative law can only be properly understood against the background, political theory which a society actually espouses, or against such a background which a particular commentator believes that a society ought to espouse'.[10]

An appreciation for the role of theory, 'the abstract principles of the subject', has been a fundamental feature of the development of EU and UK public law.[11]

[9] Craig, 'Six Dimensions of Public Law: Pressure' (Chapter 20, this volume).

[10] Paul Craig, *Public Law and Democracy in the UK and USA* (Clarendon 1990).

[11] See also Paul Craig, 'Theory, 'Pure Theory' and Values in Public Law' [2005] PL 440; Paul Craig, 'Theory and Values in Public Law: A Response' in Paul Craig and Richard Rawlings (eds), *Law and Administration in Europe: Essays in Honour of Carol Harlow* (OUP 2003); Paul Craig, 'Public Law, Political Theory and Legal Theory' [2000] PL 211; Paul Craig, 'Integration, Democracy and Legitimacy' in Paul Craig and Grainne de Burca (eds), *The Evolution of EU Law* (1st edn, OUP 2011).

Theoretical inquiry however, does not typically yield a neat and harmonious set of ideas, nor even converge on an appropriate methodology.

The second foundation explored is that of case law with chapters by Alison Young, Gráinne de Búrca, and Timothy Endicott (Chapters 5, 6, and 7). Much of Craig's writing has focused on the development of legal doctrine by courts. As he stated in 1994, the 'capacity of the common law to develop and evolve' is 'one of its enduring qualities'.[12] Not only has he made important contributions to the debate over the theoretical foundations of judicial review,[13] Craig also has charted the cutting edge of UK law doctrine as new grounds of review have emerged and older grounds have evolved.[14] In regards to EU law, his scholarship has likewise made many important contributions,[15] including strengthening understanding about direct effect and the relationship between national courts and the European Court of Justice (CJEU).[16]

Legislation and delegated legislation are examined in separate chapters by Jeff King, Advocate General Eleanor Sharpston, and Lord Sales (Chapters 8, 9, and 10). Through his work, Craig has explored the substantive nature of UK and EU legislation in detail including how it structures legal relationships and the rights and obligations it creates.[17] His painstaking analysis brings discussion down to legal realities. As he noted about the EU: 'It is important to dispel any illusion that the primary legislation captures issues of principle, while secondary norms address insignificant points of detail.'[18]

The nature of public institutions, specifically administrative institutions, and the questions they create for public lawyers are pondered by Elizabeth Fisher, Deirdre Curtin, and Anne Davies (Chapters 11, 12, and 13). The landscape of public law and EU law is scattered with institutions, some of which are fully constituted and limited by law and many which are not. It is also the case that these institutions lie on both sides of the public/private divide. Much of Craig's work has been about

12 Paul Craig 'The Common Law, Reasons and Administrative Justice' (1994) 53 CLJ 282.

13 For example, Paul Craig, 'Ultra Vires and the Foundations of Judicial Review' (1998) 57 CLJ 63; Paul Craig, 'The Common Law, Shared Power and Judicial Review' (2004) 24 OJLS 237.

14 Besides his textbook (n 4), also see as other examples Paul Craig, 'The Nature of Reasonableness Review' (2013) 66 CLP 1; Paul Craig, 'Judicial Review, Appeal and Factual Error' [2004] PL 788; and Paul Craig, 'Legitimate Expectations: A Conceptual Analysis' (1995) 108 LQR 79.

15 Besides his two EU textbooks (notes 5–6), other examples include Paul Craig, 'Once More Unto the Breach: The Community, the State and Damages Liability' (1997) 113 LQR 67; Paul Craig, 'Competence: Clarity, Conferral, Containment and Consideration' (2004) 29 European Law Rev 323; and Paul Craig, 'Subsidiarity: A Political and Legal Analysis' (2012) 50 JCMS 72.

16 Paul Craig, 'The Legal Effect of Directives: Policy, Rules and Exceptions' (2009) 34 European Law Rev 349; and Paul Craig, 'The Jurisdiction of the Community Courts Reconsidered' (2001) Texas Int'l LJ 555.

17 For example, Paul Craig, 'Constitutional Principle, the Rule of Law and Political Reality: The European Union (Withdrawal) Act 2018' (2019) 82 MLR 319; Paul Craig, 'Delegated Acts, Implementing Acts and the New Comitology Regulation' (2011) 36 European Law Rev 671; Paul Craig, 'The European Union Act 2011: Locks, Limits and Legality' (2011) 48 CMLR 1881; and Paul Craig, 'Contracting Out, the Human Rights Act and the Scope of Judicial Review' (2002) 118 LQR 55.

18 For example, Paul Craig, *The Lisbon Treaty: Law, Politics, and Treaty Reform* (OUP 2010) 49.

exploring the significance of these institutional arrangements for both EU law and public law and how they evolve over time and under different ideological influences.[19] He has been insistent on stressing the importance of providing coherent accounts that do justice to the complexity and detail of these institutions. As he noted in regards to the EU: 'From the very inception of the EEC it has been difficult to fit the principal institutions within any neat ordering that corresponds to that within a nation state.'[20]

The fifth foundation explored is that of process and procedure with three chapters by Carol Harlow and Rick Rawlings, Joana Mendes, and Mark Freedland respectively (Chapters 14, 15, and 16). Concerns about ensuring legitimate and robust process and procedure are central in both public law and EU law. Legislation, constitutions, and case law all focus on this issue. As governing institutions evolve, the issue remains a live one. It is also an issue that requires an engagement with fine technical detail. Craig's work has constantly been mapping these phenomena to make sense of them.[21]

The sixth foundation is arguably the most fundamental of them all: constitutionalism. It contributes to the legitimacy and stability of legal orders, although what is 'constitutional' is not always easy to delineate.[22] Moreover, while 'denominating' an issue as constitutional takes it 'off the agenda of normal politics',[23] constitutionalism is often a contested concept. It also evolves. Cheryl Saunders, Sionaidh Douglas-Scott, and Miguel Poires Maduro and Benedita Menezes Queiroz explore constitutionalism from different perspectives (Chapters 17, 18, and 19).

II. Foundations

Although this volume is arranged around these aforementioned foundational themes, there is another sense of 'foundation' to which the contributors' essays also speak. If we understand the term, with Martin Loughlin, as referring to 'the architectonic structuring of modern governmental ordering',[24] or perhaps the 'social

[19] Some examples include: Paul Craig, 'Public Law and Control Over Private Power' in Michael Taggart (ed), *The Province of Administrative Law* (Hart 1997); Paul Craig, 'The Fall and Renewal of the Commission: Accountability, Contract and Administrative Organisation' (2000) 6 ELJ 98; Paul Craig, 'The Constitutionalisation of Community Administration' (2003) 28 European Law Rev 840; and Paul Craig, 'European Governance: Executive and Administrative Power under the New Constitutional Settlement' (2005) 3(2–3) Int'l J of Constitutional L 407.

[20] Paul Craig, 'Institutions, Power and Institutional Balance' in Craig and de Burca (eds), *The Evolution of EU Law* (2nd edn, OUP 2011).

[21] Paul Craig, *EU Administrative Law* (2nd edn, OUP 2012) 321 and Paul Craig, 'Perspectives on Process: Common Law, Statutory and Political' [2010] PL 279.

[22] Paul Craig, 'Constitutionalising Constitutional Law: *HS2*' [2014] PL 373, 389.

[23] Paul Craig, 'Constitutions, Constitutionalism, and the European Union' (2001) 7 ELJ 125.

[24] Martin Loughlin, *The Foundations of Public Law* (OUP 2011) 94.

and political foundations'[25] of contemporary legal orders, then a different set of themes emerges. Among the more material or political foundations of public law in this sense, we will find the ideas of sovereignty and the state, the process of law-making, the executive, and the rule of law. The collection of chapters presented here offers exceptional insight into each of these.

We can begin by considering the idea of *sovereignty*.[26] The state is an important foundation for the very idea of modern constitutionalism, however much marginalized in Anglo-American constitutional thought.[27] The idea of sovereignty is essential to the understanding of the state in the international order, and also of national legal systems, and above all that of the United Kingdom.[28] Barber's Chapter 4 puts the state front and centre, arguing that understanding the point of the classically conceived state helps us to understand the point of public law itself. In some contrast, the chapters by Walker (Chapter 2), Douglas-Scott (Chapter 19), and Saunders (Chapter 17) illuminate the uncertain relationship between political sovereignty and the classical, Westphalian, or Weberian notion of the nation state. Douglas-Scott sketches the long-running decline of the Westphalian model of the full political and legal independence of national states and the rise of transnational law. This is exemplified in the project of EU integration and indeed in the national politics of the United Kingdom, both being examples of the 'post-sovereign' world. Walker looks at the essence of the European Union, a legal entity having state-like characteristics but which in his view differs fundamentally from nation states in a manner that creates four significant paradoxes for its current project of integration. Whereas Douglas-Scott warns that the classical picture of sovereignty is belied by legal and political pluralism, Walker's unintended rejoinder is that the distinctiveness of the state remains salient for understanding the EU's current predicaments. Saunders' chapter explores a different dimension: multi-level government which sits chiefly 'below' rather than 'above' the nation state. She outlines the rise and significance of diverse forms of multi-level government, extending well beyond federalism and devolution. She argues that multi-level constitutionalism is crucial for realizing the value that lies at the heart of modern constitutionalism itself—democracy. Indeed, we see the idea of democracy take on importance in each of the chapters that touch centrally on the idea of sovereignty, whether in relating the point of the state to the interests of its citizens (Barber), or being the political rationale for multi-level constitutionalism (Saunders), being a problematic hurdle

[25] Dennis Galligan and Mila Versteeg (eds), *The Social and Political Foundations of Constitutions* (OUP 2013).

[26] Loughlin (n 24) Part III. For an account of the constitutional relationship between sovereignty and government, see Richard Tuck, *The Sleeping Sovereign* (CUP 2016).

[27] Janet McLean, *Searching for the State in British Legal Thought: Competing Conceptions of the Public Sphere* (CUP 2012).

[28] Paul Craig, 'The United Kingdom, the European Union, and Sovereignty' in Richard Rawlings, Peter Leyland, and Alison Young (eds), *Sovereignty and Law: Domestic, European and International Perspectives* (Hart Publishing 2013).

for the project of integration (Walker), and, more critically, being the dubious rallying cry implicit in the politics of UK independence from the European Union, one which may well hasten the departure of Scotland and hence the disintegration of the British state (Douglas-Scott).

Talk of democracy, in the perspective of public law, turns attention to the *law-making power*, a second foundation.[29] Hans Kelsen located the law-making power at the centre of the material (as opposed to formal) constitution, which he considered to be 'those rules which regulate the creation of the general legal norms, in particular the creation of statutes'.[30] Sharpston (Chapter 9) and King (Chapter 8) each invite an illuminating reply from Lord Sales, who has elsewhere observed with regret that 'statutory interpretation languishes as a subject of study'.[31] Sharpston explores the unique challenges of complex law-making at the centre of the European Union. Legislation is the result of a challenging bureaucratic effort in a multi-lingual, national, and jurisdictional exercise of drafting and compromise, issued textually in all the EU's official languages. Such a process inevitably gives adjudication a unique role in completing the task of giving legislation its meaning. The court must not just clarify what the legislation said but what it was *trying to say*. King shows that the flaws in parliamentary oversight of delegated legislation in the United Kingdom are of old pedigree, are unresolved, and have predictably led to the impending crisis of legitimacy in respect of delegated legislation made at breakneck pace under the European Union (Withdrawal) Act 2018. Relying on considerable experience, Lord Sales adopts a more sanguine view of the politics of delegated legislation, and a more modest view of the judicial role in respect of any legal challenges to Brexit-related statutory instruments made under the 2018 Act. In Chapter 7, Endicott is also preoccupied with law-making but under the common law rather than in legislation (a distinction explored in both his and Young's chapters). He aims to explain how there is no paradox in how judges who are tasked with applying the law can also make law, provided we understand their law-making role as incidental to the judgment rather than purposive in the manner evident in legislation.[32]

As with the interrelated ideas of sovereignty and the state, *the executive* is certainly a foundation of public law.[33] The relationship between the state, democracy, and sovereign authority is at the centre of the historical exploration of

[29] See eg Paul Craig and Carol Harlow (eds), *Lawmaking in the European Union* (Kluwer 1997); and for a careful study of a very important UK statute, Paul Craig, 'Constitutional Principle, the Rule of Law and Political Reality: The European Union (Withdrawal) Act 2018' (2019) 82 MLR 319.

[30] Hans Kelsen, *General Theory of Law and State* (trans Anders Wedberg, Harvard UP 1945) 124.

[31] Rt Hon Lord Justice Philip Sales, 'Modern Statutory Interpretation' (2017) 38 Statute L Rev 125, 125.

[32] While different in significant respects, compare Friedrich A Hayek, *Law, Liberty and Legislation: A New Statement of the Liberal Principles of Justice and Political Economy* Vols 1–3 (Routledge, 1993 [1973]) ch 5 ('Nomos').

[33] Paul Craig and Adam Tomkins (eds), *The Executive in Public Law: Power and Accountability in Comparative Perspective* (OUP 2006).

administration in McLean's Chapter 3. Building on her important previous work,[34] McLean examines the dominant authority and legitimacy claims that underpinned British public administration successively between the seventeenth and twentieth centuries. She illustrates how the ideas of independence, public trust, efficiency, and democracy shaped common law doctrine in different ways across the centuries.

The interplay between law and the administrative state is also central to Chapter 11 by Fisher and Chapter 13 by Davies. Fisher's historical chapter examines two would-be watershed legal moments in the relationship between law and administration in the United Kingdom and the United States. Both moments failed in their aspirations due to the inability to grasp fully the complex institutional topography of administration as well as the inability to get past thinking of administrative law in ideological terms. While Fisher explores twentieth-century administrative law thought, Davies focuses in detail on a highly significant site of administrative reform in the contemporary British administrative state. Davies explores how the UK Health and Social Care Act 2012 embodied a statutory policy of marketisation, whereas ministers had gradually made a shift towards a different policy—of offering integrated care—when implementing the Act. Davies argues that two important legal challenges to this change resulted in judgments 'marked by very close attention to the technical details of the statutory provisions',[35] but which nevertheless failed to stop ministers from wandering away from the object and purposes of the 2012 Act. Here, formalistic judicial deference and the failure to take *ultra vires* challenges seriously was a disservice rather than service to democracy. Chapter 14 by Harlow and Rawlings and Chapter 15 by Mendes also illustrate how law and administration cannot be understood in isolation from one another, due to their complex interactional effects. Harlow and Rawlings show how at first proceduralisation of administration takes on rule of law-like (or better, *Rechtsstaat*-like) dimensions. But as such proceduralisation has in places increasingly tended towards automation, the gulf between proceduralisation and the common law understanding of procedural fairness has become substantial and troubling. Mendes explores how the duty to give reasons manifests itself both as an internal norm applied by the administrative institutions of the European Union, as well as an adjudicative norm developed in the jurisprudence of the CJEU. In her focus on the 'power of the executive to orient society', Mendes demonstrates how executive bodies become crucial agents, guardians, and interpreters of constitutional norms and principles.

While Loughlin doubts whether the rule of law can properly be considered a foundation of public law,[36] another view is possible, particularly if one believes that

[34] McLean (n 27).
[35] Davies, 'The Administrative State and the Fundamentals of Public Law' (Chapter 13 this volume).
[36] Loughlin (n 24) ch 11.

a polity in which the rule of law is substantially absent can exhibit public power but not public *law* in any meaningful sense.[37] At any rate, the rule of law is of concern throughout this collection, in ways that continue to connect law and adjudication to the other important foundations of public law. Maduro and Queiroz's Chapter 18 illustrates how increasing interdependence between Member States of the European Union has meant that observance of the rule of law and fundamental rights at the national level is a bona fide constitutional concern to the entire EU legal order, as is reflected in Articles 2 and 7 of the Treaty of the European Union. Crucial to their argument is that a gross failure of the rule of law in one state not only generates externalities in others but also poses a central challenge to the constitutional legitimacy of the entire Union. De Búrca, in Chapter 6, methodically explores the attempted, actual, and probable influence of UK court judgments on decision-making at the CJEU, when the former gives judgment under preliminary reference procedures. Her chapter is an important contribution to the literature on dialogue between national and supranational courts,[38] in effect a discussion about the relationship between public law and political sovereignty. Chapter 16 by Freedland is also concerned about the rule of law, but not so much in its adjudicative capacity. His contention is that the rule of law properly conceived presupposes sustainable governance, and that the Brexit process is creating a 'disordered state' in which the constitutional fundamental of the rule of law is at patent risk.

While the chapters by Davies (Chapter 13), Fisher (Chapter 11), King (Chapter 8), McLean (Chapter 3), and Mendes (Chapter 15) are each concerned indirectly with judging in the administrative state, it is in the fine chapters by Young (Chapter 5) and Endicott (Chapter 7) in which the very essence of common law adjudication is given close study. Both chapters recognise that the analogical reasoning evident in common law judging is different from legislative law-making and invites deep explanation of the relationship between law-making and law application. In recognising the institutional difficulties of judges focusing on analogical reasoning alone in the context of public law, Young argues that a solution may be found in a modest shift towards either more inductive or deductive judicial reasoning. She argues in favour of moving towards the former for public law cases, though not as a hard and fast rule. The more inductive approach entails greater reliance on standards and first principles, in preference to the ossification of precedents into taxonomical categories that are to be applied in a rule-like fashion to future cases.[39] Endicott's analysis extends deeper still, as noted earlier, showing

[37] This is true whether one adopts a formal or substantive conception: Paul Craig, 'Formal and Substantive Conceptions of the Rule of Law' [1997] Public Law 467.

[38] Nicolas Bratza, 'The Relationship Between the UK Courts and Strasbourg' [2011] EHRLR 505; Dean Spielmann, 'Wither Judicial Dialogue?' (Sir Thomas More Lecture, Lincoln's Inn, London, 12 October 2015). Available at: http://echrblog.blogspot.com/2015/10/lecture-by-courts-president-on-judicial.html, accessed 15 July 2019.

[39] Jason Varuhas, 'Taxonomy and Public Law' in Mark Elliott, Jason Varuhas, and Shona Wilson Stark (eds), *The Unity of Public Law? Doctrinal, Theoretical and Comparative Perspectives* (Hart 2018); Paul Craig, 'Taxonomy and Public Law: A Response' [2019] PL 281.

how in common law adjudication judges are part of a diffuse and unintentional law-making process, 'a process in which each judge needs to take account of what others have decided, and each has an influence on the future that will be mediated in the future by the judgment of others'.

III. Future

Endicott's meditation in Chapter 7 on how the past, present, and future come together in common law judgments returns us to our introduction. As we have stressed, this book is not just about revisiting the foundations of public law. It also examines the potential challenges to these foundations posed by recent and current events. The chapters together pose a more general question: how firm are these foundations and will they need to be modified, or even replaced with other foundations, as we move forward? Three specific challenges are illustrated in this collection: Brexit; the growing rise of the use of technology and automation to perform public law functions; and the role of public law in the face of austerity.

It is hardly astonishing that Brexit is a theme of this collection. The outcome of the UK referendum in favour of exiting the European Union sent shock waves through the United Kingdom, the European Union, and beyond. It poses deep issues for public law, placing pressure on its foundations and its ability to regulate the exit of the United Kingdom from the European Union, given the extent to which their laws, legal systems, and institutions have been entangled over the last forty years and more. It is therefore no surprise that Craig would choose this as his theme through which to explain how Brexit illustrates a series of pressure points in the UK constitution. Craig's chapter clearly illustrates how the UK's decision to leave the European Union has had an impact on the theoretical foundations of public law, case law, legislation, process and procedure, institutions and constitutions.

Other contributions to this collection drill down on some of the more specific challenges posed by Brexit. King's chapter (Chapter 8) illuminates how preparations for facilitating the UK's exit from the European Union has provided further illustration of the ever-growing use of delegated legislation, and the ensuing difficulties that may arise when delegated legislation is used to create rather than implement policy. The European Union (Withdrawal) Act 2018 brings this issue into stark relief through its transfer of a broad power to the executive to enact delegated legislation when ministers consider it 'appropriate'.[40] In addition, it includes Henry VIII clauses, where delegated legislation 'may make any provision that could be made by an Act of Parliament'.[41] Both King's chapter and Lord Sales' response in

[40] European Union (Withdrawal) Act 2018, s 8 (1).
[41] European Union (Withdrawal) Act 2018, s 8 (5).

Chapter 10 critically evaluate the growing use of delegated legislation through the Brexit process and beyond.

Brexit also has an impact on the European Union. Douglas-Scott's Chapter 19 examines how Brexit may lead to further fragmentation in the United Kingdom and potentially even in the European Union. Whilst there is evidence of the EU 27 working together in their negotiations with the United Kingdom through the Article 50 process, it is hard to deny that the example of one state expressing its intention to leave the European Union may lead other Member States to question their continued membership and the value of the EU project. De Búrca's Chapter 6 illustrates a further future loss following the UK's exit from the European Union; the UK's influence on the development of EU law through both article 267 references and the membership of the court's institutions by UK nationals.

It would be wrong, however, to dwell only on the potential negative impact of Brexit on the European Union. Chapter 18, Maduro and Queiroz's chapter, draws attention to the recent decision of the CJEU in *Commission v Poland*, which may mark a move towards a stronger, more systemic protection of fundamental rights and the rule of law across the European Union.[42] They argue in favour of broadening the scope of the protection of fundamental rights in the European Union so as to recognise how this protection of rights is needed to support the supranational nature of the European Union and the interconnections between the legal systems of the Member States and the European Union. Brexit may provide more of an impetus for the EU institutions to focus on providing a strong foundation of the protection of democracy and the rule of law across Europe in the face of further threats based, in part, on populist movements and nationalism.

The continuing saga of Brexit can only continue to place pressure on its unique nature. In Chapter 2, Walker analyses the theoretical foundations of the European Union, work which may well play a crucial role as the European Union continues to evolve. Such an esoteric organisation may require a more novel analysis, perhaps through an application of the concept of compound constitutionalism, developed by Saunders in Chapter 17. She focuses on a range of forms of multi-level governance, reimagining the interrelationship between their component parts. This approach may have great utility not just in the European Union but also, as Douglas-Scott further notes in Chapter 19, as regards the future relationship between England, Scotland, Wales, and Northern Ireland following Brexit. Walker's analysis of the European Union may also play a role here. Brexit may well require a reimagining of the conception of the state as it applies to the United Kingdom, with a call for greater collaboration between its component nations when negotiating international trade agreements, and a need for an understanding of shared competences and common frameworks to regulate the UK's internal market. All three

[42] Case C-619/18 *Commission v Poland* EU:C:2019:531.

chapters provide illuminating insight into how to traverse these complicated issues in the future.

The second challenge for the future of public law is found in the growing use of technology and computers in administration. New technologies are used to share data across the European Union and across institutions of a particular state. This may lead to integration of a range of administrative agencies. Moreover, administrative decisions are no longer merely taken by a front-facing administrator. Rather, computer programmes and algorithms are developed to perform public functions, particularly through allocating social and welfare rights, or implementing immigration policies. These issues are the focus of Chapter 12 by Curtin, Chapter 14 by Harlow and Rawlings, and Chapter 15 by Mendes.

Curtin focuses on the issues that arise from data sharing across the European Union. There is a growing use of private bodies to collect data, which can then be distributed across regulators in the different Member States. Whilst this may facilitate public administration, concerns arise as to data mining, in addition to the problem of ensuring effective judicial review over the collection and sharing of data. Harlow and Rawlings share these concerns but focus on a different aspect of the growth of digitalisation and proceduralisation in administrative law. How can we ensure that this growing use of technology does not exacerbate inherent bias in administrative decision-making, or lead to a lack of transparency in decision-making processes? In particular, the increasing use of technology is reducing the role of face-to-face processes which can provide an effective corrective mechanism. Mendes' chapter illustrates how new technologies impact on EU financial regulations and the interconnected nature of both public and private institutions across the European Union and the Member States. All three authors question how far traditional legal and political controls over administrative institutions and decision-making may need to adapt to a digital age. They recognise a need to draw on foundations in the face of a new problem.

A third problematic issue concerns the reaction of administrative bodies and the judiciary to measures of austerity. As charted by McLean (Chapter 3), the role of the administration, and the means through which states have justified the legitimacy of administrative bodies, have modified over time. The role of the state and of the European Union has grown, particularly as concerns the definition of public services and the provision of social and economic rights. However, as both Davies (Chapter 13) and Freedland (Chapter 16) point out in their contributions to the book, the growth in public services has seen a change in direction following the recent times of austerity. The judiciary in both the United Kingdom and the European Union have been reluctant to interfere with policy decisions, seeing these as better taken by politically accountable institutions. However, as Davies' analysis of recent decisions on healthcare illustrate, a failure to take legality seriously may undermine the rule of law and democracy, enabling administrative bodies to modify the policy choice establishing in legislation without democratic oversight by the legislature. As the legislative agenda becomes crowded in difficult times, whether caused by

Brexit or other difficulties, this is a lesson which applies across the entirety of the administrative state. The correct balance between the role of the courts, administrators, and legislatures in times of austerity continues to pose a problem for public law, one which no doubt will continue into the near future.

In addition to these specific issues, it is also important to realise how the contributions to this volume raise a more fundamental issue for public law scholarship and public law in the future. Public law focuses on the regulation of the state and of public power. In doing so, public law scholars often draw on key concepts, or on perceived dichotomies. These dichotomies, in turn, influence public law scholars to reach divergent conclusions as to the nature and purpose of public law, and the extent to which public law should rely on legal or political controls. Barber connects conceptions of the state with principles of constitutionalism, with Walker's work in Chapter 2 challenging how far these foundations apply to the European Union. As we face ever greater globalisation, and the creation of further international and supranational institutions, connected in myriad new ways in a digital age, we may need to question how far these traditional concepts can and should continue to shape public law in the future. This is particularly true when considering how public law can and should regulate these new organisations and interconnected relations between governmental institutions. This is not to question our use of foundational concepts but is rather a call to continued re-evaluation of their legitimacy; of these concepts' ability to adapt to the modern era of public law in an age of artificial intelligence, the growing use of computer data and algorithms, and globalisation.

This contribution has also challenged traditional dichotomies which may continue to be questioned in the future. Both McLean (Chapter 3) and Barber (Chapter 4) challenge traditional dichotomies between common law and modified *ultra vires* accounts of judicial review, themselves relying on deeper dichotomies between legal and political controls. Fisher's Chapter 11 explains the problems that have arisen in administrative law from adopting a bifurcated approach. Schools of administrative law scholarship have been formed around this bifurcation, with preferences for legal or administrative controls, and the ensuing focus on either courts or administrative bodies in public law scholarship. Chapter 9 by Sharpston criticises traditional understandings of the division between legislating and adjudicating, drawing on the complex realities of enacting EU legislation. Young, in Chapter 5, questions how far analogical reasoning in case law is being challenged by new forms of legal challenge to administrative decisions. McLean, Saunders, and Douglas-Scott all question how far traditional understandings of the state and multi-level governance are relevant in an ever-evolving world, particularly in the light of globalisation, the development of international and supranational institutions, and calls for more localised decision-making.

However, other chapters reflect on how some dichotomies need to be maintained. King (Chapter 8) reflects on the distinction between delegated and primary legislation, focusing in particular on the relative lack of democratic scrutiny over delegated legislation. Ignoring this distinction could give rise to a democratic deficit, particularly in the light of a broad transfer of power to the executive following Brexit. Nevertheless, as Lord Sales, in Chapter 10, remarks, it does not follow automatically that the courts should step in when legislatures are inactive, be that through their scrutiny of delegated legislation, or the enactment of broadly worded legislative provisions. He argues that there is still a need to maintain the distinct functions of the legislature and the judiciary. Endicott reflects on the differences between law-making by the judiciary and by the legislature, again suggesting a preservation of their distinct functions. Davies recognises how ignoring more traditional heads of judicial review may lead to an undermining of legitimate judicial control over the executive. Harlow and Rawlings draw on understandings of administrative procedure and its relationship with administrative law to evaluate the challenges faced in administrative law in a digital age. Barber draws on a traditional understanding of the state as a source of constitutional principles.

A further theme emerges from what may appear to be divergent approaches to traditional understandings of public law and their application to future challenges: the need to adopt a contextualised approach. Fisher explains how relying on traditional bifurcations in public law scholarship fails to adopt a contextualised approach and urges public law scholars of the future to consider choosing a new path. Endicott recognises the importance of context when exploring common law reasoning. Young argues that the choice between a more principled or taxonomical approach to previous cases depends on a range of features, focusing on the relative importance of legal certainty, accuracy, and the distribution of authority between rule-makers and rule-appliers. All these chapters show how the public law of the future will require continual reflection on foundations and dichotomies, applying these in a contextually sensitive manner. The public law of the future may adopt a further understanding of the legitimacy of the state and administrative bodies, and of courts, as their relative roles evolve over time. These modifications may undermine traditional dichotomies and require public law scholars both to draw on and potentially alter the foundations of public law.

IV. Conclusion

It is clear that coming to terms with the future of public law requires critical engagement with its foundations. This will be essential if that future will accommodate rather than be overwhelmed by profound changes in the nature of the state, technology, the natural environment, and political fragmentation. If there is an emerging theme through all the contributions in this book, it is to recognise that UK and EU public law scholarship and practice needs to tackle its future in both a principled and contextual manner. Saying that does not, of course, provide a simple formula for tackling the current challenges of the subject, but by focusing on the building blocks of public law, this collection shows how a principled and contextual approach requires critical and reflexive engagement with the foundations of the subject. Sometime this may require us to interrogate what are understood as traditional concepts and dichotomies. It may also ask us to remind ourselves of the importance of forgotten understandings and distinctions. It may also require us to face the enduring nature of some of the challenges of the subject. Overall, it demands that we have a fidelity to the materials of public law. In other words, it needs to adopt the approach that Craig has continually perfected throughout his career.

PART I
THEORY

2. The Diverse Objects of Public Law: Taking Theory to the Next Level
Neil Walker

3. The Authority of the Administration
Janet McLean

4. Law and The Point of The State
NW Barber

2

The Diverse Objects of Public Law

Taking Theory to the Next Level

Neil Walker

I. Beyond the State

Reflecting on Paul Craig's immense body of work prompts me to consider anew certain theoretical questions concerning the ever-extending reach of public law under the changing conditions of late modernity. The high modern age—on which late modernity builds—saw the development of territorially located political societies of unprecedented size, complexity, and integrative ambition whose coordination depended on a variety of steering mechanisms. Alongside economics, culture, and science, law offered one such steering mechanism. So, we tend to think of modern law (even more so than its predecessors), and in particular modern public law, in suitably society-encompassing and systemic terms, as a complexly interconnected whole geared to the complexly interconnected whole of its host territorial political society. To adopt law's own language, modern public law is a 'jurisdictionally-relative concept'[1] and, it follows, since the paradigmatic political society—or polity—of modernity has been the modern state, the jurisdiction relative to which public law took shape and revealed its systemic character was that of the state.

When we consider how and why public law operates as it does today, therefore, we do so within an inherited state-centred framework. Our very sense of the 'publicness' of public law, not to mention our appreciation of the aims and methods of the constitutional law, administrative law, and human rights law parts of public law, is closely informed by the self-conception and practice of the modern state. For the state presents itself as the dominant source and container (if not the originator)[2] of the distinction between public and private goods, values, relations, and identities, as well as supplying the legal architecture and the institutional forms—often framed by a written constitution—through which that distinction is articulated. Public law, in brief, serves mutually supportive normative and expressive functions in the steering work of state-building and state maintenance.

[1] Neil MacCormick, *Questioning Sovereignty* (OUP 1999) 14.
[2] See eg Raymond Geuss, *Public Goods, Private Goods* (Princeton UP 2003).

Neil Walker, *The Diverse Objects of Public Law* In: *The Foundations and Future of Public Law*. Edited by: Elizabeth Fisher, Jeff King, Alison L Young, Oxford University Press (2020). © Oxford University Press.
DOI: 10.1093/oso/9780198845249.003.0002

It both designs a machinery of governance and, at least in some measure, supplies (through the generation of narratives of identity and sentiments of belonging associated with the constitution—the commemoration of its emergence, its textual highlights, its record of development—as well as with Parliament, the higher courts and other legally coded polity-identifying institutions) a symbolic resource for the development and sustenance of a framework for putting things in common—a fabric of shared meaning that is both shaped by and facilitates the implementation of the architectural design.[3]

In today's late modern age, however, as Paul Craig has spent much intellectual energy elucidating, public law, considered in such systemic terms, has more diverse objects on which it performs its societally integrative normative and expressive functions, albeit that such non-state legal orders no longer supply the exclusive or dominant jurisdiction for a particular territory. Beyond the state there is now the supranational level of the European Union with its own dense jurisprudence, and its own incipient European political society and associated public functions. Many other international organisations carry out more limited general or sector-specific 'public' functions and possess more modest legal jurisdictions to that end;[4] and there are, in addition, increasingly strong claims for a broader globally pervasive and territorially unbounded level of public law, and especially administrative law.[5]

For reasons of space, and in recognition of the intensity of Craig's own focus, in the present chapter we restrict ourselves to an investigation of the European Union. In so doing, we begin with the reasonable—indeed unchallenged—assumption that it is the most 'state-like' level of law—and consequently of legal-theoretical investigation—beyond the state in terms of functional range, penetration, and integrative ambition. And in making that reasonable assumption, I would contend, it becomes methodologically appropriate for us to view the state template as a point of departure and comparison for our investigation. Crucial questions follow from this in the exploration of what is distinctive to the European Union as a polity and what is distinctive to the law of the EU polity. To what extent, first, do the deep assumptions we make about the very nature and justification of the form of organised living-in-common peculiar to the state translate to the EU polity level? These concern matters such as the EU's actual or potential democratic credentials, its self-understanding as a distinct political community with a capacity to develop a distinct (rather than merely state-dependent and state-supporting) conception of its public good, and its claim to a domain of final and exclusive authority. And,

[3] See eg Neil Walker, 'Beyond the Holistic Constitution?' in Petra Dobner and Martin Loughlin (eds), *The Twilight of Constitutionalism?* (OUP 2010) 291–308.

[4] See eg Guy Fiti Sinclair, *To Reform the World: International Organizations and the Making of Modern States* (OUP 2018).

[5] See eg Neil Walker, *Intimations of Global Law* (CUP 2015).

second, to what extent do the deep assumptions we make about the capacity and proper role of the fundamental ordering mechanism known as public law (with its associated normative and expressive functions) in mediating these deep political assumptions translate to the EU level? Otherwise put, given the kind of functions that public law performs in the case of the state, as the bearer, modifier, corrective, or other mediating influence upon the basic political premises of its host polity, does public law perform the same or similar functions where the European Union is its host?

It is here that 'theory' and, more specifically, the notion of 'theoretical foundations' enter the picture. For the two sets of 'deep assumptions' referred to are themselves, at least in an elementary sense, theoretical in nature; they are so just by dint of their making or implying speculative claims and hypotheses about how we account for—whether by explanation or justification—the emergence or sustenance of a particular state of affairs. And so we might say that the two fundamental and interconnected questions of the nature and justification of polity-specific law beyond the state (and in the European Union in particular), namely those concerning our deep assumptions about the very nature and purpose of the arrangements of living in common fashioned under a polity, and those concerning our deep assumptions about the capacity and proper role of law in ordering and articulating these polity-specific arrangements for living in common, together in either case with the associated methodological question of the extent to which we might rely on a state-centred template in accessing these deep assumptions, lie within the associated domain of political theory and legal theory respectively.

These are by no means new questions.[6] But in revisiting them together in the EU context, I will argue that we can improve our understanding of the relationship between the particular vulnerability of the European Union today in terms of its overall legitimacy and the particular vulnerability of its legal order. In particular, I will contend that the relative scarcity of traditional democratic and cultural supports for the EU polity, and an emphasis instead on the attainment of results, have placed a greater burden on the autonomous role of law—especially as understood in pragmatic vein—in legitimating supranationalism. It is a burden, furthermore, that law finds increasingly difficult to discharge.

Before pursuing these matters, however, and to provide more context for my inquiry, I want to say something about the contribution that Paul Craig has made to these and related matters.

[6] Although in comparing state with non-state sites, there is a tendency, at least in Anglophone literature, to take for granted and treat only cursorily the paradigmatic qualities of the state and to focus instead on the peculiarities (or otherwise) of newer non-state sites. Notable exceptions include Martin Loughlin, *Foundations of Public Law* (OUP 2010); Nick Barber, *The Constitutional State* (OUP 2010).

II. The Consummate All-Rounder

In any straw poll of the best UK public law 'all-rounder' of his generation, Paul Craig would probably come out on top. The all-rounder accreditation would, for many, be about scope of coverage, referring to the range of doctrinal fields within the wide terrain of public law in which the candidate professes expertise. A noted and prodigiously published UK constitutional lawyer and administrative lawyer, EU constitutional and administrative lawyer, and, more recently, global administrative lawyer, it is difficult to argue that Professor Craig would not prevail in that contest.

Others might argue for a different definition, or at least an additional criterion. They might ask who takes the most rounded—in the sense of the most holistic—view of the subject. Here too, Craig excels. The very 'foundational' theme of the celebratory conference from which this collection has emerged suggests why. In many works, including his 2014 Hamlyn Lectures on *UK, EU and Global Administrative Law: Foundations and Challenges*, he has advertised his curiosity in the broadest terms to include 'conceptual, judicial, theoretical, administrative and regulatory foundations'.[7] Craig remains first and foremost a doctrinal lawyer. In most of his work, including his major textbooks,[8] his primary objective is to give a lucid, considered, coherent, comprehensive, and persuasive account of the law and its development. Yet he understands that part and parcel of that full account has always been the provision of historical, social, and political background, as well as the teasing out of the law's deeper philosophical meaning, and contestation over that meaning. These concerns are always present, even in his most apparently 'black letter' contributions. Indeed, in certain publications, notably his book-length comparative study of public law and democracy in the United Kingdom and the United States,[9] these broader contextual and philosophical considerations have even dominated.

So, on either version Craig would be a strong contender for the prize of most accomplished all-rounder. But if we focus on the second sense of all-rounder, as relating most directly to our present concerns, what, more specifically, might he mean by philosophical or 'theoretical' foundations, and how does he understand the contribution of theory to public law, and his own contribution to that contribution?

Craig's theoretical interests are typically wide-ranging and broadly pursued, but there are common threads. First, he is primarily interested in law as the

[7] Paul Craig, *UK, EU and Global Administrative Law: Foundations and Challenges* (CUP 2015) 3–4.

[8] In particular, his seven editions of *Administrative Law* (Sweet & Maxwell), his six editions (with Gráinne de Búrca) of *EU Law: Text, Cases and Materials* (OUP), as well as his *EU Administrative Law* (OUP 2012).

[9] Paul Craig, *Public Law and Democracy in the United Kingdom and the United States of America* (Clarendon 1990).

explanandum rather than the *explanans*—as the thing to be explained rather than the thing explaining other things. As we might expect of someone whose primary reference point is legal doctrine, he is most interested in the best understanding of law as it is and on its own terms, rather than—as a social scientist might be particularly concerned with—in tracing the significant consequences for other aspects of social and political life of law being as it is. Second, when exploring the meaning and justification of law as it is, he is as interested in detailed questions—the sense of this or that rule of constitutional or administrative law, as he is in 'big picture' themes such as the rule of law or parliamentary sovereignty, although he is undoubtedly interested in both.[10]

Third, again setting Craig apart from social science perspectives, he is mainly interested in accounts of law at the level of justificatory ideas rather than material background and causality. This brings us directly to the conception of theory set out in our introductory remarks. For rather than simply tracing the chain of historical cause and effect, Craig wants to inquire what model(s), or set(s) of 'deep assumptions', of how things should be arranged within our frameworks of organised communal living provides the *best* account of what the law is and how it has come to be as it is, however explicitly or implicitly such models are endorsed. And he is interested in the answers given to that question both over the course of the law's development and in contemporary rationalisations by commentators, courts, politicians, and government officials.[11] It is in seeking and elucidating these conceptual models—these justificatory ideas of how law fits the broader background picture—that Craig is drawn to theory.

Finally, in the fourth place, and providing a deeper rationale for these other threads, Craig's theoretical work is always *normatively engaged*. While as a basic point of departure he wants to give a disinterested account of the law, in the way that he uses theory to deepen and defend that account there is *both* a recognition that law typically occupies contested normative terrain *and* a commitment to the view that it matters that, in negotiating that contested terrain, law takes the right path, whatever that path might be.[12]

The theme of normative engagement, indeed, lends coherence to the various aspects of his interest in and use of theory. Theory, in the core sense that he is (and we are) concerned with, as the explication of the unexplicated assumptions driving a trend or underpinning a state of affairs, is an explanatory, evaluative, and practical resource in his work. Different theories are invoked first to identify and explain the normative stakes invested in the development of legal doctrine; what

[10] See eg Paul Craig, 'Constitutional Foundations, the Rule of Law and Supremacy' [2003] PL 92.

[11] See eg Paul Craig, 'Public Law, Political Theory and Legal Theory' [2000] PL 211, 238.

[12] It would be possible from a relativist standpoint to acknowledge contestation while dismissing the search for the right path as inherently subjective. Or it would be possible to dogmatically assert the right path without conceding the existence of a domain of justified contestation. But Craig is neither relativist nor dogmatist.

living theories have influenced the making of law from the inside, so to speak? Second, these theories also allow us to evaluate the adequacy of the development of doctrine from the outside; regardless of how the law actually came to pass and how it might even be conventionally understood from the inside, what theory or combination of theories provides the most attractive account for the law as it now stands? Third, theory, in terms of an elaborated set of beliefs about how law might work in its particular polity context, can be a resource for persuasive intervention in the course of legal and political development—in the crucial task of favouring one interpretation or mode of extrapolation from existing doctrine or structural arrangements over another. This may occur at the level of first-order preferences, where Craig wants to lend support for or against a particular development in law.[13] More commonly, however, and also more subtly and more distinctively, the practical point of his concern with theory registers at a second-order level. This is because Craig shows a consistent preference for the very idea of a theoretically informed development of legal doctrine,[14] for a style of legal reasoning and justification that is theoretically explicit and transparent; one that, just because it brings its preconceptions and reasons for choices into the open thereby both demands greater reflection on the part of those making these choices and exposes them to the force of the better argument. On this view, over and above any specific commitment to the content and implications of a particular theory, a general commitment to taking theory seriously as a way of achieving argumentative candour and rigor becomes a vital resource for a more enlightened and enlightening approach, and so also a more seriously normatively engaged approach to the development of the law.

How does Paul Craig's theoretical approach chime with the inquiry of this chapter? Most basically, the task he sees theory performing is also central to the task here undertaken; namely, rendering explicit the kind of candidate frameworks of collective living, and of the ordering of collective living within a political community, that are often left implicit but would account for how the law has come to figure in the way that it does. And, indeed, Craig's work, as we have seen, suggests a particularly expansive justification of this approach, showing that it can pay explanatory, evaluative, and practical dividends, and is generally consistent with a normatively engaged stance.

Second, Craig takes a balanced and quite ecumenical position on the question of the relevance of the state paradigm to public law at European and wider non-state levels. On the one hand, there is a universal strain in his justification of some of the

[13] See his interventions on (and, indeed, against) Brexit; eg Paul Craig, 'The Process: Brexit and the Anatomy of Article 50' in Federico Fabrinni (ed), *The Law and Politics of Brexit* (OUP 2017) 49–67.

[14] This emerges both as a general theme and in his interventions in more specific debates; for example, in his qualified preference for a common law approach, with its greater readiness to look for independent foundational principles, against a narrowly positivistic *ultra vires* approach to judicial review; see eg Craig, 'Constitutional Foundations' (n 10); and Paul Craig, 'Ultra Vires and the Foundations of Judicial Review' (1998) 57 CLJ 63–90.

normative methods and techniques of public law, especially in the administrative law field. We should not be surprised that the kind of strong commitment to explicit forms of reasoned justification of particular normative approaches in law that he espouses be consistent with a belief in the translatability of key principles, and the good reasons that underpin them, from one jurisdictional context to another. On the other hand, he is keenly aware of the importance of context, and, adopting his own term, that much of the historical pedigree and institutional form of the European Union is 'singular'[15] and distinctive.

Third and finally, on what I have signalled as the key matter of taking both legal theory and political theory seriously within the one framework of inquiry—treating the deep assumptions of how the law works in a particular polity framework as being as important and contentious as the deep assumptions about the polity framework itself—Craig shows the way by grasping this point in principle even if he does not fully develop it in practice.[16] Consistent with his core preoccupations as a 'doctrinal constructivist',[17] Craig may remain more interested in law as *explanandum* than as *explanans*, but he also recognises that the role law plays in articulating the wider political order is not uniform but can differ significantly according to context. And, particularly where he draws and pursues a distinction between positivist and anti-positivist models of law's functioning in the political order,[18] he demonstrates an awareness of the complex linkage between the modelling of the basic nature and purpose of the polity and the modelling of the capacity and ordering role of law within that polity that, as we will see, is key to an understanding of the distinctive properties of public law in the EU environment.

III. Candidate Conceptions of (Public) Law

What, then, are the different conceptions of the capacity and role of law, and public law in particular, in articulating and giving effect to any particular vision of the polity? After treating that preliminary issue, we proceed to ask what is distinctive (from the state) about the political form and structure—the basic conditions of and for living-in-common—of the European Union. Then, putting these two pieces together, we ask which of the candidate conceptions of the role of law or, rather, which combination of conceptions has become most prominent in the EU context, in light of the development of its distinctive political structural tendencies. Finally, we consider what the resulting pattern of legal authority today, with its emphasis

[15] Paul Craig, 'Institutions, Power and Institutional Balance' in Paul Craig and Gráinne de Búrca (eds), *The Evolution of EU Law* (2nd edn, OUP 2011) 41–84, 41.

[16] Craig, 'Public Law, Political Theory and Legal Theory' (n 11) 211, 238.

[17] Armin Von Bogdandy, 'The Past and Promise of Doctrinal Constructivism: A Strategy for Responding to the Challenges Facing Constitutional Scholarship in Europe' (2009) 7 ICON 364–400.

[18] See eg Craig, 'Public Law, Political Theory and Legal Theory' (n 11) 235–39.

on legal pragmatism, tells us more generally about the legitimacy problems and prospects of the European Union.

Our candidate conceptions of law, as earlier noted, should be understood as involving different deep assumptions about the capacity and role of law in the generation and maintenance of a polity. These assumptions connect and roughly correspond to different frameworks of legal theory, and can be elaborated by reference to these. Those who have pursued this line and developed typologies of different operational conceptions of law within the polity and of their underlying theoretical presuppositions have cut the conceptual cake somewhat differently, although some variation of Craig's positivist/non-positivist distinction can typically be discerned.[19] My own approach draws on earlier efforts in identifying four ideal typical categories. These are in turn, *positivism, idealism, culturalism*, and *pragmatism*. Each theoretical model is associated with a particular mindset, a particular sense of the basis upon and standard by which law is framed and received within the political order. For the positivist, the focus is on 'the *authorised* law'; for the idealist, it is 'the *good* law'; for the culturalist, 'the *appropriate* law'; and for the pragmatist, 'the law *that works*'. Let us explore each of these.

The positivist narrative is concerned with pedigree—with the identification of an agreed set of social sources upon which the authority of law depends and from which all law should emanate. Positivism offers itself as the most or only plausible version of how law, as a human construct dealing with matters over which human subjects have differing and sometimes conflicting interests and values, may nevertheless be successfully devised and applied according to collectively acknowledged and accepted standards of validity. For those who subscribe to some version of 'ethical legal positivism',[20] the focus on authoritative sources identifies various more specific benefits and forms of legitimation, both 'input' and 'output'. First, on the input side, the pedigree rule shows how the content and direction of law can be tied to and legitimized through a particular political will or authorising convention, including (but not restricted to) the democratic determination of the collective citizenry represented in an elected Parliament or through some other constitutionally prescribed law-making procedure. Second, on the output side, the emphasis on law as a purposive intervention available from a determinate authoritative source indicates a consistency and concentration of law-making means that can aid rational planning and coordination of legal policy. Third, also on the output side, positivism's certainty over law-making sources provides a basis for the legibility,

[19] See eg Ronald Dworkin, *Law's Empire* (Harvard UP 1986) (distinguishing conventionalism, pragmatism, and his own law-as-integrity); Sean Coyle, 'Positivism, Idealism and the Rule of Law' (2006) 26 OJLS 257–88; Martin Loughlin, *Sword and Scales: An Examination of the Relationship Between Law and Politics* (OUP 2000) chs 1 and 14 (distinguishing law as command, law as custom, and law as right); Brian Tamanaha, *Law as a Means to an End* (CUP 2006) (distinguishing non-instrumental conceptions of law (natural law and law as custom) from instrumental conceptions); Kaarlo Tuori, *Ratio and Voluntas: The Tension Between Reason and Will in Law* (Ashgate 2011).

[20] See eg Tom Campbell, *The Legal Theory of Ethical Positivism* (Routledge 1996).

transparency, calculability, predictability, and reliable effectiveness of law; that is to say, certainty and clarity of input enables, but by no means ensures, certainty and clarity of output—features allowing individuals and groups to orient their conduct towards the law and its coordinating properties and also to hold law-makers and law-executors to account for the quality of their laws and the fidelity of their execution respectively. Fourth and finally, as one more significant output feature linked to legal positivism, we can indicate a connection to the virtues of legal formalism, understood as a commitment to 'autonomous conceptualism'[21] in judicial and broader legal decision-making. Legal formalism models law as a self-contained, internally consistent system, one where correct legal answers may be given to any question by reference to the logic of that system, and where resort need not be had to morally or socially controversial external values. While there is certainly no necessary connection between positivism's source-based foundationalism and a legal system displaying formal properties,[22] there are significant complementarities that facilitate their coexistence. Legal positivism's disciplined approach to the proper sources of law provides one important way in which the formalist distinction between system-internal and system-external factors can be sustained. More concretely, while their reasons differ, the two approaches share a preference for the legal system to be inhabited by a dense structure of rules or other general precepts organised in a clear internal hierarchy. For the positivist, this protects the 'input-legitimacy'-conferring connection between the foundational rule or convention and the particular legal disposition, while for the formalist it prevents 'gaps' that would require to be filled by politically and morally contentious considerations external to the system.

The idealist narrative supplies the most obvious contrast with the positivist narrative. Justifying law according to general moral standards, legal idealism is most prominently associated with the natural law tradition. For the idealist, law should reflect, reward, or be otherwise conducive to ways of communal living according to criteria of moral excellence or defensibility. These criteria may be discovered by reference to the immutable precepts of religious or other metaphysical belief systems or developed through other forms of ethical insight, reasoning, or communication. In any case, the legitimate authority of law depends upon its pursuit of a generally affirmable conception of the good life.

The culturalist narrative values law as an expression of custom or tradition particular to the political community in question. Unlike the positivist narrative, law is not just a jurisdiction-specific activity as a matter of authoritative design but also because it reflects a jurisdiction-specific background culture. Evolving over generations, and supplying an adjustable, experience-led practice that becomes a

[21] Paul Cox, 'An Interpretation (and Partial Defense) of Legal Formalism' (2003) 36 Indiana L Rev 56, 59.

[22] See eg Brian Leiter, 'Positivism, Formalism, Realism' (1999) 99 Columbia L Rev 1138.

key part of the societal matrix, law-as-culture distils, refines, and contributes to the ethical life of the community. Yet unlike the idealist narrative, law's legitimacy under the culturalist narrative is not connected to universalisable conceptions of the good but depends on its appropriateness as an expression of the way of social being peculiar to its host community.

The pragmatic narrative distances itself from the foundationalist assumptions associated with the first three narratives. It turns away from the positivist reliance on the insuperability of a broadly acknowledged pedigree rule, and turns too from the universal moral foundations of the idealist and the societal foundations of the culturalist. For pragmatists, the contribution of law depends instead on particular context and on the capacity of legal regulation to grasp and offer secure and reliable solutions to problems in light of the contingencies and uncertainties peculiar to that context. So understood, pragmatism is a broad church. It includes a wide range of contemporary schools of thought from legal realism to the economic analysis of law, and, for those for whom pragmatism's vital contextual knowledge base is intimately tied to the inclusiveness of its law-generative procedures, even democratic experimentalism.[23] The pragmatist's orientation is towards effect rather than cause, future rather than past. Looking forward, the claims of pragmatism bear some resemblance to those output criteria of the positivist centred on the precision, purposiveness, and wide-ranging remit and adaptability of law. Yet, unlike the positivist, the pragmatist is not primarily interested in the general 'rule of law' goods of certainty and consistency of regulation across the community as a whole, but in its more issue-specific benefits as a tool which is flexible in form, versatile in purpose, yet also stably reliable in its effects. For the pragmatist, the worth of law is instrumental rather than intrinsic, as a secure yet supple and adaptable means to a specific end. Law is technique, defined in terms of 'what works' rather than a code of higher norms elevated in accordance with the various foundational premises.[24] And while many would concede a pragmatic 'engineering'[25] or problem-solving role for law, with its pliant and highly versatile capacity for normative design, at the micro-level of contemporary public policy, a key question—nowhere more so, as we shall see, than in the circumstances of the European Union—concerns the terms on which a more root-and-branch pragmatism might come to coexist with or displace law's more common foundational narratives.

[23] See eg Michael Dorf and Charles Sabel, 'A Constitution of Democratic Experimentalism' (1998) 98 Columbia L Rev 267; Oliver Gerstenberg, *Euroconstitutionalism and its Discontents* (OUP 2018) esp ch 1.

[24] See eg Brian Butler, 'Legal Pragmatism: Banal or Beneficial as a Jurisprudential Position?' (2002) 3(2) Essays in Philosophy 14; for an explanation of the roots of modern legal instrumentalism and a thoroughgoing account of its problems, see Tamanaha (n 19).

[25] David Howarth, *Law as Engineering* (Elgar 2013).

IV. The State and the European Union: Structural Variation

The identification and assessment of these background circumstances brings us to the question of the distinctive assumptions associated with the European Union as a supranational polity, and so to the prior domain of political theory. If political theory is the primary locus of conceptions of how we conduct and should organise our living together in political communities, we can draw a further distinction between *substantive* and *structural* questions. Substantive questions concern normative assumptions and choices about the priority to be given to particular values and aspirations in the making of political community in, for example, the distinction between liberalism and republicanism, or between secular and theocratic states, or between Marxism and social democracy. Structural questions concern not the basis in terms of human values and aspirations of our living together but the basic shape and locus of the political community in which we conduct our living together, including the concentration or dispersal of authority, jurisdictional scope, and the terms of overlap or intersection with other political communities. These latter questions already arise within the state, in particular through the federal question, but they are more salient in the context of post-state polities, where variation from the statist norm in polity shape and in inter-polity relations can become much more pronounced. These structural arrangements inform conceptions of the capacity and role of law within the polity more directly than do substantive purposes and aspirations. For that reason, we will focus here on structural questions, taking the state as a key point of departure and comparison.

In basic structural terms, the European Union is *not* a state, at least not in any of our familiar registers of legal or political thought. Although it may seek to develop functional equivalents, the European Union lacks the crucial aspects of *unlimited final authority*, *originality of collective agency*, and *primacy of political identity*[26] associated with the mature character of the constitutional state, most emphatically in the high modern phase of the global system of states. The idea of a final authority not subject to limits beyond itself refers to the classical notion of state sovereignty. This holds that there exists one supreme ordering authority for a territorially located polity, an authority that defers to and is limited by no other internal or external authority and to which all other authorities must instead defer. Originality of collective agency refers to the idea of such state sovereignty as the product of an irreducible *pouvoir constituant* or constituent power; a power, typically residing in 'the people' or a similar abstract collective such as 'the nation', itself conceived of as a non-derivative and unencumbered source. Primacy of political identity refers to a deep aspect of political culture, to the idea that the framing political

[26] For an earlier treatment, see Neil Walker, 'The European Union's Unresolved Constitution' in Michel Rosenfeld and Andras Sajo (eds), *The Oxford Handbook of Comparative Constitutional Law* (OUP 2012) 1185–208.

persona of the subject is citizenship of the state polity, and that such citizenship announces the general associative bond through which any more particular political commitments and loyalties, interests, and beliefs are articulated and negotiated and in terms of which other commitments, loyalties, interests, and beliefs are circumscribed.

The system of public law is key to the articulation and sustenance of these three 'peaks' of unlimited final authority, original collective agency, and primary political identity. Unlimited final authority is a function of the interlocking of an autonomous legal order possessing an unchallenged and unfettered jurisdictional range, and a set of authoritative political institutions tailored to the pursuit of that legal mandate. Original collective agency is a function of an act or process of self-authorisation by which the constituent power is deemed to generate authorship or assume control of these sovereign institutions. Primacy of political identity depends, on the one hand, upon these constitutionally sourced legal measures and institutional orientations that designate the citizen *qua* citizen, and on the other, a socio-political culture, itself part product of the symbolic power of the constitutional order as a fount of common meaning, which encourages the *self*-identification of citizens as political community members. What is more, these three elements stand in a relationship of circular support and reinforcement. Sufficient affinity at the socio-cultural level is required to develop and sustain recognition of these sovereign legal and political institutions as self-authorised artefacts, which institutional accomplishment and event history in turn reinforce the common bond of citizenship.[27]

How does the European Union compare? Precisely because the European Union exists alongside and in relation to states, it does not and cannot possess these statist features of unlimited authority, original agency, and primary political identity, or at least not in the fullest sense associated with high modern statehood. While states themselves are challenged, altered, and somewhat diluted in their constitutional character by the rise of non-state political entities such as sub-state nations or the European Union, the fact that states still continue to claim and, in some measure, to possess attributes that are by their nature exclusive, precludes the European Union from possessing them.

But, how might we elaborate the comparative attributes of the European Union in more positive terms? In so doing in the somewhat stylised manner, summarised in Table 2.1, I emphatically do not suggest that these structural questions are resolved at the EU level. The sheer range and variation of theoretical output dealing with structural matters in the European Union, work which tends to go by the (somewhat one-sided) name of 'integration theory',[28] indicates otherwise. The aim

[27] See eg Dieter Grimm, 'The Achievement of Constitutionalism and its Prospects in a Changed World' in Petra Dobner and Martin Loughlin (eds), *Light of Constitutionalism?* (OUP 2010) 3–22.

[28] The three most significant schools of structural thought within integration theory are federalism, neofunctionalism, and intergovernmentalism, but there are countless nuances and variations.

instead is to show the conditions of possibility out of which the structural form of the European Union has evolved and may continue to do so. Within these parameters, there is much scope for choice, controversy, disagreement, and reformation in line with rather different visions of the scope and potential of the European Union as a polity type—which visions in turn may be connected to different preferences as to the substantive aims of the European Union.

Our comparative structural exercise can be organised under three general headings—*capacity*, *spatiality*, and *temporality*—each with more specific subheadings. We begin with the fundamental matter of *capacity*, and so with the more restricted breadth and depth of the EU polity horizon. The extent and intensity achievable through the high modern state in terms of its peaks of sovereignty, constituent power, and primary citizenship implies a claim to be the source and container of collective action for a political community which is only *self*-limiting in jurisdictional reach, asserts comprehensive normative capacity to deliver within that range, and provides the primary political frame of reference for its members. This is reflected in the self-referential character of the state's constitutional posture—its self-orientation as a *comprehensively* self-sufficient and *elementary* form of political organisation made up of individuals for whom it provides a *prior* political identity. In comparison, the European Union possesses both a narrower competence and a less penetrative reach within that narrower competence, and so a jurisdiction only *partial* in scope and effective capacity. The European Union is also a polity that, at least as understood in chronological terms, is constituted through and *derivative* of the states as the most elementary expression of constituent power, so attracting a political identity secondary and *accessory* to that of state citizenship.

The more restricted capacity of the EU polity finds a deeper explanation in terms of the very rationale of the entity in question. A useful starting point is Michael Oakeshott's understanding of the history of modern political thought and practice as a tension between two kinds of political association, each characterised with terms he draws from Roman private law: between *societas*, or civil association, on the one hand, and *universitas*, or enterprise association on the other.[29] Or to use Hayek's similar and derivative terminology, the distinction lies between *nomocracy* and *teleocracy*.[30] Put simply, the *societas* or nomocracy is based on the acceptance of common rules as grounding a notion of political society as a domain of relatively free-floating relationships without prior specification of common ends, while the *universitas* or teleocracy stands for a form of cooperation animated by some

For a good recent overview, see Sabine Saurugger, *Theoretical Approaches to European Integration* (Palgrave 2014).

[29] Michael Oakeshott, *On Human Conduct* (Clarendon 1975).
[30] Friedrich Von Hayek, *Law, Legislation and Liberty Vol.1—Rules and Order* (University of Chicago 1976).

specified collective purpose. As Oakeshott insists, there are no pure cases of either type, only hybrids variously placed along a continuum. Yet, based on this distinction, the state provides the more encompassing project, the settled framework for the organisation of a common form of life rather than, as in the European Union, at least in earlier incarnations, a bespoke tool for the pursuit of particular shared ends. Otherwise put, the state claims to embody a general public *good* of political community, whereas the European Union has been a vehicle for the pursuit of discrete public *goods*.[31]

The more limited perspective of the European Union, in turn, has implications for its spatiality—for how it relates to other polities implicated in the same territorial and jurisdictional space. The only *self*-limiting state polity treats other law-sites either as its (mutually exclusive) fully sovereign counterparts, or, at the other extreme, as entities to whom certain limited powers are delegated or that perform strictly demarcated functions. In contrast, the partial EU polity is also perforce a polity whose jurisdiction and capacity may, from one perspective, overlap the boundaries of other polities, and, from another perspective, represent the 'crowded space' or point of intersection of various different polities. These two perspectives on its situation—'inside-out' boundary overlap and 'outside-in' interlocking—indicate four further distinguishing features of the European Union as a structurally complex constitutional polity.

The first 'inside-out' perspective accounts for two contrasting features of the EU's open and overlapping boundaries—though here the caveat applies with particular force that the European Union has transformed the state itself in ways that soften its 'ideal typical' contrast with the European Union. On the one hand, as a limited polity in terms of scope and capacity, the EU's orientation towards states and other polities is not that of the modern state classically understood as the comprehensive and *exclusive* source of final authority, but instead often that of a collaborative and *complementary* polity, seeking through various inter-systemic normative 'bridging mechanisms'[32]—from the preliminary reference procedure to the use of the Open Method of Coordination—to coordinate its objectives and its means for realising its objectives with these other polities. On the other hand, the shift from self-reference to external reference also has a less harmonious connotation, and again the contrast with the system of high modern states, at least as conventionally understood, is marked. The exclusively empowered and self-sufficient state tends to treat its domain of authority, and the domain of authority of other exclusively empowered and self-sufficient states, in *monopolistic* terms. For its part, given its extensive overlap with other polities, primarily state polities, alongside and in tension with its collaborative approach to these other polities, the European

[31] See Neil Walker, 'The European Public Good and European Public Goods', manuscript available from the author.

[32] Stephen Weatherill, *Law and Integration in the European Union* (OUP 1995) chs 4 and 5.

Union can also find itself in a rivalrous and *competitive* relationship with these same polities over their respective domains of authority.[33]

The situation is further complicated by the third and fourth 'outside-in' relational dimensions of the EU polity. Here the logic of polity interpenetration extends a stage further, the environment of polity diversity understood not just to affect the margins of the EU polity but to shape its internal composition. Whereas the comprehensively and exclusively authorised state polity grounded in the unitary collective agency of the 'people' or 'nation' possesses a *simple* form of structural integrity, in which all institutional parts contribute to and are resolved in terms of one and the same polity whole, the European Union may instead be viewed as a *composite* entity. It is a hybrid—a 'mixed'[34] or 'compound'[35] structure—which through its different institutions (Council, European Council, Commission, Parliament, Court) with their different normative emphases reflects and interlocks its different polity-sourced parts.

As a further consequence of its unitary source, the state polity also possesses a basic *singularity* of normative design. It is based on a set of common commitments in which norms are either generally applicable across the polity as a whole, or where a measure of diversity is allowed to different territorial, ethnic, or functional parts, this is the product of a single, multilaterally negotiated, collectively endorsed and largely symmetrical design. In contrast, the European Union, reflected in and encouraged by five waves of enlargement, has increasingly come to permit a more *differentiated* normative arrangement where the separate national parts engage in bilateral negotiation with the supranational polity in pursuit of optimal arrangements. The most prominent cases are Economic and Monetary Union, with membership of the Eurozone gradually increasing from eleven to nineteen, and the Schengen Agreement on open borders, signed by five out of the then ten members thirty years ago and today comprising twenty-six parties, only twenty-two of them EU members. Yet this is the tip of the iceberg, with as many as fifty types of differentiation provided under the treaties.[36] Moreover, as in the abortive pre-Brexit agreement to exclude the United Kingdom from the *telos* of 'ever closer Union', discussions of the future of the European Union increasingly place a more differentiated architecture centre stage.[37]

[33] These other polities include other transnational organisations and non-EU states. For discussion of a range of complementary and competitive techniques in the EU's external relations, see Joanne Scott, 'Extraterritoriality and Territorial Extension in EU Law' (2013) 62 American J of Comparative L 87–125.

[34] See eg Giandomenico Majone, 'Delegation of Regulatory Powers in a Mixed Polity' (2002) 8 ELJ 319; MacCormick (n 1) ch 9.

[35] Sergio Fabbrini, *Compound Democracies: Why the United States and Europe are Becoming Similar* (OUP 2007).

[36] See eg Dirk Leuffen, Berthold Rittberger, and Frank Schimmelfennig, *Differentiated Integration: Explaining Variation in the European Union* (Palgrave 2013).

[37] General Secretariat of the Council, *European Council meeting (18–19 February 2016)—Conclusions* (EUCO 1/16); available at: https://www.consilium.europa.eu/media/21787/0216-euco-conclusions.pdf, accessed 28 June 2019.

Alongside these four spatial features of the constitutional particularity of the European Union there are two distinguishing features of its *temporality*. Although their resilience is highly variable[38] and their sequence of development differs[39]—we encounter the vast majority of enduring state constitutions and associated systems of public law as achieved states of affairs. We typically confront them as always/already 'thickly' *accomplished* projects whose dynamic is one of consolidation or adaptation. In contrast, the European Union today remains a constitutional work in progress—an *incipient* structure still self-consciously under construction rather than a fully realised form. Moreover, the EU's unfinished condition is not just empirical but also conceptual. Whereas the completeness of the state constitutional model presupposes a recognisable template for its mature form, and so a *determinacy* and finality of conception, the incompleteness of the European Union and its irreducibility to these state-centred terms suggests the absence of any such settled model of its mature form; an *indeterminacy* and open-endedness of conception that remains subject to contestation in terms of different general polity visions.

A final distinctive characteristic of EU constitutionalism flows from—indeed, summarises—all previous features. The state constitutional polity is a *settled* political form. Such is its embeddedness, self-sufficiency, self-containment, and structural unity, its typical manifestation as an already accomplished state and conformity to a familiar template that neither its basic eligibility as a constitutional polity nor the general terms on which that eligibility depends are the subject of serious contestation. That does not mean that its basic status *qua* constitutional state will not be challenged. The very identity of the state or, more commonly, its satisfaction of basic constitutional standards, may be contested, both externally and internally. But however sharply engaged, the contest is about specific cases rather than the general type. The European Union is instead a constitutionally unsettled and disputable polity. In light of its limited jurisdiction, its secondary form of political identity and agency, its open and unsettled relationship with states and other polities, its hybrid structure, its still emergent status and provisional conception, both its basic eligibility as a constitutional polity and the terms on which that eligibility rest are subject to continuing uncertainty and contestation.

In a nutshell, as set out in Table 2.1, whereas the state, at least in its dominant high modern form, has generally been considered as a comprehensive, elementary, prior, nomocratic, exclusive, monopolistic, relatively simple, singular,

[38] See eg Zachary Elkins, Tom Ginsburg, and James Melton, *The Endurance of National Constitutions* (CUP 2009) chs 2 and 4.

[39] See Michel Rosenfeld, *The Identity of the Constitutional Subject: Selfhood, Citizenship, Culture and Community* (Routledge 2010) chs 5–7.

Table 2.1 Structural comparison of state and European Union

STATE	EUROPEAN UNION
capacity	
comprehensive	partial
elementary	derivative
prior	accessory
nomocratic	teleocratic
spatiality	
exclusive	complementary
monopolistic	competitive
unitary	composite
singular	differentiated
temporality	
accomplished	incipient
determinate	indeterminate
settled	**unsettled**

accomplished, determinate, and settled political form and constitutional polity, the European Union remains a partial, derivative, accessory, teleocratic, complementary, competitive, composite, differentiated, incipient, indeterminate ,and unsettled political form and constitutional polity.

V. The Special Place of Public Law in the European Union

When we come to evaluate the role of public law and legal actors in the European Union in light of these structural features, we face a basic conundrum. On the one hand, EU law appears to lack many of the supportive conditions we are familiar with in the context of the state. On the other hand, that weakness notwithstanding, law appears even more central to the operation of the EU polity than to the national polity. Only by looking closely at how the deep assumptions associated with the different candidate schools of legal theory might apply in the case of the European Union, with its distinctive structural features, can we unlock this conundrum.

What of the absent supportive conditions? Jürgen Habermas has recently revived and reinforced a line of thinking that holds the EU legal order to be novel in its mode of articulation of the political order since, unlike the state, it is effectively underpinned neither by a sovereign political will nor by *sittlichkeit*—the idea of a prior common ethical framework.[40] These features often hang together in the state context, democratic foundations reflecting and reinforcing the existence of elements of a common societal culture, and law providing a medium to channel and express both. EU law, in contrast, cannot rely heavily on the claims of legal efficacy associated either with common will or with a strong cultural affinity, and so cannot draw unreservedly on the resources either of the positivist or the culturalist tradition of legal theory.

As regards the positivist tradition, the European Union today has no clear line of 'input legitimacy'.[41] Unlike the state, there is no single undisputed *voluntas*, whether the undifferentiated European citizenry, the European states—or 'peoples'—in perpetual combination, each national sovereign people considered separately, or some variation or mix of the above.[42] Importantly, however, in earlier phases of European integration, there was a case for arguing that, in pedigree terms, the European Union was merely a special form of delegate of each of the national sovereignties considered separately, their continuing mandate supplied by a rolling programme of international agreements. It was a delegated authority possessed of an unusually extensive but still clearly demarcated jurisdiction, fundamentally more concerned with the administrative implementation of prior Treaty objectives than the articulation of its own agenda.[43] Writing in the early 1980s, Weiler teased out the implications of this by drawing attention to the 'dual character of supranationalism'.[44] At that point, developed legal supranationalism in the internal market, framed by the European Court of Justice's (CJEU's) gradual assertion of the vigorous formal properties of the European Union as an autonomous legal system with a distinct Treaty pedigree, complete with supremacy, direct effect, pre-emptive authority, and independent standards of rights protection, stood in contrast to a modestly conceived political supranationalism. Yet the two were symbiotically related. The early prominence of legal supranationalism was encouraged or acquiesced in precisely *because* political supranationalism remained so modest, with a relatively limited jurisdiction and the Member States retaining a veto power in most areas of European policy-making within that jurisdiction.

[40] Jurgen Habermas, 'Plea for a Constitutionalization of International Law' (2014) 40 Philosophy and Social Criticism 5. For an influential earlier version of this argument, see Walter Hallstein, *Europe in the Making* (Allen and Unwin 1972).

[41] Fritz Scharpf, *Governing in Europe: Effective and Democratic?* (OUP 1999) ch 1.

[42] For discussion of options, see Mattias Patberg, 'Challenging the Masters of the Treaties: Emerging Narratives of Constituent Power in the European Union' (2018) 7 Global Constitutionalism 263.

[43] See eg Peter Lindseth, *Power and Legitimacy: Reconciling Europe and the Nation State* (OUP 2010).

[44] Joseph Weiler 'The Community System: The Dual Character of Supranationalism' (1981) Yearbook of European Law 267.

This element of input legitimacy was important not only in its own terms—as an assertion of an authoritative source—but also because it provided strong support for some of the 'output' benefits associated with positivism. The virtues of a coherent framework of legislative planning for the world's largest single market, and of certainty and predictability for those operating within the market, flowed more easily from a positivist baseline. So too, as regards the emergence of a prominent supranational judiciary, a cadre largely drawn from the civilian jurisdictions of Europe with their strong tradition of legal formalism; their confidently legalistic mindset and self-presentation was facilitated by a stable consensus over the clearly delineated sources of EU law, as well as by the emphasis within the first generation of EU law of a philosophy of individual economic right-centred 'negative integration'[45] with which the tradition of legal formalism had long been familiar. They were able to populate their newly autonomous legal order with rules and concepts that could themselves be treated as the autonomous product of that new order, and so insulated from the controversies of everyday politics and disputed long-term objectives.

But the conditions which allowed the EU's legislative product to be treated as an attenuated form of national sovereignty of each member state in aggregate did not last. From the Single European Act onwards, expansion of legislative jurisdiction beyond the positive-sum market-making core towards areas of security, economic, and social policy that were more transparently controversial or involved an uneven distribution of winners and losers across national boundaries, as well as the gradual development of Qualified Majority Voting in the Council and the greater involvement of the European Parliament in the legislative process in response to this extended jurisdiction, tended towards a more multi-polar balance of power. The pedigree question thus became more contentious—with the intensification of clashes between the CJEU and national apex courts about the division of competence before increasingly overlapping policy domains only the most obvious manifestation of this[46]—and the legitimacy dividend of law's connection to a democratic source of authority becoming ever more depleted.

As regards the culturalist tradition, the picture is no more encouraging. Claims linking EU to a common continental heritage have always been of limited strength and carried some unwanted connotations. There is a well-known narrative of 'common constitutional traditions' woven through the EU's attachment to fundamental rights, both in its case-law,[47] and later, its Treaty sources.[48] Additionally, many so-called general principles of EU law, such as proportionality, subsidiarity, legal certainty and the protection of fundamental rights, present both as the

[45] Scharpf (n 41) ch 2.

[46] See eg Neil Walker, 'Constitutional Pluralism Revisited' (2016) 23 ELJ 333.

[47] Case 11/70 *Internationale Handelsgesellschaft* [1970] ECR 1125 (*Solange 1*).

[48] Consolidated Version of the Treaty on European Union [2008] OJ C115/13, art 6.

consolidation of strands of a common legal culture and as the platform for new forms of mutual learning and convergence. Yet these claims are selective, arguably superficial, and in some cases carry imperialistic pretentions—conveying a sense of the innate superiority of the European legal cultural tradition.[49] They also run against the grain of successive Enlargements and the adoption of the motto of 'unity in diversity'.[50] More generally, they can be criticised as elitist—the product, at best, of a common judicial and administrative and diplomatic culture rather than a shared *popular* European culture.[51] The German-inspired idea of a *europäischer Verfassungsgerichtsverbund*—'A European Club of Constitutional Courts'[52]—may speak to the development of a common judicial vernacular amongst national constitutional courts and the CJEU that can deflect or moderate conflict arising from increasing jurisdictional overlap. But the very idea of 'club government' projects a sense of a closed circle of privilege, a contemplative arena distant from the material conditions and sentiments of ordinary Europeans.

The imperialist and elitist tendency is reinforced if we look to the relevance of the broader idealist tradition of legal theory in the development of EU law. In the grand claims made for EU law in the Preambles and common provisions of the key treaties, the emphasis upon universal morality is at least as strong as is the emphasis on continental cultural distinctiveness. This may reflect the inherent weakness of any claim to shared cultural distinctiveness. It may also reflects a sense that the two are convergent—that the universalism of values is proof of their European-ness and, equally, the European-ness of values is proof of their universalism.[53] In turn, this 'particular universalism'[54] finds an amplifying presence, but has also drawn a strong anti-imperial reaction, in the context of the EU's efforts to export its ethical

[49] As in the reference to a 'Special area of human hope' in the Preamble to the 2004 Draft Constitutional Treaty (2004/C 310).

[50] Which became the EU's motto in 2000.

[51] The German notion of a European *Rechtsgemeinschaft* (community of law)—influential in the early legal culture of integration through figures such as Walter Hallstein, the first President of the EEC (see n 40)—has been criticised as increasingly divorced from national legal-cultural concerns and sensibilities; see Armin von Bogdandy, 'Beyond the Rechtsgemeinschaft, with Trust—Reframing the Concept of European Rule of Law' Max Planck Institute for Comparative Public Law & International Law (MPIL Research Paper No. 2018-02); available at: https://ssrn.com/abstract=3103691, accessed 28 June 2019, On the foundational influence of European legal elites more generally, see, Antoine Vauchez, *Brokering Europe. Euro-Lawyers and the Making of a Transnational Policy* (CUP 2015).

[52] See eg Max Steinbas, 'Piercing the Hull' (*Verfassungsblog*, 12 January 2019); available at: https://verfassungsblog.de/piercing-the-hull/, accessed 28 June 2019.

[53] See eg the blend of implicit universalism and distinctiveness of origins evident in the statement of common founding values, Article 2 TEU. This blending is even more explicit in the Preamble to the 2004 Draft Constitutional Treaty, later reproduced in Art 1 of the 2007 Treaty of Lisbon (2007/C 306/01): 'Drawing inspiration from the cultural, religious and humanist inheritance of Europe, from which have developed the universal values of the inviolable and inalienable rights of the human person, freedom, democracy, equality and the rule of law. . . .'

[54] See eg Neil Walker 'The Place of European Law' in Grainne de Búrca and Joseph Weiler (eds), *The Worlds of EU Constitutionalism* (OUP 2012) 57–104.

standards and aspects of its legal *acquis*—whether through its Enlargement policy, its Neighbourhood Policy or in its external relations more broadly.[55]

If EU public law today represents neither a strong instrumental good tied to and backed by political will and a clear democratic voice, nor a strong symbolic good tied to and reflecting and reinforcing a particular cultural way of life, how might this apparent weakness underscore rather than undermine its functioning? The answer involves distilling virtue from necessity. The key lies in understanding EU law's *less supported* situation, compared to state law, as also one of *lesser dependence*, and so as also somehow requiring and enabling a more robustly autonomous role.

Renaud Dehousse and Joseph Weiler once alluded to this in describing EU law as the 'agent and object of integration';[56] both the means and end of the European project, each element supporting the other.[57] We may hold, more strongly, that EU law has established itself as the *primary* 'agent and object of integration' in the supranational context. The core technique of integration could not be to offer law as an instrument of political will backed by force, treating law as a *secondary* and derivative agent of political accomplishment—as in the positivist understanding of the state tradition. Nor could the object of integration be to sustain a thick political community of which law would be a trace and expression, so treating law as *secondary* object of integration—as in the context of the state and national culture. Rather, EU law was conceived of a new type of *primary* means and end—a division of legal labour that recalls and recasts the duality of law's normative and expressive functions. And crucially, in pursuing this double track EU law was bound to draw heavily upon the assets of legal pragmatism.

As regards, first, the question of agency, EU law is not an instrument for channelling the agency of a prior general political authority and its integrated sense of the public good; rather it is a primary means for stabilising our mutual commitments to achieve various complex public goods under a new transnational political authority. The lack of clear prior underpinnings of democratic authority together with other structural features of the EU—the emphasis on a plural, shifting and incomplete telos, the need to find optimal ways of interfacing with and adding value to other polities, and the complexities of managing internal

[55] For example, Article 3(1) TEU states that the Union's aim 'is to promote peace, its values and the well-being of its peoples'; these aims are reproduced in Article 3(5) (international promotion), and Article 49 (accession). For analysis, see eg Ian Manners, 'Normative Power Europe: A Contradiction in Terms?' (2002) 40 JCMS 235; Elisabeth Johansson-Nogues, 'The (Non) Normative Power EU and the European Neighbourhood Policy: An Exceptional Policy for an Exceptional Actor' (2007) 7 European Journal of Political Economy 181. See also Rachel Kleinfeld and Kalypso Nicolaidis 'Can a Post-Colonial Power Export the Rule of Law? Elements of a General Framework' in Gianluigi Palombella and Neil Walker (eds), *Relocating the Rule of Law* (Hart 2008) 139–69.

[56] Renaud Dehousse and Joseph Weiler, 'The Legal Dimension' in William Wallace (ed), *The Dynamics of European Integration* (Pinter 1990) 242–60, 244.

[57] See further, Daniel Augenstein and Mark Dawson, 'What Law for What Polity? "Integration Through Law" in the European Union Revisited' in Daniel Augenstein (ed), *'Integration through Law' Revisited: The Making of the European Polity* (CUP 2012) 1–10.

differentiation and of resolving the tensions within a composite institutional structure oriented towards different constituencies, combine to place a premium on the twin pragmatic virtues; both *security* and *versatility* of legal technique. Law matters so much precisely because of its capacity to 'get things done' where other steering mechanisms cannot—a capacity also associated with the 'output' side of legal positivism, but in the case of pragmatism, importantly, with the focus more on its dependable contextual adaptability and less on its steady generality and uniformity of coverage.

On the one hand, as we see from the earliest polity-defining cases of *Van Gend en Loos*[58] and *Costa*,[59] the clarity and certainty that law can deliver, especially as regards the 'four freedoms' with their emphasis upon the kinds of individual rights and obligations that law is effective at registering and protecting, secures against free-riding in a context of highly provisional trust where other underpinnings of commonality may be absent. In an environment of market-making where the temptation for each national member of the continental trade-liberalising cartel to engage in protectionism while exploiting the general opening of the markets of other national members posed a significant collective action problem, law performed a vital disciplining function. The reliable application and enforcement of the rules of the game by independent legal institutions, with the CJEU at the apex of the system, was crucial in rendering common commitments more credible.[60] On the other hand, the increasing need to track a shifting horizon of policy goals and to do so in a crowded regulatory space and in a context of multi-polar governance with high levels of internal plurality and polity overlap, has meant that law's versatility is repeatedly called upon. Throughout the history of EU law we see successive new waves of legally innovative methods of governance, from the basic form of directives, to the New Approach to Harmonization, to mutual recognition,[61] to Comitology, to Open Method of Co-ordination, to ever more complex forms of differentiated integration and ever more diverse methods of conditionality in external relations.[62] Where a different and changing legal ecosystem has required ever-altering methods, law's flexibility as a tool has been at a premium.

As regards EU law as an object of integration, again virtue has been a function of necessity. In the absence—or only flickering presence—of other 'sacred' objects on which it can reflect, whether a clear affirmation of continental popular will, a dimension of popular European culture, or a universal good, law, and

[58] Case 26/62 *Van Gend en Loos v Nederlandse Administratie der Belastingen* [1963] ECR 1.

[59] Case 6/64 *Flaminio Costa* v *ENEL* [1964] ECR 1141.

[60] Martin Shapiro, 'The European Court of Justice' in Paul Craig and Gráinne de Búrca (eds), *The Evolution of EU Law* (1st edn, OUP 1999) 321–41..

[61] Case 120/78 *Rewe-Zentral v Bundesmonopolverwaltung für Branntwein* [1979] ECR 649 *(Cassis de Dijon)*.

[62] See eg Grainne de Búrca and Joanne Scott (eds), *Law and New Governance in the EU and US* (Hart 2006).

often in ways that showcase its pragmatic achievements of securing piecemeal coordinated gains and displaying an agile aptitude for innovative design and adaptation, has often been projected as *itself* a prominent mark and symbol of community at the EU level. The Single Market, the Customs Union, the '1992' Project, the Area of Freedom Security and Justice, the Eurozone, European Monetary Union, the Euro itself, European citizenship, the Central and Eastern European Enlargement, and perhaps most vividly (if least successfully) of all, the Constitutional Treaty project of 2003–05,[63] are amongst the key artefacts presented as strongly legally coded measures of community. Separately and in combination these events, processes, and achievements are cast as cultural objects—manifestations of a shared world of meaning and accomplishment—that are legible and primarily expressible in legal form. They have become prominent *self-signifiers*, pointing to the significance of their own achievement, rather than being merely or mainly of secondly and derivative import in signifying other and prior cultural features of the polity, as is often the case with polity-evocative legal symbols in the national context.[64]

A similar point about the prominently legal coding of the EU's achievements can be made about its legal institutions, in particular the CJEU. As noted earlier, a posture of judicial neutrality has been assiduously cultivated by a Court composed of senior jurists from all member states and delivering judgment in a typically laconic and scrupulously non-partisan 'legalese' that draws heavily on the legal formalism of civilian national roots.[65] For all that it possessed a considerable margin of discretion in the early polity-building phase, the fact that the CJEU could nevertheless lay the constitutional foundation stones in a manner closely harmonised with its own ostensibly apolitical authority as an adjudicatory organ—in the language of individual rights and remedies familiar from the modern lexicon of European domestic adjudication[66]—helped cement its place as perhaps the key exhibit within the narrative of the EU as a pronouncedly *legal* accomplishment.

[63] For a retrospective, see Neil Walker, 'Europe's Constitutional Overture' in NW Barber, Maria Cahill, and Richard Ekins (eds), *The Rise and Fall of the European Constitution* (Hart 2018) 177–96; see also Miguel Maduro, 'The Importance of Being Called a Constitution: Constitutional Authority and the Authority of Constitutionalism' (2005) 3 ICON 332.

[64] As noted in Section I of the present chapter, public law always possesses expressive functions alongside its instrumental functions, but it is unusual for it to have such a prominent signifying function as in the EU case. The partial exception is as regards written constitutions. Even in the state context, constitutions, particularly those of long duration, can become key tokens of community in their own right. At the same time, however, more so than in the case of the legal symbols of the European Union, they remain powerful ways of projecting other accomplishments of common culture.

[65] See eg Joseph Weiler, *The Constitution of Europe* (CUP 1999) ch 5.

[66] See eg Alec Stone Sweet, 'The European Court of Justice' in Paul Craig and Gráinne de Búrca (eds), *The Evolution of EU Law* (2nd edn, OUP 2011) 121–54; Fritz Scharpf, 'Legitimacy in the Multilevel European Polity' in Petra Dobner and Martin Loughlin (eds), *The Twilight of Constitutionalism?* (OUP 2010) 89–119; Shapiro (n 60).

VI. Conclusion

Just how sustainable is the pragmatic turn in EU law? The lack of strong democratic and cultural supports that has led to a gradually greater emphasis on a pragmatic approach to EU law in the first place only encourages its continued expansion, yet this exposes both certain inherent weaknesses in the pragmatic approach and growing tensions in its relationship with other supporting legal narratives. We conclude by presenting these difficulties synoptically in terms of four paradoxes.

First, there is the *paradox of support*. The more we lack the democratic and cultural underpinnings familiar from state law, the more we rely on EU law to achieve progressive 'outputs' (that would be consistent with such sustained underpinnings) *without the support of* these underpinnings. Law has to do more pragmatic work just when it increasingly lacks the foundational supports that bolster legal pragmatism's virtue of security of delivery, and the more it strives to do so the more distant it becomes from these foundational supports. Examples include the raft of institutional responses to actual or anticipated political resistance to the lack of democratic undergirding in the supply of financial crisis relief measures that have involved attenuating power further from popular sources—in particular the centralising of executive authority in elite entities such as the European Central Bank, the Ecofin Council, and European Stability Mechanism (ESM).[67] This has been summarised as the problem of 'post-democratic executive federalism'.[68]

Second, and closely related, there is the *paradox of deformalisation*. The more we rely on law to achieve progressive results with unstable democratic and cultural underpinnings the more we depart from certain key virtues of legal formality that also underpin legal certainty and security. Examples include, again in the context of the financial crisis, the exploitation of the 'liminal' legal space of intergovernmental (rather than full EU) treaty option for the ESM Treaty, discretionary financial sanctions for deficit management failures, and the use of discretionary forms of conditionality for bail-outs—here including 'memoranda of understanding' only loosely related to legal competences and rights.[69] In other words, the security aspect of the post-foundational pragmatic justification of law may be further compromised by anti-formalist pressure in the teleocratic order demanding greater innovation and a departure from general norms.

Third, there is the *paradox of blocked progress*. Given the struggle to develop new policy agendas in a framework of partial competence, EU law confronts situations of blocked progress where it is exposed by its 'half-way house' jurisdiction, which

[67] See eg Damian Chalmers, 'The Retransformation of Europe' in Damien Chalmers, Markus Jachtenfuchs, and Christian Joerges (eds), *The End of the Eurocrats' Dream: Adjusting to European Diversity* (CUP 2016) 1–28..

[68] See Jurgen Habermas, *The Crisis of the European Union: A Response* (Polity 2012).

[69] See eg Menelaos Markakis and Paul Dermine, 'Bailouts, The Legal Status of Memoranda of Understanding and The Scope of Application of the EU Charter: *Florescu*' (2018) 55 CMLR 643–71.

in turn constrains and compromises legal pragmatism's other great virtue, its flexible capacity to deliver workable solutions. Recent examples include the crab-like development of citizenship law, where free movement rights are not consistently complemented by economically supported residence rights,[70] and in the context of the Eurozone, the absence of instruments of fiscal competence necessary to stabilise monetary policy.[71] In short, the lack of 'joined-up' competence can deprive EU law of the context-specific dexterity and room for manoeuvre on which its pragmatic credentials depend.

Fourthly, there is the *paradox of differentiation*. In a broader constitutional horizon, we can view the many-faceted post-Maastricht trend towards greater differentiation as a strategy of accommodation designed to safeguard the underlying integrity of the whole.[72] It speaks to a greater emphasis on optimal sector-specific outputs, and the pragmatic flexibility required for this, and lays less stress on the core idea (still less the uncontentious pedigree) of a singular jurisdictional foundation for the European Union as whole. We see the intensification of this approach in recent moves to revive the idea of multi-speed Europe, and similar models of flexible integration.[73] But as the Brexit process indicates, the idea of bespoke membership not only undermines the residual sense of a common cultural foundation but also the very sense of a basic unity of transnational discipline whose preservation is the ultimate strategic purpose of differentiation. And so we observe the endangering of an idea of generality and equality of treatment *across* sectors to match the endangering of the idea of generality and equality of treatment *within* sectors produced by the paradox of deformalisation. The corrosive effects of this danger can be seen both in the increasing indifference of Eurosceptic voices, both Brexiteer and more generally, to the very idea of a common project, and in the defensive reaction of an EU establishment concerned at the possible spread of a culture of disinvestment in the legal order.[74]

Law's pragmatic role, *in nuce*, depends on certain positive underpinnings, formal attributes, instrumental flexibilities, and a residual sense of a common cultural investment in a single project which come under increasing strain because of the very tendencies which made pragmatism such an attractive approach in the first place. Given this, what other resources if any, might EU law draw on or develop, and how in particular might it reinforce its own claim to legitimacy? What

[70] See in particular Case C-333/13 *Dano v Jobcenter Leipzig* ECLI:EU:C:2014:2358. See further Ronan McCrea, 'Forward or Back: The Future of European Integration and The Impossibility of the Status Quo' (2017) 3 ELJ 66–93.

[71] See McCrea (n 70); see also Alicia Hinarejos, *The Euro Area Crisis in Constitutional Perspective* (OUP 2015).

[72] See Leuffen, Rittberger, and Schimmelfennig (n 36).

[73] See eg European Commission, *White Paper on the Future of Europe* (2017) COM 2025.

[74] See eg Simon Hix and Nick Sitter 'Svexit or Huxit? How another country could follow the UK out of the EU' (*#LSE Thinks*, 30 January 2018); available at: http://eprints.lse.ac.uk/88244/1/brexit-2018-01-30-svexit-or-huxit-how-another-country-could-follow.pdf, accessed 28 June 2019.

of a more basic *framing* role? Can a renewed process of constitution-making, or its functional equivalent, help address the legitimacy deficits of EU law? Such a project should not embrace the constitution as a *merely* rhetorical device—involving the legally self-signifying projection of a new 'object' and mark of Community standing onto what was mainly the consolidation of 'old' text, which was part of the problem of the failed Draft Constitution of 2003–05.[75] Rather, it should envisage a new constitutional order as signalling and reflecting something more substantively polity-generative, which, perhaps through giving greater emphasis to the legitimising pedigree of the undifferentiated European citizenry alongside the traditional national constituencies, would help irrigate the democratic and cultural supports of which the European Union has always—and increasingly in recent years—been in short supply. Can EU law both continue to pursue an approach which explores an alternative pragmatic seam of legitimacy and, at the same time, bootstrap the very foundations on which public law has traditionally relied in the context of 'thick' polities? A vital question, but one for another day.[76]

[75] See Walker, 'Europe's Constitutional Overture' (n 63).

[76] See eg ibid; see also Paul Craig, 'Treaty Amendment, the Draft Constitution and European Integration' in NW Barber, Maria Cahill, and Richard Ekins (eds), *The Rise and Fall of the European Constitution* (Hart 2018) 51–72.

3

The Authority of the Administration

*Janet McLean**

I. Introduction

Administrative lawyers have for decades been concerned to provide justifications for the courts' supervisory jurisdiction in judicial review. Increasingly too, there has been renewed interest in the authority, or perhaps limited authority, of Parliament. I choose a different starting point for my discussion of justificatory authority in administrative law, and that is the authority claims of the administration itself in the British legal tradition.

Starting with the administration[1] instead of the courts or Parliament sheds new light on a number of issues which have long troubled administrative lawyers.[2] First, it helps us to explore the relationship between constitutional and administrative law in careful and subtle ways. Second, it avoids the thorny question of what counts as 'administrative law'. Third, it demonstrates the contingency of many of the authority claims which have been considered to animate judicial review doctrines in the modern era. The *ultra vires* theory, for example, which renders the administration the means by which Parliament transmits its will, can only apply to particular administrative forms, structures, and ways in which authority is conceived and allocated. Its claims to being *foundational* must be rejected.[3] Framing the analysis around the authority claims of the administration also challenges common law constitutionalism. The idea that the common law's role is to limit government power and protect individual rights has been criticised by Loughlin and others as privileging certain liberal values and hence 'peddling an ideology'.[4] By focusing on the authority claims of the administration itself, the central role of the common law in *constituting* as well as controlling authority is made plain.

[1] The term is anachronistic. I mean the officials who provide the interface between the government and the ordinary citizen. At times this has included the judges.

[2] See also Sidney Shapiro, Elizabeth Fisher, and Wendy Wagner, 'The Enlightenment of Administrative Law: Looking Inside the Agency for Legitimacy' (2012) 47 Wake Forest L Rev 463.

[3] On the difficulties and challenges in ascertaining 'foundations' see Samuel Moyn, *The Last Utopia: Human Rights In History* (Harvard UP 2012).

[4] Martin Loughlin, *Political Jurisprudence* (OUP 2017) 9.

Janet McLean, *The Authority of the Administration* In: *The Foundations and Future of Public Law.* Edited by: Elizabeth Fisher, Jeff King, Alison L Young, Oxford University Press (2020). © Oxford University Press.
DOI: 10.1093/oso/9780198845249.003.0003

I approach the authority claims of the administration more as a historian of thought than as a common lawyer for these purposes. That is, I attempt to understand the history of administration in light of contemporary self-understandings and not in order to establish the pedigree of a particular doctrinal approach or set of values,[5] or, as some have recently attempted, to unseat the contemporary administrative state altogether.[6] This is not the common law story of the inexorable progress of the law of the administration or of judicial review doctrine. No fully autonomous rendering of the common law is possible even if the common law's *claims* to autonomy are an important part of the story. Such an approach helps us to identify epochal change as well as path dependency and continuity. The fit between particular judicial review, tortious, and other doctrines depends in part on the logic of the authority claims of the administration itself. This may help to explain some of the ways in which judicial review has developed over time, account for its current 'theoretical turn', and provide a different theoretical starting point for conceptualising contemporary judicial review.

The bases of the authority claims of the administration have radically changed over the course of centuries. The concept from which the authority claims of administration were traditionally derived was that of 'office', and it is with the concept of office I propose to start. The dominant twentieth-century idea of a centralised administrative hierarchy which operates collectively and under direction from statute or the Minister is a relatively recent phenomenon and one that has only partially survived the advent of new public management and new administrative techniques.

I identify four distinct periods in which the authority claims of the administration have been significant for the broader narrative of administrative law in the British legal tradition: the seventeenth century in which the concept of office helped to limit Kingly power and secure the independence of the subordinate official; the eighteenth century in which the concept of office was imbued with the idea of public trust; the nineteenth century in which independent office-holding gradually gave way to a more centralised bureaucratic hierarchy staffed by civil servants; and the democratic justifications for administration in the twentieth century. In each era, the authority claims of the administration are reflected in the frameworks for juridical supervision and control. In the present day we are in the process of rethinking whence administrators derive their legitimacy, and the appropriate juridical responses are being adjusted accordingly.

[5] See eg Paul Craig, *UK, EU and Global Administrative Law: Foundations and Challenges* (CUP 2015) 36 ff discussing proportionality.

[6] Philip Hamburger, *Is Administrative Law Unlawful?* (University of Chicago Press 2014).

II. Office in the High and Low Politics of the Seventeenth Century

Understandably, modern common law constitutionalists tend to look to the seventeenth century for their foundations. It is to the high constitutional politics of the seventeenth century concerning the prerogatives of the King and powers of Parliament to which they tend to turn.[7] Paul Craig, for example, liberally cites the cases which attempted to limit the King's prerogative as providing the foundations of judicial review.[8] Trevor Allan cites Coke CJ's dicta in *Dr Bonham's* case about the power in the judges to control Acts of Parliament.[9] This is indeed the era which sought to establish the distinct and putatively superior modes of reasoning of the common law despite the plaintive rejoinder of Charles I that he too had the capacity for reason.[10] Liberal readings by contemporary common law constitutionalists (not necessarily authentically Lockean but claiming his theories nonetheless) tend to cast the whole era as one in which the liberties of the people were asserted and upheld against the sovereign (though those liberty claims mostly took the form of rhetoric and legal dicta).[11]

My reading of the seventeenth century does not start with high constitutional politics, but rather with the local administration. This is because the interface between government and the ordinary citizen took place primarily at the local level through corporations, townships, parishes, chartered boroughs, and hundreds. The relationship between central and local government was mediated by local gentry who took up the roles of county officials, sheriffs and under-sheriffs, and Justices of the Peace. The authority of such people depended as much upon their local social standing as it did upon their appointment by the King. Charles I found to his chagrin that his replacements for uncooperative Justices of the Peace were often no more obedient than their predecessors.

[7] Hamburger (n 6) and see Paul Craig 'The Legitimacy of US Administrative Law and the Foundations of English Administrative Law: Setting the Historical Record Straight' (Oxford Legal Studies Research Paper No 44/2016); available at: https://papers.ssrn.com/sol3/papers.cfm?abstract_id=2802784, accessed 28 June 2019; Phillip Hamburger, 'Early Prerogative and Administrative Power: A Response to Paul Craig' (2016) 81 Mo L Rev 939 and Adrian Vermuele, 'No: Review of Philip Hamburger, Is Administrative law Unlawful?' (2014) 93 Texas L Rev 1521.

[8] Paul Craig, 'Ultra Vires and the Foundations of Judicial Review' (1998) 57 CLJ 63, 81, 88.

[9] TRS Allan, *The Sovereignty of Law* (OUP 2013) 155; TRS Allan, 'Constitutional Foundations of Judicial Review' (2002) 61 CLJ 88, 90.

[10] Jonathan Scott, *Commonwealth Principles: Republican Writing of the English Revolution* (CUP 2004) 25.

[11] There was, for example, a loss of confidence in the courts after *Hampden's* case (ship money) in which the judges ruled seven to five in favour of the Crown, and again after the later decision in *Godden v Hales* which favoured King James II. It has been suggested that the dicta in *Dr Bonham's* case was ignored until 1765 when it was invoked by the Massachusetts Assembly to declare the Stamp Act void see Howard Nenner, 'Law, Liberty, and Property: The Constitution in Retrospect from 1689' in JR Jones (ed), *Liberty Secured? Britain Before and After 1688* (Stanford UP 1992) 88–121, 98. However, Holt CJ referred to it in 1701 in *City of London v Wood* as 'far from any extravagancy' 88 Eng Rep 1602.

The significance of local control accounts for the surprising degree of administrative continuity despite the disruptions of the seventeenth century.[12] The Independents of the Long Parliament and Commonwealth actively fostered such local authority.[13] The excise system which funded the Parliament's army, for example, has been credited with success because it levied a fixed total of excise but left it to local officials to work out how the tax burden would be distributed.[14]

Edith Henderson argues that the doctrine of limited judicial review was worked out in the seventeenth and eighteenth centuries in connection with these agencies of local government. The seminal case which is usually taken to be the forerunner of the writ of mandamus involves just such a local dispute. James Bagg[15] was a burgess at Plymouth who had criticised the mayor and his fellow burgesses and was consequently removed from office. The King's Bench regarded him as having been unlawfully deprived of office and reinstated him. Henderson identifies the case as one of a number of disputes out of which a distinction between 'sedition or contempt for authority and legitimate disagreement' was beginning to emerge.[16] While *Bagg's* case can be read in this way as fitting squarely within a liberal constitutionalist concern for liberty, it also concerns how authority is constituted and how sovereignty is to be discharged.

In *Bagg's* case, Coke CJ asserted the power in the King's courts not only to correct errors in judicial proceedings but also in relation to extra-judicial misdemeanours. Property was the basis on which the courts could intervene against arbitrary removal in this matter of public concern: Coke CJ characterised the public office of a burgesse as a *freehold* consisting of Bagg's interest in the lands of the corporation. The most directly challenging aspect of his judgment, in terms of the high politics of the day, was Coke CJ's claim that the King's prerogative to do justice had now passed to the courts.

The seventeenth century was undoubtedly a critical time in reinforcing the authority and autonomy of the common law and simultaneously of the judges as independent office-holders. Indeed, in certain writings and speeches of the period, the laws too were treated as property and a part of the ancient titles inherited by Englishmen: 'Laws, when made, were to become the joint property of those who made them, and henceforth not to be altered or repealed except by consent of all the property holders involved.'[17]

[12] Michael Braddick, *God's Fury, England's Fire* (Penguin 2008); Jonathan Scott, *Commonwealth Principles: Republican Writing of the English Revolution* (CUP 2004) 8.

[13] GE Aylmer, *The State's Servants: The Civil Service of the English Republic 1649–1660* (Routledge 1961) 29.

[14] Ibid.

[15] *James Bagg's Case* 11 Co Rep 93b, 95–7.

[16] Edith Henderson *Foundation of English Administrative Law: Certiorari and Mandamus in the Seventeenth Century* (William Hein 1963) 74.

[17] Nenner (n 11) 88, 93.

Bodin's political theory from the previous century, with which Coke CJ was fully conversant, offered some support for this approach. Bodin was read and admired by James I as an apologist for absolute sovereignty. But Bodin also warned of the inadvisability of a sovereign Prince governing by way of personal rule. Some of these warnings were prudential. It was better for the Prince to bestow awards and honours and to leave potentially unpopular tasks such as adjudication to officials.[18] More fundamentally, personal or direct rule tends to tyranny.[19]

Bodin's absolute version of sovereignty was mitigated by his recognition of officials who were neither sovereigns nor subjects. Bodin's understanding was that office-holding *by definition* conferred a jural status: an officer (properly so called) 'is a public person who has an ordinary charge defined by law';[20] 'Office is a thing borrowed . . . which the owner cannot demand again before the time it was lent for be expired.'[21]

It was through such officials who mediated between sovereigns and subjects that some of the earlier medieval juristic tradition could continue to apply even in the face of an absolute sovereign. An official could by varying degrees be independent of a sovereign's arbitrary will. It was this idea of office that would make government by law and administrative law possible.[22] Law helped initially to define the independence of the official from the King, and later the obligations of office to the public.

In recognising the property in office in *Bagg's* case, and using it as the basis of protection against arbitrary removal, Coke CJ was asserting the independence of office, including (albeit indirectly) the office of the judge. Of course, as Coke CJ was all too aware, independence in practice depended on two interrelated things: tenure and the terms of delegation of authority. At the time, English judges held office at the King's pleasure (and in Bodin's terms were technically commissioners rather than officers). By contrast, many of the Crown's executive agents, more directly under the King's command, held positions for life.

How authority was conferred on officials differed markedly. In the language of the time, all authority was *delegated* from the King. But delegation could be used to refer to a general mandate to act (jurisdiction conferring, if you will) or it could connote authorising an agent to act on behalf of the principal channelling the principal's wishes (a puppet tethered to its master's will),[23] or even as an agent acting in the principal's interests (a concept closer to trust).[24] Bodin distinguished

[18] Jean Bodin, *Six Books of the Commonwealth* (M J Tooley trans, Basil Blackwell, 1967 [1586]) 134.

[19] Ibid 129.

[20] Ibid 84.

[21] J Bodin, *Commonweale*, 282 [iii, 2] quoted in Daniel Lee, '"Office is a Thing Borrowed": Jean Bodin on Offices and Seigneurial Government' (2013) 41 Political Theory 420.

[22] Lee (n 21) 428Cf J Franklin 'Introduction' in *Jean Bodin On Sovereignty* (Franklin trans CUP 1992) xiv.

[23] Lee (n 21) 423.

[24] Farrah Ahmed, 'The Delegation Theory of Judicial Review', Paper to the Melbourne Oxford Biennial Public Law Conference (July 2018) (cited with permission).

between different kinds of conferrals of power and the discretion they conferred.[25] Strikingly, he viewed the conferral of discretion or general jurisdiction as the least problematic, and regarded them as subject to law and equity. He was more exercised about the circumstances in which the sovereign commanded an official directly and when an official should remonstrate with a sovereign or resign in the face of a particular command.[26]

Bagg's case concerned the independence of office, not only with clear implications for the judges themselves but for the range of other offices too. There is another, more subtle, connection between *Bagg's* case and high constitutional politics. The aim of much of the Parliamentary rhetoric in the first half of the century

> was to draw a distinction between the natural person of the King and the public authority of his office, and to suggest that one could exist independently of the other... Separating that authority [of institutions and officials] from the person of Charles I ... allowed [officials] to defy the King's commands while claiming to defend the integrity of his royal office.[27]

Throughout Europe, at the time, offices for profit were regarded as a species of private property which could be sold and exchanged. Bodin objected to this idea: '[T]here is no doubt, but that all estates, magistrats, and offices, do in propertie belong unto the Commonweale [republique], rest and remaine in the possession and propertie of the Commonweale [republique], as a thing put in trust.'[28] They should not be treated as the private property of the sovereign, but rather as 'depersonalized state sovereignty'.[29] These ideas are clearly reflected in some of the parliamentary speeches during the reign of Charles I:

> His Majesty's towns are no more his own than his Kingdom is his own, and his Kingdom is no more his own than his people are his own ... This erroneous maxim being infused into Princes, that their Kingdoms are their own and that they may do with them what they will ... is the root of all the subjects' misery, and of all the invading of their just rights and liberties. Whereas, indeed they are only entrusted with their Kingdoms and with their towns and with their people and with the public treasure of the commonwealth and whatsoever is brought therewith.[30]

25 Lee (n 21) 420.
26 Bodin, *Six Books of the Commonwealth* (n 18) iii, iv, and v, 85–91.
27 James Hart, *The Rule of Law 1603–1660: Crowns, Courts and Judges* (Routledge 2014) 208.
28 Lee (n 21) 427 *Commonweale* 330, 333 [111, 5].
29 Lee (n 21) 427.
30 J Hart (n 28) quoting William Cobbett (ed), *The Parliamentary History of England* 36 Vols (1806–20) vol ii, 1310.

These legal struggles to discipline the personal rule of Kings involved the invocation of the concept of office in relation to the King himself. Central to the political struggles of the period was the claim that the office of the King then, like other offices including those of the judges, was an invention of law and reason rather than personal will. The Crown was not to be considered an estate in fee but rather a property in trust—an office 'not in property but in care'.[31] Once an office is constituted and regulated by law as legally separate from the person and the state, it is but a short step to suggest it could be relinquished or forfeited. The 1689 Scottish Claim of Right would indeed describe James II as having 'forfeited' the Crown.

The relationship between the nascent ideas of office in *Bagg's* case and the high politics of the period concerning the nature and extent of the King's prerogative, has a number of layers. Central concepts travelled in both directions between administration and constitutional law. There were issues relating to delegation—but unlike the *ultra vires* arguments of the late nineteenth and twentieth centuries, the delegation of duties to officers was used in significant part to *resist* the transfer of the sovereign's will to his officials.[32] There were issues of liberty at stake but in important ways it was the liberty to participate in politics that was valued and thus the controversies involved the constitution of authority. This was a republican moment as well as a natural law one.

III. Propriety and the Official

The guaranteed tenure and independence of the judges would be part of the revolutionary constitutional settlement. Other issues surrounding office, and particularly the relationship of office to property, continued into the long eighteenth century but took on new political and legal forms. The eighteenth century is a period very much studied by American constitutional lawyers,[33] but a typical public lawyer from the United Kingdom and its former dominions today is likely only to recall cases such as *Entick v Carrington* (1765)[34] which continue the seventeenth-century common law constitutionalist theme that the common law's role is to protect the individual from the state. Pocock suggests that such a liberal reading is wildly out of step with the political preoccupations of English politics during the eighteenth century:

[31] Nenner (n 11) 120.

[32] Throughout the Commonwealth period more offices were created by statute than by patent and were salaried. For the first time the question was raised whether a statute could override a patent. Aylmer (n 14), 59, 83.

[33] For example, Nicholas Parrillo, *Against the Profit Motive: The Salary Revolution in American Government 1780–1940* (Yale UP 2013).

[34] 1765 19 Howell's State Trials 1029, 95 ER 807.

> From 1688 to 1776 (and after), the central question in Anglophone political theory was not whether a ruler could be resisted for misconduct, but whether a regime founded on patronage, public debt, and professionalization of the armed forces, did not corrupt both governors and governed; and corruption was a problem in virtue, not in right, which could never be solved by asserting a right of resistance. Political thought therefore moves decisively, though never irrevocably, out of the law-centred paradigm and into the paradigm of virtue and corruption.[35]

Even if Pocock's reading is an overly republican one, he is surely correct that the common law constitutionalist 'rights' story does not fully capture many of the important issues confronting government in the eighteenth century. The administration was notoriously a patchwork of old and new—many parts still dating from Tudor times.[36] Aspects of central administration—such as excise, the navy, the treasury—were becoming more centralised and hierarchical even in the eighteenth century, but even then much of the administration still depended on individual office-holders such as Post Master General who employed his own servants, and took fees to cover his expenses, or like Justices of the Peace, were unpaid. Officials, such as Justices of the Peace, were sometimes subject to specific direction conveyed in the terms of their appointment, or by Parliament (their jurisdiction expanded enormously during this period and there were instructions about when they had to decide in pairs etc). In general, it seems that delegations continued to be much more in the form of a mandate to act rather than in the form of the transmission of the will of a political principal. Statutes sometimes conferred duties or more often jurisdiction upon such officials, but public duties were as often treated as the creations of the common law. In any event, the distinction between statute and the common law was not of the same import as it would be today given that statutes were generally regarded at that time as declaratory of the common law—a view that can be traced back to Coke CJ.[37]

There is admittedly a level of controversy about the extent to which elements of republican thought from the seventeenth century continued to have a general influence into the eighteenth century.[38] There is at least some evidence that Whigs were often regarded as proto-republicans, and country Tories accepted some of republicanism's basic tenets in their defence of local self-government.[39] Many of republicanism's central concerns about the encouragement of virtue, the elimination of corruption, and particularly the participation and self-government of the

[35] JGA Pocock, *Virtue, Commerce and History, Essays on Political Thought and History Chiefly in the Eighteenth Century* (CUP 2010) 48.

[36] John Brewer, *The Sinews of Power: War, Money and the English State 1688–1783* (Harvard UP 1990) quoting Alymer (n 13) 71.

[37] Nenner (n 11) 99–100.

[38] See Martin Loughlin, 'Towards a Republican Revival?' (2006) 26 OJLS 425, 434.

[39] See Nenner (n 11) 275.

independent propertied citizen can be traced into the legal sources. I disagree with Pocock that there is no law-centred narrative of this century to be told, though admittedly it is a complex and hitherto obscure one. The need to separate public office from the person remained as urgent as ever as a matter of high as well as low politics. And while the cultivation of public trust tended to be treated as a matter for personal morality and even politeness for citizens and office-holders alike, law was central in defining, protecting, and constraining office-holding in particular. There is a juristic story to be told and that juristic story is inextricably linked to the bases on which the administration sought to maintain its legitimacy. I take three aspects of that story in turn: the enforcement of virtue, upholding independence of office, and the regulation of the property interest.

A. Reinforcing civic virtue

In the eighteenth century, the problem of corruption was endemic and anxiety about a want of virtue was widespread. Citizens, voters, Members of Parliament, as well as officials were all tempted by corrupt practices. The practice of Aristotelian virtue positively required citizens to engage in public life, ruling for the public good rather than for private interest, and being ruled by turns. The purpose of politics was to make men better:[40] to throw off the government of will, sin, and passion, and to be governed by reason. Therein lay a set of inherent tensions: at the same time as taking up the duties of public office was a quintessential example of participation in public life, in so doing office-holders were exposed to some of the worse temptations of venality and self-interest.[41] If office-holders were willing to exert themselves, the possibilities for exploiting the profit-making potential of offices were manifold (bribery, extortion, perquisites, and misappropriation were rife); the more indolent or incompetent could neglect their duties or seek passive income from sinecures. As a justification for authority, the cultivation of virtue appears unrealistic not least during such a venal age. The common law and, by the end of the century, increasingly statute, had an important, if mainly symbolic role in enforcing virtue. Attempts at the enforcement of civic duty included the requirement to take up particular offices upon pain of a fine for refusal (a common law offence), the use of oaths of office as a form of moral commitment, and the payment of bonds in advance of taking appointment as sureties.

[40] These ideas had surfaced earlier during the Commonwealth in the writings of Sydney and Milton (but not Harrington), see Scott (n 10) 187.

[41] See eg Mark Latham, '"The City Has Been Wronged and Abused": Institutional Corruption in the Eighteenth Century' (2015) 68 Economic History Review 1038; A Graham, 'Auditing Leviathan: Corruption and State Formation in Early Eighteenth Century Britain' (2013) CXXVIII No 533 English Historical Review, 806.

Administrative law, broadly conceived, during this period, was calibrated to the perceived problems in public administration. What is striking to modern eyes is the use of the criminal law as an important public law control mechanism against public officials specifically. The more serious issues of maladministration could be dealt with by the common law criminal offences of 'misconduct in public office' and 'wilful neglect of public office' (ie offences of both misfeasance and nonfeasance). There was also an extensive case law which finely distinguished between extortion and bribery (which were criminal offences), and the fees, perquisites, and gifts properly given and taken according to 'ancient customs of the office'.[42] There was sometimes substantive overlap in the content of the misconduct offences and the prerogative writ of certiorari and the fledgling doctrine of misfeasance in public office (*Ashby v White*).[43]

Both criminal and civilian procedures were concerned to ensure that a decision-maker ought not to be a judge in his own cause,[44] and ought not to misuse his powers. But unlike the prerogative writs which were instruments of centralising control, the criminal offences were in theory, if not in practice, oriented to enforcing *public-facing* accountabilities. The offence of misconduct in public office was defined as applying to 'offices of trust concerning the public'.[45] Moreover, unlike the prerogative writs, their *central* focus was on an individual official's motives and intentions.[46]

Over the eighteenth century these public trust offences evolved into a mechanism by which superior officials could control their subordinates.[47] More specific statutory offences which supplemented the common law became much more prevalent by the beginning of the nineteenth century.[48] By then too there were more centrally appointed officials more directly answerable to the centre rather than to local communities. It is difficult to assess the relative importance of these different means of defining and constraining the duties of public office, but the offence

[42] Quantum meruit actions by officials for unpaid fees were used to control the other side of the ledger. The judges had a potentially large role in monitoring 'decentralised negotiations' about fee taking and consequently profit making in office. Of course, the judicial system itself was riven with the same practices. One striking example comes from the Seal Office at the Court which operated a 'special holiday' system. On those 'special' days officers attended but the door would be closed and the work would only be performed after a special payment was made. De Grey CJ said 'I do by no means approve of these self-made holidays. The public offices ought to be open, and justice ought to be unbought.' The court said that the practice of taking a pretended holiday for thirty-five years was not sufficient to be an ancient custom but was, rather, a 'modern encroachment' (*Figgins v Willie* (1777) 3 Black W 1186).

[43] [1790] Eng Rep 55;(1703) 2 Ld Raym 938; 1 Smith LC (13th edn) 253; [1790] Eng R 55; 92 ER 126 discussed in Mark Aronson, 'Misfeasance in Public Office: A Very Peculiar Tort' (2011) 35 Melb ULR 1.

[44] Jeremy Horder, *Criminal Misconduct in Office* (OUP 2018) 63 referencing *R v Burdett* (1697) 1 Ld Raym 148 as a case outside the judicial context. See also *City of London v Wood* 12 Mod 669, 88 Eng Rep 1592 (1702) and *Dr Bonham's* Case.

[45] Horder (n 44) 53 citing *R v Bembridge* (1783) 3 Doug 327.

[46] Ibid 55, 67.

[47] Ibid 77ff

[48] Fines were calibrated to the office for example in *Warne v Varley* 6 TR 443 (1795) the default of the supervisor of leather manufacture default was satisfied by the payment of a £10 fine.

of neglect of duty at least seems to have been significant and frequently used.[49] Functionally they performed a very similar purpose to the prerogative writs.

The fact that vicarious liability often resided in the office-holder for the acts of his servants goes some way towards explaining why high officials were often regarded as *victims* of the misconduct of their inferiors rather than as perpetrators.[50] This may have been one reason for the increasing desire for stronger controls by superiors over their subordinates as the eighteenth century wore on. The rules of vicarious liability varied according to the laws of the particular office. In *Lane v Cotton* (1701)[51] three judges found only the salaried employee and not the Post Master General was answerable for an exchequer bill lost in the post. They found that it would have been impossible to oversee everyone in his service 'at such distant places ... and by so many hands'. In at least one report they also gave the reason that there was a clause in the Post Master General's patent which said he would not be answerable for under offices. Holt CJ was loud in his dissent that the 'law makes an officer, whoever he may be, answerable both for himself and his deputy for the act of the deputy is adjudged as the act of the principal, who may displace him at pleasure, and there is no need for a contract, because the law makes him answerable' as a consequence of taking up public employment. He is the Post Master General, to whom 'the care of the whole is committed ... and the rest are but his deputies ... for his undertaking is in proportion to his power and convenience'.[52]

Holt CJ's view later in the century prevailed in relation to sheriffs. In *Woodgate v Knatchbull* [53] a sheriff *was* held to be vicariously liable for the wrongdoing of his bailiff in the wrongful taking of fees.[54] The sheriff was indemnified by his employees by way of the sureties taken at their appointment for their good behaviour. The court was more doubtful about whether a sheriff would have to answer for all *criminal* wrongdoing, suggesting that he could not be imprisoned or indicted but could be liable for damages and fines and could be required to make pecuniary satisfaction.[55] For civil liability purposes Buller J suggests '[t]he sheriff is the only officer known to this Court; he may employ whom he pleases; but he is answerable civiliter for the acts of all those employed by him'.[56]

49 Horder (n 44) 75.

50 As Horder observes, ibid 53

51 91 Eng Rep 1701.

52 Holt KB 583.

53 2 TR 155 (1787). But see by contrast, *Whitfield v Lord Le Despencer* 2 Cowp 762 (1778) in which Lord Mansfield stated in a categorical fashion that the Post Master 'like all other Public officers, such as the Lords Commissioners of the Treasury, The Commissioners of Customs and Excise, The Auditors of the Exchequer &c. who were never thought liable for any negligence or misconduct of the inferior officers of their several departments' (766). He overstates the case. By the late eighteenth century these were the most centralised departments and office was held by several commissioners jointly.

54 A Sheriff was also civilly liable for false imprisonment and trespass. By contrast a Deputy could enforce the non-payment of fees by way of a quantum meruit action.

55 See (n 51) 156.

56 Ibid [155–56]. The accountability of the individual office-holder was here viewed as more important than enforcing any internal hierarchy of command. An officer who levied a tax illegally was liable in damages even though his warrant was regular in form. A lowly constable too could be distrained

There was a range of common law rules, alongside the prerogative writs, which was specifically public in nature and whose primary concern was to promote the sense of public duty and virtue in administration. Once the worst misconduct had been controlled and eliminated, the discretion left to the decision-maker was not viewed with the same alarm as it would attract later in the twentieth century because personal standing and social authority were its justification.

B. Upholding independence

The use of the language of independence in the legal sources is the most direct connection with republican thought. Certain kinds of office-holding were considered corrupting in the eighteenth-century sense that they had the potential to destroy the 'independence' essential for republican virtue. Aristotle emphasised the importance of material independence as the proper basis for citizenship. Offices held of the Crown were viewed as particularly harmful:

> [They potentially] destroyed the balance of the constitution by destroying that personal independence which could only belong to men whose property was their own and did not consist in expectations from the men in government; and the moral quality which only propertied independence could confer, and which became almost indistinguishable from property itself, was known as virtue.[57]

Anxiety to secure the independence of office, at least from *Crown* patronage, was renewed from about 1675. Concerns about the independence of office-holders from the sovereign in Parliament began to take practical statutory form. The Act of Settlement protected the independence of judicial officers by requiring cause for their removal. According to its original terms, intended to take effect when the Hanoverians came to the throne, the Act also laid down that no person who held an office or place of profit under the Crown was able to serve as a member of the Commons. Before the provision came into effect it was changed to disqualify from the House of Commons only a person having an office or a place of profit created after 25 October 1705.[58] Accepting such an office voided election to the House, although a person was capable of standing for re-election. Effectively the provision divided offices into new and old. Each time a new office was created by statute, its effects on parliamentary qualification were considered. Numerous further statutes

on a warrant regular in form for a wrong that was not his—effectively acting as the insurer. JPs were liable in damages under an unlawful warrant for actions outside the record.

[57] Pocock (n 35) 66.

[58] See 4 Anne c 8 (1705) and 6 Anne c 41 (1707).

followed with lists of disqualifications.[59] The practice which has emerged even to the present day owes its origins to this period: holders of high office (tending to be older offices) can sit in the Commons, while holders of subordinate offices are generally disqualified from sitting.[60] The distinction between high political and subordinate offices (which we would now call the public/civil service) was a thin and originally an arbitrary one.

Administrators, for their part, sought to distance themselves from parliamentary politics. The Whig purges of Jacobite (1694–95) and later Tory officials alleged to be disloyal to the Hanoverian Crown (1715–17), were widely condemned as 'extremely obstructive of good government'.[61] According to a contemporary account, excessive politicking was regarded as leading to 'administrative confusion, low morale, and uncertain prospects for employment . . . emboldening the bad and terrifying the good' and 'limiting security of tenure'.[62] The same excise officers collected taxes for Jacobite and Hanoverian Kings alike.

Although holding offices from the crown attracted the most disquiet, in fact *all* office-holding affected independence because every office was in someone's gift and its grant required the exercise of patronage which created relationships of dependence. Without a patron one could not obtain office or do much else.

Patronage reflected social standing and cut across political party lines. A client would be accountable to his patron and could sometimes be sanctioned by him or her for poor conduct.[63] Such ties were at first a substitute for party loyalty and later became absorbed by party. Despite Pitt's attempts to do something about patronage later in the eighteenth century, it survived the reform and departmentalisation of certain parts of the state and reinforced departmental loyalties and rivalries between different departments. The reach of the common law into questions about the improper uses of patronage took the form of regulating the property interest in office.

C. Restoring independence in property

Property was the fulcrum of tensions between independence and dependence. Offices were themselves treated as a form of property protected by the common law (as Coke CJ had affirmed in the previous century).[64] Even the holders of the most

[59] Clerke's Act, 1784 for example, later disqualified contractors.

[60] FM Maitland, *The Constitutional History of England* (CUP 1961 [1908]) 326, 368–69.

[61] Brewer (n 36) 74.

[62] Ibid.

[63] JW Croker, Secretary to the Admiralty, wrote to a consul suspected of jobbery (the use of public service for private profit) in 1826: 'As I placed you in your present office for public benefit so I shall take care to have you removed the moment I learn you are meddling in private jobs.' John Bourne, *Patronage and Society in Nineteenth Century England* (Edward Arnold 1986) 61.

[64] Not all positions attracted the duties of office properly so-called see *Garforth v Fearon* 1 H Bl Rep 327 (1787).

notorious sinecures were compensated when their offices were eventually abolished. On the one hand, this supported the independence of office-holders from arbitrary removal and reinforced their authority and the stability of the administration and existing social structures based on landed property. On the other hand, offices could be vehicles for the creation of new and moveable sources of property which created and exploited dependence. Fortunes could be gained from them—including through the plunders of prize money and the East India Company but also in apparently innocuous positions such as judicial office.[65] As the nature of property itself undergoes change, the property basis for the claims of administrative authority become seriously eroded toward the end of the eighteenth century.

Both the courts and the legislature were beginning to place limits on the nature of the property interest in offices, to preserve it from corruption by appealing to the values which the property interest, properly exercised, was intended to support viz., stability and independence, personal accountability, and public trust. Among such attempts were statutes prohibiting the sale of particular offices. These were treated by the courts as if they were declarations of the common law and were subject to numerous judicial embellishments.[66]

The rules about the delegation of office are particularly revealing of the system of authority in place, a system that appears to be coming increasingly under scrutiny and strain. The use of deputies was widespread and to be expected given that gentlemen often held numerous offices. There were, however, common law limits to what could be delegated or devised and on the proper uses of patronage.

The Office of the Marshal of the Marshelsea, for example, had long been considered by the common law to be an office of great trust concerning the administration of justice and the life of the law.[67] As such it attached to an individual person and could not be the subject of disposition in a will: 'The law will not repose confidence in the administration of justice in persons unknown.' In this and many other cases, the courts found there to be important limits to the property interest in office-holding. Matters concerning the King's revenue, for example, could not be executed by deputy at all.[68]

Offices requiring only common skill and diligence, however, could be executed by way of deputy and also could be granted for years.[69] The facts of a widely reported case brought in 1787[70] are illustrative of the kinds of practices at large and

[65] Lord Eldon rose from relatively modest circumstances to leave 1,300,000 in his will (Douglas Allen, 'Purchase, Patronage, and the Professions: Incentives and the Evolution of Public Office in Pre-Modern Britain' (2005) 161 Journal of Institutional and Theoretical Economics 57, 67).

[66] Sale of Offices Prevention Act 1809. *Richardson v Mellish* 2 Bing 224 (1824) cited *Blachford v Preston* 8 T R 89 (1799) to the effect that the statutes prohibiting the sale of offices were merely declaratory of the common law position that 'the sale of an office of trust has always been deemed illegal'.

[67] *Sir George Raynel's Case* 9 Co Rep 96 a and see *Robarts v Mayor* 1882 46 LT 627.

[68] *Law v Law* Cases T Talbot 142 [141] (1735).

[69] *Sir George Raynel's Case* 9 Co Rep 97 a 874.

[70] *Garforth v Fearon* 126 Eng Rep 193 (1787). See also *Law v Law* 3 P WMS 390 (1735). A contract entered into to pay for the recommendation of a place in the excise was unenforceable and equity would relieve against it. It was argued 'that it could be no objection that the whole salary or profits belonging to

the attempts of the judges in Chancery to protect the notion of a propertied office-holder exercising a free and independent will. A Mr Garforth recommended the appointment of a Mr Fearon for an office in the customs department. Garforth also appointed Fearon's deputies and contracted that all the profits, salaries, and wages and fees should be held in trust to be paid by Fearon to him and his successors. In an action Garforth brought against Fearon in assumpsit for money had and received, Lord Loughborough found that such an arrangement was unenforceable. Effectively the arrangement would have made Garforth the real authority but:

> not accountable for the due execution of [the office], he may enjoy it without being subject to the public restraints imposed by law on such officers, he may vote in elections, he may exercise inconsistent trades, he may act as magistrate in affairs concerning the revenue, he may sit in Parliament, and will be safe if he remains undiscovered. If extortion be committed in the office by those appointed, the profits redound to him, but he escapes prosecution [because his name does not appear on the Court of Exchequer's register of offices] and is not liable to the disabilities imposed by statute on officers guilty of extortion who are incapacitated to hold any office relating to the Revenue.

This passage reveals the numerous public law controls on an office-holder personally. It is he who has supervisory and legal responsibility. It is his conflicts of interests with which the law is primarily concerned. The case is also an example of judicial control of the unacceptable use of patronage, and of an arrangement tending to circumvent the rules prohibiting the sales of offices concerning customs and excise. The problem at the heart of the arrangement is that Fearon is not in fact able to act as an independent person with a will of his own. That is one of the very things that property in office was meant to protect.

A number of cases concerned attempts to circumvent the statutes about the sale of offices and the courts were vigilant in regulating these arrangements. The Joint Keep of the Register of Sasines (Scottish land registry) was found not to be able to assign future emoluments of his office, the implication being that assigning future profits would create the wrong incentives and could impair the provision of services to the public, or result in excessive fees.[71] In another case a court suggested that 'any salary paid for the performance of a public duty ought not to be perverted to

an office ought to be received by him who executed it, for this was frequently otherwise, and yet tolerated in law and equity'. But the Lord Chancellor's objection was that 'merit, industry and fidelity ought to recommend persons to these places and not interest with the commissioners, who, it is presumed, had they known from what motive the plaintiff at law applied to them on behalf of his brother, would have rejected him... It is a fraud on the public, and would open the door for the sale of offices relating to the revenue.'

[71] *Hill v Paul* 8 Cl & Fin 295 (1841). The judges also found that agreement to assign future profits was void in *Palmer v Bate* 2 Brod 7 B 673 (1821).

other uses than for those which it was intended'.[72] That case concerned whether an insolvent clergyman could assign the income from his living in trust for his creditors. The court ruled that the clergyman should not be able to divest himself of his income because doing so would also divest himself of his ability to serve the church (he was required by the Bishop to increase the curate's pay). Not only did such a rule protect the clergyman and his successors from his own imprudence but also, by delineating the property interest that attached to public office in this way, the judges were concerned to sustain the capacity of the official to provide public services and to maintain continuity of public services at a reasonable price. An office-holder could not serve two purposes or masters and could not enter into an enforceable arrangement which might undermine the public trust.

These are but a few of the instances in which the common law played a crucial role in reinforcing and superintending the virtues and the independence of office-holders and the related nature of the property interest in office. Such cases also have a good claim to be part of the administrative law broadly understood in a pre-democratic era, bolstering the authority claims of, at the same time as potentially controlling, the official.

In retrospect, these claims to authority by the administration look pretty fragile. The common law could not effectively quell concerns about corruption in public life or effectively enforce duties of public trust. Scandals proliferated. There were numerous public inquiries.[73] John Wade's *Red* and *Black* books detailing the sinecures, pensions and corruption of named members of the clergy and aristocracy added fuel to the campaigns for parliamentary and administrative reform.[74] Of more lasting and profound impact was the philosophical abandonment of the pursuit of virtue understood as the objective conformity to reason. Hume's important insight was that people were by nature neither intrinsically wholly good nor wholly bad. Virtue did not derive from objective reason but rather from artificial reason, education, and social conventions. The abstract public interest was too remote a motive to operate with any force against the private interest. It would be better to consult our common and shared interests in order to encourage virtue.[75] This refocus on institutions and the incentives that surround them would be taken up in the work of Adam Smith and Jeremy Bentham. At the same time, Adam Smith's work made the pursuit of commerce and moveable property morally respectable just as landed wealth was becoming less important economically. Blackstone's views about authority and landed property were beginning to be seen as belonging

[72] *Arbuckle v Cowtan* (3B and P 321) 328 (1803).

[73] See eg John Torrance, 'Social Class and Bureaucratic Innovation: The Commissioners for Examining the Public Accounts 1780-87'(1978) 78 Past and Present 56.

[74] John Wade, *Extraordinary Red Book* 1816; John Wade, *The Black Book or Corruption Unmasked* (Fairburn 1819).

[75] David Hume, *A Treatise on Human Nature Book II of Morals*, Part I Of Virtue and Vice in General and ff (Kindle edition).

to a past age. Parliamentary democracy was coming and it would be the new basis for political as well as administrative authority.

IV. Democracy

In *Searching for the State*, I trace how the Reform Act 1832 and related measures effected changes in administration.[76] Local government, which had previously derived its authority from charters and the common law, was brought gradually under statute and increasingly centralised political control. It was also gradually empowered with new functions and conferred with new duties. Individual office-holding gave way to a more bureaucratic hierarchy where everyone except for political and statutory office-holders came to be treated in law as a servant of the Crown. Public servants came to be conceived of as agents for their political superiors. This represented epochal change and it brought with it much greater efficiency, the expansion of social services, and rationalisation of organisation. It also brought with it a loss of common law resources as well as adaptation and innovation in common law doctrines and forms of control.

We get some sense of the element of *loss* in Lord Hewart's outpouring against the new administrative state in the *New Despotism* 1929. Much of his complaint is about the erosion of individual rights, the rule of law, and the role of the ordinary courts, and the 'anaesthetisation'[77] of Parliament. He goes further to draw implicit comparisons between present and past systems of administration. Gains by way of the new 'scientific and benevolent'[78] expertise in the civil service may have been made, he grudgingly admits,[79] but some of the merits of the old system have also been lost and replaced by 'anonymous' and 'unascertainable' civil servants,[80] who 'lack independence',[81] 'further the instructions of superiors'[82] under a 'secrecy which is inveterate',[83] lack personal responsibility,[84] and operate under a 'cloak of obscurity'.[85] He does not go quite so far as to say that there is now even the absence of a record, but it is implied.[86] Whatever the gains on former centuries in terms of efficiency and responsiveness to social need, administration had undoubtedly become less local, less personal, and less participatory. Lord Hewart's attacks both

[76] Janet McLean, *Searching for the State in British Legal Thought* (CUP 2012).
[77] Gordon Hewart, *The New Despotism* (Ernest Benn 1929) 17.
[78] Ibid 14.
[79] Ibid 14.
[80] Ibid 43.
[81] Ibid 46.
[82] Ibid 46.
[83] Ibid 48.
[84] Ibid 43.
[85] Ibid 12.
[86] Ibid 47.

signalled and sustained a crisis in legitimacy for the administrative state especially post war. A new narrative was needed as the basis for its legitimacy.

One rationale would be provided by the functionalists such as William Robson who viewed the efficiency and utility of the new social service state as authority and legitimacy-generating. On its own, however, that idea did not do enough to help resolve disputes about administrative overreach. The judges offered an alternative justification which sought to square the new administration with Parliamentary sovereignty and to lend the support of law to the authority of the administration. The executive bureaucracy would be conceived as an extension of the law-making power of Parliament.[87] That legislative work would involve transmitting the legislative will into policy and detailed rules. The existence of discretion would pose a particularly difficult problem in this era because the administrator could no longer derive independent authority from his or her personal standing. Exercises of discretion, too, would come to be viewed as bounded by Parliament's inferred expectation. A certain latitude would be allowed to the policies of the government of the day. The bureaucracy would be imagined as the alter ego of the legislature, and of Ministers. The judges, now in the role of supertending whether civil servants were acting as the faithful agents of Parliament, both helped to constituted bureaucratic authority and control it.

The common law, this time through *ultra vires* doctrines in judicial review, reinforced the authority of the bureaucracy and supplied its essential underpinning and justification. This was so even when the judges were not actively intervening to control or limit administrative power. It served everyone to treat administrators as 'transmission belts'[88] of the will of the legislature, at least so long as administrators confined themselves to findings of fact and to applying policy and did not stray into making binding interpretations of law. Strikingly, through such *ultra vires* doctrines, democratic legitimacy would come to form the bases for both the administration's claims to authority and the courts' authority to engage in judicial review. Democracy would be the central pillar.

There were always tensions in this narrative. Just as judicial review was having its 'renaissance' in the 1960s, the immediate logical problem became how to account for the judiciary's reluctance to enforce ouster clauses. One could view an ouster clause as a democratically authorised conferral of a carte blanche to the administration, and hence one that the courts should respect and uphold. Or one could attack the very democratic authority of Parliament to enact such an ouster clause and then the bureaucrat could not enjoy the freedom it confers either—a step which courts have not been prepared to take directly. There is, however, a middle way.[89]

[87] Peter Cane, *Controlling Administrative Power: An Historical Comparison* (CUP 2016) 277.

[88] Richard Stewart 'The Reformation of American Administrative Law' (1975) 88 Harv L Rev 1667.

[89] TRS Allan suggests that people engaged in the ultra vires debate must take a stand on whether Parliament has unqualified sovereignty. See Allan (n 9) 211.

It is made possible because the authority claims of the bureaucracy are distinct from and more tenuous than the authority claims of the legislature. The expression of a Parliamentary intention *not* to allow judicial control over its delegates is not authority-conferring in the same way as the expression of a Parliamentary intention to define and constrain administrative power and implicitly to enlist the aid of the courts in so doing. Even in a democratic age, the administration often needs *both* Parliamentary *and* judicial support as the basis for its authority. Indeed, the judicial non-enforcement of an ouster clause may actually enhance the authority of the administration in the longer term. Without the potential for supervision of the courts or Parliament the legitimacy of authority claims of the bureaucracy often appear to be pretty thin. Administration has long needed the support of the authority of law even when that law has not been *effectively* controlling.

We currently find ourselves on the verge of epochal change once again.[90] The democratic basis for the legitimacy of the administration is facing fundamental disruption from two directions: the rise of more technocratic, privatised, and transnational forms of administration; and a new era of human rights. The first, in part, rejects the democratic rationale for administrative authority; the second, human rights protection, requires more substantive understandings of what is required by democracy.

The claims of democratic authority in the bureaucracy have become increasingly weak and attenuated as the bureaucracy has become increasingly insulated from Parliament and often from its political masters in Cabinet. This has occurred by design. More general empowering legislation, the structural reorganisations of the 1990s (including the creation of next steps agencies and contracting out) have all contributed. In many cases, authority can no longer be traced to precise legislative mandates or only tangentially so (the power to enter a contract, for example, has been treated as merely ancillary to the functions and purposes of the statute). Although the *ultra vires* doctrine still works to explain many parts of public administration, its explanatory power is increasingly partial.

New bases of authority are sometimes claimed—notoriously in the language of efficiency, effectiveness, and economy—but such claims based on technical expertise and functionality, with little more by way of democratic underpinning to boost them, are hard to treat as legitimating when something demonstrably appears to have gone wrong. In some cases, regulatory regimes have attempted to ameliorate these apparent democratic deficits by consultation and participation processes. These are ambiguous. It is not clear whether they reproduce democratic processes on a smaller scale, or whether they actually work to augment the technical expertise claims of the decision-makers.[91] Often they do both.[92] In either

[90] See Thomas Poole, 'Back to the Future? Unearthing the Theory of Common Law Constitutionalism' (2003) 23 OJLS 435.

[91] Thanks to Ed Willis for this insight.

[92] For example in the case of *R (ex parte Begum) v Denbigh High* [2006] UKHL 15; [2007] 1 AC 100.

event they pose a challenge to the modern rationales for and doctrines of judicial review.

It is hardly surprising that the assertion of technical expertise, rationality, and efficiency as rationales for the authority of the administration has tended to attract more penetrating substantive judicial supervision in order to test such rationality claims.[93] This draws us into new territory in which we are required to consider issues about competing models of rationality[94] and relative institutional competence.[95]

At the same time as the democratic rationale for certain kinds of administrative power has decreased, the judges have been bolstering the democratic rationale for judicial review, by arguing about the substantive commitments of democracy, particularly in relation to the rule of law and human rights.[96] In other words, the judicial response has still largely been framed by the *ultra vires* democratic language but on a basis which allows judges to be drawn further into the substance.

V. Conclusion

In this chapter I have suggested that one way we can think about the historical and conceptual foundations of administrative law is by tracing the authority claims of the administration itself. Using the administration as the starting point complicates and enriches our accounts of: the relationship between high constitutional politics and administrative law; the *ultra vires* debate; and common law constitutionalism. The concept of delegation has indeed been critical, depending on the period, but delegation has been understood as both enabling officials to resist the will of the sovereign and as transmitting the will of a sovereign to a civil servant. The source of the authority of an official over the eighteenth century was a combination of social standing and the common law (statute, patent, and charter playing a relatively peripheral role).

[93] See eg *R (on the application of Mott) v Environmental Agency* [2018] UKSC 10, [2016] EWCA Civ 564.

[94] See eg Adrian Vermeule, 'Rationally Arbitrary decisions in Administrative Law' Harvard Working Paper Series SSRN; https://papers.ssrn.com/sol3/papers.cfm?abstract_id=2239155, 25 March 2013.

[95] See eg Jeff King, 'Institutional Approaches to Judicial Restraint' (2008) 28 OJLS 409, and ch 3 and Part II of his *Judging Social Rights* (CUP 2012); Aileen Kavanagh, 'Judicial Restraint in the Pursuit of Justice' (2010) 60 University of Toronto LJ 23 and Part II of Aileen Kavanagh, *Constitutional Review under the UK Human Rights Act* (CUP 2009). See further, Cass R Sunstein and Adrian Vermeule, 'Institutions and Interpretation' (2003) 101 Michigan L Rev 885; Neil Komesar, *Law's Limits: The Rule of Law and the Supply and Demand of Rights* (CUP 2001); Neil Komesar, *Imperfect Alternatives: Choosing Institutions in Law, Economics and Public Policy* (University of Chicago Press 1997).

[96] See eg Lords Steyn, Hope, and Baroness Hale in *R (Jackson) v Attorney-General* [2005] UKHL 56; [2005] 1 AC 262. See also David Dyzenhaus, 'Form and Substance in the Rule of Law: A Democratic Justification for Judicial Review' in Christopher Forsyth (ed), *Judicial Review and the Constitution* (CUP 1999) 141–72.

The long thread of the common law is ever present. It is, however, a thread with many strands. The common law has not only been concerned with protecting individual rights against the sovereign but, crucially, with supporting the authority claims of the administration. Judges, themselves officials, used accounts of the independence of office, to reinforce their own autonomy and that of their discipline, against the sovereign. In the eighteenth century, the common law had a critical, if not always effective, role to play in upholding the virtue and independence of the official and the idea of public trust. It used a range of public law tools to do so, including common law offences, rules about property in public office, and tortious liability rules alongside the prerogative writs. As independent office-holding and its claims to legitimacy gradually gave way to a bureaucratic hierarchy and more centralised parliamentary democracy, a new rationale for the authority of the administration was needed. Both authority and control appeared to have been lost. Democracy would provide that legitimacy and *ultra vires* doctrine would be the means of putting it into effect.

We now find ourselves at the cusp of a new era when once again the authority claims of the administration are being challenged and reset. That presents new challenges for the common law, for administrative lawyers, and for the administration. Theorising and framing a judicial response which is at once *reflective* of the new authority claims of the administration while at the same time *testing* of such claims, would be a good place to start.

4

Law and the Point of the State

*NW Barber**

On the face of it, Janet McLean and Neil Walker have written very different chapters. McLean's Chapter 3 examines the claimed source for the authority of the administration, principally focusing on the seventeenth, eighteenth, and nineteenth centuries. Walker's Chapter 2, in sharp contrast, focuses on the contemporary problems faced by the European Union; its uncertain nature and legitimacy. But under the surface, these chapters address a shared set of questions. They are meditations on the connections between the state and law. They ask whether the purpose we ascribe, or should ascribe, to the state shapes the purpose we ascribe, or should ascribe, to public law. They engage a core question of legal scholarship: does public law have a point, and, if so, what is it?

This chapter will engage with these questions—and with McLean's and Walker's answers to them—in two parts. First, the point of the state will be considered; what it means to claim that the state exists for a purpose, and the implications of this claim for the nature of the state. Second, the chapter reflects on the connection between the point of the state and the point of law in general and public law in particular. Not all law is state law, so, if it is accepted that states have a defining point, state law may have a different purpose to other forms of law because of its connection to the state.

I. The Point of the State

The question of the point of the state arises in both McLean's and Walker's chapters. In McLean's chapter, this is treated as a historical question: she examines the development in understandings of the state over a few hundred years, principally the move from a view of the state as an institution dominated by an individual, a single person vested with sovereignty, to the state as an institution in which sovereignty is vested in the state as a whole. This shift was accompanied by a refinement in the understanding of the point of the state, moving from the state, through the

* This chapter was originally written as a reply to McLean's and Walker's papers. Although it has been expanded, it retains the format of a response. I am grateful to Liz Fisher, Jeff King, and Dorota Leczykiewicz for comments on an earlier draft.

NW Barber, *Law and the Point of the State* In: *The Foundations and Future of Public Law*. Edited by: Elizabeth Fisher, Jeff King, Alison L Young, Oxford University Press (2020). © Oxford University Press. DOI: 10.1093/oso/9780198845249.003.0004

person of the sovereign, as the protector of its members, through to the state as an institution that facilitates the flourishing of its members, supporting and enabling them to act together. Walker's chapter starts where McLean's stops: given that the state exists for the general good of its community, what does this tell us about the European Union, which has a narrower range of concern to that of the state? Whilst it is common to talk of the state as having a purpose, there is an ambiguity about the claim. It is undeniably the case that many states have sought many different objectives throughout history, some of which have been defensible, some of which are plainly immoral. Given this, what does it mean to talk of the state possessing a point that some manifestations of that institution have plainly failed to pursue?

In this section, three possible meanings will be examined. First, there is a functionalist version of the claim, drawn from sociology. On this account, the state's purpose is found in the reasons for its flourishing and persistence; perhaps it is the state's capacity to advance people's well-being that explains its ubiquity in the modern world. Second, there is an interpretivist claim, grounded in the capacities of the state and the reasons we have for creating this institution. Given that it is a morally significant feature of the state that it has the capacity to advance people's well-being, and given that, in communities like ours, we have need of an institution like the state to achieve this end, we have reason to create the state. Third, building on this second argument, there is a claim grounded in the identity of the state as a social institution constituted by rules. It could be that states, like hospitals, prisons, schools, and so forth, of necessity include a rule identifying the pursuit of its members' well-being as its goal. Like many, perhaps like all, social institutions, a rule of the institution defines its point, determining what the state exists to achieve. An institution that did not include such a rule would not be a state. In my work I have argued in support of the second and third of these propositions, and I suspect that the first is plausible as well.

Functionalists argued that institutions within society should be understood by reference to the part they played in maintaining the stability of that community.[1] It was this role that explained their origin and flourishing; by looking at their function, we could come to understand the reasons for their existence. To draw a frequently used analogy from biology, the function of the heart is to pump blood around the body; this function provides an explanation both of the existence of the heart and the form that the organ takes. When applied to social sciences, functionalism aspired to provide explanations of social institutions and practices that mimic these biological accounts.[2] Unfortunately, with institutions such as the state, it seems likely that there is a range of different historical stories to be told about

[1] Durkheim's work is a classic example of functionalism in sociology: see Whitney Pope, 'Durkheim as a Functionalist' (1975) 16 TSQ 361.

[2] Philip Pettit, *Rules, Reasons, and Norms* (OUP 2002) 246–48. For an early attempt to provide a simple Darwinian account of the emergence of the state, see Walter Bagehot, *Physics and Politics* (2nd edn, Henry S King 1872) 39–48.

its origins and development, with states emerging for different reasons at different times.[3] Indeed, a strength of the state as an institution is its flexibility—it is capable of undertaking and supporting a very wide range of tasks—and it would be surprising if it had not fulfilled different roles in different times and places. Given this diversity, any attempt to claim that the state emerged for a single reason is likely to fail. But even if functionalism cannot explain the emergence of the state, it might yet be able to explain the state's persistence. Perhaps the most sophisticated modern account of functionalism is found in the work of Philip Pettit. Pettit argues that whilst functionalism in the social sciences fails to provide a convincing explanation of the origins of institutions it can provide an explanation of their resilience.[4] The capacity of the state to advance the well-being of its people might not explain its origin, but might explain, in part, why the institution persists.

The invocation of the point of the state by constitutional scholars is, normally, both less and more ambitious than the claims made by the functionalists.[5] It is less ambitious in that it is not an assertion of a causal explanation of the emergence or even the persistence of the state; the state may exist to advance the well-being of its people, but it does not follow from this that the founders of any particular state wished to achieve this end, or even that this factor led the community, unknowingly, to create the institution. But the claim is more ambitious than those of the functionalists in that it moves beyond attempting to describe the state and requires the theorist to engage in an explicit moral assessment of that institution.

John Finnis has provided a powerful articulation of this methodology: the task of social science is interpretive; it should aim to illuminate significance of social phenomena.[6] A successful interpretation of phenomena such as the state is one that brings forward its important features, explaining the part it plays within the life of a community. Finnis argues that a successful interpretation of a social institution requires it to be placed within a normative context; it is the process of moral assessment that allows us to pick out its important features.[7] Social scientists will, then, have to be both empirically alert and morally sensitive; able to identify how an institution affects the world and, also, which of those effects is of moral significance. Finnis pushes the argument one stage further: to understand a social institution, like law or the state, we start by asking *why* we have the institution, the

[3] Ted Lewellen, *Political Anthropology: An Introduction* (3rd edn Westport 2003), ch 3; J Elster, *Ulysses and the Sirens* (CUP 1979) 28–35.

[4] Pettit (n 2) 248–53.

[5] I discuss the methodology of constitutional theory at far greater length in NW Barber, *The Constitutional State* (OUP 2010) ch 1.

[6] John Finnis, *Natural Law and Natural Rights* (2nd edn, OUP 2011) ch 1. Contrast the similar but distinct approach of Charles Taylor: Charles Taylor, 'Interpretation and the Sciences of Man' in Charles Taylor (ed), *Philosophy and the Human Sciences: Philosophical Papers Volume 2* (CUP 1985).

[7] Finnis (n 6); Charles Taylor, 'Neutrality in Political Science' in Charles Taylor (ed), *Philosophy and the Human Sciences: Philosophical Papers Volume 2* (CUP 1985) 86–90.

reasons we have for its creation.[8] On this methodology, the central case of an institution is always positive; the product of rational people acting on valid reasons.[9] This approach struggles when faced with a wholly bad institution—explaining genocide or slavery by reference to some positive analogue appears contrived—but when applied to an institution that brings a distinct benefit to the community, Finnis' methodology provides us with a second way of understanding claims about the point of the state.[10] Now claims about the point of the state are claims about the (valid) reasons we have for wanting the state to exist. That the state has the capacity to advance its people's well-being and, moreover, can advance that well-being in ways other social institutions cannot, is a reason to create the state.[11]

The claim that moral evaluation is needed in order to produce a successful account of a social institution leads to a worry: perhaps this builds into the account an unhelpful subjectivity, with accounts of the state turning on the expounder's moral beliefs. There is a strand of thought in writings on the state that, perhaps in response to this uncertainty, attempts to ignore the point of the state and, instead, focuses on its capacity to exert power and the particular form that this exertion of power takes. These accounts examine the characteristic mode of state action rather than the ends to which this action is directed. Max Weber's classic account of the state takes this form. Weber described the state as 'a human community that (successfully) claims the *monopoly of the legitimate use of physical force* within a given territory'.[12] His account of the state brought forward the characteristic techniques of the state: its assertion of a form of authority, coupled with a capacity to exercise force to back up these claims.[13] Some contemporary accounts of the state take Weber as their starting point.[14] One way of interpreting accounts of the state that include a purpose is to treat them as supplementary to Weber's account; given that the state has the capacity to act in a certain way, this capacity should be directed towards a particular goal. Theorists might argue over what this goal is, whilst conceding that Weber's account captures the core of the nature of the state.

It might be thought that reflection on the point of the state is, then, something that comes second: we start with description, we then move to moral evaluation. But this would be a mistake. The features that Weber identified as important

[8] John Finnis, 'Law and What I Truly Should Decide' (2003) 48 Am J Juris 108, 115. It is at this point that Taylor and Finnis diverge.

[9] John Finnis, *Aquinas* (OUP 1998) 11.

[10] On the problems with Finnis' requirement that the central case of an institution be morally positive, see Barber (n 5) ch 1 and Timothy Endicott, 'The Irony of Law' in John Keown and Robert P. George (eds), *Reason, Morality, and Law: The Philosophy of John Finnis* (OUP 2013). For Finnis' problematic attempt to provide an interpretation of slavery, see Finnis, *Aquinas* (n 9) 49–50.

[11] I argue for these points in NW Barber, *The Principles of Constitutionalism* (OUP 2018), ch 2.

[12] Max Weber 'Politics as a Vocation' in Hans Gerth and C Wright Mills (eds), *From Max Weber: Essays in Sociology* (Routledge 1991) 78.

[13] Barber, *The Constitutional State* (n 5) ch 2, and Barber, *The Principles of Constitutionalism* (n 11) ch 2.

[14] Leslie Green, *The Authority of the State* (OUP 1990) 60–64.

structural aspects of the state can only be so identified because of their relationship with the point of the state. It is the identification of the point of the state that allows us to identify its important features.[15] We know, for example, that the capacity to hand out medicines and conduct operations are important features of a hospital *because* the point of a hospital is to cure the sick. As I have argued elsewhere, the claims and capacities that Weber rightly identified as important features of the state are important precisely *because* they enable the state to achieve its purpose.[16] There is, then, a circularity here: the point of the state is partly deduced from its characteristic structure, but we identify its characteristic structure partly from its point.

Given that the identification of the point of an institution depends on both empirical and moral assessment, either of which may be impaired, it is possible for those within an institution to be unaware of the true point of that entity. Our account of that institution may then diverge from that of the participants. The rain dance is the classic example of this: those who engage in this practice believe its point is to produce rain, but, given that rain cannot be generated through dance, if the practice has a point, it must be found elsewhere.[17] It could be, perhaps, that the rain dance serves to bring together the community in times of crisis. If this is correct, the practice has two points: an ostensible purpose and an actual purpose. The ostensible purpose, grounded in the beliefs of its practitioners, is to produce rain. The actual purpose, grounded in the beneficial product of the institution, is the unity of the community. A belief in the ostensible purpose is necessary for the existence of the practice—a community that has ceased to believe that the dance will produce rain can no longer perform the rain dance—but it is community cohesion that gives the practice its actual purpose. This claim can either be understood in Pettit's terms, that community cohesion is the reason the dance persists and flourishes, or in Finnis' terms, that community cohesion is the reason the participants have for engaging in the dance.

Lots of social institutions have effects of which its participants are unaware, but it seems unlikely that many have quite as sharp a divide between the ostensible purpose and the actual purpose as the rain dance. But might the state be an institution of this type: could the state exist in a society that recognised it as a discrete social entity, but was systematically confused as to its point?

The apparent diversity of candidates for the point of the state might appear to suggest this. McLean's chapter charts the development of understandings of the state over a number of centuries, with a shift from a model of the state as guardian, with authority vested in the head of the state, to a republican model, in which state power is diffused throughout the state, and the state becomes an instrument for the

[15] Finnis, *Natural Law and Natural Rights* (n 6) ch 1.
[16] Barber, *The Principles of Constitutionalism* (n 11) ch 2.
[17] Carl Hempel, 'The Logic of Functional Analysis' in Michael Martin and Lee McIntyre (eds), *Readings in the Philosophy of Social Science* (MIT Press 1994). See also Pettit (n 2) 250–51.

common projects of its people. There is a corresponding shift in an understanding of what the state should do, from a belief that the state should confine itself to protecting the property and person of its members to a belief that the state should ensure that a wide range of social benefits are available to its people.

McLean's story might be taken to chart a shift in the understanding of the purpose of the state but perhaps these different accounts embody different understandings of how the state should advance the well-being of its members rather than a disagreement about the ultimate ends of the state. They reflect a varying level of confidence in the capacity of the state to support its members. Those who think the state is poorly placed to help its people, either because they will be better off looking after themselves or because the risk of abuse of state power means a minimalist state is less likely to cause harm, will think that the state better advances the well-being of its people by doing less than those who have greater confidence in the state's capacities. Which of these is correct will depend on the local circumstances of the state; at some times and in some places, the minimalists might be right. Underneath this superficial disagreement lies a deeper consensus: there is a broad and longstanding recognition that the state, as an institution, is partly defined by its purpose, and this purpose is found in the well-being of its people.

This consensus directs our attention towards the rules that construct the state. Social institutions are created by rules, and those rules must be oriented towards some objective, even if this objective is simply the creation of the capacity for the group to act in concert.[18] The content of these rules lies, more or less directly, in the beliefs of those within the institutions and the wider communities in which those institutions exist. It is their beliefs that fashion the rules that, in turn, attribute a purpose to the institution. Though the social forms in which institutions exist are often very flexible, allowing for a broad range of refinement and interpretation of the institution's purpose, they are not infinitely flexible. There are some purposes that cannot be combined with some institutions—a 'hospital' that gave up treating the sick and instead focused on playing football would be an example of a mischaracterised institution; it is no longer, if it ever was, a form of hospital. The state is no exception: states cannot exist unless its participants, or at least a sizable number of its participants, acknowledge that the state's purpose is to advance the well-being of its members. Like a hospital that has ceased to take treatment of the sick as its defining goal, a purported state whose members did not acknowledge this purpose would not be a state; it would have become some other type of social entity.

This point requires qualification: whilst those within the state will have a particular view as to the purpose of that institution, a community could possess the institution of the state without being aware of its existence as a distinct social entity,

[18] Finnis, *Natural Law and Natural Rights* (n 6) 150–53.

they might lack the conceptual apparatus to single it out.[19] Just as the social institution of, for example, a bank could pre-exist people's awareness of banking—people might not distinguish banks from trading corporations or friendship groups—so too a community could possess the state but not identify it as such. Like other social institutions, the state can emerge from similar entities, growing out of religious groups, tribes, villages, or even commercial corporations.[20] In these communities the state might be conflated with these entities: we, as observers, may determine that there is a state present within the community, but members of that community may still think of the state as an aspect of a religious entity, or persist in labelling it a corporation. Nevertheless, for us to identify these entities as states, those participating in them must, on the whole, whether sincerely or not, acknowledge that the entity exists to advance the well-being of its members rather than to make a profit for its owners or to provide an institutional context for the worship of a deity.

This leaves open the possibility that those within the state are systematically confused about the state's actual, as opposed to ostensible, purpose; the beliefs required for the existence of the state may, in fact, be a collective delusion. To return to the rain dance, the actual purpose of this institution was, it was contended, to bring the community together in a time of crisis; its participants, though, believed that its purpose was to alter the weather. Lenin's account of the state took this form: participants in the state might believe the state had the virtuous purpose discussed in previous paragraphs, but, in actuality, its point was to facilitate and maintain class oppression.[21] Two responses can be made to claims that there is systematic confusion about the actual point of the state. The first would challenge the claim head on: those who deny that the state exists to advance the well-being of its people are making a mistake. Given the type of communities we live in, there is a need for a body such as the state to coordinate and regulate power within society; the existence of the state is necessary for people's lives to flourish.[22] Those who believe the state can and should play this role are correct; it is telling that even Lenin, once in power, found that the state could not be abandoned. Not only do people within the state generally believe the state exists to work for the good of its members, they are also right to believe this. The second response steers around the challenge. In the example of the rain dance, the belief that the dance will bring rain is integral to the practice, even if mistaken. A community that abandoned this belief

[19] Raz, writing on the nature of law, makes a similar point: Joseph Raz, 'On the Nature of Law' in Joseph Raz (ed), *Between Authority and Interpretation* (OUP 2009) 91–106. There are some aspects of law of which people must be aware (such as the existence of rules) but other aspects of which they could be unaware (such as the wider existence of a legal order).

[20] Barber, *The Principles of Constitutionalism* (n 11) 44–45, 129–30; Daniel Greenwood, 'The Semi-Sovereign Corporation' in James Smith (ed), *Property and Sovereignty: Legal and Cultural Perspectives* (Routledge 2013) 41–43.

[21] Vladmir Lenin, *The State and Revolution* (trans Robert Service, Penguin 1992) 7–9. See further, Kenneth Dyson, *The State Tradition in Western Europe: A Study of an Idea and Institution* (OUP 1979) 104–07.

[22] I explore this further in Barber, *The Principles of Constitutionalism* (n 11) especially ch 2.

but kept the communal dancing for fun would no longer be performing the rain dance: the institution would have changed. Similarly, if Lenin had proved persuasive, if people had come to believe the state's point was to oppress and had abandoned the belief the state existed for positive ends, this institution would change. It would no longer be the state as we understand that entity.

This second response builds on the claim that the acknowledgement of the point of the state is an aspect of that institution. Not only should the state work towards advancing the well-being of its members, the recognition of this obligation by state members is also part of the nature of the state. A social institution that does not acknowledge this is not a state: a gang of people who issued orders over others with the clear and ostensible aim of enriching themselves, for example, would not have constituted a state but, instead, be a criminal gang engaged in a protection racket.

This discussion has led us to a third sense in which we can talk of the state having a point. Where the existence of a social institution requires that the members of the group believe that the institution is committed to a particular goal, the pursuit of that goal becomes a necessary rule of the group. If those directing the group fail to orient their actions towards that goal (or a sub-goal of that goal) they act contrary to the rules of the group. Consequently, a state that acts against the well-being of its people is not just acting badly, it is failing by its own terms, failing to succeed as a state, and acting contrary to one of its constituent rules; the point of the state is a constitutive, and necessary, rule of that institution.

We have, then, three senses in which we might talk of the state having a point or a purpose. First, there is the functionalist claim: the purpose of the state is the effect it has on society that has caused it to flourish as a type of social institution. Second, there is a claim grounded in the interpretation of social institutions: a good account of an institution like the state identifies the (moral) reasons we have for its creation and operation. Third, there is a claim grounded in the constituent rules of the state: the state is partly constituted by its acknowledged purpose; its participants, or at least a significant proportion of its participants, recognise this objective as the end the institution should be seeking to achieve. Here, the purpose of the state is set by one of the foundational rules of that institution. Of course, all three of these claims may be true: an appreciation of the capacity of the state to advance the well-being of its people may have motivated people to create and support the state, and may also underpin the rule defining the state's purpose.

II. The Point of the State and the Point of Public Law

Should public lawyers be interested in the point of the state? After all, law exists inside and outside of states; there is state law, and there are other types of law. Law certainly should pursue the good—it is an action-guiding institution, after all—but the aspects of the good it pursues will depend on the area in which the law operates.

Where law exists within groups that pursue a subset of the good—the law of religious organisations, the internal rules of companies or sporting bodies—the point of those legal orders will be similarly constrained. But when law is the law of the state, law is the instrument of that institution and, as such, its point is determined by the point of the state.

The relationship between the point of state law and the points of particular parts of state law is complicated: parts of state law can have a narrower focus than state law taken as a whole. For example, it could be argued that the purpose of tort law is to restore balance to relationships unsettled by a wrong, whilst the purpose of property law could be to enable people to make use of land and objects. Public law comprises those rules that set the legal framework that constitutes state institutions and in so doing, constitutes the legal relationship between those institutions. Public law is a subset of state law and, like contract and land, its point need not be synonymous with the point of state law taken as a whole. Is it possible to identify a distinctive point for public law and, if so, what will the connection be between the point of public law and the broader point of state law?

One of Paul Craig's many contributions to public law theory has been to clarify the foundations of public law. Over a number of years Craig has argued that public law, in particular administrative law, is grounded in the Common Law. In part, this account of the basis of public law is a reaction against a school of thought that has been labelled the *ultra vires* theory of judicial review. Early versions of this doctrine contended that Parliament had willed the application of specific rules of administrative law, and the content of administrative law could be linked back to statutes.[23] The recent modified *ultra vires* theory, in contrast, advances the more plausible argument that Parliament should be taken to intend that judges should apply the rules of good administration they have developed. In Mark Elliott's ingenious reformulation, Parliament is presumed to have intended the powers it confers are to be exercised in accordance with the rule of law, and this conception of the rule of law is flexible enough to include the principles of judicial review formulated by the judges at any point in time.[24]

Craig has demonstrated, in a series of articles, that the *ultra vires* theory of judicial review is mistaken.[25] It rests on the erroneous assumption that, in the United Kingdom constitution, whatever Parliament has not prohibited it must have authorised, either expressly or by implication.[26] But, as Craig contends, this is a

[23] See the discussion in Christopher Forsyth, 'Heat and Light: A Plea for Reconciliation' in Christopher Forsyth (ed), *Judicial Review and the Constitution* (Hart 2000).

[24] Mark Elliott, 'The *Ultra Vires* Doctrine in a Constitutional Setting: Still the Central Principle of Administrative Law' in Christopher Forsyth (ed), *Judicial Review and the Constitution* (Hart 2000).

[25] Paul Craig, 'Competing Models of Judicial Review' [1999] PL 428. See also Paul Craig, 'Ultra Vires and the Foundations of Judicial Review' (1998) 57 CLJ 63 and Paul Craig, *UK, EU, and Global Administrative Law: Foundations and Challenges* (CUP 2015) ch 1.

[26] Craig, 'Competing Models of Judicial Review' (n 25) 438–40. This is the same error made by Austin: John Austin, *The Province of Jurisprudence Determined* (Weidenfeld & Nicholson 1954) 31–22; NW Barber, 'The Academic Mythologians' (2001) 21 OJLS 369.

misreading of the constitutional order: the Common Law's validity does not turn on the implicit authorisation of Parliament; it is a distinct source of law with independent legal legitimacy.[27] Like other areas of law, public law contains a mix of statutory and Common Law rules, and other sorts of rules too. And the bulk of the law relating to judicial review has been developed by the Common Law, and cannot be traced back to decisions of Parliament.[28]

The resolution of the *ultra vires* debate clears the ground for an account of the point of public law, but it does not provide an account in itself. Even once we recognise that public law is drawn from a mix of legal sources, the question of what those rules are seeking to achieve, or should be seeking to achieve, is left open. The question of the point of public law is important and complex—there is clearly not enough space in this chapter to attempt its resolution—but McLean's and Walker's chapters indicate how a shifting understanding of the nature and needs of the state has led to a shift in our understanding of the purpose of public law.

Walker's chapter illustrates how a developed appreciation of the point of the state allows us to avoid some mistaken models of public law. The Weberian account of the state, one which focused narrowly on the state's exercise of power and assertion of authority may sometimes, knowingly or unknowingly, lie behind accounts of public law. These approaches to public law treat that area of law as a set of constraints imposed upon the state to protect its people from the exercise of state power.[29] On these accounts, the constitution exists separate from the state and is applied to that body in order to limit its capacity to act. The role of the courts is to police the state, demanding that the state show that its actions are compatible with the rights of citizens. On this model, public law becomes rights-focused, with emphasis placed on bills of rights, and judicial review of administrative action presented as a set of rules that preserve the autonomy of the individual when facing the might of state bureaucracy. As Walker notes, this is overly reductionist. Public law exists to create and empower, as well as to constrain and limit. Indeed, seeing public law purely as a constraint cuts against the point of the state; stopping the state from achieving its objectives.[30] A richer account of the state, one that brings forward the obligation of the state to help and support its people, brings with it a richer understanding of the point of public law.

Walker's chapter brings forward the ways in which a changing understanding of the nature of the state may result in a changed understanding of the objectives

[27] Craig, 'Competing Models' (n 25).

[28] Craig, *UK, EU, and Global Administrative Law* (n 25) 22–25.

[29] See Harlow and Rawlings on 'red-light' theories of public law: Carol Harlow and Rick Rawlings, *Law and Administration* (3rd edn, CUP 2009) ch 1. Although note Craig's cautionary remarks: Craig, *UK, EU and Global Administrative Law* (n 25) 98–103.

[30] Jeremy Waldron, 'Constitutionalism: A Sceptical View' in Jeremy Waldron (ed), *Political Theory* (Harvard UP 2016); Barber (n 12) ch 1.

of public law. McLean's chapter, in contrast, charts a development in the techniques used by public law in response to the needs of the state. McLean identifies a shift away from a property-based concept of public law: from the notion that offices of state were, in some sense, the property of those who held them, to a model of public law that is grounded in democratic values. In each case, the underlying conception of the state was compatible with the model advanced in the first part of this chapter. Public offices might be 'owned' by the king or officials, but these officers were expected to act to advance the public good.[31] On this understanding of public law, public law functions like the law of trusts: protecting the office-holder from third-party interference with her property whilst, potentially, requiring her to use that property for the advantage of its beneficiaries. Traces of this conception of public law remain within judicial review. We still sometimes use language that is related to trust law: when a person exceeds their powers they act *ultra vires*, state officials who make a decision are expected to act in good faith and, sometimes, the notion of a fiduciary relationship between the state official and the citizens they engage with is invoked. Indeed, some recent scholarship, building on these points of similarity, has used the idea of the trust as the foundational idea of public law, with the state depicted as having a fiduciary relationship with its people.[32]

Treating public offices like property will always prove problematic. As our appreciation of the purpose of the state shapes the ways the techniques and aims of public law are fashioned, the notion of public office as property becomes increasingly artificial and contrived. It is, after all, rare that holders of public office are permitted to destroy or trade those posts. Furthermore, in contrast to owners of private property, state officials cannot, or should not, extract value from the office to enrich themselves; public offices exist for the benefit of the people of the state, not for the benefit of those who occupy them. The invocation of the idea of the trust as the property base for public office brings public law more closely in line with the point of the state—now, at least, the property benefits the right set of people—but the analogy remains inexact.[33] In trust law the legal owners of the property decide, within the bounds set by the trust, on the best interests of the beneficiaries. In the state, a significant part of the role of public law is to establish structures through which the citizens—the beneficiaries, on the trust account—can exercise control over state officials. It is public law, when public law is working well, that constrains officials to statutes enacted by elected legislatures and in so doing, helps instantiate the principle of democracy within the constitution. Consequently, whilst in trust law the beneficiaries of the trust instrument have a significantly restricted capacity

[31] Robert Filmer, *Patriarcha* (CUP 1991) 12; Thomas Hobbes, *On the Citizen* (CUP 1998) ch 13.
[32] Evan Fox-Decent, *Sovereignty's Promise: The State as Fiduciary* (OUP 2011).
[33] Timothy Endicott, 'The Public Trust' in Evan Criddle et al (eds), *Fiduciary Government* (CUP 2018).

to shape or revise the framework under which the legal owners act, in the public realm the citizenry can and should revise the framework conditioning the actions of state officials. In a well-functioning state, citizens are a central part of the governance of the state, both by occupying offices of state and by engaging with those offices in the political realm.[34] If a division in the state exists between beneficiaries and rulers, even those acting under fiduciary obligations, the state has failed to turn its members into citizens, failed to give them the types of control over the institutions of the state that they are entitled to exercise. Resting as it does on this problematic distinction, the property law analogy for public law will always be partial and risks being misleading.

If the point of judicial review is not to be found in the will of Parliament, as the *ultra vires* theorists contended, nor in the transposition of ideas of property law into the constitutional realm, as argued by those tempted by the fiduciary model, we are still left with the question of what public law is seeking to achieve.[35] Moving beyond Walker's and McLean's chapters, there is a broad range of candidates on offer. Martin Loughlin, for example, contends that the point of public law is to maintain the stability and autonomy of the public realm.[36] Judicial review, on this account, becomes a collection of devices that aim to encourage people to accept the decisions of political institutions. Trevor Allan, in sharp distinction, sees public law as a justificatory practice, one that requires the state to justify its use of power over its people to the judges.[37]

There is not enough space here to survey and critique these different accounts of public law. But our earlier discussion of the point of the state provides some indications of the form that an attractive account of the purpose of public law might take. Elsewhere, I have written about the connection between the point of the state and citizenship.[38] To achieve its defining purpose in full the state needs to instantiate its members as citizens, enabling them to share in the government of the state, both ruling and being ruled.[39] There are lots of good instrumental arguments for citizenship. It is likely that a democratic state will be governed better, and less corruptly, than a non-democratic state.[40] But there is also an

[34] Ibid 325–29.

[35] Indeed, given that the *ultra vires* theory had, by the end of its academic evolution, become a cipher for underlying constitutional principles, even if the *ultra vires* doctrine were endorsed its supporters would still have had to explain the ends to which those principles were oriented.

[36] Martin Loughlin, *The Idea of Public Law* (OUP 2003) 115; I discuss Loughlin's work at greater length in NW Barber, 'Professor Loughlin's Idea of Public Law' (2005) 25 OJLS 157.

[37] TRS Allan, *Constitutional Justice* (OUP 2001) and Alison L Young, *Democratic Dialogue and the Constitution* (OUP 2017) 74–80.

[38] I discuss the connection between states and citizenship in Barber, *The Constitutional State* (n 5) ch 3.

[39] Aristotle, *The Politics and Constitution of Athens* (Stephen Everson (ed), CUP 1996) III.IV, 1277b13–22.

[40] See Daron Acemoglu and James Robinson, *Why Nations Fail: The Origins of Power, Prosperity, and Poverty* (Profile Books 2012); Robert A Dahl, *On Democracy* (Yale UP 1998) ch 4.

intrinsic value to citizenship. Creating structures that enable government by the people is the only way in which state decisions can be made whilst respecting the moral equality of persons, and realising that moral equality within the structures of the state.[41] When state membership is not characterised by possession of citizenship, state members are, instead, subjects, passive recipients of the state's commands. In such a situation the state has failed to constitute itself in a manner that respects the moral equality of its people, and has failed to give them the share in control over collective decision-making that they are entitled to exercise. By denying them this recognition and failing to vindicate this right, the state fails to realise their well-being.

A core task of public law—perhaps *the* core task—is to create a set of institutions and relationships that permits the realisation of citizenship. Part of this is achieved indirectly. Public law establishes, at least in part, the institutions that enable the democratic process to function; legislatures, the executive, and the courts all have a role to play in enabling members of the state to share in governance. For citizenship to be realised in the state, these institutions need to work effectively. But public law also pursues this task directly by endowing state members with rights and claims they can exercise in their engagement with state institutions. Some of these legal rights are obvious. For a state member to be a citizen, she must possess and be able to exercise the right to vote, to stand for election, and to hold public offices. Others are, perhaps, less obvious. Many of the principles of administrative law lead state officials to treat people as citizens. For example, the principles relating to the rationality of decision-making require that the decision-maker regard those they make decisions about as people whose interests matter; a person affected by the decision can challenge it if the decision-maker has ignored considerations that should have been taken into account or if their assessment of the importance of those considerations has been deficient. Similarly, administrative law often requires that people affected by a decision are included in the process by which that decision is produced.[42] Natural justice can impose an obligation on the decision-maker to consult those likely to be affected by a decision and, sometimes, to explain the decision once it is made. Administrative law has long been a part of public law, but the rise of the welfare state, which brought with it an expansion of the administrative branch, has served to increase its significance and visibility. Administrative law should be seen as a vital part of the realisation of the office of citizenship in the modern state, and as a working through of the implications of the point of the state for the aims of public law.

[41] Ronald Dworkin, *Justice for Hedgehogs* (Harvard UP 2011) 388–92; Jeremy Waldron, 'Participation: The Right of Rights' in Jeremy Waldron (ed), *Law and Disagreement* (OUP 1999).

[42] Mark Seidenfeld, 'A Civic Republican Justification for the Bureaucratic State' (1992) 105 Harvard L Rev 1512, 1529–33.

PART II

CASE LAW

5. Public Law Cases and the Common Law: A Unique Relationship?
Alison L Young

6. The Mutual Judicial Influence of National Courts and the European Court of Justice through the Preliminary Rulings Mechanism: Evidence from the United Kingdom
Gráinne de Búrca

7. How Judges Make Law
Timothy Endicott

5

Public Law Cases and the Common Law

A Unique Relationship?

*Alison L Young**

It is hard to deny that case law has played a crucial role in the development of English public law. So much so, that we tend to mark the development of public law through references to famous case names, with *Anisminic*,[1] *Privacy International Limited*,[2] *Wednesbury*,[3] the *GCHQ*[4] case, and *Miller*[5] marking important milestones. It is also undeniable that case law has played a key role in what Paul Craig refers to as the second and third levels of English administrative law; the development of a specific category of administrative law and the detailed specification of the heads of judicial review.[6] Craig also regards case law as playing a crucial role at his first level of analysis of English administrative law, providing the imperative for, and justification of, the role of the judiciary in resolving problems that arise in the regulation of public authorities.[7] This is evident in his common law model of judicial review, which Craig describes as

> based on the premise that the principles of judicial review, and their application, are created by the courts. It is the courts that have fashioned these principles in accord with the principles of justice and the rule of law in the manner explicated above.[8]

Perhaps unsurprisingly, Craig's account of his common law model of judicial review has prompted detailed critical analysis, initiating the debate between 'common law' theorists and 'modified *ultra vires*' theorists.[9] Rather, than revisiting

* Alison L Young, Sir David Williams Professor of Public Law, University of Cambridge and a Fellow of Robinson College. With thanks to David Feldman, Liz Fisher, Hayley J Hooper, and Jeff King for comments on an earlier version and to Timothy Endicott for his extremely insightful response to this chapter.

1 *Anisminic v Foreign Compensation Commission* [1969] 2 AC 147 (HL).
2 *R (Privacy International Ltd) v Investigatory Powers Tribunal* [2019] UKSC 22.
3 *Associated Provincial Picture Houses Ltd v Wednesbury Corporation* [1948] 1 KB 223 (CA).
4 *Council for Civil Service Unions v Minister for the Civil Service* [1985] AC 374 (HL).
5 *R (Miller) v Secretary of State for Exiting the European Union* [2017] UKSC 5, [2017] 2 WLR 583.
6 Paul Craig, *UK, EU and Global Administrative Law: Foundations and Futures* (CUP 2015) ch 1.
7 Ibid.
8 Ibid 22–23.
9 See Christopher Forsyth (ed), *Judicial Review and the Constitution* (Hart 2000) and Craig (n 6).

Alison L Young, *Public Law Cases and the Common Law* In: *The Foundations and Future of Public Law*. Edited by: Elizabeth Fisher, Jeff King, Alison L Young, Oxford University Press (2020). © Oxford University Press.
DOI: 10.1093/oso/9780198845249.003.0005

this debate, I want to ask a deeper question: is the common law method of developing legal controls through case law well suited to the development of principles of judicial review?

My quest is motivated by my growing suspicion that the common law method is not necessarily suited to public law. This chapter will focus on three aspects of common law reasoning. First, common law develops principles of judicial review on a case-by-case basis, building on specific cases brought before the courts. Second, common law reasoning is best described as reasoning by analogy. In any particular case, courts look to past case law to see if there are comparable previous cases. The judiciary then examine these cases, looking for relevant similarities and differences. It is through this process of looking back, examining the specific facts of the case before the court, and looking forward, that courts develop the common law. Third, common law reasoning often leads to the development of taxonomies—the heads of judicial review. Applicants for judicial review need to demonstrate that their case falls within one of these heads of review, using the criteria of that head of review to establish their claim that a public body has acted unlawfully.

This chapter will examine recent examples that appear to challenge these characteristics of common law reasoning. Are they mere peculiarities of public, as opposed to private law, or do they demonstrate a deeper problem with case law? I will argue that these examples illustrate weaknesses in common law methodology which may arise equally in both public law and private law cases. However, I will also argue that, at a very abstract and general level, there is a tendency for these weaknesses in the analogical reasoning employed in the common law to be resolved differently in public law and in private law cases. These weaknesses may be remedied either by moving towards more inductive or deductive reasoning, both of which are more likely to provide logically correct answers than the use of analogical reasoning. The chapter will propose the modest argument that there may be greater justification for private law cases to answer the problems of analogical reasoning by moving more towards deductive reasoning, and for public law cases to move towards inductive reasoning. This is not to argue for a difference in kind, but one of degree; a general tendency as opposed to a definitive distinction. In addition, I will argue that background constitutional principles may play a greater role in public law than in private law when it comes to determining whether to move towards deductive or inductive reasoning. As such, the weaknesses of common law reasoning may have more serious consequences and may be resolved in a different manner in public law cases.

This inquiry will focus on UK law, focusing on judicial review cases as opposed to human rights controls through the Human Rights Act 1998. Nor will it examine the role of the ombudsman and tribunals, or the way in which case law has evolved as regards torts committed, or contracts entered into, by public authorities. It will also not examine the interpretation of legislation. These restrictions are due to issues of space. It is hoped that this analysis of the role of case law in English public law will also have resonance in other common law jurisdictions, as well as beyond the case law on judicial review.

I. Why Common Law Reasoning May Not Suit Public Law

If we are to understand why case law may not be the ideal mechanism through which to develop principles of public law, then we need to understand what we mean by reasoning through case law and how case law differs from other forms of rule-making. Although we frequently deploy the phrase 'common law reasoning' to describe how the legal community reasons in a distinctive manner, we often do so without paying full attention to how lawyers and judges reason, or why this reasoning is distinct from other forms of reasoning.

The common law appears to be a form of artificial reasoning.[10] It is referred to as analogical reasoning, where judges look back to past cases, examining possible similarities and differences between a series of case and the specific facts of the case before the court.[11] It is in this sense that common law reasoning is referred to as 'bottom-up' as opposed to 'top-down'.[12] Sir John Laws, for example, describes common law reasoning as having four distinct features: evolution, experimentation, history, and distillation.[13] Evolution occurs as rules and principles of the common law are developed through time, honed by a series of precedents. Experimentation refers to how the common law reasons from a series of hypotheses, these being discarded or adopted over time as the common law evolves. History refers to the power of continuity of the common law, with current rules and principles of the common law established through a series of historical precedents. Distillation refers to the process of the modification of the common law, as precedents are adopted over time to meet new conditions. Legal hypotheses are normative. They stand the test of time until they are challenged and potentially modified by good normative justifications for change.

[10] *Prohibitions del Roy* (1607) 12 Co Rep 63, at 64 (Coke), quoted by Craig in Craig, *UK, EU and Global Administrative Law: Foundations and Challenges* (n 6) 45.

[11] Larry Alexander and Emily Sherwin *Demystifying Legal Reason* (CUP 2008) ch 3, Adam Rigoni, 'Common-Law Judicial Reasoning and Analogy' (2014) 20 Legal Theory 133, Gerald Postema, 'A Similibus ad Similia: Analogical Thinking in Law' in Douglas Edlin (ed), *Common Law Theory* (CUP 2007) 102, Charles Fried, 'Artificial Reason of the Law or: What Lawyers Know' (1981) 60 Texas L Rev 35, Gerald Postema, 'Philosophy of the Common Law' in Jules Coleman, Kenneth Einar Himma, and Scott Shapiro (eds), *The Oxford Handbook of Jurisprudence* (OUP 2004) 5888, Edward Hirsch Levi, 'The Nature of Judicial Reasoning' (1965) 32 University of Chicago Law Review 395 and Cass Sunstein 'On Analogical Reasoning' (1993) 106 Harvard L Rev 741.

[12] Jeffrey Rachlinski, 'Bottom-up Versus Top-down Reasoning' (2006) 73 University of Chicago L Rev 993.

[13] Sir John Laws, 'Lecture One—the Common Law and State Power' in *The Common Law Constitution* (CUP 2014) 3.

John Gardner's work distinguishing between the common law and legislation provides a further means of honing the definition of common law reasoning. He argues that there are three main differences between legislation and case law. First, legislation is expressed. The content of legislation is determined by examining legislative provisions; words containing the expression of the legislature as set out in legislation. Legal doctrines found in case law, on the other hand, tend to emerge not from expression but from argumentation and discussion. For the purposes of this chapter, I interpret this to mean that whilst judges may express their decision in a particular case, the resolution of a specific case may not be sufficient to establish a legal rule of the common law. This may happen. But the content of a rule of the common law may not stem merely from one case. It may be further forged through later cases. The rules relating to precedent, the search for possible principles running through a series of cases, and concerns as to the proper constitutional role of the judge all play a role in the development of rules of the common law from a series of cases.[14]

Second, legislation is intentionally made. Set forms and procedures are required to enact legislation. The use of these forms and procedures demonstrates a clear intention to enact legislation. The same may, but need not, be true of case law. Case law may be intentionally made. Courts may intend to make the law when they decide a particular legal issue in a specific case. However, there is no requirement of this intention. Rather, case law develops as a decision in an earlier case is recognised and applied in a later case, leading to the formation of a rule or principle of case law.

Third, legislation is made by more than one agent, requiring a form of joint agency to enact legislation. Each Member of Parliament (MP) acts individually when voting for legislation. However, in doing so they create a joint intention of Parliament—at least for the purposes of the law.[15] This is not the same for case law. Although case law is also made by more than one agent, the judges who make up the judiciary do not work as joint agents in the same way as the legislature. Rather, they work in common. They rely on earlier judgments of their colleagues, working together to reinforce case law through these references to earlier judgments and their application and refinement in later cases.[16]

These characteristics of case law cast light on the case-by-case reasoning adopted by the common law. Case law develops by reasoning from like to like, looking at aspects of earlier cases and assessing how they apply to the specific facts before the court in a future case.[17] There is no reasoning or speculation in a legal vacuum.

[14] I am grateful to Timothy Endicott for challenging me on this point and helping me to refine my argument. For an alternative account of how common law rules develop, see the work of TRS Allan, particularly *The Sovereignty of Law: Freedom, Constitution and Common Law* (OUP 2013) ch 1, where he discusses 'internal' and 'external' approaches to legal reasoning.

[15] Richard Ekins, *The Nature of Legislative Intent* (OUP 2012).

[16] John Gardner, 'Some Types of Law' in Douglas Edlin (ed), *Common Law Theory* (CUP 2007) 51.

[17] Postema, 'A Similibus ad Similia' (n 11).

Rather, general principles emerge from a series of similar cases, each case developing the principle in relation to its own specific facts.[18] Moreover, case law reasoning is pragmatic, looking for a solution to a specific case before the court rather than focusing on developing general principles.[19] It demonstrates a preference for reaching an agreement at a lower level, rather than engaging in higher-level abstract theory which aims to reach a fully theorised argument according to abstract principles.[20]

From this more abstract discussion, three features appear to emerge. First, common law reasoning is concrete as opposed to abstract. This concrete nature has two features: ripeness and specificity.[21] Ripeness refers to the characteristic that common law reasoning applies to an actual decision or action that has taken place, or that will take place in the future. Specificity explains how common law reasoning focuses on a particular set of facts, assessing how this factual situation presented to the court will be determined by the court. Second, common law reasoning tends to be bottom up as opposed to top down. Principles and rules of the common law emerge from a series of cases, rather than common law reasoning applying general principles to particular facts. Third, common law reasoning tends to develop taxonomies, adopting a taxonomical approach as specific cases solidify into rules or principles over time. However, there are examples which question the existence of these features of common law reasoning in public law, particularly, though not restricted to, litigation surrounding Brexit. [22] This, in turn, questions the value of common law reasoning in public law.[23]

Examples exist of more abstract, unripe forms of review, where the courts appear to be being asked to determine legal issues without this being linked to the assessment of a particular decision or action that has taken place, or that will occur in the near future. The clearest example of this form of abstract review is *Wightman*, a case which arose in the Scottish courts.[24] Andy Wightman, a Member of the Scottish Parliament, and others brought an action requesting the Scottish courts to refer a question to the Court of Justice of the European Union (CJEU), using the preliminary reference procedure under Article 267 Treaty on the Functioning of the European Union (TFEU). They wished to know whether it would be legally possible for the United Kingdom to revoke Article 50 unilaterally. Difficulties arose

[18] Fred Schauer, 'Do Cases Make Bad Law?' (2006) 73 University of Chicago L Rev 883 and Rachlinski (n 12).

[19] Postema 'A Similibus ad Similia' (n 11).

[20] Sunstein (n 11).

[21] I am grateful to David Feldman for helping me to refine my thoughts on this point.

[22] This is one of the many impacts of *R (Miller) v Secretary of State for Exiting the European Union* (n 5). See Mark Elliott, Jack Williams, and Alison L Young 'The *Miller* Tale' and Alison L Young, '*Miller* and the Future of Constitutional Adjudication', both in Mark Elliott, Jack Williams, and Alison L Young (eds), *The UK Constitution After Miller: Brexit and Beyond* (Hart 2018).

[23] Paul Craig, 'Taxonomy and Public Law: A Response' [2019] Public Law 281.

[24] *Andy Wightman MSP v The Advocate General* [2018] CSIH 18, 2018 SLT 356, [2018] CSOH 61, and *Andy Wightman MSP v Secretary of State for Exiting the European Union* [2018] CSIH 62.

given that, at the time, the UK Government had made it clear that it had no plans to revoke Article 50, so the issue of whether this was legally possible or not was moot. In the words of the Outer House, the court was being asked to issue 'what is in effect an advisory declarator'; whilst this was possible in 'appropriate (and exceptional) circumstances', they were not met in this case.[25] As such, the Outer House refused to grant permission for judicial review. Nevertheless, following an appeal to the Inner House, permission was confirmed, due to the constitutional importance of the issue and given that this was information that would be relevant to MPs exercising the 'meaningful vote' under section 13 of the European Union (Withdrawal) Act 2018.[26] The court's decision has been criticised for referring an issue before it was ripe, essentially asking the CJEU to answer a moot question. [27]

There are also examples of abstract review where courts review administrative rules or legislation in general without focusing on a specific example setting out why these provisions are unlawful, that is, where there is a lack of specificity. The recent *Northern Irish Abortion Case* provides an interesting example.[28] The Northern Ireland Human Rights Commission (NIHC) wished to challenge the Convention compatibility of the Criminal Justice Act (Northern Ireland) 1945 which criminalises abortion in Northern Ireland. A majority of the Supreme Court concluded that the NIHC did not have standing. It was not a victim of the abortion laws and Convention challenges could only be brought by victims of a human rights abuse. Nevertheless, some of the judges who refused to grant standing discussed whether the legislation breached Convention rights. In doing so, the court drew on a range of possible circumstances under which abortion would be prohibited which might breach Convention rights; for example, where abortion was prohibited as a result of rape or incest, or where it prohibited the abortion of a foetus with serious or fatal foetal abnormalities.[29] These examples had been brought to the attention of the court by the NIHC. Rather than waiting for a particular victim with a specific case, the Supreme Court considered the Convention compatibility of the legislation against these hypothetical situations.

Second, examples also exist of courts adopting a top-down as opposed to a bottom-up approach to cases in public law. This is particularly true of cases reaching the Supreme Court, often where it can be hard to discern the extent to

[25] *Andy Wightman MSP v The Advocate General* [2018] CSOH 61, [37].

[26] The Court of Justice of the European Union concluded that it was possible for the United Kingdom to unilaterally revoke Article 50. C-621/18 *Wightman v Secretary of State for Exiting the European Union* [2018] 3 WLR 1965.

[27] Stephen Laws, 'Judicial Intervention in Parliamentary Proceedings'(Policy Exchange, 19 Nov 2018). Available at: https://policyexchange.org.uk/publication/judicial-intervention-in-parliamentary-proceedings/, accessed 28 June 2019.

[28] *In the matter of an application by the Northern Irish Human Rights Commission for Judicial Review (Northern Ireland)* [2018] UKSC 27, [2019] 1 All ER 173.

[29] See Shona Wilson Stark 'In re Northern Ireland Human Rights Commission's Application for Judicial Review [2018] UKSC 27: A Declaration in All But Name?' UK Const L Blog (12 June 2018); available at https://ukconstitutionallaw.org/, accessed 28 June 2019.

which the Supreme Court is establishing a new, general principle, or is providing an alternative justification for its outcome, or merely providing *obiter dicta*. One such example of courts' reasoning in a more top-down manner is *Miller*.[30] This is particularly true of what Mark Elliott refers to as the 'constitutional scale' argument,[31] where the court refused to accept

> that a major change to UK constitutional arrangements can be achieved by ministers alone; it must be affected in the only way that the UK constitution recognises, namely by Parliamentary legislation. This conclusion appears to us to follow from the ordinary application of basic concepts of constitutional law to the present issue.[32]

In reaching this conclusion, the Supreme Court did not draw on a series of past cases, setting out the origins of this long-standing principle of the common law. The conclusion that Ministerial action alone would not suffice arose from the application of general principles of the UK constitution to the specific situation of the use of the prerogative power to trigger Article 50 Treaty on European Union (TEU).[33] Whilst there are constitutional principles that could justify this principle of the law, including background principles referred to by the Supreme Court, there was no detailed argument setting out this justification, or the scope of its application.[34]

Similar patterns can be found in the case law discussing parliamentary sovereignty. In *Jackson v Attorney General*, Lord Steyn predominantly reasoned from first principles when justifying his statement that there could be principles of the UK constitution that were so fundamental that they could not be repealed by ordinary legislation, such that were Parliament to purport to abolish such principles, the courts would refuse to recognise such legislation.[35] Similar reasoning is found in the judgments of Lord Neuberger and Lord Mance in *HS2*.[36] In *AXA General Insurance*, Lord Hope also appeared to reason in a top-down manner when concluding that there were common law limits on the law-making powers of the Scottish Assembly and, by analogy, the other devolved legislatures.[37] In reaching this conclusion, Lord Hope explained that the issue of parliamentary sovereignty, and its precise balance with the rule of law, 'has to be addressed as one of principle'.[38] Nor is this restricted to Supreme Court cases. Another clear example can be

[30] *R (Miller) v Secretary of State for Exiting the European Union* (n 5).

[31] Mark Elliott, 'The Supreme Court's Judgment in *Miller*: In Search of Constitutional Principle' (2017) 76 CLJ 257.

[32] Ibid [82].

[33] For a criticism of this principle, see Ibid 263–68.

[34] See Alison L Young, '*R (Miller) v Secretary of State for Exiting the European Union*: Thriller or Vanilla?' (2017) 42 European L Review 280.

[35] *Jackson v Attorney General* [2005] UKHL 56, [2006] 1 AC 262, [102]–[103].

[36] *R (HS2 Alliance) v The Secretary of State for Transport* [2014] UKSC 3, [2014] 1 WLR 324, [207].

[37] *AXA General Insurance v Lord Advocate* [2011] UKSC 46, [2012] 1 AC 868.

[38] Ibid [207].

found in the key judgment of Sir John Laws in the *Thoburn* case, which established the separate category of constitutional statutes, instruments, and measures, whose terms could not be impliedly repealed, their repeal requiring express or specific words.[39]

Third, there is evidence of an emerging trend away from approaching public law in a taxonomical manner. Courts adopt a taxonomical approach when they first identify a particular head of review and apply the rules and principles found under this head of review when determining whether an application for judicial review succeeds on the facts. This can be contrasted with a balancing approach, where the courts reason from first principles and general concepts rather than focusing on a particular head of review.[40]

Perhaps paradoxically, this is best illustrated through reference to a recent decision of the Supreme Court that attempted to push back against this trend. In *Gallaher*, the Supreme Court was asked to determine issues of equality and fairness which arose in response to competition law proceedings, following allegations of price-fixing in the tobacco market.[41] What is important is the way in which barristers argued on behalf of Gallaher and the way in which Lord Carnwath treated their argument. Both Gallaher and TMR had entered into Early Resolution Agreements with the Competition and Markets Authority (CMA), paying reduced fines in return for cooperation in the CMA's investigation into price-fixing in the tobacco market. However, TMR had received an assurance that, were others to successfully appeal the outcome of this investigation, their fine would be waived. Gallaher did not receive this assurance. The barristers for Gallaher claimed that failing to apply the same reduction to Gallaher as was applied to TMR breached the principles of equal treatment and substantive fairness. This breach of equal treatment and fairness was in itself a breach of public law.[42] Their argument drew on general principles underpinning English administrative law, applying them to Gallaher's situation.

Lord Carnwath, however, refused to accept that a breach of fairness or equal treatment in and of itself was a breach of public law. Although both equal treatment and fairness are general principles of English law, neither are grounds of judicial review.[43] He was also critical of approaches to legal reasoning where phrases and expressions were taken, 'out of context', from judgments and then used to create 'free-standing principles of law'.[44] Lord Carnwath's judgment takes a more taxonomical approach. He looks to established heads of judicial review, such as

[39] *Thoburn v Sunderland City Council* [2002] EWHC 195 (Admin), [2003] QB 151.
[40] See Kathleen Sullivan, 'Foreword: The Justice of Rules and Standards' (1991) 106 Harvard L Rev 22, 56–95.
[41] *R (Gallaher Group) v The Competition and Markets Authority* [2018] UKSC 25, [2018] 2 WLR 1583.
[42] Ibid [19]–[23] and [31].
[43] Ibid [24] and [32].
[44] Ibid [40].

Wednesbury unreasonableness,[45] rather than applying general principles. This is not to dismiss the role of principles. These can be used to help determine the content of heads of judicial review. Rather, it is to reason in a different manner. Courts do not apply general principles to specific facts. Rather they look to clear legal doctrines and heads of review. Each of these heads of review then requires the application of a specific set of tests. General principles may help to determine the scope of these tests, but the role of the court is to interpret and apply rules in a deductive manner, not to inductively apply general principles to specific facts.

Given these examples, the question arises as to whether common law reasoning works for public law cases. Is it too restrictive for public law cases always to focus on ripe events that have happened or definitely will happen? Should public law cases allow for more abstract challenges, which do not require specific facts to determine whether general provisions breach public law standards? Moreover, is public law more suited to top-down as opposed to bottom-up reasoning, applying general principles free from the constraints of legal taxonomies and specific heads of judicial review? The next section will argue that these examples are best understood more broadly. They illustrate difficulties with common law reasoning more generally, not merely issues that arise in public law cases.

II. Evaluating Common Law Reasoning

Common law reasoning is similar to analogical reasoning. It relies on an analysis of similarities and differences between specific examples. If the circumstances raised in case B are sufficiently similar to those which arose in an earlier case (case A) then analogical reasoning will conclude that case B should be decided in the same way as case A. However, if there are relevant differences between case B and case A, analogical reasoning would argue that these differences would mean that case B need not be decided in the same way as case A. These differences mean that case B requires a distinct solution. This search for similarities and differences may occur between specific cases and may also occur at a more abstract level, between different principles or rules of the common law, or different values and principles relied upon to justify different rules or principles of the common law. However, this section will argue that this process of analogical reasoning is flawed. It does not provide the same logically correct or justifiable outcomes as occur when we apply deductive or inductive reasoning. This suggests that, to the extent that we can find examples of public law cases which appear to reject aspects of common law reasoning, this may be due to deeper flaws in analogical reasoning as a whole rather

[45] *Associated Provincial Picture Houses Ltd v Wednesbury Corporation* (n 3).

than due to specific issues that arise in public law. This can be seen by investigating analogical reasoning in more depth.

Analogical reasoning can best be explained by means of an example. We referred earlier to the *Northern Ireland Abortion* case.[46] When discussing the compatibility of legislation with Convention rights, the Supreme Court discussed a range of possible circumstances where the law would prevent a woman from seeking an abortion in a manner that would harm her Convention rights. One example was serious foetal abnormality. Another example was fatal foetal abnormality. Case A, an earlier case, could reach the conclusion that Convention rights were breached as the legislation prevented abortion for fatal foetal abnormality. Case B then arises before the court, which concerns a case of serious, but not fatal, foetal abnormality. Analogical reasoning requires the court in case B to look for relevant similarities and differences between case A and case B. Both concern issues where the foetus has abnormalities. However, there are differences between the two. In case A, the foetus will die of these abnormalities. In case B, the foetal abnormalities in and of themselves are not fatal, but they may significantly impede the quality of life of the child once born, or shorten life expectancy, perhaps making the child more prone to other potentially fatal illnesses, with consequences for both the child and the child's parents.

This example both illustrates analogical reasoning and demonstrates its weaknesses. When do these similarities or differences mean that the courts should reach the same or a different conclusion? These problems lead some to question whether analogical reasoning is a form of reasoning or logic at all, as its application does not reach clear logical conclusions in the same way as deductive and inductive reasoning.[47] In order to determine whether courts should conclude that Convention rights are breached when the law prevents abortions for serious foetal abnormality, more needs to be known about the distinction between fatal and serious foetal abnormality and whether these mean that the law should treat the two cases differently. In the *Northern Irish Abortion Case*, Lady Black concluded that the Northern Ireland abortion regulations did breach Convention rights in situations of fatal foetal abnormality, but she was not prepared to reach the same conclusion for serious foetal abnormality. Lady Hale, Lord Kerr, Lord Mance, and Lord Wilson reached the opposite conclusion.[48] If we are to regard analogical reasoning as providing a clear, logical conclusion, then we would have to regard either Lady Black, or Lady Hale and Lords Kerr, Mance, and Wilson, as having reached a logical mistake. They must have failed to reason correctly. What was probably influencing the different conclusions in the *Northern Irish Abortion* case was the use of an analysis

[46] *In the matter of an application by the Northern Irish Human Rights Commission for Judicial Review (Northern Ireland)* (n 28).

[47] Postema, 'Philosophy of the Common Law' (n 11).

[48] *In the matter of an application by the Northern Irish Human Rights Commission for Judicial Review (Northern Ireland)* (n 28).

of Convention rights to ascertain whether different outcomes should be reached in cases of fatal or serious foetal abnormalities. Perhaps for Lady Black, the right to life had more importance than the right to autonomy, such that only the prevention of abortions for fatal foetal abnormality would breach Convention rights. The other judges of the Supreme Court who concluded that Convention rights had been breached arguably placed more value on the right to autonomy than the right to life. Whilst analogical reasoning requires us to look for similarities and differences, it does not provide a framework from which to determine which of these similarities and differences are relevant in order to determine whether a later case should follow the outcome of an earlier case.[49] However, the process of analogical reasoning is silent as to whether this use of Convention rights was necessary or sufficient to determine whether the two cases should be treated in the same manner. It is also silent as to the relative weight to be given to differences and similarities between the cases. Which begs the question: is analogical reasoning doing anything in this case at all?

Further difficulties arise from adopting a case-by-case approach. Frederick Schauer's work provides a clear illustration of the problems that arise when judges focus too greatly on the circumstances of the case before the court. This may lead them to fail fully to take account of other information. As such, the rule developed by the courts fails to recognise all of the future circumstances in which the rule may be applied. Drawing on work in behavioural psychology, Schauer argues that there are three particular heuristics—understood as short-cuts in our reasoning process akin to rules of thumb—that could influence case-by-case decision-making and lead to flawed conclusions: the availability heuristic, the anchoring heuristic, and the issue-framing heuristic.[50] The availability heuristic occurs as courts focus so much on the case before them, they see this as more representative of the typical or common case that may arise in the future than is realistic. To apply this to the *Northern Irish Abortion Case*, a future case could arise regarding abortion for children conceived through incest. When determining whether an abortion should be permitted in these circumstances, the court may be influenced by the case of incest before it and overestimate the extent to which incestuous relationships occur and when pregnancies arise as a result of these relationships. This may lead to a restriction of abortions to incest or exceptional circumstances, to the detriment of other situations where abortion may be justified such as rape outside of incest.

The anchoring heuristic occurs when the properties in the case before the court influence the estimation of properties in future events. When applied to abortion,

[49] See Alexander and Sherwin (n 11), chs 1–3, Rigoni (n 11), Postema, 'A Similibus ad Similia' (n 11), Sunstein (n 11), and Scott Brewer, 'Exemplary Reasoning: Semantics, Pragmatics and the Rational Force of Legal Argument by Analogy' (1996) 109 Harvard L Rev 923.

[50] Schauer (n 18) See also Rachlinski (n 12).

the anchoring heuristic would focus on the properties of incest and why this particular set of circumstances would merit an abortion, perhaps focusing on the particular circumstances of the abuse of the pregnant woman concerned, or her age. These circumstances would then anchor abortion to such instances, limiting future possible expansion of the law to permit abortion in other circumstances. The issue-framing heuristic occurs when the circumstances of the case before the court frame future issues. For example, this would occur were the example of an abusive incestuous relationship to frame the issues for future abortion cases, requiring the court to focus too greatly on the relationship between the parents of the foetus and whether this was abusive towards the mother. This may mean that the court overlooks other issues relevant to whether an abortion should be permitted such as in the case of serious or fatal foetal abnormalities. [51]

These heuristics may mean that case-by-case reasoning is less likely to develop the best rule or principle of the common law. When combined with the weaknesses of analogical reasoning, they provide a powerful criticism of the extent to which common law reasoning provides a means through which courts reach the right outcome. These difficulties are exacerbated when common law reasoning applied in one particular case may establish a more general precedent, yet the specific case in which the general principle is developed may be unable to take account of the application of this principle to possible future circumstances.[52] When faced with these difficulties, advocates of common law reasoning face a number of possible responses.[53]

One option is to reject analogical reasoning as part of the common law. Those who choose to reject analogical reasoning could advocate instead that the courts should adopt an 'all things considered' reasoning process.[54] Whilst this may mean that courts look to past cases when determining decisions, these past cases are merely evidence that courts could use. If the court concludes that abortion law should treat serious foetal abnormalities in the same way as fatal foetal abnormalities, it does so because there are good reasons for concluding that a law which prohibits abortion for serious foetal abnormalities breaches Convention rights, not because the courts are led to this conclusion by contemplating the similarities and differences between serious and fatal foetal abnormalities. Examples of this approach include Dworkin's theory of adjudication, using a combination of fit and integrity, drawing on principles running through the common law.[55] Trevor Allan's

[51] Schauer (n 18).

[52] Richard Buxton, 'How The Common Law Gets Made: Hedley Byrne and Other Cautionary Tales' (2009) 125 LQR 60.

[53] See Charles Barzun, 'Justice Souter's Common Law' (2018) 104 Virginia L Rev 655, Scott Brewer, 'Exemplary Reasoning: Semantics, Pragmatics and the Rational Force of Legal Argument by Analogy' (1996) 109 Harvard L Rev 923 and Postema 'Philosophy of the Common Law' (n 11).

[54] Alexander and Sherwin refer to this as the 'natural law model', see Alexander and Sherwin (n 11) ch 2.

[55] Ronald Dworkin, *Law's Empire* (Fontana 1986).

approach is similar to that of Dworkin, however Allan focuses predominantly on integrity as opposed to fit.[56]

An alternative response is to accept analogical reasoning as part of the common law, despite its flaws. This may merely be a matter of trust or faith in the artificial reasoning of the common law.[57] Or it may be because there are other reasons for adopting the common law approach. For example, common law reasoning may restrict judicial activism.[58] It may also enable judges to reach incompletely theorised agreements, such that judges can agree as to the outcome in a particular case even when they disagree as to why this is the right outcome.[59] Moreover, judges should gain expertise in legal reasoning, potentially avoiding some of the flaws of analogical reasoning.[60] Whilst imperfect, it may be the best form of reasoning suited to the constitutional role of the common law judge.

Analogical reasoning may also have value as a distinct form of reasoning. Brewer, for example, argues that analogical reasoning is best understood as a form of abductive reasoning.[61] Courts look at past cases and abduct possible legal principles that can be applied to future cases. These legal principles are abductions as they form hypotheses as to the most likely explanation for the results of legal cases. However, abductions differ from deductions. They are not logical arguments which lead to the truth. Rather, they give rise to probabilities, with an accompanying selection of the most probable hypothesis being used to support a particular outcome. Having abducted these possible principles, based on a selection of relevant similarities and differences between cases, the court then confirms or disapplies these possible principles, selecting the most likely hypothesis. It then applies these principles to the case before the court.

Alternatively, there may be value in the dynamic aspect of common law reasoning, based on the value of dialogue and reasoning by argument. Courts may devise a means of ascertaining the relevance of similarities and differences through a dynamic process, before using these differences and similarities to determine the case before the court.[62] This dynamic process places restraints on the court: from history; the need for judges to reach collective solutions; and the ensuing creation of different legal taxonomies combined with background principles. Schauer also argues that this dynamic process may reduce the impact of the heuristics that develop in case-by-case reasoning.[63] These possible responses to the weaknesses of

[56] See TRS Allan, 'Text, Context, and Constitution: The Common Law as Public Reason' in Douglas Edlin (ed), *Common Law Theory* (CUP 2007) 185.

[57] See, for example, Lord Coke (n 10) and Levi (n 11).

[58] Schauer (n 18) and Emily Sherwin, 'Judges as Rulemakers' (2006) 73 University of Chicago L Rev 919.

[59] See Sunstein (n 11) and Cass Sunstein, 'Incompletely Theorized Agreements' (1995) 108 Harvard L Rev 1733.

[60] Frederick Schauer and Barbara Spellman, 'Analogy, Expertise and Experience' (2017) 84 University of Chicago L Rev 249.

[61] Brewer, 'Exemplary Reasoning (n 53).

[62] Postema, 'A Similibus ad Similia' (n 11).

[63] Schauer (n 18) 906–18.

analogical and case-by-case reasoning do not argue that analogical reasoning will have the same value as deductive or inductive reasoning. Nevertheless, they aim to explain the value of adopting analogical reasoning in the common law, showing in particular how this may be suited to the judiciary, justifying their role in the development of the common law.

An alternative response to the weaknesses of analogical and case-by-case reasoning is to develop rules to ascertain the relevant similarities and differences between cases. These rules are then applied, enabling courts to establish relevant similarities and differences. These rules, in turn, are deduced from previous cases.[64] This is where we see the development of legal taxonomies playing a role. Legal taxonomies can provide categories from previous cases, whose provisions are then applied in a rule-like manner. As such, they aim to provide a form of deductive logic. Courts look to the rules which are derived from a series of past cases, applying these to current cases before the court. These rules are established within particular legal doctrines. In English public law, this means that we focus on determining specific heads of judicial review, with the case law establishing the rules of these heads of judicial review. This can be contrasted with approaches that focus on standards as opposed to rules, where courts are less constrained by legal doctrines, and focus more on reaching what they perceive to be the right conclusion in a particular case, or focus on applying general standards that run through public law.

This analysis of common law reasoning suggests that examples of public law cases which do not fit common law approaches to case law are explained as reactions to flaws in analogical reasoning more generally, rather than specific to public law. This, in turn, may suggest that there is nothing special or distinct about public law. However, the following section suggests that things may not be so simple. This current section has hinted at two possible responses to the weaknesses of analogical reasoning, the inductive turn and the deductive turn. The inductive turn aims to correct flaws in analogical reasoning by applying inductive reasoning in case law. This is illustrated by the use of top-down as opposed to bottom-up reasoning in public law cases, as well as a willingness to consider unripe, non-specific cases. The deductive turn is illustrated by a greater use of taxonomies to provide sets of rules to determine necessary and sufficient differences between different cases when using bottom-up common law reasoning.

Less work has been done on producing a taxonomy of public law as a whole than there has been in the field of private law.[65] This might suggest that taxonomies are less suited to public law, although it may also be caused by alternative explanations.[66] This, in turn, could suggest that public law is different as it is more suited

[64] Alexander and Sherwin (n 11) ch 3.

[65] See Jason Varuhas, 'Taxonomy and Public Law' in Mark Elliott, Jason Varuhas, and Shona Wilson Stark (eds), *The Unity of Public Law? Doctrinal, Theoretical and Comparative Perspectives* (Hart 2018) 39.

[66] Ibid 40–48.

to a move towards inductive as opposed to deductive reasoning to correct flaws in analogical reasoning. The next section will develop this argument further. It will do so by re-examining the difference between developing a taxonomical approach, the deductive turn, and a balancing approach to legal reasoning, the inductive turn. It will not argue that public law cases and private law cases provide a different type of case which is more or less suited to taxonomical approaches. However, it does argue that there is a difference in degree between public and private law, whereby public law is slightly more suited to inductive reasoning. This can be illustrated by revisiting what it means to adopt a taxonomical as opposed to a balancing approach and how this connects to rules and standards.

III. Is Public Law More Suited to Inductive Reasoning?

Whether the law moves towards adopting a taxonomical approach to legal reasoning, focusing on deductive reasoning, or a balancing approach to reasoning, based on inductive reasoning, is linked to differences between rules and standards. When courts apply rules, they respond in a set way to a series of triggers or facts. When courts apply standards, they apply background principles to the facts to reach a particular conclusion.[67] This distinction is one of degree, and it may not be possible to draw a definitive line between the two in practice.[68] This section explores the relative advantages and disadvantages of adopting a more taxonomical or balancing approach to explore whether this points to a difference between public law and private law, arguing that public law may be less likely to adopt a taxonomical approach, given the existence of reasons for public law cases to use standards as opposed to rules. Moreover, background constitutional principles can be more influential when evaluating the use of common law reasoning in public law cases than in private law cases. This is not to argue for a difference in type, but for one of degree. However, it is nevertheless important when assessing whether common law reasoning should be lauded for its ability creatively to keep public bodies in check, and to preserve the rule of law and individual rights, without undermining their ability to achieve the public good, or whether common law reasoning should be criticised for its tendency to undermine democracy and to cripple public authorities, preventing them from achieving the public good.

The choice between rules and standards depends, in part, on a choice between accuracy and certainty and predictability. Rules make generalisations, meaning

[67] Frederick Schauer, *Playing by the Rules: a Philosophical Examination of Rule-based Decision-making in Law and in Life* (Clarendon Press 1991), Frederick Schauer, 'The Convergence of Rules and Standards' (2003) New Zealand L Rev 303, Sullivan (n 40) Duncan Kennedy, 'Form and Substance in Private Law Adjudication' (1976) 89 Harvard L Rev 1685, Cass Sunstein, 'Problems with Rules' (1995) 83 California L Rev 953.

[68] Schauer, 'The Convergence of Rules and Standards' (n 67).

that they can be over- and under-inclusive. Rules promote formal equality, whereas standards promote substantive equality. Also, the application of rules and standards assigns different power to the person making or applying the rule or standard. A classic example used to explain these differences is a rule prohibiting all dogs in cafés, except assistance dogs. The purpose behind the rule may be to prevent disruption in cafés whilst ensuring equal access. But the rule would also allow badly trained assistance dogs and other pets into the café, causing disruption. Standards set looser guidelines, for example preventing all animals from the café, except when required to ensure the equal treatment of all visitors to the café. However, they create inefficiency. Each prospective café visitor with a pet would have to be talked to, their pet assessed, and their justification for the need for their pet evaluated to determine whether the pet should be allowed to enter the café in order to ensure equal treatment for all.[69] Rules provide formal equality. All those with dogs and with other pets are treated in the same way. Standards facilitates substantive equality, remedying situations where treating all those with dogs or other pets in the same way can give rise to unequal treatment such as preventing those with other types of assistance animal from enjoying the hospitality of the café. If the café manageress sets a rule, she determines the content of the rule. Very little discretion is left to the waitress. She merely has to determine whether an animal is a certified assistance dog. When the café manageress sets a standard, far more decision-making power is given to the waitress. She has to assess what is meant by disruptive and how to ensure that all are treated equally. This requires an evaluation of each pet, the needs of its owner, the needs of those in the café, and permissible levels of disruption.

These differences point to a possible distinction between the use of case law in public law and private law, which may suggest that the problems of analogical reasoning may be more likely to be resolved in public law cases by a move towards inductive reasoning, whereas they may be more likely to be resolved in private law cases by a move towards more deductive reasoning. A move towards taxonomical reasoning, focusing on deductive reasoning, is more likely to occur when there are good reasons to prefer rules over standards; for example, when there is a stronger need for certainty over accuracy, a preference for formal over substantive equality, and a need to place more power in the rule-maker as opposed to the person or institution empowered to interpret and apply the rule. A move away from taxonomical reasoning towards balancing, applying first principles to specific cases in a top-down manner, is more likely to occur when the area of law values accuracy over certainty, substantive over formal equality, and is less likely to be concerned about placing greater power in the hands of the institution interpreting and applying the law as opposed to the institution making the law.

[69] Schauer, *Playing by the Rules* (n 67).

An argument could be made that, at a very abstract level, certainty is more valuable than accuracy for private law cases, and that accuracy is more important than certainty for public law cases. First, this is because of a difference between the purposes of private and public law. Private law often aims to provide a framework of rules, enabling individuals to carry out their lives and regulate their relationships with other individuals. The more this framework produces clear and certain rules, the more the framework is able to achieve its purpose of facilitating individuals to regulate their relationships with others. We can see this, for example, when we look at contract law or property law. Clear, certain, predictable rules mean that individuals can enter into contracts or purchase and lease land. Without certainty, individuals may be deterred from entering into these negotiations, particularly when concerned with large sums of money or when trust is needed, such as in international trade relationships. Public law is different. It is concerned less with providing a framework within which individuals can enter into relationships with others and concerned more with regulating public bodies. Public law both facilitates public bodies to achieve the public good and restricts the powers of public bodies to ensure that their authority is kept within legal bounds. Accuracy—understood as ensuring these purposes are achieved—may be more important in public law than certainty and predictability.

These concerns are exacerbated by the requirement of the common law that the courts reach a decision in a particular case. This reinforces the focus of the court on the particular circumstances before it, requiring a correct outcome in that case, regardless of its impact on future decisions. If we see public law cases as placing greater importance on developing the right answer to general issues that arise in public law, unencumbered by a focus on the specific features of the case before the court, we may be more willing to allow the courts to entertain abstract review, reasoning from general principles as opposed to reasoning from case to case.

This is not to suggest that these are the only purposes of public law. Nor is there any suggestion that private law is solely concerned with regulating individuals. Rather, it serves as a broad generalisation, suggesting not that there is a difference in kind between private and public law but a difference of degree. Moreover, this suggestion is not meant to undermine the place of certainty and predictability in public law. Indeed, certainty and predictability are important in upholding the rule of law. However, it may be that these values are better achieved in a different manner. When public bodies are given broad discretionary powers, these bodies may create policies or guidelines to help them exercise this discretion. These policies can be developed in an incremental manner, or they can be added to through the development of administrative rules, practices, guidelines, and standards.[70] The development of administrative rules in this manner helps to provide a balance

[70] Kenneth Culp Davis, *Discretionary Justice: A Preliminary Inquiry* (Louisiana State University Press 1969).

between certainty, stability, and predictability. This, in turn, may require public law to interpret administrative policies more as rules than as standards to achieve a better balance between accuracy and certainty in public law.[71] It may also require courts to treat common law precedents more as standards than rules, to correct the inevitable inaccuracies that will arise through the application of rules given that rules are over- and under-inclusive. Common law heads of review may act as a check on the application of administrative rules which no longer achieve their purpose.

Similar arguments may apply to an assessment of whether specific areas of the law prioritise formal or substantive equality. Public law may be more likely to focus on human rights, where there is often a preference for substantive over formal equality. Again, this is not to argue that formal equality is not relevant to public law, or that human rights do not play an important role in private law as well as in public law. Rather, it is to point to a matter of degree. Whilst formal equality may suffice to ensure that those who enter into similar contracts are treated in a similar manner, as well as preserving freedom of contract, for example, the same may not be true of public law issues which may require greater substantive equality in the distribution of public goods or the protection of human rights.

Differences between private law and public law cases may also emerge when we evaluate the way in which a choice between rules and standards allocates decision-making power. When applying a rule, greater decision-making power is given to the rule-maker. When applying a standard, greater decision-making power is given to the rule-applier. When courts adopt a taxonomical approach, applying previous case law in a more rule-like manner, greater certainty is created for administrative bodies as to the scope of their powers, facilitating their ability to achieve the public good. Taxonomies also provide a greater discretionary area of judgment to public authorities. The opposite is true of the application of standards and reasoning from first principles. To return to *Gallaher*, establishing clear rules as to when legitimate expectations are created, and when public authorities can go back on these expectations, provides clearer guidance to the CMA than instructing it that it must act fairly and respect equality in all cases. This, in turn, may enable the CMA a greater discretionary area of judgment when determining how to police price-fixing cartels.

Public law cases may also require the balancing of different rights and interests, as illustrated in the *Northern Irish Abortion Case*. The balancing of these rights and interests may be contestable. It can be reasonable to disagree as to the relative merits of the protection of the right to life of the unborn child and the protection of the autonomy of the mother. In these circumstances, finality is needed and institutions may be required to provide a clear determination, setting a precise rule that

[71] Julia Black, '"Which Arrow?" Rule Type and Regulatory Policy' [1995] PL 94.

is adhered to in order to provide clarity and certainty. We may, therefore, want the Supreme Court to set a clear rule, which is then applied in a taxonomical manner in lower courts. The concern to uphold the rule of law may justify the adoption of a more top-down approach to reasoning by the Supreme Court, allowing the Court to provide for as good a protection of rights as it can, taking account of all of the relevant interests. It may also justify the adoption of more abstract reasoning, providing clearer guidance to lower courts.

However, we also want this balancing of competing rights and interests to be made in a legitimate manner. Democratically elected and accountable bodies may be a more legitimate institution to perform this balance. Some public authorities have greater democratic legitimacy and may make decisions in a more democratically accountable manner than the courts. For example, local councils may make planning and licensing decisions in a democratic manner, with locally elected councillors voting to approve or reject specific committee decisions.[72] Administrative bodies may also have indirect democratic legitimacy, with public authorities being held to account for the decisions they make—for example the decisions of Ministers—or through arguments that public authorities are performing the public good, having had delegated to them the power to exercise functions that would otherwise be performed by Parliament. This is not true of all administrative bodies; for example, individual immigration officers taking specific decisions, or Housing Officers determining whether to allocate a home to someone who is unintentionally homeless.

These concerns as to the relative institutional composition, and constitutional legitimacy of courts, legislatures, and the administration, may also be relevant to our assessment of whether applying standards as opposed to rules really is more likely to produce the right answer. Whilst an application of standards may be better able to reach the right outcome in theory, this may not be the case if the relative institutional features of the body making and applying the law are different. If there are good reasons to suggest that the institutional features of the court mean that they are more likely to reach the best answer than the administration, then there remain good reasons to apply standards as opposed to rules. However, if the relative institutional features of the legislature and the court suggest that the administration is better placed to reach the right decision, then there may be good reasons for applying rules as opposed to standards. In the *Northern Irish Abortion Case*, we could argue that courts are better placed to ensure that legislation protects Convention rights, given that courts develop relative expertise in the interpretation of human rights. However, the CMA may be better able to reach the right conclusion as to whether a particular business practice is anti-competitive, given its greater knowledge of and expertise in economic analysis. As such, we may want

72 The UK courts have shown themselves to be sensitive to this issue, giving deference to such decisions. See, for example, *Miss Behavin' Ltd v Belfast City Council* [2007] UKHL 19, [2007] 3 All ER 1007.

courts to adopt standards when determining whether legislation regulating abortion breaches Convention rights, but to apply clear taxonomies when evaluating anti-competitive practices.

Two conclusions emerge from this analysis. First, it suggests that there may be differences in degree as to whether public law is more likely to take an inductive as opposed to a deductive turn in order to correct flaws in analogical reasoning. However, this is contextual and depends upon the specific nature of the case before the court. Second, background constitutional principles may play more of a role in determining the approach to case law in public law than in private law. There may be good constitutional reasons for courts to reason in a top-down as opposed to a bottom-up manner and perhaps even adopting abstract judicial review in public law cases.[73] Such an approach is taken where background constitutional theory dictates that substantive principles of the rule of law and substantive equality is more important than formal equality, or where courts are better able to reach the right answer as to the resolution of a specific case. In contrast, when courts are faced with more contestable issues there may be good constitutional reasons to adopt a more case-specific, taxonomical approach, transferring more decision-making authority to directly or indirectly accountable institutions.[74] These examples represent opposite ends of a broad spectrum. There is a range of positions in between these extremes which aim to reconcile the rule of law and democracy,[75] or which advocate a more contextually specific role for courts.[76] The modest argument made here is not that these concerns are specific to public law but merely that this constitutional dimension may be more apparent in public law cases than in private law cases.

IV. Conclusion

'Would that it were so simple'.[77]Since writing this chapter, the Supreme Court delivered its judgment in the *Privacy International* case.[78] The case illustrates the deficiencies of analogical reasoning. This chapter has argued that reasoning by analogy does not provide a logically correct answer. Rather, it relies on other factors to determine whether previous cases are sufficient similar to, or different from, the case before the court. In *Privacy International*, the Supreme Court had to decide whether

[73] See TRS Allan, 'Principle, Practice and Precedent: Vindicating Justice, According to the Law' (2018) 77 CLJ 269.

[74] See Philip Sales, 'Partnership and Challenge: The Court's Role in Managing the Integration of Rights and Democracy' [2016] PL 456.

[75] Elliott (n 31).

[76] Sunstein, 'Incompletely Theorised Agreements' (n 59) and Sunstein, 'On Analogical Reasoning' (n 11) and Alison L Young *Democratic Dialogue and the Constitution* (OUP 2017).

[77] Joel Cohen and Ethan Cohen, *Hail, Caesar!* (Working Title Films 2016).

[78] *R (Privacy International Ltd) v Investigatory Powers Tribunal* (n 2).

the decision of *Anisminic* was sufficiently similar to that in *Privacy International*.[79] Both involved an ouster clause over decisions of a tribunal. However, whilst the clause in *Anisminic* stated that 'determinations … shall not be called in question in any court of law', the clause in *Privacy International* stated that 'determinations (including any decisions as to their jurisdiction)' shall not to be 'questioned in any court'. The High Court, the Court of Appeal, and Lord Wilson in the Supreme Court concluded that this difference was sufficient to distinguish *Anisminic* from *Privacy International*. However, Lord Carnwath, with whom Lord Kerr and Lady Hale agreed, and Lord Lloyd-Jones, reached the opposite conclusion. They read *Anisminic* as concluding that a 'determination' did not include a 'purported determination', a determination by the tribunal that had made a legal error. Similarly, the ouster clause in *Privacy International* did not included 'purported determinations' made by a tribunal as to whether it had jurisdiction.[80] The distinct wording was insufficient to distinguish the ouster clause in *Privacy International* from the clause in *Anisminic*.

The court also divided over its treatment of other similarities and differences between the two cases. *Anisminic* concerned determinations of the Foreign Compensation Commission. *Privacy International* concerned decisions of the Investigatory Powers Tribunal (IPT). Yet these bodies had different compositions and functions. The IPT performed a judicial function and its membership included members of the high court. The minority in the Supreme Court placed more emphasis on these differences. In particular, they argued that there was a better justification for removing judicial review over decisions of the IPT, given that the IPT may be just as capable of upholding the rule of law as the high court. Lord Sumption, drawing on a similarity between *Privacy International* and *Lee v Ashers Baking Co Ltd* that was not mentioned by Lord Carnwath,[81] concluded that the ouster clause in *Privacy International* did not remove judicial review of jurisdictional determinations where the IPT made a procedural error, but did oust judicial review for other determinations of the IPT. How can we argue that analogical reasoning provides a logically correct answer to a specific case when we can point to these differences in the assessment of the similarities and differences between *Anisminic* and *Privacy International*?

Additionally, the majority and minority in *Privacy International* adopt different approaches to judicial reasoning. The majority judgment of Lord Carnwath reasons from first principles. Lord Carnwath relies on *Cart*,[82] which he interprets as a move away from the more 'technical' approach exemplified in *Anisminic*.[83]

[79] *Anisminic v Foreign Compensation Commission* (n 1).

[80] *R (Privacy International Ltd) v Investigatory Powers Tribunal* (n 2), [104]–[112] (Lord Carnwath) and [164]–[165] (Lord Lloyd-Jones).

[81] [2018] UKSC 49, [2018] 3 WLR 1294.

[82] *R (Cart) v Upper Tribunal* [2011] UKSC 28, [2012] 1 AC 663.

[83] *R (Privacy International Ltd) v Investigatory Powers Tribunal* (n 2) [98]–[99].

Lord Carnwath regards the case law on ouster clauses as an application of the principle of legality.[84] Rather than focusing on the difference in wording between the two ouster clauses,[85] he reasons from first principles to determine the extent to which the high court should be able to review decisions of the IPT, focusing on the relative institutional features of the IPT and the high court, and the need to ensure that the high court upholds the rule of law and ensures that the IPT is not able to create its own distinctive enclave whose law deviates from the law as established by the high court.

Lord Wilson, however, adopts a more technical approach, focusing specifically on the legal taxonomies created by earlier case law. Although he 'deprecates' the reinterpretation of *Anisminic* in later cases,[86] Lord Wilson nevertheless concludes that *Anisminic* now means that clauses stating that determinations are final do not oust judicial review of jurisdictional errors, with all errors of law deemed to be jurisdictional errors. As such, a clause which purported to oust judicial review for jurisdictional issues as well would be capable of removing judicial review of the court. Lord Sumption also adopts a more taxonomical approach, drawing on *Anisminic* and *Lee v Ashers Baking Co Ltd*.[87] He derives three principles from these cases as to how to interpret the ouster clause in *Privacy International*: 'the character of the Tribunal's functions, the nature of the error of law of which it is accused by the appellant, and the construction of section 67(8) as applied to alleged errors of that kind'.[88] The difference between Lord Sumption and Lord Wilson is best understood as one of degree as opposed to a difference in kind. Lord Sumption derives his principles from an analysis of the case law. Lord Wilson, however, is less willing to read the case law in order to find general principles of application, focusing instead on the more technical approach illustrated in *Anisminic*.

This chapter argued that, at a general abstract level, there may be good reasons for public law cases to move towards inductive as opposed to deductive reasoning, whilst recognising that this argument is both modest and abstract. In addition, background constitutional principles may be more relevant to public law than to private law when determining whether the courts should adopt a more inductive, abstract approach to judicial review as opposed to adopting a more deductive, taxonomical approach. This reasoning would tend to suggest that the approach of Lord Carnwath is more suited to public law reasoning than that of Lord Sumption. However, this presumption could be rebutted if there was a greater need for legal certainty as to whether such clauses can oust the jurisdiction of tribunals than there was a need for a right answer to such issues, or if it were felt that Parliament, as opposed to the courts, were best placed to determine this issue. The question

[84] Ibid [100]–[101].
[85] Ibid [107].
[86] Ibid [219].
[87] See (n 81).
[88] *R (Privacy International Ltd) v Investigatory Powers Tribunal* (n 2) [193].

before the Supreme Court in *Privacy International* not only determined the relative powers of tribunals and courts, it also raised deeper constitutional issues concerning the separation of powers, parliamentary sovereignty, and the rule of law. These deep issues of constitutional law are best resolved by a use of first principles rather than the development of technical taxonomies that may fail to take account of constitutional implications. Lord Carnwath concluded that there were strong constitutional reasons for the court to make these determinations, with a smaller role for Parliament.[89] Lord Sumption felt that Parliament should play a stronger role.[90]

The problems with analogical reasoning that we identified are not unique to the use of case law in public law. Nor do they provide a strong challenge to the use of case law as a means of developing principles of public law. As such, they are insufficient to challenge Craig's assertion that case law does and should shape the content of judicial review. Rather, the challenge is more subtle. It questions the extent to which we can make generalisations about the role of case law in public law. A range of factors will influence how cases should be used in English administrative law, influenced by the relative importance of certainty and accuracy, the specific institutional features of the administration and the judiciary, and background constitutional theories. Case law is foundational to English administrative law. However, we cannot generalise about its role. The extent to which it legitimately grounds English public law, and the specific role it should play, is contextually sensitive. Perhaps in this sense, we can only conclude that an assessment of the extent to which case law is foundational, and the extent to which case law should be used to ground principles of judicial review, can itself only be determined on a case-by-case basis.

89 Ibid [122]–[132].
90 Ibid [208]–[210].

6

The Mutual Judicial Influence of National Courts and the European Court of Justice through the Preliminary Rulings Mechanism

Evidence from the United Kingdom

*Gráinne de Búrca**

I. Introduction

Amongst the many topics on which Paul Craig has written authoritatively and thoughtfully is the relationship between national courts and the European Court of Justice (CJEU). In one of his classic articles on EU law, he suggested that the relationship between national courts and the CJEU can tell us much about the nature of the EU legal order, and he surveyed a range of proposals that were made at that time for the reform of the famous preliminary reference procedure.[1] This chapter takes as its starting point his suggestion about what the relationship between national courts and the CJEU can reveal, and examines the relationship between the UK courts and the CJEU through the lens of the preliminary reference procedure. While this topic has been studied before, the prospect of Brexit gives cause to reflect anew on the mutual influence of the British courts on the CJEU. In that vein, and drawing on Craig's reflection about the preliminary reference procedure, the chapter asks to what extent and in what ways did UK membership of the European Union influence the CJEU and vice versa? In addition to addressing the questions themselves, the study provides a basis for reflecting on what might be lost, from the perspective of the judicial role, on the departure of the United Kingdom from the European Union.

* I would like to thank the participants at the conference at St John's College Oxford in September 2018, and the EU law roundtable in New York in November 2018 for their comments and critiques. Particular thanks are due to Francis Jacobs and Oke Odudu for their suggestions, and to Markos Volikas and Isobel D'Arcy for their valuable research assistance.

[1] Paul Craig 'The Jurisdiction of the Community Courts Reconsidered' (2001) 36 Texas Intl LJ 555.

Gráinne de Búrca, *The Mutual Judicial Influence of National Courts and the European Court of Justice through the Preliminary Rulings Mechanism* In: *The Foundations and Future of Public Law*. Edited by: Elizabeth Fisher, Jeff King, Alison L Young, Oxford University Press (2020). © Oxford University Press.
DOI: 10.1093/oso/9780198845249.003.0006

The chapter begins by summarising some of the aspects of UK judicial influence on the CJEU that have previously been analysed, and moves on to examine an additional aspect of legal influence—the extent to which UK courts, through the preliminary reference procedure, seem to have influenced the CJEU in its interpretation of EU law—that has not yet been the subject of much analysis. It concludes by reflecting on what these aspects of the relationship shaped by the preliminary reference procedure between the CJEU and the British courts tell us about the EU judicial order.

The chapter finds that there is a remarkable lack of information available about what happens after a preliminary ruling is given by the Luxembourg Court, which makes it difficult to assess the extent to which the preliminary rulings of the CJEU were implemented by the referring UK courts. On the question of the possible influence of British courts on the CJEU through the preliminary reference procedure, however, the findings of the study suggest that in the substantial number of references in which the British courts advanced a proposed interpretation of EU law, the CJEU adopted that interpretation in a majority of those cases. The unwillingness of the CJEU to refer expressly to the proposed interpretation of the referring court, however, means that this influence must be inferred rather than clearly demonstrated.

II. The Influence of UK Membership on the European Court of Justice: A Summary

Earlier scholarship has examined specific dimensions of the topic of the influence of UK membership on the CJEU. One important aspect has been the influence of the British judges and Advocates General of the CJEU on the reasoning and judgments of the Court.[2] Another has been the impact of UK membership on the practice and style of argument before the Court.[3] A more basic but fundamental dimension of the UK's influence on the Court to which attention has recently been drawn is the fact that English is the most common spoken language amongst those working at or with the Court, even if French remains the working language of the judges.[4] It has been pointed out that despite the United Kingdom's likely exit from the EU, the common usage of English as a working language amongst many of

[2] Fernanda Nicola 'National Legal Traditions at Work in the Jurisprudence of the Court of Justice of the European Union' (2016) 64 American J of Comp Law 865.

[3] David Edward 'The British Contribution to the Development of Law and Legal Process in the European Union' in Basil Markesinis (ed), The British Contribution to the Europe of the Twenty-First Century (Hart 2002) 25–35.

[4] See Fernanda Nicola 'Luxembourg Judicial Style With or Without the UK' (2017) 40 Fordham Intl LJ 1505.

those at the court is likely to remain one of the key lasting contributions to the CJEU of Britain's EU membership.[5]

Some years ago David Edward, a former UK judge of the CJEU, outlined a number of the different ways in which British lawyers and law had influenced the European Court.[6] He pointed to the individual influence of the various Advocates General from the United Kingdom, all of whom had been highly distinguished and notable lawyers, and whose opinions in many cases were persuasive.[7] At the time he was writing, the three British Advocates General had been Jean-Pierre Warner, Gordon Slynn, and Francis Jacobs. These were since joined by the equally distinguished and influential Advocate General Eleanor Sharpston, whose opinions in a range of key EU cases—including *Ruiz Zambrano*,[8] *Bougnaoui*,[9] and the *Singapore Free Trade* Opinion,[10] to name just three—have been much discussed in recent years. Edward also referred to the impact that the UK Judge Mackenzie Stuart had while he was president of the CJEU, particularly on the productivity of the Court, and through his efforts to impress on Member States the importance of taking seriously the process of selection and appointment of CJEU judges.[11] And while the influence of the British judges on the Court is less visible than that of the Advocates General due to the collegiate nature of CJEU judgments and the absence of concurring or dissenting opinions, it seems likely that they had an impact on decision-making and the drafting of judgments, particularly given that the four British judges selected for membership of the CJEU were already prominent and respected advocates and judges from the domestic system.

Pointing to a second kind of influence apart from that of specific judges and Advocates General, Edward also mentioned the practice adopted by the CJEU after British accession of asking questions of lawyers during the oral hearing before the Court.[12] This had apparently not been part of the Court's practice before accession, and Edwards suggests that British lawyers had brought to the Court 'a greater awareness of the help that judges can derive from good advocacy, both in defining the factual context of the case and in arguing the law'.[13] A third kind of influence he mentioned was the practice first introduced by the Court after British accession of explicitly citing its previous judgments as a form of precedent.[14] While the CJEU

[5] Ibid.

[6] Edward (n 3).

[7] Ibid 30.

[8] C-34/09, *Zambrano v ONEM* [2011] ECR I-1177.

[9] C-188/15, *Bougnaoui v Micropole SA* ECLI:EU:C:2016:553.

[10] Opinion 2/15 *(EU-Singapore Free Trade Agreement)* EU:C:2017:376.

[11] Edward (n 3) 30.

[12] Ibid 31–32.

[13] Ibid.

[14] Ibid at 32. See also Takis Tridimas 'Precedent and the Court of Justice: A Jurisprudence of Doubt?' in Julie Dickson and Pavlos Eleftheriadis (eds), *Philosophical Foundations of European Union Law* (OUP 2012) 307–30, who does not explicitly mention the influence of UK accession but notes that the practice of the Court of citing to its previous rulings began in the 1970s and continued apace in the 1980s. For

prior to the 1973 accession did frequently repeat large chunks of reasoning drawn from its earlier cases and used them again in later cases, it did not draw attention to the origin of these passages nor cite those earlier cases. And while it is difficult to point to causal effect with any certainty, the Court's move towards making explicit reference to its previous case law is likely to have been influenced by the presence of UK lawyers on the Court who were familiar with the domestic system of precedent, and by the presence of British lawyers arguing cases before the CJEU. Other academic commentators have pointed to a change in the style of reasoning of the CJEU, following the accession of the United Kingdom, Ireland, and Denmark in 1973, away from its earlier and more formal style influenced by the civil law background of its judges at the outset, to a more eclectic and argumentative style.[15]

A further source of British influence on the Court cited by David Edward was the willingness of British courts to send preliminary references to the CJEU, as well as the kinds of preliminary references they chose to send. He pointed to the fact that many of the cases referred to Luxembourg by UK courts—such as *Van Duyn*,[16] *Factortame*,[17] and *Courage v Crehan*[18]—became influential and important in the development of EU law more generally. In other words, the legal issues and the questions of EU law posed in the references sent by British courts gave the European Court the opportunity to deliver a range of rulings with widespread impact and importance for the EU legal order.[19] Others have suggested that the United Kingdom played a significant part in influencing the approach of the CJEU towards EU anti-discrimination law through the role of the British Advocates General as well as through the preliminary references made by UK courts and the participation of British lawyers in arguing these cases before the Luxembourg Court.[20] A less obvious but highly significant source of influence of UK membership on the CJEU, according to empirical research carried out, has been the very active practice of

a full-length treatment of the use of precedent before the CJEU, see Mark Jacob, *Precedents and Case-based Reasoning in the European Court of Justice: Unfinished Business* (CUP 2014).

[15] Nicola, 'Luxembourg Judicial Style' (n 4). For an earlier analysis at the time the United Kingdom joined the European Economic Community, see Valerio Grementieri and Cornelius Joseph Golden, 'The United Kingdom and the European Court of Justice: An Encounter Between Common and Civil Law Traditions' (1973) 21 American J of Comparative L 664.

[16] Case 41/74 *Van Duyn v Home Office* [2014] ECR 1337.

[17] Case C-213/89 *R v Secretary of State for Transport, ex parte Factortame* [1990] ECR I-2433.

[18] Case C-453/99 *Courage v Crehan* [2001] ECR I-6297.

[19] A somewhat similar observation was made by Carl Otto Lenz (an Advocate General of the CJEU) in discussing the references made by British courts to the CJEU: 'I think it can fairly be said that references from British courts nearly always raise substantial points concerning the interpretation of European law.' See Carl Otto Lenz and Gerhard Grill, 'The Preliminary Ruling Procedure and the United Kingdom' (1995) 19 Fordham Intl LJ 844, 856. For an analysis of the relationship between UK courts and the CJEU in relation to the preliminary reference procedure, see Jonathan Golub 'The Politics of Judicial Discretion: Rethinking the Interaction between National Courts and the European Court of Justice' (1996) 19 West European Politics 360.

[20] Julie Suk 'Equality after Brexit: Evaluating British Contributions to EU Anti-discrimination Law' (2017) 40 Fordham Intl LJ 1535

British government lawyers intervening to make observations in cases (including non-UK-originating preliminary reference cases) before the CJEU.[21] Finally, it has recently been suggested that the end of the productive stream of British court references to the CJEU could be the most significant impact of Brexit on the Court.[22]

It is clear from this brief summary that UK membership of the European Union had a clear and significant impact on the CJEU, on the content of the cases that came before the Court, on the nature of the oral stage and the development of a practice of advocacy before the Court and questioning by the Luxembourg judges, on the style of drafting and reasoning of the CJEU, the use of English by many of those working at the Court, and the active intervention by British government lawyers in all kinds of preliminary reference cases.

III. Mutual Influence of the UK Courts and the Court of Justice via the Preliminary Reference Procedure?

Apart from the presence of UK judges and Advocates General in the European Court, and the existence of informal judicial meetings and judicial networks,[23] the most obvious channel for the mutual influence of British Courts and the CJEU was the steady flow of preliminary references from the former to the latter. The preliminary reference mechanism was described by Paul Craig as the 'jewel in the crown' of the CJEU's jurisdiction,[24] and is widely accepted as a major source of its influence and a direct channel into the legal and judicial life of the member states. A great deal has been written about the importance of the preliminary reference mechanism, including by Craig in a number of articles and book chapters, outlining the ways in which the CJEU advanced the effectiveness of EU law in the Member States, and drew national courts into the process to act as decentralised EU courts participating in domestic enforcement.[25] The most obvious and

[21] Marie Pierre Granger 'When Governments go to Luxembourg: The Influence of Governments on the European Court of Justice' (2004) 29 European L Rev 3, who quotes the UK Treasury solicitor's department in 1996 in the following terms, at p 10: 'It is the policy of the United Kingdom to take an active part in proceedings. It is thought that the direction of case law can be best influenced by good quality arguments presented by Member States.' More recently Julian Dederke and Daniel Naurin have noted that the United Kingdom 'was the most active member state during [the 2004–2007] period, with observations recorded in almost every third case': Julian Dederke and Daniel Naurin, 'Friends of the Court? Why EU Governments File Observations before the Court of Justice' (2018) 57 European J of Political Research 867, 870. According to former Advocate General Francis Jacobs, the United Kingdom was alone amongst Member States in its early years as an EU Member State in systematically reviewing all preliminary references made to the CJEU with a view to determining whether or not to submit an observation in the case: email correspondence, November 2018.

[22] Ibid 1506.

[23] Monica Claes and Maartje de Visser 'Are you Networked Yet? On Dialogues between European Judicial Networks' (2012) 8 Utrecht L Rev 100.

[24] Paul Craig, *EU Administrative Law* (3rd edn, OUP 2018) Craig, 'The Jurisdiction of the Community Courts Reconsidered' (n 1).

[25] See eg Paul Craig 'Once Upon a Time in the West: Direct Effect and the Federalization of EEC Law' (1992) 12 OJLS 453.

widely discussed aspect of influence is the impact of the rulings of the CJEU on domestic UK courts, while the possible influence or impact of domestic courts on the CJEU has not often been studied. Each of the two aspects is addressed in the next section.

A. The influence of the CJEU on UK courts through preliminary rulings

By the time the United Kingdom joined the European Economic Community in 1973, the primacy and direct effectiveness of EU law were already established (via the preliminary reference procedure) as fundamental principles of EU law. This meant that British courts found themselves confronting not an optional source of judicial influence but a legal obligation to give immediate and overriding effect to EU law even when faced with conflicting domestic law. UK courts were—according to the doctrine of the Luxembourg Court—obliged to give immediate effect to EU law as interpreted by the CJEU in relevant cases. This legal position was not generally contested, even if in practice the British courts—like the domestic courts of many other Member States—often resisted or avoided this conclusion, for example by failing to cite relevant points of EU law, by not making preliminary references in cases which raised clear questions of EU law, or by opting for an interpretation of EU law which would avoid conflict with domestic law.[26]

It is at any rate clear that the UK courts applied and followed the rulings of the CJEU in a range of high-profile and important cases.[27] Cases such as *Factortame*,[28] *Macarthys v Smith*,[29] and *Marshall*[30] have been closely observed, and the responses of the referring British courts to the rulings of the CJEU tracked and noted by academic scholars. Commentators have also pointed to the more diffuse influence of EU law and of the preliminary rulings of the CJEU on the interpretative approaches of the British courts, and to the adoption by the latter not just of European concepts and principles such as proportionality[31] but also to a teleological or purposive style

[26] See eg Andreas Hoffman 'Resistance against the Court of Justice of the European Union' (2018) 14 Intl J of L in Context 258; Gareth Davies 'Activism Relocated: The Self-restraint of the European Court of Justice in its National Context' (2012) 19 JEPP 76, and Golub (n 19).

[27] For an analysis of a select number of more recent preliminary references in key cases made by the UK Supreme Court, see Alessia Fusco 'The Supreme Court of the United Kingdom and Preliminary References to the European Court of Justice: An Opencast Constitutional Lab' (2015) 16 German LJ 1529.

[28] C-213/89, *R v Secretary of State for Transport ex parte Factortame*, [1990] I-2433.

[29] Case 129/79 *Macarthys v Smith* [1980] ECR I-1275.

[30] C-152/84, *Marshall v Southampton and South West Hampshire Area Health Authority* [1986] ECR 723.

[31] Francis Jacobs 'Judicial Dialogue and the Cross-Fertilization of Legal Systems: The European Court of Justice' (2003) 38 Texas Intl LJ 547, 549.

of interpretation (rather than a more literal approach) in a range of cases involving EU law.[32]

However, it is less easy to determine to what extent the rulings of the CJEU have been applied and followed in many other cases in which preliminary references have been made by the British courts, rather than in the relatively small number of high-profile and closely followed cases. Most of the academic literature dealing with the preliminary reference procedure has focused on the stage at which the preliminary ruling is given by the CJEU, and particularly on the substantive content of that ruling. A good deal of scholarly attention has also been devoted to the stage at which domestic courts decide whether or not to send a case for a preliminary ruling to Luxembourg, to the circumstances in which they have been willing to refer, and to the procedure surrounding the practice of referrals. Less attention, however, has been devoted to the final stage of the procedure, that is to the stage at which the ruling is received by the national court and how the ruling is applied (or not) by the national court at that stage.[33] Even the CJEU has paid relatively little attention to this final stage, which could arguably be said to be the most important stage of the procedure from the point of view of the domestic effectiveness of EU law and indeed of the preliminary reference procedure.

Following almost thirty years of preliminary references, in 1996 the CJEU for the first time published some basic guidance for national courts on the preliminary ruling procedure.[34] Since then, the Court has updated the guidance on three occasions, most recently in 2016. In its 2016 guidance, which is significantly longer and more detailed than the original guidance of 1995, the Court devoted just one paragraph out of thirty-eight (in addition to a seven-paragraph annex) to the final decision of the national court after receiving the preliminary ruling. This paragraph specifies that the registry of the Court will send the preliminary ruling 'to the referring court or tribunal, which is invited to inform the Court of the action taken upon that decision in the case in the main proceedings and to communicate to the Court its final decision in that case'.[35]

[32] For an overview, see Tom de la Mare 'The Use of EU Law in English Courts' (2012) 17 Judicial Review 111, 112–14, Compare Lord Neuberger, 'Has the Identity of the English Common Law Been Eroded by EU Laws and the European Convention on Human Rights?' (Speech, Faculty of Law, National University of Singapore, 18 August 2016; available at: https://www.supremecourt.uk/docs/speech-160818-01.pdf, accessed 28 June 2019) who considers that the UK courts were much more influenced in their reasoning by the ECHR system and the Strasbourg court than by EU law and the Court of Justice.

[33] See however Davies (n 26). For a study of the implementation of CJEU rulings by the Swedish courts in a selection of environmental cases, see Sanja Bogojević 'Judicial Dialogue Unpacked: Twenty Years of Preliminary References on Environmental Matters Initiated by the Swedish Judiciary' (2017) 29 JEL 263.

[34] European Court of Justice, *Note for Guidance on References by National Courts for Preliminary Rulings* (1996), reproduced in (1997) 34 CML Rev 1319.

[35] *Recommendations to National Courts and Tribunals, in Relation to the Initiation of Preliminary Ruling Proceedings* [2016] OJ C 439/1, para 29.

The Luxembourg Court maintains a database which logs the decisions taken by national courts following a preliminary ruling, but in true transparent fashion, Court personnel have indicated that 'this is an internal resource of the Court and as such is in principle accessible only to its personnel'.[36] Due to an agreement between the CJEU and the Association of the Councils of State and Supreme Administrative Jurisdictions of the European Union, however, a certain number of these decisions are referred to in a publicly accessible database maintained by the Association, but it contains only references to decisions and not the actual national decisions themselves nor links to them.[37] A range of 'notable cases' from national courts is summarised and publicised by the Court's research division through its 'Suivi des Décisions Préjudicielles' on the Association's website, but again these appear to be highly selective.[38] Indeed, it seems that in practice many eventual decisions of national courts following preliminary rulings are not communicated to the CJEU so that the database in any case is far from being comprehensive. In relation to the United Kingdom in particular, the Research and Documentation division of the CJEU indicated that 'a relatively low percentage of national decisions from the UK have been sent to the Court in recent years'.[39]

Thus, despite the fact that national courts are encouraged to inform the CJEU about their final decisions, it is not easy to trace these 'return' judgments, and hence it is difficult to establish how the rulings of the CJEU were applied by British courts when they were sent back from Luxembourg. The general assumption seems to be, absent evidence of judicial resistance or clear refusal to apply rulings, that the UK courts have been broadly compliant with the rulings of the CJEU.[40] This has been referred to as the 'implementation prejudice' in the scholarly literature; that is, the assumption that national courts do in general comply with the rulings of the CJEU.[41] Nevertheless, it is difficult to state with confidence what exactly the influence of preliminary rulings of the Luxembourg court on UK courts has been without being able to examine each of the cases in which a preliminary ruling was sent back by the CJEU to the referring court, and was subject to a final ruling by the referring court or led to a settlement between the parties to the case.

[36] Email exchange with the Director of the Research and Documentation Directorate of the Court of Justice of 27 September 2018.

[37] http://www.aca-europe.eu/index.php/en/dec-nat-en, accessed 28 June 2019.

[38] http://www.aca-europe.eu/index.php/fr/flash-cjue/suivi-des-decisions-prejudicielles, accessed 28 June 2019.

[39] See (n 38).

[40] An early set of (partly unpublished) studies carried out at the EUI, Florence by Joseph Weiler and Renaud Dehousse, in the early 1990s provided some evidence for this assumption in several member states. For the Netherlands case study see Alfred Kellermann, Wilhelmina Levelt-Overmas, and Francisens Possen (eds), *Primus Inter Pares: The European Court and National Courts: The Follow-up by National Courts of Preliminary Rulings ex Art 177 of the Treaty of Rome: A Report on the Situation in the Netherlands* (Nomos 1991).

[41] Stacy Nyikos 'The Preliminary Reference Process: National Court Implementation, Changing Opportunity Structures and Litigant Desistment' (2003) 4 Eur Union Pol 397.

In the study carried out for this chapter, for example, a search was conducted for all preliminary references sent by UK courts to the CJEU between January 2008 and August 2018. The search found 174 preliminary references sent by all UK courts (including tax, immigration, employment tribunals, etc). For the purposes of manageability, this was narrowed down to focus only on the references made by the higher English courts, namely the High Court, Court of Appeal, House of Lords, and Supreme Court. The search found 113 references made by those courts during the same 10-year period. Of those 113 cases, the return judgment of the referring court could be found in only 26 cases. Even given the likelihood that many litigants may have chosen to discontinue proceedings and to settle after the ruling from the CJEU was received,[42] the number of cases in which information can be found about the final decision of the referring court is remarkably low, meaning that an accurate assessment of what kind of immediate influence or effect the preliminary rulings of the Luxembourg Court have had in the large majority of cases referred cannot readily be made.

B. The influence of UK courts on the CJEU through preliminary references

What then of the other direction of influence? What kind of influence, if any, have the UK courts had on the CJEU through the preliminary reference procedure? This question raises the more general inquiry as to whether national courts really do have an opportunity to influence the CJEU via the mechanism of the preliminary reference procedure, or whether the procedure is primarily a one-way channel. An initial and perhaps obvious answer is that national courts certainly have an impact on the CJEU in the context of the Article 267 TFEU procedure: we know that national courts are extremely important to the CJEU, and that without the active cooperation and engagement of national courts the preliminary reference mechanism would remain a formality without much practical significance. It is common knowledge that the CJEU is entirely reliant on national courts, and on the domestic advocates arguing cases before those courts, to identify relevant points of EU law and to send suitable questions to Luxembourg via the preliminary reference procedure.[43] Without a stream of cases sent by national courts on the issues being raised by the application of EU law in the domestic legal system, the preliminary reference mechanism would have no impact. And the Luxembourg Court is also

[42] Stacy Nyikos, ibid, has described how litigants have regularly chosen not to continue the litigation following receipt of the ruling of the CJEU, thereby pre-empting the risk of incurring further costs in terms of time and money by waiting for the domestic court to implement that ruling. In such cases, there will be no final decision of the national court.

[43] George Tridimas and Takis Tridimas, 'National Courts and the European Court of Justice: A Public Choice Analysis of the Preliminary Reference Procedure' (2004) 24 Int Rev Law Econ 134.

reliant on national courts in the second way described earlier, in the sense that it relies on them to follow and to apply its preliminary rulings in those cases in which the Court delivers a ruling relevant to the facts before the domestic court. On the other hand, this double dependency of the CJEU in the preliminary reference procedure—the fact that it relies on national courts both to make references and to implement its rulings when the case returns—does not necessarily amount to the same thing as national courts being in a position to *influence* the CJEU through the procedure.

What would it mean for national courts to influence the CJEU through the preliminary reference procedure, other than by the fact that they send references to Luxembourg and subsequently apply the rulings on their return? One potentially important way in which UK courts, and other domestic courts, could influence the CJEU would be if their proposed interpretations of EU law were persuasive to the Luxembourg Court, such that the Court would follow or adopt the same interpretation as that proposed by the national court. Having the opportunity to influence the interpretation of EU law, which has broader and ongoing relevance not just for the referring court and the dispute before it but for the whole of the European Union, is a potentially important dimension of the preliminary reference procedure. Yet while there is a substantial academic literature on the extent and quality of 'dialogue' or conversation between national courts and the CJEU, little of it—with the exception of specific high-profile cases such as *Gauweiler*[44]—has focused much on the question whether the CJEU takes account of or follows the interpretation of EU law offered or suggested by national courts. There is also an interesting literature on the likely influence or impact of *government* submissions made to the CJEU during the preliminary reference procedure, but no systematic research appears to have been done on the potential impact of national court proposed interpretations.[45] Most of the emphasis in the literature on 'judicial dialogue' and 'constitutional pluralism' has been on the engagement between national constitutional courts and the CJEU in relation to the primacy of EU law, and on the issue of who if anyone has the final say on the question of the compatibility

[44] In a small number of very high-profile and high-stakes cases such as the *OMT* case referred by the German Constitutional Court, close attention has been paid to the question whether the Court of Justice was influenced by the proposed interpretation or solution suggested by the domestic court: see C-62/14 *Gauweiler v Deutsche Bundestag*, EU:C:2015:400. However, such cases are the exception and the emphasis is usually on whether the national court is willing to accord precedence to EU law over domestic law, rather than on whether the national court has offered an interpretation of EU law and if so whether the CJEU accepts that interpretation. Stacy Nyikos has also mentioned the well-known case of Case 14/83 *Von Colson* [1984] ECR I-1891 concerning remedies for sex discrimination as another such case in which the national court's proposed interpretation of EU law appeared to influence the Court of Justice: see Stacey Nyikos 'Strategic Interaction Among Courts Within the Preliminary Reference Process—Stage 1: National Court Preemptive Opinions' (2006) 45 European J of Political Research 527, 530.

[45] See Dederke and Naurin (n 21) and Clifford Carrubba, Matthew Gabel, and Charles Hankla, 'Judicial Behavior Under Political Constraints: Evidence from the European Court of Justice' (2008) 102 Am Polit Sci Rev 435.

of domestic law with EU law, or whether national law must be set aside in order to comply with EU law.[46]

One possible response to the paucity of scholarly attention devoted to the extent to which the Court may be influenced by the interpretations of EU law offered by domestic courts would be to suggest that it is not really the role of national courts to offer their interpretation of EU law when they make a reference asking the CJEU for a ruling.[47] After all, the whole purpose of the reference is to seek an authoritative ruling on a point of EU law—usually on an issue of interpretation, though sometimes on the issue of validity—from the Luxembourg Court because the domestic court is unsure of the answer and feels ill-equipped to provide one.

(i) Encouragement from the CJEU to national courts to adopt provisional views

However, the reality is that the CJEU has, for several decades now, encouraged national courts precisely to include their own proposed answer to the question of interpretation they have posed when making a preliminary reference under Article 267. No such encouragement was included in the first guidance note issued by the CJEU for national courts in 1996—a spontaneous initiative of the Court to flesh out the somewhat sparse provisions of what was then Article 177 of the EC Treaty with non-binding guidance for domestic courts, based on the experience of the Court with almost thirty years of preliminary references.[48] Published in what was then the Court's weekly report in 1996, this first guidance note was rather brief and contained recommendations to the national courts as to when and what they should include in making a preliminary reference to the Court, but made no mention of the national court's own view as to what the answer to the question referred should be. In the next iteration of the guidelines in 2005, however, this suggestion first appears: 'Finally, the referring court may, if it considers itself to be in a position to do so, briefly state its view on the answer to be given to the questions referred

[46] The very large literature on constitutional pluralism in the EU, launched in part by Neil MacCormick's influential book, *Questioning Sovereignty: Law State and Nation in the European Commonwealth* (OUP 1999), focuses significantly on these issues.

[47] There are two notable exceptions to the relative lack of scholarly attention to this question. The first is the study published by Stacy Nyikos in 2006 of the incidence of what she calls 'preemptive opinions' by national courts: Nyikos, 'Strategic Interaction' (n 46). However, her interest was not so much in whether the national courts managed to influence the CJEU through their opinions but rather in the circumstances under which national courts chose to include a proposed interpretation of EU law or a proposed resolution to the question they posed in the file they sent to the CJEU. The second consists of a study by Karin Leijon 'The Choices Courts Make: Explaining When and Why Domestic Courts express Opinions in the Preliminary Ruling Procedure', (General ECPR Conference, Montréal, 26–29 August 2015). The focus of Leijon's interest is also not on whether the national courts managed to influence the CJEU through their proposed interpretations, but rather on the reasons why domestic judges did or did not propose an interpretation, and what position the domestic courts took on the question they referred, particularly on whether their position could be said to 'support EU law' or to 'support national legislation'.

[48] *Note for Guidance on References by National Courts for Preliminary Rulings* (n 36).

for a preliminary ruling.'[49] The same advice was included in the Court's updated 2009 guidance[50] and in its 2012 guidance.[51] In the 2012 iteration, the Court added a reason for this request, suggesting that 'that information may be useful to the Court, particularly where it is called upon to give a preliminary ruling in an expedited or urgent procedure'.[52] In the fourth and most recent iteration of the guidance to national courts, published in 2016, the Court this time switched from its previous voluntarist language which had suggested that the referring national court 'may, if it considers itself in a position to do so' to more mandatory language indicating that 'in so far as it is able to do so, the referring court *should* briefly state its view on the answer to be given to the questions referred' (emphasis added).[53] While the guidance remains non-binding, the change in emphasis to indicate that national courts should express their views on the questions referred clearly indicates that the Court is keen to hear the interpretation proposed by national courts, and that its interest in so doing has grown stronger over the years.

In recent years Francis Jacobs, former Advocate General of the Court, repeated the suggestion in a public lecture that national courts should include in their references to the CJEU a provisional answer to the question being referred.[54] Referring to the increasing expertise in EU law of national courts, and the maturity of the EU legal system, he stated:

> I would raise the suggestion that the time has now come when national courts ... should (as some do already) consider carefully the reasons for their decision to refer (and perhaps set them out in their judgment); and should also (as is sometimes already done) include in the reference their own provisional views on the answers to the questions they refer.[55]

He proposed the introduction of a 'green light' procedure whereby the CJEU, rather than giving a ruling on the point referred or even endorsing the interpretation

[49] *Note for Guidance on References by National Courts for Preliminary Rulings* [2005] OJ C143/1, para 23.

[50] *Note for Guidance on References by National Courts for Preliminary Rulings* [2009] OJ C297/01, para 23.

[51] *Note for Guidance on References by National Courts for Preliminary Rulings* [2012] OJ C338/1, para 24.

[52] In the part of the guidance dealing with the urgent preliminary reference procedure, the Court elaborated further, declaring that such a statement on the part of the national court 'makes it easier for the parties to the main proceedings and the other interested persons participating in the procedure to define their positions and facilitates the Court's decision, thereby contributing to the rapidity of the procedure'. OJ [2012] C 338/1, para 42.

[53] *Recommendations to National Courts and Tribunals, in Relation to the Initiation of Preliminary Ruling Proceedings* [2016] (n 37) para 6 of the Annex.

[54] Francis Jacobs 'The European Courts and the UK—What Future? A New Role for English Courts' (Bar Council Law Reform Committee Lecture 2014); available at: https://www.barcouncil.org.uk/media/313255/lecture_delivered_by_professor_sir_francis_jacobs_3_11_14.pdf, accessed 28 June 2019.

[55] Ibid 4.

proposed by the national court, could simply give a positive signal to the national court that it could proceed to apply that interpretation in the case in question.[56] Jacobs concluded by noting that even if this suggested green light procedure did not materialise, there is plenty of opportunity for national courts to use the possibility of indicating their proposed interpretation of EU law in order to develop a dialogue with the CJEU, to assist it in its task and to improve the case law.

Even if a significant part of the motivation of the Court and of former Advocate General Jacobs in pressing national courts to include a provisional answer to the question referred reflects concerns about efficiency, and specifically the concern to expedite proceedings by clarifying the issues at stake and soliciting the different positions of the parties on the issue,[57] the encouragement to national courts to offer their own views on the question of EU law at issue is interesting also from the perspective of the potential influence of national courts over the interpretation and evolution of EU law.

In an early study, Stacy Nyikos examined 574 preliminary reference cases decided by the CJEU between 1961 and 1995 in the fields of free movement of goods and workers, and equal treatment/equal pay, to assess how many cases included a provisional interpretation by the national court when making its reference to the CJEU.[58] She found that provisional opinions were included by national courts in a remarkably high proportion of these cases, namely 41 per cent of them. In a study conducted by Karin Leijon of fifteen Member States (those which were members prior to the Eastwards enlargement of 2004) over the ten year period from 2002 to 2012, the author found that provisional opinions were included by national courts in 50.4 per cent of the cases, amounting to 181 of 359 preliminary references.[59] While these studies do not focus on the question of whether and if so how the CJEU responded to these provisional opinions, the statistics are interesting and suggest that the practice of including a proposed answer to the question referred may be far more common than often realised.

[56] The European Parliament some years earlier had also voiced its support for such a 'green light' procedure for national courts in the preliminary reference procedure. See European Parliament, 'Resolution of 9 July 2008 on the role of the national judge in the European judicial system (2007/2027(INI)), [2009] OJ C294/E/27, para 31.

[57] These are the reasons which the CJEU has explicitly given in its guidance notes: see (n 54).

[58] The Nyikos study was conducted only on cases decided before 1995, because that was the year in which the CJEU discontinued (for reasons of expense of translation) the inclusion of a section entitled 'Facts of the Case' within its published reports. Since 1994, a summary of the facts of the case, which used to include the observations of all participating Member States and a description of any position taken by the national court, is no longer included in the report of the case. This means that it is only possible to find the provisional opinion of a national court if it has been specifically included in the terms of the actual reference made by the national court (as the CJEU in its guidance to national courts is encouraging them to do), or specifically referred to in the ruling of the CJEU, or if the full decision of the referring court is available and accessible. For the current study of UK courts, I have relied on the decisions of the referring courts to determine whether a provisional opinion on the question of EU law was included.

[59] Leijon (n 49).

(ii) Influence of the provisional views of the UK courts?

The analysis carried out for this chapter aimed to examine whether and if so to what extent the higher UK courts in recent years may have had an influence on the CJEU by means of the interpretations they proposed on the questions they referred to the Court.

It can of course be argued that we do not know why particular national courts included a proposed interpretation of EU law in the reference they sent, nor even whether in doing so they sought to influence the CJEU or not.[60] Nevertheless, the opportunity to suggest an interpretation of EU law to the Luxembourg Court, particularly when the Court welcomes and encourages this, does offer the possibility to national courts to influence the Court in its own eventual ruling. And this is so even if the national court is not specifically seeking to persuade the CJEU of the correctness of its own proposed interpretation. If the CJEU adopts the same interpretation as that proposed by the national court, the inference may be drawn that the Luxembourg court agreed with the stance of the referring court and that it may have been influenced by the referring court in adopting this interpretation. It is of course not possible to know this with any certainty, since the CJEU only very rarely indicates expressly that it agrees with the view proposed by the referring court, but it is nonetheless a reasonable inference to make in those cases in which the Court reaches the same conclusion on the point of EU law as the national court had suggested.

The reasons why the CJEU might be influenced by the proposed interpretation of EU law advanced by the national court may be somewhat different from the kinds of reasons the Court might be influenced by the observations of Member State governments in the preliminary reference procedure, although in each case, the likelihood of compliance with and enforcement of its preliminary ruling will be enhanced by adopting the interpretation preferred by its interlocutor, whether the national court or an intervening government. Carrubba and others have suggested that fear of legislative or other override by governments is likely to induce the Court to lean in favour of the observations submitted by intervening governments,[61] but arguably the Court is as likely to be concerned about the risk of non-application of its rulings by the referring national court if that national court has expressed a clear view about the appropriate interpretation of EU law.

It could also be argued that the number of cases referred from the United Kingdom and the percentage of those in which the British courts offered their own

[60] For an attempt by Karin Leijon, by means of a qualitative study, to identify some of the reasons why Swedish courts chose to include or not to include a provisional interpretation in their preliminary reference to the CJEU, see 'National Judges as Gatekeepers in European Integration: Supporting Further Integration, Protecting National Sovereignty or Following Professional Norms?' (ECPR General Conference, University of Oslo, September 2017).

[61] Clifford Carrubba, Matthew Gabel, and Charles Hankla, 'Judicial Behavior Under Political Constraints: Evidence from the European Court of Justice' (2008) 102 Am Polit Sci Rev 435.

interpretation of the question of EU law are statistically too low to tell us anything significant, and indeed that the questions referred to the CJEU may have been in many cases minor and unimportant. Nevertheless, the numbers are interesting, and the array of questions referred by the British courts during the period studied, while they include some technical and relatively mundane issues, also cover a whole range of important legal issues including anti-terrorist sanctions, the rights of residence of workers, EU citizenship, environmental law, competition law, the patentability of human embryos as well as a range of cases on intellectual property and taxation issues.

Based on the cases examined, I suggest below a spectrum of degrees and types of influence that national courts may exert on the Luxembourg court via the preliminary reference procedure on the question of the interpretation of EU law referred.

A first and strongest form is that of *clear influence* where the Court agrees with and expressly adopts or follows the proposed interpretation of the national court. A second type of influence which is less clear or direct but nonetheless significant is that of *probable influence*, where the CJEU eventually adopts the same interpretation of EU law as that proposed by the national court but without expressly acknowledging that it is doing so or that it has taken account of the national court's view. The next category, which does not involve the same kind of influence on the substantive outcome of the ruling, is that of *unsuccessful attempted influence* where the national court advances a provisional view but the Court does not eventually follow the proposed interpretation. In some of these cases of attempted influence, the CJEU acknowledges that the national court has advanced a provisional view, but in many others, it makes no mention of that fact and simply adopts its own preferred interpretation without reference to the stance of the national court. A final category concerns those cases which do not reveal any form of influence or any attempt at influence by the national court, that is, where the national court does not advance a provisional view: I have referred to this category as *no attempted influence*.

Most of the 113 preliminary references made by the High Court, Court of Appeal, House of Lords, and Supreme Court between January 2008 and August 2018 can be grouped into the four clusters just described: (i) strong influence, (ii) probable influence, (iii) (unsuccessful) attempted influence, and (iv) no attempted influence. Only four references, one from the House of Lords, two from the Court of Appeal and one from the High Court, can be described as instances of *strong influence*.[62] A further twenty-two cases can be described as instances of *probable*

[62] These are (i) the House of Lords reference in the case of C-340/08, *M and Others v Her Majesty's Treasury*, ECLI:EU:C:2010:232, concerning the scope of financial sanctions imposed on individuals associated with Al-Qaeda, and in particular whether the reach of the sanctions extended to welfare benefits paid to a family member of an individual; (ii) the Court of Appeal case of C-325/09, *Secretary of State for Work and Pensions v Maria Dias* [2011] ECR I-6387 concerning free movement and the conditions governing the acquisition of a right of permanent residence of EU nationals in another member state; (iii) the Court of Appeal case of C-533/06, *O2 Holdings Ltd v Hutchinson 3G UK Ltd*

influence, in which the CJEU adopted broadly the same interpretation as that proposed by the UK court but without acknowledging it as such. Twenty cases can be described as instances of *unsuccessful attempted influence*, in which the referring court adopted a provisional view on the interpretation but the CJEU did not follow this view. In some of these twenty cases the Court mentioned the provisional interpretation of the referring court without expressing its own view on it, while in others it did not mention the provisional interpretation at all. Finally, in fifty-eight cases, the referring court did not adopt a view on the question of European law before making the reference, hence these may be categorised as cases involving *no attempted influence*. The remaining nine cases have not been categorised since the original judgment of the UK court could not be located and it was not possible to determine from the judgment of the CJEU or the Advocate General's Opinion whether the national court had proposed an interpretation or not.

Overall, therefore, the UK courts advanced a provisional view on the question of European law in 46 out of 113 cases, thus arguably having an opportunity to influence the outcome of the rulings in 41 per cent of the cases referred. And in twenty-six of those forty-six cases, namely in 56.5 per cent of the cases in which a provisional view was advanced, the inference can be drawn that the opinion of the national court had an influence on the ruling of the CJEU, even though that influence was explicitly acknowledged by the Court in only four cases, namely in just 8.7 per cent of the cases where the national court advanced its own view.

IV. Conclusion

Returning to Paul Craig's reflection at the outset of this chapter that the relationship between national courts and the CJEU can tell us a good deal about the nature of the EU legal order,[63] what does the interaction between the higher UK Courts and the Luxembourg Court over the past decade in the context of the preliminary rulings procedure tell us about the EU legal order today?

A first observation is that one of the possible reasons for the 'implementation prejudice' in the literature (ie the assumption that referring national courts generally comply with and implement the rulings of the Court of Justice) is that very little information is actually available about what happens to the rulings given by the CJEU in preliminary reference cases because only a small percentage of 'return

[2008] ECR I-4231 concerning an interpretation of the provisions of the EU Directive on comparative advertising and its interaction with trademark protection, and the High Court case of C-72/15, *Rosneft v Her Majesty's Treasury* ECLI:EU:C:2017:236 concerning the extent of the CJEU's jurisdiction to review EU economic sanctions against Russia which had been adopted in the scope of the Common Foreign and Security Policy.

[63] See Craig (n 1).

judgments' can be found. It seems plausible that many of these cases are settled in light of the CJEU ruling, but absent further information it is difficult to tell.

A second interesting observation is that the higher UK courts have fairly frequently (in approximately 41 per cent of cases referred) sought to influence the interpretation of EU law by the CJEU insofar as they have offered their own provisional view as to the answer to the question referred. Third, it seems that the CJEU has followed—or at least adopted the same view as—the UK courts on the question referred in more than 56 per cent of the cases in which the national courts offered their provisional view. This suggests that the UK higher courts may well have influenced the CJEU and its interpretation of EU law in the majority of those cases in which they sought to express a view on the question of interpretation.

Equally notable, however, is the fact that in only a tiny number of cases—just four out of the forty-six cases in which the UK higher courts expressed their view on the answer to the question referred—did the CJEU acknowledge that it had taken note of the national court's stance in reaching its own ruling. Hence the Luxembourg Court has been reluctant to acknowledge any influence on the part of the national court, and it has also chosen not to engage with the views proposed by the UK courts in cases in which the Court decided not to follow those views, and has not explained why it chose a different interpretation.

One response to this unwillingness or failure to engage explicitly with the arguments advanced by national courts is simply to note that it is typical of the CJEU's style. Judgments of the Court, unlike opinions of the Advocates General, and despite significant criticism, have tended to remain brief, non-discursive, formal, and often minimalist. Commentators may argue that the Court might not like to deter or embarrass a national court by pointing out why their proposed interpretation was wrong, or that to include such an explanation in the ruling would be time-consuming and that the explanation should in any case be implicit in the Court's eventual ruling. Yet there are surely good reasons for the Court to have engaged more actively with the UK courts when they proposed a view as to the interpretation of EU law in the cases they referred to Luxembourg, and arguably good reasons that outweigh the considerations mentioned in the previous paragraph. The CJEU itself regularly refers to the preliminary reference procedure as a 'dialogue' between itself and the national referring court.[64]

Further, the extensive academic literature on the subject of dialogue between the CJEU and national courts reflects not just a scholarly fashion but a growing sense of the desirability of genuine dialogue taking place between national courts and the CJEU, rather than just the one-way delivery of authoritative answers from

[64] For recent examples see cases C-234/17 *XC, YB, ZA*, ECLI:EU:C:2018:853, para 41 and C-284/16, *Achmea*, ECLI:EU:C:2018:158, para 37: 'The judicial system as thus conceived has as its keystone the preliminary ruling procedure provided for in Article 267 TFEU, which, by setting up a dialogue between one court and another, specifically between the Court of Justice and the courts and tribunals of the Member States, has the objective of securing uniform interpretation of EU law.'

Luxembourg to the national courts which maintain a supply of questions. While the Court for many years emphasised almost exclusively the importance of the uniformity and supremacy of EU law, and the preliminary rulings procedure developed a significantly hierarchical rather than horizontal character,[65] the more recent era of crisis, contestation, and questioning of the EU, including questioning the legitimacy of the CJEU, might be thought to have brought with it a recognition of the importance of greater sensitivity on the Court's part to the need for a more reciprocal and mutually responsive partnership and dialogue with national courts.

If the CJEU is to rely on national courts to make preliminary references in suitable cases, and to implement the rulings after they are given, and has begun to encourage national courts strongly to offer their own proposed answers to the questions referred, would it not be appropriate for the Court to engage with and respond to the proposed answers of the national courts and to explain why it has or has not chosen to follow them? Yet despite the Court's own use of the term dialogue in relation to the preliminary reference procedure, and the approval of particular CJEU judges of this idea of dialogue,[66] with one prominent judge declaring that 'a genuine dialogue requires some reciprocity and an exchange of views and experiences',[67] it does not appear that the Court as an institution has taken this view.

Far from a reciprocal dialogue or a back-and-forth exchange of views between the national courts and the CJEU on the proper interpretation of EU law, the study of UK cases undertaken for this chapter suggests that even though the UK courts in practice appear to have influenced the CJEU in its interpretation of EU law in a majority of the cases in which they expressed their view on the issue, the CJEU's conception of 'dialogue' nonetheless has remained a formal one in which national courts send suitably formulated questions to Luxembourg, and any views they offer as to how the question should be answered require no acknowledgement, engagement, or response on the Court's part.

Hence the investigation conducted in this chapter into the mutual influence of the British courts and the CJEU over a recent ten-year period suggests that the nature and extent of the mutual influence of the Luxembourg and the national courts is not easy to capture with any certainty. The lack of available information about domestic implementation of CJEU rulings by referring domestic courts and the lack of express acknowledgement by the CJEU of the interpretations advanced by domestic courts mean that their influence on one another cannot be unequivocally

[65] See Paul Craig and Gráinne de Búrca, *EU Law: Text, Cases and Materials* (6th edn, OUP 2015) ch 13.

[66] See eg Sacha Prechal, 'Communication within the Preliminary Rulings Procedure: Responsibilities of the National Courts' (2014) 21 Maastricht J of European and Comparative L 754; Allan Rosas, 'The European Court of Justice in Context: Forms and Patterns of Judicial Dialogue' (2007) 1 European J of Legal Studies 1; and Jacobs (n 27) above proposing a more advanced and structured form of dialogue in the shape of a 'green light' procedure.

[67] Rosas (n 68).

demonstrated but has to be inferred. Nevertheless, at a moment when the United Kingdom has chosen to leave the European Union, it is notable that another likely loss—in addition to the loss of political influence of the United Kingdom over EU decision-making—will be the influence of British courts over the interpretation of EU law by the CJEU.

7
How Judges Make Law

*Timothy Endicott**

As you open the door every day when you come home, you may make a groove in the wood, as the keys on your keyring rub against the door. Or a carpenter may make a groove in a strip of wood for a picture frame, to hold the glass. The latter mode—the purposive mode—is the primary way of making something. The groove is not only the result of the carpenter's action; making it is the carpenter's purpose. Both modes really are *ways of making* a groove. But making a groove in the door with your keys is incidental to your purpose, even if you know you are doing it.

A legislature makes law in the purposive mode, as a carpenter makes a groove. The standard mode of law-making by *judges* is incidental. The fact that it is incidental does not make it unimportant. And although judicial law-making bears a similarity to making a groove in the door with your keys, it also bears a dissimilarity. The action to which it is incidental is judgment in a case. Giving judgment is a reflective and articulate activity that ought to be carried out according to law. I will address the reciprocal relationship between judicial rulings and the law, and the seeming paradox that the court can only change the law for the future if it does not give effect to the existing law in the case at hand. I hope to clarify the nature of judicial law-making by attending to the nature of a judgment. To do that, it will be necessary to explain why it is so difficult to distinguish between a judgment that gives effect to the law and a judgment that breaks new ground.

I. Case Law is Source-Based

Statute law has its source in the enactment of statutes; case law has its source in judicial decisions.[1] Those forms of law depend on the authoritative effect that the law gives to legislative decisions and to judgments of the courts.

* Fellow in Law, Balliol College; Professor of Legal Philosophy, University of Oxford. I am grateful to Alison Young; this chapter originated as a response to her remarks on the role of intention in case law in 'Public Law Cases and the Common Law: A Unique Relationship?' I am also grateful to Alison, to Jeff King, and to Sebastian Lewis for extraordinarily useful comments on a draft.

[1] By 'sources' of law I mean, as Joseph Raz put it, 'facts by virtue of which [a law] is valid and which identify its content'—*The Authority of Law* (2nd edn, OUP 2009) 47–48. There may be many sources in this sense for a single proposition of law, as its validity and content may depend on many such facts, or (in case law) on the complex fact of a pattern of decisions.

Timothy Endicott, *How Judges Make Law* In: *The Foundations and Future of Public Law*. Edited by: Elizabeth Fisher, Jeff King, Alison L Young, Oxford University Press (2020). © Oxford University Press.
DOI: 10.1093/oso/9780198845249.003.0007

It may seem that even if statute law is a set of norms made by a law-making agency, the common law is different, and that the decisions of the judges are the epiphenomena of a practice in which the judges themselves do not treat the law as source-based, but as an array of principles (which can be seen as principles *of their law* because judges have acted on them in past cases).[2] But I will argue that all case law is source-based. That may sound as if I am trying to say that judges lay down the law in cases in the same way that legislatures lay down the law in statutes. On the contrary, the modalities are crucially different. I aim to explain why it is still true (and to explain the sense in which it is true) that case law is made by judicial decisions, and to explain the value of the practice.

To understand judicial law-making and its value, we have to understand what it is incidental to. It is incidental to the exercise of the judges' primary role.

II. The Primary Role of a Court is to Give Judgment

Resolution is the central purpose of courts and they achieve it by giving judgment.[3] We tend to think of the purpose of a court as *dispute* resolution, resolving a *lis* between parties such as a disputed claim in tort. The dispute resolution role captivates lawyers and everyone else. There would be no courtroom dramas without disputes. Moreover, there are two ways in which dispute resolution is crucial to law-making in the common law. First, it is in dispute resolution that adversarial advocacy thrives, and advocacy is the engine of judicial law-making. The source of much legal innovation is the lateral thinking of a gifted lawyer whose case ought to be a loser. Second, a dispute typically calls for the giving of reasons (which may be unnecessary where there is no dispute), and we will see that the giving of reasons is one of the two techniques of judicial law-making.

But a legal dispute is just one reason why the purposes of the law may require judicial resolution. The court has a role that is *no less central* in issuing a default judgment against a party who, after proper service, makes no response to a claim in tort or in debt. Even without a dispute, the court needs to give judgment and to issue an order giving effect to the judgment. The rule of law forbids:

[2] So, in Ronald Dworkin's theory of case law, the 'gravitational force of earlier decisions' is determined by 'the extension of the arguments of principle necessary to justify those decisions' (*Taking Rights Seriously* (Duckworth 1977) 113, and see generally 110–23).

[3] I will use the term 'ruling' to refer to the authoritative determination of any issue by a court. I will use 'judgment' to refer to a ruling on the operative issue of a proceeding, such as whether a claim is to be allowed or not (or in a criminal prosecution, the issue of whether to acquit or convict, combined with the sentence on a conviction). I will use 'order' for the directive action of a court on the basis of a judgment (eg discharging a prisoner on an acquittal, or making an award of damages). I have benefited from the discussion in chapter 1 of Stephen A Smith's ground-breaking book, *Rights, Wrongs, and Injustices: The Structure of Remedial Law* (OUP 2019).

1. self-help to enforce a valid claim (subject to contingencies such as lawful set-off), and
2. state action to enforce a valid claim, or to punish an offender, without the judgment of a court.

Even if you have an undisputed, legally valid right of *action*, you have no right to *execution* unless the court gives judgment. And a defendant cannot be treated as guilty of a criminal offence without the judgment of a court, even if the defendant admits the offence and accepts the prosecution's proposals as to sentence, and would prefer that there were no judicial proceedings. There is a categorical difference between being liable to a penalty and being penalised, whether or not there is any dispute over the liability. And the lawful imposition of the penalty depends not directly on the liability but on a *ruling as to the liability*; the liability is part of the justification for the ruling. The ruling gives resolution, so that an order imposing the punishment accords with the rule of law.

There are many other aspects of legal ordering that can be accomplished only by judicial order, even where there is no dispute: in English law, probate of wills and divorce decrees and legal adoption of children are examples. These judicial measures may involve no dispute and are central because they reflect the purpose of instituting courts: to give the law effect in a particular case, where resolution is needed for the purposes of the law. The common feature in all these diverse instances of the judicial role—the centre of the judicial role—is a judgment: a ruling on the legal position of the parties that is the basis for an order of the court. That is, the court creates a particular legal norm (that *this* person is to be imprisoned for *this* offence, that *this* defendant is to compensate the claimant, that *this* will is to be executed, that *this* parent is to have legal custody of a child etc). The making of a particular norm is a crucial technique for giving effect to the general law.

III. Giving Judgment is Making a Particular Norm

Hans Kelsen opposed the legal realist idea 'that all law is judge-made law, that no general legal norms exist, but only individual legal norms'.[4] But he replaced it with his own form of scepticism: 'the court of last instance is authorised to create either an individual legal norm whose content is predetermined by the general norm, *or* an individual norm whose content is not so predetermined, but is to be determined by the court of last instance itself'.[5]

[4] Hans Kelsen, *Pure Theory of Law* (Max Knight trans, U of California Press 1967) 270. I will use the term 'particular norm' instead of 'individual norm'.

[5] Ibid 269. HLA Hart's brilliant discussion of the distinction between 'finality and infallibility in judicial decision' in *The Concept of Law* (3rd edn, OUP 2012) ch VII.3 supported the view that a decision of a court may be valid and final even if the court had a legal duty to make a different decision.

Kelsen's theory dissolved the possibility of a judicial duty to give effect to the law. Where there is no appeal from the ruling of a court, he ascribed to the court an arbitrary discretion to make any order. The fallacy is the presumption that if the system treats a decision as final, the decision must have been *authorised*. It may indeed seem that way because the law, by treating the decision as final, treats the particular norm (the ruling) as valid whether it was made according to law or in a departure from the law. And then, Kelsen concluded, the court is authorised either to create an individual legal norm according to the general law ('the general norm') or to give a ruling that does not accord with the general law.

But there can be very good reason for the system to treat a decision as valid, and final, even if it was contrary to the law, and even if the court was not authorised to make it. The reason is the rule of law requirement of resolution, which depends on finality in the creation of particular norms. There is a standing tension within the rule of law: it requires both fidelity to the law (or legal accuracy, as it is sometimes called) and also resolution. And ironic as it may seem, the requirement of resolution takes primacy over fidelity to law. If the court of last instance gets the law wrong, the rule of law does not require a judicial remedy, or it would require an infinite regress of judicial proceedings. That would be a negation of the rule of law because if a ruling could always be lawfully challenged, the law would never actually *rule*—that is, determine, on behalf of the political community, what is to be done.

The resolution accomplished by the order of a court, and based on the judgment of the court, is one of the most important ways in which law is reflexive (others being that law regulates what counts as a source of law, and that it regulates its own interpretation). The law needs to secure its own application. Rulings of a court are, therefore, an essential feature of a legal system. They are an answer to the community's need for the law to be effective, and to regulate its own effect. The complex point of giving judgment includes meeting whatever need arose for a ruling, and giving that resolution with finality (subject to lawful appeal), and doing what is just and convenient in the case, and doing so lawfully.

The need for resolution can arise whether or not the law requires one particular resolution. Although Kelsen was wrong to suggest that a court is *always* free to give one ruling or another, it *can* be the case. The law may be indeterminate on the point in issue. The court may have lawful power to depart from the law on equitable grounds, or to change it (eg by distinguishing a precedent). Or the court may depart from the law without any authorisation, either through mere mistake, or taking advantage of the unreviewability of its decisions to make what it sees as an improvement in the law. While the general law regulates the rulings of courts, the need for a ruling does not at all depend on whether the law requires one particular ruling. The court must determine the law whether the law is determinate or indeterminate. Resolution is a standing need in any political community, if it is to be ruled by law. So it is a fundamental principle of legal ordering that there should be an institution authorised to determine the law and to give effect to it by the creation of a particular norm. The purity of Kelsen's theory disabled him from accounting for the juridical principle of resolution and led to absurdity: the absurdity of concluding that a court of last instance is legally authorised to do what it will.

IV. The Two Aspects of the Legal Effect of a Judgment: Ostensive and Explanatory

When preparing to give argument, there are two things that an advocate loves to find in the reports of previous decisions:

1. a case with the same facts that was decided in a way that favours the client, and
2. statements of law that favour the client's case.

When the two come apart, a favourable statement of law is *obiter*, but may still be useful; an earlier case with a favourable outcome is still useful, even apart from any statement of the law, because the advocate can point to it as an example for the court to follow in the new case. The statements of law and the ruling come together in the *ratio*, when the favourable statement of law is the ground on which the court in the earlier case justified the result. The effect of judicial decisions in the common law has two distinct, corresponding aspects: (i) the precedential effect of the judgment itself (*stare decisis*),[6] and (ii) the authority that the common law gives to the court's reasoning.

Because a judicial decision creates a particular legal norm, the common law treats it as *prima facie* an instance of the application of the general law. That instance can then be used in an ostensive explanation of the law. After a judicial decision, you can point to the outcome and say, '*This* is how *this* kind of case is decided.' I will call that aspect of precedent the ostensive aspect. Precedent also has an explanatory aspect, because you can cite the reasons of the court in the previous case, and say, 'This is *why* this kind of case is decided in this way.'

Case law depends on both of its aspects; it is a set of norms made valid by (i) the legal force that the common law gives to the fact that cases have been decided as they have, and (ii) the legal force that the common law gives to the reasons the courts have given for deciding them as they have.

Why might it be a good idea for a community to be governed in this way? The question is important for understanding both the nature of judicial law-making,

[6] We could of course use the phrase '*stare decisis*' to include standing by the court's reasons for judgment in an earlier case, since the reasons as well as the judgment are part of what was decided. But I will use '*stare decisis*' as a term for standing by the judgment given as to the outcome of an earlier case with the same facts; I am using the term in what Cross and Harris called 'the narrow sense': Rupert Cross and James Harris, *Precedent in English Law* (4th edn, OUP 1991) 101.

and its proper limits. We can give two answers that correspond to the two aspects of case law.

A. The value of the ostensive aspect of case law: coordination

The value promoted by the first aspect of case law is the value of treating like cases alike. Treating like cases alike is commonly thought of as a requirement of fairness or justice.[7] I think that is a mistake. *Stare decisis* is a good doctrine not because justice requires that like cases be treated alike but because of the need for the rule of law. The doctrine imposes a rule-governed form of control on the wide discretions of judges in applying the common law and statute law.

The judgment in a case solves a coordination problem: the problem of resolution in a particular case. And then *stare decisis* solves another coordination problem: how is the law generally to treat cases like this? Deciding a new case in the same way that an earlier case was decided may do justice, or may perpetuate injustice. But either way, the coordination imposed by *stare decisis* secures a form of responsibility in decision making that is essential to good governance.

Responsible government isn't everything, I hasten to add, and there is an obvious tension between *stare decisis* and justice. It is an instance of the tension between justice and the rule of law. *Stare decisis* yields controlled decision making that is less arbitrary because it is regulated according to a consideration, or a pattern of considerations, distinguishable from the mere say-so of the judge in a new case. And *stare decisis*, as a result, has a coordination value, insofar as it is valuable to have a non-optional determination of an issue as to the content of the law, where the court would otherwise have more than one option.

B. The value of the explanatory aspect of case law: expertise

The value promoted by the second, explanatory aspect of case law depends not on the ruling in an earlier decision but on the court's reasoning. Case law does not simply subject the current judge to the opinions of earlier judges; it presumes that they are *all* expert (and that judges in appellate courts are pre-eminently expert). Judicial reasoning binds future judges because judicial reasoning in general is treated as a good ground of law. The presumption that the court's reasoning is

[7] For example, Ronald Dworkin suggested that 'The gravitational force of a precedent may be explained by appeal ... to the fairness of treating like cases alike' (*Taking Rights Seriously* (Duckworth 1977) 113), and HLA Hart wrote concerning justice that 'its leading precept is often formulated as "Treat like cases alike"' (*The Concept of Law* (3rd edn, OUP 2012) 159).

sound has some coordinating effect, too, but its rationale depends on whether judicial reasoning *is* generally sound. That depends on the expertise and the wisdom of the judges. And it depends on whether they benefit from good advocacy.

In their earliest days, the common law courts quickly developed a prestige that has been very significantly sustained and perhaps increased over centuries in very diverse political and cultural conditions in England. The judges have managed the same political feat in many other common law and civil law countries. That prestige reflects all sorts of complex aspects of political and social and commercial culture, and reflects a diffuse perception that the courts can do well at developing the law, and also at restraining themselves.

Their prestige as oracles must sometimes go the judges' heads. And prestige tends to involve non-rational currents that have the result, no doubt, that the value of the explanatory aspect of case law is sometimes exaggerated, and along with it the wisdom of the common law. Yet the perception is undeniably partly accurate. There is something to be gained for the community from institutional and cultural phenomena that support judicial law-making, such as:

- the sense that serving as a judge counts as a form of career success for lawyers;
- practices of appointing highly regarded advocates to the bench in a competitive process;
- promotions designed to get especially accomplished judges onto the appellate courts;
- the giving of reasons and the potential for a judge to gain distinction by giving compelling reasons; and
- the practice of dissenting judgments (and multiple concurring judgments), creating a form of competition among the judges.

The value of giving legal effect to the judges' reasoning depends on their background and training and is supported—and limited—by their forensic techniques and by adversarial advocacy. Good advocacy is a terrific support for good judicial reasoning, as it gives the judge the benefit of perspective. It can equip the judges with arguments for the conclusions they reach, and it can equip them to respond to the strongest arguments against their conclusions.

V. Equity

The court's primary function of giving judgment yields one further, significant value in case law, distinguishable from the court's coordination function and its expertise. It is the opportunity of a court to administer equity. There are gains to be made through the making of law based on an equitable response to a particular case. I am referring not to English equity, but to the older, simpler, related,

Aristotelian idea of particularised grounds of justice that may justify a departure from a general rule.[8] We think of equity in this sense as *particular*, and a court is well placed to respond to particularities of a case that a legislature might not have been able to provide for in advance.

Whenever the *particularities* of an individual's case give grounds for departure from a general rule, those grounds of equity can be stated *generally*. If the intervention of equity is justified in a particular situation, it is justified in other, similar cases. And then the equitable grounds identified in a particular case may be fit to be adopted as general rules. Case law enables judges to achieve a nexus between the particulars of a case (vividly put to the court by a party to litigation) and the general law.

All law involves a tension between the community's needs for rigidity and for flexibility. If the rules are made by legislation, courts can manage the tension through interpretation, and by resolving indeterminacies in the rules and inconsistencies between rules. Case law gives the courts a particularly supple way of managing the tension: the self-correcting revisability of the common law, associated with its aptitude for equitable decision making, enables the judges to manage the tension case by case, intending primarily to craft a good ruling for the case, but mindful of the implications for the law in general. The resulting flexibility is so striking that it is easy to exaggerate; it is not unlimited, and it need not be excessive. Case law enables courts not only to develop the law but also to give the law the elements of rigidity that are demanded by the rule of law and good public policy and justice.

VI. The Paradox of Judicial Law-Making, and the Incidental Jurisdiction to Change the Law

But it may seem impossible for judges to make law unless they are authorised to change it, and then, it seems, the court is not bound to apply the law. How can we reconcile the possibility of judicial law-making with a judicial duty to apply the law? I think that the fact that change in case law is incidental to rulings in particular cases is actually the starting point for a non-paradoxical account of the limited but significant authority of courts to change the law.

No court has unlimited authority to depart from the law in a particular case (even if there are no limits on the final, lawfully binding effect of its rulings). But on the other hand, it would be futile to try to prohibit courts from giving a judgment that departs from the law. If it could be done, it would involve a crude ban on equitable decision making. The courts' authority to act equitably in giving judgment is

[8] Aristotle, *Nicomachean Ethics* V.10.

tightly constrained by rules of law on some points, and is loosely constrained by political culture, but is to some significant extent unspecified. And if the court of last instance goes *beyond* its authority, it is an urgent demand of the rule of law that no other agency should have authority to correct their judgments (although the legislature may have the authority to change the resulting law). It is a remarkable fact about judicial law-making power that there is generally no authority for its limits. It is open-ended, by which I mean that it is the responsibility of the judges themselves to determine how far it goes.

In *M v Home Office*, Lord Donaldson established the sound proposition that a government minister cannot lawfully ignore a court order on the ground that it was made without jurisdiction. But in order to do so, he thought he had to assert an unlimited jurisdiction: 'The High Court is a court of unlimited jurisdiction. The judges of that court, acting as such, can make any order which is not illegal, the sole question on a reconsideration of the order or on appeal being whether the order should have been made.'[9] I think that the rider, '. . . which is not illegal . . .' contradicts his assertion of unlimited jurisdiction.

Like Kelsen, he evidently thought that an order of the Court could only have legal force if the Court was authorised to make it. And since a Minister of the Crown does not have lawful authority to depart from a judicial order on the ground that there was no authority for the order, he came to the conclusion that the High Court must have unlimited jurisdiction. But a doctrine that government Ministers cannot pass judgment on the lawfulness of an order of the High Court does not depend on the High Court having unlimited lawful authority to issue any order.

The incidental nature of judicial law-making supports a sound account of the lawful jurisdiction of the court to change the law. Its authority to change the law is incidental to its role of giving judgment, and therefore it has no such authority in any case in which there is a judicial duty to give judgment in one way rather than another in the particular case.

What are the resulting limits? No-one has ever had to decide what changes common law courts do and do not have authority to make. This is one of the great unexplored questions of the common law. Although Lord Donaldson implicitly claimed authority to change everything, I am sure he would not have done so expressly; the Law Lords certainly did not claim such a power in their 1966 announcement that they would 'depart from a previous decision when it appears right to do so'.[10]

The judges have no authority to abolish the doctrine of precedent, or to abolish the law-making power of Parliament. I would go further and say that they have no authority to create new criminal offences, or to abolish the law of contract, or to give direct effect to unincorporated UK treaties. I say they have no authority to do

[9] *M v Home Office* [1992] QB 270 (CA).
[10] Practice Statement [1966] 1 WLR 1234.

it because in any particular case they are duty-bound to give effect to contracts, and not to convict a person for an offence that was not known to law at the time of the offence, and not to usurp Parliament's authority to decide whether to give domestic legal effect to a treaty.

I do not mean that it is uncontroversial that they have no such authority![11] I am sure that no one could give a good account of the limits of the judges' authority to change the law, without saying something controversial. The limits of their authority are determined by the answers to controversial questions as to what, as a matter of legal duty, the law requires them to do in any individual case. And it is the judges who have the jurisdiction to answer those questions. But for the reasons I have explained concerning Kelsen's theory of judicial authority, the judges' unreviewable jurisdiction cannot mean that they have unlimited authority to change the common law.

VII. Judicial Law-Making: The Standard Case and the Heroic Case

The model I have proposed suggests the following account of judicial law-making. I think it is *almost* right, except that it needs a critically important and far-reaching caveat.

1. The law may require a particular judgment in a case; if the court gives that judgment, it makes law only in the sense that it makes a particular legal norm for the case;[12] or
2. the law may not require a judgment one way or another, or it may be indeterminate whether it does so; the court must resolve the question, and its resolution has legal effect as a precedent; or
3. the law may require a particular judgment, and the court may give another judgment instead. Then, if its decision is unreviewable, the court's decision changes the law.

The standard form of judicial law-making results from situation (2). The judgment of a court resolves the matter by determining the answer to the question of law (with incidental, ostensive effect through *stare decisis*). It can be done without any intention to make law.

[11] See for example Lord Kerr's dissenting opinion in *R (SG) v Secretary of State for Work and Pensions* [2015] UKSC 16 that some provisions of unincorporated treaties are 'directly enforceable in domestic law' [254–56].

[12] In a certain sense, the decision may change the law for the future by providing new support for a proposition of law that was already true; the new support may make a disputable proposition indisputably true, and bind lower courts, and affect rights of appeal, and so on.

Let us call situation (3) the 'heroic' case. It is *prima facie* contrary to the judges' duty, because they ought to respect the rule of law. It can, however, right an injustice between the parties and make an improvement in the law. And it may not be unfair to the losing party.[13] It can be an act of statecraft for a judge to go against the law in giving judgment and thereby, incidentally, to change it. That is the heroic form of judicial law-making.

But here is the critically important caveat to this picture: there is no uncontroversial, general criterion to distinguish the standard case from the heroic case because there is no uncontroversial, general limit to the court's legal duty in a particular case. For that matter, there is no general criterion to distinguish either the standard or the heroic case of judicial law-making from situation (1), in which the judgment of a court simply gives effect to the determinate law that the court was *duty-bound to apply*.

Think of any great judicial improvement in the law: prohibiting the King from raising taxes without Parliamentary approval, or holding that the King's Ministers cannot authorise a trespass to property on grounds of state necessity, or imposing on manufacturers a duty of care in negligence toward a consumer who had no contract with the manufacturer, or holding that the exercise of the Royal prerogative can be subject to judicial review on grounds developed for the control of the exercise of statutory powers, or holding that the status of the victim as the wife of the accused does not give the accused a defence to a charge of rape.[14] In none of these cases did the judges say that they had decided to change the law, rather than to give effect to the law as it was on the morning of the day of the judgment. It would not be unreasonable to view each of those decisions as an instance of heroic law-making. But the judges described each as if they were giving the judgment that the law required. They took the view, in each of those cases, that they were only doing what the law already required of them.

VIII. The Open-Endedness of the Common Law

Why is it hard to distinguish making new law from giving effect to the existing case law? The reason is the open-endedness of the legal effect of precedents. It would take a vast study of common law method to give a complete diagnosis. I will illustrate, instead, using one example of the sort of judicial technique that makes case law open-ended in its effect. It is the technique of abstraction, and the example is a

[13] See Timothy Endicott, 'Adjudication and the Law' (2007) OJLS 311.

[14] *Case of Proclamations* (1611) 12 Co Rep 74; *Entick v Carrington* (1765) 19 St Tr 1030; *Donoghue v Stevenson* [1932] AC 562; *Council of Civil Service Unions v Minister for the Civil Service ('the GCHQ case')* [1984] 3 All ER 935; *R v R* [1992] 1 AC 599.

classic case on the judicial law-making role from Lord Denning's career of innovation in the Court of Appeal: *Morgans v Launchbury*.[15]

Mrs Morgans' husband was using her car for the day. Having had too much to drink, he asked Mr Cawfield to drive him home. Lord Denning held that Mrs Morgans was vicariously liable for Mr Cawfield's negligent driving.

Lord Wilberforce and the unanimous House of Lords overturned the decision on the ground that it departed from the 'established law', [16] which imposed vicarious liability only where a driver was acting as the agent of the owner of the car. Lord Wilberforce pointed out that if liability was to be extended further, there was more than one potential basis for it (including treating a car as a matrimonial car or a family car, or imposing vicarious liability wherever the driver had the owner's permission). He concluded,

> I do not know on what principle your Lordships acting judicially can prefer one of these systems ... The choice is one of social policy ... I am unable to state with any precision a rational (as opposed to a policy) preference for drawing a line at either of the alternative points, the spouses or the family.[17]

The important point for our purposes is the form of Lord Denning's argument, which enabled him to see what he was doing as giving effect to the law, rather than changing it. Concerning the undisputed liability of a car owner for *her agent's* use of the car, he held,

> The reason behind this principle is at bottom the principle which lies behind all vicarious liability. It is to put the responsibility on to the person who ought in justice to bear it. Now the owner or hirer of the vehicle is in most cases the person who ought to bear the responsibility ... He ought, therefore, at common law to shoulder the responsibility.[18]

The chain of reasoning works as follows:

- There is precedent for vicarious liability for the negligence of an agent.
- That established doctrine puts responsibility on the person who ought in justice to bear it.

[15] [1972] AC 127 (HL).

[16] Ibid at 137.

[17] Ibid at 136–37. With respect, a policy preference is rational insofar as there are reasons for or against a policy. Lord Wilberforce must have meant that there are aspects of policy making that are not *justiciable*. But the idea of policy is incomplete as a criterion of justiciability. Any choice of public action is a policy, and some policies (eg a policy of subsidising the automobile insurance industry) are not for judges, while other policies (eg a policy of shooting suspects to kill at the scene of a crime) are merely unlawful and entirely within the judges' limited responsibility for justice and the rule of law.

[18] *Launchbury v Morgans* [1971] 2 QB 245, 255.

- An owner who allows anyone to use the car is a person who ought in justice to bear responsibility.
- Therefore, the principle puts responsibility on the owner if the driver has her permission.

Understood as an application of the established doctrine, it would be a fallacy: from the fact that a legal liability gives effect to a principle, it does not follow that the law imposes all liabilities that give effect to the principle (or the law would impose all just taxes, if it imposes any just tax). But we should understand the argument, instead, as a form of abstraction, in which the principle behind a rule is identified and then used as the justification for imposing an unprecedented liability. It is no more fallacious than drawing an analogy. And in fact, every analogy is an instance of abstraction.[19]

Abstraction is a very important technique of judicial law-making. It explains the apparent attraction of Ronald Dworkin's theory of law. I think it was the basis of the landmark *GCHQ* decision,[20] which demonstrates that it is used in public law as in private law.[21]

This common law method of abstraction—the method of Lord Denning—has two noteworthy aspects for our purpose. First, I propose, it is a *good* method just insofar as the broad principle identified by abstraction is itself a good principle for judgment in the case at hand (and, incidentally, a good ground for making new law), even though the application of the broad principle in the new case is not required by the precedent. Second, where the *ratio* of a precedent does not apply to the new case, the method of abstraction may still offer a way of seeing the precedent as support for the decision in the new case. A dynamic tool for innovating in the case, and incidentally for law-making, takes on the appearance of case-based support for the new decision. Reasoning by abstraction involves a heroic form of law-making because it does not apply the rule in a precedent; it creates a new rule for a case that bears some similarity to the earlier case. Case law enables law-making, in part, because of the plausibility of seeing abstraction as supporting the judgment in a particular case.

Case law gives an open-ended authority to the judges. That is, they can depart from the existing law in giving judgment, and they themselves have the responsibility to determine the extent to which they can do so. That sometimes makes it

[19] By 'analogy' I mean a ground of decision in a case in which the rule in a precedent does not apply, but the precedent is similar in a way that the court treats as justifying the same outcome in the new case. The difference between the rule in the precedent *applying* and *forming the ground for an analogy* is the difference between the new case being *the same* and being *similar in a way that justifies giving the same result*. That defining aspect of analogy—the tenuous distinction between sameness and similarity—makes it a technique of decision making that is notoriously difficult to theorise.

[20] *Council of Civil Service Unions v Minister for the Civil Service* [1984] 3 All ER 935.

[21] On the role of case law in public law and private law, see Alison Young, 'Public Law Cases and the Common Law: A Unique Relationship?' (Chapter 5, this volume).

look as if it is not law at all. Or if you call it 'law', you may end up thinking that the source of law is the judicial imagination. But I propose that its open-endedness is compatible with the view I have defended: that case law is a set of rules that have their sources in previous decisions. This is not simply because, for example, the Lord Wilberforce approach prevailed over the Lord Denning approach, so that Mrs Morgans won her appeal to the House of Lords. It is because where the Lord Denning approach prevails, it is possible to understand the decision of the court *as changing the law*.

The open-endedness of case law does not arise from any mysterious feature of the doctrine of precedent; it arises because:

1. the common law's ostensive technique ('*this* is how we decide *this* sort of case') is vague in its effect, because of the potential for doubt and disagreement as to whether the facts of a new case are the same as the facts of the earlier case; and
2. the common law's explanatory technique gives legal effect to the judges' expression of their reasons,[22] and controversy and the resulting leeway for judicial creativity may arise where the reasons are complex and unclear; and
3. the doctrine gives legal effect to *many* decisions, which may themselves form complex patterns, and which may conflict; and
4. a court may have authority to distinguish an earlier decision, or to overrule it.

The advocates' and the judges' techniques for identifying legal rights, duties, and liabilities in the individual case (such as the method of abstraction) can make it difficult to distinguish between a ruling that the court is duty-bound to make, and an innovative ruling that is an instance of heroic law-making. But case law is not entirely open-ended; sometimes the court really is duty-bound to decide one way. The system has techniques not only of law-making but of closure. The paradigm, of course, is a case like *Morgans v Launchbury*: an unequivocal decision of the highest court, closing off a line of argument for lower courts, as a matter of duty (with only a remote—perhaps vanishingly remote—prospect of persuading the highest court to overrule itself on the point).

Legislation may seem more law-like. It has law-making as its purpose. To legislate is not to issue a ruling but to make rules. A legislature can provide exceptions to a rule, but cannot administer equity. It is a legislature's enactment of a bill (the formulation of a proposal for law) that has legal effect, while the legal effect of judicial decision is a complex of the ostensive and explanatory uses that courts make of earlier judicial decisions.

But I think it would be a mistake to think that case law is generally less law-like than statute law. In case law, because of indeterminacies in the applicability of

[22] See Joseph Raz's bracingly simple account of the *ratio decidendi* as 'the reason(s) by which the court justifies its decision': *The Authority of Law* (OUP 1979) 183–84.

precedents in a new case, and because of judicial techniques such as abstraction, it can be plausible to see a judgment *either* as a departure from the law *or* as if it were giving effect to the law. But statute law gains its own open-endedness from indeterminacies in the applicability of vague legislation to particular cases, and from creative judicial techniques of interpretation.

IX. Conclusion

There is a distinctive tension in case law that does not arise in statute law between the duty of a court to give effect to the law and its capacity to make new law. That standing tension between adhering to the law and developing the law has a structural value that explains the continued use of case law over centuries, and in all areas of the law, and in diverse jurisdictions. The legal effect of a particular decision is a creative way for a legal system to deal with the tensions between the value of stability and the value of innovation, and between justice and the rule of law. Judges can manage the tensions, and where they mismanage them, the courts in future cases may be able to put things right, and the legislature can reverse the judges' innovations if it sees fit.

When a court gives a judgment that departs from what has gone before, the judges make law without necessarily failing in the respect that they owe to the rule of law. This possibility resolves the paradox of judicial law-making into a mere tension. The common law's ostensive technique treats the fact of decision as a source of law, and the explanatory technique gives legal force to the court's reasons for decision. But neither technique depends on whether the court intended to make law. The focus and the defining point of the court's law-making power result from its role in the case. And for that very reason, judicial decisions generally make law by purporting to identify the already-existing law. *Entick v Carrington* is a great example: a case of heroic law-making by Lord Camden, who innovated by appealing to the 'ancient venerable edifice' of the constitution.[23]

The dynamics of judicial law-making do not commit the development of the law to one single judge's view, but to a process in which each judge needs to take account of what others have decided, and in which the influence of each judge on the future will be mediated in the future by the judgment of others. That process enhances the rule of law by providing a complex discipline against arbitrary law-making by any individual judge. It is not exactly the wisdom of a crowd; it is an ongoing, argumentative reconciliation of the decision-making results of the response of judges with diverse inclinations (like Lord Wilberforce and Lord Denning) to creative advocacy, through the continual on-the-hoof revisability of the common

[23] (1765) 2 Wils KB 275, 292.

law. And the revisability of a scheme of rules is entirely compatible with the fact that it is a scheme of rules. Any scheme of case law is a scheme of rules, unless the behaviour of the judges is unconstrained, so that it becomes impossible to see anything that is capable of being revised, or applied, in a new case.[24] Lord Wilberforce was right to insist that the judges' power to innovate ought to be exercised responsibly. But even he did not claim that they should not innovate.

In *Darnel's Case* in 1621,[25] Lord Chief Justice Hyde had a ground of case law for refusing to issue *habeas corpus* where a prisoner had been detained by special order of the King. His ground was that it would be unprecedented: 'we find none, no, not one, that hath been delivered by bail in the like cases, but by the hand of the King or his direction ... what can we do but walk in the steps of our forefathers?'

Suppose the court had, instead, delivered the prisoners. As the Chief Justice pointed out, there was no precedent for the proposition that the judges could inquire into the lawfulness of the detention. But it would have been heroic if he had done so in that case. It would, incidentally, have been good law making. The judicial duty does not restrict the judges to walking in the steps of their forefathers.

Darnel's Case was the common law's own disaster. Those who love the common law should remember this. *Habeas corpus*—a rather beautiful product of incremental judicial law-making—was destined to become a protection against arbitrary executive detention by the state itself. But that destiny was only achieved by the Habeas Corpus Act 1640.

[24] Grant Lamond argues, to the contrary, that the doctrine of precedent constrains courts 'to treat earlier cases as correctly decided', without creating rules: 'Do Precedents Create Rules?' (2005) 11 Legal Theory 1–26.

[25] (1627) 3 Howell's State Trials 1.

PART III
LEGISLATION

8. The Province of Delegated Legislation
   Jeff King
9. Legislating and Adjudicating—Where and How to Strike the Balance
   Eleanor Sharpston
10. Law, Democracy, and the Absent Legislator
   Philip Sales

8

The Province of Delegated Legislation

*Jeff King**

In its comments on the European Union (Withdrawal) Bill 2017–19, the House of Lords Constitution Committee claimed that the bill 'weaves a tapestry of delegated powers that are breath-taking in terms of both their scope and potency' constituting 'an unprecedented and extraordinary portmanteau of effectively unlimited powers upon which the Government could draw'.[1] The Delegated Powers and Regulatory Reform Committee announced it as 'one of the most important Bills in the constitutional history of the United Kingdom', one that it contains 'wider Henry VIII powers than we have ever seen', and that the principal clause on delegated powers is 'notable for its width, novelty and uncertainty'.[2] As we shall see further in this chapter, the resulting Act was passed, in the main, riding roughshod over the recommendations that were made by these committees to attenuate these shortcomings.

The origins of this chapter lie in a baseline of deep interest in the growth of the use of delegated legislation, which I favour on the whole, and morbid curiosity over how the constitution could nevertheless arrive at such a situation. I commence by examining the all-important 1932 report of the Donoughmore Committee on Ministers' Powers and its context. I conclude that surprisingly there was more agreement in substance on the subject between that report and Lord Hewart's (in) famous *The New Despotism* than the authors might have liked to acknowledge. The consensus view that emerged was that delegated powers were essential for modern government, that there was a catalogue of principal abuses, and a need for safeguards. Yet in section II I show that the problems identified by the Committee have grown in significance, and the success of the safeguards remains in serious doubt. In section III I explore the mechanism of parliamentary accountability and then consider the passage of the European Union (Withdrawal) Act 2018 in some detail,

* Professor of Law, University College London and Legal Adviser to the House of Lords Select Committee on the Constitution. I would like to thank Gabrielle Appleby, Joel Blackwell, Elizabeth Fisher, Daniel Greenberg, Tom Hickman, Jack Simson Caird, Alexandra Sinclair, Hannah White, and Alison Young for helpful discussions or comments on previous drafts, as well as to Lord Sales for his penetrating observations on the day an earlier draft of this paper was presented. I furthermore thank Clement Cheung and in particular Abe Chauhan for outstanding research assistance. The usual disclaimer applies.

1 Constitution Committee, *European Union (Withdrawal) Bill: Interim Report* (HL 2017–19, 19-I) 2.

2 Delegated Powers and Regulatory Reform Committee, *European Union (Withdrawal) Bill* (HL 2017-2019, 22-I) [1], [9], [15].

Jeff King, *The Province of Delegated Legislation* In: *The Foundations and Future of Public Law*. Edited by: Elizabeth Fisher, Jeff King, Alison L Young, Oxford University Press (2020). © Oxford University Press. DOI: 10.1093/oso/9780198845249.003.0008

as well as the initial exercise of powers under that Act. The story on the whole suggests that the road to the sweeping powers in the Act was long but predictable, and the constitutional lurch towards the significant growth in executive power comes just as the role of judicial accountability, both generally and on this subject specifically, has become more robust. On the whole it is an area that may become an explosive site of public law litigation in the coming years.

I. The Origins and Rationale for Delegated Powers

'In mere bulk', Cecil T Carr observed of the relationship between primary and secondary legislation in 1921, 'the child now dwarfs the parent'.[3] And the child has grown yet larger, while the parent has shrunk. Carr was a barrister who in 1919 commenced editorial duties in respect of the Revised Statutes and of the Statutory Rules and Orders, work essentially consolidating the statutes and statutory instruments (SIs) then in effect. He would in 1921 deliver a set of lectures on delegated legislation at the University of Cambridge, his alma mater, which were a seminal statement on the role and function, and defence of, the practice of delegated legislation.[4] His editorial overview of the field would give him a distinct tone of authority on the question of propriety, allowing him to remark that

> [n]o one who looks at a collection of the annual output of delegated legislation can seriously propose that Parliament should now cancel the concession of legislative power and should undertake for the future under its own direct authority all the legislative activities which at present are left to His Majesty in Council or to the various public Departments... If it did not exist, it would be necessary to invent it. [5]

Continuing in this same vein, Carr set out three core arguments for delegated legislation.[6] They were necessitated by limitations on parliamentary time, the need for expertise in specialised policy-making, and the need for flexibility and expeditiousness to govern, in emergencies and in daily life. Carr also gave evidence to, and was highly regarded and quoted liberally by, the Donoughmore Committee on Minister's Powers, established in 1932. That Committee was charged with an overview of the legitimacy and operation of delegated legislation and administrative adjudication.

[3] Cecil T Carr, *Delegated Legislation; Three Lectures* (CUP 1921) 2.

[4] The lectures are quoted liberally in the Report of the Committee on Ministers' Powers, *Report* (Cmd 4060 1932) 14, 21–23. Biographical information about Carr and about Lord Hewart (below) is drawn from the Dictionary of National Biography.

[5] Carr (n 3) 20.

[6] Ibid 19–21.

The Committee would expand slightly on Carr's list, offering the following reasons for the necessity of delegated legislation:[7]

1. Pressures on parliamentary time
2. The technicality of the subject matter
3. Dealing with unforeseen contingencies
4. The need for flexibility
5. Opportunity for experimentation
6. The requirement for emergency powers

It is striking that the list adopted by the Committee is in matters of substance very similar to the list accepted by the House of Lords Constitution Committee in 2019, which did not include emergency powers but did include reference to the need to enable consultation to take place on the detailed implementation of policy.[8]

Of course, this list in many ways begs the question of exactly *why* there was a need for so much legislative action in the first place. Whether prompted by the expanding franchise or not,[9] in Britain the need for delegated legislation seemed more or less assumed by reference to the almost spontaneously developing practice, emerging in a 'haphazard way'.[10] However, at the time the need for delegated legislation was far from fully established in the public mind, neither fully among Members of Parliament (MPs), the media, and above all not in the legal profession.[11] The most prominent attack on delegated legislation in the inter-war period was *The New Despotism*, a collection of essays published by Gordon Hewart in 1928. Hewart was a Liberal MP, Solicitor General, and Attorney General before becoming the Lord Chief Justice of England and Wales in 1922. His book had a sensational impact on the United Kingdom and was the direct cause of the creation of the Donoughmore Committee on Ministers' Powers. The book adopted a sardonic tone, castigating the growth of bureaucracy and its underlying rationale. He caricatured the 'creed' of the 'ardent bureaucrat, the amateur of the new despotism', the one who 'clothe[s] himself with despotic power'. The creed entails the belief that 'the only persons fit to govern are experts', and that the only obstacles in their way are the 'Sovereignty of Parliament' and the 'Rule of Law'.[12] Due to a 'kind of fetish-worship' of these ideals, 'prevalent among an ignorant public' he clarifies, '[t]he expert … must make use of the first in order to frustrate the second'.[13] Here,

[7] Committee on Ministers' Powers (n 4) 51–52.
[8] Constitution Committee, *The Legislative Process: Delegated Legislation* (HL 2017–19, 225) [9].
[9] AV Dicey, *Lectures on the Relation between Law & Public Opinion in England during the Nineteenth Century* (1st edn, Macmillan 1905).
[10] Committee on Ministers' Powers (n 4).
[11] William A Robson, 'The Report of the Committee on Ministers' Powers' (1932) 3 Polit Quart 346, 349: 'It is not too much to say that Lord Hewart's attitude represents 99 per cent of the opinion of the bench, the bar and the solicitors' profession.'
[12] Gordon Hewart, *The New Despotism* (Ernest Benn Limited 1929) 20–21.
[13] Ibid.

Hewart pits the fledgling idea of the emerging administrative state against the two fundamental principles of the constitution, only freshly minted by AV Dicey. Hewart's distinguished contemporary, the law and public administration scholar William A Robson, would describe it as a 'violent and undisguised attack upon Civil Servants'.[14]

Yet a close look at Hewart's actual claims about delegated legislation in *The New Despotism* suggests that the tone of the book and its attack on civil servants was more vitriolic or 'exaggerated'[15] than were its concrete statements and proposals. For instance, he would observe that

> It is tolerably obvious that the system of delegation by Parliament of powers of legislation is within certain limits necessary, at least as regards matters of detail, because it is impossible, if only for want to time, for Parliament to deal adequately and in detail with all the matters calling, or supposed to call, for legislation. Indeed, without a drastic alteration of its methods of procedure, it would be impossible for Parliament to deal adequately with even a comparatively small part of the present-day volume of departmental legislation. It may also be conceded that the system, if not abused, and subject to proper safeguards, may have its uses. It is the abuse of the system that calls for criticism, and perhaps the greatest abuse, and the one most likely to lead to arbitrary and unreasonable legislation, is the ousting of the jurisdiction of the Courts.[16]

Though telling in its acceptance of delegated legislation, Hewart's discussion, as with Carr's, skated around the deep reason such powers were needed in the first place—the need for a modern regulatory and growing welfare state. Such a discussion was prominent in the United States at the time, where the administrative state required its own constitutional theory.[17] The Donoughmore Committee took note of the American discussion, quoting the distinguished US lawyer and statesman, Elihu Root, who in 1916 outlined the case for agency government in a speech to the American Bar Association. Root explained that

> [b]efore these agencies, the old doctrine prohibiting the delegation of legislative powers has virtually retired from the field and given up the fight. There will be no withdrawal from these experiments. We shall go on; we shall expand them, whether we approve theoretically or not, because such agencies furnish protection

[14] Robson (n 11) 348. Committee on Ministers' Powers (n 4) 59–60, found Hewart's view 'unsupported by the smallest shred of evidence'.

[15] The official view in the Committee on Ministers' Powers (n 4) 7.

[16] Hewart (n 12) 80–81.

[17] James O Freedman, *Crisis and Legitimacy: The Administrative Process and American Government* (CUP 1978); G Edward White, *The Constitution and the New Deal* (Harvard UP 2000) (a revisionist account).

> to right, and obstacles to wrong-doing, which under our new social and industrial conditions cannot be practically accomplished by the old and simple procedure of legislatures and courts as in the last generation.

The Committee simply observed without additional comment that '[i]n our opinion these words are as applicable to-day in the United Kingdom as they were in the United States in 1916'.[18] The national context might explain the perfunctory nature of this observation, which was not expounded and had great significance. The relationship between the British state, society, and the economy was completely transformed during the First World War (which indirectly furnished 'the greatest argument for State Socialism ever produced'),[19] and the Committee itself reported in the midst of a severe national economic crisis prompting Britain's first National Government. This was soon followed by the consolidation of a managerial economic policy and development of the post-war Beveridge welfare state.[20] Delegated legislation, as with rule-making in the United States, has been seen as a core feature of the regulatory and welfare state ever since. It would be a mistake to think, furthermore, that criticism of broad delegated powers somehow entails a failure to appreciate the welfare state.[21] The most significant expansions of delegated powers in post-Second World War Britain, in terms of number and substance of SIs, have been part of programmes of deregulation carried out by governments of each major persuasion.[22]

A. The problems of wide delegation

The Donoughmore Committee shed light on the principal abuses of delegated legislation by distinguishing between what it called the 'normal' use of such powers, and their 'exceptional' use.[23] The normal cases involve (i) a clear delineation of

[18] Committee on Ministers' Powers (n 4) 24.

[19] Chris Renwick, *Bread for All: The Origins of the Welfare State* (Allen Lane 2017) ch 6, quoting Winston Churchill's description of the Ministry of Munitions' wartime role.

[20] Robert Skidelsky, *John Maynard Keynes: The Economist as Saviour 1920–1937* (Viking 1994); *Report of the Inter-Departmental Committee on Social Insurance and Allied Services* (Cmd 6404 1942) (the 'Beveridge Report').

[21] Cf. Jeff King, *Judging Social Rights* (CUP 2012) esp ch 2, and Jeff King, 'The Future of Social Rights: Social Rights as Capstone' in Katharine Young (ed), *The Future of Economic and Social Rights* (CUP 2019) for my view of the intimate connection between human rights and the welfare state.

[22] See Vyara Apostolova, *Acts and Statutory Instruments: The Volume of UK Legislation 1950 to 2016* (House of Commons Library, Commons Briefing papers CBP-7438 2017) 6 for the overall numbers. Notable instances of substance include the Deregulation and Contracting Out Act 1994 (Conservative Party), extended in the Regulatory Reform Act 2001 and Legislative and Regulatory Reform Act 2006 (Labour Party), and still further under the draft Deregulation Bill 2013 (Coalition, Con-Lib), which was significantly pared back in the Deregulation Act 2015, and the European Union (Withdrawal) Act 2018 (Conservative Party).

[23] Committee on Minister's Powers (n 4) 30–31ff.

powers, (ii) easy access to courts to enforce the *vires* of the SIs, (iii) the making of SIs that are transparent and easily accessible to citizens and public officials, but which (iv) do not confer powers to legislate on matters of principle, raise taxes, or amend or repeal primary legislation (i.e. Henry VIII powers). The 'exceptional' cases include powers to legislate on matters of principle, create Henry VIII powers, confer 'so wide a discretion on a Minister that it is almost impossible to know what limit Parliament did intend to impose', and the ousting of judicial review. It discussed the problem of 'skeleton legislation' in some depth.[24] '[H]aving only the barest general principles', such legislation permitted 'matters which closely affect the rights and property of the subject [to] be left to be worked out in the Departments, with the result that laws are ... [not] made by, and get little supervision from, Parliament.'[25] Skeleton legislation was as such a symptom of the broader problem of (i) 'loosely defined powers', (ii) 'inadequate scrutiny in Parliament', (iii) broad powers being used to 'deprive the citizen of the protection of the Courts against action by the Executive which is harsh, or unreasonable', and (iv) lack of transparency and publicity about the extent or even existence of such powers.[26] The Committee found each of these to be 'important criticisms' which nevertheless 'do not destroy the case for delegated legislation',[27] but rather call for safeguards.

B. A question of safeguards

The Donoughmore Committee was optimistic about the potential for corrective safeguards:

> [W]e venture to express a hope that in the future Parliament will be more conscious both of the principles at stake and of the safeguards needed; that whenever legislative power is delegated, the limits of the power will be clearly defined in the statute by which it is delegated; that Parliament will not depart from the normal into the exceptional type of delegated legislation without special need, nor without conscious consideration of the special grounds put forward as constituting the need; and that it will grant delegated powers of the exceptional type—e.g. powers to legislate on matters of principle or to impose taxation—only on exceptional grounds.[28]

Turning to such safeguards, the Committee spelled out its hopes in greater detail. The most important but also most nebulous proposed safeguard was

[24] A term also employed in Carr (n 3) 16; Hewart (n 12) 20–21.
[25] Committee on Minister's Powers (n 4) 53.
[26] Ibid 54.
[27] Ibid 54.
[28] Committee on Ministers' Powers (n 4) 58–59.

a requirement of clarity about the extent and limits of proposed powers: 'The precise limits of the law-making power which Parliament intends to confer on a Minister should always be expressly defined in clear language by the statute which confers it: when discretion is conferred, its limits should be defined with equal clearness.'[29]

It will be seen in the analysis in section II.D following that this concern for clarity and non-delegation of policy-making decisions remains acutely relevant in current parliamentary practice.

The Committee's other proposed safeguards were less vague. Three of them deserve attention here. The first was a quite attenuated role for Henry VIII clauses.[30] It was highly critical of their use, but accepted them grudgingly after exploring their undeniable role in securing passage of the National Insurance Act 1911. It nevertheless noted the 'extreme convenience' to Government of such powers, proposed that each use of the clause must be justified by the Minister 'up to the hilt', and that they 'should be abandoned in all but the most exceptional cases'.[31] Such cases would be limited to those uses essential for bringing an Act into operation, what we now refer to as 'technical' or 'consequential' or 'incidental' amendments (ie tidying up amendments that flow implicitly from giving operation to the requirements of the new Act),[32] bound by a sunset clause causing them to expire after one year.[33]

The second safeguard was to emphasise the importance of judicial control of the vires of delegated legislation and criticise the use of ouster clauses. It argued the latter should be highly exceptional and that 'there should not be anything in the language of the statute even to suggest a doubt as to the right and duty of the Courts of Law to decide in any particular case whether the Minister has acted within the limits of his power'.[34] The third safeguard concerned the role of standing parliamentary committees in respect both of bills proposing the creation of statutory powers and for draft SIs.[35] Such committees would perform oversight, drawing the two Houses' attention to, among other things, whether the powers are 'clearly defined' and whether they relate to a 'matter of principle', involve Henry VIII powers, or the ouster of judicial review.[36] The Committee was nevertheless emphatic that such committees would report on the form and not the merits of the proposed powers or instruments.

29 Ibid 65.
30 Ibid 59ff.
31 Ibid 61.
32 Ibid 5. See further Delegated Powers and Regulatory Reform Committee, *Special Report: Henry VIII Powers to make Incidental, Consequential and Similar Provision* (HL 2002–13, 19).
33 Committee on Ministers' Powers (n 4) 59–61.
34 Ibid 65.
35 Ibid 62–64.
36 Ibid 67–69.

II. The Current Practice

The conclusions of the Donoughmore Committee on the subject of delegated legislation were largely welcomed, including with surprise and relief by some progressive lawyers.[37] However, its recommendations concerning delegated legislation were adopted by successive governments and Parliament only very gradually, if at all. Its recommendations concerning publication were partly fulfilled in the Statutory Instruments Act 1946. Scrutiny by standing committees proceeded slowly, first in the commons in 1944, later through the creation of the Joint Committee on Statutory Instruments in 1973; it would take until 1992 to create the Delegated Powers and Regulatory Reform Committee. Yet the Committee's optimism about parliamentary restraint in respect of skeleton legislation, Henry VIII clauses, and attentive judicial oversight would prove unfounded over the subsequent seventy years.

A. The structure of parliamentary oversight

The overall volume of delegated legislation has increased significantly, and in recent years the volume of primary legislation has declined. The number of SIs made hovered at around 2,000 a year between 1950 and 1980, swiftly rising until reaching around 3,500 a year in 1992, since which time it the volume of instruments has fluctuated on average between 3,000 and 4,000 a year. [38] In comparing the number of pages, the more accurate comparison of volume, it remains the case that secondary legislation exceeds primary legislation (which also increased in length) by anywhere between two- and fivefold annually over the last two decades, which is actually comparable to what Cecil Carr noticed in 1921.[39]

Table 8.1 illustrates the extent and character of the main forms of parliamentary scrutiny in respect of SIs.

Parliamentary committees assist both houses with (i) scrutinising the proposed creation of delegated powers, (ii) technical scrutiny (including drafting, general sense, and *vires* questions), and (iii) policy scrutiny of the substance of particular (draft or made) SIs. The distribution of Committees along these lines can be seen in Table 8.2.

The involvement of the committees above typically depends on whether the delegated powers issue is contained in a bill or is a draft SI. When the powers are outlined in a bill, it must be accompanied by a Delegated Powers Memorandum

[37] Robson (n 11) at 351 'a far better piece of work than might have been expected' and 355 'exceedingly good'.

[38] Apostolova (n 22) 6–7.

[39] Ibid 9 (Table 3). Cf Carr (n 3) 2 (five times as more pages of secondary than primary legislation).

Table 8.1 Levels of delegation

Complete	Negative Instruments	Affirmative Instruments	Super Affirmative Instruments
Minister can make law on his own authority, eg closing a road, commencement orders.	Must lay before Parliament for 40 days- can be rejected by a prayer motion.	Laid as draft. Cannot come into effect until both Houses have debated and approved it.	Laid as SIs with specific scrutiny procedure set out in Act, eg Legislative Reform Orders, Public Body Orders.
Approx. 2,200 a year	Approx. 800 a year	Approx. 200–250 a year	Less than 10 per year

Note: This table is almost verbatim, though adapted slightly, from Delegated Powers and Regulatory Reform Committee (n 47) Appendix C. No dates are given in the table. There are at least eighteen sub-variations under these four forms. The 'made affirmative' procedure, used in connection with the EU (Withdrawal) Act 2018 among other Acts, allows instruments to come into force either before or when laid, but which will lapse if not approved affirmatively by one or both Houses.

Table 8.2 Parliamentary committees concerned with scrutiny of SIs

House of Commons	House of Lords	Joint Committee
Delegated Legislation Committees (ad hoc, policy scrutiny of instruments subject to affirmative procedure)	Secondary Legislation Scrutiny Committee (policy scrutiny)	Joint Committee on Statutory Instruments (technical scrutiny)
Select Committee on Statutory Instruments (technical scrutiny for instruments laid before or subject to proceedings in HoC only).	Delegated Powers and Regulatory Reform Committee (scrutiny of proposed delegation)	Joint Committee on Human Rights (irregular) (policy scrutiny)
	HL Constitution Committee (irregular) (scrutiny of proposed delegation, sometimes policy scrutiny)	

setting out the formal justification of such powers and have regard to committee guidance when writing it.[40] Wherever there is a concern, such committees report to their respective House and will almost invariably receive and publish

[40] DPRRC, *Guidance for Departments on the role and requirements of the Committee*, July 2004. From the same Committee, see *Special Report: Quality of Delegated Powers Memoranda* (HL 2014–15, 39).

a formal Government response to concerns they have raised. In some cases, the Committees carry on a more or less direct dialogue with Government, which will frequently withdraw and reissue instruments found to be wanting by committees before relaying them.

B. The steady expansion of delegated powers

Edward C Page's *Governing by Numbers* remains the best empirical exploration of the world of what he calls 'everyday policymaking' through SIs in Britain.[41] His careful overview of the genesis, drafting, and execution of forty-six randomly selected non-controversial SIs illustrates the workings of a system not far from that appreciated by the Donoughmore Committee.[42] His more recent study largely confirms the same view.[43] While he did not conclude it was perfect, neither did he find it chronically dysfunctional.

Nevertheless, Professor David Williams would observe in a 1982 retrospective on the Donoughmore Committee's report that 'there must be few people who could speak with confidence of the system' by reference to the Committee's principal recommendations, a fact he suggested might justify another Donoughmore-style inquiry.[44] And Ruth Fox and Joel Blackwell point out that much of the criticism of delegated legislation today is 'exactly the same' as those identified by the Donoughmore Committee.[45] There is an unmistakable trend towards the expanded use of delegated powers to deal with questions of sometimes quite substantial policy. Based on extensive research interviewing dozens of persons including MPs and Peers, civil servants, parliamentary counsel, and others, Fox and Blackwell concluded that

> delegated legislation is used extensively, for example in areas such as the criminal law—with clear implications for civil liberties—that in the view of many parliamentarians and external observers can hardly be regarded as technical or inconsequential... Indeed, there has been such an expansion in the scope and application of powers and procedures that a precedent could arguably be found to justify almost any form of delegation a minister might now desire.[46]

[41] Edward Page, *Governing by Numbers: Delegated Legislation and Everyday Policy Making* (Hart 2001) 6.

[42] Ibid ch 4.

[43] Edward Page, *Policy without Politicians: Bureaucratic Influence in Comparative Perspective* (OUP 2012).

[44] DGT Williams, 'The Donoughmore Committee Report in Retrospective' (1982) 60 Pub Adm 273, 284.

[45] Ruth Fox and Joel Blackwell, *Devil is in the Detail: Parliament and Delegated Legislation* (Hansard Society 2014), 33.

[46] Ibid 219. To similar effect, see Adam Tucker, 'The Parliamentary Scrutiny of Delegated Legislation' in Alexander Horne and Gavin Drewry (eds), *Parliament and the Law* (Hart 2018).

The House of Lords' Delegated Powers and Regulatory Reform Committee (the 'DPRRC')—created in 1992 and tasked chiefly with oversight of the attempt to create delegated powers—observed in a recent report that

> Our reports on bills ... indicate that time and again successive governments have attempted to relegate too many important policies to delegated legislation, leaving too little on the face of the bill. Of particular concern to the Committee is the use of skeleton bills or skeleton provisions in bills, and Henry VIII powers.[47]

The House of Lords Constitution Committee (the 'Constitution Committee') observed recently that '[t]here has been an upward trend in the seeking of delegated powers in recent years and this should cease'.[48] Neither is the issue purely about attempts by governments; it is also about results. In his evidence to the Constitution Committee, Lord Lisvane, the former Clerk of the House of Commons and member of the DPRRC, observed that '[t]he threshold between secondary and primary legislation has moved upwards, and delegated legislation is used for matters of policy and principle, which 20 or 30 years ago would not have been thought appropriate'.[49]

Indeed, the proliferation of Henry VIII clauses is (only slightly) more easily quantifiable, and hence illustrates the trend in a more striking fashion. While the Donoughmore Committee could find only nine examples prior to 1932, Lord Rippon would complain in 1989 of four in the previous parliamentary session alone. Lord Justice Judge would identify over 100 in the session prior to 2010.[50] And even at a relatively early point in the Brexit-process, the Hansard Society has identified that between June 2018 (when the European Union (Withdrawal) Act 2018 was given Royal Assent) and 8 April 2019, fully 128 of the 515 Brexit-related SIs laid were an application of Henry VIII powers.[51] Perhaps most worrying, as I shortly explain, the existence of a 'precedent' is a formal rationale in the Cabinet Office *Guide for Making Legislation* for the resort to delegated legislation.

[47] Delegated Powers and Regulatory Reform Committee, *Special Report: Response to the Strathclyde Review* (HL 2015–16, 119) [22].

[48] Constitution Committee, *The Delegation of Powers* (n 8) [25].

[49] Ibid [17].

[50] Committee on Ministers' Powers (n 4) Annex III; Lord Rippon, 'Henry VII Clauses' (1989) 10 Statute L Rev 205, 206; Lord Judge, 'Ceding Power to the Executive: the Resurrection of Henry VIII' (KCL 12 April 2014).

[51] Hansard Society, *Statutory Instrument Tracker*; available at: https://www.hansardsociety.org.uk/services/statutory-instrument-tracker (date accessed 28 June 2019). The SI Tracker is available by subscription-service, but the Hansard Society also periodically publishes data relating to Brexit Statutory Instruments on its website.

C. Reasons for seeking delegated powers

Delegated powers are exceptionally convenient for a government.[52] The Cabinet Office *Guide to Making Legislation* provides a formal set of reasons that it uses in seeking such powers: the need for flexibility and adjustment, the accumulation of experience in a particular policy area, or the existence of a 'strong precedent' which is 'uncontroversial', as well as for transitional or technical matters suitable for delegated powers.[53] Apart from over-reliance on precedent,[54] these are often sensible grounds. Yet reasons of convenience and political strategy will often overwhelm good legislative practice.[55] For the most part, such reasons revolve around the legislative timetabling priorities of the Government, and the schedule set by the Parliamentary and Legislative Business Committee (PBL Committee) of the Cabinet. If the policy process is incomplete before the applicable timetable set by the PBL Committee takes effect, then parliamentary counsel will often be required to allocate matters that might have been put through in the bill to delegated legislation instead. As Baroness Fookes, a Conservative Party MP for twenty-three years prior to taking her peerage in the Lords, and later Chair of the DPRRC, observed:

> Governments go into Bills in too much of a rush, without adequate preparation. This is for two reasons, Governments like to have as much play as they can through the use of delegated legislation, and very often they have not worked out what they want in the regulations in the first place.[56]

Such delays can arise either because policy thinking is incomplete, there is a need to be seen to respond decisively to some problem, or there is a simple desire among business managers to keep legislation short. More darkly, resort to delegated powers makes it easier to give effect to controversial or 'difficult' policy decisions with little scrutiny.[57] The latter point was a major issue in the furore caused by the attempted use of delegated powers by the Conservative Government to reduce entitlements to tax credit in 2015. In considering the issue of obscurity and scrutiny, the Shadow Secretary of State for Pensions, Seema Malhotra (Labour), observed that

> [t]he original intention had been to implement these changes with the scantiest possible parliamentary scrutiny—through a statutory instrument not debated by the whole House, but considered by a short Committee session of no more than

52 See generally Fox and Blackwell (n 45) 57–61 and Page, *Governing by Numbers* (n 41) chs 3 and 4.
53 Cabinet Office, *Guide to Making Legislation* (July 2017) 124.
54 Rightly criticised by Fox and Blackwell (n 45) 219.
55 Ibid 57–61, 221–22.
56 Constitution Committee, *The Delegation of Powers* (n 8) [20].
57 Page, *Governing by Numbers* (n 41) 186 (highlighting the attractiveness of political obscurity).

> 15 MPs and without scrutiny in the House of Lords... [T]hey were to be sneaked in through the back door.[58]

The House of Lords refused to approve the measure. In outrage, the Government appointed a review inquiry having the goal of taming the upstart House of Lords, whose report was shelved and the resulting inquiry if anything led to the general recognition of the Lords' role as one of the stronger points of a very weak system of parliamentary scrutiny.[59]

D. Criteria for deciding between primary and secondary legislation

The difference between primary and secondary legislation is very significant. Primary legislation is often preceded by green or white papers; the discussion, across a typically lengthy timeframe, is more protracted, iterative and episodic; the principles of the legislation are discussed at second reading and the detail thrashed out in committees; and the whole of that is duplicated in the other house, with reconciliation between them (ping pong stage) yet another layer for accommodation. Most importantly, amendments can be and often are made at various stages. Secondary legislation laid before Parliament has a lower profile and is unamendable (though draft instruments can be withdrawn), and often is effective or 'made' at the time it is laid. This depth of attention and flexibility of response makes a significant practical difference, over and above any principled grounds for an important distinction between primary and secondary legislation.

Despite that, the criteria for deciding between them have remained vague even though there has been a vast amount of scrutiny of delegated legislation since the Report of the Donoughmore Committee. Although the Committee advised that powers should not be too wide, and 'matters of principle' should be reserved for primary legislation, such matters are frequently addressed by way of delegated legislation, many of them unobjectionable.[60]

In recent years, the Constitution Committee and DPRRC have sought to flesh out when the resort to delegated powers over primary legislation is a cause for concern. Jack Simson Caird, Robert Hazell, and Dawn Oliver produced a code of the constitutional standards derived from the reports of the Constitution Committee,

[58] HC Deb 15 September 2015, vol 599, cols 967–968.

[59] *Strathclyde Review: Secondary legislation and the primacy of the House of Commons* (Cmnd 9177, 2015). The proposals backfired and were shelved. See Constitution Committee, *Delegated Legislation and Parliament: A response to the Strathclyde Review* (HL 2015–16, 116); Delegated Powers and Regulatory Reform Committee, *Response to the Strathclyde Review* (n 47); Delegated Legislation Scrutiny Committee, *Response to the Strathclyde Review: Effective parliamentary scrutiny of secondary legislation* (HL 2015–16, 128).

[60] Page, *Governing by Numbers* (n 41) ch 3.

section 2 of which concerns the use of delegated legislation.[61] Twelve such standards relate to appropriate uses of delegated powers. Among these, three relate to not using delegated legislation to alter constitutional arrangements,[62] three to the inappropriate use of Henry VIII clauses, two to avoiding using secondary legislation to create new criminal offences,[63] and two to the use of delegated powers in a way that would impact on certain rights.[64] One standard is that '[t]he most important aspects of a policy should be included on the face of a bill and not left to be decided through delegated legislation'.[65]

The DPRRC was established in 1992 and its terms of reference stipulate that it is to report on, among other things, 'whether the provisions of any bill inappropriately delegate legislative power or whether they subject the exercise of legislative power to an inappropriate degree of parliamentary scrutiny'.[66] Fox and Blackwell conclude that the Committee has built up a 'formidable reputation', and is 'perhaps the biggest success story in the delegated legislative process' in recent decades.[67] The DPRRC itself estimates that about 66 per cent of its recommendations have been accepted by Government.[68] In 1997 the DPRRC reported that it would apply the principle that delegation would be unsuitable for a power 'so important that it should only be one granted by primary legislation' and it pays special regard also to whether a proposed power 'sufficiently particularises the principles on which, and the circumstances in which, secondary legislation may be passed, and so avoids being characterised as a "skeleton bill"'.[69] However, the Committee has deliberately avoided framing specific criteria, preferring to use a case-by-case approach. It addressed the subject of principles in a Special Report in 2000,[70] but only identified three areas in which it found that matters should better be regulated by primary legislation: provisions designed to ensure that legislation is clearly compatible with the European Convention on Human Rights; substantial changes to electoral law; and the power to increase the severity of the sentencing power.[71] In a 2013 report, the Committee indicated further what principles it would apply in

[61] *The Constitutional Standards of the House of Lords Select Committee on the Constitution* (Constitution Unit 2015).

[62] Ibid 2.3.1, 2.3.9, 2.3.10.

[63] Ibid 2.3.5, 2.3.6.

[64] Ibid 2.3.4 (respect for private life), 2.3.11 (right of appeal).

[65] Ibid 2.3.8, citing three reports of the Committee which used this standard.

[66] *Companion to the Standing Orders of the House of Lords* (2015) 195 [11.51]. The origins of the Committee are traceable to the report of Jellicoe Committee: Select Committee on the Committee Work of the House (HL 1991–92, 35-I).

[67] Fox and Blackwell (n 45) 71.

[68] Constitution Committee, *The Delegation of Powers* (n 8) [30]; Fox and Blackwell (n 45) 71 report an estimated acceptance rate of between 80–85 per cent. No method is offered for determining either number, and there is no formal record.

[69] Delegated Powers and Regulatory Reform Committee, *Special Report* (HL 1997–98, 158) [12].

[70] Delegated Powers and Regulatory Reform Committee, *Special Report: The Committee's Work* (HL 1999–2000, 130) esp [31]–[36].

[71] Ibid [36].

scrutiny of the Delegated Powers Memoranda produced by Departments seeking delegated powers in bills. Henry VIII clauses, skeleton bills, the power to make incidental, consequential, and similar provision, and where a bill creates a criminal offence and the power to set the penalty is by delegated legislation would come in for very close scrutiny and must be carefully justified in the Delegated Powers Memorandum.[72] Yet it affirmed its view that 'it was not possible to set out a list of criteria which would give precision to the test of appropriateness'[73] and the House of Lords Constitution Committee has endorsed that same conclusion.[74]

The refusal of both committees to specify a more concrete standard is one of the few complaints the Fox and Blackwell study makes about the operation of the DPRRC.[75] I agree with the complaint. While the Constitution Committee and the DPRRC refer to the principles in the latter's document providing guidance for the preparation of delegated powers memoranda to accompany bills,[76] such principles only indicate where *justification* of the powers must be produced. In other words, while the explanatory burden is enhanced, there is nothing to suggest that such powers should be avoided or cannot be routinely justified—neither for Henry VIII clauses, nor even skeleton legislation. The sole exception is the proposal that the maximum penalty for any criminal offense should be specified on the face of a bill, and (typically) 'where this is not the case, the memorandum should explain why not, and at the very least the Committee would expect the instrument to be subject to affirmative procedure'.[77] Whatever the difficulty of specifying concrete standards, it is clear that such guidance rules out virtually nothing in advance. While that may sound wise, there are good reasons to doubt it, given the tendency of such powers to swell over time. Indeed, in both committees, one sees a tendency to prevaricate over whether broad delegated powers can be justified (i) only exceptionally, (ii) if accompanied by enhanced scrutiny procedures, or (iii) not at all. The first of these is not particularly helpful because the exceptions become precedents. The third is used rather infrequently, it appears (no-one knows the full extent). And the second is used all too frequently. It is too frequent because, as noted by Fox and Blackwell, there is a belief that enhanced scrutiny will deal with the underlying problem. In fact, as these authors say, 'rather than ameliorating the problems with delegated legislation it is feeding the beast'.[78] The concession of enhanced scrutiny is taken to justify the grant of increasingly wide powers, but such additional

72 Delegated Powers and Regulatory Reform Committee, *Special Report: Quality of Delegated Powers Memoranda* (HL 2014–15, 39).

73 Ibid Annex 4.

74 Constitution Committee, *The Delegation of Powers* (n 8) [36]–[39].

75 Fox and Blackwell (n 45) 198.

76 Delegated Powers and Regulatory Reform Committee, *Guidance for Departments on the Role and Requirements of the Committee* (July 2004).

77 Ibid [38].

78 Ibid 220.

scrutiny almost invariably fails to provide meaningful accountability or control over such measures anyway.

Perhaps the committees are concerned not only with the limits of what they can know about how extensive a particular practice is or what knock on effects stopping it might produce (epistemic uncertainty), but also with institutional self-defence.[79] They no doubt wish to use their political capital sparingly, since the Government can refuse their suggestions and ordinarily prevail on the floor of either House. One example can illustrate both points. The Constitution Committee has maintained that delegated legislation should not be used to create criminal offences. However, as James Chalmers notes, 'the vast majority of offences ... are created by secondary legislation'[80] including serious offences that carry heavy maximum penalties.[81] Assuming the Constitution Committee is right in principle about its claim, insisting on it will force it to confront the inertia of a routine practice, and probably back down from it. The natural course for a parliamentary committee here, when faced with a burgeoning practice, is to play safe by declaring that a power 'should' be used 'exceptionally' or be subject to greater scrutiny.

In my view, part of the problem is that it is not only difficult to trace a workable dividing line between policy-making and policy implementation under delegated powers but also, and more importantly, that there are many SIs that plainly involve important policy-making and some of which are steered through by ministers.[82] Indeed, in the existential moment of 1943, Ivor Jennings would observe without complaint that '[i]n large measure the legislative powers of Parliament have been superseded by the legislative powers of the Crown under the Emergency Powers (Defence) Acts'.[83] It is I think part of the problem that 'everyday policy-making'[84] is plainly expected under delegated powers, and that makes untenable in practice statements such as the Constitution Committee's headline claim that '[i]t is essential that primary legislation is used to legislate for policy and other major objectives'.[85] While the gist of that claim seems intuitively attractive, it is neither routinely observed in practice nor arguably even required, so baldly stated, as a matter of

[79] NW Barber, 'Self-Defence for Institutions' (2013) 72 CLJ 558.

[80] James Chalmers, '"Frenzied Law Making": Overcriminalization by Numbers' (2014) 67 CLP 483, 489.

[81] James Chalmers and Fiona Leverick, 'Criminal Law in the Shadows: Creating Offences in Delegated Legislation' (2018) 38 LS 221.

[82] The present chapter is not comparative, but a similar difficulty has bedevilled all the foreign versions of the non-delegation doctrine that I have examined. See Susan Rose-Ackerman, Stefanie Egidy, and James Fowkes, *Due Process of Law-Making: The United States, South Africa, Germany and the European Union* (CUP 2014); Hermann Pünder, 'Democratic Legitimation of Delegated Legislation: A Comparative View on the American, German and British Law' (2009) 58 ICLQ 353, 357–58; Robert Schütze, '"Delegated" Legislation in the (new) European Union: A Constitutional Analysis' (2011) 74 MLR 661 (contrasting non-delegation doctrines in the European Union and the United States).

[83] Ivor Jennings, *The Law and the Constitution* (University of London 1943) 'Introduction'.

[84] The sub-title of Page's book, *Governing by Numbers* (n 41).

[85] Constitution Committee, *The Delegation of Powers* (n 8) [3], [25].

principle. The development of a more specific standard is urgent business if the good sense underlying that statement is not to be lost.[86]

III. Parliamentary Accountability and the 2018 Withdrawal Act

A. The inadequacy of parliamentary scrutiny

While the parliamentary system of scrutiny is impressive in outline, and aspects have been appreciated as a model abroad,[87] it remains the case that even Erskine May is candid in admitting that '[c]riticism of the volume of delegated legislation and its lack of scrutiny by Parliament has frequently been made by committees of both Houses and by outsiders'.[88] Even the ordinarily restrained Supreme Court was prepared to find, in the case of *Public Law Project*, that '[w]hether subject to the negative or affirmative resolution procedure, [subordinate legislation] is subject to much briefer, if any, examination by Parliament and cannot be amended'.[89]

How have we reached the point where the Supreme Court could openly dismiss the effectiveness of a procedure in a constitution where comity is the leitmotif of relations between the branches? The most oft-noted problem is that less than 0.001 of all SIs have been voted down by Parliament.[90] The importance of that figure can be and probably has been exaggerated. Contemporary scholarship on Parliament has tended to explore the way in which government accommodates parliamentary concerns upstream rather than in a showdown on the floors of either House.[91] In exploring the reports of the DPRRC and the Joint Committee on Statutory Instruments, one can find a significant level of government accommodation of Committee recommendations through amendments to draft SIs or bills. Nevertheless, even accounting for the influence of 'anticipated reactions' or modifications to draft instruments,[92] the general mood among

86 The development of such a standard is an aspect of the broader research project from which this chapter results.

87 Lorne Neudorf, 'Rule by Regulation: Revitalizing Parliament's Supervisory Role in the Making of Subordinate Legislation' (2016) (Spring) Canadian Parliamentary Review 29.

88 Malcolm Jack et al (eds), *Erskine May's Treatise on The Law, Privileges, Proceedings and Usage of Parliament* (24th edn, LexisNexis 2011) 667.

89 *McKiernon v Secretary of State for Social Security*' (1989) 2 Admin LR 133 (CA) 140 (Lord Donaldson MR), cited with approval in *R (on the application of Public Law Project) v Lord Chancellor* [2016] UKSC 39, [2016] AC 1531, [27].

90 Judge (n 51) notes, however, that the statistic was 17 out of 170,000.

91 Meg Russell and Philip Cowley, 'The Policy Power of Westminster Parliament: The "Parliamentary State" and Empirical Evidence' (2016) 29 Governance 121; Louise Thompson, 'More of the Same or a Period of Change? The Impact of Bill Committees in the Twenty-First Century House of Commons' (2013) 66 Parliamentary Affairs 459. Page (n 41) ch 8 and especially 172ff observes a similar phenomenon at work.

92 To my knowledge, based on discussions with researchers and parliamentary staff, there is no quantitative empirical research on this question.

parliamentarians and commentators is that the process is a wholly inadequate safeguard.[93]

Once the measures move past the committees to the floors of each House, one finds that 'debates are rare, and defeats are all but unheard of'.[94] Instruments subject to negative procedures rely on MPs and Peers tabling a 'prayer' against the measure to obtain any form of debate on them. Since the 1997–98 session, there have been prayer motions against only 2.5 per cent of the total, with steeply declining numbers of late—in the 2013–14 session only 10 prayer motions were tabled against 882 negative instruments. A prayer motion is generally tabled as an Early Day Motion, namely ones 'for which no time for debate has been fixed and, in the vast majority of cases, for which no time is likely to be available'.[95] If the motion is put down by the Official Opposition it is likely, though not certain, to be debated. For example, in 2013–14 only two of the ten motions tabled were debated, and in the 2010–12 session, eight of twenty-seven were considered, albeit all in committee rather than on the floor of the House. The last successful motion to annul in the House of Commons was in 1979.[96] The scrutiny situation is improved in the House of Lords but due to the primacy of the Commons, restraint is shown. Between the 2004–05 and 2013–14 sessions, for example, there were seventy-nine non-fatal motions, twelve of which led to a Government defeat. In roughly the same period, twenty-one fatal motions were put down and two led to defeats. Since the Second World War the House of Lords has not approved five affirmative instruments and has annulled only one.[97]

The consideration of instruments subject to the affirmative procedure by the House of Commons is somewhere between 90–95 per cent of the time conducted in Committees rather than on the floor of the House. The debates in the Delegated Legislation Committees were described in interviews with Fox and Blackwell as 'farcical', 'an absolute joke', and 'a waste of time', with one MP adding that serving on such committees is seen as 'punishment' within a party.[98] The average time for these committees, which are considered a form of enhanced scrutiny, is twenty-six minutes.[99] Party whips tend to dominate the outcomes in advance of debate.

Whatever work may or may not be done in encouraging the Government to amend draft SIs, the time spent on the floor of the House of Commons debating both primary and secondary legislation has been calculated. And it is telling.

[93] The 'mood' was conveyed to me in discussion with Joel Blackwell, co-author of *The Devil is in the Detail* (n 45).

[94] Page, *Governing by Numbers* (n 41) 175.

[95] Richard Kelly, *Statutory Instruments* (Commons Library Briefing, 15 December 2016) 9.

[96] Ibid, citing Paraffin (Maximum Retail Prices) (Revocation) Order 1979 (SI 1979/797)

[97] Kelly (n 96) 24.

[98] Fox and Blackwell (n 45) 182.

[99] Ibid 80.

Table 8.3 Percentage of time debating legislation in the House of Commons

Year	Hours Debating SIs	Hours Debating All Legislation	SIs as Percentage of Total	All Legislative Debate as Percentage of Sitting Time
2004–05	10	228	4.4	42.5
2005–06	18	705	2.6	44.9
2006–07	18	380	4.7	34
2007–08	28	471	5.9	36.1
2008–09	20	342	5.8	32.5
2009–10	16	204	7.8	37.8
2010–12	30	774	3.9	33
2012–13	11	363	3.0	32
2013–14	6	412	1.5	32.4
2014–15	17	278	6.1	28.1
2015–16	8	361	2.2	39.8

Note: Table adapted from Apostolova (n 22) 13 (Table 7). Hour numbers are rounded to the hour and so percentages are not exact. There are no data furnished in respect of the House of Lords.

The average percentage of legislative debate time spent on SIs across this range is 4.35 per cent. Thus, despite the fact that 'the child dwarfs the parent', SIs still receive a quite low profile in the Commons.

The point here is manifestly not that parliamentary procedures are a waste of time or that they have no impact on the content of instruments or the scope of scrutiny procedures of particular delegated powers.[100] Perusing one session's reports of the DPRRC or Joint Committee on Statutory Instruments, and Government responses thereto, will disabuse an observer of any such view. It is rather that while necessary, they are widely perceived *by parliamentarians* as insufficient or at any rate unable to cure the problems of the system. The road to the EU Withdrawal Act 2018 was long but predictable.

B. The European Union (Withdrawal) Act 2018: a case in point

The 2018 Act is of course unusual and monumental, and it is all too tempting to say no conclusions can be drawn about a desperate measure at a desperate time.[101]

[100] Page, *Governing by Numbers* (n 41) ch 8 is positive about the interstitial, or 'discreet' impact of Parliament on the SIs.

[101] For a superb overview of the Act, see Paul Craig, 'Constitutional Principle, the Rule of Law and Political Reality: The European Union (Withdrawal) Act 2018' (2019) 82 MLR 319.

But the curious feature of the Act is that it exhibits precisely the faults surveyed above. And it manifests them at a time, as I show by way of conclusion, when the courts have become much more willing to quash delegated legislation or declare it to be *ultra vires*. We can consider the significance of the delegated powers under the 2018 Act in terms of the scope of the created powers, the reaction in Parliament during the bill's passage, the Government's assurances given during that time, and initial indications about the volume, character and scrutiny of SIs passed under the Act thus far.

(i) Remit

The 'main powers in connection with withdrawal', as the title of the relevant part of the 2018 Act clarifies, are found in sections 8 (correcting deficiencies in EU Law) and 9 (implementation of the withdrawal agreement). Similar powers are provided in respect of the devolved regions in sections 10–12. Section 8(1) provides:

> (1) A Minister of the Crown may by regulations make such provision as the Minister considers appropriate to prevent, remedy or mitigate—
> (a) any failure of retained EU law to operate effectively, or
> (b) any other deficiency in retained EU law,
> arising from the withdrawal of the United Kingdom from the EU.

The terms 'appropriate', 'remedy', 'operate effectively', 'deficiency', and 'arising from the withdrawal' are vague and on their face confer broad power, and hence the cause of much of the critical commentary during the bill's passage. There is an indicative list of what constitutes deficiencies arising from withdrawal in sub-section 8(2). However, sub-section 8(3) confirms that there will also be a deficiency if it is analogous to those in sub-section 8(2) *or*, crucially, if it is of any kind 'described, or provided for, in regulations made by a Minister of the Crown'. This means, effectively, that the power is wide open for ministers, subject to a limited number of exceptions specified in sub-section 8(7), to make any changes that can be approved by statutory instrument. Section 8(5) clarifies that any regulation under 8(1) can be a Henry VIII power (see also sections 9(2) and 23(2)), and the Government confirms that it not only can enact further, so-called tertiary secondary legislation under the instruments created under this power, but that such tertiary secondary legislation intentionally will not itself be subject to parliamentary scrutiny.[102] Despite the outrage expressed in various parliamentary reports, a redline copy of

[102] Such was a concern for the DPRRC and subject of an amendment to the bill moved by Lord Lisvane, HL Deb 12 March 2018 col 1472, but the Government held to its initial position: Delegated Powers and Regulatory Reform Committee, *European Union (Withdrawal)Bill: Government Response* (HL 2017–19, 119) Appendix 1.

the final act against the bill as introduced shows very few changes of importance to what was Clause 7 and became section 8 of the Act.[103]

Schedule 7 provides for additional limitations and parliamentary scrutiny of the SIs adopted under sections 7–12. Of particular note, it provides that outside some limited exceptions,[104] the default scrutiny procedure is the negative resolution procedure.[105] Notably, Henry VIII powers are not uniformly subject to the affirmative procedure.[106] Furthermore, any provision in the Act that a regulation be subject to the affirmative resolution procedure can be made effective immediately by a Minister or devolved authority if he or they think that it is 'urgent', subject to nullification afterwards.

(ii) Reaction

The constitutional significance of a bill can best be discerned by looking at reactions from committees charged with such matters as well as peers known for non-partisanship. As noted in the introduction of this chapter, the Constitution Committee reported in striking terms on the bill ('breath-taking', 'unprecedented', 'extraordinary', 'effectively unlimited', 'unacceptable') as did the DPPRC ('wider Henry VIII powers than we have ever seen' and 'notable for its width, novelty and uncertainty'). Lord Wilson of Dinton (Crossbench), who was Cabinet Secretary and Head of the Home Civil Service before taking up a peerage in 2002, explained in the Lords that the powers were 'the dream of tyrants through the ages. It is something which is repugnant to the history of this country and the development of our legal system.'[107] Lord Lisvane, the former Clerk of the House of Commons, would play a key role in the DPRRC and in moving amendments in the Lords to attenuate the scope of the powers in the bill. Many such comments among MPs would be made in debates in the House of Commons as well.

Despite this kind of resistance, the Government made fairly few important concessions during the passage of the bill. That is not to say no concessions of importance were made. In the area of delegated powers alone, the Government conceded to recommendations made by the Committees on a few issues, including

- That the powers under section 8(1) expire after two years. This was conceded and a sunset clause provision added (section 8(8));[108]

[103] The document I refer to is available on the EU Withdrawal Act 2018—Bill Documents page at http://www.legislation.gov.uk.

[104] Principally those identified in Schedule 7, paras 1(2) (transfer of EU functions to UK public authority, fees, offences, and creating or amending power to legislate), 1 (5) (ministerial specification of 'deficiency'), 2(3) (similar to para.1(2)), and miscellaneous situations detailed in Schedule 7, Part II.

[105] EU (Withdrawal) Act 2018, Schedule 7, para 1(3).

[106] As the Explanatory Notes to Schedule 7, para 1(1) and (3) make clear at [295].

[107] HL Deb 7 March 2018 col 1178.

[108] Constitution Committee, *European Union (Withdrawal) Bill: Interim Report* (HL 2017–19, 19) [49]–[50]. The clauses were introduced in respect of other provisions of the bill and resulting Act.

- That a sifting mechanism be created, namely, a parliamentary committee charged with sifting draft regulations to be laid under the negative procedure recommending some for affirmative scrutiny (accepted in Schedule 7);[109]
- That the power to amend the 2018 Act itself by regulation be removed.[110]

On the other hand, several quite substantial recommendations were not accepted

- That the sifting committee's recommendations to upgrade scrutiny be binding rather than advisory;[111]
- That the powers to use regulations to implement the withdrawal agreement were removed altogether and be located within a withdrawal bill that was anyway necessary;[112]
- That the capacity to enact tertiary legislation (the sub-delegation of delegated law-making powers) which would not itself be subject to scrutiny in Parliament be prohibited;[113]
- That the power to make regulations under section 8 that remedy deficiencies in retained EU law be limited to those changes that are 'necessary' rather than those 'the Minister considers appropriate'.

The last point deserves closer attention, as the breadth of power created by the statute has a direct impact on the capacity of the law courts to find an instrument to be *ultra vires*. A major site of disagreement was on the language in the bill (and section 8(1) of the Act) providing the power to make such provision as 'the Minister considers appropriate' to correct a deficiency. The Constitution Committee considered the standard 'subjective and inappropriately wide', with the DPRRC agreeing and offering draft text for amendment which would substitute a test of necessity.[114] The Government refused the recommendation. In the result, Yvette Cooper MP (Labour) tabled an amendment to effect the change recommended by both committees. She argued that '"necessary" is a much higher legal threshold', effectively requiring Ministers to 'to satisfy the courts that the regulation was in fact

[109] The suggestion originated with the DPPRC (n 2)[107]. The Government tabled an amendment at Committee stage in the Commons, as explained in sources cited in (n 111) following.

[110] Constitution Committee, *European Union (Withdrawal) Bill* (HL 2017–19, 69) [196]; Delegated Powers and Regulatory Reform Committee (DPRRC), *European Union (Withdrawal) Bill* (HL 2017–19, 73) [24]. The wording 'including modifying this Act' was dropped from what became section 9(2).

[111] Constitution Committee, ibid [227]; HL Deb 19 March 2018 cols 143–144 (amendment tabled by Lord Lisvane and passed by the Lords but rejected by the Commons at ping-pong stage: Charley Coleman and Nicola Newson, *European Union (Withdrawal) Bill: Commons Consideration of Lords Amendments*, House of Lords Library Briefing Paper, LLN-2018-0067, 15 June 2018, 30 (Appendix 1)); Delegated Powers and Regulatory Reform Committee, *European Union (Withdrawal) Bill: Further Government Amendments* (HL 2017–19, 128) [6].

[112] Constitution Committee (n 111) [196]; DPRRC (n 1102) [24].

[113] DPRRC (n 110) [16]; HL Deb 12 March 2018 col 1472 (Lord Lisvane, moving an amendment).

[114] Constitution Committee (n 111) [167]; DPRRC (n 110) [12], note 20.

required to address the deficiency'.[115] In reply, Steven Baker MP (Conservative) clarified that the clause conferred an 'intrinsically limited' power but that a necessity test was too strict because it implied only one possible option when two or more may be appropriate.[116] The amendment was defeated narrowly (295 in favour, 311 against).[117] A similar amendment was moved successfully by Lord Lisvane. Yet it was narrowly rejected by the Commons during the Commons Considerations of Lords Amendments (ping-pong) stage.[118]

(iii) Reassurances

Within the cut and thrust of the bill's passage, two assurances of some substance were made to Parliament. The first is that the Government affirmed repeatedly that the powers sought were to implement technical changes and not make major policy decisions. In its White Paper introducing the 'Great Repeal Bill', it claimed '[t]he Great Repeal Bill will not aim to make major changes to policy or establish new legal frameworks in the UK beyond those which are necessary to ensure the law continues to function properly from day one'.[119] Such assurances were noted and relied on by committees without any qualification from Government. The second is that notwithstanding the breadth of the powers conferred, there was no suggestion that this intended to oust the supervision of the courts. To the contrary, Lord Callaghan would indicate in his Government response to a report of the DPRRC that

> It is certainly true that 'appropriate' is a broader term than 'necessary', but when the courts turn to interpret broad discretions, they construe them in the context in which the powers have been conferred by Parliament. As *Craies on Legislation* notes, the more apparently wide a power is, the more the courts will feel obliged to impose some kind of limitation based on the context and probable legislative intent.[120]

These two reassurances were in all likelihood the only way to maintain a semblance of constitutional respectability during the bill's passage, for without them the bill would plainly justify the outrage it provoked. What it may portend for the future is something I consider by way of conclusion.

[115] HC Deb 12 December 2017 c253. See a similar amendment (rejected without division) in respect of the devolved powers by Joanna Cherry MP: HC Deb 16 January 2018 col 801.

[116] HC Deb 12 December 2017 col 283.

[117] Lucinda Maer, *The European Union (Withdrawal) Bill 2017–19: Summary of Commons Committee Stage* (House of Commons Library Briefing Paper, CBP-8192 1 January 2018) 20.

[118] Newson and Coleman (n 111) 30.

[119] White Paper, *Legislating for the United Kingdom's Withdrawal from the European Union* (Cm 9446), March 2017, para 1.21. See also [3.7] for a similar commitment.

[120] Delegated Powers and Regulatory Reform Committee, *European Union (Withdrawal) Bill: Government Response* (HL 2017–19, 119) Appendix 1.

(iv) Realisation

It is too soon to assess the operations of the 2018 Act, however it remains the case that the vast majority of the projected pre-exit day Brexit-related SIs under section 8(1) have been made at the time of writing. They merit brief comment as they give some indication of what has resulted. As of 8 April 2019, 515 Brexit-related SIs had been laid, 421 using powers under the 2018 Act, and the remainder using powers in other Acts of Parliament.[121] They are on average 20 pages in length, and the total volume of pages is 10,269, which makes them significantly longer on average that regular SIs in previous parliamentary sessions. It suggests that there was consolidation of measures that were initially projected to be in different instruments into longer regulations.[122] Of the 515, which are considered to be near the total expected number prior to exit day, roughly 25 per cent are regulations that amend an Act of Parliament (Henry VIII powers). Approximately 47 per cent of the Brexit-related instruments laid under the 2018 Act, and 25 per cent of those laid under other Acts of Parliament, are subject to the affirmative procedure.[123] The sifting committees in the Commons and Lords recommended either separately or concurrently that a total of 28 per cent (63) of draft negative instruments (222) be upgraded to affirmative scrutiny—with the Government accepting the recommendation in approximately 86 per cent of the cases (54).[124]

The experience thus holds out something for critics and defenders of the Act's offering. Defenders can point to the frequent use of the affirmative scrutiny procedure and the concessions during the bill's passage having a tangible post-enactment impact on its operation. Critics will decry the soaring use of Henry VIII powers, and that the conferral of subjective power on ministers remains breathtaking. The key question is, are such measures being used to make 'major changes of policy' which the Government promised they would not? No qualitative analysis of that question is now complete, and it would anyway be premature as there will be more to come. Nevertheless, a group of organisations has created a network, the SIFT Project, to assist with precisely that kind of enquiry.[125] In two blog posts, the coordinators of this project have drawn attention to two ways in which major policy decisions have been undertaken in the exercise of delegated powers. The first is to simply observe that in fact some major policy change have been occurring.[126] As they observe—being

[121] Hansard Society, *Statutory Instruments Tracker* (n 52).

[122] As noted ibid, cf Apostolova (n 22) 9 for annual page volume across the twentieth century. This point matters because even under the affirmative procedure the scrutiny in committee is very brief.

[123] Hansard Society, *Statutory Instruments Tracker* (n 52).

[124] Ibid.

[125] It is run jointly by the Hansard Society and the Public Law Project, in conjunction with other organisations.

[126] Alexandra Sinclair and Joe Tomlinson, 'Brexit, Primary Legislation, and Statutory Instruments: Everything in Its Right Place?' UK Const L Blog (25 Mar 2019); available at: https://ukconstitutionallaw.org/.

those most centrally concerned with the bulk of the substance of these draft instruments—'[i]t is clear … that the approach to EUWA powers is, at least in multiple important places, inconsistent with the promised course of action'. The second, and more subtle point is that such policy changes are occurring, among other ways, by simply deleting functions previously performed by the European Union when the functions are transferred into UK law.[127] This illustrates the commencement of deregulation by stealth, much feared by liberal and left-leaning critics of Brexit.

Another important point is that the mechanism of parliamentary oversight for the measures is not well adapted to rejecting something on the grounds that it is a 'major policy choice'. While the sifting committee can only recommend upgrading the scrutiny level, the Lords' Secondary Legislation Scrutiny Committee (SLSC) and the ad hoc Commons' Delegated Legislation Committees are those tasked with scrutiny of policy. In the latter case, as discussed,[128] the discussions are brief and rarely iterative on points of detail. The Minister presents the case; the other parties respond for a few minutes; the minister replies briefly. Either the instrument is agreed without dissent or there is a division which the Government invariably wins. This is usually within a half-hour envelope, on what is on average a piece of twenty or more pages of densely structured legislation. The SLSC can bring the measure to the House's attention. But as noted, defeats there are still rare, and in this session, unheard of (though a few instruments have been withdrawn and re-laid). In other words, once the delegated powers genie was let out of the bottle, there was no effective way of controlling it, still less of putting it back in.

IV. Conclusion

Louis Blom Cooper QC spoke at an important Commonwealth conference in 1989 about the judicial control of delegated legislation, noting that even on questions of vires, the courts 'on past record, remain[ed] remote and seldom … [were] used for that purpose'.[129] Yet he added, with prescience, that 'if we do not do something about scrutinising delegated legislation within the parliamentary process, the courts may well begin to flex their muscles'.[130] Just that has occurred. The longer story will need to be told a different day, but it is clear that the courts

[127] Alexandra Sinclair and Joe Tomlinson, 'Deleting the Administrative State?' UK Const L Blog (7 Feb 2019); available at: https://ukconstitutionallaw.org/.

[128] Nn 99–100 earlier and accompanying text.

[129] Louis Blom-Cooper, 'Delegated Legislation in the Courts' in *Third Commonwealth Conference on Delegated Legislation: Record of Proceedings* (HMSO 1990) 48, 50.

[130] Ibid 51.

will quash regulations for inadequate consultation,[131] frustration of a legitimate expectation,[132] vagueness,[133] unreasonableness,[134] breach of common law fundamental rights,[135] *Padfield* inconsistency with the scheme of the parent Act.[136] Essentially a claimant can in principle plead any ground of public law illegality.[137] In the landmark *Public Law Project* case, the Supreme Court relied on the inadequate scrutiny in parliament in concluding that 'a delegation to the Executive of power to modify primary legislation must be an exceptional course and that, *if there is any doubt about the scope of the power conferred upon the Executive or upon whether it has been exercised, it should be resolved by a restrictive approach*'.[138] This trajectory has corrected the mismatch observed previously between the doctrinal legal position that full judicial control of the vires of delegated legislation is beyond doubt, and the practice of pronounced judicial restraint. As with other areas of public law, whether or not the judges had already found their voice, it has certainly become much louder.[139]

It is an unfortunate development for the Government at the present time. As we have seen, the European Union (Withdrawal) Act 2018 contains broad powers which have been used to pass many measures of policy substance, a large number of which are Henry VIII clauses, at a time when the courts have asserted their readiness to control them and the Government itself acknowledged the importance of the judicial role during the passage of the bill. Furthermore, such measures will affect a large number of well-resourced persons who will have much on the line and thus good reason to pursue legal challenges. The many vague provisions in the 2018 Act will come in for interpretation, and narrow readings will be suggested at every opportunity. While it seems clear that the courts cannot but recognise the fundamentally important and unique circumstances in which the Act came to be passed, neither can they deny their role in supervising the legality of its implementation. No-one doubted that during the passage of the bill. On the whole, it seems likely that there will be a storm of litigation brewing on the horizon. It is just the

[131] *Agricultural, Horticultural and Forestry Industry Trading Board v Aylesbury Mushrooms Limited*, [1972] 1 WLR 190; *Bank Mellat v HM Treasury* [2013] UKSC 39, [2014] AC 700.

[132] *R (BAPIO) v Secretary of State for the Home Department* [2008] UKHL 27, [2008] 1 AC 1003.

[133] *Tabernacle v Secretary of State for Defence* [2008] EWHC 416 (Admin); *Commissioners of Customs and Excise v Cure & Deeley Ltd* [1961] 3 All ER 641 (QB).

[134] *R (on the application of Asif Javed) v Secretary of State for the Home Department and Another* [2001] EWCA Civ 789, [2002] QB 129.

[135] *(UNISON) v Lord Chancellor* [2017] UKSC 51, [2017] 3 WLR 409.

[136] *R (on the application of Rights of Women) v Secretary of State for Justice* [2016] EWCA Civ 91, [2016] 1 WLR 2513.

[137] Paul Craig, *Administrative Law* (8th edn, Sweet & Maxwell 2016) ch 15. The chapter is a masterfully succinct overview of the law.

[138] *R (on the application of Public Law Project) v Lord Chancellor* (n 90), [27] (emphasis added).

[139] For a persuasive argument suggesting such a development is appropriate, see Gabrielle Appleby, 'Challenging the Orthodoxy: Giving the Court a Role in Scrutiny of Delegated Legislation' (2015) 69 Parliamentary Affairs 269 (considering in particular the Australian example).

kind of storm in which many are likely to turn to Paul Craig for advice on how to stabilise the ship of state. Extremely few know the institutional and legal shorelines of both the European Union and the United Kingdom quite so well. And as every contributor to this volume doubtless knows, Paul Craig is a man who gives exceptionally good advice.

9

Legislating and Adjudicating

Where and How to Strike the Balance

*Eleanor Sharpston**

I. Introduction

This chapter focuses on the role played by the Court of Justice of the European Union (the CJEU or 'the Court') in ruling authoritatively on the meaning of EU legislation. The CJEU is often accused—and not only by belligerent Brexiteers—of being an activist court: of legislating rather than merely adjudicating. Hence the title of the chapter.

Over the years, EU legislation has often had a bad press for incomprehensibility. As counsel before the English courts, I became fairly inured to the exasperated judicial comment, 'What on earth is this meant to mean, Miss Sharpston?' With approximately equal frequency, the CJEU has been castigated for ignoring, in its judgments, the 'plain text' of the measures that it is called upon to interpret and instead taking an interventionist approach to promote its hidden federalist agenda.

Well, as to the federalist agenda: possibly I am unobservant, but I confess that I have not come across anything approximating to a federalist agenda in the thirteen years that I have been serving at the Court. The CJEU is a court of law. Like many other courts, it is preoccupied above all with getting through its caseload with reasonable despatch and producing judgments that give succinct answers to practical legal problems. However, I have *certainly* come across instances where the Court has deviated from the literal wording of the text in its judgments—often, at my instigation as Advocate General. Let me therefore try to set out my understanding of *why* EU legislation is the way it is, and *why* the CJEU approaches its task of interpreting that legislation in the way that it does.

If one starts from the premise that respecting Montesquieu's separation of powers is a Good Thing,[1] the immediate temptation is to ask, 'Why should the

* The views expressed are personal and do not of course bind the Court of Justice of the European Union, in which I serve as an Advocate General. I am very grateful to Peter Gjørtler in my chambers for finding time, in between helping to draft Opinions, to read through and comment on this text in draft form. All remaining errors and infelicities should be laid at my door.

[1] To borrow the excellent classification system of WC Sellar and RJ Yeatman, *1066 and All That* (Methuen 1930).

Eleanor Sharpston, *Legislating and Adjudicating* In: *The Foundations and Future of Public Law*. Edited by: Elizabeth Fisher, Jeff King, Alison L Young, Oxford University Press (2020). © Oxford UniversityPress.
DOI: 10.1093/oso/9780198845249.003.0009

CJEU ever need to do more than just take the literal meaning of the text as promulgated by the EU legislator and give effect to it? Isn't that what all right-thinking judges do?'

The short answer is that that question starts from an Anglo-centric view of the world, in which the text of any statute is drawn up in copious detail by Parliamentary counsel, and statutory instruments are prepared with similar loving attention to detail by lawyers within the civil service. The English common law tradition is to frame legislation in that way: to try to use terminology which is as sharply focused and comprehensive as possible and to seek to anticipate every conceivable permutation that might arise (even, perhaps, at the risk of over-elaboration). That is complemented by a judicial tradition of interpretation that pays great attention and deference to the precise wording of the text that has emerged from the legislative process. The extensive case law nevertheless demonstrates that that technique of statutory drafting does not automatically generate perfect results, not least because it is in practice impossible to foresee all eventualities.

That English common law tradition is not, however, the tradition of every other Member State. Other, *equally valid* ways of approaching legislative drafting are alive and well within the diversity that is both the strength and the challenge of the European Union. One has only to look at the French Code Civil, or the German Bürgerliches Gesetzbuch, to realise that civilised and highly developed legal systems may (perfectly legitimately) *choose* to write their legislative instruments in a way that is much more abstract than a UK statute. Along with the more abstract drafting comes a slightly different, and equally permissible, role for the judicature.

Each legal system, in other words, has its own perception of what *precisely* respecting Montesquieu's separation of powers entails. (We also tend, despite our best endeavours, to retain a subconscious reflex that our own system is the 'natural' starting point for that analysis!) Within a unitary national legal system, what matters is that the constitutional balance between the different legal powers—executive, legislature, and judiciary—is appropriate, understood by the different actors and respected.

But the EU's legal system is not unitary. It is an extraordinary experiment in supra-national legislating. EU law has to operate as a single uniform system of law that intertwines and meshes perfectly with twenty-eight different national legal systems and traditions. It is created by representatives of Member States (in the Council) and elected representatives (in the European Parliament) who negotiate and frame EU law texts against that rich tapestry of disparate backgrounds.

Even were everyone responsible for legislating in the European Union suddenly to agree in principle to 'do things in the British way', the actual process of generating EU legislation, the multinationalism (more reminiscent of public international law than of law-making within a single nation state) and the multilingualism that permeates the European Union would together make it impossible to proceed in that neat and (to UK-trained lawyers) convenient fashion.

Let us begin with the legislative process itself. The Edinburgh European Council in 1992 recognised the need for better law-making in the shape of clearer, simpler acts complying with the principles of good legislative drafting. The Council and the Commission both duly took steps to meet that need.[2] Political commitment to that objective was reaffirmed by Declaration No 39 on the quality of the drafting of Community legislation, annexed to the final act of the Amsterdam Treaty. The three institutions involved in the procedure for the adoption of Community acts (the European Parliament, the Council, and the Commission) then adopted common guidelines intended to improve the quality of drafting of Community legislation by the Interinstitutional Agreement of 22 December 1998.[3] The first edition of the 'Joint Practical Guide of the European Parliament, the Council and the Commission for persons involved in the drafting of European Union legislation' (the JPG) appeared in 2000. A think tank was created in 2010 to facilitate cooperation between the three institutions on matters of legislative drafting.[4]

Currently, there is no shortage of sensible guidance on the topic of how to draft EU measures. The 2013 edition of the JPG[5] lays down, with commendable clarity, a set of 'general principles', together with guidelines for different parts of the legislative act and internal and external references. Amending acts are specifically dealt with, as are final provisions, repeals, and annexes.

It would be exceptionally difficult to take issue with those general guidelines. Thus, for example, the first guideline states that 'Legal acts of the Union shall be drafted clearly, simply and precisely.' The fourth guideline stipulates that 'Provisions of acts shall be concise and their content should be as homogeneous as possible. Overly long articles and sentences, unnecessarily convoluted wording and excessive use of abbreviations should be avoided.' Moreover, the JPG is intended to be used in conjunction with other more specific instruments (of which there is no dearth), such as the Council's Manual of Precedents, the Commission's Manual on Legislative Drafting, and the Interinstitutional style guide published by the Publications Office of the European Union.[6] With such a plethora of good models, what could possibly go wrong?

Unfortunately, for practical reasons that have next to nothing to do with either the competence or the good faith of those engaged in the process, the reality of EU drafting does not always manage to live up to those worthy aspirations.

[2] 'Council Resolution of 8 June 1993 on the Quality of Drafting of Community Legislation' [1993] OJ C166/1. European Commission, 'General Guidelines for Legislative Policy' SEC (1995) 2255/7, 18 January 1996.

[3] Interinstitutional Agreement of 22 December 1998 on common guidelines for the quality of drafting of Community legislation [1999] OJ C73/1.

[4] See footnote 2 to the preface to the second (2013) edition of the Joint Practical Guide.

[5] Available at: https://eur-lex.europa.eu/content/techleg/KB0213228ENN.pdf.

[6] See the Preface to the first (2000) edition of the *Joint Practical Guide*, reproduced in the 2013 edition.

By way of illustration, let's look at the progress of the legislative proposal for an (imaginary) new directive to improve trans-border measures to combat people trafficking. As with many measures in the Area of Freedom, Security and Justice (AFSJ),[7] there is surely going to be general agreement about the desirability of doing *something* at EU level but probably much less agreement between the Member States as to precisely what should be done.

Work starts within the Commission on the preparation of the first draft and accompanying explanatory memorandum. A Latvian (Ligita) and a Portuguese (Bernadete) are the two Commission officials responsible for putting electronic pen to paper. They are drafting in English—now, the usual internal working language of the Commission.[8] They present the first draft to their team leader, a studious and conscientious German called Dieter. He goes through it line by line, commenting, making suggestions. Ligita and Bernadete have another go. The review process is repeated a couple of times and then the draft goes up the line for further scrutiny, by a Pole (Krzysztof) and a Belgian (Ignace). Further adjustments are made to the proposed text in the light of their comments.

The Commission's proposal is then presented to a working party within the Council, composed of delegates from all Member States. Each has arrived in Brussels with a briefcase containing red lines: points to which their government will emphatically *not* agree. The ensuing meeting produces comments, objections, sticking points, mild encouragement. The directive is, they all agree, a desirable measure; it's just that they cannot accept *that* particular formulation of a key definition in Article 1(2) (etc). The Commission is instructed to go away and produce a revised proposal for further consideration.

Back at the Commission, the nice Portuguese (Bernadete) is now on maternity leave and Ligita's hands are rather full with a different, very urgent, project. So, an energetic and talented Greek former stagiaire/intern who is now on a temporary agent's contract, initially only for six months but then subsequently extended (Pangiota—'Penny' to her non-Greek colleagues), takes over the file and eagerly drives it forwards, liaising with Ligita as much as time allows. They mull over the comments from the Council working party and try to craft suitable amendments. Occasionally, when they sense that they are really getting bogged down in

[7] Once memorably rechristened by one of my référendaires—now a distinguished judge at the General Court—as the 'Area of Peace, Love and Understanding'. Judge Geert de Baere was entirely right that the title of the AFSJ is aspirational but that beneath it lurk hidden tensions. Promoting 'freedom' may not always imply the same priorities as promoting 'security'; and occasionally Member States adopt positions that suggest that they consider that promoting 'justice' would only be possible at the price of undermining one or both of the other aims.

[8] When I began my career as an EU lawyer in 1981 with a five-month stint as an eager young stagiaire (intern) in the Commission's legal service (courtesy of the Middle Temple's generous Sir Peter Bristow award), the language of that institution was emphatically and unquestionably French. That remains the position in the CJEU; but—particularly after the major wave of accessions in 2004—it has ceased to be the case in the other institutions, where the special sub-variant of the language of Shakespeare known as 'international English' reigns supreme.

a linguistic morass, they touch base with their UK colleague down the corridor (Ben) to ask for his help. Ben, of course, has his own work to be getting on with and is also understandably distracted by (and agitated about) Brexit, so they try not to bother him too often with linguistic queries.

The Commission's revised proposal goes back to the Council. In due course the European Parliament becomes drawn into the process with counter-suggestions and textual tweaks. I'll spare you the full gory details of the co-legislator process. The final, much chewed-over compromise text—replete with constructive ambiguities to deal with the points where various Member States' red lines collided—receives a linguistic 'toilettage' and is then translated into all the EU languages and published in the Official Journal.

The example I have just given is perfectly plausible, I assure you. I used it recently in a teaching seminar whose objective was to improve the clarity of EU legislative drafting. The mixed-nationality group of experienced, competent, and hard-working Commission officials attending dissolved into rueful, appreciative laughter. But the serious point behind my illustration is this: even though everyone is doing their honest best, there is ample scope for the text that emerges from the legislative process to be a text that may not read as smoothly, and may not be as precise, as would be desirable in an ideal world. 'Doing' law in a language which is not one's mother tongue is, to be honest, pretty daunting anyway. Accommodating the need for intentional ambiguity—yes, slightly less precision is occasionally required in order to negotiate the necessary consensus between sovereign States—merely adds a further layer to the challenge. It is not fair or realistic to expect a perfect result. If that is true of any individual language version, it is true in spades when considering the various different linguistic versions, *all of which are equally authentic.*[9] Approaching such a text as though every comma is of immense significance will simply not work as an interpretative technique. The English text of (let us say) Article 27 has, perhaps, four commas. The French text has five. The Spanish text has three. And that is before we hit any major divergence in drafting between linguistic versions.

The perils of multilingualism can neatly be illustrated by the reference for a preliminary ruling in *Emirates Airlines*.[10] Dr Schenkel had bought a return air ticket for a trip to Manila with Emirates Airlines, flying out of Düsseldorf (Germany) via Dubai. On the outbound journey, all went according to plan. Alas, his inbound (return) flight was cancelled and he arrived back in Düsseldorf two days later than scheduled.

[9] See (amongst many examples) C-100/90 *Commission v Denmark*, ECLI:EU:C:1991:395, [1991] ECR I-5089.

[10] C-173/07, *Emirates Airlines v Schenkel*. My Opinion of 6 March 2008 is available at ECLI:EU:C:2008:145; the Judgment of 10 July 2008 at ECLI:EU:C:2008:400, [2008] ECR I-5237.

The Air Passengers Regulation[11]—I dare to suggest, one of the EU's more popular pieces of legislation, at least among the travelling public—makes express provision for passengers who have had their flight cancelled or who have been denied boarding to be paid compensation. But it imposes different obligations on 'Community carriers'[12] and non-Community carriers. Thus, Article 3 ('Scope') makes it clear that the Regulation always applies 'to passengers departing from an airport located in the territory of a Member State to which the Treaty applies' (Article 3(1)(a)). In contrast, it *only* applies 'to passengers departing from an airport located in a third country to an airport situated in the territory of a Member State to which the Treaty applies … *if the operating air carrier of the flight concerned is a Community carrier*' (Article 3(1)(b), emphasis added).

Emirates Airlines (as its name perhaps indicates) is no Community carrier. So how did Dr Schenkel's claim for compensation for his cancelled *inbound* flight ever get off the ground?

The key lies in the difference between the wording of Article 3(1) in most language versions of the regulation and the text of the German version, which formed the basis of the referring court's question. Most language versions use a construction similar to the phrase 'passengers departing from an airport', which appears in the English version of Article 3(1)(a) and (b).[13] The German version however includes the word 'flight', rendering the phrase as 'passengers who embark on a flight at airports'.[14] Dr Schenkel argued that the outward and return flights were non-independent parts of a single flight, for which he had purchased a return ticket. Since the point of departure for that single flight was Düsseldorf, he was thus a passenger 'departing from an airport located in the territory of the Member States'. It followed that he was covered. Dr Schenkel won at first instance. The appeal court was inclined to consider that a journey out and back did constitute a single flight for the purposes of the Air Passengers Regulation, but out of caution it made a reference for a preliminary ruling under Article 267 TFEU (Treaty on the Functioning of the European Union).

You might have thought that this was a storm in a teacup. As France correctly pointed out in its written observations, the difference in wording between the German and other language versions does not alter the actual sense of the

[11] Regulation (EC) No 261/2004 of the European Parliament and of the Council of 11 February 2004 establishing common rules on compensation and assistance to passengers in the event of denied boarding and of cancellation or long delay of flights, and repealing Regulation (EEC) No 291/91 [2004] OJ L47/1.

[12] A 'Community carrier' is defined in Article 2(c) as 'an air carrier with a valid operating licence granted by a Member State in accordance with the provisions of Council Regulation (EEC) No 2407/92 of 23 July 1992 on licensing of air carriers'.

[13] The French wording is '*passagers au départ d'un aéroport*', and the Spanish, '*pasajeros que partan de un aeropuerto*'. Equivalent formulations are found, for example, in the Dutch, Italian, and Portuguese versions.

[14] '*Fluggäste, die auf Flughäfen … einen Flug antreten*.' Similar wording is used in the German version of recital 6. See my Opinion (n 10) points 6 and 7.

provision. Embarkation on a flight is the normal preliminary to departure. When passengers depart from an airport, it is understood and obvious that they do so by embarking on a flight.[15]

It nevertheless took a chamber of five judges, a hearing, and an Advocate General's Opinion[16] to unscramble the linguistic mess and to decide that the EU legislator had *not* intended to obliterate the difference ostensibly drawn in Article 3 between Community carriers and non-Community carriers.[17]

A further, more recent, and perhaps even more striking example is provided by *Teglgaard and Fløstrupgard I/S v Fødevareministeriets Klagecenter*.[18] The national court was seised with 173 cases concerning payments of aid under direct support schemes for farmers and deductions therefrom to sanction failure to respect 'cross-compliance requirements' (ie obligations in other EU legislation that farmers are required to respect as a condition for receiving that EU funding, such as limitations on the use of fertiliser).[19] The key question was, when a breach of the rules occurs, should the reduction in the direct support granted be applied to the payment due for the year in which the breach occurred, or to that applicable in the year in which the breach was discovered? In apparently opting for the latter, the French text of the Council Regulation[20] said the opposite to what was laid down in the English text. Linguistically, there is no way of 'reconciling' these two diametrically opposed versions of what the legislator intended to write. A painstaking comparison of the different language versions confirmed that the 'odd man out' was indeed the French text. Despite that, the Commission had (apparently) taken the French text as the

[15] Ibid point 8.

[16] When I began as a practitioner before the Court, every case had a hearing and an Opinion from the Advocate General. As the case load and the pressure upon finite resources has increased, the Court has become more parsimonious. Thus, since the entry into force of the Treaty of Nice the Court has been able to dispense with an Advocate General's Opinion if the case 'raises no new point of law': see Article 20, para 5 of the Statute of the Court of Justice. Likewise, the Court may now in principle decide to dispense with a hearing if it 'considers that it has sufficient information to give a ruling'. There is a solitary exception, within the procedure governing references for a preliminary ruling, namely where a hearing is requested with reasons by an 'interested person' (as referred to in Article 23 of the Statute) who did not participate in the written part of the procedure: see Article 76 of the Rules of Procedure.

[17] See, in particular, points 49–64 and 87–94 of my Opinion (n 10). I am very happy to record that the Court followed its Advocate General.

[18] Case C-239/17, Opinion ECLI:EU:C:2018:328, judgment ECLI:EU:C:2018:597.

[19] The amounts of fertiliser used had released excess quantities of nitrates, thus contravening Council Directive 91/676/EEC.

[20] Article 6 of Council Regulation (EC) No 1782/2003 of 29 September 2003 establishing common rules for direct support schemes under the Common Agricultural Policy and establishing certain support schemes for farmers and amending Regulations (EEC) No 2019/93, (EC) No 1452/2001, (EC) No 1453/2001, (EC) No 1454/2001, (EC) 1868/94, (EC) No 1251/1999, (EC) No 1254/1999, (EC) No 1673/2000, (EEC) No 2358/71, and (EC) No 2529/2001 [2003] OJ L270/1. The French text reads, 'le montant total des paiements directs à octroyer au titre de *l'année civile au cours de laquelle le non-respect est constaté*, est réduit ou supprimé'. All the other language versions have 'the total amount of direct payments to be granted *in the year in which the non-compliance occurs* ... shall be reduced or cancelled'.

basis for its subsequent detailed implementing regulation, to the great detriment of the Danish farmers who brought the test actions before the national court.[21]

Unsurprisingly, the national court made a reference asking the Court how the EU legislation was to be interpreted. The case went to a chamber of five, again with hearing and Opinion. At the hearing, the Commission was peppered with questions not only from the reporting judge (Judge Vilaras) and the Advocate General (myself) but also from the President of the Court, Koen Lenaerts, who was substituting for a colleague in the chamber who could not take part in the case. (This happens, if not regularly, at least with sufficient frequency for it not to be entirely untoward. It is probably a little disconcerting for the lawyers who turn up to a five-judge chamber hearing and find themselves being grilled by the President of the Court, who would normally only sit in Grand Chamber cases.)[22]

The Court—I am tempted to say, hunting as a pack—established that, if the sanction were calculated on the basis of the payment due for the year of discovery, the result might bear no relation whatsoever to the breach. Depending on whether the size of holding farmed had increased or diminished, the offending farmer might be punished much more severely, or on the contrary get off scot free.[23] The Opinion painstakingly unpicked the legislation, drawing a distinction between the *computation* of a reduction and its *imputation* to the aid payment that would otherwise be due and invoking the principle of equality of treatment. I recommended that the Court should rule that the sanction should be *calculated* on the basis of the payment due in the year of the breach, but that the sanction so calculated should then be *imputed* (ie applied) to the aid payment due in the year of discovery. The judgment firmly endorsed that approach.[24] The result was eminently just. It was not, however, arrived at by a literal application of the Commission's preferred version of the applicable texts.

As these two examples demonstrate, there are cogent reasons why the Court cannot 'just' use the literal text of an EU legislative measure to arrive at its judgment. For many years, it has therefore applied a purposive—or, as it is known in Euro-jargon, a 'teleological'—approach. As the Court put it in *Teglgaard and Fløstrupgard I/S v Fødevareministeriets Klagecenter*:

[21] Aid paid under the direct support scheme is based, essentially, on the area farmed. Both farmers had increased their holdings between the year of the breach and the year of its discovery. Sanctions are calculated as a *percentage* reduction of the aid that would otherwise be payable; so the offending farmers were therefore faced with greater sanctions. See point 33 of my Opinion (n 18).

[22] A recent example of exactly this happening is the infringement proceedings against three Member States for failure to give effect to the provisional measures taken at the height of the refugee crisis to relocate thousands of applicants for international protection so as to share out the administrative burden of considering their applications more equitably between the Member States. See Case C-715/17 *Commission v Poland*, Case C-718/17 *Commission v Hungary*, and Case C-719/17 *Commission v Czech Republic* (all pending; Opinion delivered on 31 October 2019).

[23] See the examples at points 60–63 and the discussion, under the 'principle of equality', at points 87–95 of the Opinion (n 18).

[24] See, notably, paras 47–55 of the judgment (n 18).

> [t]he provisions of EU law must be interpreted and applied uniformly in the light of the versions existing in all the languages of the European Union and, in the case of divergence between those versions, the provision in question must be interpreted by reference to the purpose and general scheme of the rules of which it forms part.[25]

II. The Court Deciding Not to Take Steps that Might Be Construed as 'Legislating'

A very well-known historical example of the Court showing judicial restraint and declining to 'redraft' (or at least nuance) the existing Treaty rules in the interests of better access to justice is *Unión de Pequeños Agricultores (UPA)*.[26] There, an association of farmers was appealing an order of the Court of First Instance (CFI) dismissing as manifestly inadmissible its application to annul a regulation that amended substantially the common organisation of the olive oil market. Applying established case law, the CFI had held that the members of the association were not 'individually concerned' by the regulation. That aspect of the 'direct and individual concern' test to establish the standing of applicants seeking the annulment of a measure that is not addressed to them had been interpreted strictly. Applicants were regarded as individually concerned by a measure only 'if it affects their legal position by reason of certain attributes peculiar to them, or by reason of a factual situation which differentiates them from all other persons and distinguishes them individually in the same way as the addressee'.[27] The members of the association were indubitably 'directly concerned' by the changes to their market. But they failed the 'individual concern' limb of the test.

Advocate General Jacobs recorded that 'this aspect of the case-law has been much criticised both by Members of the Court of Justice in their individual capacity and by commentators and is often regarded as creating a serious gap in the system of judicial remedies created by the EC Treaty'.[28] He indicated that he would 'argue that locus standi must ... be determined independently and that ... the only solution which provides adequate judicial protection is to change the case-law on individual concern'.[29] He went on to do so in a devastatingly clear and magisterial analysis.

[25] At para 38 of the judgment (n 18), citing C-230/09 and C-231/09 *Kurt und Thomas Etling and Others*, EU:C:2011:271, [2011] ECR-I-3097, para 60, and C-112/15, *Kødbranchens Fællesråd*, EU:C:2016:185, [2016] All ER (D) 175 (Mar), para 36.

[26] Case C-50/00 P. The Opinion of Advocate General Jacobs is at ECLI:EU:C:2002:197; the judgment of the Court at ECLI:EU:C:2002:462, [2002] ECR-I-6677.

[27] See point 2 of the Opinion (n 26), citing 25/62 *Plaumann v Commission* ECLI:EU:C:1963:17 and judgment of 22 November 2001, C-451/98 *Antillean Rice Mills*, ECLI:EU:C:2001:622, [2001] ECR I-8949.

[28] At point 2 of the Opinion (n 26).

[29] At point 4 of the Opinion (n 26).

So convincing was the Opinion that during the four-month interval between the Opinion and the judgment, whilst *UPA* was in *délibéré*, the General Court decided that Advocate General Jacobs was obviously right and followed him (thus departing from established case law) in its judgment in *Jégo Quéré*.[30]

Intellectually attractive though Francis Jacobs' arguments were, the Court decided that following them would be a bridge too far. It held that, whilst the individual concern condition for *locus standi*

> must be interpreted in the light of the principle of effective judicial protection by taking account of the various circumstances that may distinguish an applicant individually ... such an interpretation cannot have the effect of setting aside the condition in question, expressly laid down in the Treaty, without going beyond the jurisdiction conferred by the Treaty on the Community Courts.[31]

Never mind that the *meaning* of 'individual concern' was the product of earlier case law. The Court shied away from grasping the nettle, concluding that,

> While it is, admittedly, possible to envisage a system of judicial review of the legality of Community measures of general application different from that established by the founding Treaty and never amended as to its principles, it is for the Member States, if necessary, in accordance with Article 48 EU, to reform the system currently in force.[32]

Following that judicial restraint, it took first the (abortive) Constitution for Europe[33] and then the reworded Article 263(4) TFEU put in place by the Treaty of Lisbon slightly to liberalise the criteria for direct access to the EU courts. The CJEU is, perhaps inevitably, now engaged in explaining precisely what the new criteria actually mean.[34] At least those following our case law can be reasonably sure that these decisions will be 'big' enough to warrant publication under the Court's new resource-saving criteria.[35]

[30] Case T-177/01, ECLI:EU:T:2002:11, [2002] ECR II-2365.

[31] Ibid at para 44 of the judgment.

[32] Ibid at para 45 of the judgment.

[33] See Article III-365(4) of the Treaty establishing a Constitution for Europe. The various different types of legal acts of the Union were defined in Articles I-33 to I-37.

[34] See eg C-398/13 P *Inuit Tapiriit Kanatami* et al *v Commission*, ECLI:EU:C:2015:535, [2016] 1 CMLR 663, C-456/13P *T & L Sugars Ltd and Sidul Açúcares, Unipessoal Lta v Commission*, ECLI:EU:C:2015:284, [2015] All ER (D) 231 (Apr) and C-236/17 P *Canadian Solar Emea*, ECLLI:EU:C:2019:258 (see in particular paras 99–104).

[35] To see precisely what the Court does (*and does not*) publish, visit the following link on the Curia website: https://curia.europa.eu/jcms/jcms/P_106308/en/.

III. The Court Going to the Limit of 'Constructive Re-Interpretation' of a Text

Probably the most striking recent illustration of a teleological interpretation being taken to its outer limits is *Sturgeon and Böck*,[36] two more (joined) cases concerning the Air Passengers Regulation. That regulation compensates passengers who have had their flight cancelled or who have been denied boarding. But where a flight is delayed, the regulation appeared merely to require the carrier to provide (depending on the destination and the length of the delay) the various kinds of 'assistance' specified in Articles 8 and 9. That is obviously a humane arrangement. But is it a sufficient arrangement? Should the passenger not also be entitled to compensation for a delayed flight?

As the Advocate General in the case, I pointed out the obvious disparity of treatment that appeared to result from the fact that the text of the regulation clearly did *not* address the question of compensation for delay. I gave examples—it was easy enough to do—in which a delayed flight might cause greater inconvenience to the passenger than a flight cancellation.[37] I summed up this part of my analysis thus:

> the Court has heard no argument as to the potential impact, on the questions referred, of the principle of equal treatment. The possibility that an examination of the distinction between delay and cancellation might lead to the conclusion that the way in which the Regulation treats these two concepts violates that fundamental principle of EC law has therefore not been dealt with in any adequate way. I am conscious that there may be counter-arguments that I have failed to identify. Both the institutions and the Member States should have the opportunity to comment on the analysis that I have advanced and to put forward arguments relating to objective justification. I therefore propose that the Court should reopen the oral procedure and invite submissions on that matter from the Member States, the Commission, the European Parliament, and the Council.[38]

In case the Court declined to do so, I went on to examine the factors that had been cited before the Court and in national case law and legal writing as providing possible indications that a flight has been cancelled. Those factors included: change of air carrier, change of aircraft, change of flight number, change of airport of departure or arrival, giving baggage back to passengers, new check-in for passengers, new seating assignment, allocation of all passengers to one or more other aircraft,

[36] Joined Cases C-402/07 and C-432/07, *Sturgeon v Condor Flugdienst Gmbh; Böck and Lepuschitz v Air France SA*, ECLI:EU:C:2009:716, [2009] ECR I-10923.

[37] Ibid see points 51–56 of my Opinion.

[38] Ibid at points 65 and 66 of my Opinion, ECLI:EU:C:2009:416.

issuing new boarding passes, and the fact that the flight was described as 'cancelled' by the pilot (or other air carrier staff) or on the departures board. I concluded that,

> Common sense suggests that all of these factors could be indications that a flight has been cancelled rather than merely delayed. The more factors that are present together, the more likely it becomes that there has indeed been a cancellation. By the same token, I do not think that any individual factor can be conclusive.[39]

Well, perhaps an 'inordinately long' delay could be deemed to become a de facto cancellation, triggering the right to compensation under Article 5(1)(c) of the Regulation?[40] However, it seemed to me impossible to identify, with any acceptable degree of precision, exactly what period of time must elapse before a delay becomes 'inordinate'. The ensuing variability of results was likely to conflict with the principle of legal certainty. As for specifying a number of hours after which a right to compensation for delay came into existence, I advised against attempting that exercise. In a passage in which I nailed my colours to the mast, I said:

> Any numerical threshold for qualification for a right delineates two groups —the fortunate and the unfortunate—and in establishing that threshold the legislator must be careful not to infringe the principle of equal treatment. The legislator has the right to pick a figure and then defend it, to the extent that its choice is challenged as infringing that principle, as objectively justifiable. The actual selection of the magic figure is a legislative prerogative. To the extent that *any* figure is to some extent arbitrary, its arbitrariness is covered by that prerogative (the margin of legislative discretion).
>
> Thus, the Community legislator can select a particular time-limit (23 and a half hours, 24 hours, 25 hours, or 48 hours – whatever it be) triggering a right to compensation. The Court cannot. Any figure one cared to pick would involve reading into the Regulation something it plainly does not contain and would be a judicial usurpation of the legislative prerogative.[41]

And, here was my conclusion:

> It seems to me that, in seeking to avoid Scylla (obvious discrimination against passengers whose flights are inordinately delayed when compared to passengers who obtain automatic compensation for their cancelled flight), one is immediately swept into Charybdis (legal uncertainty). Moreover, the underlying difficulties that I have identified earlier in relation to the principle of equal treatment are

[39] Ibid, see points 68 and 69 of my Opinion.
[40] Ibid, see points 77–95 of my Opinion.
[41] Ibid at points 93 and 94 of my Opinion.

> unfortunately not solved by adopting a teleological approach towards 'inordinate delay'. They appear to me to be inherent in the structure of the Regulation as it presently stands.
>
> It is because I do not think that the underlying problem can be 'fixed' by interpretation, however constructive, that I suggest that the Court should reopen the oral procedure pursuant to Article 61 of the Rules of Procedure of the Court of Justice and invite submissions from the Member States, the Commission, the European Parliament, and the Council on whether Articles 5 and 7 of the Regulation and Article 6 of the Regulation, and specifically the distinction they introduce between cancellation and delay, are invalid in the light of the principle of equal treatment.[42]

Seldom have I been so comprehensively wrong about what the Court might decide to do in the light of an Opinion.

The five-judge chamber examined the notions of 'delay' and 'cancellation' in the Air Passengers Regulation and concluded that 'a flight which is delayed, irrespective of the duration of the delay, even if it is long, cannot be regarded as cancelled where there is a departure in accordance with the original planning'.[43] It then turned to the possibility of compensation in the event of a delay.[44] After accepting at the outset that 'it does not expressly follow from the wording of Regulation No 261/2004 that passengers whose flights are delayed have such a right',[45] the Court moved on to the aim and objective of the regulation (a high level of protection for air passengers) and seized gratefully upon my analysis of equal treatment. Passengers who were denied boarding or whose flights were cancelled or delayed all were all caused 'similar serious trouble and inconvenience connected with air transport'.[46] According to a general principle of interpretation, a Community act must be interpreted, as far as possible, in such a way as not to affect its validity; and the principle of equal treatment is a principle of primary law. Passengers whose flights have been cancelled and passengers affected by a flight delay suffer similar damage (a loss of time): they thus find themselves in comparable situations for the purposes of the application of the right to compensation laid down in Article 7 of Regulation No 261/2004. With considerable ingenuity, the Court then attached the right to compensation for delay to the three-hour period that triggers the right to compensation under Article 5(1)(c)(iii) of Regulation No 261/2004 for passengers who are re-routed. It then held that passengers whose flights are delayed and passengers whose flights are cancelled could not be treated differently without the principle of equal treatment being infringed (in the process ruling out any objective

[42] Ibid at points 96 and 97 of my Opinion.
[43] Ibid at para 34 of the judgment.
[44] Ibid see paras 40–69 of the judgment.
[45] Ibid at para 41 of the judgment.
[46] Ibid at para 44 of the judgment.

justification for that difference in treatment). Air carriers would not, however, be obliged to pay compensation if they could show that the flight cancellation or long delay was caused by extraordinary circumstances.[47]

The Fourth Chamber's ruling in *Sturgeon* was subsequently confirmed by the Grand Chamber in *Nelson and TUI Travel*.[48] The extreme teleology of the Court in these cases has provoked both fervent defence and heavyweight academic scorn.[49] I merely add that from a consumer protection perspective, the decision in *Sturgeon* is probably one of the most popular rulings the Court has ever made.

IV. How Far Should the Court '*Bend*' a Text?

The 'Dublin III' Regulation[50] contains the rules that determine which participating State[51] should take responsibility for examining an application for asylum. It contains, in Chapter III, a series of criteria which are to be applied in turn, the intention being that—in a logical and orderly way—the administrative burden of applying the (same) procedural and substantive rules and the subsequent obligation to accept, shelter, and integrate persons qualifying for international protection should be shared out fairly and equitably between the participating States.[52]

[47] Unsurprisingly, an extensive case law has grown up as to what do and do not constitute such 'extraordinary circumstances'. See e.g. C-302/16 *Krijgsman*, ECLI:EU:C:2017:359, [2017] 3 CMLR 1395 (communication to a travel agent), C-195/17 etc *Krüsemann* et al, ECLI:EU:C:2018:258, [2018] 3 CMLR 698 (strikes) and C-501/17 P *Germanwings*, ECLI:EU:C:2019:288 (air traffic security).

[48] Joined Cases C-581/10 and C-629/10, *Nelson v Deutsche Lufthansa AG; TUI Travel and Others v Civil Aviation Authority* ECLI:EU:C:2012:657, [2013] 1 CMLR 1191. Given the firmness of the line that I had espoused in *Sturgeon*, I recused myself from involvement in the Grand Chamber follow-up and my colleague Yves Bot took the case. His Opinion is at ECLI:EU:C:2012:295.

[49] See for example the two 'bookends', by Koen Lenaerts and Joseph Weiler respectively, in the essay collection published in Maurice Adams and others, *Judging Europe's Judges: The Legitimacy of the Case Law of the European Court of Justice* (Hart 2013).

[50] Regulation (EU) No 604/2013 of the European Parliament and of the Council of 26 June 2013 establishing the criteria and mechanisms for determining the Member State responsible for examining an application for international protection lodged in one of the Member States by a third-country national or a stateless person (recast) [2013] OJ L180/31). The Dublin III Regulation is the successor to Council Regulation (EC) No 343/2003 of 18 February 2003 establishing the criteria and mechanisms for determining the Member State responsible for examining an asylum application lodged in one of the Member States by a third-country national (the 'Dublin II Regulation') [2003] OJ L50/1), as amended by Regulation (EC) No 1103/2008 (OJ 2008 L 304, p 80). The Dublin II Regulation itself replaced the Dublin Convention (Convention determining the State responsible for examining an application for asylum lodged in one of the Member States of the European Communities ([1997] OJ L254/1)).

[51] The Dublin III Regulation automatically covers twenty-five of the twenty-eight EU Member States. Recital 41 states that Ireland and the United Kingdom have both opted in under Protocol 21 to the EU Treaties. Recital 22 states that, in accordance with Protocol 22, Denmark is not covered. However, Denmark made an agreement with the European Union to be covered by the Dublin II Regulation, which Denmark was entitled to continue for the Dublin III Regulation. Similar agreements have been concluded between the European Union and Iceland, Liechtenstein, Norway, and Switzerland.

[52] For a reasonably full description of the relevant parts of the Dublin III Regulation, see my Opinion in Case C-490/16 *A.S. v Slovenia* ECLI:EU:C:2017:585, [2018] 1 WLR 852 and Case C-646/16 *Jafari* ECLI:EU:C:2017:443, [2018] 1 WLR 773 ('the Opinion in *A.S. and Jafari*'), points 22–42.

The Dublin III Regulation starts from the premise that—roughly speaking, of course—asylum seekers are likely to present themselves in approximately equal numbers to the authorities of each of the various Member States. Given the physical geography of Europe, that is a rather heroic assumption to make even in ordinary times.[53]

Between September 2015 and March 2016, the times were anything but normal. Over that period, in addition to the (repeated) summer-time tragedies of overcrowded semi-inflatable boats foundering in the Mediterranean there was the seemingly endless stream of displaced persons crossing over the land bridge into Europe from Turkey and trudging up the 'West Balkans Route'.[54] And then they poured over the external frontier of the European Union and entered Croatia. They did not slip under the border fence or climb it clandestinely at dead of night. In pursuance of various ad hoc agreements made between Member States seeking to deal with the refugee crisis, they were waved through by the border guards, given basic care (such as bottles of water), ushered onto buses, and transported onwards across Croatia en route towards other Member States, notably Germany. Was this an 'irregular crossing of an external border' within the meaning of Article 13 of the Dublin III Regulation? If so, the Member State of first entry (Croatia) would become responsible for examining the substantive applications for asylum made by those claimants.

Croatia had a total population of 4.154 million in 2017.[55] How was it meant to cope, as the first point of call and therefore responsible Member State, with up to three-quarters of a million potential refugees?

Once the human tide of refugees reached its final destination (often, but by no means invariably, Germany), there were inevitably delays in processing the subsequent asylum claims. No immigration system, however efficient, could deal with so many applications all at once. But the Dublin III Regulation lays down strict time limits for requests between Member States to 'take charge' of a particular claimant. If Member State B (where the claimant is) feels that Member State A is responsible (most frequently, because that Member State allowed the claimant to cross irregularly over its frontier into the territory of the European Union), that request has to be made within three months of the date on which the application was 'lodged'. The period is reduced to two months if there is a 'Eurodac hit' (fingerprint trace in the Eurodac system) identifying the applicant as having earlier been present in another Member State.

That, in a nutshell, was the background to the highly sensitive Grand Chamber decisions in *A.S.*[56] and *Jafari*,[57] on the one hand, and in *Mengesteab*,[58] on the other

[53] See the Opinion in *A.S. and Jafari* (n 52) points 1–3.
[54] See ibid points 5–18.
[55] Source: Eurostat.
[56] *A.S. v Republic of Slovenia* (n 52).
[57] *Jafari* (n 52).
[58] Case C-670/16, *Tsegezab Mengesteab v Bundesrepublik Deutschland*, ECLI:EU:C:2017:587, [2018] 1 WLR 865. My Opinion is at ECLI:EU:C:2017:480.

hand. It was abundantly clear, both to the Grand Chamber and to its Advocate General (myself) that the applicable law—the Dublin III Regulation—had never been designed with the refugee crisis in mind. How could one craft answers which would avoid triggering a melt-down of the EU's asylum system?

The Advocate General's solution was to apply robust common sense. A border crossing in exceptional circumstances that is actively assisted by officials in peaked caps, with the necessary humanitarian assistance and transport laid on, may not be 'regular' (in the sense of, 'following the standard procedures'), but I found it impossible to conclude that it was 'irregular' in the sense of 'unlawful' (or that the crossings were the result of the kind of lax behaviour by the frontier Member State that means that it 'should' then become responsible for dealing with the subsequent asylum paperwork). Had Croatia not opened its border, there would have been a humanitarian crisis on the EU's doorstep.[59] The fact that Croatia had done so surely did not mean that it should then be penalised by being swamped with all the substantive applications for refugee status on the grounds that there had been irregular border crossings?

By the same token, I was prepared to take a substantive, rather than formal, view of when an asylum application is actually 'lodged' under Article 20(2) of the Dublin III Regulation and therefore of the point from which the time limit in Article 21(1) begins to run for the purpose of issuing a take charge request.[60] In the process, I also drew attention to the underlying issue of whether Mr Mengesteab's arrival in Italy by sea should really be equated to an irregular frontier crossing under Article 13 of the Dublin III Regulation, whilst recognising that the Court would probably not wish to drink from that poisoned chalice in that particular case. (In that prediction, at least, I was proved entirely right.)

Informally, there was praise for the thoughtfulness and the passion of my two Opinions. But the Court was not prepared to adopt the solutions that I had put forward.[61] In *A.S.* and *Jafari*, it held that the frontier crossings were indeed 'irregular' within the meaning of Article 13 of the Dublin III Regulation, so that Croatia became the Member State responsible for examining the asylum applications. In *Mengesteab*, it held that time did begin to run from the initial (bare) certificate of registration as an asylum seeker: it followed that Germany was out of time in

[59] Ibid, see points 155–190 of the Opinion, in particular point 182.

[60] 'German law distinguishes the first request for asylum, which is generally made at an authority other than the Office, from lodging a formal application for asylum at the Office. A third-country national requesting asylum is referred to a reception centre where he receives a certificate of registration as an asylum seeker. That centre must then inform the Office without delay of the fact that the person concerned has requested asylum. However, the authorities responsible for that information have often failed to fulfil that obligation, particularly in the second half of 2015, due to the unusual increase in the number of asylum seekers who entered Germany during that period. In that context, many asylum seekers have had to wait several months to lodge their formal applications for asylum, without being able to expedite that procedure.' *Tsegezab Mengesteab v Bundesrepublik Deutschland* (n 58) para 37.

[61] The Court did follow my Opinion in relation to other aspects of those cases.

making its take charge request to Italy and would have to examine Mr Mengesteab's asylum application.

The important point is, I suggest, that neither I nor the Court could make the wording of the Dublin III Regulation fit the facts of the cases before us with any real degree of comfort. Possibly, the net result of the different solutions we explored was not so very dissimilar. Who really knows? As the old joke about asking for road directions in Ireland has it, 'Well, if I were you, I wouldn't be starting from here.'

The saga does not, of course, end with *A.S./Jafari* and *Mengesteab*. At the height of the refugee crisis, two decisions[62] were adopted with the aim of easing the pressure on Italy and Greece, as the obvious 'frontline' Member States in the Mediterranean. Those decisions put in place a temporary mechanism to effect the relocation, in a spirit of solidarity between Member States, initially of 40,000 persons (Decision (EU) 2015/1523) and (a week later) of 120,000 persons (Decision (EU) 2015/1601). Two of the 'Visegrád' Member States,[63] Slovakia and Hungary, unsuccessfully challenged the validity of the latter decision.[64] There are now infringement proceedings pending against three Visegrád Member States—Poland,[65] Hungary,[66] and the Czech Republic[67]—for failing to notify to the Commission the numbers of applicants for international protection that they were prepared to accept (and then, by necessary implication, failing to take their share of those applicants). A problem of the magnitude of the refugee crisis will inevitably engage both EU legislature and the EU judiciary repetitively over an extended period of time, as national courts grapple with individual cases whilst Member States hunt for a solution to an unwelcome political conundrum.

V. Conclusion

These examples serve, I hope, to demonstrate that the intrinsic parameters within which cases arising under EU law are decided do not always permit a nice clean

[62] Council Decision (EU) 2015/1523 of 14 September 2015 establishing provisional measures in the area of international protection for the benefit of Italy and of Greece [2015] OJ L 239/146) and Council Decision (EU) 2017/1601 of 22 September 2015 establishing provisional measures in the area of international protection for the benefit of Italy and of Greece [2015] OJ L248/80).

[63] The 'Visegrád group' (or the 'Visegrád Four') is a cultural and political alliance that traces its origins to a summit meeting between the leaders of Czechoslovakia, Hungary, and Poland in 1991. The meeting was held in the Hungarian castle town of Visegrád as a deliberate allusion to the Congress of Visegrád (1335) between John I of Bohemia, Charles I of Hungary, and Casimir III of Poland.

[64] See Joined Cases C-643/15 and C-647/15, *Slovakia and Hungary v Council*, ECLI:EU:C:2017:631, [2018] 1 CLMR 895.

[65] Case C-715/17, *Commission v Poland* (pending), Opinion delivered 31 October 2019.

[66] Case C-718/17, *Commission v Hungary* (pending), Opinion delivered 31 October 2019.

[67] Case C-719/17, *Commission v Czech Republic* (pending), Opinion delivered 31 October 2019.

distinction to be drawn between adjudicating and legislating. Many more could be found.

Within a national legal system, there is a more straightforward and immediate relationship between the different branches of government. The legislative process is working within simpler parameters in terms of policy, language, and legal tradition. It is easier for the executive to react to a clearly unjust result thrown up by the case law by bringing forward proposals to amend the statute that the national supreme court has just reluctantly construed in a restrictive and literal way. If a major crisis breaks, emergency legislation can be put in place very swiftly. Gap-patching sometimes does not even require legislation but can be done by the executive using delegated powers.

In contrast, the EU legislative machinery is—*by its very nature*—much more complex and elaborate. Like the oil tanker steaming down the Channel, it can change course but will probably have travelled two further miles, after the lookout's initial alert to the bridge, before the course alteration actually becomes effective. And on the rare occasions that it does act swiftly, full multilateral compliance with what was (probably) intended is not necessarily a given.

During the earlier decades of the 'European project', the Court took a number of decisions that were in no sense political, but that were indubitably teleological and that helped to move technical economic integration forward. Many of those 'choices' have now been made and form an uncontroversial part of established case law. That unobtrusive process continues today.[68]

It is no coincidence, I think, that many of the recent cases with which the Grand Chamber has had to grapple concern legal instruments in the AFSJ. Without wishing to sound polemical, the Court does not *enjoy* having to make a 'call' on the scope of a provision that should have been made during the legislative process. However, when a problem must imperatively be addressed at EU level, the reality is that the Member States in the Council sometimes avoid dealing definitively with a particularly thorny aspect of that problem in order to reach the necessary agreement to get the measure adopted at all. When that happens—when the text can be explained back home in whatever manner is expedient—you are looking at a Grand Chamber case five years down the line.

At that point, the Court cannot duck. Unlike, for example, the UK Supreme Court or the US Supreme Court, we have no system of 'docket control'. Provided

[68] See, for example, Case 120/78, *Rewe Zentrale v Bundesmonopolverwaltung für Branntwein* ('*Cassis de Dijon*'), ECLI:EU:C:1979:42 (mandatory requirements and mutual recognition) or C-302/86, *Commission v Denmark* ('*Danish bottles*'), ECLI:EU:C:1988:421 (trade restrictions and environmental protection). A slightly wider list of significant but ultimately uncontroversial judicial innovations over time would include C-109/88, *Danfoss*, ECLI:EU:C:1989:383 (reversal of burden of proof in equal pay claims); C-324/98, *Telaustria* ECLI:EU:C:2000:669 [2000] ECR I-10745 (unwritten principles of public procurement); C-345/06, *Heinrich*, ECLI:EU:C:2009:140, [2009] 3 CMLR 219 (unenforceability of unpublished legislation—my (rather fiery) Opinion is at ECLI:EU:C:2008:212) and C-549/14, *Frogne*, ECLI:EU:C:2016:634, [2016] All ER (D) 41 (Sep) (contract amendment within public procurement).

that an order for reference from a national court satisfies the rather basic requirements of Article 94 of the Court's Rules of Procedure,[69] it will be admissible, and the Court will have to fulfil its duty of cooperation with the national court and adjudicate on it.

In trying to strike the balance between judicial adjudication and impermissible legislating, the Court will cast the net far wider than an English national court. It will take account not only the text of the substantive provisions but also (always) the legal Treaty base for the measure and the recitals forming its preamble and (often) the 'travaux préparatoires' leading to its adoption. It will try to find an interpretation that, without doing actual violence to the text, respects the teleology of the measure ('why is it there?' 'what is it meant to be achieving?') and that fits intelligently into the overall mosaic of EU law.

And, in an imperfect world, that is probably the best that we can aim for.

[69] Article 94 Rules of Procedure of the Court of Justice states, 'In addition to the text of the questions referred to the Court for a preliminary ruling, the request for a preliminary ruling shall contain: (a) a summary of the subject matter of the dispute and the relevant findings of fact as determined by the referring court or tribunal, or, at least, an account of the facts on which the questions are based; (b) the tenor of any national provisions applicable in the case and, where appropriate, the relevant national case-law; (c) a statement of the reasons which prompted the referring court or tribunal to inquire about the interpretation or validity of certain provisions of European Union law, and the relationship between those provisions and the national legislation applicable to the main proceedings.'

10
Law, Democracy, and the Absent Legislator

Philip Sales[*]

In the age of democracy, how should a legal system respond to the practical non-availability of a democratic legislature as an effective agent of legal change?[1] What implications does the absence of the legislator have for law? This is the theme for this essay, prompted by reflection on the chapters by Jeff King (Chapter 8) and Eleanor Sharpston (Chapter 9). Both chapters arise from the problem of the absent legislator, albeit moving in different directions from that unspoken premise.

King's chapter is prompted by what he regards as the distortion of the legislative process when legislative activity is pushed downwards from Parliament into delegated forms. His particular focus is the major recourse to delegated legislation which is likely to occur in the context of Brexit. I will argue that this is an understandable and necessary—and hence, by and large legitimate—response to Parliament being overwhelmed by the political demands of Brexit and the challenge of recasting a substantial part of the existing legal system in the light of it. It is a response at the legislative level to the absent legislator, in the shape of Parliament producing law in the form of primary legislation.

Sharpston's chapter reports on the judicial function of a court—the European Court of Justice (ECJ), now the Court of Justice of the European Union (CJEU)[2] acting in an environment where democratic input into legislation is weak[3] and where, moreover, the legislator works in a slow and unwieldy way. Further, legislation is often produced in a form which reflects awkward compromises between relevant stakeholders in the drafting process, leaving gaps or using vague expressions where necessary to secure agreement. The judicial style of the CJEU is notable for its strongly purposive or

* Lord Sales, Justice of the Supreme Court.

[1] I write primarily with reference to the legal systems in the United Kingdom and the European Union, but many of the points made are capable of being generalised across jurisdictions.

[2] Hereafter, for ease of reference I will use the term CJEU to refer to the Luxembourg court in all its instantiations. Similarly, I will use European Union or EU to refer to the European Communities in all their instantiations.

[3] The democratic credentials for EU legislation are attenuated: there is no effective cross-jurisdictional system of political parties appealing directly to national electorates in relation to clear EU-wide electoral programmes, and the Council operates on the basis of inter-governmental negotiations at one remove from citizens, and hence supplies only limited and indirect democratic authorisation for the EU's activities.

Philip Sales, *Law, Democracy, and the Absent Legislator* In: *The Foundations and Future of Public Law*. Edited by: Elizabeth Fisher, Jeff King, Alison L Young, Oxford University Press (2020). © Oxford University Press.
DOI: 10.1093/oso/9780198845249.003.0010

teleological approach to interpretation both of the Treaties and of European Union (EU) legislation. The CJEU's judicial approach has often been characterised as one of judicial activism, and this has often been ascribed to a sense of political mission on the part of the Court.[4] The CJEU has been described as being an active agent in promoting the agenda of 'ever closer union' by the interpretations given in its judgments. These are sometimes perceived as being strongly *communautaire*, favouring the interests and collective perspective of the European Union against those of Member States. This has been so despite political efforts to counter the CJEU's centripetal approach by declarations appealing to the principle of subsidiarity.

It may be that this was true of the CJEU's self-conscious role at one period of its existence, and at a particular stage of development of the European Union. However, Sharpston offers a different account of and explanation for the CJEU's approach to its judicial role. This is the explanation, true to a degree for most if not all courts, that, faced with a difficult practical problem cast in legal terms, the CJEU will be disposed to try to resolve it in a fair manner which gives effect to its perception of the underlying logic or purpose of the law in issue. According to Sharpston, the CJEU's approach is not self-consciously political, at any rate in the current phase of its history.

I think that this explanation from a practising judge (Advocate General) at the heart of the CJEU should be taken seriously. In particular, it rings true when assessed against the background of the EU's constitutional arrangements and in light of wider reflection on the behaviour of courts coping with an absent legislator. The absence of the legislator tends to lead to an expansion of the law-creating or law-developing role of courts, in part for practical reasons and in part for reasons of legitimacy. In practical terms, when the legislator is absent, the courts see problems and know that they will not be addressed or resolved through legislative action any time soon; so the moral pressure on the courts to find a fair and workable solution themselves is increased. In legitimacy terms, the courts know that public respect for the law depends in the long term to a considerable degree on the fairness and defensibility of outcomes which the law produces.[5] If the legislator is absent, a court will tend to feel that it is (more) legitimate for it to act to develop or apply the law in an imaginative way.

[4] See eg Sir Patrick Neill, *The European Court of Justice: A Case Study in Judicial Activism* (European Policy Forum 1995); Paul Craig and Gráinne de Búrca, *EU Law: Text, Cases and Materials* (6th edn, OUP 2015) 63–65; Joseph Weiler, *The Constitution of Europe: 'Do the New Clothes Have an Emperor?' and Other Essays on European Integration* (CUP 1999) ch 5.

[5] *Per* GWF Hegel: 'How blind they are who may hope that institutions, constitutions, laws which no longer correspond to human manners, needs and opinions, from which the spirit has flown, can subsist any longer; or that forms in which intellect and feeling now take no interest are powerful enough to be any longer the bond of a nation!'—ZA Pełczyński (ed), *Hegel's Political Writings* (TM Knox trans, Clarendon Press 1964) 243–44.

I. Courts' Response to the Absent Legislator

The standard basic model for legal change in a modern Western democratic polity is a simple one. The democratic, representative legislature is constituted with authority to change laws and make new ones, and the courts loyally enforce those laws in legal disputes which come before them. There are strong reasons of principle underlying this model, based on democratic ideas of equal respect and equal rights of participation and control by citizens.[6] Admittedly, there is often a gap between the canonical statement of a law in a statute and the application of the statute to the facts of a particular case, so the model accepts an interpretive role for the courts which is in practice inevitable. As Denning LJ succinctly put it:

> it is not within human powers to foresee the manifold sets of facts which may arise, and, even if it were, it is not possible to provide for them in terms free from all ambiguity. The English language is not an instrument of mathematical precision.[7]

It may nonetheless be pointed out that the normal interpretive role for the courts is itself a function at a basic level of an absent legislator. In theory, if the legislator which passed the statute whose meaning is in doubt in legal proceedings were immediately on hand to answer questions, the courts could adopt a procedure of referring questions of interpretation back to it in order to ensure that the outcome had democratic legitimacy to the fullest possible extent.[8] That is not viable, both because the relevant legislature which passed the law may have ceased to exist[9] and because no legislature has the time to devote to doing this, given the many other calls upon its attention.

However, the extent to which the legislator is absent has different degrees. The legislator may be absent, unavailable, in a more acute way, beyond the basic level assumed in the standard model. There is a body of scholarly commentary which calls attention to the effect that this can have on judicial attitudes as to how adventurous it is legitimate for judges to be in making or developing law themselves, without leaving it to the legislature. The effects may be subtle, but still real. The practice of the courts may gradually come to change as it reflects developments

6 See eg Jeremy Waldron, *Law and Disagreement* (OUP 1999).

7 Quoted in Carleton Kemp Allen, *Law in the Making* (Clarendon Press 1951) 462.

8 Bentham thought that any disputes on interpretation of statutes should be referred back to the legislature: John Dinwiddy, *Bentham: Selected Writings of John Dinwiddy* (William Twining ed, Stanford UP 2004) 63–64; Cf the reference procedure under Article 267 TFEU whereby national courts are obliged to seek answers from the CJEU on doubtful points of EU law, thereby ensuring legitimacy of legal interpretations; this is according to a different principle of authorisation, namely that given by the EU Treaties.

9 A statute is, of course, passed by a particular parliament (composed of particular MPs voted into office on a particular occasion), which will be dissolved after a period and replaced with a new parliament.

within a background legal culture. The change may occur without adoption of clearly defined doctrinal statements to explain what is happening. The more absent the legislator, the more the courts may feel they have to be imaginative or activist in their interpretations of the law. The point has been made in temporal terms, by making comparisons across time within a jurisdiction. It has also been made by making comparisons across jurisdictions.

As regards temporal comparison, Benjamin Cardozo made the point in 1921. As he observed, the relationship of judges and the legislature varies over time; the ready availability of the legislative process to effect change in more recent times affects the willingness of judges to make law themselves.[10] Conversely, in another work he argued that courts should be prepared to be creative in their judgments in keeping the law in line with social expectations, since the legislature would come on the scene too late in the day to achieve this.[11]

Attention has been called to the same issue of interaction of judicial attitudes towards developing the law and the availability of the legislature to do this, by comparisons across jurisdictions; in particular by comparison of German legal and political culture (particularly in the nineteenth century) with that of the United Kingdom, and by comparison of England and the United States in the latter part of the twentieth century.

Franz Neumann, writing in the 1930s, observed that in the British doctrine of the rule of law associated with Dicey, 'the centre of gravity lies in the determination of the content of the laws by Parliament', while the German theory of the *Rechtsstaat* as developed in the nineteenth century 'is uninterested in the genesis of the law, and is immediately concerned with the interpretation of a positive law, somehow and somewhere arisen'; as he put it, '[t]he German theory is liberal-constitutional; the English, democratic-constitutional'.[12] The role of eminent jurists and judges in establishing the law was critical in Germany.[13] Parliament's role was more important in Britain. The difference in culture reflected the long

[10] Benjamin Cardozo, *The Nature of the Judicial Process* (Yale UP 1921) 28 and 60. Since legislative change had become more readily available, judges should legislate only cautiously and interstitially: 68–69. See also Learned Hand, *The Spirit of Liberty: Papers and Addresses of Learned Hand* (Irving Dilliard (ed), Knopf 1954) 158: previously judicial law-making was tolerated because the legislature was slow and judges represented the governing classes; but now legislative change is relatively easy and the judges are not representative in any relevant sense, so only interstitial advances by the judiciary are legitimate.

[11] Benjamin Cardozo, *The Growth of the Law* (Yale UP 1924) 133–35.

[12] Franz Neumann, *The Rule of Law: Political Theory and the Legal System in Modern Society* ([1935–6]; Berg 1986) 185.

[13] Kaarlo Tuori, *Ratio and Voluntas: The Tension Between Reason and Will in Law* (Routledge 2011) ch 3, esp 99–101: in politically fragmented Germany positivism was based on legal doctrine rather than legislation; legal science's doctrinal system grew increasingly logical and autonomous in the form of *Begriffsjurisprudenz*. This cultural framework continued into the Imperial and Weimar periods and beyond: see Michael Stolleis, *Public Law in Germany: A Historical Introduction from the 16th to the 21st Century* ([2014] trans. Thomas Dunlap, OUP 2017) esp 51, 57, 61–62, 69, and (for discussion of the gradual dismantling of anti-democratic and anti-parliamentary biases in the period after the Second World War) 144–49.

tradition of parliamentary sovereignty in a highly centralised British state, by comparison with the unified juristic tradition which grew up in Germany, applicable across the many disparate jurisdictions which existed there prior to unification in 1871. In Britain, Parliament was available to make laws. In Germany prior to 1871, there was no single legislature available, and even after 1871 the legislature was weaker than its British equivalent. These cultural differences continue to be reflected in different approaches to statutory interpretation in Germany and the United Kingdom to this day.[14]

The differing approaches of judges in England and the United States to statutory interpretation—with the English being more formalist and loyal to the semantic meaning of a statutory text and the US judges being more creative in terms of extracting coherent meaning from statutes—was emphasised by Louis Jaffe writing in 1969[15] and, still further, by Patrick Atiyah and Robert Summers writing in the 1980s.[16] Jaffe noted that Parliament might be better able to respond to changing circumstances than US legislatures—albeit he was doubtful how true that really was—and '[i]f so, the demand for judicial lawmaking in England may be to that extent less'.[17]

Atiyah and Summers elaborated this point as part of their explanation for what they saw as a major difference between legal culture generally in the United Kingdom and that in the United States. On their account, English judges tend to adopt a more textual, literal approach to statutory interpretation, while American courts tend to take a more purposive and substantive approach.[18] The reasons for this difference lie in the contrast in institutional context, including that in England the drafting of statutes is done well and with technical proficiency by experts (by contrast with the United States) and a feeling that an incorrect or unsatisfactory construction can in England readily be put right by legislative amendment (again by contrast with the position in the United States).[19]

Writing to provide an historical perspective, SFC Milsom reviewed the past and future of judicial law-making across the sweep of the history of the common law, noting the modern view of legislation as a democratic activity based on utilitarian and managerial ideas as a result of which the courts are reluctant to intervene to change the law themselves.[20] He contrasted this modern approach with their attitude in the nineteenth century, in which they felt more confident to make law

[14] See Robert Alexy and Ralf Dreier, 'Statutory Interpretation in the Federal Republic of Germany' in Neil MacCormick and Robert Summers (eds), *Interpreting Statutes: A Comparative Study* (Dartmouth 1991) 73–122; Martin Brenncke, *Judicial Law-making in English and German Courts: Techniques and Limits of Statutory Interpretation* (Intersentia 2018) ch 2.

[15] Louis Jaffe, *English and American Judges as Lawmakers* (Clarendon 1969) esp ch 3.

[16] Patrick Atiyah and Robert Summers, *Form and Substance in Anglo-American Law* (Clarendon 1987).

[17] Jaffe (n 15) 69.

[18] Atiyah and Summers (n 16) ch 4, in particular at 100–01.

[19] Ibid 104–07.

[20] SFC Milsom 'The Past and the Future of Judge-made Law' (1981) 8 Monash UL Rev 1.

themselves because they sensed they were articulating discoveries of how basic, timeless principles of right and wrong (different from rules given by the democratic process) worked themselves out in the legal sphere. However, the change to a more democratically sensitive style of judging had, in Milsom's view, major drawbacks. There was a choice to be made between seeing judges as making law or as just applying it, but in England at the beginning of the 1980s Milsom thought we might have ended up with the worst of both worlds: judges do have some role in making law, but do not regard its adjustment as their business, thinking that this was something for the legislature. However, '[l]egislative resources, in time and otherwise, are insufficient. And the great apparatus of case law remains in being although it can do little more than refine authority into yet further detail'; the value of such increased complexity at a decreasing level of generality being very doubtful, in his view.[21]

Atiyah and Summers also recognise that the assumption in England of ready access to Parliament for statutory amendment may not accurately reflect reality.[22] Consequently, they suggest that in England the courts may be 'a little too ready to pass the buck for some statutory error to Parliament', shirking 'what would more reasonably be their responsibility to reach the proper result in the case at hand'.[23]

So, it is not only European lawyers who regard judicial interpretive activity to develop and, as necessary, change the law the better to reflect social values and coherent principles of reason and justice as potentially legitimate under certain conditions in a democratic society. This may be justified where the legislator is absent in some way from the process of the creation of the law. Legislature and courts are engaged in a joint enterprise in which 'the judges complete the law promulgated by Parliament by applying it',[24] and the more the legislator is withdrawn from that enterprise the greater the role the courts tend to feel they should assume. To similar effect, Nick Barber notes that the failure of one organ in the constitution can lead to 'constitutional inflation' in relation to the usual role of other organs; the most common example being that

> when the legislature is malfunctioning in some way—perhaps it lacks democratic legitimacy for some reason or it has become deadlocked and unable to legislate—this sometimes leads to the courts modifying their law-making role in response, becoming more willing to radically interpret existing legislation or make decisions that depart from existing law.[25]

[21] Ibid, 12–13.
[22] Atiyah and Summers (n 16) 105–06.
[23] Ibid 106–07.
[24] Philip Sales, 'Judges and Legislature: Values into Law' (2012) 71 CLJ 287, 292.
[25] NW Barber, *The Principles of Constitutionalism* (OUP 2018) 232–33.

One can use this insight as part of an explanatory framework for the teleological interpretive approach employed by the CJEU in the current phase of EU law. It is possible to argue for the legitimacy of the Court's interventionist, quasi-legislative interpretive approach as being based upon the absent legislator in the EU context. The legislator is absent to a degree even when making EU legislation, by reason of the need for compromise in the formulation of the law at that stage, leaving the detail to be filled in by the CJEU later at the stage of interpretation. This absence can be contrasted with the active and controlling presence of the legislator when the UK Parliament promulgates a statute, acting on the basis of highly refined legislative proposals[26] put forward by a centralised government which (typically) controls the legislative process via its majority in the House of Commons. The legislator is also absent in EU law after legislation has been promulgated, if problems in its application come to light. There is no easy recourse to EU law-making mechanisms to make corrections. The CJEU has to produce interpretations of the legislation which resolve such issues as best it can, recognising that there is no other agent on hand to put things right.

The fact that the CJEU is left, to a degree, to act as a law-maker in place of the legislator, as the agent for promulgating legal content not clearly inherent in the legislation itself, means that one can draw a parallel between it and bodies which produce delegated legislation in domestic jurisdictions. On that note, I turn to the issue of delegated legislation in the context of Brexit and Jeff King's chapter.

II. The Absent Legislator and Brexit

King's paper for the conference had two aspects. The first related to control of delegated legislation through parliamentary procedure; the second to control of delegated legislation by the courts.[27]

My comments in relation to each aspect have to be qualified in different ways. As to the first, I am not a parliamentarian. I do not have in-depth knowledge about how Parliament works and how its workings might be improved. As to the second, I am a judge. Nothing written below indicates any firm view about the law. I address the issues discussed by King in a rather abstract and general way, without commenting on the interpretation of specific provisions to which he refers. Obviously,

[26] Drafted by expert drafters in the Office of Parliamentary Counsel acting on the basis of direct instructions from government departments: see Philip Sales, 'The Contribution of Legislative Drafting to the Rule of Law' (2018) 77 CLJ 630. As I note there, in relation to poorly drafted domestic legislation dating from before the creation of the Office, the effect of such drafting is to transfer practical law-making power from Parliament to the courts which have to strive to make sense of it at the interpretive stage.

[27] King's truncated paper in this volume is focused on the first aspect.

as and when cases arise, a judge's decisions will depend on the detailed arguments in those cases.

Reading King's chapter, it is striking how little about the abstract scheme regarding the relationship between primary and delegated legislation is really in doubt. There is general recognition that parliamentary time is in short supply, so the use of delegated legislation in appropriate circumstances is legitimate and necessary. Cecil Carr's basic justifications for delegated legislation, as referred to by King, remain valid: (i) use of delegated legislation is necessary because of the limits on parliamentary time for creating primary legislation; (ii) use of delegated legislation may be necessary where it is desirable for laws to be drafted by reference to specialist expertise which may more readily be available within a Government department; and (iii) delegated legislation may more readily meet the need for flexibility and expedition on occasion in the interests of effective government.

It also seems broadly desirable, again uncontroversially, that big picture policy issues for legislation should usually be set out in primary legislation, debated in Parliament, and subject to amendment procedures in the usual way, whereas it is more appropriate for fine detail to be pushed down into delegated legislation.

Again, it also seems sensible to allow for different levels of oversight by Parliament of delegated legislation. This allows for more finely calibrated accommodations between democratic oversight by Parliament and the values promoted by use of delegated legislation and parliamentary time-saving made possible by such use. This is what the various gradations of parliamentary oversight described by King are designed to achieve, moving from the simple laying of some forms of delegated rules before Parliament[28] (so that Parliament is afforded an opportunity to intervene, if it chooses), through the negative resolution procedure and the affirmative resolution procedure, and on to the super-affirmative resolution procedure for certain kinds of delegated legislation. It should be noted that there has been a movement towards graduated parliamentary involvement at the level of primary legislation level as well, with special truncated parliamentary procedures for certain kinds of uncontroversial legislation or legislation proposed by the Law Commission.

Putting it like this makes it sound as though there is a coherent scheme which governs law-making and the relationship between primary and secondary legislation. The problem is that this scheme, like a battle plan, does not really survive first contact with the enemy, in the form of the real world of politics. On King's account, based on a range of sources, it does not appear to work very well at the parliamentary end. Some of the statistics deployed by King regarding the rarity of the occasions on which proposed delegated legislation is voted down, if taken at face value, give a somewhat misleading picture. This is because, as King acknowledges,

[28] The Immigration Rules are an example of this.

they do not capture the effect of strategic bargaining by parliamentarians against the backdrop of the opportunities for disruption of the government's programme of delegated legislation created by the rules governing the creation of such legislation. Determined parliamentarians may be able to extract concessions from government and secure the amendment of proposed delegated legislation before it comes to be placed before Parliament in its final form. Thus, a simple record of what happens in Parliament at the end of the day does not reflect the full value of such graduated law-making procedural rules. Nonetheless, the effectiveness of detailed review even of primary legislation in Parliament is open to serious doubt in many cases, and that picture of lack of effective review by Parliament seems inevitably to be more pronounced in the case of delegated legislation.[29]

The principal reasons for this, I suggest, are twofold. First, there is the increase in governmental activity since the nineteenth century. Rule by central government has massively expanded due to the demands made on the state for welfare protection, provision of health services, management of the economy, management of various security risks and so forth as a result of the democratisation of our political system.[30] To this must be added the boost to centralisation through the experience of two World Wars, to which King particularly refers.[31] It is noticeable how even in the course of the nineteenth century the form of legislation changed, with fewer and fewer Acts of Parliament to regulate purely local matters than had previously been the case.[32] How much more so is that true in the twentieth and twenty-first centuries.

The second reason, which is connected with the first, is the limits on parliamentary time and the demands made on that limited time. Sometimes it seems that the debate criticising the extent to which things are done by delegated legislation does not take sufficient account of this factor.

In our system, Parliament is an instrument of government as well as a legislature. It is the site for political debate and theatre, providing a focus for democratic engagement and scrutiny. It is the place for important government announcements, for debate over government policy, for holding the government to account

[29] For another recent critical account from a close observer of Parliament, see Isabel Hardman, *Why We Get the Wrong Politicians* (Atlantic Books 2018); also Stephanie Pywell, 'Something Old, Something New: Busting Some Myths About Statutory Instruments and Brexit' [2019] PL 102.

[30] For where we have ended up, see Thomas Poole, *Reason of State: Law, Prerogative and Empire* (CUP 2015) ch 8: the state has acquired new responsibilities to manage risks in order to guarantee the security of individuals. For a graphic representation of the growth in social welfare spending in Western democracies, see Steven Pinker, *Enlightenment Now* (Penguin 2018) 108. For a philosophical account of how the liberal tradition originating in the seventeenth century has paradoxically led to an extension of law and provision by the state, see Patrick Deneen, *Why Liberalism Failed* (Yale UP 2018) ch 2.

[31] See also on this, James C Scott, *Seeing Like a State: How Certain Schemes to Improve the Human Condition Have Failed* (Yale UP 1998) 97–98, who identifies the paradigm of centralised state planning as Germany in the First World War.

[32] Cf Frederic William Maitland, *The Constitutional History of England* ([1909] CUP 1941) 383; Philip Sales and Ben Hooper, 'Proportionality and the Form of Law' (2003) 119 LQR 426, 453–54.

and, ultimately, for testing the ability of governments to rule, by holding votes of confidence. It is the hurly burly of the political contest which, unsurprisingly, tends to capture the time and attention of politicians and the wider public, rather than the legal minutiae of legislation. The attention of Members of Parliament is most concentrated on legislation at those points where the legislation itself becomes the focus for more general public discussion and attention. None of this is wrong or necessarily bad. The profile and focus which the more theatrical elements of politics give to public debate regarding the general policy direction of government are an important concomitant of an effectively functioning representative democracy. They provide a salient demonstration of what is being done in society's name and help connect public opinion to the political and law-making process. They assist the formation of public opinion into coherent patterns, stable across time, which in turn provide guidance for politicians in offering policy solutions, standards against which their performance in serving the public can be judged and a degree of transparency for the public to monitor the performance of their representatives.[33]

So, although the abstract scheme for graduated parliamentary scrutiny and control of delegated legislation seems coherent enough, it does not work well in practice. The different grades of parliamentary oversight do not seem to act as triggers for increasing levels of scrutiny. The impression one gets from the statistics—which whilst not a completely fair picture is not a completely unfair picture either—is that there is close to being one level of scrutiny, which is none.

Brexit has highlighted and compounded the problem. The parliamentary political theatre around this issue has sucked up large amounts of parliamentary time and is likely to continue to do so. It absorbs vast amounts of politicians' time and attention outside parliamentary procedures, as they try to explain their competing visions and compete for public support. This is entirely understandable, given the strategic importance of working out a new path forward for the country. Further, coming after years of cutting back government departments through sustained austerity policies, Brexit also puts special strain on the limited resources of government to work out the detail of policy and give proper instructions for the drafting of primary legislation. The Office of Parliamentary Counsel, responsible for the drafting of primary legislation, has likewise been subject to cuts.

Parliament itself plainly could not cope, in addition, with the huge amount of detailed and often technical legislation which is likely to be needed to achieve the unscrambling of the UK's laws from the EU's after a period of more than forty years of their being increasingly entwined.[34] Given the extent of the task of this unscrambling and its importance for providing legal stability and the predictability

[33] Nadia Urbinati, *Representative Democracy: Principles and Genealogy* (University of Chicago Press 2006); Barber (n 25) ch 6; Nancy Rosenblum, *On the Side of the Angels: An Appreciation of Parties and Partisanship* (Princeton UP 2008) 143–60.

[34] For commentary on the scale of the task, see Pywell (n 29).

necessary for individuals and businesses to plan their affairs, it is not altogether hyperbolic to characterise the situation as one of a national legal emergency. In the airless vacuum created by Brexit, Parliament cannot even cope with ordinary legislative activity.[35] The position is worse if proposals to make any changes to primary legislation are remotely controversial—as many measures for effective government have to be—because that would create an even greater demand for parliamentary time for the debate necessary to carry them through Parliament. The legislator, in the form of Parliament making primary legislation, is absent because the time and other resources needed for legislating are highly constrained and its attention is elsewhere.

In light of the major volume of legislative work to be done to implement Brexit and the great substantive significance of many of the areas of law which will need to be recast, there is a strong argument in favour of the creation within Parliament of some clearer form of half-way house procedure for some types of primary legislation to cope with the overload. This might involve assigning laws of mid-level importance to some kind of truncated primary legislative procedure, perhaps after expert assessment and recommendation, for a sort of 'quick and dirty' response mechanism which retains more parliamentary involvement than promulgation of delegated legislation. The truncated procedure for Law Commission-sponsored legislation might provide the beginnings of such a model. At the moment, however, there do not appear to be any signs that this is likely to happen. It seems that we are going to be stuck with our existing model of primary and delegated legislation and will have to cope with that.

At the conference, King proposed a possible criterion for allocation of matters to be dealt with via primary legislation rather than delegated legislation; that is, where the legislation concerns matters of high policy on which there is partisan disagreement. This was proposed both as a criterion for use in parliamentary procedure (as a matter of political practice and morality)[36] and as a legal criterion in the interpretation of provisions creating the power to promulgate delegated legislation, to be implied according to the principle of legality. As a legal criterion, it could be developed and fleshed out case by case.

Attractive as the proposal might sound, it is fraught with difficulties from both the political and the legal perspectives. From the political perspective, there appears to be no political appetite to spell out such a criterion and allow it to govern parliamentary procedure. The Select Committee on Delegated Legislation has refused to articulate criteria for the allocation of law-making to primary or to

[35] This appears to be the common experience across government departments. For instance, working parties on court procedures have proposed sensible minor reforms of primary legislation, which Government agrees with, only to be told that they cannot be implemented because of lack of Parliamentary time.

[36] Presumably enforced in some way by the Parliamentary authorities and the House of Lords Select Committees on the Constitution and on Delegated Legislation.

delegated legislation.[37] Politics is a messy and sometimes brutal business, and use (and sometimes abuse) of parliamentary procedures is inevitably bound up with the raw exercise of political power on the ground. I fear that King's proposal is too idealistic to find much purchase within Parliament; that is particularly so in the House of Commons, where ultimate political power resides.

So, should the courts supply what Parliament will not, by devising and adopting King's criterion and using it to police the exercise of the power to promulgate delegated legislation? Delegated legislation can of course be struck down as being *ultra vires* the enabling power. In some important cases the principle of legality has been employed as an interpretive tool to read down such powers, leading to the conclusion that delegated legislation is *ultra vires*: see in particular *R v Secretary of State for the Home Department, ex p Leech*,[38] *R v Lord Chancellor, ex p Witham*,[39] and *R (UNISON) v Lord Chancellor*.[40]

However, these were cases where reasonably determinate and accepted individual rights could be identified as the foundation for that interpretive approach. By contrast, there are significant problems with King's proposed criterion.

First, it concerns a matter of parliamentary procedure, where courts are typically reluctant to become involved. The subject matter to which the criterion is directed is different from the individual rights which are usually the subject matter of the principle of legality.

Second, the relevant parliamentary bodies have declined to identify such a criterion, so it will be difficult for the courts to say that such a criterion in fact exists and is sufficiently recognised in such a concrete way as to feed the principle of legality. The conceptual legitimacy of the principle of legality requires, I suggest, joint recognition by courts and parliament of some constitutional rule or principle, such that the courts can say that Parliament legislated on the unspoken assumption that such a rule or principle would continue to apply.[41] Just as much as the courts, Parliament needs to know where it stands with unwritten fundamental rights and constitutional principles which are going to affect the meaning of legislation, otherwise its ability to exercise effective political choice in making law will be undermined.[42] But such joint recognition does not exist here. The courts cannot suddenly say that delegated legislation is *ultra vires* on the basis of some

[37] See Section IID of King's paper.

[38] [1994] QB 198.

[39] [1998] QB 575.

[40] [2017] UKSC 51, [2017] 3 WLR 409.

[41] I have presented the argument for this view at greater length elsewhere: see Philip Sales, 'Rights and Fundamental Rights in English Law' (2016) 75 CLJ 86.

[42] This point was made forcefully by the Supreme Court in *R (Black) v Secretary of State for Justice* [2017] UKSC 81, [2018] AC 215, in which it declined to abrogate the presumption that a statute does not bind the Crown, since Parliament had repeatedly exercised its legislative power on the footing that such a presumption existed, so that to abrogate it would distort Parliament's true intention in relevant statutes.

new principle dreamed up by them for the first time, of which Parliament was not on fair notice when it legislated.

Third, the vagueness and highly contestable nature of the elements in King's proposed test may make it unattractive to the courts for adoption by them. It is not just that this will make the law very uncertain where it is critical that it should be highly certain, since what is in issue is whole schemes of legislation, not one-off decisions in individual cases. It is also that both elements within the test—what counts as a matter of high policy? what counts as disagreement which is sufficiently partisan?—would involve the courts in making political-type judgments of their own in a highly charged and highly contested field.

No doubt arguments will be presented to attack the *vires* of Brexit delegated legislation promulgated under widely drafted powers in the principal Brexit Acts, and no doubt cases like *R (Public Law Project) v Lord Chancellor*[43] will be prominent in those arguments. But ultimately, as is accepted in these cases, parliamentary sovereignty means that widely drafted powers, if written sufficiently clearly, should be given effect. The clear scale of the Brexit law rewrite, the absence from the scene of Parliament as a legislator with capacity to deal with the full range of challenges which Brexit poses, and the critical importance of achieving legal certainty as law in the United Kingdom undergoes transition from EU law to domestic law, will be contextual factors which also have a part to play in determining how the powers to make delegated legislation should be construed.

III. Conclusion

Society needs law. It needs it in positive and determinate forms. This is required to resolve problems of coordination of action, to promote individual well-being, and to specify and enforce just standards of behaviour.

For various reasons, the principal democratic law-giver may not be able to provide all the law that society requires. Such an absence of the legislator means that alternative sources of law-generation are required. Within limits which are liable to be affected by the extent of the absence of the legislator, the interpretive work done by the courts provides an important additional source of concrete normative content for law. The courts can be seen as working in a constitutional partnership with Parliament to meet society's need for law, from high-level concepts to low-level justice in the adjudication of concrete cases. The more absent the legislator, the more the courts may feel an obligation to work to make good deficiencies in the law which come to their attention.

43 [2016] UKSC 39, [2016] AC 1531, in particular at [26]. See also *R (Ingenious Media Holdings Plc) v HM Revenue and Customs* [2016] UKSC 54, [2016] 1 WLR 4164, [21].

Delegation of the law-making function is the route to providing another source of law, which may have greater capacity than Parliament to provide legal content, albeit with lesser directly democratic credentials. Again, the extent of the absence of the legislator is important. The more absent the legislator, the more it may be appropriate to construe wide delegations of rule-making authority at face value.

Thomas Hobbes addressed the problem of what happened to sovereignty when the sovereign was asleep. His solution to the sleeping sovereign was to draw a distinction between the sovereign and the executive government, and to say that government continues while the sovereign sleeps; but the sovereign remains sovereign and can resume authority whenever he wakes.[44] Something similar happens with the absent legislator. It has to let others carry on some of the day-to-day business of norm creation, while retaining its democratic authority to intervene as and when its attention can be focused on some particular subject matter.

[44] See the discussion in Richard Tuck, *The Sleeping Sovereign: The Invention of Modern Democracy* (CUP 2016). Tuck ties Hobbes' image of the sleeping sovereign to the development of the idea of popular sovereignty, given expression in the form of constitutional documents. The constitution is distinct from, but a framework for, executive government; and it is open to amendment by the sovereign people.

PART IV
INSTITUTIONS

11. The Open Road? Navigating Public Administration and the Failed Promise of Administrative Law
Elizabeth Fisher

12. The EU Automated State Disassembled
Deirdre Curtin

13. The Administrative State and the Fundamentals of Public Law
ACL Davies

11

The Open Road?

Navigating Public Administration and the Failed Promise of Administrative Law

*Elizabeth Fisher**

In December 1933, Jerome Frank, as General Counsel of the US Agricultural Adjustment Administration, made a speech in which he argued that the rise of the administrative state meant that lawyers had 'taken to the open road ... in seeking the welfare of the great majority of our people and not in merely preserving, unmodified, certain traditions and folkways'.[1] Frank's 'open road' was an exercise in what he called 'experimentalist jurisprudence'.[2] Frank's stance at that time stood in contrast to those lawyers who argued that the administrative state violated fundamental legal principles.[3] For Frank, experimentalists were 'critical students of institutions',[4] doubted the 'efficacy of legal thinking',[5] and thought that 'legal institutions and devices' were to be 'judged by their everyday consequences'.[6] From Frank's perspective, you were either for the administrative state (and thus a 'new' jurisprudence) or for established legal ideas such as legal reasoning[7] and the adjudicative method.[8] You could not be for both.

He was, and is, not alone in thinking this[9] and this is just one example of the unhelpful binary that has framed Anglo-American administrative law for over a century. In the United States its latest manifestation has been the crude wars over the

* I would like to thank Sanja Bogojević, Sid Shapiro, Jeff King, and Alison Young, and attendees at the Foundations and Future of Public Law: A Conference in Honour of Paul Craig, 27–28 September 2018 for comments on an earlier draft of this chapter. Any errors or omissions remain my own.

[1] Jerome Frank, 'Experimental Jurisprudence and the "New Deal"' (Address Before the Association of American Law Schools, Chicago, 30 December 1933).

[2] For a further discussion of Franks' work see Neil Duxbury, 'Jerome Frank and the Legacy of Legal Realism' (1991) 18 JLS 175.

[3] See the account in Daniel Ernst, *Tocqueville's Nightmare: The Administrative State Emerges in America, 1900–1940* (OUP 2014).

[4] Frank (n 1).

[5] Ibid 3.

[6] Ibid 5.

[7] Ibid, illustrated with his tale of Mr Try-it and Mr Absolute, two different types of government lawyers.

[8] Jerome Frank, *If Men Were Angels: Some Aspects of Government in a Democracy* (Harper & Bros 1942) 109–23.

[9] Robert Gordon, 'Willis's American Counterparts: The Legal Realists' Defence of Administration' (2005) 55 University of Toronto LJ 405.

Elizabeth Fisher, *The Open Road?* In: *The Foundations and Future of Public Law*. Edited by: Elizabeth Fisher, Jeff King, Alison L Young, Oxford University Press (2020). © Oxford University Press.
DOI: 10.1093/oso/9780198845249.003.0011

Chevron doctrine, a battle between those who wish to ensure that all questions of law are determined by courts and those who argue the need for deference to agency expertise.[10] In the United Kingdom it has been the enduring appeal of Harlow and Rawling's red light/green light models of administrative law, a descriptive account that depicts this binary with a loving attention to detail.[11] Red light theorists focus on the importance of upholding common law ideals and green light theorists focus on the function of public administration and what it delivers.

The dominance of this binary is far from ideal. Law and administration are not only seen at odds with each, but the choice in administrative law appears a dismal one—you are either for 'law' and what it preserves or for 'administration' and what it delivers.[12] As Louis Jaffe noted in 1942, it is also a discourse that is 'so pompous, so self-satisfied, so humourless, and so uncompromising', and ultimately a debate between 'straw men'.[13]

The binary nature of the debate is due to the struggles of administrative lawyers to foster a body of law that constitutes administrative institutions, limits them, and holds them to account *as administrative institutions*. The either/or choice between law and administration comes about because it is perceived such a body of law is not possible. The end result is that administrative law is not, and has never been, primarily understood as what it axiomatically should be: the law of public administration.[14] Reading those statements, you may be readying yourself for a self-righteous lesson in the need for administrative lawyers to be far more devoted in their attention to administrative institutions, something akin to a 'eat your greens, drink lots of water, and floss' lecture for administrative lawyers. That is not the purpose of this chapter is, however.

Rather, the purpose of this chapter is to map out why it has been so difficult for Anglo-American administrative law to break out of the binary it has found itself in. I do that by examining two 'administrative moments' in the history of administrative law: the Committee on Ministers' Powers Report (the Donoughmore Committee Report) published in 1932 in the United Kingdom[15] and the Attorney General Committee's Report on Administrative Procedure 1941 (Attorney General's Committee Report)[16] in the United States. While

[10] *Chevron USA Inc v NRDC* 467 US 837 (1984). For a flavour of the debate see William Bumpers and others, 'The Debate: Is Deference Dying? Our Panel Holds a Vigil Over the Chevron Precedent' The Environmental Forum (Sept/Oct 2017) 54.

[11] Carol Harlow and Richard Rawlings, *Law and Administration* (3rd edn, CUP 2009).

[12] This binary is explored in more detail in Elizabeth Fisher and Sidney Shapiro, *Administrative Competence: Reimagining Administrative Law* (CUP forthcoming) ch 1.

[13] Louis Jaffe, 'The Reform of Federal Administrative Procedure' (1942) 2 Public Administration Rev 141, 141.

[14] This is an argument explored in length in Fisher and Shapiro (n 12).

[15] Committee on Ministers' Powers, *Report of Committee of Ministers' Powers* (Cmd 4060, HMSO 1932).

[16] Attorney General's Committee on Administrative Procedure, *Final Report of the Attorney General's Committee on Administrative Procedure* (Government Printing Office 1941).

both were partly instigated by an appreciation of the need to forge a body of law grounded on a robust understanding of public administration, neither ultimately achieved that aim. My argument is that this was because they never surmounted three structural challenges inherent in developing administrative law: engaging with administrative material; fostering administrative law expertise; and not reducing the legal reasoning inherent in administrative law to a battle between ideologies. Overall, the experience of both reports shows the need for the opening up of the collective administrative law imagination. As Jasanoff states, imagination unites 'members of a social community in shared perceptions of futures that should or should not be realised'.[17] In administrative law, that imagination has remained limited.

This chapter is structured as follows. In section I, I briefly sketch the development of public administration in the late nineteenth century and early twentieth century and show how a major reason for the growth of administrative institutions was that they provided the capacity for evaluating facts in specific areas. In section II, I examine three intertwined legal discourses that emerged around these developments: the growth of administrative law as a discipline; debate over the legitimacy of non-adjudicative structures; and the evolution of judicial review doctrine by the courts. In section III, I examine two high-profile attempts to take stock of all of this: the Donoughmore Committee Report and the Attorney General Committee's Report. While both rejected a rigid vision of public administration and administrative law, neither provided a robust framework for the fostering of administrative law as the law of public administration. In section IV, I ponder why this was the case, show how neither report surmounted the three challenges just identified, and consider the implications of my analysis for the current way we imagine administrative law.

Three points should be made before starting. First, this chapter is part of a larger intellectual project I have been carrying out over the last several years, particularly with Sid Shapiro, about reimagining administrative law.[18] Second, this chapter is not just an indulgent exercise in looking back into the past. The narratives we tell about the history of administrative law are fundamental to how we make sense of the present. The New Deal is invariably cast as an era which pitted 'expertise' against 'law'.[19] The 1930s in the United Kingdom is understood as a 'deserted territory' in administrative law terms and the Donoughmore Committee as a major contributor to that state of affairs.[20] This chapter questions both these accounts.

[17] Sheila Jassanoff, 'Future Imperfect: Science, Technology and the Imaginations of Modernity' in Sheila Jassanoff and Sang-Hyun Kim (eds), *Dreamscapes of Modernity: Sociotechnical Imaginaries and the Fabrication of Power* (University of Chicago Press 2015) 5–6.

[18] On the US side see Fisher and Shapiro (n 12). In the United Kingdom, see Elizabeth Fisher, 'Law and Energy Transitions: Wind Turbines and Planning Law in the UK' (2018) 38 OJLS 528.

[19] Ernst (n 3).

[20] Bernard Schwartz and William Wade, *Legal Control of Government* (Clarendon Press 1972) 4.

More significantly, it highlights just how challenging administrative law is to master. Finally, it is important to note that during the 1920s and the 1930s there was an ongoing dialogue between American and British administrative lawyers,[21] as both wrestled with the same set of issues in their distinctive socio-political and legal cultures. That is a very different state of affairs from today where, besides a few exceptions (including the work of Paul Craig),[22] there has been little transatlantic dialogue about the nature of administrative law.

I. Public Administration and Factual Evaluation

Public administration does, and has done many things, but one of its most common activities is factual evaluation. The emergence of modern constitutionalism in the wake of the Enlightenment saw a dramatic evolution in both the role and nature of executive power. Not only was there an expectation it would be intimately connected to democratic processes but, more importantly, the need for public administration reflected a commitment to reasoned decision-making grounded in rigorous knowledge.[23] Administrative institutions, such as the war pensions regime in the United States[24] or the Alkali Inspectorate in the United Kingdom,[25] were created to provide frameworks for systematised and informed decision-making. Other administrative institutions reflected a 'philosophy that government should be actively involved in the production and interpretation of knowledge'.[26] The nineteenth-century public health regimes in the United Kingdom[27] and the Interstate Commerce Commission (ICC) in the United States are examples.[28] Civil service reform in the latter half of the nineteenth century in both the United Kingdom and United States cemented the importance of administrative institutions grounded in reasoning capacity. In the United Kingdom, there was a commitment to the permanent civil service, an institution providing a 'generalist' resource

[21] Ralph Fuchs, 'Concepts and Policies in Anglo-American Administrative Law Theory' (1937) 47 Yale LJ 538.

[22] Paul Craig, *Public Law and Democracy in the United Kingdom and the United States of America* (Clarendon Press 1990). See also Peter Cane, *Controlling Administrative Power: An Historical Comparison* (CUP 2016) and Susan Rose-Ackerman, Peter Lindseth, and Blake Emerson (eds), *Comparative Administrative Law* (2nd edn, Edward Elgar 2017).

[23] On the relationship between science and democracy see Stephen Shapin, *A Social History of Truth: Civility and Science in Seventeenth Century England* (University of Chicago Press 1994).

[24] Theda Skocpol, *Protecting Soldiers and Mothers: The Political Origins of Social Policy in the United States* (The Belknap Press of Harvard UP 1992).

[25] Roy Macleod, 'The Alkali Acts Administration 1863–84: The Emergence of the Civil Scientists' in R Macleod (ed), *Public Science and Public Policy in Victorian England* (Variorum Press 1996).

[26] Sheila Jasanoff, *The Fifth Branch: Science Advisers as Policy Makers* (Harvard UP 1990) 42.

[27] Christopher Hamlin, *Public Health and Social Justice in the Age of Chadwick, Britain 1800–1854* (CUP 1998).

[28] Thomas McGraw, *Prophets of Regulation* (The Belknap Press 1984) ch 2.

for government.[29] The United States initiated a system of appointment on the basis of examined merit for particular posts.[30]

This description may suggest I am retelling the well-worn account of the rise of a strict model of rationalised Weberian bureaucracy[31] and/or the Progressive faith in 'expertise'. But while there is no doubt that public administration was evolving to incorporate new forms of skills and specialised knowledge, that does not necessarily mean that it resulted in a singular model of 'expert public administration'. Weber's account was of Prussian institutions and it remained untranslated into English well into the twentieth century, and Wilson's work, which is invariably understood as promoting ideas of Progressive neutral expertise, only became popular in the 1920s.[32] The preoccupations of different writers in presenting descriptive and prescriptive account of public administration also varied. Take for example Fry and Raadschelders' description of the concerns of different public administration theorists:

> Weber and Waldo were intrigued by, and concerned about, the survival of democracy in the face of a burgeoning bureaucracy. Taylor and Gulick sought to discover general principles of management. Mayo and Barnard sought to balance managerial prerogatives with employee needs. Weber, Simon, and Lindblom attempted to make sense of rationality, by exploring its limits. Follett and Barnard delved into the nature of authority in co-operative social systems. And that is only the beginning.[33]

Thus, while there was a general commitment to more informed government, there were differences of opinion over what that actually was.[34] It was also the case that public administration as an object of study only emerged at the end of the nineteenth century,[35] and the first public administration textbooks did not appear until the 1920s.[36]

More importantly, while the need for expert capacity in factual evaluation was a catalyst for administrative development, expertise came in many different forms.

29 *Report on the Organization of the Permanent Civil Service* (House of Commons 1854) (known as the Northcote–Trevelyan Report).

30 Pendleton Act 1883, 22 Stat 27 (16 Jan 1883). See Ari Hoogenboom, *Outlawing the Spoils: A History of the Civil Service Reform Movement 1865-1883* (University of Illinois Press 1961).

31 Max Weber, *From Max Weber: Essays in Sociology* (Routledge 1991).

32 Paul van Riper, 'Some Anomalies in the Deep History of US Public Administration' (1997) 57 Public Administration Rev 218, 219.

33 Brian Fry and Jos Raadschelders, *Mastering Public Administration: From Max Weber to Dwight Waldo* (3rd edn, CQ Press 2013) 447

34 For overviews see Fisher and Shapiro (n 12) ch 5 and Elizabeth Fisher, 'The Enigma of Expertise' (2016) 28 JEL 551.

35 Woodrow Wilson, 'The Study of Administration' (1887) 2 Polit Sci Quart 197.

36 For example, Lloyd Milton Short, *The Development of National Administrative Capacity* (John Hopkins Press, 1923). For an overview see Wallace Sayre, 'Premises of Public Administration: Past and Emerging' (1958) 18 Public Administration Rev 102.

Administrative growth was organic and not patterned along a single model. In the United States, there was the development of independent regulatory commissions such as the ICC, but also the development of new offices in old departments[37] and/or legislative requirements for the appointment of people with particular expertise.[38] There was also general administrative expansion. The staff of the Departments of Agriculture and Commerce, for example, grew fourfold between 1915 and 1930.[39]

In the United Kingdom, the deployment of specialist officers, and thus expertise was less wholesale, reflecting an anxiety about experts being too narrow in their outlook.[40] Specialists were never fully integrated into departmental structures, with much of their work of an advisory nature.[41] Alternatively, expertise was clustered into inspectorates,[42] or structured into evolving local/national structures to address the consequences of crowded cities.[43] There was also a significant decentralised tribunal system.[44]

The First World War saw a greater need for administrative expertise and growth in the central executive. But as the Haldane Committee noted in 1918 about the United Kingdom, there was much 'overlapping and consequent obscurity and confusion in the functions of the Departments and Executive Government'.[45] While the Committee called for greater expertise, it explicitly stated, despite the formal title of its report, that bureaucracy was not a 'machine' and pointed to the 'living forces' supplied by Parliament.[46] In promoting expertise, it also focused upon deliberation and 'the duty of investigation and thought as preliminary to action'.[47]

An important legal dimension of these developments was the creation of specific legislative frameworks for making decisions involving some form of factual evaluation, often involving some form of administrative regime. These frameworks were diverse but all were quite distinct from the adjudicative method that

[37] For example, Bureau of Chemistry in Department of Agriculture, s 4, Pure Food and Drug Act 1906 34 Stat. 768 (30 June 1906).

[38] Meat Inspection Act 1906 34 Stat. 1256 (5 March 1906).

[39] Theda Skocpol and Kenneth Finegold, 'State Capacity and Economic Intervention in the Early New Deal' (1982) 97 Polit Sci Quart 272.

[40] Fisher, 'The Enigma of Expertise' (n 34).

[41] JR Howard Roberts, 'The Professional Expert and Administrative Control' (1929) 7 Pub Adm 247, 248.

[42] Roy Macleod (ed), *Government and Expertise: Specialists, Administrators, and Professionals 1860–1919* (CUP 1988).

[43] Peter Hall, *Cities of Tomorrow: An Intellectual History of Urban Planning and Design in the Twentieth Century* (4th edn, Wiley-Blackwell Publishing 2014) 47.

[44] Chantal Stebbings, *Legal Foundations of Tribunals in Nineteenth Century England* (CUP 2006) and Harry Arthurs, '*Without the Law': Administrative Justice and Legal Pluralism in Nineteenth Century England* (University of Toronto Press 1985).

[45] Ministry of Reconstruction, Report of the Machinery of Government Committee (Cd 9230, 1918) 4.

[46] Ibid 16.

[47] Ibid 6.

courts used to find facts.[48] As Lord Loreburn LC noted in *Board of Education v Rice*, '[c]omparatively recent statutes have extended, if they have not originated, the practice of imposing upon departments or officers of State the duty of deciding or determining questions of various kinds'.[49]

In some cases, this represented a new form of decision-making. Take for example, the ICC in the United States. The ICC Act 1887 laid down a number of standards for carriers that shippers could enforce by taking them to the ICC. The ICC was vested with considerable powers to 'inquire into the management of the business of all common carriers subject to the provisions of the [ICC] Act'.[50] That included having the power 'to require the attendance and testimony of witnesses and the production of all books, papers. tariffs, contracts, agreements, and documents relating to any matter under investigation'.[51] The ICC's duty was to

> make a report in writing in respect thereto, which shall include the findings of fact upon which the conclusions of the Commission are based, together with its recommendation as to what reparation, if any, should be made by the common carrier to any party or parties who may be found to have been injured.[52]

Moreover, 'such findings so made shall thereafter, in all judicial proceedings, to be recorded, be deemed prima facie evidence as to each and every fact found'.[53] Thus, while the ICC did not initiate these actions or have any simple prospective rule-making authority, its rulings served as the basis for future action.[54]

In other cases, the development of new fact-finding processes was more evolutionary. The Housing of the Working Classes Act 1890[55] empowered local authorities to apply to Justices of the Peace to summons a property owner so as to enforce sanitary and nuisance legislation, a process that had adjudicative procedure at its heart. But that process evolved with legislative amendment. For example, the Housing, Town Planning, &c Act, 1909 vested the power of enforcement in the local government authority, with an appeal process to the Local Government Board which included a 'public local inquiry'.[56]

[48] John Wigmore, 'Administrative Boards and Commissions: Are the Jury-Trial Rules of Evidence in Force for Their Inquiries?' (1922) 17 Ill Law Rev 263 and Paul Vinogradoff, 'Some Problems of Public Law' (1924) 12 Calif Law Rev 443.
[49] [1911] AC 179, 182.
[50] S 12.
[51] S 12.
[52] S 14.
[53] S 14.
[54] Jaffe (n 13) 148.
[55] S 5.
[56] S 39(1)(b).

II. Emerging Legal Discourses

The discussion in section I provides only a glimpse of the significant evolution in administrative practices. This evolution was in direct response to the changing needs of urbanising, capitalist democracies which created a shift in the normal expectations of government and collective practices.[57] By the 1920s, and after at least half a century of unsystematic administrative growth, the legal validity of these new administrative structures became a matter of legal debate and scrutiny. This had three significant and overlapping dimensions: discourses around what form administrative law should take as a distinct legal discipline; legal polemic over the use of non-adjudicative procedures in decision-making; and doctrines that courts developed in reviewing decisions made as part of these new administrative frameworks. Let me consider each of them briefly here.

The first set of debates was over what form administrative law should take as a distinct legal sub-discipline. This was part of a more general discussion about the study of law as an academic discipline, particularly in the United States where strands of legal realist thinking began to emerge.[58] The late nineteenth-century accounts of administrative law were written primarily by non-lawyers or those straddling law and political science,[59] but by the early twentieth century, the study of law and the study of public administration were going their separate ways.[60] The first significant administrative law textbooks emerged during the 1920s, but it is clear in reading them that administrative law was in search of an intellectual framework. Frankfurter and Davison used a separation of powers analysis to structure their textbook[61] while Robson approached administrative law through a more rationalised bureaucratic lens.[62] Others took a more methodical, albeit not necessarily easily readable approach to the subject.[63]

Around the edges there was also much academic comment,[64] and Fuchs in 1938 commented that over 20,000 pages on Anglo-American administrative law had

[57] Taylor describes these expectations as 'social imaginaries'. See Charles Taylor, *A Secular Age* (Belknap Press 2007) 172.

[58] Laura Kalman, *Legal Realism at Yale, 1927–1960* (University of North Carolina Press 1986).

[59] Take Goodnow who was a political scientist writing about law—Frank Goodnow, *Comparative Administrative Law: An Analysis of the Administrative Systems National and Local of the US, England, France and Germany* (GP Putnam & Sons 1893). Likewise, Wilson was working both in the fields of law and public administration. For an overview of his work see Brian Cook, *Democracy and Administration: Woodrow Wilson's Ideas and the Challenges of Public Management* (Johns Hopkins UP 2007). Also, Bruce Wyman, *The Principles of Administrative Law: Governing the Relations of Public Officers* (Davidson Company 1903).

[60] Sidney Shapiro, 'Why Administrative Law Misunderstands How Government Works: The Missing Institutional Analysis' (2013) 53 Washburn LJ 1.

[61] Felix Frankfurter and J Forrester Davison, *Cases and Other Materials on Administrative Law* (Commerce Clearing House Inc. 1931).

[62] William Robson, *Justice and Administrative Law* (Steven & Sons 1928).

[63] Frederick Port, *Administrative Law* (Longmans 1929).

[64] A Berle, 'The Expansion of American Administrative Law' (1917) 30 Harvard LR 430; Ernst Freund and others, *The Growth of American Administrative Law* (Thomas Law Book Company 1923);

been published.[65] Dicey even recognised the emergence of administrative law, but did little to provide a positive vision of it beyond stressing the importance of legislative frameworks and to doubt the ability of ministerial responsibility to work as an accountability mechanism.[66] Others, such as Frank and Robson, focused more on what administrative law could achieve.[67] Many in the United States promoted the idea that public administration harnessed expertise so as to address social problems, but what expertise actually entailed was not elaborated upon.[68]

The second strand of debate was primarily polemical, albeit a form of legal polemic. While much of this debate was carried on at a relatively high level of abstraction,[69] fact evaluation processes attracted considerable attention. As noted in section I, there was no common template for factual evaluation, but in all cases these new processes represented departures from what lawyers understood as a classic approach to fact-finding: an adjudicative trial. In the main, these modes of evaluation were harnessing evaluative processes from other disciplines. But for lawyers, as Wigmore noted, 'the jury trial system of rules is the only safe method of investigation when liberty and property may be at stake'.[70] Stephens noted in 1933 that this assumption 'lurks in almost every judicial opinion' and 'echoes instantly in the breast of the orthodox legal practitioner'.[71]

Not all lawyers thought this way. Some saw the limits of the adjudicative model. Felix Frankfurter, for example, endorsed commissions of inquiry as important vehicles for 'defining issues, sifting evidence, posing problems and enlightening the public mind'.[72] Smellie rhetorically asked, 'Can the technique developed to decide conflicts between plaintiff and defendant be adapted to the weighing of social values or the choosing of expedients?'[73] Even Dicey grudgingly admitted that 'the management of business, in short, is not the same thing as the conduct of a trial. The two things must in many respects be governed by totally different rules.'[74] Lord Sankey noted that 'disputes between individuals no longer only concern the individuals themselves'[75] and Robson commented that 'a kind of interlocking mesh

John Dickinson, *Administrative Justice and the Supremacy of Law* (Harvard UP 1927); Sir John Marriott, 'Liberty and Law' (1929) 250 Edinburgh Review 3; CT Carr, 'Administrative Law' (1935) 51 LQR 58.

65 Fuchs (n 21) 538.
66 AV Dicey, 'The Development of Administrative Law in England' (1915) 31 LQR 148.
67 Frank (n 1) and Robson (n 62).
68 James Landis, *The Administrative Process* (Yale UP 1938).
69 A point often made. Jaffe (n 13) and Gordon (n 9).
70 As quoted in Harold Stephens, *Administrative Tribunals and the Rules of Evidence* (Harvard UP 1933) 3. See also Wigmore (n 48).
71 Stephens (n 70) 3.
72 Felix Frankfurter, *The Public and Its Government* (Yale UP 1930) 162–63.
73 KB Smellie, 'Some Aspects of English Administrative Law' (1927) 5 J Pub Adm 276, 277.
74 Dicey (n 66) 151.
75 Lord Sankey 'Foreword' in Port (n 63) ix.

of decisions can be seen to exist'.[76] Administration was perceived as more able to blend the viewpoints of expertise and amateurs than could a court.[77]

But others saw these non-adjudicative models of fact-finding and evaluation as *prime facie* illegitimate and voiced their objections in strident terms. The Lord Chief Justice of England and Wales, Lord Hewart, was the most high-profile critic of administrative factual evaluation practices. In a number of cases he noted with disdain new administrative developments.[78] In 1929 he published a series of newspaper articles in the *Daily Telegraph* in which he attacked the growth of administrative power. These were also published as a book, *The New Despotism*, by the conservative Member of Parliament, Ernest Benn.[79]

Hewart's work is as much a rousing manifesto for adjudicative procedure as it is an attack on administrative discretion. For him such a procedure was the only way for administration to proceed. One of Hewart's objections to public administration was the fact that officials were not bound by rules of evidence.[80] For him, '[e]vidence not tested by cross examination is nearly always misleading and practically valueless'.[81] Judges in engaging with fact-finding were doing so in the concrete context of legal disputes which also meant they were not considering abstract questions.[82] Hewart reinforced his argument with his vigorous advocacy of Dicey's rule of law, particularly its third limb. Hewart was keen to stress that 'supremacy of law means something more than the exclusion of arbitrary power'.[83]

Many reviewers criticised Hewart's book at the time as overstating the problem, relying on 'old prejudices', and being concerned with the form rather than the substance of justice.[84] Others dismissed his book as being simply akin to 'trade unionism',[85] a fact backed up by the popularity of the book among the legal profession of both England[86] and the United States.[87] Hewart's criticism of what he called 'administrative lawlessness' also chimed well with Pound's censure of 'administrative absolutism'.[88] What Hewart's work highlights is the way in which adjudicative procedure dominated the legal imagination. That meant it was very difficult for lawyers to engage with these new evaluation procedures and make legal sense of them.

[76] Robson (n 62) 1.

[77] XYZ (Laski) 'Book Review: The New Despotism' (1930) 1 Polit Quart 125, 130.

[78] For example, *R v Minister of Health ex parte Worthley Rural Council* [1927] 2 KB 229, 236; *R v Minister for Health, ex parte Davis* [1929] 1 KB 619, 625.

[79] Gordon Hewart, *The New Despotism* (Ernest Benn Ltd 1929). For an American version inspired by Hewart see James Beck, *Our Wonderland of Bureaucracy* (Macmillan 1932).

[80] Hewart (n 79) 44.

[81] Ibid 47.

[82] Ibid 125–26.

[83] Ibid 23.

[84] Richard Joyce Smith, 'Book Review: The New Despotism' (1930) 39 Yale LJ 763, 754–55.

[85] XYZ (Laski) (n 77) 130.

[86] Book Review, 'The New Despotism' (1929) 168 Law Times 364.

[87] Thomas James Norton, 'Book Review: The New Despotism' (1929) 16 Am Bar Assoc J 254, 255.

[88] Roscoe Pound, 'The Growth of Administrative Justice' (1924) 2 Wisconsin L Rev 321.

The third dimension of emerging debates was the very opposite of this state of affairs. The courts were, by necessity, developing legal doctrines concerning the judicial review of these new administrative institutions due to the cases coming before them. Judicial review has deep historical roots, but from the end of the nineteenth century the courts were involved in evolving doctrine in reviewing these new institutions. In some cases, this represented an exercise of common law powers, and in other cases was due to review powers included in legislation.[89] What is striking in both jurisdictions is that a complex and nuanced body of administrative law doctrine emerged.

Take, for example, the US Supreme Court's review of ICC action. The Supreme Court ('the Court') was aware that the ICC had been created to incorporate different types of practical and disciplinary expertise.[90] The Court emphasised the importance of flexibility in the solving of problems and was not concerned that the ICC did not fit into a tripartite separation of powers model.[91] The Supreme Court also perceived railroad rate-setting to be a highly complex and difficult exercise, involving some element of future assessment and requiring consideration of multiple interests.[92]

In light of all this the Court found its task in carrying out judicial review difficult. On the one hand, the ICC was carrying out a sort of adjudicative process and thus the relationship between the Court and the agency could be likened to that between a lower court and a court of appeal. For example, from early on the Supreme Court divided any decision of the Commission along the lines of the fact/law distinction as it would a decision on appeal.[93] The Court soon realised that the lower court/court of appeal analogy was not a very helpful one because it ultimately cast the ICC simply as a fact-finder when clearly the agency's role was far more complex. As a result, the Court's application of the fact/law distinction was an extremely loose one. The 'facts' it referred to were not technical issues but rather socio-political events and factors which the ICC may or may not take into account.[94] The Court noted that fact-finding in rate making had to be based on judgement rather than just empirical analysis.[95] In deciding whether the construction of an Act was the correct one, the courts would refer in an expansive fashion to the type of problems that the ICC was trying to solve.[96] As long as the ICC had

[89] For example, s 18, Federal Trade Commission Act 1914 38 Stat 717 (26 Sept 1914).

[90] *ICC v Louisville & Nashville Railway Co.* 227 US 88, 98 (1913); *New York N.H. & H.R. Co. v ICC* 200 US 361, 401–2 (1906).

[91] *Texas P. Ry Co. v ICC* 162 US 197, 219 (1896).

[92] *Cincinnati N.O. & T.P. Ry Co. v ICC* 162 US 184, 194 (1896) and *ICC v Illinois Central Railroad Co.* 215 US 452, 478 (1910).

[93] There was nothing in the ICC Act to require such an approach.

[94] *ICC v Chicago Burlington & Quincy Railway Co.* 186 US 320, 338 (1902).

[95] *ICC v Alabama Midland Ry Co.* 168 US 144, 163 (1897); *Illinois Central Railroad Co. v ICC* 206 US 441, 455 (1906) *Tennessee, V. & G. R. Co. v ICC* 181 US 1, 27 (1901) and *ICC v Clyde Steamship Co.* 181 US 29, 33 (1901).

[96] *Texas P. Ry Co* (n 91) 211.

considered all the relevant factors, and at least some testimony supported its viewpoint, the decision would stand.[97] This formula became known as the 'substantial evidence test', a test borrowed from an upper court's approach to reviewing jury deliberations. The test required that an agency had some evidence because otherwise the decision was felt to be 'inconsistent with formal justice'.[98] This was not to say that a decision-maker had to adhere strictly to the rules of trial process[99] or that the decision would be a perfect example of methodological rigor.[100] Overall, what can be seen is the way in which the courts, in reviewing decisions, were engaged in a bottom-up approach that was concerned with understanding the administrative nature of these new structures and reviewing them on that basis. Review was being crafted to the institutional context.

A similar pattern can be seen in regards to the UK courts. Courts in reviewing decisions were trying to make sense of decision-making structures, often incorporating tribunals, and how they applied specialised knowledge.[101] The infamous case of *Arlidge* is a case in point.[102] That case dealt with an appeal to the Local Government Board against a borough council order prohibiting the use of a house for habitation under section 17 of the Housing and Town Planning Act 1909. As noted in section I of this chapter, that Act represented a steady evolution in decision-making procedures. Much of the reasoning in the case of the different Law Lords rested on their understanding of the legislative and administrative framework for decision-making. Two judges referred to the helpfulness of an affidavit put before the Court of Appeal by the Secretary of the Local Government Board, Sir Horace Munro.[103] Viscount Haldane noted:

> In accordance with that practice the Board, in order to obtain materials with which to decide, appointed one of its health inspectors to hold a public inquiry. This was in accordance with the rules it had made under the section of the statute which I have quoted and with its usual practice. It is said that the report of the inspector should have been disclosed. It might or might not have been useful to disclose this report, but I do not think that the Board was bound to do so, any more than it would have been bound to disclose all the minutes made on the papers in the office before a decision was come to. It is plain from Sir Horace Monro's affidavit that the order made was the order of the Board, and so long as the Board

[97] *Prentis v Atlantic Coast Line Company* 211 US 210 (1908); *Pennsylvania Co. v US* 236 US 351, 361 (1915); *Northern Pacific Railway Co. v M.J. Solum* 247 US 477, 478 (1918); and *Manufacturers Railway Co. v US* 246 US 457, 481(1918).

[98] *Louisville & Nashville Railway Co.* (n 90) 94.

[99] Ibid.

[100] *FTC v Klesner* 280 US 19, 29 (1929); and *Pennsylvania* (n 97) 361.

[101] For example, *Swift v Board of Trade* [1926] 2 KB 131 and *Northwood v London City Council* [1926] 2 KB 411.

[102] *Local Government Board v Arlidge* [1915] AC 120.

[103] Ibid 128 (Viscount Haldane) 142–43 (Lord Parmoor).

> followed a procedure which was usual, and not calculated to violate the tests to which I have already referred, I think that the Board was discharging the duty imposed on it in the fashion Parliament must be taken to have contemplated when it deliberately transferred the jurisdiction, first, from a Court of summary jurisdiction to the local authority, and then, for the purposes of all appeals, from quarter sessions to an administrative department of the State.[104]

In other words, the House of Lords was trying to determine the standards of action being created by the legislative framework which should be used to assess the legal validity of the Board's decision.

Or consider the even more notorious case of *Roberts v Hopwood.*[105] That case concerned the interplay between two legislative provisions. The first was section 62 of the Metropolis Management Act 1855 which stated that a metropolitan borough council 'may allow to such clerks, treasurers, surveyors, officers, and servants respectively such salaries and wages as [they] may think fit'. The second was section 247(7) of the Public Health Act 1875 which stipulated '[a]ny auditor acting in pursuance of this section shall disallow every item of account contrary to law'. As Lord Atkinson noted:

> The decision of these questions involves the consideration of first, whether it is the duty of a district auditor to consider the reasonableness of the charges and payments appearing in the account of local authorities, and also whether he has power to disallow unreasonable charges and payments, or whether his duty in dealing with any payment purporting ex facie to have been made for an authorized purpose is confined to merely vouching the payment of the sum appearing to have been expended, without questioning the reasonableness of the amount; and second, the question as to the scope of the discretion vested by Parliament in the metropolitan borough councils in connection with the payment of salaries and wages.[106]

The issue of the reasonableness of the auditor's decision turned on what was understood to be the purpose of audit in the legislative regime and how that then related to the assessment of the reasonableness of how wages were set.[107] That was neither an isolated nor straightforward legal inquiry and different judges varied in their approach.[108]

104 Ibid 137.

105 *Roberts v Hopwood* [1923] AC 578.

106 Ibid 591.

107 Ibid 604.

108 Ibid. Compare Lord Buckmaster's focus on the nature of what the legislative provisions empower 585, 588; Lord Atkinson evoking ideas of trustee's duties (596); Lord Sumner looking at the temporal relationship between the provision (603); Lord Wrenbury analysing the definition of 'fit and proper' wages (613); and Lord Carson giving emphasis to the idea of decision-making in good faith.

A standard account of these cases, based primarily on responses to their outcomes at the time, is that *Arlidge* represented a progressive ushering of administrative law,[109] and *Roberts* a conservative backlash against a new labour politics.[110] But what can be seen in these two cases, and can also be seen in the United States, are judges, on the whole, making attempts in good faith to make sense of the new administrative regimes being created. That reasoning was often quite nuanced; an understanding of its significance required an understanding of the legal and institutional context in which it was operating. This also meant the cases did not create easily transferable precedents. They also did not fit easily into discourses focused on overarching constitutional principles. The question for the courts was how to craft their review and that rested on how they understood the particular administrative process.

III. Attempts at Navigation

By the 1930s, there was thus a heady mixture of administrative law coalescing as a discipline, strident polemic, and a steady flow of case law. Given this, it was inevitable in both jurisdictions that there would be calls for taking stock and making sense of these developments. The publication of administrative law textbooks could partially be understood as one attempt to chart and evaluate these developments, but in both the United Kingdom and the United States, there was a perceived need for more official accounts.[111] For example, Claud Schuster, Permanent Secretary to the Lord Chancellor's Office, in a confidential memorandum in March 1929 stated that 'the time has arrived for a serious and deliberate consideration' of the issues raised by administrative growth.[112]

In 1929, the new Labour government, with Sankey as its Lord Chancellor, initiated such consideration. But even after the decision was made to have an inquiry, there was a process of writing and rewriting the Committee's terms of reference. An early internal draft of the terms of reference for such an inquiry reflected its possibly wide-ranging nature:

> A. To examine the origin of the development of the practice of entrusting to public departments the exercise of functions of a legislative and of a judicial character respectively, and to consider and report, what additional checks and safeguards, if

[109] Dicey (n 66).

[110] Harold Laski, 'Judicial Review of Social Policy in England: A Study of Roberts v. Hopwood et al' (1926) 39 Harvard L Rev 832.

[111] Lord Justice Sankey 'The Principles and the Practice of the Law Today' (1928) 72 Solicitors Journal 184, 197.

[112] Claud Schuster, Confidential Memorandum, March 1929, Lord Chancellor's Office, PRO/LCO/2/1133, 1–2. See also Letter from Sankey to the Chancellor of the exchequer, 11/10/29, PRO/LCO/2/1133.

any, should in the public interest be applied to the assignment to and the exercise by public departments of such functions, due regard being had on the one hand to public business and on the other hand to the necessity of preserving in fact as well as in form the constitutional principles of the Sovereignty of Parliament and the supremacy of the law.

B. To consider and report upon the limits within which and the conditions subject to which the exercise of the functions of a legislative and a judicial character may with advantage/without prejudice to the public interest be entrusted to departments of the Executive Government.[113]

While these reflect the importance of evaluating administrative growth against certain legal principles, they also emphasised the importance of making sense of these developments. There was some criticism of the narrowness of these terms of reference. Maurice Gwyer, the Treasury Solicitor, did not like the phrase 'supremacy of law' because it suggested the validity of Hewart's argument. Rather, he argued the phrase should be 'justice is done between the parties'.[114]

The direct impact of Hewart's work and the perceived political necessity to counteract it is evidenced in the final terms of reference which stated that the Committee was:

> To be a Committee to consider the powers exercised by or under the direction of (or by persons or bodies appointed specially by) Ministers of the Crown by way of (a) delegated legislation and (b) judicial or quasi-judicial decision, and to report what safeguards are desirable to secure the constitutional principles of the sovereignty of Parliament and the supremacy of the Law.[115]

These terms of reference were direct replies to Hewart's attacks and were published two days before the publication of the *New Despotism*. They were also immediately identified as being very narrow and overtly legalistic. Viscount Bridgeman on being invited to join the Committee wrote: 'I am unable from the terms of reference to understand what we are asked to do. In any case, it seems to me to be a question of a highly technical and legal character.'[116] From its outset the Committee's terms of reference thus limited the scope of analysis.

One example of this limited scope is the questionnaire sent to each government department asking it to classify its legal powers in the ways framed by the terms of reference. There was little in the way of engagement with institutional frameworks. The limited nature of the inquiry is reflected in the answers that were sent back that

[113] Seemingly from Sir John Anderson of the Home Office. See PCO/LCO/2/1133 and PCO/TS/27/782. Correspondence between Sir Claud Schuster and Maurice Gwyer, 9 October 1929.

[114] Letter, 9 October 1929, see PCO/LCO/2/1133 and PCO/TS/27/782.

[115] Committee on Ministers' Powers (n 15).

[116] Letter from Bridgeman to Schuster, 30 October 1929.

expressed frustration with the questions being asked.[117] This questionnaire along with a number of other legislative collection exercises was the extent of inquiry into the administrative process.

An early draft of the report was made in January 1931,[118] but the final report was not published until April 1932. Maurice Gwyer, the Treasury Solicitor, was asked to comment on one draft. He sent back a long and quite fervent letter in which he was critical of the Committee's obsession with the Rule of Law. He argued 'Why should the interests of Mr Arlidge be so tenderly regarded and those of his unhappy tenants who live in his water-logged houses be forgotten?'[119] The final report remained diffident on the questions put before it. The committee recognised the dangers of rigidity,[120] the 'opportunistic' nature of administrative development,[121] and the inevitability of delegation.[122] Hewart's criticisms were also found to be exaggerated.[123] With that said, there was little in the way of a positive template for administrative law emerging from the Report. Sir Leslie Scott, who had chaired the Committee after Donoughmore had retired, writing shortly after publication, noted: 'I for one view with suspicion the abstract logic of extreme systemisation; the factors of human progress are too complex.'[124]

The New Deal created a very different set of political and institutional developments in the United States, but there were similar calls for a review of administrative growth and reform and rationalisation. Throughout the 1930s there was a plethora of reports. The American Bar Association (ABA)[125] stressed the importance of adjudicative procedure and the Brownlow Commission argued the need to streamline public administration along managerial lines.[126] After vetoing Congressional attempts to introduce legislation to reform administrative procedure to make it more adjudicative,[127] President Roosevelt appointed a committee—the Attorney General's Committee on Administrative Procedure—to conduct a 'thorough and comprehensive study... of existing practices and procedures with a view to detecting any existing deficiencies and pointing the way to improvement'.[128]

The Committee was thus not harnessed with the narrow terms of reference that shackled the Donoughmore Committee. At the core of the Committee's activities

[117] PCO/T/162/282/E22987. See also Committee on Ministers' Powers (n 15), Register of Friendly Societies and Office of the Industrial Assurance Commission, 72 and War Office 110.
[118] PRO/MH/71/1
[119] Letter from Gwyer to Fraser, 7 January 1932, PRO/TS/27/782
[120] Committee on Ministers' Powers (n 15) 4.
[121] Ibid 16.
[122] Ibid 51.
[123] Ibid 7
[124] Leslie Scott, 'Evolution of Public Law' (1932) 14 (3rd Ser) J Comp Leg 163, 170.
[125] For example, Report of the Special Committee on Administrative Law (1934), 57 ABA Annual Reports, 539, 543–44.
[126] President's Committee on Administrative Management, *Report of the Committee* (1937).
[127] For an overview see James Landis, 'Crucial Issues in Administrative Law. The Walter-Logan Bill' (1940) 53 Harvard L Rev 1077.
[128] Attorney General's Committee on Administrative Procedure (n 16) 1.

was a series of reviews of different administrative practices in different agencies. The Committee recognised that the growth of administration had been 'pragmatic' and had been due to the need to have a flexible approach to preventative regulation.[129] They saw expert agencies were important because their 'continuity of attention' and expertise could allow for the more effective solving of problems.[130] With that said there was also a need to ensure an 'understandable record for decision' was developed.[131]

In discussing procedure, the Committee also recognised the varied tasks carried out by expert public administration and the need to ensure procedure related to those tasks and to 'constantly checking the skill and integrity' of the relevant expert.[132] They also recognised the importance of administrative traditions and culture.[133] On adjudicative procedure they stated: 'The full utilization of concentrated experience may be frustrated if administrative hearing procedure must be shaped to an inflexible pattern which has just evolved with an eye to the frailties of inexperienced jurors.'[134] That was not to say that they thought hearings were not appropriate but that they saw them as serving the purpose of being both fact-finding forums and opportunities for discussion about relevant issues.[135] The Committee also viewed formal methods of adjudication as problematic, particularly because such methods encouraged excessive analysis of the evidence, whether or not such evidence was relevant.[136]

The Committee also noted that the relationship between procedure and scope of review doctrine was a close one and they stated: 'Dissatisfaction with the existing standards as to scope of judicial review derives largely from dissatisfaction with the fact-finding procedures now employed by administrative agencies.'[137] The Committee argued that judicial review should check but not supplant the administrative process.[138] It argued that to engage in *de novo* judicial review of the facts would be contradictory to the reasons for having expert administration.[139] The courts should not be concerned with ensuring that a decision was 'correct' but that it was the product of 'fair consideration'.[140] The Committee stressed the importance of a flexible and conscientious approach to the scope of review depending on both the body being reviewed and the nature of the decision.[141] It also thought that a

129 Ibid 13.
130 Ibid 19.
131 Ibid 19.
132 Ibid 37–38.
133 Ibid 59.
134 Ibid 61.
135 Ibid 19.
136 Ibid 46.
137 Ibid 92.
138 Ibid 77.
139 Ibid 91.
140 Ibid 78–79.
141 Ibid 91.

Court needed to 'judge the fundamental soundness of the details of the administrative reasoning process'.[142]

The Committee thus engaged far more with the nature of these new evaluation processes than the Donoughmore Committee did. With that said, in the final report ideas of adjudicative rule-making and adjudication framed the analysis, and these concepts were not related to the detailed maps of administrative process that the Committee had completed. The Report did have legal consequences in that its thinking can be seen in the Administrative Procedure Act 1946 which introduced informal 'notice and comment' rulemaking procedures.[143] Informal rule-making, as it became known, represented an important step away from adjudicative procedure and it could accommodate a range of different fact evaluation processes, but it was never accompanied with a positive vision of administrative process. Adjudicative procedure continued to haunt the legal imagination.

IV. Learning from History

The brief sketch above is a reminder of just how rich administrative law discourse was during the 1920s and 1930s. But discourse was not enough. While both the Donoughmore Committee Report and the Attorney General's Committee Report pushed back against adjudicative procedure as the universal template for administrative action, they both failed to generate a way of assessing the legitimacy of factual evaluation process grounded in the new administrative reality. That failure led them to not foster what administrative law should ideally be: a law of public administration. Adjudicative procedure was not replaced with a robust understanding of what administrative procedure does and should look like. To put the matter another way, while these were attempts to put public administration front and centre in legal imagination, they were not successful in doing so.

It is easy to dismiss both reports and to argue that administrative lawyers know better now, but I am not sure we do. Many administrative lawyers tend to be remarkably vague when it comes to administrative detail. Doctrinal analysis often focuses on general principles. Public administration is described as 'bureaucratic', 'technocratic', and 'expert' with little engagement with what these terms mean. Theoretical accounts often focus on the 'state' writ large, rather than public administration specifically. There are of course exceptions and the keen-eyed observer will note I do not footnote the statements above. That is because I am not interested in pointing fingers. The overall point is, as Brian Tamanaha has recently noted, '[n]o existing theory of law adequately accounts for government entities that utilise legal mechanisms in myriad ways in their activities'.[144]

142 Ibid 117.
143 5 USC §553.
144 Brian Tamanaha, *A Realistic Theory of Law* (CUP 2017) 126.

Given the genuine scholarly talent of administrative lawyers, this lack of engagement is not for want of ability (the same is true of the 1920s and 1930s). Nor is it for want of people pointing out the problem. Many wise administrative lawyers argue that it is important for administrative lawyers to know something about public administration.[145] Sometimes this is an argument from theory,[146] sometimes an argument from empirical study,[147] and sometimes an argument about how to teach the subject.[148]

Given all of this, something deeper and more structural is going on. What both the Donoughmore Committee Report and the Attorney General's Committee Report highlight is just how difficult it is to foster a true administrative law as a law of public administration. In particular, the experience with the two reports highlights three structural challenges inherent in administrative law. Identifying these challenges not only helps us make sense of the early twentieth century but also our current times. Specifically, it helps makes sense of the limits of the current collective imagination of administrative lawyers.

The first and most obvious challenge is with engaging with the diversity of administrative material and institutions. As Port stated in his 1929 textbook on UK administrative law, understanding administrative practice required understanding the 1,001 places it is embedded.[149] As noted in section II, many judges were wrestling with the nature of these new regimes, but overall there was a struggle to provide a comprehensive picture of these developments. The Donoughmore Committee's questionnaire did little to engage with that detail, and while the Attorney General's Committee was more comprehensive in its survey, it struggled to build on its analysis. Furthermore, the legal realism of the type that Frank promoted[150] tended to focus on the consequences of administrative action rather than the processes it entailed. Claims to expertise tended to also not explain exactly what expertise entailed.[151] This lack of engagement with administrative institutions is not just about not doing one's homework properly. Without providing an account of the administrative landscape, it becomes very difficult to imagine what that landscape is and what it can be. More significantly, it becomes difficult to imagine the possible roles for law. This lack of engagement, by itself, results in a limiting of the legal imagination.[152]

145 Shapiro (n 60).

146 And different types of theory at that. See Gerald Frug, 'The Ideology of Bureaucracy in American Law' (1984) 97 Harvard L Rev 1276 and Colin Diver, 'Policy-Making Paradigms in Administrative Law' (1981) 95 Harvard L Rev 393.

147 Jerry Mashaw, *Bureaucratic Justice: Managing Social Security Disability Claims* (Yale UP 1983).

148 For an overview of these types of arguments see Peter Strauss, 'Jerry L Mashaw and the Public Law Curriculum' in Nicholas Parillo (ed), *Administrative Law from the Inside Out: Essays on Themes in the Work of Jerry L Mashaw* (CUP 2017).

149 Port (n 63) 2.

150 Frank, 'Experimental Jurisprudence' (n 1).

151 But see William Butler, 'The Rising Tide of Expertise' (1946) 15 Fordham L Rev 19.

152 See also Elizabeth Fisher, *Environmental Law: A Very Short Introduction* (OUP 2017) chs 5 and 10.

The Internet and freedom of information legislation has made the material of administrative law far more accessible, but the problems created by the rich diversity of legal material remain, particularly given the technical and specific nature of many administrative processes.[153] Take, for example, the setting of the national ambient air-quality standards under the Clean Air Act in the United States, which involves a rolling and evolving assessment process for a set of pollutants that integrates both specific data about those pollutants with techniques for assessment: understanding the law requires understanding those processes.[154] Even now, much administrative law scholarship is disembodied from administrative practices, such as the *Chevron* doctrine.[155] That two-step 'test' explicitly rests on an idea of agency expertise and understandings of expertise inform doctrinal reasoning, and yet very little of the academic discussion explores concepts of expertise.[156]

The lack of engagement with administrative material and the subsequent impoverishment of the legal imagination overlap with the second structural challenge: the difficulties in fostering administrative law expertise. To be an 'administrative lawyer' you need skills, experience, and knowledge both about administrative law and that which administrative law applies to: public administration.[157] As we saw earlier, during the first half of the twentieth century, the former expertise was dominated by understanding law in terms of adjudicative procedure. Separation of powers thinking also reinforced this vision of law. Studying administrative institutions did not sit easily with legal expertise which had been fostered through the study of laws and legal reasoning. But without expanding understanding of administrative processes, administrative law expertise could never be nurtured. Claims by scholars that administrators were 'experts' or that what they did was beneficial did not do this either.

The problems of administrative law expertise have in many ways become worse. In both jurisdictions, there has been a tendency to ground legal expertise in other legal disciplines such as constitutional law or ideas of property law.[158] A focus on rights also diverts attention from fostering an understanding of administrative institutions. A further challenge now is it is hard to know where to start in the study of public administration.[159] Not only does public administration take many divergent institutional forms but it can be studied through a range of different disciplinary

[153] Elizabeth Fisher, Pasky Pascual, and Wendy Wagner, 'Understanding Environmental Models in Their Legal and Regulatory Context' (2010) 22 JEL 251.

[154] Elizabeth Fisher, Pasky Pascual, and Wendy Wagner, 'Rethinking Judicial Review of Expert Agencies' (2015) 93 Texas L Rev 1681.

[155] *Chevron* (n 10).

[156] Sidney Shapiro and Elizabeth Fisher, 'Chevron and the Legitimacy of Public Administration' (2013) 22 William and Mary Bill of Rights LJ 465.

[157] This is the distinction between contributory and interactional expertise developed by Harry Collins and Robert Evans, *Rethinking Expertise* (University of Chicago Press 2007).

[158] Richard Epstein, *The Classic Liberal Constitution: The Uncertain Quest for Limited Government* (Harvard UP 2014).

[159] Fry and Raadschelders (n 33).

lenses and the focus of study can be a range of different levels. Is it best to study public administration as Weberian bureaucracy?[160] From the perspective of public choice theory?[161] As a series of socio-legal studies?[162] Should you study organisational flow charts, individual decisions, high-level policy, or something else?

This set of scholarly challenges lies at the heart of administrative law. For administrative law to be a true law of public administration, it needs to take the institutional competence of public administration seriously.[163] These are also a very dynamic set of challenges. A good example is how both environmental problems and environmental law force an expansion of both the legal and institutional imagination.[164] Again, what is striking is how much courts are often at the coalface of this process.[165] It is also conspicuous how many of those judgments are often overlooked.

This relates to the third structural challenge that the history of the Donoughmore Committee Report and the Attorney General's Committee Report highlights: that it is far too easy to turn administrative law into a narrative about competing ideologies. As the analysis in sections II and III show, it was understood by some in such terms at the time and it is still understood in such terms today.[166] Furthermore, accounts of administrative law history have tended to reinforce the ideological narrative of administrative law. The history of the APA for example, has largely been understood in political terms, a compromise between right-wing lawyers and left-wing idealists.[167] A similar pattern can be seen in UK administrative law.[168] There are important exceptions,[169] but often scholars find it hard to know what to do with histories that do not fit neatly into the binary of being for or against the administrative state.

[160] Compare Stephen Skowronek, *Building A New American State: The Expansion of National Administrative Capacities 1877–1920* (CUP 1982) and William Novak, 'The Concept of the State in American History' in James Sparrow, William Novak, and Stephen Sawyer (eds), *Boundaries of the State in US History* (University of Chicago Press 2015).

[161] Jerry Mashaw, *Greed, Chaos and Governance: Using Public Choice to Improve Public Law* (Yale UP 1997).

[162] Jerry Mashaw, *Bureaucratic Justice: Managing Social Security Disability Claims* (Yale UP 1983) and Keith Hawkins, *Environment and Enforcement* (OUP 1984).

[163] Elizabeth Fisher, *Risk Regulation and Administrative Constitutionalism* (Hart Publishing 2007). See also Fisher and Shapiro (n 12).

[164] Elizabeth Fisher, 'Environmental Law as "Hot" Law' (2013) 25 Journal of Environmental Law 347 and Elizabeth Fisher, Eloise Scotford, and Emily Barritt, 'The Legally Disruptive Nature of Climate Change' (2017) 80 MLR 173.

[165] Fisher, 'Law and Energy Transitions: Wind Turbines and Planning Law in the UK' (n 12) and Fisher, Pascual, and Wagner, 'Rethinking Judicial Review of Expert Agencies' (n 154).

[166] Fisher and Shapiro (n 12) ch 1 and Harlow and Rawlings (n 11).

[167] Martin Shapiro, 'APA: Past Present and Future' (1986) 72 Va LR 447 and McNollgast, 'The Political Origins of the Administrative Procedure Act' (1999) 15 JLEO 180.

[168] Patrick McAuslan, 'Administrative Law, Collective Consumption and Judicial Policy' (1983) 46 MLR 1.

[169] Jerry Mashaw, *Creating the Administrative Constitution: The Lost One Hundred Years of American Administrative Law* (Yale UP 2012).

Public administration and hence administrative law clearly are normatively inflected. That is evidenced in high theory[170] and also the lived experience of public administration.[171] As Woodrow Wilson once noted, public administration 'rests its whole front along the line which is drawn . . . between Interference and Laissez faire'.[172] In being so, its actions reflect prescriptions about the role of state in society. As Wilson also noted '[a]dministration... *is always in contact with the present*: it is the State's experiencing organ'.[173] It must make decisions (either general or individual) that will create new winners and losers, and thus awaken resentment and disagreement,[174] as does any process of development. As Sir Claude Schuster noted in a confidential memorandum recommending the creation of the Donoughmore Committee, administrative development, had caused a 'feeling of helplessness' on the part of citizens' and the subsequent controversy a 'feeling of injury and soreness' on the part of civil servants'.[175]

Given all this it is very tempting to understand administrative law as simply political action in another guise. But administrative law is very much law, and it was always so as the legislation and the case law that I have discussed illustrate. The real challenge for both the Donoughmore Committee Report and the Attorney General's Committee Report was addressing this fact. That required the appropriate expertise, but as we saw, that expertise was not forthcoming. Nor is it still in many cases. The narrative of ideologies reinforces the idea that the choice in administrative law is a binary one based on political preference rather than understanding public administration.

V. Conclusion

Overall, administrative law as the law of public law administration requires the opening up of the legal imagination to realise the legal and institutional possibilities in taking public administration seriously.[176] This is not about taking to the 'open road'. As Daniel Ernst has recently noted about Frank's time at the Agricultural Adjustment Administration, it was an 'object lesson

[170] Craig (n 22).

[171] Arlie Russell Hochschild, *Strangers in Their Own Land: Anger and Mourning on the American Right* (The New Press 2016).

[172] Quoted in Brian Cook, *Bureaucracy and Self-Government: Reconsidering the Role of Public Administration in American Politics* (John Hopkins UP 2014) 122.

[173] Woodrow Wilson, 'Notes for Lectures at the John Hopkins (First Year Course)' (*c.* Jan 26 1891–Feb 27 1894) in Arthur Link (ed), *Papers of Woodrow Wilson: Volume 7 1890–1892* (Princeton UP 1969) 138 (emphasis in the original).

[174] Louis Jaffe, *Judicial Control of Administrative Action* (Little, Brown & Co 1965) 323.

[175] PRO/LCO/2/1133, 4.

[176] Fisher and Shapiro (n 12).

on how not to be a general counsel'.[177] This was because, on Ernst's reckoning, Frank failed to take the statutory frameworks and concepts of legal authority seriously.

As this chapter has shown, opening up legal imagination is difficult, however. The Donoughmore Committee Report and the Attorney General's Committee Report were ultimately failed promises, but the analysis here does also point to a way forward. Specifically, it identified three structural challenges that need to be overcome in opening up that imagination, the challenges that arise from: the diversity of administrative institutions; the need for administrative law expertise; and the tendency towards ideological binaries. Identifying those challenges is an important first step in fostering a law of public administration. Such a conclusion may frustrate as it provides few easy answers, but it does open up new lines of debate for fostering a true administrative law.[178]

177 Daniel Ernst, 'Mr. Try-It Goes to Washington: Law and Policy at the Agricultural Adjustment Administration' (2019) 87 Fordham Law Review 1795.

178 Ibid.

12

The EU Automated State Disassembled

Deirdre Curtin

I. Introduction

The EU institutions have always been 'singular[,] ... any neat ordering that corresponds to that within a nation state' has remained elusive.[1] Yet, the depth of integration as a result of the European Union, its institutions, laws, and practices is unparalleled. Much explanatory scholarship has focused on the EU's formal rules delegating substantial powers to supranational institutions such as the European Commission and the power of majority voting in the intergovernmental Council of Ministers.[2] Part of this account has highlighted the growth of executive power in this context, also as a result of many Treaty revisions over the decades, and in parallel, the putting in place of formal accountability structures that range wider than traditional legal and political accountability.[3] The wide-ranging narrative of constitutionalisation in this context has bolstered the conclusion that gradually the political system of the European Union has become more akin to that of its Member States.[4] In parallel, the administration of the European Union has evolved both through its core, newer institutions (the European Commission and the host of EU agencies that now exist) and risk regulation instruments in areas such as genetically modified organisms (GMOs), pharmaceuticals, food safety as well as the customs union. Over time, the equivalent of an EU administrative state has been constructed, albeit intricately connected to that of the Member States.[5]

The administrative state is undergoing significant transformations at the national level. Those transformations have transferred to the European level in a manner that arguably goes way beyond how the formal rules of the EU institutions

[1] Paul Craig, 'Institutions, Power and Institutional Balance' in Paul Craig and Gráinne de Búrca (eds), *The Evolution of EU Law* (OUP 2011) 41–84.

[2] Ibid and the literature cited.

[3] Paul Craig, 'The Locus and Accountability of the Executive in the European Union' in Paul Craig and Adam Tomkins, *The Executive and Public Law. Power and Accountability in Comparative Perspective* (OUP 2006) 316–46; see further, Mark Bovens, Deirdre Curtin, and Paul 't Hart, *What Deficit? The Real World of EU Accountability* (OUP 2010).

[4] Simon Hix, 'The Study of the European Community: The Challenge to Comparative Politics' (1994) 17 West European Politics 1.

[5] Filipe Brito Bastos, *Beyond Executive Federalism. The Judicial Crafting of the Law of Composite Administrative Decision-Making* (unpublished Ph.D. thesis, European University Institute, Florence 2018); Deirdre Curtin, 'Executive Power' in Denis Patterson and Anna Södersten (eds), *A Companion to European Law and International Law* (Blackwell 2016) 109–18.

Deirdre Curtin, *The EU Automated State Disassembled* In: *The Foundations and Future of Public Law*. Edited by: Elizabeth Fisher, Jeff King, Alison L Young, Oxford University Press (2020). © Oxford University Press.
DOI: 10.1093/oso/9780198845249.003.0012

and their accountability structures were conceived. Automated personal information collection systems, introduced by states, have gradually succeeded more traditional and ad hoc ways of collecting, storing, and processing information.[6] Automation is catalysed by the supranational level from its informal inception in particular in the Area of Freedom, Security and Justice (AFSJ) through a host of separately conceived databases. Automation as a term comes from the word automatic and refers to the technology by which a process or procedure is performed with minimum human assistance.[7] Automation implies something self-moving without human will or discretion and can be applied to software and hardware in the private as well as the public domains. The key feature of an automated administrative system is the capacity to automate and embed administrative decision logic into a computer system.[8] The contemporary administrative state is not replaced by modern information and communication technologies (ICT) but core parts of the traditional administrative state have been automated, resulting in a significant impact on both institutions and their accountability.

In the past decades, an intensified growth has taken place of personal record collection also in non-routine state interactions such as policing and border control. Governments around the world build databases and deploy new data analysis techniques to mine law enforcement, communications, and intelligence data.[9] Electronic databases and their interlinks form 'the nervous system of contemporary criminal justice operations... The risk of error stemming from these databases is not slim.'[10] The expansive use of ICT and the growing automation of administrative decision-making systems including law enforcement arguably brings about radical change in the administrative state that is difficult to link with the procedural norms of the last century.[11] Automated systems not only jeopardise due process norms but also negate the possibility of participatory rule-making in any meaningful sense. Code not rules become largely determinative and code is drafted by computer programmers, not public officials with individual discretion.

Automation goes hand in hand with interoperability. This term refers to the ability of different information systems to communicate, exchange data, and use

[6] Colin Bennett, *Regulating Privacy: Data Protection and Public Policy in Europe and the United States* (Cornell UP 1992) 18.

[7] 'Automation' (*Wikipedia*, last edited 22 January 2019); available at: https://en.wikipedia.org/wiki/Automation, accessed 24 January 2019.

[8] Australian Government, *Automated Assistance in Administrative Decision-Making: Better Practice Guide* (Australian Government 2007); available at: https://www.ombudsman.gov.au/__data/assets/pdf_file/0032/29399/Automated-Assistance-in-Administrative-Decision-Making.pdf, accessed 13 November 2019.

[9] See further, Liane Colonna, *Legal Implications of Data Mining. Assessing the European Union's Data Protection Principles in Light of the United States Government's National Intelligence Data Mining Practices* (Ragulka Press 2016) 96.

[10] *Herring v United States* (2009) 555 US 135, Justice Ginsburg dissenting, 155.

[11] See, for example, Giacinto della Cananea, *Due Process of Law Beyond the State: Requirements of Administrative Procedure* (OUP 2016).

the information that has been exchanged.[12] Interoperability implies not only full availability but also interconnections between different systems and actors. It does not mean the creation of 'an enormous database where everything is interconnected'.[13] It refers rather to the ability of information systems to exchange (personal) data and to enable the sharing of information.[14] It fits within an accentuated trend in recent years towards more institutional and organisational interoperability in law enforcement and intelligence both in the European Union and globally. From the very beginning, interoperability, especially in the context of the European Union, has been presented as a technical matter; a matter of protocols and interfaces.[15] Its legitimacy in political and legal terms has been downplayed, not to say ignored and disconnected from mainstream thinking about EU processes. Yet, as de Hert and Gutwirth put it more than a decade ago on this very subject: 'there is a lot of wisdom in taking seriously the political dimension of technical things'.[16] The Hague programme of 2004 placed considerable emphasis on the informal exchange of information between EU agencies and the so-called interoperability of databases,[17] particularly in the context of migration management.[18] Interoperability is an ambitious and widespread policy at the European level that, up until now, has taken shape in scattered bits and pieces and has not been the subject of much legal or institutional analysis beyond data protection. However, 2019 sees the adoption of specific EU legislation regulating the principle of interoperability in a specific context, thus linking formally the supranational and the national.[19]

[12] Julia Ballaschk, *Interoperability of Intelligence Networks in the European Union: An Analysis of the Policy of Interoperability in the EU's Area of Freedom, Security and Justice and Its Compatibility with the Right to Data Protection* (unpublished PhD thesis, University of Copenhagen 2015) 51; Commission, 'High-level Expert Group on Information Systems and Interoperability: Final Report' (Ref Ares(2017)2412067 May 2017); available at: http://ec.europa.eu/transparency/regexpert/index.cfm?do=groupDetail.groupDetailDoc&id=32600&no=1, accessed 28 June 2019.

[13] Julian King, 'Commissioner King's Remarks on Interoperability', Presentation of the final HLEG report for the LIBE Committee at the European Parliament (Brussels 29 May 2017) ; available at: https://ec.europa.eu/commission/commissioners/2014-2019/king/announcements/commissioner-kings-remarks-interoperability-presentation-final-hleg-report-libe-committee-european_en, accessed 28 June 2019.

[14] Commission, 'High Level Expert Group on Information Systems and Interoperability: Scoping Paper' (Activity Report, 20 June 2016).

[15] Paul de Hert and Serge Gutwirth, 'Interoperability of Police Databases within The EU: An Accountable Political Choice?' (2006) 20 International Rev of L, Computers and Technology 21.

[16] Ibid 32.

[17] Franziska Boehm, *Information Sharing and Data Protection in the Area of Freedom, Security and Justice, towards Harmonized Data Protection Principles for Information Exchange at EU-Level* (Springer 2012) 7.

[18] Valsamis Mitsilegas, 'The Borders Paradox: The Surveillance of Movement in a Union without Internal Frontiers' in Hans Lindahl (ed), *A Right to Inclusion and Exclusion? Normative Fault Lines of the EU's Area of Freedom, Security and Justice* (Hart Publishing 2015) 33–64, 55.

[19] Commission, 'Amended proposal for a Regulation of the European Parliament and of the Council on establishing a framework for interoperability between EU information systems (police and judicial cooperation, asylum and migration)' COM (2018) 480 final.

The aim of this chapter is to shed light on the fragmented way in which automation and its handmaiden, 'interoperability', are put in place in the European Union in a distinct area—police and security cooperation—and the ensuing risk of disassembling the traditional mechanisms of administrative law and public accountability. The joining up of private and public actors and of different public actors through interoperability, in particular for the purpose of law enforcement, arguably results in a disassembling of existing accountability mechanisms. Section II highlights the fragmented manner in which institutions and actors have evolved in the AFSJ context. The sharing of information across institutions and governance levels has over time moved partially from the largely informal realm to being formally regulated in legislation. Section III discusses the informal and formal joining up of private and public actors to fuel the collection of data, and the way in which the Court of Justice of the European Union (CJEU) addresses this challenge. Section IV discusses in more detail the actual joining up of European databases and highlights the hub function of Europol, the most established agency in the field. Section V emphasises the centrality of information to the exercise of power and to understanding how accountability can be operationalised. Section VI draws some preliminary conclusions that emphasise that on the spectrum of automation there is a conjoining or pooling of information with low threshold access and opacity how personal data is used in actual concrete decision-making processes. Disassembled describes the current state of accountability, ill-fitted to the nature of the challenges facing public law in the twenty-first century.

II. A Web of (In)formal Institutions and Officials

The interaction of novel systems of information collection under construction in the European Union is complex from a legal perspective. This is due not only to the data protection challenges but particularly because of the interaction of the many different legal frameworks and instruments that set up the respective databases and grant powers to European agencies and national authorities.[20] There is what has been called an 'inflation' of EU databases under amendment or construction at present,[21] and virtually no attempt has been made to see the bigger picture either in terms of the type of composite administration being created nor to position empirical practice on a broader map of normativity. A highly fragmented legal and institutional framework has been present since prioritising, early on, information sharing as a core part of transnational law enforcement agencies in Europe. In the

[20] Fundamental Rights Agency, *Fundamental Rights Interoperability* (2017); available at: http://fra.europa.eu/en/publication/2017/fundamental-rights-interoperability, accessed 28 June 2019.

[21] Heiner Busch and Matthias Monroy, *Counter-Terrorism and the Inflation of Databases* (Statewatch 2018); available at: http://statewatch.org/analyses/no-316-ct-and-inflation-eu-databases.pdf, accessed 28 June 2019.

era of automated technology, data sharing takes place through constructing and accessing databases and linking separate databases so that the reach is increased very significantly. Both the Schengen Convention[22] and the original Europol Convention[23] were instruments of public international law, conceived and applied outside the EU legal framework before being eventually incorporated (in 1999 and 2016, respectively). Eurodac[24] and the Visa Information System (VIS)[25] started off as intergovernmental instruments of the 'third pillar', established with the Treaty of Maastricht (1992), and were formally transferred to the EU system only with the Treaty of Amsterdam (1999). Access to these databases for law enforcement remained within the third pillar until the Treaty of Lisbon (2009). Now, in 2019, we also have a new, more horizontal interoperability regulation that at the same time sets up new databases.

In the past, automated computer systems helped humans (in this case civil servants) to apply rules to individual cases but we are now moving increasingly to the blurring of assistance and actual decision-making by automated systems, in particular with the help of artificial intelligence. Public officials traditionally had direct contact with citizens or clients in the execution of their work and a large degree of discretion.[26] With the aid of modern computer systems and databases, they may still exercise significant discretion in dealings with individuals and decisions, but they now operate alongside system analysts and software designers who become key systemic decision-makers.[27] In most policy fields, the European Union does not adopt decisions immediately in respect of individuals but rather serves as a kind of intermediary between different national administrations.[28] This 'second-order administration'[29] exists, however, alongside ongoing operational expansion of supranational agencies with some direct relations with individuals. This expansion is a response to what has been identified as significant dangers to public security or crisis situations, as in the case of the strengthening of Frontex's (European Border and Coast Guard) operational capacity with a view to address

22 Convention Implementing the Schengen Agreement between the Governments of the States of the Benelux Economic Union, the Federal Republic of Germany and the French Republic on the gradual abolition of checks at their common borders [1985] OJ L239/19.

23 Convention on the establishment of a European Police Office [1995] OJ C316/2.

24 Council Regulation 2725/2000 concerning the establishment of 'Eurodac' for the comparison of fingerprints for the effective application of the Dublin Convention (no longer in force) [2000] OJ L316/1.

25 Council Decision 512/2004 establishing the Visa Information System (VIS) (no longer in force) [2004] OJ L213/5.

26 Ig Snellen, 'Street Level Bureaucrats' in Ig Snellen, Marcel Thaens, and Wim van de Donk (eds), *Public Administration in the Information Age: Revisited* (IOS Press 2012) 264–80.

27 Marc Bovens and Stavros Zouridis, 'From Street-Level to System-Level Bureaucracies: How Information and Communication Technology is Transforming Administrative Discretion and Constitutional Control' (2002) 62 Public Administrative Rev 174; Danielle Keats Citron, 'Technological Due Process' (2008) 85 Washington University L Rev 1249.

28 Brito Bastos (n 5); see also, Curtin (n 5).

29 Ibid.

increased migration. Visible on the horizon are the 10,000 more European border guards promised by President Juncker in his 2018 State of the Union speech.[30] Law enforcement agencies at national and EU level are, moreover, utilizing migration control practices to abet counterterrorism activities. In particular, there is evidence that systems for monitoring and gathering data on migrants have been harnessed as part of the EU's anti-terrorism strategy.

A single-issue focus (policing, visas etc) may miss how surveillance capacity is intensifying as a result of the combination and integration of systems.[31] One of the dominant underlying drivers is the desire to bring technological systems together, to combine practices and technologies, and to integrate them into a larger whole.[32] It is in this sense that Haggerty and Ericson speak of surveillance as an assemblage 'with such combinations providing for exponential increases in the degree of surveillance capacity. Rather than exemplifying Orwell's totalitarian state-centred Oceana, this assemblage operates across both state and extra-state institutions.'[33]

The interlinking of police as state institutions at different governance levels is increasingly supplemented in practice by private actors and institutions that are not part of the state or any formal law enforcement function. They are commercial actors such as banks, airline companies, mobile phone operators, and Internet intermediaries.[34] They are mandatorily required, through instruments of public law, often at the EU level and supplemented by national law, to retain personal data from their clients and customers and pass it on to public law enforcement for access, sharing, data mining, and use in individual cases. Private actors in the European Union but also globally are being made responsible for datasets that fuel law enforcement activity in an incremental fashion.[35] Across different governance levels a fundamental security paradigm underlying European integration processes is becoming visible and taking further shape.[36] At the political level, EU laws have imposed obligations on private actors to retain personal data of different types, such as communications, financial, and travel information.[37] At the external level, international agreements with third countries have included information sharing of retained data.[38]

[30] See, Jean-Claude Juncker, 'Keynote Address' ('State of the Union' Conference, 12 September 2018, Florence).

[31] Kevin Haggerty and Richard Ericson, 'The Surveillant Assemblage' (2000) 51 British Journal of Sociology 605, 618.

[32] Ibid 610.

[33] Ibid.

[34] See further, Deirdre Curtin, 'Data Privacy Rights and Democracy: Ireland, European and Beyond' (2015) 18 Irish Journal of European Law 5.

[35] Joel Reidenberg, 'The Data Surveillance State in the United States and Europe' (2014) 49 Wake Forest L Rev 583, 600.

[36] Massimo Fichera, *The Foundations of the EU as a Polity* (Edward Elgar 2018).

[37] See further, Curtin, 'Data Privacy Rights' (n 34).

[38] Ibid 11.

These assemblages do not create an EU-level administrative state as such, but they empower national administrative states and ensure that retained information is available to them and most probably placed in European databases or otherwise available for information sharing by the police. In Europe, the manner in which EU regulation 'deputises' private actors is part of a wider law enforcement assemblage involving the mandatory collection of data by private actors and its sharing with public actors. The manner in which private actors are deputised for law enforcement through institutional structures will now be explored largely through the case of passenger name records (PNR). PNR present a striking example revealing how internal security has become intertwined with external security, nationally, in Europe, as well as globally.

III. The Deputisation of Private Actors

A. Data assemblages and private actors

Passenger name records (PNR) are an example of privately gathered big data, mandatorily collected by airline and travel companies and then transferred to public authorities for processing (and potentially data mining). A key strand in US counterterrorism efforts after 9/11 was the requirement for airlines to collect detailed personal data from their passengers in advance of travel so that such data could be made available to the US Department of Homeland Security. Parallel efforts were made to instigate a European system of PNR over many years and the EU 'internalised' to some extent US border security norms[39] in the EU–US PNR international agreement.[40] An ambitious Europe-wide PNR system was prioritised in 2015 after terrorist attacks in France. On 27 April 2016, in the immediate aftermath of the Brussels terrorist attacks of 22 March, a Directive on PNR for passengers of EU flights was approved.[41] Member States are now able to process, that is, collect, use, and retain information previously gathered in the computerised reservation systems of air carriers for commercial reasons[42] for the 'purposes of preventing, detecting, investigating and prosecuting terrorist offences and serious crime'.[43] Thus, Member States have the capacity to 'connect the dots' through a pre-emptive surveillance of travel arrangements.[44]

[39] Javier Argomaniz, 'When the EU is the "Norm-Taker": The Passenger Name Records Agreement and the EU's Internalization of US Border Security Norms' (2009) 31 J of European Integration 119.

[40] Agreement between the European Union and the United States of America on the processing and transfer of passenger name records to the United States Department of Homeland Security [2012] OJ L204/16.

[41] Directive 2016/681 on the use of passenger name record (PNR) data for the prevention, detection, investigation and prosecution of terrorist offences and serious crime [2016] OJ L119/132.

[42] Andreas Busch, 'The Regulation of Transborder Data Traffic: Disputes across the Atlantic' (2013) 23 Security and Human Rights 313.

[43] Directive 2016/681 (n 41) art 1(2).

[44] David Lyon, *Surveillance after Snowden* (Polity Press 2015) 10.

Once the PNR data are obtained by the authorities, the data are subject to methods relating to the identification of passengers who have not hitherto been known to law enforcement. These methods emerge from data mining and seek to reveal patterns of behaviour of 'concern' or presenting an 'interest'. One of the key features of data mining is the fact that it is not clear what patterns will be revealed. A system of algorithms searches the database for relevant patterns by formulating hypotheses of its own. In this way, 'interesting' patterns can be discovered in huge amounts of data. This makes it well-nigh impossible to specify the exact purpose of the intended use of the data and notify the data subjects in advance.[45] If individuals are not aware that their personal information/knowledge is being collected or how it will be used, they have no opportunity to consent or withhold consent for its collection and use. In the words of the Danish Advocate General, Saugmandsgaard Øe: 'the power to catalogue the private lives of individuals and to catalogue a population in its entirety' causes serious risks for a democratic society. This is a system of power based on personal information.[46] What can be done about it either institutionally or individually in order to prevent domination in an undemocratic fashion that also may breach privacy requirements?

B. Legality challenges

To trigger legality review mechanisms, an authorised applicant must clearly indicate a specific act or action which allegedly breach laws of a higher rank.[47] The interested person's knowledge of a potentially unlawful act or action is a precondition of holding its author to account before a court. But thanks to technology, new forms of administrative action, such as data sharing—which may involve a breach of law—have become continuous and invisible, more scattered, and less palpable. This is why more systemic challenges may be the only ones possible to challenge the legality of new systems of information gathering and retention pre-operationally—when the new system is instigated, or shortly thereafter. At this moment, a claim can be made before a national or European court that the systems are in violation of fundamental rights; in particular, that of privacy and of data protection in its specifically European understanding. Such a pre-emptive judicial review does not concern actual use of the shared information but rather its potential use and the presumed risks it entails.

[45] Frank Pasquale, *The Black Box Society. The Secret Algorithms That Control Money and Information* (Harvard UP 2015).

[46] Berthold Rittberger and Klaus H Getz, *Secrecy in Europe* (2018) 41 West European Politics 825.

[47] For instance, the Article 263 TFEU action for annulment is focused on a specifically identified legal act, as indicated by the applicant, and the Article 268 TFEU action for damages is focused on a specific act or action allegedly causing damage to the applicant.

With regard to the specific regulation of PNR, the CJEU could engage with systemic legality because specific legislation was challenged, both at the EU[48] and national levels.[49] It specified the requirements stemming from Articles 7 and 8 of the EU Charter of Fundamental Rights, regarding privacy and data protection, in particular in the recent Opinion of the CJEU on the legality of the draft international agreement on the transfer of PNR data from the European Union to Canada.[50] The European Parliament had asked the Court for an opinion on the compatibility of the envisaged agreement with the provisions of the Treaty on European Union and the EU Charter of Fundamental Rights. The draft agreement sought to provide the Canadian authorities with a legal framework allowing the mandatory transfer of PNR data from the airlines to the Canadian authorities, including information on identified individuals (passengers flying between the European Union and Canada). In terms of the private lives of individuals, the data transferred:

> may, inter alia, reveal a complete travel itinerary, travel habits, relationships existing between air passengers and the financial situation of air passengers, their dietary habits or state of health, and may even provide sensitive information about those passengers, as defined in Article 2 (e) of the envisaged agreement.[51]

That data must be transferred to the Canadian authorities as an 'intelligence tool'.[52] This is part of the contemporary security derivative which 'is not centred on who we are, nor even on what our data say about us, but on what can be imagined and inferred about who we might be –on our very proclivities and potentialities'.[53]

Once the PNR data are obtained by the Canadian authorities, the data are subject to methods relating to the identification of passengers who have not hitherto been known to law enforcement. One major problem for the Court (and Advocate General) was that none of the terms of the draft agreement actually deal with the establishment of the methods of what effectively amounts to data mining: the so-called conditions and circumstances for authorities to handle the data are not defined.[54] The lack of specificity in terms of the actual methods to be used and the fact that each 'targeted' passenger has no right to be informed of the methods used nor is assured that such 'targeting' methods are subject to administrative and/or judicial control meant that the draft agreement interfered with the rights of privacy and data protection as guaranteed by Articles 7 and 8 of the EU Charter.[55]

[48] Joined Cases C-293/12 and C-594/12 *Digital Rights Ireland and Seitlinger* [2014] ECLI:EU:C:2014:238.

[49] Joined Cases C-203/15 and C-698/15, *Tele 2 Sverige* [2016] ECLI:EU:C:2016:970.

[50] Opinion 1/15 *EU-Canada PNR Agreement* [2017] ECLI:EU:C:2017:592.

[51] Ibid para 128.

[52] Ibid para 130.

[53] Louise Amoore, 'Data Derivatives: On The Emergence of a Security Risk Calculus for Our Times' (2011) 28 Theory, Culture & Society 24.

[54] Opinion 1/15 (n 50) paras 190–191.

[55] Ibid paras 202 and 208.

Another problematic issue for the Court was the period of retention of the personal data. The retention period of five years is regarded as a particularly long period for information on the private lives of passengers to be available. Although the framing of the agreement seems to suggest that only through such retention can the Canadian authorities effectively undertake counterterrorism activities, at the end of the day, all passengers are very much 'transformed into potential suspects'.[56] The problem with PNR schemes is that suspicion is not raised prior to the collection and processing of the data (and thus targeted in some manner) but is discovered as a result of the *conduct* of collection, processing, and mining. Advocate General Mengozzi considered that masking the records would be unsatisfactory in terms of guaranteeing that personal details were blocked from unwanted access. The Court also ruled that the draft agreement was illegal because of insufficient guarantees of strictly necessary retention. There is a lack of clarity as to the irreversibility of the obligations placed on the Canadian authorities to destroy the information retained after the five-year period as well as the possibility of use by the authorities after the departure from Canada of those passengers 'in respect of whom there is no objective evidence from which it may be inferred that they may present a risk in terms of the fight against terrorism and serious transnational crime'.[57]

Thus, by using the general concept of privacy, data protection, and the principle of proportionality rooted in the EU Charter of Fundamental Rights, the Court operates as an accountability facilitator. The Court requires that the use of data, except in cases of validly established urgency, be subject to a prior review carried out either by a court or by an independent administrative body and must strictly follow a valid reason such as the prevention, detection, or prosecution of crime.[58] Thus, the Court provides tools to combat increased government (and private) surveillance in Europe. The conceptual generality of 'privacy' and 'data protection' gives them the potential to evolve in a flexible manner that addresses technological developments in, for example, pre-emptive surveillance.[59] Privately retained data that is shared with public law enforcement and other public authorities in the Member States may be assembled with other data in various EU and other databases and then accessed and used by public actors other than the data originators in different Member States or by new 'operational' actors at the supranational level (eg the new European Border Guards). EU databases and EU agencies are linked up and connected through the principle of 'interoperability', assembling information better in order to make available for actual use. Interoperability significantly enhances the surveillance powers of the European Union by enlarging the number (and types) of national authorities that can have access to personal data and arguably nullifies the

[56] Ibid para 176.
[57] Ibid para 232.2(d).
[58] Ibid para 208.
[59] Valsamis Mitsilegas, 'The Transformation of Privacy in an Era of Pre-emptive Surveillance' (2015) 20 Tilburg L Rev 35.

limited purposes for which European level databases have originally been set up. As Vavoula put it: 'through the aggregation of information from different systems, a brand powerful system might emerge'.[60]

IV. Interoperable Public Platforms in Europe

A. Regulating interoperability

Interoperability as it is used and applied in the EU context means a blurring and a joining up when it comes to the sources of information (personal data) that are used to support decisions that exist either in the supranational no man's land or in the discrete national domains. The fact is that the component parts remain active and operationally powerful. In a context of interoperable police and other databases (eg migration and border control), the local (or maybe soon-to-be supranational) street-level bureaucrats are the ones who 'use' the information acquired or shared at the supranational level but act upon it generally at the national level. The push to be more interoperable—the drive to create assemblages of data—reveals at the same time a lack of consciousness as to the fundamental challenge and necessity to reconfigure accountability in an era of composite interoperability that is rendered ever more possible by advancing technologies. The existing European regulations on data protection do not address this complex interface across systems, governance levels, and legal systems.[61]

The policy of interoperability has incrementally created a whole networked web of interlinkages among EU level databases and European and national law enforcement actors. Recently part of this interoperability was regulated by two pieces of ordinary legislation;[62] considerable pressure was exerted for agreement to be reached in final form before the end of the term of the European Parliament and new elections.[63] This is the first time that the subject matter of interoperability in the Area of Freedom Security and Justice is being dealt with by the EU co-legislators. However, it represents only a slice of the fabric of interoperability which is also advanced incrementally and less visibly in lower-level rules and practices among agencies through actual processes of granting access and sharing information. The fact is

[60] Niovi Vavoula, 'EU Immigration under Scrutiny: Towards the Normalisation of Surveillance of Movement in an Era of "Privacy Spring"' in Gert Vermeulen and Eva Lievens (eds), *Data Protection and Privacy under Pressure: Transatlantic Tensions, EU Surveillance and Big Data* (Makly 2017) 215–51, 246–47.

[61] See, Paul de Hert and Vagelis Papakonstantinou, 'The New Police and Criminal Justice Data Protection Directive. A First Analysis' (2016) 7 New Journal of European Criminal Law 7.

[62] Commission (n 19); Commission, 'Proposal for a Regulation of the European Parliament and of the Council establishing a centralised system for the identification of Member States holding conviction information on third country nationals and stateless persons (TCN) to supplement and support the European Criminal Records Information System (ECRISTCN system) and amending Regulation 1077/2011' COM(2017) 344 final.

[63] European Council, Meeting (22 and 23 June 2017)—Conclusions, EUCO 8/17, para 3.

that a policy of interoperability, however partial, is made visible in new legislation that creates yet more data bases without linking them up to the host of agencies and other databases that were also created at the level of secondary EU legislation. None of these databases or agencies are formally part of the EU treaties (with the exception of the mention made of Schengen and Europol) and the institutional structure established in that context.

The specifics of the new legislation intend to create more and new institutions: a centralised database for the first time through the construction of four new components: a European search portal; a shared biometric matching service; a common identity repository; and a multiple identity detector. These are in effect three new databases that will combine data from different sources. In Vavoula's words: 'the fancy wording that is used (component and repository) should not distract from the dangerous reality, which is the creation of massive catalogues of third-country nationals at EU level'.[64] As the language of these four components already reveals the intention is to enable authorised users (including police officers in the Member States and border officials) to, for example, carry out a single search and receive results from all the systems they are authorised to access, rather than searching each system individually. In the first stage, the new EU interoperable database will include the Schengen Information System (SIS), Eurodac (fingerprints of asylum seekers and, under new proposals, third-country nationals who have entered 'irregularly'), and the Visa Information System (VIS, personal data, and fingerprints of recipients of short-stay visas), plus three new systems currently being negotiated and/or developed: the Entry/Exit System (EES),[65] European Travel Information and Authorisation System (ETIAS, for visa-free arrivals),[66] and the European Criminal Records Information System for third-country nationals (ECRIS-TCN)[67]. The new interoperability databases will also be linked to Europol data and Interpol's Stolen and Lost Travel Documents database.

The present legislative drafts are explicitly worded so as mainly to affect non-EU citizens but once the centralised EU database is set up it will most likely be extended to include Prüm (vehicle registration, DNA, and fingerprint data), ECRIS (criminal records), and the EU Passenger Name Record system (PNR, which will cover internal flights as well as those in and out of the EU), affecting many EU citizens.

[64] Niovi Vavoula, 'Databases for Non-EU Nationals and the Right to Private Life: Towards a System of Generalized Surveillance of Movement?' in Francesca Bignami (ed), *EU Law in Populist Times: Crises and Prospects* (CUP 2019) 227–66.

[65] Regulation 2017/2226 of the European Parliament and of the Council establishing an Entry/Exit System (EES) to register entry and exit data and refusal of entry data of third-country nationals crossing the external borders of the Member States and determining the conditions for access to the EES for law enforcement purposes, and amending the Convention implementing the Schengen Agreement and Regulations 767/2008 and 1077/2011 [2017] OJ L327/20.

[66] Regulation 2018/1240 of the European Parliament and of the Council establishing a European Travel Information and Authorisation System (ETIAS) and amending Regulations 1077/2011, 515/2014, 2016/399, 2016/1624 and 2017/2226 [2018] OJ L236/1.

[67] Commission (n 62).

The plan is seemingly to include all existing, planned, and future AFSJ databases. The European Union Agency for the Operational Management of Large-Scale IT Systems in the Area of Freedom, Security and Justice (EU-LISA) is an EU agency that was founded in 2012 to ensure the uninterrupted operation of large-scale IT systems within AFSJ. It has specific tasks to 'manage operations of the second-generation Schengen Information System (SIS II), the Visa Information System (VIS) and EURODAC'.[68]

The question of interoperability has been most sensitive regarding access to VIS and Eurodac since both databases were primarily designed as instruments of migration control. Law enforcement agencies at national and EU level have attempted to utilise migration control practices to abet counterterrorism activities. In particular, there is evidence that systems for monitoring and gathering data on migrants have been harnessed as part of the EU's anti-terrorism strategy.[69] Moreover, Brouwer argues that all these measures of data processing may result in new forms of 'digital entry bans' on third-country nationals without a realistic prospect of access to justice.[70]

Beyond the creation of new agencies and the creation of new centralised databases, Europol stands out because of its pivotal position as a matter of embedded institutional practice at the centre of the web of networked databases and actors. The idea behind the very notion of the interoperability of police databases is that the data are collected locally and may be maintained locally or uploaded in a common 'database' ready for circulation or sharing upon a certain number of triggers. It does not necessarily require new or overarching integrated databases as such but rather that national information may be uploaded and made interoperable through a hit/no-hit system, so that it is easily known whether data on a suspect (or migrant) are held on the database of a sister organisation.[71]

In its report of 11 May 2017, the high-level expert group on information systems and interoperability concluded that the European Union has already made substantial steps towards granting Europol wider access to relevant EU databases.[72] Europol already has the right to access and directly search data entered into the Schengen Information System (SIS)[73] for arrests, for discreet and specific

[68] See further https://www.eulisa.europa.eu/, accessed 28 June 2019.

[69] Niovi Vavoula, *Immigration and Privacy in the Law of the European Union—The Case of Databases* (Brill Nijhoff 2019); Valsamis Mitsilegas and Niovi Vavoula, 'The Normalisation of Surveillance of Movement in an Era of Reinforcing Privacy Standards' in Phillippe Bourbeau (ed), *Handbook on Migration and Security* (Edward Elgar 2017) 232–51.

[70] Evelien Brouwer, 'A Very Hungry Caterpillar. Entry Bans and Information-sharing in the Field of Migration and Security: Revitalising the Non-discriminatory Approach of Data Protection' (unpublished paper on file with the author).

[71] Marieke de Goede, 'From Justice and Home Affairs to Security Union, Platform Integration?' (unpublished manuscript 2018) 9.

[72] Commission (n 14) 35.

[73] Council Decision 2007/533/JHA on the establishment, operation and use of the second generation Schengen Information System (SIS II) [2007] OJ L205/63, art 41.

checks, and for objects for seizure. So far, Europol 'has carried out a relatively limited number of searches in SIS'.[74] The Memorandum of Understanding between Europol and EU-LISA also reflects upon the access of other databases by Europol. Access by Europol to large-scale IT systems operated by EU-LISA, such as SIS II, VIS, and Eurodac provide Europol, when required for the performance of its tasks and within the limits of its mandate, 'with input to its analytical and investigative work in preventing and combating organised crime, terrorism and other forms of serious crime'.[75] The recently installed capability to launch automated batch searches facilitates more structured cross-checking of large amounts of relevant Europol data against the SIS.[76]

SIS II 'has been progressively morphed from a reporting system into a powerful intelligence database'.[77] The use by Europol of SIS II grew significantly with searches increasing from 630 in 2016 to 21,951 from 1 January until 11 September 2017.[78] The success of SIS II 'lies in its flexibility, vague wording and wide discretion to define the outer limits of who constitutes part of the risk population and be subject to surveillance of movement'.[79] Creating links between alerts may lead to situations where persons who were previously innocent become connected with crime or criminal networks, with adverse effects on their status.[80] Given the size and nature of SIS II this is of concern. On 31 December 2016, there were over 70 million alerts stored in the system, showing a net increase of over 7 million (12 per cent) compared with 31 December 2015. Since the second generation of the system was brought into operation on 9 April 2013—when there were almost 47 million alerts stored in the database—there was a net increase of 51 per cent in alerts stored. Regarding the data reported by Member States, in 2016 SIS II was searched almost 4 billion times, 1 billion more than in 2015—an increase of 39 per cent—when the number of reported queries was 2.8 billion. Searches performed in 2016 increased by 81 per cent compared with searches in 2014, the first year with full reporting available. Along with the increase in searches, there was also an increase in the number of reported hits on foreign alerts. In 2016, 200,788 hits were reported, showing an increase of 30 per cent compared with hits reported for 2015.[81]

[74] High-level Expert Group (n 14) 35. 32,000 searches in 2017 does not seem 'relatively limited'.

[75] Memorandum of Understanding between Europol and EU-LISA, preamble (3) 2–3 and legal acts cited therein which regulate the access by Europol.

[76] Europol, *Europol Programming Document 2018-2020* (22 January 2018) 37–38; Europol, *2017 Consolidated Annual Activity Report* (Europol 2018, 3 May 2018) 20, where it says: 'Schengen Information System (SIS) II: the batch search functionality was installed at the end of 2016. The efficiency of the process had a positive impact on the ability of Europol to utilise the system in supporting operations, with searches moving from 630 in 2016 to 21,951 from 1 January until 11 September 2017.'

[77] Vavoula (n 69) 134.

[78] Europol, *2017 Consolidated Annual Activity Report* (n 76) 20. Unfortunately, 'SIS II—2017 Statistics' (February 2018) do not cover Europol;https://www.eulisa.europa.eu/Publications/Reports/2017%20SIS%20II%20Statistics.pdf, accessed 28 June 2019.

[79] Vavoula (n 69) 135.

[80] See Boehm (n 17) 266.

[81] EU-LISA, 'Report on the technical functioning of Central SIS II and the Communication infrastructure, including the security therefore and the bilateral and multilateral exchange of supplementary

B. Policing by hits

Europol was designed as the European Policing Office that was formed to promote and strengthen cooperation among law enforcement agencies in the EU.[82] Europol has no executive operational authority as such. All arrest and policing functions are carried out by competent law enforcement authorities within Member States and third countries. In Europol's own words, it acts as a support centre for law enforcement operations primarily through analysing information to act as an intelligence hub and a centre for law enforcement expertise.[83] It gradually transformed into an intelligence network and a real hub for sharing information and intelligence exchange with national liaison officers from police and intelligence services and later with police forces from third states.[84] This represents a considerable evolution from its initial position where Member States did not share enough of their police files with it. It now has a strong added benefit in terms of the analysis of local data it can offer. It has deepened and intensified its internal relations not only with the police forces of the various Member States but also with other agencies and associated databases as they have come into being (eg Eurodac and Schengen) and a host of third countries.[85] Most importantly, it has direct relations and agreements with private parties in terms of information collection as well. Europol's network of liaison officers, the platforms that Europol provides for information exchange with and between Member States and its specialty criminal intelligence analysis provide added value.[86]

Europol processes personal data in three ways: in the Europol Information System (EIS), the analysis work files, and the index system. In addition, a secure information exchange tool, SIENA, connects the Member States via the Europol national units and the Europol liaison bureaus but does not routinely involve Europol.[87] The EIS interconnects the databases of the national police of the Member States with Europol and allows introducing and accessing data from it. According to the new Europol Regulation,[88] the data introduced in the EIS must be necessary for the performance of Europol's tasks. It may be processed only to

information between Member States' (July 2017) 6–7; available at: https://www.eulisa.europa.eu/Publications/Reports/EL-AE-17-001-EN-N.pdf, accessed 28 June 2019.

[82] See Emma Disley et al, *Evaluation of the Implementation of the Europol Council Decision and of Europol's activities* (RAND Europe 2012) xv.

[83] Ibid 3; Boehm (n 17) 177.

[84] Ballaschk (n 12) 51.

[85] For the lists of agreements with third countries, see https://www.europol.europa.eu/partners-agreements/operational-agreements and https://www.europol.europa.eu/partners-agreements/strategic-agreements, accessed 28 June 2019.

[86] Disley et al (n 82) xvi.

[87] Boehm (n 17) 182.

[88] Regulation 2016/794 of the European Parliament and of the Council on the European Union Agency for Law Enforcement Cooperation (Europol) and replacing and repealing Council Decisions 2009/371/JHA, 2009/934/JHA, 2009/935/JHA, 2009/936/JHA, and 2009/968/JHA [2016] OJ L 135/53.

identify persons who are suspected or convicted of criminal offences in respect of which Europol is competent; to carry out strategic, thematic, or operational analyses; and to facilitate information exchange between the Member States, Europol, other Union bodies, third countries, and international organisations.[89] This represents a considerable broadening from the original Europol Convention and later Decision.[90] It includes the fact that an individual might one day commit a crime. Data stored in the EIS can be accessed by all Member States and liaison officers from third states. Creating links between alerts may lead to situations where persons who were previously innocent become connected with crime or criminal networks with obvious adverse effects on their status.

Statistics provide evidence of ever-increasing information sharing by the Member States with Europol.[91] The most recent numbers regarding Europol can be found in its 2017 Consolidated Annual Activity Report.[92] The use of the EIS reached an all-time peak by the end of 2017, represented by the number of objects stored[93] and of searches[94]. This far exceeded forecast results, largely due to intense communication activities and the systematic use of EIS in business processes across Member States' competent authorities. The area of counterterrorism experienced the most important increase in terms of number of objects in EIS.[95] In 2017, the number of EIS objects related to terrorism increased mainly due to the massive upload of data from the FBI Terrorist Screening Centre.[96] There was an increase of 442 per cent in the number of persons linked to terrorism in the EIS, compared to the previous year. With this increase, terrorism became the biggest crime area in the EIS with terrorism-related data covering more than 50 per cent of all objects. The number of SIENA messages exchanged by counterterrorism units almost quadrupled in 2017 compared to 2016.[97] More than half of these were exchanged by third parties. The number of contributors of data linked to terrorism increased: in total, twenty-two Member States and fifteen third parties contributed via the Europol Operational Centre to this data. The increase of communication volume over the last four years more than doubled. The number of SIENA messages exchanged with third parties was almost 13 per cent of the total in 2017, an increase of around 35 per cent compared to the previous year.[98] Forty-five EU Member States/third-party counterterrorism units were configured to SIENA. This includes key US law enforcement agencies such as the Federal Bureau of Investigation (FBI), Customs

[89] Ibid art 18(2).
[90] Boehm (n 17) 183.
[91] Disley et al (n 82) xxiii.
[92] Europol, *2017 Consolidated Annual Activity Report* (n 76). The figures following are all unless otherwise stated taken from this report.
[93] 1,062,236 objects in 2017; in 2009 it included 135,489 objects; Boehm (n 17) 193.
[94] 2,478,825 searches in 2017.
[95] Europol, *2017 Consolidated Annual Activity Report* (n 76) 9.
[96] Ibid 33.
[97] Ibid 4.
[98] Ibid 23.

and Border Protection, Immigration and Customs Enforcement (ICE), and the US Secret Service (USSS), who were provided with the possibility to connect to SIENA directly from their own headquarters.[99]

Europol has deepened and intensified its internal relations with the police forces of the various Member States. It has also deepened and intensified its external relations with other agencies and associated databases as they have come into being (Eurodac, Frontex)[100] and a host of third countries. Europol also closely cooperates with other EU agencies and satellite organisations.[101]

Europol now has direct relations and agreements with private parties in terms of information collection as well. What we see is significant expansion across the board in terms of cooperation agreements and working arrangements in particular with the private sector. Eight new strategic partnerships were seemingly signed between Europol and the private sector in 2017 and Europol supported forty-nine operations in which private partners were involved.[102] The new possibilities for cooperation with private parties are considerable and include the ability to receive (bulk) personal data from any private party, as long as Europol processes it only to identify the Member State concerned. Europol may also send personal data to private parties in individual cases.[103] This is a substantial evolution in the old position that was considered too restrictive where information from private parties had to be routed through a Europol National Unit.[104] The public information available on the nature of the cooperation with private parties is, however, very patchy.

Interoperability, as it is used and applied in this European context, means a blurring and a joining up when it comes to the sources of information (personal data) that are used to support decisions in one way or another that exist either in the supranational no man's land or in the discrete national domains. At the same time, it counterintuitively implies uncoupling or disconnection from mechanisms of accountability that are themselves neither conjoined nor composite. The fact is that the component parts remain active and operationally powerful. In a context of interoperable police and other databases (eg migration and border control), the local (and soon supranational) public officials on the ground or at the border are

[99] Europol, *Europol Review 2016–2017* (Europol 2017) 68.

[100] Disley et al (n 82) xxxii; See further, Agreement on Operational Cooperation between the European Police Office (Europol) and the European Agency for the Management of Operational Cooperation at the External Borders of the Member States of the European Union (Frontex) [2015], available at: https://www.europol.europa.eu/agreements/frontex, accessed 28 June 2019; see also on operations with Frontex: https://www.europol.europa.eu/organisations/european-border-and-coast-guard-agency-frontex, accessed 28 June 2019; Europol, *2017 Consolidated Annual Activity Report* (n 76) 22.

[101] Examples cited include EUNAVFOR MED, EEAS/CSDP, EUROGENDFOR, EMSA, SatCen, EASO, and EU INTCEN, ibid 26 (no further specificities provided).

[102] Ibid 23.

[103] Commission, 'Stronger and Smarter Information Systems for Borders and Security' (Communication) COM (2017) 205 final.

[104] Disley et al (n 82) xxxiv.

the ones who 'use' the information acquired or shared at the supranational level but act upon it generally at the national level. The disassembling is arguably a side effect of a push to be more interoperable, a lack of consciousness as to the fundamental challenge and necessity to reconfigure accountability in an era of composite interoperability that is rendered ever more possible by advancing technologies.

V. Disassembled Accountability

A. Information disconnect

The modern capacity to process personal information automatically is generally considered a game-changer for the administrative state. The resulting technological imperative has been described as a driver for public officials to 'seek data on individuals to design and evaluate programs, to augment their prestige and power, and, as a product of a supposed technological imperative, to enable them to use the latest hardware and software programs'.[105] A citizen is seen, but does not see; she is 'an object of information, never a subject in communication'.[106] If she does not see, does not know, and is not consulted or informed then activation of traditional administrative law procedural remedies may be difficult, not to say impossible, except when a clearly defined decision can be the subject of adjudication. Automation may, however, generate significant problems for the adjudication of important procedural rights. Secrecy surrounding the data input into the systems and the way it is validated, accessed, shared, and used make review of the facts supporting a system's decision very difficult. The very opacity of automated systems entails disassembling traditional mechanisms of accountability which imply access to information as a first step.

It is indeed from the opacity of power that the demand for accountability arises.[107] The very function of accountability is to hold those public institutions who exercise power to account for their use of that power.[108] According to the definition of accountability by Bovens, the provision of information is the first stage of the accountability process upon which all further stages rest.[109] For an accountability relationship to exist overall there needs to be an actor (the power holder) and a forum to hold to account. Information sharing arrangements are key to

[105] Michael Flaherty, *Protecting Privacy in Surveillance Societies: The Federal Republic of Germany, Sweden, France, Canada, and the United States* (University of North Carolina Press 2014) 13.

[106] Michel Foucault, *Discipline and Punishment* (Alan Sheridan trans, Vintage 1975) 200.

[107] See Andreas Schedler, 'Conceptualising Accountability' in Andreas Schedler et al (eds), *The Self-Restraining State: Power and Accountability in New Democracies* (Lynne Riener Publishers 1999) 13–28, 20.

[108] Ibid; Carol Harlow, *Accountability in the EU* (OUP 2002) 8.

[109] Marc Bovens, 'Analysing and Assessing Accountability: A Conceptual Framework' (2007) 13 ELJ 447.

access power.[110] Providing information changes the allocation of power both for those who take decisions (the power holders) and those who want to hold them to account for use of that information. Without information, the power holders cannot have the basis for their decision and its accuracy or otherwise challenged. In this sense, information is both an instrument of empowerment and its withholding to those outside the enclave a source of dis-empowerment.

In the national law enforcement arena, executives enjoy a wide strategic and operational discretion where 'normal' accountability mechanisms do not traditionally apply. At the level of EU databases, the information holder is formally at the European level and subject to its rules and regulations and the data are transferred/shared with an information recipient that is different to the (Member State) information provider. In this information triangle, the common outsider is the individual whose data are at stake. Without information to hold the power holder to account, the individual cannot hope to attain accountability for the actual decision taken which may well be of a transient nature—for example exclusion from the territory of a Member State/EU—and thus in many cases, will not lead to a full judicial hearing where the data relied on is scrutinised at the national level. In the area of police cooperation and shared information in interoperable databases, there are a number of characteristics that are quite specific and might lead to the conclusion that mechanisms of accountability are quite simply 'unplugged' or disconnected from the content and use of the data in question (as opposed to its retention and collection). This customisation of existing notions of accountability to interoperable AFSJ databases and agency cooperation may have to lead to novel conceptualisations of what accountability can mean in this context. This is beyond the scope of the present chapter; here the focus is as a first cut confined to the secrecy rules and the manner in which they result in a roadblock that hinders any progress down the road of any accountability mechanism.

B. Secrecy road-blocks

The secrecy rules that apply in the arena of security and police cooperation are 'meta-paradigmatic'.[111] In terms of 'ownership' of the original data collected, the Member State is all-powerful in a manner that is not plugged in to the actual access and subsequent use of the data at the European or trans-governmental level. This reality is not addressed by administrative law as the formal principle that applies in this context is that of originator control. Interoperability as a principle exacerbates

[110] Albert Meijer, 'Transparency' in Marc Bovens et al (eds), *The Oxford Handbook of Public Accountability* (OUP 2014) 507–24, 517–18.

[111] Liora Lazarus, 'Secrecy as a Meta-Paradigmatic Challenge' in Benjamin Goold and Liora Lazarus (eds), *Security and Human Rights* (Hart Publishing 2019).

the obscurity and difficult accountability that results from the fragmented character of composite administration, where the EU administration enjoys the status of a 'second-order' administration that is only answerable to other administrations, if at all. It becomes hard to pinpoint at exactly what level of administration, EU or national, mistakes are made. It is also close to impossible for the public or for institutions not involved in the interoperable (law enforcement) networks to demand access to them and the data processing. Increased digital sharing of information creates new possibilities of error, in particular with wrong or outdated data. The effect of error is greatly amplified as a matter of fact because interoperability and sharing enables the data to seep out and across a wide variety of systems including those where data is relied upon and used for potentially very different purposes. A database that generates bad information may not have a formal record of error, making legal challenge very difficult. It may only be in exceptional circumstances that the existence of such errors and their consequences may reach the light of day.[112]

The requirement to share information as part of an accountability arrangement can derive either from rights held by the accountability forum in the Bovens definition—such as access to information rights—or from obligations incumbent on the forum including the delivery of annual reports or the required appearance in a public hearing.[113] Potential accountability forums will generally have no automatic access to the actual data in databases and are reliant on the information they are actually given by the executive power in question (either European or national). This means that they may be structurally short of information with a greater information asymmetry than normally applies in this context. The courts may of course be significant accountability facilitators, as we saw in section II on the 'legality workarounds' but only at specific regulatory moments, for example, when data retention or other legislation being adopted or indirectly challenged.[114] When it comes to national courts, their role is with regard to their own executives use of data but any accountability they exercise is unplugged from the databases themselves, which exist at the European level.[115] It is not clear to what extent supervisors such as the European Ombudsman and the European Data Protection Supervisor may in some circumstances operate as potential 'information multipliers';[116] this requires further empirical study and is beyond the scope of this chapter.

[112] Also picked up by the House of Lords in an earlier report: House of Lords, 'Europol: Coordinating the Fight Against Serious and Organised Crime' (European Union Committee, 29th Report of Sessions 2007–08); available at: http://www.publications.parliament.uk/pa/ld200708/ldselect/ldeucom/183/183.pdf, accessed 28 June 2019.

[113] Carolyn Moser, *EU Civilian Crisis Management. Law and Practice of Accountability* (unpublished PhD thesis, Utrecht University 2018) 135.

[114] Deirdre Curtin, 'Second Order Secrecy and Europe's Legality Mosaics' (2018) 41 West European Politics 846, 858.

[115] Moser (n 113) 244.

[116] The term coined by Moser (n 115) 278.

The optimal moment for legality challenges as part of wider ambient accountability in practice is indeed when new systems of information gathering and retention are instigated—or shortly thereafter—although as the *Schrems* case[117] shows claims of illegality can be raised before national courts many years after the entry into operation of the new system. A claim can be made before a national or European court that the systems are in violation of fundamental rights—in particular, that of privacy and of data protection in its specifically European understanding. This does not concern actual use of the shared information but rather its potential use and the risks it entails in terms of actual use and conduct. But what of actual use of the data accessed in the decisions or actions of law enforcement or other public officials? The link between access to information and actual administrative or other public decision making is itself shrouded in secrecy both systemically and operationally.

C. Decisional opacity

Who actually takes the decisions or actions in the intricate set-up that is information sharing on an interoperable basis? As Cuellár put it: 'increasingly, agencies and entire governments will face the challenge of how to instruct complex machines so routinely guiding human decisions that it becomes exceedingly difficult to tell where an algorithm's nudge ends and an accountable individual's choice begins'.[118] Complex questions arise regarding knowing who prepares the information, making it possible to search on it and achieve 'hits'. Moreover, the actual use of that information to take decisions of whatever kind concerning individuals is not necessarily documented in a manner that is shared. The manner and way in which the private actors (airline companies, mobile phone operators, Internet intermediaries, banks etc) input into data that are ultimately shared will often be blurred, with a resulting impact on the possibility of an accountability relationship. There is no single actor that can be held to account in informational terms. That is clear too from the schematic discussion on Europol in section IV. At best, there are different actors at different governance levels and subject to different rules and practices that come into play in terms of the possibility of accountability. It seems inevitable that various types of accountability fora may be relevant but in relation to different 'bits' of the whole. Moreover, how can Europol or any actor be held to account for information that is both informal and largely invisible?[119]

[117] C-362/14 *Schrems* [2015] ECLI:EU:C:2015:650.

[118] Mariano-Florentino Cuellár, '*Cyberdelegation and the Administrative State*' (Stanford Public Law Working Paper No 2754385 2016) 134 and 159.

[119] This question is also posed in a different context in Moser (n 113) 120.

The secrecy that protects databases from abuse may facilitate abuse of power from within.[120] At the very least, responsibilities are hidden and dispersed.[121] Predictive and information-guided policing 'creates relationships between information sources and decision-making processes that were previously separate'.[122] Challenges to legality or even political accountability by parliaments are ill-equipped to deal with fundamental issues of database administration. They may (weakly) assist at foundational moments when systems for the retention or acquisition of information are put in place but it is difficult to see a role for parliamentary scrutiny relating to the subsequent maintenance, sharing, and actual use of that information. Focusing on the latter moments of the information process may require more administrative-type solutions, also in the area of criminal law, and is part of a future-orientated research agenda.

VI. Conclusion

The contours I have discussed in this chapter are not about the 'deep' secrets of states, either individually or collectively, but rather about administrative systems and institutions that are quietly and incrementally being put in place at various levels but in a coordinated fashion in a context that very largely escapes existing contours of administrative law at any level, as well as at the level of individual states. More substantively, it is on the likely significance of automation for accountability and democracy beyond the state, both European and global. There is of course neither a full-blown automated and interoperable (police) state in Europe, nor is accountability disassembled. There is no fully automated system at the European level in the sense that policy is applied and decisions taken without any human intervention. Nor could there be; in the arena of law enforcement there can never be full automation as human intervention and discretion will be required as a matter of course (one hopes). On the spectrum of automation there is rather a conjoining or pooling of information with low threshold access and opacity or blurring of use in actual concrete decision-making processes. In this sense, there is no *de jure* delegation of rule-making power as such, but public officials cannot detect when rules in an automated system depart from policies precisely because of their opacity. In the law enforcement context, the investigatory capacity of national law enforcement improves when multiple databases are connected and the aggregate data made searchable (inter-operability). In linking the data to identifiable human beings, decisions will follow (eg expulsion of migrants at borders). An interoperable system

[120] Projectgroep Visie op de politiefunctie, *Politie in ontwikkeling. Visie op de politiefunctie* (Raad van Hoofd-Commissarissen, NPI, 2005) 21, cited by Bert-Jaap Koops, 'Technology and the Crime Society: Rethinking Legal Protection' (2009) 1 Law, Innovation and Technology 93, 113.

[121] Projectgroep (n 120) 16.

[122] De Goede (n 71) 9.

of data requires accurate and up-to-date data that has systems in place for originators and accessors of data to correct and delete data. This is exactly what is lacking at the European level with the very real risk that inaccurate data simply continue to circulate and spread with no way of stopping this or remedying against a careless or negligent originator of data.

My chapter goes beyond a discussion of how accountability has evolved for certain distinct actors such as Europol, to highlight the fuzziness and disconnection with accountability mechanisms that result from the collection, sharing, and use of shared data both at the European level and at the joined-up national level. We observe in the process how the Area of Freedom, Security and Justice is at the cutting edge of understanding where some European integration processes are moving: not simply supranational, not simply intergovernmental, but towards something much more conjoined. The European administrative state is to be understood in a very broad sense as also including those supranational agencies and databases in the field of law enforcement and flanking areas (eg migration and border control). A system based on shared data requires accurate, up-to-date information and quality controls that go beyond the non- compulsory obligation for the originator of data to correct or delete wrong data. Shared data and interoperable databases arguably need to develop a broader culture that includes the auditing of data, standards for record collection, and perhaps, as some have more radically discussed, even notice requirements for targeted suspects.[123] Databases in any event require structural oversight which might involve transparency of access and logs,[124] at least for specialised supervisors. The challenge more broadly may well be to develop administrative oversight, considering what Koops calls the 'paradigm shift' in criminal law with its increasing footprint into more architectural and preventative approaches to crime.[125] Shoehorning interoperable databases into existing forms of individual legal protections is unlikely to work, or at least only in highly specific and limited circumstances.

Much of the discussion underlying this chapter consists in the pursuit of non-public information and in attempting to see beyond the black box of operational activities in sensitive areas of national policy-making such as law enforcement and security cooperation. In making visible the missing link between information and accountability forums of whatever kind, a conversation can hopefully begin about how to link information provision within the contours of assembled accountability and its future operationalisation. Disassembled accountability implies the exact opposite: a form of accountability that is assembled to match the data assemblages and networks of police and intelligence, adapted to the nature of automation and

123 Andrew Guthrie Ferguson, 'Big Data and Predictive Reasonable Suspicion' (2016) 163 University of Pennsylvania L Rev 327, 393.

124 Reidenberg (n 35) 607.

125 Koops (n 120) 94 and 115.

artificial intelligence. Assembled accountability would, on the other hand, overcome the current divide between the originator of the data and the user who are for now left pulled apart, embedded in different legal systems, and with no obvious remedies in terms of inaccurate information and its correction. A new research agenda involves a more sustained and comprehensive reflection on the adaptation of the existing parameters of accountability to the automated administrative state. This is no easy task, but the contours of the systemic as opposed to operational challenges are a basis on which Europe's public lawyers can move towards a vista of more assembled accountability—hopefully, no mirage.

13

The Administrative State and the Fundamentals of Public Law

*ACL Davies**

It can sometimes seem as if the day-to-day workings of the administrative state are far removed from the fundamentals of public law. The legal details of the immigration regime, the welfare state or the National Health Service (NHS) might be viewed as topics in their own right—as the preserve of specialist immigration, social security, or healthcare lawyers, where the generalist administrative lawyer might, and might reasonably, fear to tread. My aim in this contribution is to illustrate the importance of applying the fundamentals of administrative law, so clearly articulated in Paul Craig's scholarship, to these areas of sometimes mind-boggling complexity, in order to uphold essential rule-of-law values in the governance and operation of administrative institutions.

I will take as an example some recent litigation about the NHS. The statute currently governing the NHS is the Health and Social Care Act 2012. This legislation, which was highly controversial at the time of its introduction, sought to promote a competitive market for service provision within the NHS, a concept I explain in more detail in the following section. This choice of structure for the NHS has since fallen out of favour, and the NHS is moving back towards a more 'integrated' model, in which a single organisation takes responsibility for all or most healthcare within a particular geographical area. It might be expected that this change—which amounts to a complete reversal of the previous policy—would be brought about by new legislation. However, there is little appetite for legislation on the NHS at the time of writing, partly because so much parliamentary time is occupied by the UK's exit from the European Union, and partly because the Government does not have a majority to force through legislation on potentially controversial topics. But the policy change is proceeding regardless. This has been challenged in two applications for judicial review, *Hutchinson*[1] and

* Professor of Law and Public Policy, Faculty of Law, University of Oxford. This contribution considers developments up to 2 February 2019. I am grateful to the editors for their comments on an earlier draft. Responsibility for errors and opinions remains my own.

[1] *R (Hutchinson) v Secretary of State for Health and Social Care* [2018] EWHC 1698 (Admin).

ACL Davies, *The Administrative State and the Fundamentals of Public Law* In: *The Foundations and Future of Public Law*. Edited by: Elizabeth Fisher, Jeff King, Alison L Young, Oxford University Press (2020). © Oxford University Press.
DOI: 10.1093/oso/9780198845249.003.0013

Shepherd,[2] in which it has been argued that different aspects of the new policy are *ultra vires* the 2012 Act. Neither application was successful.

In this short contribution, I explain the legislative background, analyse the decisions in the two cases, and offer a critique of the judges' reasoning. I conclude by emphasising the importance from a rule-of-law perspective of taking challenges to the *vires* of administrative decisions and actions seriously, even in complex cases.

I. Context

The UK NHS has long been a central focus of national political debate. While it enjoys cross-party support—and, indeed, it would be politically disastrous for a mainstream party to propose its abolition—there are ongoing concerns about its resourcing. On the one hand, there is general political pressure against raising taxes and a variety of other demands on the public purse. On the other hand, it is clear that a combination of advances in medical treatment and an ageing population are placing greater strain on the NHS because more treatment options are theoretically available and patients tend to have more complex, long-term needs.

One superficially attractive solution to this conundrum has been to search for ways of making the NHS more efficient. In theory at least, this would enable the service to cut out wastage and to make the best use of available resources. Most people who have spent time in hospital or engaging with other health services have anecdotal evidence of inefficiencies of some kind, so efficiency drives can capture the public imagination, too.

Probably the most radical example of this was the introduction of the 'internal market' into the NHS in the 1990s, under the National Health Service and Community Care Act 1990.[3] Part of the thinking behind this legislation was that the creation of 'purchasers' and 'providers' within the NHS would drive efficiency savings and quality improvements as providers competed with each other for 'business' (patient referrals and funding) from purchasers. It involved the application of many of the ideas of a school of thought known as 'New Public Management' (NPM) to the NHS.[4] Of course, this change was also highly controversial on a political level. Some critics thought that the idea of creating a competitive market within the NHS (and other public services) would be contrary to the public service ethos and to core values of equity and fairness. Others perceived the policy as a

[2] *R (Shepherd) v NHS Commissioning Board* [2018] EWCA Civ 2849.

[3] See Department of Health, *Working for Patients* (Cm 555, 1989), and for commentary, ACL Davies, *Accountability: A Public Law Analysis of Government by Contract* (OUP 2001); Rob Flynn and Gareth Williams (eds), *Contracting for Health: Quasi-Markets and the National Health Service* (OUP 1997).

[4] The foundational text of the NPM movement was David Osborne and Ted Gaebler, *Reinventing Government: How the Entrepreneurial Spirit is Transforming the Public Sector* (Plume 1993). For a more critical account, see Christopher Foster and Francis Plowden, *The State Under Stress: Can the Hollow State be Good Government?* (Open UP 1996) ch 3.

move towards privatisation, because of the possibility that private providers might compete alongside NHS entities for contracts from purchasers.[5] The political controversy made it difficult to evaluate the policy effectively.

The 'internal market' went through a variety of more or less radical reforms over the years. The Labour Government elected in 1997 purported to abolish the market but in fact kept it in place, albeit with some important changes that tackled what might have been seen as the 'worst excesses' of the market.[6] For example, a tariff pricing system was introduced so that prices for particular services were set centrally and were no longer the subject of competition on the part of providers. The original system in which General Practitioners' (GPs') practices could opt to become 'fundholders' with the power to purchase some non-emergency services (with Health Authorities purchasing everything else) was replaced with unified local organisations called 'Primary Care Trusts' which purchased secondary care and provided primary care. This was intended to reduce some of the transaction costs associated with having large numbers of small-scale purchasers in the market.

In 2012, the Health and Social Care Act (HSCA), introduced by the Coalition Government, took the reform of the market in a different direction.[7] As I wrote at the time, the aim of the Act was to make the market more 'real'.[8] This objective was pursued in two different but complementary respects. On the one hand, purchasers and providers were to be freed from central government control, so that those who were keen to innovate and explore opportunities in the market would be free to do so. On the other hand, market behaviour was to be enforced by subjecting purchasers and providers to competition and procurement law. This would require purchasers and providers who were more sceptical about the market to act commercially because of the prospect of legal challenges if they did not. It is worth examining the 2012 Act in a little more detail.

Under the regime put in place by the 2012 Act, the concept of 'provision' covered all health services except those provided by GPs, who were placed on the 'purchaser' side of the purchaser/provider split. Providers could be NHS bodies, private firms, or charities. NHS providers could take one of two legal forms: NHS Trusts or NHS Foundation Trusts, neither of which is a trust in the legal sense. NHS Trust was the default status, but an NHS Trust could acquire Foundation status if it could meet a set of financial and governance criteria and would then

5 The 'contracts' under this regime were not legally enforceable: NHS and Community Care Act 1990, s 4.

6 Health Act 1999, and see Department of Health, *The New NHS: Modern, Dependable* (Cm 3807, 1997). For comment on some aspects of these and subsequent developments, see ACL Davies, 'Foundation Hospitals: A New Approach to Autonomy in the Delivery of Public Services?' [2004] PL 807; ACL Davies, 'A Tangled Web? Accountability and the Commissioning Role in the "New" NHS' (2007) 18 King's LJ 387.

7 See Department of Health, *Equity and Excellence: Liberating the NHS* (Cm 7881 July 2010), and NHS Future Forum, *Summary Report on Proposed Changes to the NHS* (Department of Health, June 2011).

8 ACL Davies, 'This Time, it's for Real: The Health and Social Care Act 2012' (2013) 76 MLR 564, 565.

enjoy greater autonomy than an ordinary NHS Trust. A key innovation in the 2012 Act was that all providers, whether public or private, had to hold a 'licence' in order to provide services to the NHS.[9] The licensing regime was operated by a regulator called 'Monitor', which became part of NHS Improvement in 2016. The licensing regime required providers to be 'fit and proper' and to undertake not to engage in anti-competitive practices, among other things. The quality of healthcare services being provided (by providers of all types) was, and continues to be, regulated separately by the Care Quality Commission.

Perhaps surprisingly, the 2012 Act retained and placed on a statutory footing the 'tariff' system in which prices for particular procedures were set nationally.[10] The task of determining the tariff was transferred from the Department of Health to Monitor. Although this appears to contradict the overall objective of making the NHS more of a market, it was argued that the tariff had the benefit of forcing more expensive providers to become more efficient in order to deliver services at the tariff price without making a loss, thus keeping costs down overall.

However, the clearest example of the 2012 Act seeking to make the market more real on the provider side was the new role for Monitor as sector regulator concurrently with the Office of Fair Trading (OFT) (now the Competition and Markets Authority (CMA)) for the purposes of Part 1 of the Competition Act 1998.[11] This enabled Monitor to tackle alleged infringements of competition law by providers, such as abuses of a dominant position or agreements to restrict competition. Monitor was also given concurrent powers with the OFT to make a market investigation reference to the Competition Commission (also now subsumed into the CMA) under Part 4 of the Enterprise Act 2002.[12] It was already arguable that NHS providers were subject to competition law prior to the 2012 Act because they fell within the Court of Justice of the European Union's (CJEU's) definition of an 'undertaking', but the Act was an important sign that the Government both accepted this and sought to encourage greater use of competition law to regulate the market.[13]

The 2012 Act also brought about changes on the 'purchasing' or 'commissioning' side. The 151 Primary Care Trusts were replaced by some 212 Clinical Commissioning Groups (CCGs).[14] Each CCG covered a particular geographical area and all NHS GPs working in that area were required to join.[15] Although much was initially made of the idea of CCGs as GP-led groups, the Regulations ultimately required a variety of other people (the finance director, lay representatives,

[9] HSCA ss 81–110.
[10] HSCA ss 115–127.
[11] HSCA ss 72–80.
[12] HSCA s 73.
[13] See Okeoghene Odudu, 'Are State Owned Healthcare Providers that are Funded by General Taxation Undertakings Subject to Competition Law?' (2011) 32 ECLR 231.
[14] HSCA s 34. On CCGs, see generally HSCA ss 10, 13–14, 25–28, and Schedule 2.
[15] HSCA s 28.

a nurse, and a clinician in secondary care) to be included on the CCG's board.[16] Some CCGs relied heavily on private firms for the day-to-day running of the commissioning process.[17] The core statutory duty of each CCG was to commission care for patients living in or visiting their local area.[18] Because CCGs did not form part of a management hierarchy and could not simply be told what to do, the 2012 Act placed them under a number of statutory duties to perform and objectives to fulfil when carrying out the commissioning role.[19] I will return to these statutory duties shortly.

As with providers, there was a greater emphasis on using the law to regulate the activities of CCGs and to force them to behave as market actors. This was a confusing mix of procurement and competition law, which are normally regarded as mutually exclusive in EU law. On the procurement side, CCGs were required to comply with the general law and with NHS-specific Regulations on public procurement when commissioning services.[20] Thus, for example, if they were proposing to place a contract the value of which exceeded the thresholds in what are now the Public Contracts Regulations 2015, they were obliged to advertise the contract and follow the appropriate tendering procedure laid down in the Regulations.[21] Any failure to do so could be the subject of litigation or a complaint to Monitor by a disappointed bidder.[22] Regulations also obliged CCGs to refrain from engaging in anti-competitive practices.[23] Again, Monitor was given the power to investigate allegations of non-compliance with these requirements in its capacity as market regulator.[24]

The performance of CCGs as commissioners was supervised by a new non-departmental public body, the NHS Commissioning Board.[25] This later became known as NHS England. Before the start of each financial year, each CCG had to publish a commissioning plan 'setting out how it proposes to exercise its functions'.[26] The CCG was required to consult its population on the plan, and the final published plan must include 'an explanation of how the group took account of

[16] HSCA s 25, inserting NHS Act 2006 ss 14L and 14N. See the National Health Service (Clinical Commissioning Groups) Regulations 2012 (SI 2012/1631), r 11. The NHS Future Forum recommended the involvement of other professionals: above n 7, 11. The government abandoned the original label 'GP consortia' in favour of CCGs to reflect this change.

[17] See ACL Davies, 'Beyond New Public Management: Problems of Accountability in the Modern Administrative State' in Nicholas Bamforth and Peter Leyland (eds), *Accountability in the Contemporary Constitution* (OUP 2013) 333–53.

[18] HSCA s 10, inserting NHS Act 2006, s 1I; HSCA s 13, amending NHS Act 2006, s 3.

[19] HSCA ss 26–27.

[20] HSCA s 75. The current regulations are the National Health Service (Procurement, Patient Choice and Competition) (No 2) Regulations 2013/500.

[21] SI 2015/102.

[22] HSCA ss 76–77.

[23] See (n 20), r 10.

[24] HSCA ss 76–77.

[25] HSCA s 9, ss 23–24.

[26] HSCA s 26, inserting NHS Act 2006, s 14Z11(1).

[the] views' expressed during the consultation.[27] After each financial year, each CCG had to produce and publish an annual report 'on how it has discharged its functions in the previous financial year'.[28] This had to be sent to NHS England and presented to the public at a meeting. NHS England was under a statutory duty to conduct an annual performance assessment of each CCG.[29] This was defined as 'an assessment of how well the [CCG] has discharged its functions during that year'.[30] NHS England had significant powers to intervene if it perceived that a CCG was failing.[31]

Given the controversy surrounding the Act, it is perhaps not surprising that the Government was at pains to emphasise that competition was not to be regarded as an aim in itself and should be used as a tool to improve services for patients. Various compromises were introduced, including a requirement on Monitor to 'enabl[e] health care services … to be provided in an integrated way' where this would benefit patients, alongside its duty to prevent anti-competitive behaviour.[32] Similarly, the second version of the Regulations applicable to CCGs maintained the obligation to avoid anti-competitive practices but made it clear that cooperation between providers was permitted when it would improve service quality.[33] Nevertheless, it was clear that, taking the various provisions of the Act together, the overall objective was to create, promote, and enforce a competitive market within the NHS.

II. A Changing Agenda

Since the 2012 Act was passed, there has been another significant shift in policy thinking around the best way to run the NHS, with the idea of 'integrated care' taking centre stage.[34] Proponents argue that there may be efficiencies to be achieved, and improvements in patients' experiences, if services are delivered in a joined-up way. As with most ideas about running the NHS, integration is not new, but it is receiving particular emphasis in current debates.

Even in 2012, there was a degree of experimentation in some areas with small-scale integrated care projects, often for patients with particular conditions. For example, an attempt might be made to integrate hospital and community services for

[27] Ibid, inserting NHS Act 2006, s 14Z13(8)(b).
[28] Ibid, inserting NHS Act 2006, s 14Z15.
[29] Ibid, inserting NHS Act 2006, ss 14Z16–14Z20.
[30] Ibid, inserting NHSA s 14Z16(2).
[31] Ibid, inserting NHSA s 14Z21.
[32] HSCA s 62(3) and (4).
[33] Compare r 10 (n 20) with National Health Service (Procurement, Patient Choice and Competition) (No 2) Regulations 2013/500, r 10.
[34] See NHS England's website: https://www.england.nhs.uk/integratedcare/integrated-care-systems/, accessed 28 June 2019. The respected think tank the King's Fund also has useful resources: https://www.kingsfund.org.uk/topics/integrated-care, accessed 28 June 2019.

people with diabetes to help them to manage their condition better at home and to avoid unnecessary hospital admissions. The move towards integrating care more generally can probably be traced to the publication of the NHS Forward View in 2014.[35] This led to the development of forty-four Sustainability and Transformation Plans (STPs) for different geographical areas of England. It is worth noting that STPs do not just bring together providers in one CCG area: rather, they cover bigger areas and generally bring together a group of CCGs too. STPs focus on how care should be organised in their geographical area and include proposals such as reorganising acute hospitals and improving preventative strategies.[36]

At the time of writing, some fourteen of the most advanced STPs have evolved into ICSs (Integrated Care Systems), ten since June 2017, and a further four since May 2018.[37] It is difficult to generalise about ICSs because they have evolved organically, but in each case, they have taken some steps towards implementing ideas from the STPs through institutional reform. For example, some ICSs have established a joint commissioning board to enable their commissioners to work together to buy services, and others have set up financial information-sharing arrangements as a step towards a single budget for the whole area.[38]

A further step along the road to integrated care would be for the commissioners within the ICS to contract with a single organisation to provide care for their whole population. This is referred to as the 'Accountable Care Organisation' (ACO) or 'Integrated Care Partnership' (ICP) model. NHS England has drafted and consulted on an ACO contract, more recently referred to as an ICP contract, but it has not yet been used.[39] I discuss this in detail shortly.

What is remarkable about these developments is that at no point has the Government published a consultation about integrated care, or a White Paper, nor has it put before Parliament legislation to authorise them. All the changes just described have occurred under the 2012 Act which, as explained earlier, pursued a competitive market policy through the institutions it created and the powers and duties they were given. The use of that same statutory framework to implement what is, in effect, the complete opposite of the competitive market policy, raises serious questions of legality.

[35] NHS England, *NHS Five Year Forward View* (October 2014).

[36] They are published here: https://www.england.nhs.uk/integratedcare/stps/view-stps/, accessed 28 June 2019.

[37] Details are available here: https://www.england.nhs.uk/integratedcare/integrated-care-systems/, accessed 28 June 2019.

[38] For analysis see Anna Charles et al, *A Year of Integrated Care Systems: Reviewing the Journey so Far* (King's Fund, September 2018).

[39] NHS England, *Integrating Care: Contracting for Accountable Models* (December 2016; revised edition August 2017), and accompanying documentation. At the time of writing, a fresh consultation on the ICP contract has closed but no results have yet emerged: https://www.engage.england.nhs.uk/consultation/proposed-contracting-arrangements-for-icps/, accessed 28 June 2019.

A. The *Hutchinson* and *Shepherd* cases

In *Hutchinson*, a group of interested NHS watchers brought an application for judicial review of the Secretary of State's and NHS England's promulgation of the ACO model contract for use by CCGs, arguing that it was not lawful under the 2012 Act, and that CCGs using it would themselves be acting *ultra vires*.[40] This challenge failed in the Administrative Court. In *Shepherd*, another campaign group brought proceedings challenging the payment mechanism proposed in the model contract, which by this time was known as the ICP contract.[41] They argued that this payment mechanism—the WPAP, or Whole Population Annual Payment—was *ultra vires* the 2012 Act because this prescribes a national tariff of payments for different types of treatment. This challenge was rejected by the judge at first instance and by the Court of Appeal. I analyse these decisions in this section, before drawing out some broader themes about administrative law and the rule of law in the next section.

The new approach at the centre of the *Hutchinson* case is referred to throughout as the Accountable Care Organisation or 'ACO model'. The idea here is that instead of commissioning care on two-year contracts from a variety of different providers, CCGs would commission perhaps just one large organisation to provide care for their district over a longer period of time, such as ten years. NHS England has published a draft ACO contract running to some 220 pages and a variety of background documents explaining how it is intended to operate.[42]

A preliminary issue in the litigation was how to define the ACO model itself because the determination of any question of *vires* obviously requires a close comparison of what is being proposed as against the provisions of the empowering statute. For these purposes, the judge focused primarily on the contract, but also took account of the background documentation. He defined what was referred to as the 'max' version of the ACO model as 'a single entity being responsible for the preponderant part of health and care services in a defined locality operating under a long-term contract pursuant to which it has responsibility for a very high proportion of resource and budgetary decision making'.[43]

The core argument about *vires* was that, under these arrangements, the ACO rather than the CCG would be performing the functions given to the CCG under the Health and Social Care Act 2012. Since these functions are non-delegable, the CCG would be acting unlawfully in setting up the arrangement and the ACO would have no proper statutory basis for its actions. It would also be *ultra vires* for the Secretary of State and NHS England to consult on the ACO model on the basis that it was permitted by the 2012 Act and could be implemented without further legislation.

[40] See (n 1).
[41] See (n 2).
[42] See (n 39).
[43] See (n 1) [62].

As explained earlier, the main statutory functions of CCGs are to determine population needs, to commission healthcare provision to meet those needs, and to do so in accordance with a list of specific requirements in the Act.[44] The judge addressed each of these in turn. First, he suggested that the task of determining population needs arose before the ACO could be appointed.[45] Although it was a continuing duty, this was dealt with by provisions in the ACO contract requiring the ACO to conduct needs assessments for the population. According to the judge, the CCG could form its own independent needs assessment based on the information supplied by the ACO, thereby continuing to discharge its own statutory duty. Second, he argued that the task of 'arranging' healthcare provision did not preclude arranging for another organisation to provide the care in ways that would involve some subcontracting, pointing out that it was already the case that a provider under contract to a CCG did not commit to fulfilling that contract by employing all necessary staff directly.[46] Finally, he held that the CCG's various duties in relation to the way in which care should be provided—which are delineated in a number of provisions in the statute—could be met by putting the ACO under a contractual obligation to fulfil them.[47] This was evidence not of improper delegation by the CCG but of efforts to ensure that the ACO supported it to fulfil its own statutory duties.

The difficulty with this analysis is that the overall effect is very different to the one Parliament originally intended. First, in general terms, the driver for efficiency savings and quality improvement under integrated care is the possibility of redesigning services by integrating them, rather than the possibility of motivating providers to improve their performance by forcing them to compete. These are fundamentally different routes to structuring interactions between NHS bodies and incentivising them to change their behaviour. Second, the role of a purchaser or commissioner is very different in a regime of three-year contracts for specific services, and a regime of (perhaps) one ten-year contract for a wide range of services. Even if there is competition prior to the award of the contract, the role of the purchaser in monitoring and managing the contract is much more important in the latter case than in the former, where there is a regular opportunity for review through retendering. Third, the role of the provider is significantly different if it has substantial discretion to decide what to provide, how to provide it and how to allocate funds as between different activities. Of course, it is true to say that under any contracting regime, particular providers will usually subcontract some aspects of their work. A contract for an ambulance service does not mean that the provider will necessarily deliver the entire activity through its own employees. But the

[44] See (n 19).
[45] See (n 1) [105].
[46] Ibid [93]–[96].
[47] Ibid [97]–[104].

ACO model hands over to the provider many aspects of the role previously carried out by commissioners. Fourth, while it is arguably still the case that under the ACO model, the commissioner can monitor the activities of the ACO, the commissioner will be dependent on the ACO for its information, making it difficult independently to verify the ACO's claims about its performance. In summary, the ACO model is an example of what I have labelled elsewhere a 'deep' or 'post-' NPM policy, in which the commissioner outsources its own role and then largely disappears from the picture, rather than engaging actively in the design of services and the running of competitive tendering exercises.[48]

In some respects, the *Shepherd* case is a smaller-scale version of the same challenge, in that it focuses on the legality of one element of the ACO model.[49] As explained earlier, one feature of the 2012 Act was that it put the tariff pricing system onto a statutory footing.[50] This requires purchasers and providers to contract for services at prices set by Monitor. The ACO model, as explained earlier, is about contracting for healthcare for the whole population of a particular geographical area, and a key element of the model is a different payment mechanism, the Whole Population Annual Payment (WPAP). Under the WPAP, the commissioner pays the provider a lump sum based on the size of the population which is intended to cover a wide variety of services. It is up to the provider to decide how to use the money to pay for different kinds of services.

Again, the key question was whether the WPAP was lawful within the 2012 Act given that the Act required Monitor to produce a tariff and purchasers and providers to use it. This necessitated detailed analysis of the operation of the tariff. Importantly, the tariff is not comprehensive. This is acknowledged by section 115, which provides that the price payable for an NHS service is the price in the tariff where one is laid down by Monitor under section 116, or a price determined in accordance with rules laid down in the tariff where no specific price has been set. There is also a degree of flexibility around the prices themselves. Under section 116(2), the tariff may set out circumstances in which commissioners and providers at the local level may agree different prices in their contracts. Monitor may also allow for 'national variations' to reflect different contexts in which a service may be delivered under section 116(4). Moreover, where it is uneconomical for a provider to deliver a service at the tariff price, it may seek a 'local modification' by agreement with the commissioner under section 124. This must be approved by Monitor. There is a mechanism for Monitor to order a modification under section 125 if the provider and commissioner cannot agree.

[48] This phenomenon has also emerged in some local authority settings, where particular councils have hired one private firm to commission or run all or most of their services, with serious implications for local democracy. See Davies, 'Beyond New Public Management' (n 17).

[49] N 2.

[50] N 10. For the current tariff, see NHS England and NHS Improvement, *2017/18 and 2018/19 National Tariff Payment System* (2017).

The core of the argument on behalf of the applicants was that the WPAP was in breach of section 115 because it was a lump sum: it did not involve working out, for example, how many hip replacements were to be provided and paying for them at the tariff price. However, the Court of Appeal held that because the tariff was not a 'price list' and instead laid down a flexible and variable pricing regime, it could be used to agree a payment on a WPAP basis by treating it as a local variation.[51]

It is perhaps unfortunate that the argument on behalf of the applicants was put in quite strong terms, wrongly suggesting that the tariff required there to be a price per treatment per patient, and that there was no material difference between local variations under section 116 and local modifications under section 124, for example. This may have made it more difficult for the court to identify the crucial point, that the WPAP is a fundamentally different approach to setting prices than the tariff regime envisaged by the Act, even though the tariff does not operate as a 'price list' and is the subject of many exceptions. Before the internal market was introduced there was a budget for healthcare provision in each local area, which translated into very simple 'block contracts' in the early years of the market, priced by population size rather than services provided. But the aim of the tariff was to become more specific about the costs of particular services and treatments over time, in order to help providers to understand their costs better and to become more efficient as a result. The WPAP is, in effect, a return to the prior system in which providers are given a sum of money for the local population and allowed to divide it up between different treatments and services as they see fit. It is difficult to see how the 2012 Act can be construed to permit this. The argument accepted by the Court of Appeal, that the ability to vary the price of 'a health care service' under section 116(2) can be used to agree a WPAP is, with respect, implausible. The term 'health care service' clearly refers to a particular type of care or treatment and does not envisage a single payment for all types of care or treatment. The Court of Appeal's construction allows the exception to be used so as to eclipse the general rule.

B. The fundamentals of administrative law

Having examined the decisions in *Hutchinson* and *Shepherd* and explained why they were wrongly decided as a matter of statutory interpretation, I turn now to the broader issues they raise. While it is easy to dismiss them as dull and technical, I argue that these cases raise important general questions of administrative law that should have been acknowledged more readily by the courts.

The concept of legality plays a central role in administrative law and, as a result, in Paul Craig's scholarship. He has recently offered a concise overview of its

[51] N 2 [70]–[86].

different meanings and roles.[52] One view of legality, now largely discredited, is that it is the 'foundational' principle of administrative law in the sense that it is the 'meta-precept for administrative law doctrine'.[53] This is the idea that the various grounds of judicial review—legitimate expectations, natural justice, and so on—can all be traced back to parliamentary intention expressed through statute and interpreted by the courts. As Craig has argued in a series of articles, this *ultra vires* theory of administrative law is implausible because there is rarely any indication in a statute creating a discretionary power as to how the courts might approach judicial review of the exercise of that power.[54] Indeed, where Parliament does express a view, as in the case of ouster clauses, the courts are usually at pains to find ways of holding decision-makers to account regardless of Parliament's apparent intention literally construed.[55]

A second sense of legality is described by Craig as 'foundational in a narrower, but nonetheless important, sense'.[56] This is the idea that the government must be able to point to some basis in statute, prerogative, or common law for its action. As Craig explains, '[i]f it cannot do so, then its action is invalid without recourse to other doctrinal grounds of challenge'.[57] In English law, this principle is perhaps somewhat weaker than it is in other legal systems, given the range of possibilities central government in particular has for identifying a source of authority. Where there is no clear statutory authority, wide-ranging prerogative powers may provide an alternative. For example, the prerogative to organise the civil service was used as the basis for comprehensive reforms to central government departments in the 1980s in particular, including the introduction of executive agencies at 'arm's length' to their parent departments.[58] Moreover, and controversially, the government may also be able to rely on non-statutory or common law powers or capacities, such as the capacity to enter into contracts.[59]

Nonetheless, in most cases, the central question is one of statutory construction: does the statute on which the government relies in fact provide it with the authority to act, properly construed? The courts have developed the basic notion of acting 'within the four corners of the Act' into a series of specific requirements,

[52] Paul Craig, 'Legality, Five Views of the Cathedral' in Peter Cane, Peter Lindseth, and Herwig Hofmann (eds), *Oxford Handbook of Comparative Administrative Law* (OUP forthcoming).

[53] Ibid 1.

[54] For example, Paul Craig, 'Ultra Vires and the Foundations of Judicial Review' (1998) 57 CLJ 63.

[55] *Anisminic Ltd v Foreign Compensation Commission* [1969] 2 AC 147 (HL).

[56] N 52 5. For completeness, it should be noted that there is a third sense of legality—the principle of statutory construction that general statutory language should not be construed to limit citizens' rights—but this need not concern us here.

[57] Ibid.

[58] Mark Freedland, 'The Rule against Delegation and the *Carltona* Doctrine in an Agency Context' [1996] PL 19.

[59] See, for example, BV Harris, 'The "Third Source" of Authority for Government Action Revisited' (2007) 123 LQR 225.

including acting in good faith, taking into account relevant considerations and disregarding irrelevant ones, and acting for proper purposes.[60] As Craig explains, because these are regarded by the courts as elements of legality, they are generally subject to a relatively intense review by the courts, in which it is regarded as appropriate to accord limited weight to the views of the decision-maker and to substitute the court's judgment.[61] This contrasts with review of the merits of a decision, where the courts generally tread more cautiously.[62] It is often argued that this distinction is given undue weight in English administrative law.[63] For example, the expert decision-maker's view on the relevance of a particular consideration may be worthy of some respect, and may in any event be difficult to distinguish in practice from the 'merits' question of the weight to be afforded to that consideration in taking the decision.

The particular 'version' of legality review at issue for present purposes is the requirement most clearly articulated in *Padfield* that discretionary powers granted by an Act should be used for the purposes of that Act.[64] As Lord Reid explained:

> Parliament must have conferred the discretion with the intention that it should be used to promote the policy and objects of the Act, the policy and objects of the Act must be determined by construing the Act as a whole and construction is always a matter of law for the court.[65]

This envisages a two-stage process in which the court determines the 'policy and objects' of the Act, and then decides whether a particular exercise (or non-exercise) of discretion by the minister promotes the 'policy and objects'. The justification for this type of legality review is clear. It ensures that decision-makers perform both no more and no less than the task they have been allocated by Parliament and fulfils the rule of law requirement that government should be in accordance with the law. It prevents ministers from using (or refusing to use) their discretionary powers in order to frustrate the operation of the Act. In turn, this ensures that a minister who disagrees with the policy of an Act must go back to Parliament and persuade it to pass new legislation to provide a statutory basis for his or her preferred course of action.[66] In quashing a decision or action for which there is no statutory authority,

[60] *Associated Provincial Picture Houses Ltd v Wednesbury Corp* [1948] 1 KB 223, 228 (Lord Greene MR).

[61] N 52, 8.

[62] A distinction drawn sharply by Lord Hoffmann in *Tesco Stores Ltd v Secretary of State for the Environment* [1995] 1 WLR 759, 780–81.

[63] N 52, 9.

[64] *Padfield v Minister of Agriculture, Fisheries and Food* [1968] AC 997.

[65] Ibid 1030 (Lord Reid).

[66] See, for example, *R (BAPIO Action Ltd) v Secretary of State for the Home Department* [2008] UKHL 27, [2008] 1 AC 1003.

the courts provide a check on the executive which protects the role of the legislature and, more broadly, of democratic debate and decision-making.

The *Hutchinson* and *Shepherd* cases are concerned with this type of 'foundational' legality: could the Secretary of State, NHS England, and Monitor use their discretionary powers under the 2012 Act to propose and implement the ACO model and the WPAP? However, the importance of the cases is scarcely recognised by the courts. There is a clear acknowledgment of the political interest in the decisions, and, quite properly, an equally clear statement that it is not for the courts to adjudicate on the merits of the different policy choices being made.[67] However, there is less acknowledgment that the task of determining the merits of the competing policy options is a matter for Parliament unless the policy options are clearly authorised by the 2012 Act. There is a strong sense of pragmatism in the decisions: it is as if the courts' task is to find a creative way to uphold the actions of ministers and NHS bodies rather than to decide on their legality.

Both judgments are also marked by very close attention to the technical details of the statutory provisions and of the policies being adopted under them. Of course, this is entirely proper too: any question of *vires* must involve a careful analysis of the statutory provisions to determine what they do and do not permit. However, *Padfield* requires a determination of the 'policy and objects' of the Act in question, which in turn requires the courts to set the technical detail in its broader context and to decide what Parliament was trying to achieve through the legislation. A reflection of this kind would have led to the conclusion that the policies now being adopted by the NHS are different not just in degree but in kind from those put into place under the 2012 Act. In one sense, it is true that the ACO model is a contract to provide healthcare services for a period of time, just like contracts placed by CCGs with providers under the 2012 Act, and that WPAP is a price variation from the tariff. But they are not variations on a theme: they are a different policy altogether. Close attention to the detail on its own does not draw this out.

Of course, on some level, there is no real harm done by the emergence of integrated care in the NHS. The 2012 Act was highly controversial, and many people are relieved to see a change of direction away from competition and markets.[68] If it was necessary to wait for Parliament to legislate, the policy change would be much harder to implement given current political circumstances. But that is not the point. It is for Parliament to decide whether policy should be changed, not for ministers, NHS England, or Monitor, and by getting bogged down in the technical details of the ACO model and the 2012 Act, the courts have failed to fulfil their role of striking down unlawful administrative action.

[67] N 1, [4].

[68] This may change if ACO contracts are awarded to private providers so that the policy becomes one of creeping privatisation, though there is no particular sign of this at the time of writing.

III. Conclusion

It seems likely that there will eventually be legislation to support the development of integrated care in the NHS. This is not because of a recognition by ministers that legislation is needed to authorise the changes, but because the 2012 Act is perceived by NHS bodies and some commentators as an obstacle to the further development of integrated care policies.[69] The NHS Long-Term Plan, published in January 2019, identifies a variety of areas in which legislation is required.[70] Tellingly, these include removing various requirements of competition and procurement law, making the tariff pricing system more flexible, and facilitating joint working between different types of NHS bodies—Trusts and CCGs—and the regulators, NHS England, and NHS Improvement. The Plan even purports to legitimate this method of proceeding with a quotation from Aneurin Bevan, the founding father of the NHS, that is taken out of context.[71]

It may seem as if arguments about legality in the administrative structures of the NHS represent the worst kind of formalism—a fuss about legal technicalities in a context that only an 'anorak' would understand—but this view is profoundly mistaken. As Craig reminds us, legality is a fundamental principle of administrative law and, ultimately, of a democratic state. It is for Parliament to debate and authorise changes to the 2012 Act, however well-intentioned, and it is for the courts to ensure that Parliament has the opportunity to do so.

[69] For example, Charles et al (n 38).

[70] NHS England, *NHS Long Term Plan* (January 2019), ch 7.

[71] Ibid 114. See Aneurin Bevan, Speech to the Institute of Hospital Administrators, 6 April 1946. Available at: https://www.sochealth.co.uk/national-health-service/the-sma-and-the-foundation-of-the-national-healthservice-dr-leslie-hilliard-1980/aneurin-bevan-and-the-foundation-of-the-nhs/bevans-speech-to-the-institute-of-hospital-administrators-6-april-1946/, accessed 28 June 2019.

PART V
PROCESS AND PROCEDURE

14. Proceduralism and Automation: Challenges to the Values of Administrative Law
    Carol Harlow and Richard Rawlings
15. The Foundations of the Duty to Give Reasons and a Normative Reconstruction
    Joana Mendes
16. Process and Procedure in a Disordered State
    Mark Freedland

14

Proceduralism and Automation

Challenges to the Values of Administrative Law

Carol Harlow and Richard Rawlings

I. Scene-setting

Our concern in this chapter is with the place of administrative procedure in the development and conceptualisation of administrative law. The chapter has three main themes. The first is the steady proceduralisation of public administration experienced in recent years. We use the term 'procedure' loosely in this chapter to mean no more than the standard dictionary definition of 'a proceeding, a way of proceeding, a mode of conducting business or performing a task or a series of actions conducted in a certain order or manner'. The term 'proceduralisation'—a word that the *Oxford English Dictionary* (*OED*) declines to acknowledge—may mean no more than the 'creation (or substitution) of a formal method or procedure for a vaguely defined process', a mechanistic and seemingly neutral definition which does not attempt to tell us whether proceduralisation is a good or a bad thing.

However, the *OED* defines proceduralism as 'a strict or rigid adherence to procedure as laid down' and warns that the word has 'negative connotations'. The same is true of the word 'bureaucracy', synonymous in the public mind with 'red tape', or proceduralism as an over-concern with procedure and inflexibility, and again with the concept of 'juridification', which Gunther Teubner once called an ugly word for the ugly reality of 'the bureaucratisation of the world'.[1] We use the term here in its simplest sense of 'the proliferation of law', which we treat as analogous to proceduralisation as the proliferation of procedure. Elsewhere, we have described contemporary administrative law in terms of a 'cycle of juridification', in which policies expressed as rules are subject to rule interpretation and rule application by the administration but referred out in case of dispute to tribunals and courts. An adjudication may call for further interpretative rules in the form of guidance or it may provoke the administrator to produce more, and more specific, rules by formal rule change. If the new rules are challenged, the cycle of juridification recurs.[2] A very

[1] Gunther Teubner, 'Juridification: Concepts, Aspects, Limits, Solutions' in Gunther Teubner (ed), *Juridification of Social Spheres* (de Gruyter 1987).

[2] Carol Harlow and Richard Rawlings, *Law and Administration* (3rd edn, CUP 2009) 195–96.

Carol Harlow and Richard Rawlings, *Proceduralism and Automation* In: *The Foundations and Future of Public Law*. Edited by: Elizabeth Fisher, Jeff King, Alison L Young, Oxford University Press (2020).

DOI: 10.1093/oso/9780198845249.003.0014

similar process of proceduralisation can occur in a given administrative process, with the term then having a negative connotation.

It is equally possible, however, to read the term 'proceduralism' more positively, as in the dictionary definition of 'belief in the importance of instituting and following an agreed procedure'. This references the continental ideal of the *Rechtsstaat*, a state that guarantees the rights of its citizens and where consequently administrative activity is 'assigned to predictable legal forms' and functions through known rules and procedures.[3] The emphasis here on administration as subject to written law,[4] which is publicly available (transparent), suggests why the *Rechtsstaat* ideal has acted in recent years as a powerful driver to codification of procedural administrative law in the European Union, both at Union level[5] and across EU Member States.[6]

The chapter's second theme is the relationship between procedures and values and the potential for dissonance but also exchange between public administration and administrative law. Procedure is not of course the primary task of administration, which is generally seen as the implementation of policy, to be carried out in a neutral and objective fashion. Public servants are precluded from holding autonomous policy preferences, making independent policy choices or engaging in politics. In the real world, however, we know that administrators are active participants in policy-making and other output functions of government including law-making and regulation. Moreover, the existence of 'a separate civil service identity, with its own professional ethos and standards' cannot be disregarded.[7]

The relationship between administrative procedure and administrative law is complex. Much administrative law consists of procedure and many of its core principles are procedural in character but although there is substantial overlap between the two, administrative procedure is not the whole of administrative law nor are the two synonymous. A simple threefold classification serves to illustrate. In the first category are internal or bureaucratic procedural norms, as in the many organisational arrangements, house rules, and practice of bureaucracies. Generically labelled 'soft law', guidance, circulars, manuals, memoranda, etc are sometimes seen as falling outside the purview of administrative law.[8] A second, intersecting

[3] See Frank van Dun 'Political Liberalism and the Formal *Rechtsstaat*' (2004); available at: http://users.ugent.be/~frvandun/Texts/Articles/Godefridi.pdf, accessed 1 July 2019.

[4] See Wolfgang Rusch, 'Administrative Procedures in EU Member States' (2009); available at: http://www.sigmaweb.org/publications/42754772.pdf, accessed 1 July 2019.

[5] Model administrative procedure rules are the work of the academic ReNeual group: http://reneual.eu/h, accessed 1 July 2019.

[6] Fifty per cent or more of EU Member States now have administrative procedure acts: see Jean-Bernard Auby and Thomas Perroud (eds), *Droit comparé de la procédure administrative* (Editions Bruylant 2016).

[7] Lorne Sossin, 'From Neutrality to Compassion: The Place of Civil Service Values and Legal Norms in the Exercise of Administrative Discretion' (2005) 55 UTLJ 427, 430–33.

[8] Richard Rawlings, 'Soft Law Never Dies' in Mark Elliott and David Feldman (eds), *The Cambridge Companion to Public Law* (CUP 2015).

category involves doses of formal law, whereby administrative procedures are imposed externally or hardened-up, most obviously by the legislature and/or courts, but sometimes by the executive through secondary—delegated—legislation. Classically demonstrated in the Civil Service Code, we also note a tendency in recent times to formalise parts of soft law, procedural and otherwise, in published documents. Third, we note those parts of administrative law which do not bear directly on administrative procedure—the classic *ultra vires* rule perhaps or the legislative mandate of an agency—while always remembering that procedures will typically be generated within, even prompted by, such parameters. In practice, boundaries will commonly be blurred through mixes of design and the day-to-day realities of policy development and delivery in a system of law and administration.

Much turns on the particular tradition of administrative law. In the absence of a generalised procedural codification—perhaps an American-style Administrative Procedure Act—the UK courts clearly have the constitutional space in which to play a creative role. They must, however, navigate multiple statutory mini-codifications, a key force for contextualism, influenced to a greater or lesser extent by judicial precepts and typically designed in pragmatic fashion for particular policy domains. We see the relationship between courts and administration as a two-way, non-hierarchical process, involving interchange. This view is reflected in the ordering of our discussion of drivers to proceduralisation, which looks first at the internal drivers to proceduralisation emanating from administration, notably the managerial reforms of the 1980s ('new public management' or NPM) and the rise of regulation as a standard governance technique (section III). Section IV looks at some evolving judicial review principles in contemporary case law, focusing on the judicial response to and stimulus for administrative proceduralism.

We must also factor into the equation the practical realities of multilevel governance with its complex set of interactive relationships and multiple players. While there is obviously much by way of shared heritage and administrative culture, devolution has naturally spawned alternative forms of administrative procedural methodology in the diverse conditions of small country governance.[9] Again, pointing up the countervailing forces for convergence and divergence as the EU epoch in British history seemingly comes to an end, there is currently much discussion of common UK frameworks and procedures in an otherwise increasingly differentiated polity.[10] Reference must also be made to the 'bureaucratic regulation' of government bodies by other government bodies.[11] The so-called integrity branch is, for example, a fertile source of procedural norms;[12] today's plethora of ombudsman in the United Kingdom provides chapter and verse.

[9] See for example, Sarah Nason, 'The "New Administrative Law" of Wales' [2019] PL 703 .

[10] Richard Rawlings, *Brexit and the Territorial Constitution: Devolution, Reregulation and Intergovernmental Relations* (Constitution Society 2017).

[11] Christopher Hood and Colin Scott, 'Bureaucratic Regulation and New Public Management in the United Kingdom: Mirror-Image Developments?' (1996) 23 JLS 321.

[12] Robin Crekye, 'An "Integrity" Branch' (2012) 70 AIAL Forum 33.

The way in which administrative law and administrative procedure are jointly shaped by situation is powerfully illustrated in the case of EU governance, which is fragmented to an unusual degree. A heavy premium is placed on so-called network governance; committees to represent Member States, more or less informal arrangements of regulatory bodies and experts, and increasingly EU agencies, clutter the landscape, magnifying many times over the demand for effective means of communication, cooperation, and coordination—the 'three Cs' of EU administration, which act as 'superglue' to hold an essentially piecemeal structure in place.[13] Proceduralisation follows dose after dose of formal EU legislation proceeding under the broad banner of 'mixed' or 'shared' and 'composite' administration,[14] with myriad complementary and supplementary soft law procedural norms supplying elements of flexibility. Although we touch occasionally on supranational developments in the European Union, the chapter deals for the most part with administration and administrative law in the United Kingdom. In both systems, though for slightly different reasons, an unremitting proceduralisation has taken place.

The chapter's third theme, which is necessarily less determinate, concerns challenges to administrative law from the technological revolution currently underway.[15] The impact of automation on public administration was at first rather modest. Recently, however, technology has taken great leaps forward, from computerisation to artificial intelligence and beyond. Alongside, the process of automating public services has advanced quite quickly. While the effects of digitalisation and artificial intelligence on administrative law are beginning to be felt, there has been until recently little discussion of the potential impact. The time may be coming when there is a need for administrative law to protect or perhaps modify its tenets and values in the light of the technological revolution.

II. Values and Tenets

The point that procedures reflect values or serve as the instruments whereby values are given tangible expression is all too easily overlooked. Values are always contestable; they may differ, overlap, and on occasion conflict. But as the history of public administration and administrative law shows, there may also be periods in which the tension—friction—is particularly strongly felt. Thus, during the 1980s, when managerialism began to dominate public administration, there was concern amongst administrative lawyers that administrative law values might

[13] Carol Harlow and Richard Rawlings, *Process and Procedure in EU Administration* (Hart 2014) ch 13.

[14] See further, Paul Craig, *EU Administrative Law* (3rd edn, OUP 2012).

[15] Klaus Schwab, *The Fourth Industrial Revolution* (Portfolio Penguin 2017).

be eroded by managerialist values.[16] A similar point arises in section IV where we record cases when judges in assessing an administrative system in the conditions of austerity measure it against (their own understanding of) the values of administrative law.

As Mark Aronson has observed, classic administrative law values relate closely to judicial review.[17] Heading the list as foundational constitutional principles accepted alike by lawyers and administrators are the central legitimising concepts of the rule of law and legality. Aronson adds good faith, fairness, impartiality, consistency, rationality, accessibility of grievance procedures, accountability, and transparency. Also central to public law is a core set of principles and procedures that reflect our traditions of administrative justice. Fairness and impartiality are two of the three Franks' values[18] widely accepted as benchmarks for procedure in administrative tribunals, while access to justice is increasingly accepted as a substantive constitutional right.[19] There is certainly room here for a clash with the managerial ideology of complaints handling, which pervades contemporary public administration ideology and is responsible for the introduction of much new procedure in which economy, efficiency, and effectiveness are the paramount goals. The trend has been to substitute administrative complaints-handling procedures for the oral and adversarial procedures of administrative justice, a shift linking to newer, 'bottom-up' conceptions of administrative justice in terms of 'getting the first decision right'.[20] This trend is of growing importance in light of the rush to digitalise the means of delivery of adjudicative systems, briefly discussed in section V .

Administrative law cannot be static, and the list of values is not immutable; it varies in different legal orders and over time. European lawyers would, for example, undoubtedly include and probably prioritise legal certainty.[21] Again, human rights have become a dominant feature of domestic public law after the passage of the Human Rights Act 1998, raising multiple questions as to the fitness of administrative procedure for their implementation, these being familiarly associated with, but not confined to, proportionality testing. The propensity for 'events' to bring particular values centre stage is illustrated by the propagation of the seven Nolan standards for conduct in public life:[22] a watershed moment in the United Kingdom for integrity-type procedures of registration, declaration of interests, and

16 See Michael Taggart (ed), *The Province of Administrative Law* (Hart 1997).

17 Mark Aronson, 'Public Law Values in the Common Law' in Mark Elliott and David Feldman (eds), *The Oxford Companion to Public Law* (CUP 2015) 144–45.

18 *Report of the Franks Committee on Tribunals and Inquiries* (Cmnd 218, 1957) para 42.

19 See latterly *R (UNISON) v Lord Chancellor* [2017] UKSC 51, [2017] 3 WLR 409.

20 Michael Adler, 'Understanding and Analysing Administrative Justice' in Michael Adler (ed), *Administrative Justice in Context* (Hart 2010) 129.

21 Takis Tridimas, *The General Principles of EU Law* (3rd edn, OUP 2017) ch 5.

22 *First Report of the Committee on Standards in Public Life* (Cm 2850, 1995).

compliance with restrictions on lobbying driven by public concern over shenanigans at Westminster.[23]

The treatment of rationality exemplifies the sense of fluidity and scope for disparity when lawyers and officials seek to operationalise particular values. Rationality is a slippery concept, used with differing meanings in different disciplines. It is notably a key element in Max Weber's account of bureaucracy[24] and in Herbert Simon's influential studies of decision-making,[25] where the resonance is one of logical reasoning and objectivity. Traditionally, English administrative law preferred the concept of reasonableness in the undemanding sense of having sound judgment and not doing things that are so immoderate that no sensible person would do them.[26] 'Rationality' gained a firm footing in 1984 as part of Lord Diplock's famous tripartite categorisation of judicial review,[27] and is today a much-invoked value in domestic common law reasoning[28] despite, or perhaps partly because of, the spread of proportionality-type methodology. Largely justified in terms of process review, it doubles as an important driver of administrative procedures in contemporary judicial review, typically requiring a decision-maker to factor in all relevant information that is available, filter out all irrelevant information, and, a significant dimension of the rationality principle considered further in section IV, give reasons for a decision.[29]

Rationality further serves as an umbrella concept to illuminate the scope for prioritisation and giving varying weights to particular values. In his pioneering work on mass decision-making in American public administration, Jerry Mashaw underlined the importance of consistency, fairness, and a right to equal treatment as essential elements of the concept of rationality.[30] Today, the UK Supreme Court asserts that 'the domestic law of this country does not recognise equal treatment as a distinct principle of administrative law', while consistency is a 'generally desirable objective' but 'not an absolute rule'.[31] Yet the agency whose (unpublished) early resolution process the Court was examining had noted fairness, transparency, and consistency as 'overriding principles' that must always be taken into account when negotiating settlements.[32] Equality itself is now a significant constitutional value,

[23] *Code of Conduct Together with The Guide to the Rules Relating to the Conduct of Members* (2005); available at: https://publications.parliament.uk/pa/cm201516/cmcode/1076/1076.pdf, accessed 1 July 2019.

[24] Max Weber, 'Bureaucracy' in *Economy and Society: An Outline of Interpretive Sociology* (Guenther Ross and Claus Wittich trans, University of California Press 1978) vol 2, ch 11.

[25] Herbert A Simon, *Reason in Human Affairs* (Blackwell 1983).

[26] *Associated Provincial Picture Houses Ltd v Wednesbury Corporation* [1948] 1 KB 223 (CA).

[27] *Council of Civil Service Unions v Minister for the Civil Service* [1985] AC 374 (HL).

[28] See latterly *R (Gallagher Group) v Competition and Markets Authority* [2018] UKSC 25, [2019] AC 96.

[29] See further Paul Craig, 'Judicial Review and Anxious Scrutiny: Foundations, Evolution and Application' [2015] PL 60.

[30] Jerry L Mashaw, *Bureaucratic Justice: Managing Social Security Claims* (Yale UP 1983). And see Nicholas R Parillo (ed), *Administrative Law from the Inside Out* (CUP 2017).

[31] *Gallagher* (n 28) [24] (Lord Carnwath).

[32] Ibid [6].

recognised in the political process and awarded legal standing in the Equality Act 2010, which lays on public sector bodies a weighty decision-making duty when exercising their functions to 'have due regard' to the need to eliminate discrimination and advance equality of opportunity and foster good relations on the basis of a wide range of protected characteristics.[33] This is a form of mainstreaming popular with activists. But the loose statutory rubric of 'due regard' in the so-called public sector equality duty leaves much scope for creative implementation by judges,[34] a form of activism to which we return in section IV.

Paul Daly identifies core values of good administration, democracy, and separation of powers as having 'normative force' and informing the doctrinal choices that courts make in the areas of process, substance, and remedial discretion. These values are 'found by interpreting legal materials' and 'immanent in the law', acting as a source of reasoned justification for judicial review doctrines and decisions and providing benchmarks for criticism when judges fail to give effect or give insufficient weight to them.[35] It is, however, questionable whether good administration is a value 'immanent in the law' outside the European Union, where it figures as a right in Article 41 of the EU Charter of Fundamental Rights. The highly legalistic nature of this text is noteworthy. It contains little that pertains to good administration as it impacts on the public at large except perhaps the right to have one's affairs handled 'impartially, fairly and within a reasonable time by the institutions and bodies of the Union'.[36]

Daly also claims transparency as a 'value long present in the common law',[37] though he admits that judicial references to transparency are relatively recent and that 'express consideration of the principles of good administration is rare'.[38] Transparency may attain legal status, as most obviously in freedom of information legislation, though the usual terminology is 'openness'. In reality, transparency is, with accountability and participation, one of a triad of 'good governance standards' highlighted by the Organisation for Economic Co-operation and Development (OECD) as core values of its public administration programmes[39] and selected by the European Commission as underpinning good governance, democracy, and the rule of law.[40] Mechanistic in the sense that they signal the need for appropriate procedures, this trilogy of closely linked values is fast emerging as normative in

[33] See Aileen McColgan, 'Litigating the Public Sector Equality Duty: The Story So Far' (2015) 35 OJLS 453.

[34] See especially *R(Bracking) v Secretary of State for Work and Pensions* [2013] EWCA Civ 1345.

[35] Paul Daly, 'Administrative Law: A Values-based Approach' in John Bell et al (eds), *Public Law Adjudication in Common Law Systems* (Hart 2016) 23, 25.

[36] Rhita Bousta, 'Who Said there is a "Right to Good Administration"? A Critical Analysis of Article 41 of the Charter of Fundamental Rights of the European Union' (2013) 19 EPL 481.

[37] Daly (n 35) 25.

[38] Ibid 27–28.

[39] OECD, 'European Principles for Public Administration', SIGMA Papers, No 27 (OECD 1999) 8.

[40] European Commission, 'European Governance: A White Paper' COM (2001) 428 final.

character, recognised as constitutional norms on a global basis.[41] This progression raises interesting questions about the relationship between the values of public administration and administrative law, pursued in later sections.

III. From Bureaucratic Rule-Making to the Age of Managerialism

The modern building blocks of public administration and administrative law were laid in response to the nineteenth-century industrial revolutions and the consequential assumption of an increasing number of welfare and regulatory functions by the state.[42] By the end of the century, the public service was largely professionalised and a 'scientific' discipline of public administration had begun to be recognised. By the mid-twentieth century, pressures from two world wars coupled with the rise of socialism as a political force and the influence of American style 'New Deal' policies had driven the growth of 'the administrative state' much further and a process of proceduralisation of administration was well underway. Linked to progressive ideals and policies, a functionalist legal theory began to inform administrative law, growing in influence in the common law world in the inter-war years.[43] Functionalists accepted the need for an activist state and viewed administration as the means of enabling society to realise collective goals. Administration was conceived as a set of processes in the framework of which procedures operated as technical devices for implementing public service programmes and administrative law provided a toolkit of instruments for completing the task. Functionalism was protective of the values of administration.[44] Thus Canadian functionalist John Willis castigated lawyers for their ideological approach to administrative procedures and failure to respect administrative concern for economy and efficiency.[45] We are not arguing that functionalism acted as a driver for proceduralism but that the general effect of functionalist theory was to draw attention to the mechanistic side of administrative law. The paradigm functionalist textbook by Griffith and Street classifies legislation as a 'function of the Administration' and gives a detailed account of the legislative process in terms of administrative procedure. Considerable space is also devoted to procedures for,

[41] Carol Harlow, 'Accountability as a Value for Global Governance and Global Administrative Law' in Gordon Anthony et al (eds), *Values in Global Administrative Law* (Hart 2011). And see Elizabeth Fisher, 'The European Union in the Age of Accountability' (2004) 24 OJLS 495.

[42] Bernardo Sordi, '*Révolution, Rechtsstaat*, and the Rule of Law: Historical Reflections on the Emergence of Administrative Law in Europe' in Susan Rose-Ackerman, Peter L Lindseth, and Blake Emerson (eds), *Comparative Administrative Law* (2nd edn, Edward Elgar 2017).

[43] Robert W Gordon, 'Willis's American Counterparts: The Legal Realists' Defence of Administration' (2005) 55 UTLJ 405.

[44] See Martin Loughlin, 'The Functional Style in Public Law' (2005) 55 UTLJ 361.

[45] John Willis, 'The McRuer Report: Lawyers' Values and Civil Servants' Values' (1968) 18 UTLJ 351.

and parliamentary control of, executive legislation with particular attention paid to the consultation of interests and consultation procedures, [46] presaging in this respect the current emphasis on impact assessment and public consultation in public administration, a point to which we return.

The American academic KC Davis, whose work would prove particularly influential in the United Kingdom, cannot be categorised as a functionalist. Davis was shocked by the amount of low-level, unlawful behaviour, especially in the areas of policing and pre-trial, parole, and immigration procedures. But although he aimed at the familiar legal target of administrative discretion, Davis rejected the Diceyan remedy of external control by judges, turning instead to internal, administrative controls and the technique of rule-making.[47] Writing against the backdrop of the American Administrative Procedure Act with its emphasis on procedures for openness and stakeholder participation, Davis saw bureaucratic rule-making as potentially a miniature democratic process. Because they were written down, rules could be made accessible to the public (transparent), allowing stakeholders to know their rights and the public to participate in change and reform. Davis believed not only that rule-making could be used to open up the administrative process to help eradicate illegal practices and procure fairer, more consistent decisions (accountability) but also, because rules were general, to encourage comprehensive solutions to problems that 'go beyond the facts of individual cases'.

Davis's work was certainly not without impact on the development of administrative law theory. It primarily dealt with *administrative* control of discretion, which became the focus of academic writing for many years.[48] Rules were conceptualised as 'rational', which sat more easily with the model of rational administration then gained ground in administration and judicial review. Davis' ideas anticipated and related directly to the good governance principles of transparency, accountability, and participation that, as emphasised earlier, today stand as guiding principles for public administration. At the practical level, Davis saw the potential of rule-making for the internal and hierarchical control of bureaucracy and as a more consistent and effective control technique than the peripheral forays of courts. He drew attention to the practice of bureaucratic rule-making, which has been called 'the most important way in which bureaucracy creates policy' and even a rival to the legislative process as a form of governmental output. Indirectly therefore, Davis's work was a driver of proceduralisation.[49]

More direct and significant drivers came in the last decades of the twentieth century. The managerial techniques for the structure and operation of public

[46] JAG Griffith and H Street, *Principles of Administrative Law* (5th edn, Pitman 1973) 118–39

[47] Kenneth Culp Davis, *Discretionary Justice: A Preliminary Inquiry* (Louisiana State UP 1969).

[48] For early discussion in the United Kingdom, see Jeffrey Jowell, 'The Legal Control of Administrative Discretion' [1973] PL 178.

[49] William West, 'Administrative Rulemaking: An Old and Emerging Literature' (2005) 65 Public Administration Rev 655.

services (conveniently labelled New Public Management (NPM))[50] were initially developed for the commercial sector but, closely identified with privatisation, were soon transmitted to public administration.[51] The twin objectives of NPM were to (re)-impose political control over public administration and to reorganise bureaucracy and push it into self-control through the use of managerialist methodology.[52] NPM meant a shift in values: from earlier ideals of public service[53] towards, in a period of increasing austerity, an ideology of 'leanness and meanness'. As envisioned by the OECD, modernisation would lead to greater openness, effective accountability, and control, to be delivered by enhanced public service performance.[54]

In the United Kingdom, government was looking to 'a culture of improvement, innovation and collaborative purpose' for modernisation of public services that should be dedicated to effectiveness and responsiveness.[55] NPM was a driver to proceduralisation at every stage of the administrative process. At the design stage of policy-making, it asked for standard-setting, benchmarking, and the setting of targets and performance indicators; at the implementation stage, cost-effectiveness analysis, multiple impact assessments and consultations; finally, compliance codes needed to be drawn up, impact had to be measured and published as league tables, and monitoring and supervision techniques such as inspections and 'value for money' (VFM) audit set in place. In this way, managerialism led to a public administration dominated by the VFM values of economy, efficiency, and effectiveness.[56] At a later stage, when the task of public administration came to be perceived predominantly in terms of risk assessment, the strategic importance of impact assessment and cost-effectiveness analysis was even greater.[57]

In the European Union, where NPM was first accepted grudgingly but later adopted enthusiastically, managerial administration remains to the present day the Commission's preference.[58] Commission policy-making, which usually starts with a Communication, is replete with the jargon of roadmaps and action plans, integrated internal control, cost–benefit analysis, pilot projects, and other 'agreed upon procedures'. The Open Method of Coordination, a model of informal or 'soft

[50] Christopher Hood, 'A Public Management for All Seasons' (1991) 69 Pub Adm 3.

[51] Hood and Scott, 'Mirror-Image Developments?' (n 11).

[52] Michael Barzelay, *Breaking through Bureaucracy: A New Vision for Managing in Government* (University of California Press 1992).

[53] Mark Freedland and Silvana Sciarra (eds), *Public Services and Citizenship in European Law* (Clarendon Press 1998).

[54] OECD, *Modernising Government: The Way Forward* (OECD 2005).

[55] Cabinet Office, *Modernising Government* (Cm 4310, 1999) 10.

[56] Irvine Lapsley and Jeremy Lonsdale, 'The Audit Society: Helping to Develop or Undermine Trust in Government?' in *Administrative Justice in Context* (n 20).

[57] See further, Elizabeth Fisher, *Risk, Regulation and Administrative Constitutionalism* (Hart 2007).

[58] Christopher Pollitt and Geert Bouckaert, *New Public Management Reform, A Comparative Analysis* (3rd edn, OUP 2011).

governance', is designed as a series of procedural steps. Soft law guidelines combined with specific timetables for achieving EU objectives are set and quantitative and qualitative indicators and benchmarks as a means of comparing best practice are established. European guidelines are translated into national and regional policies by setting specific targets, taking into account national and regional differences. Implementing measures are adopted. All this is followed up by periodic monitoring, evaluation, and peer review organised as mutual learning processes.[59] This illustrates how the European Union, which operates as a regulatory bureaucracy, is in a position to act as a 'conduit for NPM-style procedural forms across the so-called "European administrative space" '[60] and as a revolving door whereby procedures travel between Member States and to the European Union and are returned as 'best practice' to the Member States.

Regulatory styles of governance are ambiguous in their effect on proceduralisation. On the one hand, regulatory toolkits contain many procedural items, such as enhanced consultation, impact assessment, risk-based regulation, and cost–benefit analysis that are standard elements in proceduralisation;[61] on the other, deregulation, regulatory simplification and 'better regulation' figure high and regularly on the political agenda.[62] Again, while economy, effectiveness, and efficiency are indispensable in the vocabulary of regulators, especially where the regulation of public service providers is concerned, regulatory theory pays much attention to the good governance values of accountability and transparency, shows concern for accessibility and consultation of stakeholders, and takes some interest in the fairness of regulatory procedures in the administrative law sense of the word.[63] Moreover, statutory public regulators are themselves in an ambiguous position, acting on the one hand as enforcers of good governance standards and fair procedures, on the other as targets for them. There have, for example, been complaints that regulators are insufficiently open and suggestions that the United Kingdom should adopt an equivalent to the US Administrative Procedure Act 1946. Regulatory style is, however, variable and much may depend on sector and size. Managerialism and regulation are closely linked phenomena that are transmissible from system to system. Facilitated by the technological revolution, public management and regulation are globalised disciplines.[64]

59 Lisbon European Council 23 and 24 March 2000, 'Presidency Conclusions' (2000) paras 37 and 38.

60 Harlow and Rawlings, *Process and Procedure* (n 13) 25.

61 Ed Humpherson, 'Auditing Regulatory Reform' in Dawn Oliver, Tony Prosser, and Richard Rawlings (eds), *The Regulatory State: Constitutional Implications* (OUP 2010) 266.

62 Ian Ayres and John Braithwaite, *Responsive Regulation: Transcending the Deregulation Debate* (OUP 1992); Stephen Weatherill (ed), *Better Regulation* (Hart Publishing 2007).

63 Robert Baldwin, Martin Cave, and Martin Lodge, *Understanding Regulation: Theory, Strategy and Practice* (2nd edn, OUP 2013).

64 John Braithwaite and Peter Drahos, *Global Business Regulation* (CUP 2000); Walter Mattli and Ngaire Woods, *The Politics of Global Regulation* (Princeton UP 2009).

IV. Judicial Engagement: Waves of Development

Turning to adjudication, the foundational case of *Ridge v Baldwin*[65] famously ushered in a more vigorous and open-ended concept of procedural fairness in the face of the extended 'administrative state'. A gradual widening and deepening of adjudicative-type requirements duly followed, though typically tailored in pragmatic fashion, together with some cautious experiments with judicial regulation of more plural types of process, including consultation.[66] At the same time, we see procedural review being increasingly framed by, and feeding off, the administrative dynamics of proceduralisation. Far from the Victorian prototype of the common law supplying 'the omission of the legislature' in sparse statutes,[67] it is commonly a case of the judges navigating, evaluating, and commenting on whole thickets of legislatively sanctioned administrative procedure. Juridification-like cycles of proceduralisation abound, centred round a mutual exchange of administrative and judicial values.

The development shows not only the continuing influence of classical rule of law precepts ('justice must not only be done but be seen to be done') but also the increased influence of dignitary values associated with enhanced rights protection,[68] and of the more generalised concerns for political and administrative legitimacy expressed in the good governance values of transparency, accountability, and participation. The contribution of the domestic courts has necessarily reflected the multistreamed nature of the judicial review process.[69] A quintessential common law tradition has met with EU requirements, often expressed in detailed sector-specific legislation, and with Convention rights, particularly the procedural regime of Article 6 of the European Convention on Human Rights (ECHR).[70] Expanding international webs of standards and of jurisdictions themselves operate as powerful drivers of proceduralisation.

'Precocious grandchild' of *Ridge v Baldwin* aptly describes the now leading case of *R (Osborn) v Parole Board*.[71] A recent tendency at appellate level to exploit common law roots in an increasingly confident assertion of home-grown judicial power—with particular resonance in terms of the deep-rooted common law concern with natural justice and due process—is reinforced. A strong form of contextualisation as the orthodoxy of procedural protection at common law, which itself reflects and reinforces the reality of judges engaging with the minute detail of myriad decision-making procedures, is confirmed. The importance of oral

65 [1964] AC 40 (HL).

66 Harlow and Rawlings, *Law and Administration* (n 2) ch 14.

67 *Cooper v Wandsworth Board of* Works (1863) 14 CB (NS) 180, 195 (Byles J).

68 Jerry L Mashaw, *Due Process in the Administrative State* (Yale UP 1985).

69 Richard Rawlings, 'Modelling Judicial Review' (2008) 61 CLP 95.

70 For the evident tensions, see latterly *Poshteh v Kensington and Chelsea Royal London Borough Council* [2017] UKSC 36, [2017] AC 624.

71 [2013] UKSC 61, [2014] AC 1115.

hearings is reasserted in the face of restricted—targeted—provision, to the extent of the UK Supreme Court issuing detailed instructions on the need for oral hearings in administrative (parole) proceedings. The proactive role of the courts in developing and pressing their own values is illuminated through a particular emphasis on the constitutional connotations of the rule of law, opening the way for further bouts of judicial interaction with administrative procedural frameworks.

Running alongside the rise of managerialism and marketisation and, latterly, austerity, the development of procedural review has picked up pace in the last few decades with successive waves of ground-breaking intervention, overlapping and mutually reinforcing and typically embracing and enhancing the forces of proceduralisation. A first wave concerns reason-giving. Intimately bound up with the quest for administrative rationality and legal control, but latterly reflecting the greater emphasis on human rights and nostrums of good governance, it is splendidly envisioned as part of a judicial effort to promote an administrative culture of justification.[72] To quote Jerry Mashaw, 'authority without reason is literally dehumanizing'.[73] More prosaically, the place of reasons as a foundational treaty obligation in the then European Community constituted a standing rebuke to the English common law, where the stunted development of a duty to give reasons reflected and reinforced the culture of official secrecy which long characterised British government. The scope for cross-fertilisation was obvious.[74]

The case law first sees the courts bring reason-giving inside the conceptual framework of procedural fairness; whereas there was no general common law duty, there was 'a perceptible trend towards an insistence on greater openness'.[75] It was left to later rulings to produce a tolerably workable template for establishment of a common law duty in particular contexts: the stuff of trigger factors and classes of decision.[76] Classic authority had established that reasons must be proper, intelligible, and adequate, dealing with the substantive points that have been made.[77] With pressures for variable intensity of review going in tandem with a more extensive duty, however, the scope for disagreement and further litigation emerged in standard judicial guidance ('the degree of particularity required depend[s] entirely on the nature of the issues falling for decision').[78] Nor can an occasional recycling of administrative concerns about cost and delay etc disguise the scope

[72] David Dyzenhaus and Michael Taggart, 'Reasoned Decisions and Legal Theory' in Douglas E Edlin (ed), *Common Law Theory* (CUP 2007).

[73] Jerry L Mashaw, 'Public Reason and Administrative Legitimacy' in *Public Law Adjudication* (n 30) 17.

[74] C-222/86 *UNECTEF v Heylens* [1987] I-ECR 4097; and see Paul Craig, 'The Common Law, Reasons and Administrative Justice' (1994) 53 CLJ 282, 301.

[75] *R v Secretary of State for the Home Department, ex parte Doody* [1994] 1 AC 531, 561 (HL) (Lord Mustill).

[76] *R v Higher Education Funding Council, ex parte Institute of Dental Surgery* [1994] 1 WLR 242 (HC).

[77] *Re Poyser and Mills' Arbitration* [1964] 2 QB 467 (HC).

[78] *South Bucks District Council v Porter (No 1)* [2004] UKHL 33, [2004] 1 WLR 1953, [36].

for ratcheting up the content of the procedural duty, effectively converting 'a very mild, essentially procedural requirement into a very draconian one'.[79]

A recent pair of planning cases confirms the sense of an ongoing expansionary dynamic in which the courts supplement already lengthy and complicated administrative procedures. In *Oakley*,[80] faced with the removal of a reason-giving requirement in delegated legislation on grounds of regulatory burden and delay, the Court of Appeal pushed beyond the previous template and founded a common law obligation to give reasons on a combination of factors such as widespread public controversy and 'significant and lasting impact', as well as citizens' 'legitimate interest' in understanding important local decisions.[81] In the *Dover* case,[82] the Supreme Court approved this while maintaining that there is no general duty to give reasons, brushing aside the open-ended nature of the considerations invoked in *Oakley*. The Court then reviewed various rules relating to the provision of reasons for planning decisions in subordinate legislation, remarking that it was hard to detect a coherent approach to their development.[83] However, although planning law was a creature of statute, 'the proper interpretation' was 'underpinned' by general common law principles, including fairness and transparency, and it was appropriate for the common law to fill the gaps in the present system of rules.[84] This is suggestive of another enervating cycle of proceduralisation.

The particular potential for this case law development to drive proceduralisation inside the administration is highlighted in the general briefing document for UK civil servants, *Judge Over Your Shoulder* (JOYS).

> The record should ... show by what process of reasoning issues were resolved, and how the various factors were weighed against each other... Decisions involving human rights are likely to be scrutinised even more intensely, and that means that they will have to be more fully reasoned.[85]

As socio-legal analysis demonstrates, however, there may well be a major disconnect between 'unified reasons' as conceived by senior judiciary and the multiple and fractured reasoning paths of front-line public administration—not least when decision-making tasks are dispersed among human and non-human actors. The high-level, formal expression of administrative law values may subtly influence a

[79] Martin Shapiro, 'The Giving Reasons Requirement' [1992] U Chi Legal F 179. And see *R (Litvinenko) v Secretary of State for the Home Department* [2014] EWHC 194 (Admin), [2014] HRLR 6.

[80] *Oakley v South Cambridgeshire District Council* [2017] EWCA Civ 71, [2017] 1 WLR 3765.

[81] Ibid [56–58] (Elias LJ).

[82] *R (CPRE Kent) v Dover District Council* [2017] UKSC 79, [2018] 1 WLR 108.

[83] Ibid [23].

[84] Ibid [54–58]. But see for a more cautious approach *R (Save Britain's Heritage) v Secretary of State for Housing, Communities and Local Government* [2018] EWCA Civ 2137.

[85] Government Legal Department, *Judge Over Your Shoulder* (5th edn, 2016) paras 2.56 and 2.60.

wide range of administrative settings and, from a ground-floor perspective, appear distinctly artificial.[86]

A second new wave of procedural review concerns decision-making inputs through consultation. Part of the explanation lies in an increase in statutory requirements as part of more extensive regulatory endeavour, where once again the EU influence has been strong, most obviously in the field of environmental protection.[87] But the domestic courts themselves have significantly extended the scope of consultation in recent times, while again rejecting a general common law duty, partly for pragmatic reasons of administrative overload etc.[88] Given authoritative recognition in the *GCHQ* case,[89] procedural legitimate expectation as a basis for the duty to consult has featured prominently in the context of austerity-driven reductions in public services. A firm insistence that the general legal standards apply where a public authority chooses to consult further underscores the substantial element of proceduralisation.[90]

We find JOYS patiently explaining how case law establishes a template for the 'proper' operation of consultation procedures. As well as the basics of input at the formative stage of proposals, sufficient information, and adequate time, civil servants should understand that 'the product of consultation must be conscientiously taken into account when the ultimate decision is taken'. Naturally this means further procedures, with a particular boost for reason-giving. 'Where a consultation has taken place, and before a decision has been made, proper weight must be given to the representations received. The decision must make it clear that this has been done.'[91] The judicial contribution to public participation here is duly explained in terms of 'fairness' and also, in terms of information flows, of 'rationality'.

A chief bone of contention is whether a public authority should be required not only to consult on its own proposals but also on alternative options. In the now leading case of *Moseley*,[92] which concerned a statutory consultation over local tax proposals, the UK Supreme Court held that the procedure was improper because the council gave a misleading impression of having little choice. As part of

[86] See Jennifer Raso, 'Unity in the Eye of the Beholder? Reasons for Decision in Theory and Practice' (1 August 2016). Proceedings of the Public Law Conference, The Unity of Public Law? University of Cambridge, UK, 12–14 September 2016, SSRN: https://ssrn.com/abstract=2840488, accessed 1 July 2019.

[87] For the legal influence of the UNECE Convention on Access to Information, Public Participation in Decision-making and Access to Justice in Environmental Matters, see Charles Banner (ed), *The Aarhus Convention* (Hart 2015).

[88] See the lengthy discussions in *R (BAPIO Action Ltd) v Secretary of State for the Home Department* [2007] EWCA Civ 1139 and *R (Plantagenet Alliance Ltd) v Justice Secretary* [2014] EWHC 1662 (QB), [2015] 3 All ER 261.

[89] *Council of Civil Service Unions v Minister for the Civil Service* [1985] AC 374 (HL).

[90] *R v Brent London Borough Council, ex parte Gunning* (1985) 84 LGR 168; *R v North Devon and East Devon Health Authority ex p Coughlan* [2001] 1 QB 213 (CA).

[91] *Judge Over Your Shoulder* (n 85) paras 2.43 and 2.44. And see Cabinet Office, *Consultation Principles* (rev edn, 2018).

[92] R *(Moseley) v Haringey London Borough Council* [2014] UKSC 56, [2014] 1 WLR 3947.

the consultation, the authority should have outlined what other possibilities it had considered and the reasons for their rejection. It may be that this new vista of judicial interaction with administrative procedure will not take us far.[93] Suffice it to add that, testimony to the clash with values of efficient and effective decision-making, the expansive approach of the courts to consultation has itself been in ministers' sights. In the Criminal Justice and Courts Act 2015 we thus see serious attempts at 'clamping down' on judicial review proceedings through a mix of doctrinal and financial devices.[94]

Yet it is a third wave of procedural review which, by its very nature, best illustrates the judges' close engagement with, and assertion of their own values in, heavily detailed administrative decision-making frameworks. First identified some ten years ago, this is 'structural procedural review', a novel development in the English common law now represented in a cluster of weighty cases at Court of Appeal level intended to achieve a wide impact. As the nomenclature suggests, the judges are seen circumnavigating the constraints of a classical form of procedural review directed at particular decisions, to consider whether the decision-making framework as a whole is inherently loaded against a class or classes of persons: 'systemic unfairness'. Judicial 'guidance' on how 'defects' might be cured is part and parcel of the enterprise.

The development further represents a step-change in the important and long-standing role of the courts in the control of delegated legislation, where the doctrine of parliamentary sovereignty does not provide a shield. Targeting this detailed formal legal means for policy delivery, structural procedural review fits the conception of rule-makers as chief decision-makers in the juridified bureaucratic state. Using test cases in this way to correct procedural inadequacies generating widespread error and injustice has obvious attractions, more especially in the case of vulnerable classes of persons and problems of access to justice. We see austerity as conditioning a clash of legal and administrative values as the courts are effectively prompted in collective, campaigning forms of litigation to maintain, as well as promote, basic procedural standards.

Two cases epitomise this novel approach. *Detention Action*[95] saw a successful challenge to a controversial system of 'fast-tracking' in asylum decisions. The case shows the close focus on the framework of rules that structural procedural review necessarily entails. This is underwritten by a template for dealing with such cases, an injection of discipline into the new judicial methodology which further serves to authorise it. Notably, the judge should look 'at the full run of cases' going through

[93] See *Rusal v London Metal Exchange* [2014] EWCA Civ 1271, [2015] 1 WLR 1375; *Kebell Developments Ltd v Leeds City Council* [2018] EWCA Civ 450, [2018] 1 WLR 4625.

[94] Carol Harlow and Richard Rawlings, '"Striking Back" and "Clamping Down": An Alternative Perspective on Judicial Review' in *Public Law Adjudication* (n 35).

[95] *R (Detention Action) v First-Tier Tribunal (Immigration and Asylum Chamber)* [2015] EWCA Civ 840, [2015] 1 WLR 5341.

the system, the 'core question' being whether 'the system has the capacity to react appropriately to ensure fairness'. The Court could hardly have sent a stronger message back to the Home Office: 'Speed and efficiency do not trump justice and fairness. Justice and fairness are paramount.'[96] The issue in the *Howard League* case[97] was the legality of changes to the criminal legal aid scheme that removed pre-tariff Parole Board reviews and a number of other areas of decision-making concerning prisoners from the scope of the scheme. Standing on traditional values, the Court of Appeal found the complaint of inherent or systemic unfairness partly satisfied and was generally unimpressed with the Lord Chancellor's reference to alternative—cheaper—means of protection such as internal complaints procedure and independent monitoring. The case also highlights the impact of proceduralisation on judicial review by greatly expanding the relevant fact base and extending judicial analysis into multiple statistics on categories of case and outcomes and staffing levels.

Notwithstanding the concerns about judicial overreach inevitably raised, including from the Bench,[98] structural procedural review has continued to gain momentum as a rapid progression through time limits, institutional independence, and legal support demonstrates.[99] Whether the UK Supreme Court acts to rein in the new methodology remains to be seen, though the recent *UNISON* case[100] concerning fees in employment tribunals, where Lord Reed propounds a similarly aggregative approach under the twin banners of rule of law and access to justice, suggests not.

V. Technological Revolution

The introduction of automated public services and use of information and communications technology (ICT) for purposes of intergovernmental communication and to interact with civil society can be loosely dated to the 1990s, when the Internet was first implemented, digital technology had begun to dominate telecommunications and a central government website was set up as 'the place to find government services and information'. The impact was at first modest; computers appeared in government offices, data began to be stored online, there were experiments with online service delivery, and so on.[101] Crucially, automation and technology were

[96] Ibid [22], [27] (Lord Dyson).

[97] *R (Howard League for Penal Reform and another) v Lord Chancellor* [2017] EWCA Civ 244, [2017] 4 WLR 92.

[98] *R (S) v Director of Legal Aid Casework* [2016] EWCA Civ 464, [2016] 1 WLR 4733 [18] (Laws LJ).

[99] Frederick Powell, 'Structural Procedural Review: An Emerging Trend in Public Law' (2017) JR 83.

[100] *R (UNISON)* (n 19). See Richard Rawlings, 'The UNISON Case: A New High-Water Mark' (2018) 29 PLR 190.

[101] Helen Margetts and Martin Partington, 'Developments in E-government' in *Administrative Justice in Context* (n. 20).

viewed in a largely positive light as valuable aids to efficiency; they did not at this stage imply wholesale changes to administrative methods and procedures. The objective was 'better government'; it was thought that automation would enable better policy outcomes, higher quality services, transparency through the provision of easy online access to information and greater engagement with citizens, all criteria against which government and public administration should be judged.[102] For the UK Government of the time, automation offered more: it was a key element in modernisation of the public service, a New Labour priority.[103] Delivery of the reforms promised through NPM and digitalisation would transform government's relationships with its citizens and permit democratic participation in the policy process through a process known as 'open policy-making', in which transparency and participation would come together.[104] In short, ICT and automation were empowering. They would help achieve government goals of economy, efficiency, and effectiveness while at the same time promoting the good governance values of transparency, accountability, and participation.[105]

It would have been hard at that time to foresee the extent of government reliance on automation for the delivery of public services some twenty years later. Today, vehicle and TV licensing is managed by online apps; delivery of welfare benefits is partly automated, with algorithmic calculation of benefits; National Health Service records are digitalised; smart cards allow for interdepartmental file sharing; and passport control is biometric.[106] A Government Digital Service (GDS) is sited within the Cabinet Office whose job is 'digital transformation of government'; by 2020, GDS is promising to 'design and deliver joined-up, end-to-end services' and extend the 'transformation' to as many as twenty services.[107] At the same time, we have become familiar with the technological ineptitude of government: the confusion caused by incompetent digitalisation of the Her Majesty's Revenue and Customs tax credit scheme, and the roll out of the Universal Credit scheme, which replaced it, are just examples.[108] Problems with data retention (as when a Royal Navy laptop containing unencrypted personal records for more than 600,000 people was lost[109] and a private contractor to the Driving Standards Agency lost

[102] OECD, *The E-Government Imperative* and *E-Government for Better Government* (OECD 2003).

[103] UK Cabinet Office, *Modernising Government* (Cm 4310, 1999). And see John Hudson, 'Designing the Structures of Government: The UK's Information Age Government Agenda' (2002) 30 Pol'y and Pol 515.

[104] Office of the e-Envoy, *In the Service of Democracy: A Consultation Paper for Electronic Democracy* (2002).

[105] John Morison, 'Modernising Government and the E-Government Revolution' in Nicholas Bamforth and Peter Leyland (eds), *Public Law in a Multi-Layered Constitution* (Hart 2003).

[106] For the multifarious uses of technology in governance, see Ignace Snellen, 'Electronic Governance; Implications for Citizens, Politicians and Public Servants' (2002) 68 Int'l Rev Admin Sci 183.

[107] GDS, *Government Transformations Strategy* (2017).

[108] Parliamentary Commissioner of Administration, *Tax Credits: Getting It Wrong?* (HC 1010, 2007/8); John Seddon and Brendan O'Donovan, 'The Achilles Heel of Scale Service Design in Social Security Administration: The Case of the United Kingdom's Universal Credit' (2013) 66 International Social Security Rev 1.

[109] Sir Edmund Burton, *Report into the Loss of MOD Personal Data* (30 April 2008).

a hard disk from its secure facility based in Iowa containing just over 3 million records including names and postal addresses) rendered wide reform of outdated data protection laws clearly necessary.

The impetus would come from the European Union, where the impact of ICT has been still greater. Easy communication between public bodies makes EU integration possible, encourages working across organisational boundaries, and fosters collaboration and cooperation across EU administration. Ever-expanding EU data banks, initially installed to combat terrorism and serious crime, drive proceduralisation at transnational, national, and regional levels. 'At each stage', complained Statewatch, 'databases become ever more intrusive as security demands cumulatively diminish freedoms and rights.'[110] Approaches to freedom of information and privacy vary across the Member States and, at Union level, data protection in the EU Charter received specific mention as a fundamental right.[111] Stringent new data protection procedures were finally delivered on a trans-EU basis in the General Data Protection Regulation (GDPR).[112] This in turn necessitated complex new national legislation with an array of powers to introduce procedural regulations and new administrative procedures.[113] A raft of complex security measures was also legislated at the domestic level.[114]

There is growing realisation of a significant interface with administrative law.[115] The motivation to promote artificial intelligence (AI) has to date been largely commercial[116] but AI is already in use in the public service, for example by the police, prisons, and probation services for risk assessment purposes. Algorithmic programmes of this type should be compatible with human rights law, due process, and good governance principles of transparency and accountability.[117] But we are learning that software may be systematically programmed to 'introduce inadvertent bias, reinforce historical discrimination, favour a political orientation or

[110] Tony Bunyan, 'The Interoperability of Justice and Home Affairs Databases' (Statewatch Briefing March 2018) 20; available at: http://www.statewatch.org/analyses/no-323-interoperability-briefing.pdf, accessed 1 July 2019.

[111] Article 8 of the European Charter of Fundamental Rights provides that '[e]veryone has the right to the protection of personal data concerning him or her'.

[112] Regulation (EU) 2016/679 of the European Parliament and of the Council of 27 April 2016 on the protection of natural persons with regard to the processing of personal data and on the free movement of such data, and repealing Directive 95/46/EC [2016] OJ L119/1. For commentary, see Christina Tikkinen-Piri et al, 'EU General Data Protection Regulation: Changes and Implications for Personal Data Collecting Companies' (2018) 34 Computer Law and Security Review 134.

[113] For the UK, the Data Protection Act 2018 is designed to carry the GDPR over post-Brexit.

[114] Notably the Regulation of Investigatory Powers Act 2000; the Data Retention and Investigatory Powers Act 2014 and Investigatory Powers Act 2016.

[115] *R (Bridges) v Chief Constable of South Wales Police* [2019] EWHC Admin 2341, [78], [2019] WLR(D) 496.

[116] House of Lords Artificial Intelligence Committee, *AI in the UK: Ready, Willing and Able?* (HL 100, 2017–19); *Government Response* (Cm 2645 2018).

[117] Roger Brownsword, 'What the World Needs Now: Techno-Regulation, Human Rights and Human Dignity' in Roger Brownsword (ed), *Human Rights* (Hart 2004).

reinforce undesired practices'.[118] Increasingly, this may occur robotically through the use of intelligent algorithms with capacity to remodel themselves in accordance with information from the programme they are operating. Challenge is made difficult by the lack of transparency, a term that takes on a new meaning in a computerised world, requiring understanding as well as access to 'the pattern or rules that have been used to create the outcome'.[119] Judges, officials, and the wider public will need to become computer savvy while computer experts will need to develop a greater understanding of law.

This seems to be understood by the Australian Federal Government which, in its comprehensive *Better Practice Guide* for those in charge of installing automated systems, insists that members of the design team must 'share an understanding of the primacy of the law and this understanding must be reinforced at all stages and levels of the project'.[120] Discussing the use by regulators of algorithmic reasoning and machine learning for risk assessment, Eva Micheler and Anna Whaley stress the need for accountability: 'decisions about identifying risk and acting on such identification involve judgement and should be subject to accountability'[121]—although whether a machine can be held accountable is questionable.

Automation is increasingly being trialled across the field of administrative justice, where automation in courts and tribunals at first received an enthusiastic welcome as likely to cut costs and delays, reduce error rates, and encourage participation and involvement on the part of appellants.[122] Early experiments with parking adjudication, where online hearings were pioneered, seemed to support these claims.[123] The heady atmosphere culminated with *Transforming Our Justice System*, which describes a new and simpler online procedure for online tribunal hearings, promising support to users who are uncomfortable with or unprepared for a digital legal experience. More adventurous, the paper envisions a process of 'continuous dispute resolution', adding to the case management functions of judges

[118] Marijn Janssen and George Kuk, 'The Challenges and Limits of Big Data Algorithms in Technocratic Governance' (2016) 33 Government Information Quarterly 371.

[119] Dave Coplin, Chief Envisioning Officer at Microsoft, in evidence to the House of Commons Science and Technology Committee, *Robotics and Artificial Intelligence* (HC 145, 2016–17) para 45. And see Cynthia Dwork et al, 'Fairness Through Awareness' in *Proceedings of the 3rd Innovations in Theoretical Computer Science Conference* (ACM Digital Library 2012) 214; Andrew D Selbst and Julia Powles, 'Meaningful Information and the Right to Explanation' (2017) 7 International Data Privacy Law 233.

[120] Australian Government, *Automated Assistance in Administrative Decision-Making: Better Practice Guide* (Commonwealth of Australia 2007). And see Melissa Perry, 'iDecide: Administrative Decision-Making in the Digital World' (2017) 91 ALJ 29.

[121] Eva Micheler and Anna Whaley 'Regulatory Technology: Replacing Law with Computer Code' (LSE Law, Society and Economy Working Papers 14/2018); available at: http://eprints.lse.ac.uk/100149/, accessed 1 July 2019.

[122] See Richard E Susskind, *The End of Lawyers? Rethinking the Nature of Legal Services* (OUP 2008).

[123] Caroline Sheppard and John Raine, 'Parking Adjudications: The Impact of New Technology' in Michael Harris and Martin Partington (eds), *Administrative Justice in the 21st Century* (Hart 1999).

power to determine 'the right point, in terms of the extent of the evidence gathered, to decide a claim'.[124]

Later studies are more probing. John Raine has questioned the way in which automation has transformed the character of parking adjudication, substituting typical administrative procedures for traditional adjudicative procedure.[125] More recently, Joe Tomlinson and Robert Thomas ask similar questions in a study of online tribunal processes for social security appeals, warning of the dangers of moving too fast in the absence of an adequate research basis.[126] At the same time, concern is expressed that as automation proceeds, the lack of computer literacy among claimants may hinder access to vital public services,[127] while a study of telephonic and face-to-face advice in social welfare legal aid suggests that serious or urgent cases are better served by the latter.[128] Moreover, it is time to think more closely about what we might we lose through the substitution of 'robo-judges' for the face-to-face oral hearings that have for many generations characterised the common law approach.[129] Computerisation is apt to change the nature of an administrative process, translating public administration from a person-based service to a dehumanised system where expert systems replace officials and routine cases are handled without human input.[130]

Looking forwards, some creative forms of judicial review litigation may be engendered. To this effect, a whole series of pressure points can be identified relating to well-known legal doctrines. Take *Wednesbury*-style process review under the twin rubrics of relevant and irrelevant considerations, a standard feature of the Administrative Court caseload, which could usefully take new significance in the face of ever-more sophisticated decision-making software. Other potential litigation 'hot spots' include the role, if any, of reason-giving in AI frameworks and, it being one thing for ministers to look to civil servants[131] and another to (be seen to) rely on machines, the place of (un)lawful delegation. The classical 'no fettering' doctrine may well provide an acid test. Is the notion that every rule may have an

[124] See Joe Tomlinson, 'The Policy and Politics of Building Tribunals for a Digital Age: How 'Design Thinking' Is Shaping the Future of the Public Law System', UK Const Law Blog (21 Jul 2017).

[125] John W Raine, 'Modernising Courts and Tribunals through ICT: Lessons from The London Parking Appeals Service' (2001) 9(2) International Journal of Law and Information Technology 115.

[126] Joe Tomlinson and Robert Thomas, 'Remodelling Social Security Appeals (Again): The Advent of Online Tribunals' (2018) 25 Journal of Social Security Law 84 and Joe Tomlinson, *Justice in the Digital State: Assessing the Next Revolution in Administrative Justice* (Policy Press 2019).

[127] Paul Larkin, 'Universal Credit, "Positive Citizenship", and the Working Poor: Squaring the Eternal Circle?' (2018) 81 MLR 114. In the single year 2015–16, HMRC's extra help team attended 23,447 appointments: see GDS, 'Background' (n 107).

[128] Marie Burton, 'Justice on the Line? A Comparison of Telephone and Face-to-face advice in Social Welfare Legal Aid' (2018) 40 Journal of Social Welfare and Family Law 195.

[129] See *R (Osborn) v Parole Board* (n 71).

[130] Mark Bovens and Stavros Zouridis, 'From Street-Level to System-Level Bureaucracies: How Information and Communication Technology Is Transforming Administrative Discretion and Constitutional Control' (2002) 62 Public Administration Rev 174.

[131] *Carltona Ltd v Commissioners of Works* [1943] 2 All ER 560 (CA); *R(Bourgass) v Secretary of State for Justice* [2015] UKSC 54, [2016] AC 384 [48–52].

exception, [132] and that discretion involves at least a limited power of free choice, wholly outdated in view of digitalisation and the emergence of AI? With the evolution of mass, ITC-based administrative systems, matched by greater judicial insistence on the formulation of, and adherence to policy,[133] such principles appear increasingly hard to apply. The argument can however be turned on its head. If with automated systems rules take over from discretion and individualisation, is there not a particular premium on legal doctrines which maintain at least a modicum of balance between values of certainty and consistency and responsiveness? An insistence, that is, on the role of judicial review as guarantor of a humanising element. Increased dependency on decision-making systems framed in terms of digitalisation and AI can again be said to place a special premium on wide-ranging external review founded on systemic values. The *Detention Action* and *Howard League* cases provide an important clue. We see significant potential in structural procedural review for judicial engagement in this brave new world.

VI. Conclusion

As laid out in the introduction, this chapter had three main themes. The first was the growth in proceduralisation of public administration in the period since the 1970s in which we have both worked. This term has been used both to denote the trend to substitute rule-based and formal procedures for 'vaguely defined' administrative processes, which has been the hallmark of our chosen period, and also the development of a form of proceduralism akin to the juridification described by Teubner as a 'bureaucratisation of the world'.

The substitution of fragmented structures of governance for highly centralised, unitary government created a need for procedures to glue together the resultant institutional networks, a phenomenon more pronounced in the sprawling development that characterises the current phase of EU governance. Machinery for control in the shape of regulation was also required. Within administration, we identified as the main driver to proceduralisation the reform programme that came to be known as NPM, which introduced a new, managerial ethos into an administration widely characterised as bureaucratic, unresponsive, and slow to take on new ideas. We identified a similar managerial ethos pervading regulatory theory, which borrowed tools and techniques from the audit model of governance. A derogatory note crept in when, ironically, the managerialism associated with these new governance styles came in time to foster bureaucracy through the complexity of the

[132] See *British Oxygen Co Ltd v Ministry of Technology* [1970] 3 WLR 488 (HL) (Lord Reid).

[133] See the trio of cases, *R(Lumba) v Secretary of State for the Home Department* [2011] UKSC 12, [2012] 1 AC 245; *Nzolameso v City of Westminster* [2015] UKSC 22, [2015] 2 All ER 942; *Mandalia v Secretary of State for the Home Department* [2015] UKSC 59, [2015] 1 WLR 4546.

legislative and regulatory framework and a too-rigid adherence to administrative procedures.

The second main theme of our chapter has been the idea of procedures as a repository for values, and of values as an important, though often subliminal, driver of administrative procedure, an aspect which we think deserves special emphasis in view of the multisourced character of our discipline and also because administrative procedure has an image problem ('dull, technical, routine' etc). We do not accept that the values that underlie the procedures are all 'immanent in the law' or to be 'found by interpreting legal materials'. There are many shared values and the trade in values is not, as it is sometimes presented, a one-way traffic. The ideals of fairness or impartiality are widely recognised across society as normative values that administrators and adjudicators must both observe. Much the same can be said of the good governance values of transparency, accountability, and participation, which in our view form the compass points for contemporary public administration. We have noted the extent to which this pervasive vocabulary is now making its appearance in the conceptual vocabulary of administrative law.

As every administrative lawyer should know, the relationship between courts and administration is complex and multifaceted. We have not presented it as essentially hierarchical or oppositional, although we have identified some fertile conditions for conflict, more especially when managerial values of economy and efficiency come up against judicial due process values as in *Detention Action* or *Howard League*. The clashes are, however, occasional rather than endemic and we should not overlook the fact that courts are not always the ultimate winner. In this chapter, our emphasis has rather been on the scope for interchange, juncture, and convergence in what we see as a 'pick and mix' relationship.

We are not in a position to say whether the rapid digitalisation of public services that characterises this last decade should be described as a new proceduralism, though its performance as a driver of administrative procedures has been strong. So far, it has generally been possible to treat the advent of ICT and electronic administration as machinery for administration and technical assistance to administrators; in other words, as back up for officialdom. In a world where computers assist in decision-making, but do not themselves take decisions, where computers are rule-bound but they do not make the rules, computerisation is a welcome aid to efficient delivery of administrative justice, but computers do not dispense justice. Viewed in this light, the process of digitalisation can be kept within legal parameters with some adaptation of legislation and judicial doctrine. But the assumptions on which these statements are based are changing quite rapidly, as we have tried to indicate. Computerised decision- and rule-making are changing the dynamics of governance and digitalisation is reshuffling the pack of values. Artificial intelligence is also moving us fast into uncharted administrative territory, one in which prior achievements in terms of rights protection and the good governance triad of transparency, accountability, and participation may be restricted, even reversed. We are, in short, facing a paradigm change, one in which administrative procedure is properly a chief focus. The advent of an increasingly 'virtual' administration, one which often shows little sense of connection with the population it purports to serve, is a real possibility. To couple it with an administrative law that shows little sense of connection with the changing realities of governance in a new era of technological revolution would be a mistake that we must guard against.

15

The Foundations of the Duty to Give Reasons and a Normative Reconstruction

*Joana Mendes**

I. Introduction

Administrative structures and procedures have been a pivotal feature of EU integration, having both supported the path towards an 'ever closer union' quite beyond legislative harmonisation and, at the same time, challenged and transformed some of its constitutional features. The last decade demonstrated once again the centrality of the administration in the European Union, as the restructuring of financial regulation led to the emergence and progressive reinforcement of the EU financial agencies (ESAs), to the creation of the Single Resolution Board (SRB) and to the attribution of a new role to the European Central Bank (ECB), now in charge of banking supervision, a task which it also shares in various degrees with the competent authorities of the Member States. At the same time, the *Short-selling* judgment may have opened the path for a deeper constitutional change, where EU agencies assume a stronger institutional role than hitherto, both in relation to the European Commission and to the Member States' administrations.[1] And yet, such increased executive prominence emerges in a period when the teleological ineluctability of the 'ever closer union' is more questioned than ever, when the balance between centralisation and the powers of national competent authorities is constitutionally more significant, and when the political and legal salience of financial regulation is greater than in the pre-crisis period. The tensions between technocratic competence and the democratic implications of executive empowerment are as present as ever.[2] Such context, combined with the significance and breadth

* Professor of Comparative Administrative Law, University of Luxembourg. I am grateful to the organizers of the Conference 'The Foundations and Future of Public Law' organised in Honour of Paul Craig in September 2018 (Oxford University) and to its participants, whose remarks have contributed to improving the quality of the paper. Jacques Ziller reminded me of the work of Paul Reuter, which pointed me to the constitutional foundations of the duty to give reasons. I am grateful too to Paul Craig, for a lengthy discussion, to Liz Fisher and Alison Young, for insightful comments.

[1] Case C-270/12, *United Kingdom v European Parliament and Council* (*Short-selling*) ECLI:EU:C:2014:18. See also Edoardo Chiti, 'Is EU Administrative Law Failing in Some of Its Crucial Tasks?' (2016) 22 ELJ 576.

[2] For example, Ronan McCrea, 'Forward of Back: The Future of European Integration and the Impossibility of the Status Quo', (2017) 23 ELJ 66; Agustín J Menéndez, 'The Crisis of Law and the

Joana Mendes, *The Foundations of the Duty to Give Reasons and a Normative Reconstruction* In: *The Foundations and Future of Public Law*. Edited by: Elizabeth Fisher, Jeff King, Alison L Young, Oxford University Press (2020).
DOI: 10.1093/oso/9780198845249.003.0015

of the powers of EU financial regulators, make those developments in financial regulation a fertile ground for a more general reflection on the tools of EU public law, and, specifically on the fundamentals of administrative procedural principles. Taking the cue from those who stress the importance of tinkering with administrative procedures in a context of contestation and constitutional change,[3] this chapter is a first approach to such analysis, focusing on the duty to give reasons.

Beyond the confines of the EU delegation doctrine, legislative mandates may give constitutive powers to EU agencies (and to other administrative entities) that allow them to give meaning to the law that they implement and, thereby, to define how public interests are realised. These powers may require revisiting and reassessing the function of the procedural principles that are guarantees of both proper administrative behaviour and legality. Procedural principles should ensure the constitutional embeddedness of the decisions taken in the exercise of constitutive powers. This function may not be only, or primarily, assured via judicial oversight. The chapter contends that procedural principles may have a different content, depending on whether they are mainly approached as norms of conduct in the processes through which executive bodies engage in giving concrete meaning to norms, or as norms of control deployed by the competent EU court when conducting judicial review (section II). Although these are two sides of the same coin, it is useful to distinguish them for analytical purposes. This chapter analyses the different facets of the duty to give reasons from this perspective. It outlines its threefold function—enabling Member States and citizens to be cognisant of the way the Treaty competences are carried out, providing support to judicial review, advocating the self-regulation of decision-makers (section III)—and investigates the origins of the giving-reasons requirement in the context of the European Coal and Steel Community (ECSC), building on a selection of early case law, on the ECSC Treaty (ECSCT) provisions, and on early doctrinal accounts thereof. Here, the duty to give reasons was one of the pillars of integration. A legal reflection of the High Authority's political role, reason-giving was systematically linked to legally binding assigned purposes of public action by force of the Treaty (section IV). This analysis provides the grounds for a reconstruction of the duty to give reasons and for a clarification of its constitutional function: the duty to give reasons has an action-guiding role that should facilitate public understanding of how executive action is shaping the public interests that EU executive bodies are mandated to pursue. Such a role is both consonant with the current constitutional framework within which EU executive bodies operate, as defined in the Treaty, and prepares the ground to establish it as a norm of conduct, alongside (and in interaction

European Crises: From the Social and Democratic *Rechtsstaat* to the Consolidating State of (Pseudo-) technocratic Governance' (2017) 44 JLS 56 (2017).

[3] Carol Harlow, 'Editorial: Transparency, Accountability and the Privileges of Power' (2016) 22 ELJ 3.

with) its judicially assigned role. If the duty needs to provide such a public understanding, reasons for executive action need to reflect how the latter results from compromises, assessments, and choices implied in shaping the public interests that EU executive bodies are legally mandated to pursue, within a political system and a legal order equally founded on legal values and on the achievement of political goals (section V).

II. The Constitutive Function of Executive Actors and its Procedural Implications

The ESAs, the SRB, and the Supervisory Body responsible for the ECB's supervisory tasks (ECB-SB) have been given direct powers of market intervention that are relatively novel outside of the limited areas of direct administration that have conventionally been the preserve of the Commission. Even if they rely on intricate schemes of separation of tasks between EU and Member States' bodies, collaboration, and participation in composite procedures, these bodies can adopt binding decisions that both condition the powers of national administrations and determine the rights and obligations of private entities.[4] Thus, for instance, the European Securities and Markets Authority (ESMA) may adopt measures that prohibit or impose conditions on short-selling activities if there is 'a threat to the orderly functioning and integrity of the financial markets or to the stability of the financial system of the Union', and possible measures adopted by national competent authorities 'do not adequately address' that threat.[5] In a similar vein, the ECB-SB may withdraw the license of a bank when it considers that 'proper actions necessary to maintain financial stability have not been implemented by national authorities'.[6] The SRB may exercise directly the powers of national competent authorities over private entities when it considers that those authorities have not 'properly addressed' its warning on non-compliance with the Single Resolution Mechanism (SRM) Regulation or with its own instructions, and the consistent application of high-resolution standards may be at stake.[7] In other cases, the decisions that they

[4] Within each of their functional domains, the powers of each of these bodies differ as do the specific ways in which the articulation between EU and national authorities is conceived. However, for the purposes of this chapter, these differences will be mitigated to focus on the functional similarities of the powers they were given.

[5] Regulation (EU) 236/2012 of the European Parliament and of the Council of 14 March 2012 on short selling and certain aspects of credit default swaps [2012] OJ L86/1, Article 28(1) and (2).

[6] Council Regulation (EU) No 1024/2013 conferring specific tasks on the European Central Bank concerning policies relating to the prudential supervision of credit institutions [2013] OJ L287/63, Article 14(6); the procedure includes consultations with national competent authorities in which they should be given the opportunity to decide on 'the necessary remedial actions' (Article 14(5)), and due process given to the parties concerned (Article 22).

[7] Regulation (EU) No 806/2014 of the European Parliament and of the Council, establishing uniform rules and a uniform procedure for the resolution of credit institutions and certain investment

address at private entities do not involve a suitability assessment of national competent authorities' action and an eventual substitution thereof. Thus, the ECB has direct supervisory powers over credit institutions to address 'relevant problems' when those entities do not comply or are likely not to comply with EU law and national law, or when supervisory review determines that credit institutions do not ensure sound management;[8] the SRB may resolve a financial institution when it is 'failing or likely to fail', when there is 'no reasonable prospect' that private sector measures could prevent that failure in a timely way, and when resolution is necessary in the public interest, in the terms further specified in the SRB Regulation.[9]

All these powers are highly regulated, reflecting also the contestation that surrounded their assignment to EU bodies.[10] Their legal mandates delimit the substantive scope of administrative action, identify the conditions that must be fulfilled for their exercise to be lawful, and set out the procedures they must follow, thereby making these powers amenable to judicial review. If one is to use the classification that has left a sharp imprint in EU law, they are 'clearly delimited executive powers'.[11] At the same time, they are goal-oriented, rely on prognostic technical assessments to achieve broadly defined outcomes, and shape continuously and in the long term the behaviour of both public and private entities. That their legal mandates are delimited, in no small part, by undetermined legal concepts such as 'threat', 'significant investment concerns, 'and 'financial stability' evidences the distinct characteristics of their powers. The meaning of legally defined conditions of executive action that rely on undetermined concepts can hardly be set in abstract. That meaning is given via the action of executive actors, assessing in each case which decision the economic and social circumstances require, whether and why they constitute a 'threat', raise 'significant investment concerns', or make a financial institution 'failing or likely to fail'. The verification of threats, investment concerns, or risks of failure has normative consequences as it may impact on the public interests that they need to pursue while delimiting the scope of legitimate action. Which interests ought to prevail in each specific circumstances for the better fulfilment of the regulatory and supervisory functions entrusted to the executive bodies is a discretionary choice that, arguably, co-determines the interpretation of undetermined legal concepts.[12] Via their practices and decisions, these bodies define how law is completed and made concrete, both filling in legal indeterminacy and defining the way public interests are protected. They have, in this sense, constitutive powers, shaping the polity of which they

firms in the framework of a Single Resolution Mechanism and a Single Resolution Fund [2014] OJ L225/1, Article 7(4).

[8] Regulation No 1024/2013 (n 6), Article 16(1).
[9] Regulation No 806/2014 (n 7), Article 18(1), (4), and (5).
[10] Niamh Moloney, *The Age of ESMA* (Hart 2018) 243 (on ESMA only).
[11] Case C-270/12 *United Kingdom v European Parliament and Council* (*Short-selling*) (n 1).
[12] Joana Mendes, 'Bounded Discretion in EU Law: A Limited Judicial Paradigm in a Changing EU' (2017) 80 MLR 443.

are agents and the meaning of the legal conditions that delimit their authority to act. No doubt this occurs under the vigilant eye of the Court of Justice of the European Union (CJEU), but in the end, it may be primarily EU executive actors, rather than the CJEU, defining the meaning of the legal conditions that delimit their authority to act. Courts may choose to defer on matters of legal interpretation, not least because of the expertise involved in determining the content of undetermined legal concepts, or because of the policy choices that legal interpretations may imply.[13] Indeed, a court's questioning of the law may amount to questioning the strategy of an administrative authority in view of the public interests that they need to fulfil,[14] which, depending on the circumstances of the case, a reviewing court may or not consider legally warranted. Prudential reasons for deference may prevail.[15]

The observation that highly constrained legal environments may not prevent the ability of executive actors to act in a constitutive capacity, through their ability to concretise and develop law, prompts a critical assessment of the role of procedural principles in ensuring the legality of EU administrative action. One should focus on the role of such principles to embed constitutionally the exercise of constitutive powers within the sphere of decision-making that may be left to executive and administrative bodies. Such constitutionally embeddedness is not only ensured via judicial review. In addition to functioning as norms of control—as norms that enable courts to verify the factual and legal correctness of discretionary assessments[16]—procedural principles function as norms of conduct; that is, those norms through which administrative and executive bodies define legal and non-legal criteria (eg economic models and parameters, efficacy, political convenience, non-binding international standards) that implement and flesh out the enabling norm by reference to the case that needs to be decided.[17] While norms of conduct

[13] For example, the definition of what is a 'normal handling or use' for purposes of classification of dangerous substances may result from the combination of guidelines drafted by the Commission's Legal Service and of the assessment of the competent technical committee, which the Court may endorse when assessing whether there were manifest errors of assessment (Case C-15/10, *Etimine v Secretary of State for Work and Pensions* [2011] ECR I-6681, Opinion AG Bot, paras 83–87; and, in the judgment, para 71). For the US context, referring to the *Chevron* doctrine, see Jerry L. Mashaw, *Reasoned Administration and Democratic Legitimacy. How Administrative Law Supports Democratic Government* (CUP 2018) 118, arguing that there is a substantial overlap between interpreting the legal provisions that ground the agency's authority to act and choosing policy.

[14] Pablo Ibañez Colomo, *The Shaping of EU Competition Law* (CUP 2018) 74–75.

[15] While the current powers of EU institutions and bodies in financial regulation expand the review of the CJEU, they also constitute a challenge to the Court. Pedro G Teixeira, 'Europeanising Prudential Banking Supervision: Legal Foundations and Implications for European Integration' in John E Fossum and Agustín J Menéndez (eds), *The European Union in Crises or the European Union as Crises*, (Arena Report No 2/14, 2014), 527–83, 557.

[16] This function was perhaps best formulated in the often quoted *Technisches Universität München* case (Case C-269/90, *Technische Universität München v Hauptzollamt München-Mitte*, [1991] ECR I-5469, para 14). See also Paul Craig, *EU Administrative Law*, (3rd edn, OUP 2018) ch 12.

[17] For this distinction between norms of control and norms of conduct, and respective concepts, see José M Rodriguez de Santiago, *Metodología del Derecho Administrativo. Reglas de racionalidad para la adopción y el control de la decisión administrativa* (Marcial Pons 2016) 24–25. See too Eberhard Schmidt-Assmann, *La Teoría General del Derecho Administrativo como Sistema* (Marcial Pons 2003)

ought to include non-legal criteria of decision-making (which may be the prevailing sources of legitimacy of the decision adopted), legal criteria, and in particular those stemming from legally assigned purposes of public action, should also steer executive action when making normative programmes concrete. At the end, the ensuing decisions should be justified also by reference to their ability to implement the constitutional commitments of the legal order which executive bodies are developing. This is what is meant here by constitutional embeddedness. Both the public interests that constitute the purposes of public action and the legal values that found the legal order which frames such action provide normative criteria for assessing EU executive action. Understood in this way, ensuring the constitutional embeddedness of executive action is not only a function of courts, who are bound to preserve a constitutionally assigned sphere of decision-making to administrative bodies, but also of executive and administrative bodies when acting.

Executive and administrative bodies need to comply with the judicially defined standards of legality and fairness. But procedural principles may have additional layers which enable them to steer executive action to ensure the constitutional embeddedness of the constitutive function of EU executive and administrative bodies. The aspects of procedural rules that may matter for a function of judicial control may not be the aspects of procedural rules that may matter for the function of normative development in which executive bodies engage. The multifaceted functions of procedural principles are well illustrated by the duty to give reasons, analysed next.

III. The Duty to Give Reasons: Constitutional Function, Norm of Control, and Norm of Conduct

The duty to give reasons has generally three related functions: it provides an understanding of why public authority has been exercised as expressed in a legal act, it enables courts to assert the legality of public action and those concerned to defend their rights and legally protected interests, and it prompts a thoughtful consideration by the decision-maker of the various legal and policy issues involved in public action. The first function has a specific constitutional significance in the context of EU law: a statement of reasons that shows 'clearly and unequivocally the reasoning of the institution which adopted the measure'—to use the standard judicial formula[18]—allows the Member States and 'all interested nationals' to be cognisant

241, pointing out that, in German administrative law, the predominance of judicial review in developing administrative law has downplayed an autonomous function that the administrative procedure may have in ensuring the correctness of administrative action.

[18] For a random illustration of judgments of different decades, see, eg Case C-350/88, *Delacre v Commission* [1990] ECR I-395, para 15; Case T-188/98, *Kuijer v Council* [2000] ECR II-1959,

of how the EU institutions, bodies, offices, and agencies are, by effect of their specific decisions, carrying out the tasks assigned to them under the Treaties. This constitutional function justifies that it is, since the 1950s, a Treaty-based duty, now extended to all legal acts of the Union (Article 296(2) Treaty on the Functioning of the European Union (TFEU)). It comes to the fore, particularly, but not exclusively, on litigation involving institutional disputes or challenges by Member States that dispute the use of, or the lack of reference to, legal bases.[19]

The duty's constitutional function is indissociable from the ability of the courts to review the legality of the acts of the EU institutions. But, in ensuring that the duty to give reasons is complied with, the courts also develop it as a norm of control. Because the duty to give reasons straddles the boundaries between procedural and substantive legality (in particular in assessments on the adequacy and consistency of the reasons given), the EU courts have sought to avoid 'substantive review in disguise' that could harm the autonomy of policy processes and restrict discretion.[20] In this vein, the EU courts consistently emphasise that the specific requirements of the duty to give reasons depend on the circumstances of each case, in particular on the substance of the measure, the nature of the reasons given, the interests the persons directly and individually concerned (in addition to the addressees) may have in obtaining explanations, the context of the measure and 'all the legal rules governing the matter'.[21] Such control may mirror the broader constitutional function of the duty,[22] but, in its guise of norm of control, the duty may become 'parasitic' on the rights of the persons concerned by the underlying act and on the necessities of judicial review.[23] Depending on the circumstances of the case, the standard of legality of the duty to give reasons in EU law can be delimited by two core factors: the statement 'must show clearly and unequivocally the reasoning of the ... authority which issued the measure, so

para 36; Case C-521/09 P *Elf Aquitaine* v *Commission* [2013] ECR I-8947, para 147; Case T-122/15, *Landeskreditbank v ECB* ECLI:EU:T:2017:337, para 123.

[19] Case 24/62, *Germany v Commission* [1963] ECR 63; Case 22/70, *Commission v Council* [1971] ECR 263, para 42; Case C-350/88 *Delacre v Commission* [1990] ECR I-395; Case C-41/93, *France v Commission* [1994] ECR I-1829, para 34; Case C-233/94, *Germany v European Parliament and Council* [1997] ECR I-2405, para 25; Case C-370/07, *Commission v Council (CITES)* [2009] ECR I-8907, para 37.

[20] Craig (n 16) 380–2; Christian Calliess and Matthias Ruffert, *EUV/AEUV: das Verfassungsrecht der Europäischen Union mit Europäischer Grundrechtecharta* (5th edn, Beck 2016) Article 296, pt 21. Indicating how the EU Court may perform substantive review when controlling compliance with the duty to give reasons, in connection to the principle of care, see Hanns Nehl, *Principles of EC Administrative Law* (Hart 1999) 143–44. Pointing out how the Court has moved away from that stance, Craig (n 16) 381.

[21] For example, *Landeskreditbank* (n 18) para 124; Case C-15/10, *Etimine v Secretary of State for Work and Pensions* [2011] ECR I-6681, paras 114 and 115.

[22] For example, Case C-221/09, *AJD Tuna* v *Direttur tal-Agrikoltura u s-Sajd and Avukat Generali* [2011] ECR I-1655, paras 57–67.

[23] The term 'parasitic' is used by Jerry L Mashaw, 'Public Reason and Administrative Legitimacy' in John Bell et al (eds), *Public Law Adjudication in Common Law Systems. Process and Substance* (Hart 2016), 11–22, 14, making this observation regarding US administrative law (with a hint at EU law, 16).

as to allow *those concerned* to take cognizance of the justification of the measure adopted and to enable *the Court* to exercise its power of review'. This standard enables the CJEU to proceduralise rationality as determined by the needs of effective judicial protection and by the constraints of litigation.[24] It may lead the Court to confine the scope of the duty accordingly. When, for instance, an applicant claims that specific aspects of an act were not sufficiently explained, or that the observations it submitted during the decision-making procedure were not sufficiently considered in the statement of reasons, the Court assesses whether that person could have reasonably understood the reasons given, whether it was in a position to bring a judicial action, and whether the Court has sufficient elements to review the measure.[25] Such assessment may be coupled with a review of the adequacy of the reasons given, irrespective of the position of the litigant,[26] but the duty to give reasons thereby acquires a subjective protective scope in so far as the Court will take into consideration the interests of those directly and individually concerned in obtaining explanations. This protective scope is limited by the caveat that the statement of reasons need not cover all the relevant matters of fact and law, whereby the Court shields the efficiency of decision-making from the demands of potential litigants and defines the boundaries of its reviewing role.[27] As a norm of control, the duty to give reasons has a specific ability constitutionally to embed the legal acts of which it is part in its quality of essential procedural requirement. It requires sufficient explanations for the specific purposes of review, but it may not enable an assessment of the extent to which the legal act at stake shapes the public interests it serves and the way these interests are protected and realised by effect of those acts. That will depend on the specific conditions of litigation. For example, the statement of reasons of a general act may be circumscribed when persons concerned have participated in the procedure (because of the information that they thereby acquire), while still indicating the essential objective of the act.[28]

The third function of this duty—a self-control mechanism during the decision-making process—is much less elaborated in the case law (if at all) for valid reasons of separation of powers. The sparse literature referring to this function in EU law appear to originate in an early reference by AG Roemer in a case concerning the Commission's competence to set lower tariff quotas for individual Member States. He stressed:

[24] Jerry Mashaw uses the term 'proceduralised rationality review' to refer to a type of review that, formally, at least strays away from a substantive assessment, given the need to preserve the sphere of policy-making that ought to remain in the purview of the administration, Mashaw, *Reasoned Administration* (n 13) 117.

[25] For example, Case T-100/15, *Dextro v Commission* ECLI:EU:T:2016:150, para 124; *Landeskreditbank* (n 18) para 129.

[26] For example, Case C-269/13 *P Acino v Commission* ECLI:EU:C:2014:255, paras 123 and 124.

[27] For example, *Etimine* (n 21) para 115; *Dextro* (n 25) paras 123 and 124; *Landeskreditbank* (n 18) para 129. See also section IVA below.

[28] For example, *Etimine* (n 21) paras 114–120.

> one must not forget the useful function which the obligation to state reasons performs for the purposes of *a logical strengthening of the protection afforded by the law*, in so far as it forces the Executives, when they formulate the statement of reasons for a decision, to *give careful consideration to the conditions giving rise to the decision*.[29]

In this formulation, this function of the duty to give reasons mirrors compliance with the principle of careful and impartial examination of the case at hand. If judicially enforced, this combination gives the Court a powerful tool to rein in the exercise of discretion, possibly disrupting the balance that it has sought to maintain in its more recent case law on the duty to give reasons.[30] But beyond the effect of strengthening judicial protection (the concern underlying AG Roemer's opinion),[31] the duty to give reasons leads the decision-maker to form a more substantiated idea of the concrete circumstances that surround a decision, of its various implications, and of the constraints to which it is subject, as well as of the legal criteria that may be relevant for the decision. This aspect of the duty as a norm of conduct was later picked up by Schwarze as follows: 'the duty to give an objectively conclusive statement of reasons forces the competent authority to consider keenly the issues and thus promotes administrative self-regulation'.[32]

Given the constitutive role of executive bodies, this third function merits further consideration; in particular, its potential capacity to anchor the constitutional function of the duty to give reasons. The way the EU administrative process is also shaped from 'within', and not only via judicial review, is often overlooked,[33] or at least, it may be taken as a matter pertaining to the way in which executive bodies organise their procedures internally. This self-regulatory function of the duty to give reasons may, however, have a deeper constitutional significance, ancillary to the protection afforded by 'the law' to public interests that decision-makers need to consider, which are normatively relevant in so far as they are the result of constitutional choices. An analysis of the origins of the duty to give reasons in EU law, going back to the text where it was first enshrined—the Treaty establishing the European Coal and Steel Community—will reveal the constitutional foundations of the duty and lay the ground for a richer normative understanding of the duty's role as a norm of conduct. As will be argued shortly, a reconsideration of the constitutional

[29] Case 24/62, *Germany v Commission* (n 19) Opinion of AG Roemer, p 73, emphasis added. The literature references are Jürgen Schwarze, *European Administrative Law* (rev 1st edn, Sweet & Maxwell 2006) 1401; Craig (n 16) 370; Calliess and Ruffert (n 20) pt 14.

[30] See the analyses of Nehl and Craig (n 20).

[31] This observation is borne out by the original version of its opinion: 'eine sinnvolle Verstärkung des Rechtsschutzes', refers to judicial protection, as evidenced in the translations ('un renforcement raisonnable de la protection jurisdictionnelle', 'un ragionevole rafforzamento della tutela giurisdizionale').

[32] Schwarze *European Administrative Law* (Sweet & Maxwell 2006) 1401.

[33] Carol Harlow and Richard Rawlings, *Process and Procedure in EU Administration* (Hart 2014) 38.

foundations of reason-giving is relevant for the current constitutional setting of the European Union.[34]

IV. The Origins of the Duty to Give Reasons in EU Law

A. Giving meaning to a novel duty

When the duty to provide reasons was enshrined in the Treaties, it constituted a novelty when compared to the legal orders of the six founding States. None of these acknowledged a general obligation to provide reasons for legal acts, applicable irrespective of the nature or content of the act. Unlike most other procedural rules, its introduction in EU law did not result from case law inspired by general principles common to the legal orders of the Member States. Rather, the innovation brought about by the Treaties provided 'an observation field for experimentation', capable of informing national debates on the desirability of introducing such a general duty in their respective administrative laws.[35]

From early on, the CJEU established the main building blocks of this novel duty, which resonate with the account given earlier of the current case law. Thus, the statement of reasons required 'mentioning those facts on which the legal justification for the measure depends, and the considerations which have led it to adopt its decision', being that 'the High Authority [was] not required to discuss all the possible objections which might be raised against the decision'.[36] Its content varied according to the nature of the act at stake, in particular the requirements being less strict for 'general decisions having the character of regulations'.[37] This scope was justified by the purpose the Court assigned to the duty. It sought 'to give an opportunity to the parties of defending their rights, to the Court of exercising its supervisory functions and to Member States and to all interested nationals of ascertaining the circumstances in which the Commission has applied the Treaty'.[38] These remain today the core building blocks of the duty to give reasons. On these grounds, early commentators concluded that the Court had been able to provide coherence to the duty, while adjusting its content to the act at stake, favouring synthesis in the statement of reasons over 'excessive analysis'.[39] Judicial flexibility—explained by the varying degree of review that the Court wished to perform in

[34] Section 5 below.

[35] Christian Hen, 'La Motivation des Actes des Institutions Communautaires' (1977) 1 Cahiers de Droit Européen 49, 50. His assessment was nuanced (89–91).

[36] Case 2/56, *Geitling v High Authority* [1957-8] ECR 3, 15

[37] Case 18/62, *Barge v High Authority* [1963] ECR 259, 280.

[38] Case 24/62, *Germany v Commission* (n 19) 69; Joined Cases 36, 37, 38–59, and 40/59, *Präsident et al. v High Authority* [1960] ECR 423, 439.

[39] Georges Le Tallec and Claus-Dieter Ehlermann, 'La Motivation des Actes des Communautés Européennes', (1966) 90 Revue du Marché Commun 179, 182 and 185.

each case—did not prevent the frequent annulment for breach of the duty to give reasons, having effective legal consequences.[40]

While the novelty of the duty called for innovation in defining its legal role, the Court gradually brought it in line with the laws of the Member States. The denser requirement for decisions of individual scope is one example of the gravitational attraction of the Member States' legal systems in defining the duty's content. There, the giving of reasons for acts of general scope was absent and reason-giving applied only to administrative acts of individual scope.[41] This requirement also reflected the subjective function that the duty to give reasons was acquiring in the law of the Community, guaranteeing legal protection to those potentially adversely affected by a legal act. This same rationale led the Court to admit that the content and depth of the reasons given could vary according to the degree of information that interested parties have, admitting even a reasoning by reference to general indications in the applicable legislation, where the addressees of a decision hold important information.[42] Where the advocate generals had opposed the relevance of such criterion, they had justified their opposition also on the grounds of procedural protection, instrumental to judicial review: persons other than the addressees of an act could also have standing to challenge the legality of the act.[43] The audience of those who needed to be persuaded by reasons coincided, therefore, with those who could have standing to challenge the relative legal act. Tallec and Elhermann were unambiguous regarding the beneficiaries of the duty to give reasons: 'interested or concerned' were the persons who could have standing, or those against whom an act could be invoked.[44] This position determined not only the function of the duty to give reasons but also, accordingly, its content. And yet, this judicial development accounted only in part for the constitutional function of the duty to give reasons.

B. The constitutional foundations of the duty to give reasons

The general duty to give reasons was meant also to enable 'Member States and ... all interested nationals [to ascertain] the circumstances in which the [institutions have] applied the Treaty'.[45] This function was independent of (even if related to)

[40] Hen (n 35) 72 and 77, referring to merger cases, where litigation abounded.

[41] The influence of the Member States' legal orders was felt also in other respects: when advising the Court on the required content of a reasoned opinion on the putative infringement of a Member State, AG Lagrange specified: 'no formalism must be demanded of this document, since ... the reasoned opinion is not an administrative act subject to review by the Court of its legality' (Case 7-61 *Commission v Italy* [1961] ECR 317, Opinion of AG Lagrange, 336).

[42] Hen (n 35) 79–82.

[43] Hen (n 35) 79, referring to the Opinion of AG Roemer in Case 24/62, *Germany v Commission* (n 19) 73.

[44] Tallec and Ehlermann (n 39) 187.

[45] Case 24/62, *Germany v Commission* (n 19) 69; Joined Cases 36, 37, 38–59, and 40/59, *Präsident et al. v High Authority* (n 38) 439.

the need to afford legal protection to those affected via judicial review.[46] It was justified by the constitutional framing of the powers of the High Authority (in the case of the ECSC), the Commission, and the Council (the only two institutions bound by the duty to give reasons in the original version of the Treaty of Rome). Such framing is known all too well: the institutions acted only within the limits of attributed competences (Article 3 ECSCT and Article 4(1) European Economic Community (EEC) Treaty); in doing so, the High Authority and the Commission took decisions in the interest of the Communities, independently of national governments, binding the Member States, subjecting them to the Court's oversight, and thereby conditioning their sovereign powers. This constitutional framing placed those institutions in a radically different position from the State administrations, who were also bound by a duty to give reasons on a limited range of legal acts. The duty to give reasons in Community law had, therefore, a specific constitutional foundation, which made it diverge from the duty as known in the administrative laws of the Member States.

In the case of the ECSC, that foundation had deeper roots. It was intrinsically linked to the very functions of the Community. Article 5 ECSCT outlined such functions, serving as a 'guide and reference point for the application of the other Treaty provisions'.[47] It determined, *inter alia*, that the Community ought to 'publish the reasons for its actions' (Article 5, 4th indent ECSCT). The duty to give reasons enshrined in Article 15 ECSCT in relation to the acts of the High Authority gave expression to this norm.[48] It was justified by the need to avoid the 'hidden actions' of an institution that 'too easily could be perceived as a "technocratic" body'.[49] Early case law confirms this systematic reading of Articles 5 and 15 ECSCT, referring to both provisions combined when adjudicating claims related to the duty to give reasons.[50] This link is significant. According to Paul Reuter, Article 5, 4th indent ECSCT embodied a general principle that underlay all the economic rules

[46] Originally, as enshrined in the European Coal and Steel Treaty, the duty to give reasons extended to the opinions of the High Authority (Article 15 ECSC), which were not reviewable acts (Article 33 ECSC). The High Authority later restricted the scope of application of this article with the purpose of aligning Article 15 ECSC with Article 190 EEC Treaty, which excluded opinions (and recommendations) from the scope of the duty to give reasons (Hen (n 35) 65–66, referring to Decision 22/60 of 7 September 1960 on the implementation of Article 15 of the Treaty [1960] OJ 61/1248).

[47] Robert Kovar, *Le Pouvoir Réglementaire de la Communauté Européenne du Charbon et de l'Acier* (LGDJ 1964) 178; Rolando Quadri, Riccardo Monaco, and Alberto Trabucchi (eds), *Trattato Istitutivo della Comunità Europea del Carbone e dell'Acciaio. Commentario*, Vol I, Art 1-45 (Giuffrè 1970) 109.

[48] Despite the different formulation in Article 5 ECSCT ('publish reasons'—'rends public les motifs', in the French version) and in Article 15 ECSCT ('state the reasons'—'les decisions . . . sont motivés'), the substance of the obligation appears to be the same (in the former case, a task of the Community, in the later, a duty of the High Authority). There is, nevertheless, a difference in scope between the two provisions: Article 5 encompassed legal acts of the High Authority that were outside of the scope of Article 15 ECSC.

[49] Quadri, Monaco, and Trabucchi (n 49) 112 (see also n 74).

[50] Case 6/54, *Netherlands v High Authority* [1954-6] ECR 103, 111; Case 2/56 *Mining Undertakings of the Ruhr Basin v High Authority* [1957-8] ECR 3; Joined Cases 1/57 and 14/57, *Société des Usines à Tubes de la Sarre v High Authority* [1957-8] ECR 105, 112.

established in the Treaty, which he expressed as follows: 'we can say without exaggeration that, according to the Treaty, the common market should be a "glass house".'[51] Fulfilling this principle was more than just a matter of giving reasons that could allow Member States and interested parties to ascertain whether the High Authority had lawfully used its conferred powers.

C. Making the common market a 'glass house': political significance and legal implications

The duty to give reasons was one of the constitutional pillars of the ECSC. A short excursus is needed to clarify this point. Article 5 ECSCT was inserted in Part I of the Treaty, its general part, together with the provisions that defined the economic ends of the Community (Article 2), the objectives that guided its actions (Article 3), and the notion of common market (Article 4).[52] Combined, these were the pegs that held together the other, more operational, provisions of the Treaty; these often included cross references to Articles 2 to 5 ECSCT. In articulation with the rest of the Treaty, these provisions of Part I both directed a course of action and defined the limits of what the Community could do.[53] Despite the general terms in which they were drafted, the Court was clear regarding the legally binding character of Articles 2 to 5 ECSCT: 'Those provisions are binding and must be read together if they are to be properly applied. These provisions can stand by themselves and accordingly, in so far as they have not been adopted in any other provision of the Treaty, they are directly applicable.'[54] The Court also confirmed the need for a systematic interpretation: 'If [those general norms] ... are governed by other provisions of the Treaty[,] words relating to the same provision must be considered as a whole and applied together.'[55]

In this reading, the duty to give reasons enshrined in the ECSC Treaty was more than a general rule justified by the limited competences of the Community and the 'supranational' powers of the High Authority, as it could result from Article 15 ECSCT. As a manifestation of a Community function—'to publish the reasons for its action' (Article 5 ECSCT)—the duty was one of the foundational blocks of the integration process. Politically, it fulfilled a core function: it enabled the High

[51] Paul Reuter, *La Communauté Européenne du Charbon et de l'Acier* (LGDJ 1953) 76.

[52] A final Article 6 on the legal personality of the Community, its legal capacity and representation (and an introductory Article 1 establishing the Community) completed this Part I.

[53] Quadri, Monaco, and Trabucchi (n 49) 40. Reuter, however, excluded Article 5 ECSCT from the Treaty provisions of constitutional relevance (Reuter (n 51) 45).

[54] Case 8/57, *Groupement des Hauts Fourneaux et Aciéries Belges v High Authority* [1957–8] ECR 245, 253, adding that: 'The exercise of powers ... conferred upon the High Authority is subject to the conditions set out in Articles 2 to 5 concerning the establishment, administration and guidance of the Common Market' (idem, 254).

[55] Ibid 253.

Authority to create allegiances with the Member States and the natural and legal persons subject to its decisions by assuring that, substantively, its decisions reflected the purposes of integration defined in the Treaty and, thereby, persuading through reasons. It was a means of ensuring the acceptance and cooperation of the states (without which the Community would fail) and of the persons who were the direct object of the Communities decisions.[56]

From this viewpoint, the systematic reading between the duty to publish reasons, on the one hand, and the provisions of the Treaty that defined the overall aim of the Community, its concrete goals, and the common market, on the other—supported by judicial interpretation[57]—was, arguably, the legal reflection of that political function. The Treaty-defined purpose or purposes were binding. According to the Court, they needed to 'be appraised as a whole and pursued exclusively in the common interest', which not only '[considerably exceeds] the sum of the individual interests of [each person] subject to the jurisdiction of the Community' but also ought to be 'defined in relation to the general aims [of integration]'.[58] Such was the legal relevance of the objectives set out in Article 3 ECSCT. By connecting them to the underlying ends of integration, the Court was stressing the deeply political role of the powers of the High Authority which gave it, *inter alia*, the possibility to 'exercise a broad influence on the market in coal and steel'.[59] The Court was, at the same time, embedding them constitutionally: the legal acts of the High Authority needed to be manifestations of the public interests related to the purposes of integration, pursued within the limits of the Treaty. Those objectives constituted, thereby, a substantive yardstick to assess the legality of Community acts. The statement of reasons was essential in so far as it enabled a judgment on whether and how those purposes were being fulfilled. The duty to give reasons was there not only to ensure the legal protection of affected parties and to facilitate judicial review, but also—and perhaps fundamentally—to enable 'Member States and ... all interested nationals [to ascertain] the circumstances in which the [institutions have] applied the Treaty';[60] that is, to assess whether they exercised their competences in a way that allowed them to pursue the fundamental goals for which those competences were attributed. Legally, it followed that reason-giving was 'not only

[56] This was the core integration challenge (see Mauro Cappelletti, Monica Seccombe, and Joseph Weiler, 'Integration Through Law: Europe and the American Federal Experience. A General Introduction' in Mauro Cappelletti, Monica Seccombe, and Joseph Weiler (eds), *Integration Through Law. A Political, Legal and Economic Overview* (De Gruyter 1985, 3–68, at 26).

[57] See (n 54).

[58] Case 8/57, *Aciéries Belges* (n 54) p 258. Article 3 introduced the objectives of the Community as follows: 'The institutions of the Community shall, within the limits of their respective powers, in the common interest.'

[59] Case 8/57, *Aciéries Belges* (n 54) p 253 (this case concerned the powers of the High Authority under Article 53 ECSCT to define the financial arrangements needed to pursue the objectives of Article 3 ECSCT, specifically its decision to equalise the prices of ferrous scrap).

[60] Case 24/62, *Germany v Commission* (n 19) 69; Joined Cases 36, 37, 38–59, and 40/59, *Präsident et al. v High Authority* (n 38) 439.

required by Articles 5 and 15 and [by specific Treaty provisions] but [it was] an essential, indeed constituent element of [the] act, with the result that in the absence of the statement of reasons the act [could not] exist'.[61]

D. Public understanding in the shade of judicial review

In an early case pertaining to a High Authority decision on cartel arrangements, Attorney General Lagrange went as far as a member of the Court ever did in spelling out the constitutional significance of the duty to give reasons beyond the legal protection of those affected. The duty to give reasons incumbent upon the High Authority had a dual role:

> First, it constitutes, from the point of view of public opinion, a guarantee against arbitrary action, by enabling the public to understand and investigate the actions of the executive invested with important powers. This is necessary, in particular, for the Assembly. It is this which explains and justifies the fact that reasons must be stated for all decisions of the High Authority, even those which would appear to be primary imputable to the exercise of discretionary power.[62]

By this last observation, AG Lagrange was pointing out that the scope of the duty to give reasons did not coincide with the scope of judicial review. In fact, Article 33 ECSC excluded from the Court's jurisdiction 'the evaluation of the situation, resulting from economic facts or circumstances, in the light of which the High Authority took its decisions or made its recommendations' (except in situations of misuse of powers or of manifest illegality).[63] The second role AG Lagrange identified was its ancillary function to judicial review: 'the duty to give reasons is also necessary to enable the decisions to be subjected to legal review *should they be contested before the Court*' (timewise, a subsidiary function).[64] The Court, in its judgment, did not echo Lagrange's opinion on that first function of the duty to give reasons, stressing instead the importance of the duty to give reasons in enabling the interested parties—'and, in the event of legal proceedings, the Court'—to assess the factual and legal correctness of a decision in cases where the Court's jurisdiction is limited.[65]

61 *Société des Usines à Tubes* (n 51) 112–13. See, further, Tallec and Ehlermann (n 40) 185.

62 Joined Cases 36, 37, 38–59, and 40/59, *Präsident et al. v High Authority* [1960] ECR 423, Opinion AG Lagrange, 451.

63 Article 33 ECSCT.

64 Joined Cases 36, 37, 38–59, and 40/59, *Präsident et al v High Authority*, Opinion AG Lagrange (n 62) 451, emphasis added.

65 Ibid 439. In a later case, in the context of the European Economic Community, AG Roemer would refer to this judgment to argue that 'it is precisely those decisions which are based upon an evaluation of the economic situation as a whole which require a very full statement of reasons' (Case C-24/62, *Germany v Commission*, [1963] ECR 63, Opinion of AG Roemer, 73). In his view, 'the novelty of the

AG Lagrange's reference to the *public* understanding of the High Authority's decisions on cartel arrangements remained an isolated reference in the case law, but it is worth expounding it here. The purpose was not only one of transparency (enabling the public to understand) but also one of control (enabling the public to investigate) as the original French version makes clearer ('contrôler' is the term translated as 'investigate'). The weak role of the parliamentary assembly in the institutional context of the ECSC was an important consideration in the AG's opinion and, at the same time, revealed the constitutional significance of the duty to give reasons beyond considerations of judicial review. As Hen suggested, 'the role of information that in internal law is fulfilled by the discussion of laws before the parliament is implemented here by the careful and detailed justification of the acts'.[66] At the same time, the recipients of such information were not only the assembly but also the public concerned by the legal acts, regarding whom the 'bodies of the Community need to make the reasons for their action clear'.[67]

Given the subject matter of the decisions of the High Authority, 'the public' mentioned by AG Lagrange was the informed public capable of understanding the logical path of decision-making that reason-giving ought to clarify, but not necessarily the range of those who, being directly and individually concerned, would have standing before the Community Court. The audience of the duty to give reasons was potentially broader, as the processes through which it could manifest its support or opposition to the acts of the Authority were not restricted to judicial review. That public should be able to check both the purpose with which the High Authority had acted (relevant also for judicial assessments of misuse of powers) and whether it had made use of its intervention powers in a limited way, as Article 5 ECSCT also determined.[68] Arguably, if seen in the light of the systematic link between Article 3 ECSCT (objectives of the Community) and Articles 5/15 ECSCT (duty to give reasons), the public understanding that the statement of reasons ought to facilitate would allow the High Authority to avert the 'hostility of certain milieus[,] [those who] had expressed an accusation all the more formidable as obscure of "technocracy", evoking the intervention of tenebrous powers, which in the modern political mythology have replaced the ancient gods'.[69]

subject matter with which the executives of the EEC have to deal' required a strengthened obligation to state reasons (ibid).

[66] Hen (n 35) 54.

[67] Ibid.

[68] Kovar (n 47) 178.

[69] Reuter (n 51) 52 (my translation), referring to objections that had been raised during the negotiations of the Treaty, ultimately leading to the creation of an Assembly not initially envisaged in the Schuman plan.

V. From Constitutional Foundations to Reconstruction

This excursus on the origins of the duty to give reasons and on its constitutional foundations provides a basis to reconstruct the meaning of the duty to give reasons in relation to the action of the EU executive. The constitutive function that EU executive bodies now perform in the area of financial regulation and the constitutional context in which EU executive actors exercise their competences[70] justify a reconstruction of the duty to give reasons that enables it to fulfil the constitutional function for which it was originally conceived, that is, to enable a judgment on whether and how the purposes of integration are being fulfilled, and thereby justify the exercise of authority by the European Union, irrespective of—and without prejudice to—how it is judicially enforced.

As much as the High Authority was an independent technocratic body, whose distinctive constitutional position derived from its ability to 'break with power politics' in a specific policy field and to 'pursue objectives and interests that are different from those of each of the participating nations',[71] so the EU financial agencies, the SRB and the ECB—notwithstanding their respective institutional differences—owe their existence to their technical competence and independence in the pursuance of public interests that transcend those of the Member States. In the 1950s, the powers of the High Authority were unprecedented in the way they limited Member States' action to create a Community; in the 2010s, the powers of the EU financial agencies and of the ECB in the context of the banking union amounted to 'the more drastic rearrangement of competences' in these fields to severe the links between financial institutions and states.[72] As much as the powers of the High Authority needed to be circumscribed by a duty to make public the reasons for its decisions, showing and accounting for how it was pursuing the Treaty objectives, so the EU financial agencies, the SRB and the ECB, are bound by a general duty to give reasons for their actions, rooted in Article 296(2) TFEU.

But in the decades in which the Coal and Steel Community slowly and discreetly died out, the legal relevance of the duty to give reasons as a constitutional norm linking public action to the founding objectives, instrumental to a public understanding of Community action (and presupposing a specific articulation of how the decision-maker gave meaning to the legally established purposes of public action), also faded in (then) Community law. As the Court progressively defined the legal content of the duty to give reasons, two reasons, at least, may explain that the

[70] Sections 1 and 2.

[71] Luuk van Middelaar, *The Passage to Europe. How a Continent became a Union* (Yale UP 2013) 15–16, citing Robert Schuman.

[72] Marco Lamandini, David Ramos, and Javier Solana, 'The European Central Bank (ECB) as a Catalyst for Change in EU Law. Part 1, The ECB's Mandates' (2016) 23 Columbia Journal of European Law 1, 22. Stripping banks of their 'nationality' was one of the purposes of the Single Supervisory Mechanism (Teixeira (n 15) 557).

systematic link between the objectives pursued and the reasons given weakened. On the one hand, the programmatic norms where such objectives are formulated tend to have an open-ended nature, hindering their weight in judicial arguments. On the other, the most immediate legal consequence of such systematic link is, arguably, the establishment of a misuse of power; but not only does this imperfectly express the constitutional significance of the duty (it implies a negative assessment, that is, whether a legal measure pursued an objective other than the one stated, thereby deviating from the legally established criteria) but it is also difficult to establish.[73] In fact, even those stressing in the context of the ECSC the legally binding nature of the objectives set in Article 3 ECSCT acknowledged the difficulties of determining how such objectives could condition the validity of legal acts. Paul Reuter alerted that it would be a mistake not to 'attach great importance to provisions whose generality somewhat irritates their strength' and forcefully argued that Article 3 conditioned the validity of the acts of the institutions.[74] But could one 'rebuke the High Authority for having achieved an inequitable compromise' between contradictory objectives?[75]

Such a possibility would appear to be a logical consequence of the binding nature of that provision combined with the constitutional function of the duty to give reasons as ensuring a public understanding of the decisions of the High Authority.[76] Such public understanding presupposed an articulation of how public action was constituting public interests. If it were to fulfil its constitutional function, the duty to give reasons should enable a judgment of the compromise achieved between competing public interests, of the choices made by the decision-maker when setting a specific course of action, defined in articulation with the legally defined purposes. This was a legal consequence of the way the duty had been enshrined in the Treaty, stemming in particular from the systematic links between the duty to give and publish reasons (Article 5, 4th indent ECSCT) and the objectives to be pursued (Article 3 ECSCT), as an expression of the general aims of integration (Article 2 ECSCT) and of its object (Article 4 ECSCT). Whether it was up to the Court to pass that judgment is another matter.

The way the Treaty today frames the duty to give reasons and, generally, the public action of the Union's institutions bodies, offices, and agencies justifies recovering these constitutional foundations. Unlike the preceding revisions of the norm originally enshrined in the Treaty of Rome, Article 296(2) TFEU broadened the scope of the duty to give reasons to 'legal acts' without specification, and is now inserted in a provision that delimits the way the EU institutions are bound in

[73] Agustín Gracia Ureta, 'Misuse of Powers as a Ground for the Annulment of Community Acts: A Case Law Approach' (2003) 3–4 Rivista italiana di diritto pubblico comunitario 775, stressing the limitations in invoking misuse of powers as a ground of annulment.

[74] Reuter (n 51) 91, 178 (my translation).

[75] Ibid 91 (my translation).

[76] See (n 62).

their choice of legal act. Much more than a formality, these modifications are manifestations of a larger reform process of the Union intended to establish a 'more institutionally solid, democratic and citizen-oriented foundation'.[77] This evolution has normative implications for the way in which executive bodies approach their decision-making procedures. Against this background, the constitutional function of the duty to give reasons, according to which it ought to inform the Member States, its citizens, residents, and registered legal persons, as well as its administrative bodies, of the way in which the EU institutions, bodies, offices, and agencies are applying, making concrete, and developing the Treaties, acquires a thicker dimension. It should be interpreted as requiring that EU actors show how, within each actor's specific role, they are ensuring the social, economic, and political integration as envisaged in the Treaties, within the limits specified therein and in the ensuing legal acts. The public interests established in secondary legislation as the ends that EU executive actors ought to pursue have arguably a legal value that is analogous to that of the objectives that Article 3 ECSCT had set for the High Authority. Despite their generality, when EU legislation determines that protecting the stability and effectiveness of financial markets (*inter alia* by ensuring proper regulation and supervision of the taking of investments, credit, and risks related to insurance, reinsurance, and occupational pensions activities) are the goals to be pursued by the financial agencies; or that the continuation of critical functions and the protection of public funds, depositors and client funds, and assets are among those that the SRB needs to attain via its resolution decisions; or that safety and soundness of the credit institutions and the financial stability are those that define the purpose of the new powers of the ECB in the context of the Single Supervisory Mechanism—then EU legislation is defining the substantive benchmarks against which the legal actions of these bodies should be normatively assessed in legal and political terms.[78]

[77] Calliess and Ruffert (n 20) pt 4. They stress also the reference in Article 296(1) TFEU to the principle of proportionality. By linking the duty to give reasons to Art 5 (4) TEU—and to the protocol on proportionality and subsidiarity—they connect the transformative function of the duty to give reasons mostly with regard to legislative acts (points 7 and 10 of the commentary). On the relevant constitutional modifications introduced by the Lisbon Treaty, see Paul Craig, *The Lisbon Treaty. Law, Politics and Treaty Reform* (OUP 2010) 71–77 and 247.

[78] See respectively Regulation (EU) No 1095/2010 of the European Parliament and of the Council of 24 November 2010 establishing a European Supervisory Authority (European Securities and Markets Authority), amending Decision No 716/2009/EC and repealing Commission Decision 2009/77/EC [2009] OJ L331/84, Article 1(5); Regulation (EU) No 1094/2010 of the European Parliament and of the Council of 24 November 2010 establishing a European Supervisory Authority (European Insurance and Occupational Pensions Authority), amending Decision No 716/2009/EC and repealing Commission Decision 2009/79/EC [2009] OJ L331/48, Article 1(6); Regulation (EU) No 1093/2010 of the European Parliament and of the Council of 24 November 2010 establishing a European Supervisory Authority (European Banking Authority), amending Decision No 716/2009/EC and repealing Commission Decision 2009/78/EC [2010] OJ L331/12, Article 1(5); Regulation (EU) No 806/2014 of the European Parliament and of the Council of 15 July 2014 establishing uniform rules and a uniform procedure for the resolution of credit institutions and certain investment firms in the framework of a Single Resolution Mechanism and a Single Resolution Fund and amending Regulation (EU) No 1093/2010 [2014] OJ 225/1, Article 14(2) (see also its Article 6(2)

Similarly to the objectives that bounded the powers of the High Authority, pursuing the public interests that define the function of the EU executive bodies in the area of financial regulation requires 'permanent reconciliation' which, on the whole and progressively, ought to enable the attainment of the common interest as it can be asserted on the basis of the pertinent aims now set out in Article 3 TEU.[79] The exercise of their powers, however dependent on the deployment of technical expertise and however limited to a specific field, ought to be constitutionally embedded when striking delicate balances between intervention and non-intervention and between national and EU action, within the boundaries of each legal regime and of the EU constitutional principles. Those are often the types of balances involved when EU executive actors make choices that define how the public interests that they are mandated to pursue are, as a result, defined in our societies. These are the type of normative choices enmeshed with their technical competence. It is the constitutional function of the duty to give reasons to show how those public interests are being made concrete, how EU executive actors reconcile the conflicts among them, the priorities they set in view of the economic facts or circumstances in the light of which they adopt legal acts, and the substantive implications of such balancing and priorities.[80] Nevertheless, failure to do so may not lead to a judicial finding of a breach of the duty to give reasons as that could lead to excessively intrusive review. This function of the duty to give reasons transcends the control function of the Court.[81] It is a guarantee against arbitrariness which, in addition to judicial review, should enable various constituencies to understand how executive decisions are constituting public interests and shaping social relationships accordingly, how, through the exercise of their power, they developing specific narratives of EU integration, vested with authority that has its ultimate foundation in the EU Treaties.

It is against such normative understanding that one should construct the self-regulatory role of the duty to give reasons as a guarantee of the good functioning of the administration: the duty enables the decision-maker to make a substantiated judgment of the conditions, criteria, and implications of the acts it adopts, in articulation with the purposes of legal action as defined in the enabling norms.

and (3)); Council Regulation (EU) No 1024/2013 of 15 October 2013 conferring specific tasks on the European Central Bank concerning policies relating to the prudential supervision of credit institutions [2013] OJ L287/63, Article 1.

[79] Case 8/57, *Aciéries Belges* (n 54) 254–55 and 258.

[80] This formulation on the function of executive actors draws on Case 8/57, *Aciéries Belges* (n 54) 255 (an almost identical formulation is found in Case 9/56, *Meroni v High Authority* [1957–8] ECR 133, 151–52).

[81] Contrarily, Calliess, and Ruffert (n 20) pt 11 and 12, who rather stress that the 'transparency-aimed, informative function of the duty to state reasons' is instrumental to judicial review.

These constitute core criteria of executive action. In that function—as a norm of conduct—the duty to give reasons ought to reflect a decision-making process that makes each legal act 'a plausible instance of rational collective action', in relation to the substantive yardsticks that the applicable norms define.[82]

The public understanding of the actions of the executive that a statement of reasons enables should be a reflection thereof. In a polity in which 'every citizen' has the right to participate in its 'democratic life' (Article 10(3) TEU), the citizen—both the 'market citizen' and the static citizen, since the way executive decisions pervade Member State action makes their effects transcend the scope of transboundary activity—emerges as a person entitled to understand, contest, or accept the way in which the institutions of that polity pursue collective goals, albeit in highly specialised fields. This requirement applies also to the EU executive and administrative institutions, bodies, offices, and agencies, as entities exercising public authority. Beyond the technocratic competence that grounds their decisions—and, to a great extent, justifies their creation—and the efficacy thereof to pursue the goals supporting their legal mandates, their decisions ought to be reasoned in a way that shows how they are contributing to shape the polity of which they are agents. The value judgments that underlie their decisions, the political reasons that, being supported by the relevant legal criteria (whether or not of constitutional nature), underlie and are enmeshed with the deployment of their (independent) expertise, should be brought to the forefront. As Jerry Mashaw pointed out, in an analysis of US administrative law, 'forcing the policymaking conversation into a technocratic mold may short-circuit meaningful conversation and debate about policy choices that are necessarily value-laden'.[83] In this understanding, an assessment of how the decisions of the EU executive are an expression of the constitutional commitments of the EU presupposes a debate about how EU executive bodies are defining the meaning of the public interests that they are mandated to pursue. The way this desideratum ought then to shape the specific content of the duty to give reasons as a norm of conduct may depend on the type of executive action at stake, on the availability of legally established criteria therefore, on the status of independence of the decision-maker or, possibly, on the way the acts at stake are defined by the combined intervention of national and EU decision-makers. It may, in addition, require the redefinition of administrative processes that support executive decision-making to channel and facilitate the development of this function of the duty to give reasons, outside the setting of judicial procedures.

[82] Mashaw, 'Public Reason' (n 23) 17. See too Mashaw, *Reasoned Administration* (n 13) 158–9, arguing that political reasons ought to be given by administrators in connection both to statutorily defined criteria of judgment and other legal sources of public values (such as the Constitution).

[83] Mashaw, *Reasoned Administration* (n 13) 159.

VI. Conclusion

In one of his ground-breaking works, Paul Craig argued: 'Lawyers have a tendency to emphasize the judicial role as being central in attaining the preferred constitutional vision. This is too narrow a focus.... [It] tends to place too much importance upon the power of the judiciary to orient society in a particular direction.'[84] Following this cue, this chapter placed its focus on the power of the executive to orient society. Drawing on the powers of direct market intervention that the EU financial agencies, the SRB and the ECB, acquired in the last decade, it argued that such powers enable them to give meaning to the legal conditions and criteria of their decisions, by interpreting undetermined legal concepts and defining how the public interests are realised in our societies. Those powers justify revisiting the role of procedural principles as criteria that should shape executive action when carrying out a constitutive function. As norms of conduct, procedural principles may have layers and dimensions that may not come to the fore in judicial review but that are equally important to ensure the constitutional embeddedness of executive action, making them an expression of the constitutional commitments that underpin the EU legal order.

The analysis of the duty to give reasons illustrated the multifaceted nature of procedural principles. The legal content of the duty to give reasons, as it currently binds the EU executive action, was defined early on by the Court, fleshing out a duty that constituted a novelty at the time it was inserted in the Communities' founding Treaties. The Court set the meaning and scope of the duty by reference to its reviewing role, considering also the legal protection that the duty affords to those who are directly and individually concerned. Both early commentators and today's scholars agree that the Court successfully struck a difficult balance between the needs of judicial protection and the autonomy of executive decision-makers in fulfilling their constitutionally assigned role. Without disputing this position, this chapter argued that the carrying out of the duty's constitutional function also depends on how executive actors, prompted to consider conscientiously the concrete circumstances and normative implications of public action, ensure a public understanding of how their action giving form to the constitutional commitments by which they are bound. The decision-maker's assessment of the conditions, criteria, and implications of the acts it adopts when performing its constitutive functions should be made against the public interests that they are mandated to pursue. These are guiding criteria of the duty to give reasons, in its function of self-regulatory mechanism. The policy and value-laden considerations that determined the legal action ought then to be reflected in the statement of reasons, enabling the public understanding for which it was originally conceived, when first enshrined in the

[84] Paul Craig, *Public Law and Democracy in the United Kingdom and the United States of America* (Clarendon Press 1990) 7.

Treaty establishing the European Coal and Steel Community, and, thereby, a judgment on the content of the compromises achieved. The difficulties of this proposition are clear if one considers the Court as the institution policing compliance with the duty to give reasons reconstructed in this way. Other paths will need to be trodden to explore how to make decision-makers comply with the duty to give reasons as a norm of conduct. The possible difficulties ahead may challenge the denser constitutional meaning of the duty to give reasons as a norm of conduct, as proposed in this chapter, but, as such, they do not deny or rule out at the outset the important role that this duty should have in embedding the constitutive powers of EU executive actors.

16
Process and Procedure in a Disordered State

Mark Freedland

The welcome invitation to contribute to the present collection by writing a commentary piece on the topic of 'The Administrative State: Process and Procedure' has brought me to a destination different from the one which I had in mind when accepting that invitation. I had initially imagined that this would simply be an opportunity to reflect specifically upon the two chapters which were being submitted on that topic, combining that with a tribute to the work of Professor Paul Craig in this and other aspects of public law and EU law. The first part or aspect of my commentary consists of just such a reflection, but the discussion of this topic at the conference which took place in September 2018 and my own subsequent thinking about that discussion have led me down a longer and steeper path into the foundations of public law—in fact, down to a level at which those foundations are, in the case of the British state at least, being shaken by deep disturbance and at which the state itself has become a disordered one. So, a second part or aspect of this commentary consists of a suggested approach to the questions of process and procedure which are being encountered at that fundamental level in the course of the Brexit process.

The argument of the piece moves from the first aspect to the second aspect; however, the question of whether and how far these two aspects are distinct ones is itself controversial, and the relationship between them is certainly a contestable one. Accordingly, the naming of the parts is more than usually difficult, and perhaps the piece should be played without a break. Nevertheless, I have separated the argument into two parts, and, in a way which will initially seem mysterious but for which the reasons will later appear, I distinguish between them by reference to a contrast between 'normal times' and 'times of crisis' in the affairs of the state.

I. The Processes and Procedures of the Administrative State in Normal Times

I begin with some redefinition—indeed, to be candid, some manipulation—of the topic of this commentary, which was specified as that of 'The Administrative

Mark Freedland, *Process and Procedure in a Disordered State* In: *The Foundations and Future of Public Law*. Edited by: Elizabeth Fisher, Jeff King, Alison L Young, Oxford University Press (2020). © Oxford University Press.
DOI: 10.1093/oso/9780198845249.003.0016

State: Process and Procedure'. The notion of the process and procedure of the administrative state, or even of process and procedure within the administrative state, is narrower than the one which I have in mind as delineating the boundaries of the present discussion. That is because my concern is really with the role of process and procedure in the government of the state, as much at a constitutional level as at an administrative one. In so saying, I follow and replicate the transition from an older idea of 'administrative law' as a distinct concern with the controlling of the processes and procedures of the administration of government (primarily by judicial review of administrative action), to a newer idea of 'public law' in which administrative law and constitutional law merge into an overarching concern with the shaping of the processes and procedures of government itself. That transition from 'administrative law' narrowly understood to 'public law' broadly understood is an intellectual and disciplinary transformation for which Paul Craig deserves quite a share of the credit. It is also one which in different ways informs and is expressed in the two chapters which are the immediate subject of my commentary.

The two chapters which I discuss are those of Professors Carol Harlow and Richard Rawlings on 'Proceduralism and Automation: Challenges to the Values of Administrative Law' (Chapter 14) and of Professor Joana Mendes on 'The Foundations of the Duty to Give Reasons and a Normative Reconstruction' (Chapter 15). The wise design of the present volume, advocated I believe by Paul Craig in conjunction with the editors, consisting in juxtaposing where possible papers primarily on British or Anglo-American public law with ones primarily on EU or more broadly European public law, has worked very fruitfully in this instance. Carol Harlow and Richard Rawlings, have contributed a chapter with the former focus, though not without extensive reference to EU Law. Joana Mendes has centred her chapter squarely on EU administrative law and administrative practice.

Both chapters instantiate a feature or phenomenon which has been elaborated in Paul Craig's work over the years, namely a growth in the complexity, coupled with an increase in the depth, of the notion of process and procedure in the exposition of administrative law.[1] Thus in British administrative law we can perceive a long evolution, from concern with a purely judicial overlay of process or procedural control upon administrative action, to a concern with process and procedure which is more deeply woven into the texture of the administrative state: and this concern is as liable to be vindicated by legislation as by case law, by administrative regulation or self-regulation as by judicial adjudication. In other words, we can discern a movement from the judicial review-centred vision of administrative law to a more multisourced and polycentric conception of public law itself.[2]

[1] See further n 5 and text attaching to it.

[2] This is an idea which I attempted to capture in a chapter on 'The Evolving Approach to the Public/Private Distinction in English Law' in Mark Freedland and Jean-Bernard Auby (eds), *The Public Law/Private Law Divide: Une entente assez cordiale?* (Hart 2006) 93–112.

This long-term movement can be traced, for British administrative law, from the foundational case of its modern history, the decision of the House of Lords in 1963 in the case of *Ridge v Baldwin*,[3] in many ways a cross-over case between the nascent administrative law and the nascent employment law of the United Kingdom of that period. It involved the recognition of the process rights of a Chief Constable of Police to a hearing before, and reasons for, his dismissal from his office and employment, a right which before then had been denied in such cases precisely on the basis that such decisions were seen as being 'administrative' ones rather than as being of a judicial or quasi-judicial character so as to bring the requirements of 'natural justice' into play.

The great procedural advance thus made in that decision was expressly contrasted by Lord Reid, in his leading judgment in the House of Lords in that case, with a totally de-proceduralised vision of the termination of the private law employment relationship:

> The law regarding master and servant is not in doubt. There cannot be specific performance of a contract of service, and the master can terminate the contract with his servant at any time and for any reason or for none. The question in a pure case of master and servant does not at all depend on whether the master has heard the servant in his own defence.[4]

I still experience a shock of surprise upon rereading that exposition, as much by reason of its egregiously archaic language as for the substantive view of the state of the law at the time which it quite accurately represents.

In the spheres both of public law and public administration and of the private law and management of employment relations, matters moved on from there towards the development of more extensive procedural protections of individual rights and legitimate expectations (though with some recent reversion to the primitive state in the private sphere).[5] In the public sphere, this moving on has consisted not just in an expansion of judicial review on the grounds of want of 'natural justice' or 'fairness' but also in what I believe has been the growth of a generally larger and more multifaceted concern with procedural regularity extending in complex ways to all three branches of the administrative state; that is to say, to the executive and the legislature as well as to the courts and tribunals. With regard to the legislature, one can cite the gradual recognition of the importance of pre- and post-legislative scrutiny: for the judiciary the creation of the Judicial Appointments Commission

[3] [1964] AC 40.

[4] [1964] AC 40, 65.

[5] I have attempted to offer a general survey of this territory in Mark Freedland, 'Reinforcing the Philosophical Foundations of Social Inclusion: The Isolated Worker in the Isolated State', which forms ch 18 of Hugh Collins, Gillian Lester, and Virginia Mantouvalou (eds), *The Philosophical Foundations of Labour Law* (OUP 2018) 322–26.

to replace the old 'tap on the shoulder' method, and for the executive the Freedom of Information Act, the duty to give reasons, internal review of decisions,[6] and the resort to publishing increasingly voluminous soft-law guidance.

It was this expansion and diversification which Paul Craig considered and charted in his article, published in 2010, 'Perspectives on Process: Common Law, Statutory and Political'.[7] There he describes a panoply of sources or locations of evolution of process rights or protections, depicted in his classic manner as falling into three divisions, those of common law, legislation, and political regulation. It is that third element of political regulation which is especially interesting. It is the least tangible of the three, but I think it can best be understood as the impulse of the administrative state to develop and regulate its own procedures and processes, and moreover to do so partly independently of the exactions of its judicial arm—thus for the executive arm to generate its own codes and regimes of process and procedure.

It is I think with that set of impulses and practices that our two chapters are essentially concerned. Carol Harlow and Richard Rawlings are justly famous for their contextual and functionalist approach to the understanding of the relationship between administrative law and the processes and practice of administration—an understanding which they have developed and nurtured with regard to the British administrative state in successive editions of their work on *Law and Administration*,[8] and which they have also brought to bear on the administration of the European Union in their monograph on that subject.[9] In this chapter, they reflect upon the implications for that relationship of 'the steady proceduralization of public administration experienced in recent years' which they think has by now become 'unremitting'.

In so doing, I think they find themselves grappling with a deep-seated problem, almost a paradox, which increasingly confronts their functionalist approach, namely that the processes and procedures which an activist administrative state devises to regulate and rationalise its pursuit of its collective goals eventually seem to distort those goals and to stultify their achievement. This is the problem traditionally understood as that of 'bureaucratisation', but these authors sense that it now seems to be presenting itself in an even more acute form in what they characterise as an 'age of managerialism'. In such an age, the paradoxical problem—which they variously refer to as that of 'proceduralisation' or 'proceduralism'—is that procedures originally vindicating the values of transparency, accountability, and

[6] See, generally, David Cowan and Simon Halliday, *The Appeal of Internal Review: Law, Administrative Justice and the (non-)Emergence of Disputes* (Hart 2003).

[7] Paul Craig, 'Perspectives on Process: Common Law, Statutory and Political' [2009] PL 275.

[8] Carol Harlow and Richard Rawlings, *Law and Administration* (3rd edn, CUP 2009), of which there is an excellent review by Robert Thomas at (2011) 74 MLR 153.

[9] Carol Harlow and Richard Rawlings, *Process and Procedure in EU Administration* (Hart 2014).

fairness in the conduct of public administration are gradually transformed into apparatuses of opacity, obfuscation, and defensive institutional surveillance.

This paradoxical problem is, at one level of understanding, a nearly universal one which is as old as the hills. At another level of analysis, it seems to present itself especially acutely at certain times, especially at the particular time in which one happens to be writing about it. That is because this essential problem assumes different specific forms, and we are acutely aware of the specific forms which the problem takes in the time and place in which we find ourselves. Thus, it is a problem which I have tended, in common I think with Carol Harlow and Richard Rawlings, specially to identify with the now quite long-lived wave of 'new public management' and the fashion for the privatisation, outsourcing, and contractualisation of the performance of public services.

Whether or not we believe that the paradoxical problem can be localised in that particular way, we can benefit from two further insights which these authors offer us into its current manifestations. First, they convincingly indicate the ways in which, in such an age of managerialism, the interaction between the value system of the administration and the value system of administrative law becomes an increasingly fraught one, apt to culminate in various forms of conflict between the government and the courts and tribunals which review its actions and its processes. As they succinctly and rightly put it in their presentation to the conference, 'We see austerity as conditioning a clash of legal and administrative values, as the courts are effectively prompted in collective, campaigning forms of litigation to maintain, as well as promote, basic procedural standards.'

Second, we can in my view readily share the alarm which these authors express at the reality that the paradoxical problem of proceduralisation is being rapidly intensified by automation, and in particular computer-driven digitalisation, of the processes and procedures of public administration with which we are concerned. They sound the warning as to how rapidly the automation and digitalisation of processes of interaction between the administration and the public, initially in the 1990s perceived as empowering the implementation of good governance values, seems to dehumanise those processes, appearing to enhance their sophistication and responsiveness but actually brutalising them to the sound of a mechanical chorus of honeyed words to the effect that 'your safety and comfort are our sole and over-riding concern'.

Joana Mendes, for her part, is equally interested in the different significance of processes and procedures as between, on the one hand, a set of requirements imposed on a public administration by its courts and, on the other hand, as a self-disciplinary regime implemented by the public administration itself. I think that she shares the normative view which underlies the functionalist approach of Carol Harlow and Richard Rawlings, and which is to the effect that a self-disciplinary procedural regime devised and maintained by a public administration is in its nature more possessed of authenticity and more robust than one which is exacted by the courts. This is essentially an application of the general argument for the superiority and preferability of self-regulation over imposed regulation: it is a powerful one as long as the risk is borne in mind that the executive arm of a public administration may become lazy about self-regulation if it feels too fully exonerated from the threat of judicial or legislative regulation.

At all events, my view is that Joana Mendes has built up a forceful argument of this kind for the welcoming and encouraging of procedural self-regulation on the part of the executive or administrative institutions of the European Union, and for contending that the development of such self-regulation, obviously as a response to political requirements and political pressures, is more promising for achieving the constitutional embeddedness of such a procedural regime than the equivalent exactions of the Court of Justice of the European Union (CJEU) would be likely to be. I think she successfully makes out this argument with regard to the idea of the duty of the EU executive or administration to give reasons for its actions, a duty of course imposed on it by the CJEU but which she contends could and should be accepted and elaborated by the executive as a self-control mechanism with an internal function in the carrying out of its decision-making processes.

Joana Mendes was and is also in my view right to point out the significance of Article 296(2) of the Treaty on the Functioning of the European Union's (TFEU's) broadening of the scope of the duty to give reasons to extend to a general category of 'legal acts', and to express the aspiration that this might provide the means whereby 'the transparency function of the duty to give reasons . . . acquires a thicker constitutional dimension'. In general, although her presentation and that of Carol Harlow and Richard Rawlings have quite a lot in common, and although they both share, as I have pointed out, a basically functionalist design, it is notable that the first of these two chapters concentrates more upon the processes and procedures of the administrative state at an administrative level, whereas the second is more focused upon their constitutional aspect. In this respect they complement each other, but the pointing up of this particular contrast between them leads on to a further line of reflection which I pursue in the next section of this commentary.

II. Constitutional Process in Times of Crisis

At this point in my contribution to the present symposium, as I did in my presentation to the preceding conference, I advance the suggestion that the foregoing discussion of the processes and procedures of the administrative state moves into a different dimension in times of major political crisis such as the one currently being experienced in the United Kingdom (and also, differently though scarcely less dramatically, in the United States). At the conference, I made this point in the form of the suggestion that the great affair of the UK's withdrawal from the European Union, known as Brexit, was, as they say, the 'elephant in the room' which could not be ignored. I meant that there was now a special need not just to follow out in its own terms the discussion of process and procedure which these two papers had introduced, but also to move it onto a different plane; that is to say to a level at which it engages with the deepest constitutional foundations of public law.

This suggestion was viewed as controversial by the participants in the conference, and a particular argument was advanced against it which should command our attention, especially now (this commentary being written in January 2019) that the sense of political crisis concerning Brexit has further intensified by comparison with the atmosphere in September 2018 when the conference took place. The objection to my suggestion was neatly encapsulated in a comment which seemed on the face of it to be a surprising one but which, I readily concede, deserves a fully reasoned response. The comment was that I was representing the present political period in the United Kingdom, dominated as it is by the Brexit controversy, as not constituting 'normal times', when in fact they are normal times and it is important to regard them as such.

The ensuing conversation made it clear that this was not, of course, raising a purely factual or descriptive question as to whether or not the Brexit controversy has or has not caused a great and exceptional perturbation in the affairs of the British state: there was general agreement that it had done so and was continuing to do so. The issue was, in truth, a more deeply evaluative one: it was opening up a debate about the normative implications of the very question of whether these are normal times. The difference was not as to whether these are *in fact* 'normal times' in Brexit Britain but as to whether these *should be regarded* as 'normal times' when we are talking about the processes and procedures of the administrative state.

It is useful to identify the nature of the contrast between the two opposing kinds of response to that question which were being advanced in the conference discussion or which are being advanced in the larger public debate which is taking place about the Brexit process both within the United Kingdom and more widely in Europe at large. On the one hand, the proposition that these should be regarded as times of crisis rather than normal times is one which doubts the adequacy of existing constitutional processes and procedures to deal with or resolve the crisis in question, and therefore asserts the necessity for novel procedural expedients and for a readiness to depart from existing procedural principles and rules. Taken to extremes, it represents an 'all bets are off' emergency approach.

On the other hand, the contrary response asserts the adequacy and robustness of existing processes and procedures, and moreover the desirability, on that set of assumptions, of sticking to existing processes and procedures in the interest of maintaining constitutional continuity and stability. It is in essence a 'business as usual' conservative approach. Of these two contrasting positions, the latter one appears on the face of it to be the less complicated and more straightforward of the two: indeed, it is apt to present itself as rather a blunt one, amounting to the view that the processes and procedures of the British administrative and governmental state have served the country well in past and can and should be relied upon to continue to do so even in the midst of the constitutional crisis associated with the Brexit process.

As the protagonist of the former, contrary, and apparently more radical position in this debate, I would develop my own version of that position in the following way. I would not be thinking in terms of a response to the Brexit crisis consisting of a formal declaration of a state of emergency: indeed, for reasons which will emerge shortly, I would be intent on avoiding that eventuality, though I can imagine that such a necessity might arise in the absence of policies and measures to pre-empt it. I would rather suggest a less extreme approach, consisting of a theoretical recognition that a situation of genuine constitutional crisis has come about with regard to Brexit, such as to command some shift of focus and some reordering of priorities in our thinking about the processes and procedures of the British administrative state as it seeks to resolve the crisis in which the Brexit process has immersed it.

The shift of focus which I have in mind, as I have indicated earlier in this chapter, would be from the administrative level of governmental processes and procedures to the fundamental constitutional level. The reordering of priorities which I have in mind would take place around and within the body of thinking about the securing of the rule of law which has such a central place in the discourse of the, still largely unwritten, British constitution—a body of thinking which was in my view wonderfully re-examined and reimagined by Lord Bingham in the monograph on that topic which he published in 2010.[10] Prominent in his re-articulation of the rule of law is the assertion of how important it is to understand the national observance of the rule of law as being located within and dependent upon the international legal order.[11]

It seems to me that the procedure which the Brexit process has hitherto followed has been at many points deficient in securing the rule of law in this international aspect. I have especially in mind the way in which Parliament, acting at the instance of the government of the day, enacted three statutes: the European Union Referendum Act 2015, the European Union (Notification of Withdrawal) Act 2017, and the European Union (Withdrawal) Act 2018 which between them instituted a Brexit process that was in many respects intrinsically heedless of the UK's place in the international legal order, that place having over the years become critically dependent, in many different aspects, upon its membership of the European Union. The devising and implementation of procedural mechanisms to retrieve and restore that place, or to secure a corresponding place for the United Kingdom in the international order after leaving the European Union, seem to me to represent a most pressing constitutional priority for the governments and Parliaments or Assemblies of the United Kingdom and its component national parts.

[10] Tom Bingham, *The Rule of Law* (Allen Lane 2010).

[11] Ibid, ch 10, 101–29.

I would also argue for another, associated but different, kind of recasting of priorities in the application of the idea of the rule of law to the constitutional processes and procedures of the British state in its time of Brexit crisis. This consists, as I have contended in an earlier paper,[12] in the recognition and vindication of a practical objective of sustainable governance. That earlier paper puts forward the view that this objective forms one of the crucial underpinnings of the rule of law, and that the constitutional foundations of public law are well and truly shaken when there is a failure to secure that objective. It seems to me that the Brexit process has reached a point at which there is a real prospective danger of outcomes which will represent or will bring about such a failure in the arrangements and procedures for the governance of the United Kingdom and the maintenance of its economy and its society.

III. Conclusion

It is tempting for me to conclude this part of my chapter at this point with the claim that the foregoing set of arguments provides a convincing and satisfactory framework for understanding and pursuing the normative debate about the proper degree of flexibility which should be accorded to constitutional processes and procedures in times of crisis such as those produced for the United Kingdom by its great Brexit controversy. Those foregoing arguments certainly seem to be apposite both at a descriptive and a normative level to account for the recent outbreak of contention about the proper procedures for regulating the relations between Government and Parliament in the conduct of the Brexit process. However, I fear that this claim might be an over-optimistic one, which would understate the tensions which are being experienced and the difficulties of resolving them by following the path of argument which I have pursued. I therefore proceed first to apply the argument in slightly greater detail to the Government versus Parliament procedural battles which are currently being fought, and then to indicate the problems which I think remain to be addressed.

The current procedural battles between Government and Parliament have of course been for some time foreshadowed or in the making. They were foreshadowed by the conflict in the courts in the *Miller* case[13] as to whether the Government required the authorisation of Parliament for the notification of the United Kingdom's intention to withdraw from the European Union. A crucial preliminary skirmish occurred in June 2018 when an amendment was secured to the Withdrawal Act to

[12] Mark Freedland, 'Brexit, the Rule of Law, and the Idea of Sustainable Governance' (Oxford Legal Studies Research Paper No 5/2018); available at: https://ssrn.com/abstract=3117471, accessed 1 July 2019.

[13] *R (on the application of Miller and another) v Secretary of State for Exiting the European Union* [2017] UKSC 5, [2018] AC 61.

guarantee a 'meaningful vote' in the House of Commons on the proposed withdrawal agreement.[14] The main battle was anticipated in December 2018, when the Prime Minister was due to put the proposed agreement to the vote but decided to postpone that vote,[15] and was widely accused of having violated the normal procedural conventions of the House of Commons by so doing. This impending battle was joined in earnest when, on 9 January 2019 the House of Commons was allowed by the Speaker to vote upon and to pass a procedural resolution requiring the Prime Minister to return very quickly to the House of Commons with an alternative 'Plan B' for further prosecution of the Brexit process[16] if the then proposed Withdrawal Agreement was rejected by the House of Commons.[17] This was a manoeuvre widely regarded as a major departure from the normal rules and conventions of procedure of the House of Commons.

The details of these continuing hostilities quickly become submerged from view beneath successive waves of debate in Parliament and in the media, but the general impression remains that the justificatory rhetoric emanating from the opposing sides in this continuing set of constitutional procedural battles largely follows the lines of normative confrontation which my arguments have sought to identify. Thus, the proponents of the radical procedural approach, supporting the exceptional freedom of procedural manoeuvre which has been asserted by Members of Parliament and permitted by the Speaker, claim that they are not basically subverting the procedural regime which normally regulates the relationship between the Government and Parliament but are simply modifying it slightly in order to respond to the exigencies of the Brexit crisis.[18] The opponents of this radical procedural approach, for their part, maintain that the Brexit debate has certainly not reached a point of crisis at which it has become legitimate to set aside the normal rules of process and procedure.[19]

To identify this normative debate in that way might appear to have contained it within a manageable framework: if we cannot quite regard ourselves as living in 'normal times' with regard to the constitutional processes and procedures of the administrative and governmental state, we can nevertheless be reassured that they are not crucially abnormal ones. However, as I have begun to indicate, I feel that this may turn out to be too sanguine a view of the gravity of what is at stake in this

[14] The amendment is embodied in Section 13 of the European Union (Withdrawal) Act 2018.

[15] See Hansard, House of Commons, Vol 651 cols 23 et seq (10 December 2018).

[16] See Hansard, House of Commons, Vol 652 cols 385 et seq (9 January 2019).

[17] This rejection was effected by a large majority of MPs in the following week; see Hansard, House of Commons, Vol 652 cols 1115 et seq (15 January 2019).

[18] See Dominic Grieve: 'Brexit Bid a "Tweak" not an "Upheaval"' (BBC Politics Live, 21 January 2019); available at: https://www.bbc.co.uk/programmes/p06ypl4c, accessed 1 July 2019.

[19] See, for example, Sir Stephen Laws, 'The Risks of the "Grieve Amendment" to Remove Precedence for Government Business' (Policy Exchange, 21 January 2019); available at: https://policyexchange.org.uk/publication/the-risks-of-the-grieve-amendment-to-remove-precedence-for-government-business,> accessed 1 July 2019.

debate, too complacent an insistence that these are normal or nearly normal times, when in fact they are deeply disordered ones in constitutional terms.

I have three reasons for expressing that fear, each one closely linked to the others. My first misgiving springs from the fact that, as so often in such disputes about constitutional process and procedure, the opposing ostensibly procedural stances are, of course, intimately linked to the respective rival positions in the underlying substantive Brexit debate itself. The procedural stances are, inevitably perhaps, by no means procedurally pure or disinterested. They are for the most partisan and instrumental ones, consciously or unconsciously taken up in pursuit of substantive positions in the main debates. The procedural stances very often function as proxies for the substantive goals which their protagonists are seeking or favouring.

This is, moreover, a kind of link which is quite a contingent and transient one. Because, at the time of writing, the default outcome of the Brexit process is to be that the United Kingdom will leave the European Union on 31 October 2019 with or without a withdrawal agreement, and because the normal rules of parliamentary procedure are tending to protect that outcome, the enthusiasts for that result have become the guardians of procedural propriety, while the opponents of that outcome, or those who wish to restrict the conditions in which that would be the outcome, figure as the radical advocates of flexibility in the procedural debates.

The assertion of this kind of link between these substantive and procedural disputes may be no more than a truism which applies almost universally to constitutional procedural debates, but it becomes a particularly problematical feature of constitutional situations where multiple substantive outcomes are actively in play and where many different procedural variants may be invoked in pursuit of those various outcomes. The Brexit debate has been allowed to shape up as one which is intractably convoluted by reason of this complex interplay between a multiplicity of substantive objectives and a multiplicity of possibilities for the respective pursuit of them. This explains, for example, the intricate procedural gaming in which the proponents of a second referendum are finding themselves obliged to engage.

My second misgiving about the prospects for a constructive and disinterested debate about the constitutional procedures which should apply to and during the Brexit process is quite closely associated with the first one. It is the fear that, especially in constitutional crises which are as complex and convoluted as the present Brexit debate, the procedural wrangles may themselves come to form the central battleground, thus diverting attention and effort from the resolution of the principal substantive issues which are at stake. It can sometimes be productive or even resolutive when tenacious substantive conflicts are channelled into procedural disputes, but it is more often the case that the disputes become generally more intractable where the contestation becomes acute in both the procedural and substantive dimensions, as threatens to happen in the present instance. In short, the procedural disputes may exert a centrifugal effect upon the substantive ones.

My third and final misgiving, as to the potential for negative and mutually self-reinforcing combinations of substantive and procedural constitutional conflicts, is one which is particular to the Brexit controversy (though not unique to it): it concerns the singularly multi-layered nature of that controversy. We should constantly remind ourselves of that which is all too readily forgotten by those in Westminster and its cyberspace, namely that this is not a contestation which is confined to the Government and Parliament of the United Kingdom in either its substantive or its procedural dimension. There have been many indications that this elaborate conflict could easily extend itself into the sub-national layer of what we might loosely term the governments of Scotland, Wales, and Northern Ireland: and it is intrinsic to the conflict that it in certain senses extends into the supranational layer of the governance of the European Union itself. On both those layers, more immediately perhaps on the supranational one, there are many possibilities for complex and counterproductive interactions between substantive and procedural elements of the Brexit process. For example, if the United Kingdom should seek a postponement of its exit from the European Union, the most complex partly procedural and partly substantive issues would present themselves concerning its participation in the elections to the European Parliament which at the time of writing were due to take place in May 2019.

The latter part of my paper has been devoted to delineating a particular and continuing crisis in the constitutional processes and procedures of the British administrative state, and to depicting the present times as, in this context, specially disordered ones rather than normal ones. It seems to me to be appropriate to conclude that discussion with a brief reflection upon the proper role of the public law scholar and academic teacher in such a crisis. For it seems to me that there are special demands at such times to which the academic public lawyer has to try to respond. These demands are partly for the provision of legal expertise and partly for the exercise of sound academic judgement. It is difficult to formulate a meaningful generalisation about the nature or sources of sound academic judgement in disordered times, but perhaps it is useful to suggest that it is more likely to be expressed in arguments which help to resolve grand constitutional conflicts than in arguments which serve to exacerbate them.

By following that particular path of reflection, I arrive at a point where I can conclude my chapter with a brief tribute to the work of Paul Craig in this particular field of study, treating that work as in a certain sense a culmination of his enormous endeavours in the whole field of public law. Paul Craig has been one of the men and women of the hour when it came to confronting the legal challenges of Brexit: already established as one of the leading exponents of public law in the world at large, he was especially well-qualified to rise to this particular challenge as an expert in the administrative law both of the United Kingdom and of the European Union, and also as one of the masters of the whole large field of EU law. Being so qualified, he has also brought to bear on the Brexit debates that quality of good academic judgement which I have denoted as being at a premium in this context.

Thus, he has been adept and insightful both in generally surveying the whole vast field of legal and political issues raised by or in the course of Brexit debate, and, on the other hand, in knowing when and how to home in on one particular legal issue or problem. On the general plane, he has, correctly in my view, perceived the Brexit debate as a drama of Shakespearean dimensions, at times tragic, comic, or historical; and he has amusingly but at the same time underlyingly seriously portrayed it in those terms.[20] In parallel with these general reflections he has also provided a number of incisive thrusts into particularly sensitive areas of the debate, in relation to which he has displayed a singular sagacity. Thus for instance, he was one of the first if not the very first of legal commentators to perceive the possibility that the United Kingdom might be judged to have an option unilaterally to revoke its notification of withdrawal from the European Union under Article 50 of the Treaty on European Union.[21] I was sceptical of this view and will admit to having been vastly impressed when this judgement call was vindicated by the decision of the CJEU in the *Wightman* case.[22] We all await his further contributions to this truly momentous discussion.

Postscript

It was clear from the outset that the content of this chapter, which was written towards the end of 2018 and submitted in February 2019, would be highly susceptible to being overtaken by events, especially with regard to the fast-moving saga of Brexit. That foreboding has been amply vindicated by the time that this Postscript is being added, that is to say in November 2019—and it is to be expected that the same fate may befall this Postscript in its turn. However, it still seems meaningful to set out the argument as it stood at that earlier time; and it does not seem too bold to claim that intervening developments have served only to substantiate it, leaving the record of how it looked at that moment as a useful one.

One piece of updating would nevertheless seem to be appropriate: to my concluding recital of Paul Craig's crucial contributions to the discussion of the legal dimension of the Brexit debate, there should surely be added a mention of his instantly-famous blog-posts on the Prorogation of Parliament,[23] which exerted a

[20] See Paul Craig, 'Brexit: A Drama in Six Acts' (2016) 41 European L Rev 447, and Paul Craig, 'Brexit, A Drama: The Interregnum' (2017) 36 Ybk of European L 3.

[21] See Paul Craig, 'The Process: Brexit and the Anatomy of Article 50' in Federico Fabbrini (ed), *The Law and Politics of Brexit* (OUP 2017).

[22] Case C-621/18 *Wightman v Secretary of State for Exiting the European Union* ECLI:EU:C:2018:999.

[23] Paul Craig, 'Prorogation: Constitutional Principle and Law, Fact and Causation', a posting on the Oxford Human Rights Hub Blog (31 August 2019) (available at: https://ohrh.law.ox.ac.uk/prorogation-constitutional-principle-and-law-fact-and-causation/), and also as a posting on the U.K. Const. L. Blog (2 September 2019) (available at: https://ukconstitutionallaw.org/).

major influence on the framing of the arguments on appeal of the applicants for judicial review in the English courts and/or interim interdict in the Scottish courts which enjoyed a resounding success in the Supreme Court in what has become known as the *Miller No. 2* case.[24] It remains only to reiterate and renew my concluding assertion that we await his further insights into the public law and EU law dimensions of this most consequential of discussions.

[24] *Miller, R (on the application of) v The Prime Minister; Cherry v Advocate-General for Scotland* [2019] UKSC 41 (24 September 2019). See also now Craig Paul P, The Supreme Court, Prorogation and Constitutional Principle (29 October 2019). Forthcoming in Public Law; Oxford Legal Studies Research Paper No. 57/2019, available at: SSRN: https://ssrn.com/abstract=3477487 or http://dx.doi.org/10.2139/ssrn.3477487.

PART VI

CONSTITUTIONS

17. Challenges of Multilevel Constitutionalism
Cheryl Saunders

18. A Hard Law Approach to States Systemic Violations of Article 2 of the Treaty of the European Union: Reasons and Means
Miguel Poiares Maduro and Benedita Menezes Queiroz

19. Brexit and The Challenges of A 'Post-Sovereign' Legal Landscape
Sionaidh Douglas Scott

17
Challenges of Multilevel Constitutionalism

Cheryl Saunders

I. Introduction

Multilevel government is a long-standing theme of Paul Craig's work on which he has made an extraordinary contribution. His scholarship on public law in the United Kingdom is highly influential. He is the leading British authority on EU law. His deep familiarity with administrative law in the United States gives his work an impressive comparative dimension. His interests extend also to global administrative law. In the Hamlyn Lectures in 2014, Craig drew his knowledge of these spheres together, under the title of *UK, EU and Global Administrative Law: Foundations and Challenges*. The lectures were subsequently expanded and published by Cambridge University Press, under the same title.[1] I reviewed the book for the Cambridge Law Journal and was filled with professional admiration for the insight and erudition with which he tackled a host of the most difficult questions for public law across such a huge canvas.[2] That work was the stimulus for the subject matter of this chapter in a volume to honour a remarkable scholar.

The last half century has been a time of rapid expansion and development of multilevel government above and below the level of the state.[3] Within states, devolution in forms that include but are not limited to federation has become *de rigeur*. The reasons for this development will be explored more fully in due course. They include the benefits of more localised decision-making, in both established and emerging democracies.[4] Above states, the institutionalisation of collective action for the purposes of international or, in some parts of the world, regional collaboration has been driven by conditions of globalisation for which, at the same time, these developments provide the vehicle. Multilevel government has been a catalyst for innovation in institutional design and for rapid change in approaches to government throughout the world. In a sense, it has offered a workaround for the

[1] Paul Craig, *UK, EU and Global Administrative Law: Foundations and Challenges* (CUP 2015).
[2] Cheryl Saunders, 'Book review of Paul Craig, *UK, EU and Global Administrative Law: Foundations and Challenges*' (2017) 76 CLJ 461.
[3] Arjan Shakel, Liesbet Hooghe, and Gary Marks, 'Multilevel Governance and the State' in Stephen Leibfried, Evelyn Huber, Jonah D Levy, and John D Stephens, *The Oxford Handbook of Transformations of the State* (OUP 2015) 269.
[4] Stephen Tierney, 'Federalism and the Plurinational Challenge' in Amnon Lev (ed), *The Federal Idea: Public Law Between Governance and Political Life* (Hart 2017) 227, 231–32.

Cheryl Saunders, *Challenges of Multilevel Constitutionalism* In: *The Foundations and Future of Public Law*. Edited by: Elizabeth Fisher, Jeff King, Alison L Young, Oxford University Press (2020).
DOI: 10.1093/oso/9780198845249.003.0017

artificial character of the international state system, providing a means to achieve a measure of more localised autonomy in large, consolidated states, to enable states to combine their efforts more effectively to deal with shared challenges and to manage the problems created by eroding state borders.

In the second decade of the twenty-first century, however, multilevel government appears to have reached a watershed of some kind. Systems of multilevel government, both within and above the level of the state, tend to drift towards centralisation, through judicial interpretation and political and bureaucratic action, often without persuasive supporting rationale.[5] For an amalgam of reasons that include reaction against central overreach, multilevel government above the level of the state in both regional and international spheres is now encountering resistance in forms that include evasion, non-compliance, withdrawal, and repudiation. Within states, the consequences typically are different, occasional attempts at secession aside.[6] Once established, multilevel government tends to persist, at least in outward form, with centralisation dissipating the advantages that it offers. Attachment to centralisation also may deter the adoption of effective multilevel government at all, as in Sri Lanka, or delay the implementation of a formal framework for multilevel government, as in Nepal.[7]

The primary focus of this chapter is multilevel government within states. It analyses the problems that appear to have emerged through the lens of constitutionalism. Multilevel government has the potential to enhance constitutionalism. At the same time, paradoxically, concepts associated with constitutionalism, of which the unity of the demos is an example, are one of the key causes for failure or underperformance of multilevel government. And failure or underperformance of multilevel government in turn puts constitutionalism at risk. These links between multilevel government and constitutionalism are justified in the sections that follow. It will be seen that examination of the interdependence of multilevel government and constitutionalism is complicated by variations in understandings of both that are prevalent across the world.[8] These understandings will be teased

[5] Corroboration of this claim in relation to the centralisation of law in federal systems can be found in Daniel Halberstam and Mathias Reimann, 'Federalism and Unification: Comparing Methods, Results, and Explanations Across 20 Systems' in Daniel Halberstam and Mathias Reimann (eds), *Federalism and Legal Unification* (Springer 2014) 3.

[6] Unsuccessful attempts at secession in the twenty-first century in states with forms of multilevel government include Scotland (from the United Kingdom); Catalonia (from Spain); Kurdistan (from Iraq); and (shortly before the turn of the century) Quebec (from Canada).

[7] Asanga Welikala (ed), *A New Devolution Settlement for Sri Lanka: Proceedings and Outcomes, Conference of Provincial Councils* (Centre for Policy Alternatives, Colombo, 2016); Prithvi Man Shrestha, 'Nepal's historic leap towards a federal system has not been as smooth as everyone expected' *Kathmandu Post* (Kathmandu 30 December 2018); available at: http://kathmandupost.ekantipur.com/news/2018-12-30/nepals-historic-leap-towards-a-federal-system-has-not-been-as-smooth-as-everyone-expected.html, accessed 1 July 2019.

[8] Compare, for example, the range of definitions within Anglo-American literature in David Feldman, '"Which In Your Case You Have Not Got": Constitutionalism at Home and Abroad' (2011) 64 CLP 117; also Dieter Grimm, 'The Achievement of Constitutionalism and its Prospects in a Changed World' in Petra Dobner and Martin Loughlin (eds), *The Twilight of Constitutionalism* (OUP 2010) 3.

out in due course. In each case, however, there is a core meaning on which the argument in the chapter builds. Multilevel government refers to any organisation of a state to provide for at least two levels of government, chosen in accordance with democratic or other legitimating principles, between which the authority to govern is divided. Constitutionalism involves compliance with rules of a constitutional kind, which derive their legitimacy from the people, in one way or another, and which create and regulate the exercise of public power by governing institutions.[9] Following Dieter Grimm, I accept that constitutionalism in this sense necessitates association with democracy as well.[10]

The next section of the chapter begins by mapping common forms of multilevel government, explaining the attractions of multilevel government in conditions of the twenty-first century and exploring its relationship with constitutionalism. As this section also notes, however, with some exceptions, centripetal forces typically prove irresistible so that multilevel systems do not adequately fulfil their promise. Where this occurs, it undermines both multilevel government and constitutionalism. Section III of the chapter explores the possibility that the cause lies in the failure to develop a sufficiently distinctive, compound conception of multilevel constitutionalism: compound in the sense that it integrates multilevel government and constitutionalism, for polities in which multilevel government is used. For any such conception to be translated into practice, cultural change would be necessary, in both politics and law. Sections IV and V examine what this would involve.

There are broadly comparable difficulties in achieving a balance between levels of government that enables the goals of multilevel government to be achieved, consistently with constitutional principle, above the level of the state. Theory, politics, and law loom large here as well. Inevitably, however, there are differences also, not least because of the different position of states in the hierarchy. A final part of the chapter sketches these similarities and differences as a basis for reflecting on whether and if so how insights drawn from the challenges and opportunities of multilevel constitutionalism within states might be useful above the level of the state as well.

II. Multilevel Government and Constitutionalism

A. Multilevel government

In the world of the twenty-first century, multilevel government within states takes a rich variety of forms. While there are often significant differences between them, all provide for at least two levels of government, each of which has legitimate authority to govern the people or a segment of the people on identified matters.

[9] The definition is adapted from Grimm (n 8).
[10] Ibid 10.

Multilevel government thus couples the opportunity for central action on matters of collective interest with arrangements for self-government on some, substantial, issues by the constituent parts.

Federation is one, formalised category of multilevel government. Federation involves the constitutional division of legislative as well as executive and, sometimes, judicial power between the levels of government. In this sense, at least, it divides 'sovereignty', to establish a distinctively federal state.[11] Typically, federation also involves arrangements whereby the institutions or people of the federated units, *qua* units, actively participate in one or more central institutions, in a manner sometimes described as 'shared rule'.[12] Usually, the vehicle for shared rule is a second chamber in the central legislature, but the design or operation of other central institutions may usefully contribute to the federal character of the state as well.[13] Shared rule offers the opportunity civil law expertise and enabling the experiences and views of all parts of a federated state to be reflected in the exercise of central authority. In most federations, constitutional amendment requires the consent of both levels of government as well, whether expressed directly, through institutions or people, or indirectly, in ways that involve a federal second chamber.[14]

There are many points of important difference in the structure and design of formal federations. Some of these affect the nature of relations between levels of government or the interpretation of the federal constitution and will be taken up in those contexts below. One key distinction is useful for present purposes, however: between federations that are formed by uniting previously distinct polities and those formed by the disaggregation of power within a previously unitary state. The terminology commonly used in the literature to describe this distinction, between 'coming together' and 'holding together' federations, is not entirely apt.[15] Unitary states may federate for reasons other than fear of secession, as in South Africa;[16] secession may be attempted in federations formed by aggregation, as in the United States;[17] apprehension of secession is a familiar justification for refusing to move from a unitary to a federal form of state, as in Sri Lanka.[18] Not all

[11] On the complexity of the debate on sovereignty in federations, across constitutional traditions, see Francesco Palermo and Karl Kossler, *Comparative Federalism* (Hart 2017) 83–92.

[12] Daniel Elazar, *Exploring Federalism* (University of Alabama Press 1987) 5.

[13] The requirement for three of the nine Justices of the Supreme Court of Canada to be drawn from the Quebec Bar or named Quebec courts is an example. It was explained by the Supreme Court majority as a means not only of securing civil law expertise but also to represent Quebec's 'legal traditions and social values' on the Court and to enhance the confidence of Quebec in the Court: *Reference re Supreme Court Act, ss 5 and 6* [2014] 1 SCC 433.

[14] Palermo and Kossler (n 11) 178–85.

[15] The terminology can be traced to the work of Alfred Stepan, 'Federalism and Democracy: Beyond the US Model' (1999) 10 J of Democracy 19, 22.

[16] Nicholas Haysom, 'The "Federalism" Debate in the South African Constitution-Making Process' (Universidad Nacional Autónoma de México—Instituto de Investigaciones Jurídicas 2005) 655; available at: https://archivos.juridicas.unam.mx/www/bjv/libros/4/1640/23.pdf, accessed 1 July 2019.

[17] David Potter, *The Impending Crisis* (HarperCollins Publishers 1976).

[18] Jayadeva Uyangoda, 'Ethnic Conflict in Sri Lanka: Changing Dynamics' (Policy Studies 32, East-West Center 2007) 10.

federations can be neatly categorised as formed by aggregation or disaggregation; many can point to elements of both, as the example of Canada shows.[19]

There is enough in the distinction to be useful, nevertheless. Typically, constituent units in a federation formed by aggregation have a prior history and identity as polities, existing institutions of government and constitutions of their own. The story of the formation of the federation is likely to involve the consent of the constituent polities, often as the basis for a compact theory of some kind. These attributes assist transition to a federal culture from the outset. They do not necessarily endure to sustain a federal culture over time, however, as the primary challenge shifts from building unity to maintaining diversity.[20]

By contrast, constituent units in a federation formed by disaggregation are less likely to have existing institutions of government, or constitutions of their own, even if they have a pre-existing identity of some kind. Their story of formation will involve devolution from the centre. Implementation of new federal arrangements may be a major exercise in establishing and empowering the constituent units, during a period of transition in which central institutions may be reluctant to relinquish power. Adaptation to a federal culture is much more difficult in these conditions. In the world of the twenty-first century, federations are overwhelmingly more likely to be formed in this way.

Other forms of multilevel government are found in states that formally are unitary, in the sense that they do not identify as federal. Multilevel government of this kind sometimes is described as regionalism. Spain, Italy, and the United Kingdom are examples, illustrating both the diversity of the forms of multilevel government in this category and the somewhat indistinct dividing line between regionalism and federalism.[21] In a variation on all formations, multilevel government may apply in only part of a state under asymmetrical arrangements for special autonomy. Aceh in Indonesia, Bangsamoro in the Philippines, and Hong Kong in China are examples. There is no standard terminology and there are no standard models.

Some generalisations may be made, even so. Forms of multilevel government that do not identify as federal nevertheless aspire to a degree of autonomy that distinguishes them from arrangements for a mere delegation of local governing power and that may be at least as significant as that in some federations. Unlike federations, these forms of multilevel government are not always enshrined in the formal constitution. Nor is there emphasis on shared rule as a design feature, although in practice regional autonomy may be reflected in central institutions in some way. Insistence on the continuing unitary form of the state often reflects

[19] Alan Siaroff, *Comparing Political Regimes* (2nd edn, University of Toronto Press 2009) 167.

[20] Palermo and Kossler (n 11) 39–40.

[21] John Loughlin, John Kincaid, and Wilfried Swenden, *Routledge Handbook of Regionalism and Federalism* (Routledge 2013).

aversion to any suggestion of divided internal sovereignty. Where the tipping point lies between permissible local autonomy and impermissible disunity varies between states. Depending on context, it may be taken to preclude allocation of law-making power to regions or the assumption by regions of other deemed indicia of sovereignty.[22]

This account does not exhaust the forms of multilevel government presently in use or which might be envisaged for the future. By way of example: models for self-government by indigenous peoples also merit understanding as multi-level government but differ in their rationale, assignment of responsibilities, and understanding of the relationship between constituent peoples and the state.[23] It is becoming increasingly clear that it would be useful for new forms of multilevel government to emerge for the governance of states in which traditional groupings of, for example, tribes or clans remain influential, rather than trying to accommodate such groups to more standardised forms of multilevel government that have been developed for use elsewhere.

There are various overlapping explanations for the trend to multilevel government over the last few decades.[24] First, it is an obvious way of organising a state in which a region or regions are distinct, in terms of language, religion, other aspects of culture or historical experience. In these circumstances, multilevel government may be a way of resolving or preventing conflict, even for discouraging dissolution of the state. Even in the absence of conflict, however, multilevel government offers a way of enabling communities with a natural sense of affinity to govern themselves for particular purposes, while also taking advantage of the possibilities offered by a larger state.[25] This explanation has some synergies with a second, which identifies multilevel government as a mechanism for more effective democratic government.[26] Multilevel government enables substantive decisions to be taken at more localised levels by representatives who are more accessible and potentially more accountable. Paradoxically, the force of the democratic argument for multilevel government is enhanced by globalisation and its present discontents, including the sense of exclusion that it fosters. The terminology of 'glocalisation' was coined decades ago but may have even more salience now.[27]

[22] Sardinia offers an example, where a law to establish a commission to draft a new basic law for 'the autonomy and sovereignty of the Sardinian People' was held invalid by the Italian Constitutional Court: Palermo and Kossler (n 11) 51.

[23] Dylan Lino, 'Towards Indigenous-Settler Federalism' (2017) 28 Public L Rev 118.

[24] On the trends towards decentralisation and innovation generally: Dorothee Allain-Dupre, 'Assigning responsibilities across levels of government' (OECD Working Papers on Fiscal Federalism No 24, September 2018).

[25] Will Kymlicka, *Federalism and Secession* (CUP 2000); James Madison, 'The Union as a Safeguard against Domestic Faction and Insurrection', *Federalist No 10* in *The Federalist* (Everyman 1992 [1788]).

[26] Palermo and Kossler (n 11) 111–22.

[27] Roland Robertson, 'Glocalization: Time-Space and Homogeneity-Heterogeneity' in Mike Featherstone, Scott Lash, and Roland Robertson (eds), *Global Modernities* (Sage 1995) 25.

Either or both of these explanations for recourse to multilevel government provide a foundation for a third: multilevel government as a means of disaggregating public power through a form of vertical checks and balances.[28] As with any arrangements for separation of powers, the distribution must be such that government also is effective, in the sense of equipped to achieve the ends that governments are designed to serve.[29] Nevertheless, a distribution of public power between competing centres of political authority that are territorially distributed is an antidote to the accumulation of power in a single capital by powerful central institutions.

To meet these or related purposes, multilevel government needs to achieve and maintain what might be described as a balance between the responsibilities of the respective levels of government, leaving each with the authority and capacity to perform its role. Where a suitable balance lies varies between states and may be contested within states. At some point, nevertheless, a shift in effective authority may be such that multilevel government is no longer performing adequately in the interests of the people it is designed to serve. The shift may occur in either direction, depriving the centre or the constituent units of appropriate authority. Overwhelmingly, however, in present conditions, imbalance tends to favour the centre at the expense of constituent unit authority. This may occur in many ways. Typically, however, it is the result of central initiatives, sometimes formalised through collaboration and often confirmed or at least condoned by judicial decision. The results have implications not only for multilevel government but also for constitutionalism, which the next section explores.

B. Constitutionalism

Constitutionalism is entwined with multilevel government in several ways. Outlining their interdependence is complicated not only by the varieties of multilevel government but also by different understandings of constitutionalism. It is necessary to unravel the relationship, nevertheless. Constitutionalism and multilevel government can be mutually supportive or mutually destructive. Some versions of constitutionalism or the assumptions on which they rest militate against effective multilevel government. If multilevel government is desirable, there is a case for reconciling the two so as to realise the advantages of both, in a compound conception of multilevel constitutionalism.

At a minimum, constitutionalism requires compliance with rules of a constitutional kind, which are deemed to derive their legitimacy from the people, are the source of public power, and regulate the exercise of public power by governing

28 James Madison, 'The Structure of the Government Must Furnish the Proper Checks and Balances Between the Different Departments', *Federalist No. 51* in *The Federalist* (Everyman 1992 [1788]).

29 Nick Barber, 'Prelude to the Separation of Powers' (2001) 60 CLJ 59.

institutions that are democratically accountable to the people.[30] Most, although not all, constitutions are codified, entrenched, and protected by judicial review. All arrangements for multilevel government must be consistent with the governing constitution. All federations and many other forms of multilevel government are positively protected by a constitution as well.

Failure to comply with arrangements for multilevel government that are protected by a constitution is a failure of constitutionalism. This sometimes happens; federal non-compliance with provisions applying to Sabah and Sarawak in the Malaysian Constitution arguably is an example.[31] Enactment of the European Union (Withdrawal) Act 2018 by the Parliament of the United Kingdom without observing the Sewel convention arguably is another, even though the convention is not enforceable through the courts.[32] More often, however, the erosion of multilevel government is not a failure of constitutionalism in this sense, because it has been adapted to formal constitutional requirements and survived any judicial challenge. In cases of this kind, there is no overt breach of the constitution.

The often elaborate steps that are taken to avoid the formal requirements of multilevel government, however, can cause other problems of a broadly constitutional kind. To demonstrate how this occurs requires immersion in the technicalities of constitutional law, which vary between states. The case of Australia, with which I am most familiar, illustrates the point.

In Australia, a very significant shift of power towards central institutions has taken place through an aggressive use of its allocated powers by the Commonwealth, unmediated by the federal chamber; an extreme fiscal imbalance in favour of the Commonwealth; expansive interpretation of Commonwealth power by the courts; a network of intergovernmental arrangements dominated by Commonwealth actors; and the effects of progressive disempowerment on the initiative and capacities of the States.[33] The result is a federation that operates in practice in a way that bears little resemblance to the text and structure of the Constitution, with all that follows in terms of elite and public understanding. More specific consequences affect aspects of the rule of law, democratic accountability, or both. Thus, an open-ended approach of the courts to the interpretation of Commonwealth legislative powers has encouraged a drafting technique whereby federal laws rest on a smorgasbord of possibly relevant powers, leaving to people to whom the laws

[30] The distinctive features of the Constitution of the United Kingdom do not fit generic descriptions of constitutionalism neatly: Feldman (n 8). Given the attribution of political, if not legal sovereignty to the people, however, this description of constitutionalism may fit even the circumstances of the United Kingdom well enough.

[31] Andrew Harding, 'Devolution of powers in Sarawak: A Dynamic Process of Redesigning Territorial Governance in a Federal System' (2017) 12 Asian Journal of Comp L 257.

[32] Kenneth Campbell, 'Constitutional Dogs that Barked and Dogs that Did Not: The Scottish Continuity Bill in the Supreme Court', UK Const L Blog (14 Jan 2019).

[33] Cheryl Saunders, *The Constitution of Australia: A Contextual Analysis* (Hart 2011).

might apply the complicated task of determining whether they do so or not.[34] Commonwealth reliance on financial powers, when the scope of legislative power fails, has skewed the instruments through which policy-making occurs, enhancing the position of the executive vis-à-vis the legislative branch, with consequences for transparency and accountability, as well as the quality of the decisions that are made.[35] Policy-making through an unstructured and constantly changing network of intergovernmental arrangements has blurred the lines of responsibility across most areas of government, without putting alternatives in their place.[36]

This account of the interdependence of multilevel government and federalism so far has focused on constitutional compliance. The two also are intertwined functionally and conceptually. In functional terms, multilevel government can enhance constitutionalism, in so far as it offers another way of disaggregating power and of deepening the responsiveness and accountability of democratic institutions. Conceptually, on the other hand, multilevel government may be considered antithetical to some traditions of constitutionalism and the assumptions on which they are based, in theory or in practice.

Almost all current accounts of constitutionalism have been developed in the context of the unitary state or against the backdrop of assumptions associated with it. The understandings of democracy to which these accounts are linked assume the superior virtue of the will of a national majority and privilege formal equality of law. Particular variations between constitutional traditions, often driven by historical experience, further affect the manner of the interaction of constitutionalism with multilevel government.

One account of constitutionalism effectively precludes multilevel government with the formality and apparent depth of federalism. This account, which stems from the French constitutional tradition, requires a unified demos in which national sovereignty resides and precludes the division of legislative power.[37] Multilevel government in states influenced by this tradition of constitutionalism typically takes the form of regionalism rather than federalism. Even in these cases, however, further limitations on what can be done in the name of multilevel

[34] An example is the Water Act 2007 (Cth), section 9, which relies on, for example, the powers in section 51 of the Constitution over posts and telegraphs (v), astronomical and meteorological observations (viii) and census and statistics (xi), as well as several more plausible powers, the reach of which also is unclear. For a highwater mark of the jurisprudence that has encouraged this approach see *New South Wales v Commonwealth (Workchoices case)* (2006) 229 CLR 1.

[35] The mode of implementation of one such policy initiative, to place 'chaplains' in schools, is examined in detail by the High Court in *Williams v Commonwealth of Australia* (2012) 248 CLR 156. In *Williams* the policy was held unconstitutional, but other examples abound.

[36] One of many very many examples is the difficulty in determining who is accountable for what in relation to the management of the Murray–Darling Basin, revealed in the *Murray–Darling Basin Royal Commission Report* (January 2019); available at: https://www.mdbrc.sa.gov.au/sites/default/files/murray-darling-basin-royal-commission-report.pdf?v=1548898371, accessed 1 July 2019.

[37] Olivier Beaud, 'Conceptions of the State' in Michel Rosenfeld and Andras Sajo (eds), *The Oxford Handbook of Comparative Constitutional Law* (OUP 2012) 269, 276.

government may be attributed to constitutionalism. Exactly what these limitations are vary between states. The issues on the basis of which the Spanish Constitutional Tribunal found the Catalan Statute of Autonomy unconstitutional in 2010, even after approval by the Spanish Congress and through referendum, offer one, instructive, example.[38]

There are some states influenced by this approach to constitutionalism that also are formal federations: Belgium and Germany are examples. In these cases, however, work must be done, either with constitutional theory, federal design, or both, to reconcile the two. In the case of Belgium, the rise of theories of 'plurinational' federalism offers one means to this end.[39] In the case of Germany, where local autonomy has long roots in any event, the relative centralisation of legislative power eases the tension.[40] Earlier attempts to reconcile federalism with theories of the state may be reflected, nevertheless, in now largely discredited arguments about the existence of a three-systems model of federalism, providing for a 'third state' of which the *Bund* and the *Länder* are part.[41]

By contrast, the understanding of constitutionalism in the British constitutional tradition and derivatives of it is relatively impervious to concerns centred on the theoretical unity of the demos, a distribution of legislative power or, at least in principle, the division of sovereignty. On the face of it, this tradition therefore is more hospitable to multilevel government, even in the form of federation.[42] It has no objection in principle to arrangements in which legislative, executive, and even judicial power is divided between at least two spheres of government, each of which has its own institutions and typically administers its own legislation. On the other hand, there are principles and practices in this tradition that have developed in tandem with constitutionalism which mitigate against federalism in practice. These include an instinctive adherence to the concept of parliamentary sovereignty, even when it patently is modified by a codified constitution, the speed and efficiency associated with parliamentary government along Westminster lines and a winner-take-all style of government, in which the views of a simple national majority are assumed to be entitled to prevail. None is compatible with genuinely multilevel government. In Australia, the tensions are manifested in a long-standing

[38] Constitutional Court Judgment No 31/2010, 28 June 2010, available in English translation through Asier Garrido Munoz, 'Catalan Independence in the Spanish Courts' (OUP Blog, 6 November 2017); available at: https://blog.oup.com/2017/11/catalan-independence-spanish-constitution-courts/, accessed 1 July 2019.

[39] Celine Romainville, 'Dynamics of Belgian Plurinational Federalism: A Small State under Pressure' (2015) 38 Boston College Int'l & Comp L Rev 225.

[40] Margaret Barber Crosby, *The Making of a German Constitution* (Berg 2008) 254.

[41] Arthur Gunlicks, *The Lander and German Federalism* (Manchester UP 2003) 55; Palermo and Kossler (n 11) 91.

[42] Beaud (n 37).

assumption that federalism and responsible government are in conflict, requiring decision-makers, including courts, to favour one or the other.[43]

These challenges to multilevel government presented by prevailing conceptions of constitutionalism are reinforced by a series of considerations that might loosely be described as practical that have developed in association with constitutionalism and taken to justify expansion of central power. Three that have been particularly influential are as follows. First, there are widespread assumptions that sub-state levels of government are inferior: less capable, less talented, more prone to faction, more susceptible to corruption, and less tolerant of minorities. These derive at least in part from the rhetoric that accompanied the founding of the United States, subsequently reinforced by the struggles against slavery and for civil rights.[44] Second, there are economic assumptions about the advantages of scale and what is needed to compete effectively in a globalised world, which tend to favour centralisation and the uniformity that accompanies it.[45] Third, international relations also, perhaps unwittingly, encourage centralisation, not only because central institutions typically exercise external sovereignty but because it is easier for other states to deal with one government than with many.

There are responses to each of these factors. None necessarily militates against multilevel government or even in favour of centralisation. Individually and collectively, however, they are part of the story of tension between constitutionalism and multilevel government, which operates to the detriment of both. They are additional considerations to be taken into account in conceptualising multilevel constitutionalism and in the design and practice of multilevel government.

III. Multilevel Constitutionalism

Multilevel government and constitutionalism have the potential to reinforce each other. This potential cannot be realised, however, if multilevel government is seen to be in conflict with aspects of the understanding of constitutionalism that prevails within the state. To reconcile the two, a compound conception of multilevel constitutionalism is required. Such a conception must retain the core attributes of constitutionalism and multilevel government, adapted to complement each other.

This is not a novel idea. A form of multilevel constitutionalism has underpinned the Swiss federation as it has evolved over time.[46] In addition, in recent decades, a burgeoning literature on 'plurinational' federalism has sought to reconcile

[43] For one formulation of the consequences see Stephen Gageler, 'Beyond the text: A Vision of the Structure and Function of the Constitution' (2009) 32 Australian Bar Rev 138.

[44] Madison (n 28).

[45] Amaresh Bagchi, 'Globalisation and Federalism: Uneasy Partners?' (2008) 43 Economic and Political Weekly 41.

[46] Palermo and Kossler (n 11) 91.

multilevel government and constitutionalism in states in which one or more sub-national units have a distinct 'national' identity.[47] Drawing on the sophisticated account of Stephen Tierney, plurinational federalism separates the construct of a nation from the state in order to justify the perception that distinct nations represent multiple *demoi* with a state, for which federalism in some form is an appropriate response.[48] It thus challenges the typically 'unitary' conception of the *demos*, around which constitutional accounts of 'justice, equality and fairness' have been framed.[49] In such a state, sovereignty also can be claimed as pluralised, reflecting the 'political bonds' between people and governance in the respective nations.[50] By implicit contrast, in 'uninational' states, the default conceptualisation of a single *demos* continues to apply.[51]

Theories of plurinational federalism do not meet the requirements for a satisfactory account of constitutionalism that is adapted to the conditions of multilevel government for several reasons. First and most obviously, they do not cover all states with multilevel government or all parts of individual states with multilevel government in which only some units qualify as 'nations' in the relevant sense.[52] Second, whether or not a sub-national grouping, territorially organised, constitutes a 'nation' for the purposes of a theory that purports to justify differential treatment is not always clear and is often contested. Third, while plurinational federalism might improve the operation of multilevel government in cases to which it applies and in which it is given practical effect, it is a defensive stance, to the extent that it presents as an exception to standard theories of constitutionalism.

Multilevel constitutionalism needs to accommodate the values of multilevel government so as to realise the positive contribution that it can make to responsive democracy and limited but effective constitutional government. It follows that it needs to accept diversity, even in legislation. It also needs to accept the finality of decisions of sub-national majorities, even when these differ from the preferences of state-wide majorities, as long as the outcomes comply with agreed constitutional norms. It must also build on the assumption of considerable interdependence between the roles and responsibilities of the respective levels of government. Interdependence needs to be managed, to preserve both the benefits of multilevel government and the expectations of accountability and transparency associated with constitutionalism.[53]

[47] Tierney (n 4).
[48] Ibid 234.
[49] Ibid 234–35.
[50] Ibid 240.
[51] Ibid 235.
[52] Canada is an example, in which Quebec, but not the rest of Canada, is a 'nation' within the meaning of plurinational federalism.
[53] Ben Rimmer, Cheryl Saunders, and Michael Crommelin, 'Working Better with Other Jurisdictions' (ANZSOG Research Paper for the Australian Public Service Review, March 2019); available at: <https://www.apsreview.gov.au/sites/default/files/resources/working-other-jurisdictions.pdf, accessed 1 July 2019.

The terminology of 'sovereignty' and, even, '*demos*' may be distractions in this context. Sovereignty has long since lost any absolute qualities it may once have possessed, and populations are more mobile than ever before. In any event, whether the people who are deemed to authorise or acquiesce in the constitutional project are conceived as singular or plural, the authority so conferred is for multilevel government. The relationship of people to each level of government can be equated with citizenship, in the sense that there are bonds of a political nature between people, and between people and the institutions that govern in their name, at each level of government. Within the state, responsibilities are divided between levels of government and the mode of their exercise is prescribed. If it matters, the state as a whole might be described as 'sovereign' against the rest of the world although even in this context, in conditions of globalisation, sovereignty is a misnomer. As with the internal organisation of a state, so with its external properties: it is more helpful to use terminology that reflects reality, acknowledging the very considerable external authority of states that is, however, not absolute.

A concept of multilevel constitutionalism might be built around the following principles. The first would require compliance with the constitutional framework for multilevel government, including the allocation of responsibilities between levels of government, until altered in accordance with procedures that also reflect the multilevel organisation of the state. Adoption of multilevel constitutionalism would not dictate the extent or the manner of the division of responsibility between the levels of government, which would vary with the context, as they do now. Multilevel constitutionalism would provide a backdrop against which design choices are made, however and, in that sense, would have indirect influence. It may also increase the incentive for greater sophistication in the design of institutions of shared rule, including legislative second chambers, so as to broaden the perspectives on which central institutions rely and strengthen buy-in from the constituent units.

A second principle would require compliance by both levels of government with other values and principles associated with constitutionalism. The constitutional framework within which this occurs varies between states. In some federations, constituent units have their own constitutions, although this is not invariably the case.[54] Where these exist, they should be subject to the federal constitution, in the interests of legal coherence and the rule of law. In turn, however, the federal constitution should leave adequate room for the constitutional preferences of individual constituent units and their people to be given effect.[55] In the absence of separate constituent unit constitutions, the federal constitution provides what in

[54] Kimana Zulueta-Fülscher and Asanga Welikala, 'Substate Constitutions in Fragile and Conflict-affected Settings' (International IDEA Policy Paper No 15, 2017); available at: https://www.idea.int/publications/catalogue/substate-constitutions-fragile-and-conflict-affected-settings, accessed 1 July 2019.

[55] Ibid.

effect are constitutional arrangements for the constituent units as well. In either case, the constitutional arrangements for each level of government should provide for limited but effective government and the rule of law. Elected branches should be accountable to the people in accordance with principles of democratic representation and, where applicable, direct democracy. Courts should be independent and capable. The value of equal citizenship should apply, across the state as a whole, in relation to state-wide responsibilities and within each of the constituent units, in relation to unit responsibilities. Quite apart from the centrality of this principle to any notion of constitutionalism, it also serves to alleviate a recurrent concern about the governance of constituent units.

Third, where responsibilities are interdependent, as often will be the case, collaboration of some kind between the levels of government should be acknowledged as integral to the multilevel arrangements. Multilevel constitutionalism must anticipate this as well, by requiring attention to the design of intergovernmental institutions and instruments that preserve democratic accountability, including transparency, and the rule of law. What this involves depends in part on the design of the system as a whole. The practical dimensions of these challenges are taken up in the next section.

Fourth, multilevel constitutionalism requires trust, respect, and mutual consideration between levels of government. Trust and respect characterise the appropriate relationship between democratic polities. Mutual consideration reflects their interdependence within a single state, requiring each government to pursue its perception of the public interest within its jurisdiction but with an eye on the public interest of the state as a whole. All three values are required for multilevel government to work effectively. Exactly what this principle involves, again, may vary with federal design. So, for example, the challenges to a harmonious working relationship and the temptations to which it is prey may vary between systems that are dualist in design and those that are integrated, in which constituent units implement federal legislation.

Multilevel constitutionalism, along these lines, has the potential to foster multilevel government that achieves the purposes for which it is designed. This is an intrinsic good in its own right, with longer-term benefits, one of which is to reduce the incentive for states to dissolve through secession. Theory is one thing, however; practice is another. Effective multilevel government also requires a culture to match, on the part of the institutions on which primary responsibility falls, at each level of government; arguably on the public, the media, and civil society as well. How such a culture can be encouraged is one of the more challenging questions for both emerging and established systems of multilevel government. The remainder of this chapter focuses on two sets of practices that are particularly important for this purpose: political actions in the exercise of intergovernmental relations and the interpretation and application of a constitution providing for multilevel government by the courts.

IV. Politics

Multilevel constitutionalism requires a corresponding political culture, at both levels of government. Institutions must accept and work within the letter and spirit of constitutional limits on their authority driven by vertical as well as horizontal constraints. Conversely, institutions must accept responsibility and accountability for the effective exercise of the responsibilities allocated to them. The difficult task of representing one's own jurisdiction while also taking account of the interests of the multilevel state as a whole must be translated into practice. In so far as collaboration is required across jurisdictional lines, techniques of negotiation and consensus building are required. Behaviour that often characterises political action in unitary states, of which the assumption that the winner takes all is an example, needs to be moderated to fit within the framework of multilevel constitutionalism. Actors in institutions of shared rule need to understand the logic of their role and respond accordingly. Those to whom and through whom the political and bureaucratic institutions of multilevel government are accountable need to share the same cultural assumptions and expectations: the people, variously organised; media; civil society.

This is not as high a hill to climb as might be thought. For many communities in many parts of the world, a state in which all power is centralised is an uncomfortable cultural fit. This is the paradigm model of the western state, however, even if it has been adapted in different ways in different constitutional traditions. The issue therefore demands attention. It may require monitoring and intervention, particularly during any phase of transition to multilevel government. During this phase and afterwards, development of a multilevel constitutional culture within each of the levels of government can be encouraged and reinforced through regular political and legal sanctions: reactions of the people from whom the legitimacy to govern is drawn and enforcement of the constitution by courts attuned to the implications of multilevel government.

Intergovernmental relations, involving bilateral or multilateral collaboration across jurisdictional lines, is a form of political action that faces additional challenges from the standpoint of multilevel constitutionalism.[56] Intergovernmental relations with varying degrees of formality are inevitable in systems of multilevel government, within and above the level of the state. The constitutional responsibilities of the respective levels of government may complement each other, generally or for particular purposes; they may overlap in some contexts; they may call for coordination or harmonisation; there may be gaps, which only intergovernmental arrangements can fill. Different levels of government may bring different contributions to the table for the design and implementation of policies generally

[56] For a comparative study spanning twelve multilevel systems see Johanne Poirier, Cheryl Saunders, and John Kincaid (eds), *Intergovernmental Relations in Federal Systems* (OUP 2015).

or in particular cases. It may be helpful for these purposes to distinguish between policy development, regulation, service delivery, the commitment of fiscal or other resources, and data collection and maintenance.[57] Different levels of government may play a role in intergovernmental arrangements in each or all of these ways.

The patterns and modalities of intergovernmental relations differ between systems of multilevel government in ways that depend on context and design. An important dividing line for this purpose lies between systems that are dualist, in which the default is that each level of government implements its own legislation unless alternative arrangements are made, consistently with the constitution, and integrated systems, in which, as a default, the constituent units of the state implement central legislation.[58] Integrated systems create a different kind of relationship between the levels of government for which principles requiring loyalty and trust already exist.[59] In Germany, a paradigm example of integration, the relationship is further effectuated by the use made of the Bundesrat, or Federal Council, in which state governments have their say on legislation that they will implement in due course. Strictly speaking, the Bundesrat is not a second chamber in a bicameral legislature but an institution that provides for *Länder* participation within the federal sphere.[60] In dualist systems of multilevel government, which often coincide with those embedded in common law legal systems, relations between levels are always intergovernmental, institutions of shared rule are weak in terms of their contribution to multilevel government, and there are no comparable principles against which the behaviour of parties can be measured.

Classic forms of intergovernmental relations in multilevel systems include meetings of members of the participating governments, in which collective decisions are made; agreements and other types of pact in which mutual undertakings are given, whether they are legally binding or not; shared institutions, to regulate or perform other functions on behalf of all participants in intergovernmental schemes; the transfer of funds from one level of government (usually the centre) to others subject to conditions of various kinds.[61] Each of these forms potentially creates difficulties for multilevel government and for constitutionalism, whether considered individually or as a compound concept. In terms of multilevel government, these forms are vehicles not only for achieving the effects of centralisation, by way of uniformity of policy, legislation, and administration, but also for securing de facto centralisation, through powers conferred on or assumed by

[57] I owe this useful point to my colleague, Michael Crommelin.

[58] The distinction is elaborated in Palermo and Kossler (n 11) 146, where 'integrated' arrangements are described as 'co-operative'. By contrast, the use of cooperation in the text spans all designs and refers to any mode of working together to achieve shared outcomes.

[59] Anna Gamper, 'On Loyalty and the (Federal) Constitution' (2010) 4 Vienna Online J on Int'l Const Law 157.

[60] Palermo and Kossler (n 11) 173; Matthias Niedobitek, 'The German *Bundesrat* and Executive Federalism' (2018) 10 Perspectives on Federalism 198.

61 Poirier, Saunders, and Kincaid (n 56).

central institutions, disempowering constituent units. These challenges are even greater where decisions are made by majority, or weighted majority voting, rather than consensus.

In terms of constitutionalism, the typical forms through which intergovernmental relations are conducted augment the powers of the executive vis-à-vis the legislative branch, lack transparency, and diminish the accountability of participants through the customary procedures within each level of government, without putting adequate alternatives in their place. This typically occurs, for example, because the effective decisions are made in interjurisdictional meetings of ministers, who as a collectivity have no practice of accounting to the respective legislatures and who commit their jurisdictions to 'agreements' that have no clear status in either politics or law.[62] Intergovernmental arrangements may also infringe the rule of law, where public decisions are difficult to enforce or review or compromise the legal interests of third parties, without means of redress. Exactly how this happens is likely to vary between states. In Australia, as an example, problems of this kind are attributable to uncertainty about the character and justiciability of intergovernmental agreements, including compliance with the conditions attached to grants, whether formal or informal.[63] Unless countered, these difficulties undermine multilevel constitutionalism directly. They undermine it indirectly as well, insofar as the lack of transparency inhibits the mechanisms for accountability on which the emergence of a multilevel constitutional culture depends.

There are ways of responding to these difficulties so as to counter their effects. Some more recently established systems of multilevel government constitutionalise procedures for 'cooperation'.[64] This has the potential advantages of requiring deliberate decision about intergovernmental system design.[65] Constitutional or even legal status can also ensure a greater measure of transparency. It is not a panacea, however. Formalised cooperative procedures equally may be vehicles for centralisation, for executive empowerment, and for the blurring of public accountability through politics or law.[66] Whether constitutionalised or not, intergovernmental relations should be organised with the requirements of multilevel constitutionalism in view. The selection of proposals for collaboration and decisions about the respective contributions of the participants to them should respect the pluralistic values of multilevel government. Appropriate standards for

[62] Ibid.

[63] Problems of this kind are suggested by, for example, *Re Peninsula Anglican Boys School v Ryan* (1985) 7 FCR 415; *Spencer v Commonwealth of Australia* (2010) 241 CLR 118, *Spencer v Commonwealth of Australia* [2018] FCAFC 17.

[64] For example, Constitution of the Republic of South Africa 1996, Ch 3.

[65] These issues were explored in House of Lords, Constitution Committee of the House of Lords, *InterGovernmental Relations in the United Kingdom* (11th Report, HL Paper 146, March 2015).

[66] Derek Powell, 'Constructing a Developmental State in South Africa: The Corporatization of Intergovernmental Relations' in Johanne Poirier, Cheryl Saunders, and John Kincaid (eds), *Intergovernmental Relations in Federal Systems* (OUP 2015) 305.

transparency and accountability must be maintained through each of the levels of government, in addition to any intergovernmental-specific processes that are put in place. Legislatures should be involved to a greater degree than they are now, to counterbalance executive authority. Where empowered, moreover, the role played by legislatures should be deliberative and inquisitive and not merely perfunctory.[67] The law should have a role, at least in ensuring compliance with the letter and spirit of the constitution and in judicial review of executive and administrative action. It may be that not all intergovernmental agreements are suitable for legal enforcement.[68] Whether they are or not should be clear, however. Either way, the rationale should be understandable and understood.

V. Law

The second set of actors who are critical to the implementation and maintenance of multilevel constitutionalism in practice is the courts, carrying out the function of interpreting and applying the constitution that frames the arrangements for multilevel government. This, too, requires a cultural shift, from a unitary mindset to the requirements of multilevel constitutionalism.

The meaning of constitutional provisions that give effect to multilevel government may arise in myriad contexts, which are not necessarily predictable in advance. Drawing on past experience with multilevel government possibilities include, but are by no means limited to, the requirements of an internal common market, in which free movement is guaranteed;[69] the composition, rights, and responsibilities of institutions of shared rule;[70] the properties of state-wide citizenship rights;[71] the positive and negative obligations of governments to each other;[72] the extent of the leverage that is permissible through fiscal transfers;[73] and the meaning of a commitment to fiscal equalisation.[74] They also include, par excellence, the scope and application of the powers allocated to the respective levels of government and the relationship between them. These issues go to the heart of a

[67] Johanne Poirier and Cheryl Saunders, 'Conclusion: Comparative Analysis of Intergovernmental Relations in Federal Systems' in Johanne Poirier, Cheryl Saunders, and John Kincaid (eds), *Intergovernmental Relations in Federal Systems* (OUP 2015) 440.

[68] Johanne Poirier, 'The Functions of Intergovernmental Agreements: Post-Devolution Concordats in a Comparative Perspective' [2015] PL 134; Richard Rawlings, 'Concordats of the Constitution' (2000) 116 LQR 257.

[69] *Cole v Whitfield* (1988) 165 CLR 360.

[70] *Queensland v Commonwealth* (1977) 139 CLR 585.

[71] The vast jurisprudence around the privileges and immunities clause in both US Constitution Article IV, section 2, clause 1 and Amendment XIV, section 1, clause 2 illustrates the point.

[72] A series of examples drawn from judicial consideration of the principle of federal loyalty are given in Palermo and Kossler (n 11) 250–51.

[73] *South Dakota v Dole* 483 US 203 (1987).

[74] *Financial Equalization I* 72 BVerfGE 330; Palermo and Kossler (n 11) 241.

multilevel governmental relationship and are amongst the most critical that are likely to fall to courts to decide.

There is considerable variation in the design of the distribution of powers in multilevel governmental systems, which affects the nature of the challenge presented to courts tasked with constitutional review. The key distinction between dualist and integrated federations throws up quite different questions concerning, for example, the extent of the executive power of the respective levels of government. Even if attention is focused purely on legislative power, variations between characterisation of power as concurrent rather than exclusive or reserved, in the treatment of residual power, or in the manner in which conflict or inconsistency is resolved, create different dynamics that affect the interpretive exercise.[75] To complicate matters further, there are differences between multilevel governmental systems in the meaning of some of these ostensibly familiar terms, including the concept of concurrency.[76] Sometimes these differences are shaped by courts; in all cases, it falls to courts to understand and give effect to the meaning that applies.

There are contextual differences between multilevel governmental systems as well which may have a bearing on the interpretation of parts of the multilevel constitutional design, including the allocation of powers. Any conditions that compelled provision for multilevel government may be relevant: plurinationalism, transformation, reconciliation, unification, antidote to secession. There is an obvious case for adding post-conflict constitutions that implement peace agreements to these examples too.[77] The legal system in which the constitution is embedded may affect interpretation, through differences in approaches to legal reasoning and in the underlying assumptions on which it is based.[78] In a loosely related point, interpretation of constitutional provision for multilevel government may be affected by the character of the reviewing court: all else being equal, a specialist Constitutional Court may take a more holistic, less doctrinal approach to the task than a court for which constitutional questions are only part of its jurisdiction.[79] The rest of a constitution forms part of the relevant interpretive context too. Variations that may affect judicial understanding of the meaning of an allocation of powers or other constitutional provisions for multilevel government include the

[75] Nicholas Aroney and John Kincaid, 'Introduction: Courts in Federal Systems' in Nicholas Aroney and John Kincaid (eds), *Courts in Federal Systems* (University of Toronto Press 2017) 3, 21

[76] Anna Dziedzic and Cheryl Saunders, 'The Meanings of Concurrency' in Nico Steytler (ed), *Concurrent Powers in Federal Systems: Meaning, Making, Managing* (Brill/Nijhoff 2017) 12.

[77] Consider, for example, the critique of the decision of the Supreme Court of Sri Lanka in *In re the Thirteenth Amendment* (1987) 2 Slr 312. The Amendment followed the Indo-Lanka Accord of 1987. The decision has been described as 'setting a monistic and centralizing paradigm': Asanga Welikala, 'More Than Meets the Eye? The Sri Lankan Supreme Court's Decision on the Proscription of the Federal Party' (ConstitutionNet, 29 August 2017); available at: http://constitutionnet.org/news/more-meets-eye-sri-lankan-supreme-courts-decision-proscription-federal-party, accessed 1 July 2019.

[78] The point is demonstrated by the several contributions in Andras Jakab, Arthur Dyevre, and Giulio Itzcovich, *Comparative Constitutional Reasoning* (CUP 2017).

[79] Aroney and Kincaid (n 75), 8, 9.

nature of the relationship between the legislative and executive branches, whether characterised as parliamentary or presidential or in some other way, and the ready availability of other checks on excessive exercise of power through the political process.

Some of these variations are more effective than others in encouraging a judicial culture that supports multilevel constitutionalism. As a generalisation, however, in most systems of multilevel government, judicial review is a significant vehicle for the centralisation of power in ways and with results that detract from multilevel constitutionalism.[80] How to counter the untoward effects of judicial review, without stymying desirable flexibility over time, is one of the more intractable challenges for many systems of multilevel government.

The assumptions of unitary constitutionalism may be reinforced for courts by a feature commonly associated with multilevel systems, that in the event of conflict between the otherwise valid actions of two levels of government, those of the centre are entitled to prevail.[81] Unitary constitutionalism also may encourage courts to consider constitutional provisions for multilevel government in isolation from the rest of the constitution, as an add-on to regular constitutional provisions, dealing with institutions and rights.

Another difficulty for courts in interpreting and enforcing constitutional provisions for multilevel government, however, is the absence of justiciable standards to determine ambiguous limits of an allocation of power that are contested between levels of government. Constitutional design may be part of the answer: competing lists of exclusive powers, for example, provide more obviously justiciable standards than a list of concurrent powers. More generally, however, judicial review in systems of multilevel government would be assisted by the development and acceptance of a concept of multilevel constitutionalism, to overcome apprehension about which standards are justiciable and which are not.

There has been some experimentation with these ideas already, in various jurisdictions, both within and above the level of the state. One, which became fashionable following its adoption for the European Union in areas outside the Union's exclusive competences in the Maastricht Treaty, is the principle of subsidiarity.[82] Subsidiarity indicates a commitment to the values of multilevel government that has some regard to where the balance of advantage lies in an exercise of power by one level of government or another.[83] It has not proved particularly successful, however, in offering a justiciable standard, although it potentially offers a useful

[80] Ibid; Halberstam and Reimann (n 5).

[81] The point is illustrated by the decision of the High Court of Australia in *Commonwealth v Cigamatic (In Liq)* (1962) 108 CLR 372. The rule about the paramountcy of central law is common, however.

[82] Treaty on European Union, Article 5(3).

[83] Michelle Evans and Augusto Zimmerman, 'The Global Relevance of Subsidiarity: An Overview' in Michelle Evans and Augusto Zimmerman (eds), *Global Perspectives on Subsidiarity* (Springer 2014) 1, 2.

trigger for political action on the part of the legislatures of participating states.[84] In addition, there are bottom line 'federal principles' already in existence in some federations, on which others might build. The requirement of *Bundestreue* or federal loyalty and its derivatives in the continental European federations is one example.[85] Implied limits on the exercise of power by one level of government to significantly burden the other, which have occasionally been invoked in the United States and Australia, generally with asymmetric effect, is another.[86] Notably, however, for present purposes, both of these sets of principles apply to actions that affect government to government relations, rather than to any more general interpretation of allocated powers.

A solution that offers greater promise draws on the relationship between multilevel government and constitutionalism. That relationship assumes and requires that a constitution providing for multilevel government is interpreted as an integrated whole. On this basis, the rest of the constitution also is a source from which understanding of the meaning, scope, and application of allocated powers can be drawn and considerations that play into methodology can be developed. The synergies between multilevel government and democracy may be particularly fruitful for these purposes. In one example of this approach in action, recent Australian jurisprudence has begun to clarify the parameters of federal executive power through recourse to arguments drawing on both multilevel government and representative democracy, in a holistic understanding of the constitution.[87] The federalism argument is obvious, drawing broadly on the constitutional distribution of legislative power to identify limits to the federal executive power to contract and to spend. In so far as these uses of executive power also avoid the legislature, including the federal second chamber, constitutional concerns based on representative democracy potentially are raised as well.[88]

VI. Conclusion

This chapter argues that a concept of multilevel constitutionalism is needed to enhance the effectiveness of multilevel government within states. Multilevel government takes a wide variety of forms, the range of which continues to expand. It is a useful construct within states, for reasons that presently include not only its more obvious applications to acknowledge identity and mitigate conflict but

[84] Katarzyna Grant, *The Principle of Subsidiarity and its Enforcement in the EU Legal Order* (Hart 2018) 2.

[85] Palermo and Kossler (n 11) 249–53.

[86] For Australia see, for example, *Austin v Commonwealth* (2003) 215 CLR 185; in the US, *Prinz v United States* 521 US 898 (1997).

[87] *Williams v Commonwealth of Australia* (2012) 248 CLR 156.

[88] Cheryl Saunders, 'Separation of Legislative and Executive Power' in Cheryl Saunders and Adrienne Stone (eds), *Oxford Handbook of the Australian Constitution* (OUP 2018) 617.

also its potential to deepen the responsiveness of representative democracy, at a time when new directions are sorely needed. It is ironic that, despite the prevalence of multilevel government, performance often is disappointing, as power and resources drift to the centre and the opportunity for effective and responsive substate government is missed. One of the principal causes of this state of affairs is that the principles and practices of unitary states remain the norm, influencing political action, judicial interpretation, and the assumptions on which many national traditions of constitutionalism rest. A compound conception of multilevel constitutionalism, harmonising the values of both multilevel government and constitutionalism, offers a much-needed theoretical solution, on which cultural change in political practice and judicial review can build.

A broadly parallel set of issues is raised by multilevel government above the level of the state. Multilevel government is common in both the regional and international spheres. Its goals include diminution of conflict, collaboration in resolving shared problems, and maximising economic competitiveness and political influence in a globalised world. At the dawn of the third decade of the twenty-first century, however, suprastate multilevel government is struggling as well, with performance, compliance, and participation. In the face of claims that globalisation has stalled, it is timely to evaluate the successes and failures of the past, in order to lay foundations for a future in which multilevel government almost certainly will be needed.

The seeds of answers to some of the problems that have emerged may lie in the elaboration of a conception of multilevel constitutionalism, one version of which has been explored in this chapter, with application to multilevel government within states. Many of the phenomena that suggest a need to rethink are shared. As within states, there is a tendency for power and authority to shift towards the higher level under both regional and international arrangements, without clear understanding of where the limits should lie in either case. There may be an associated assumption that the lower level, in this context the state, is lacking in capacity or otherwise unreliable. Consequential problems affect the performance of multilevel government, through overreach by higher levels of government at the expense of accountable action by the lower level. As with multilevel government within states, the vehicles through which these developments occur are broadly the same: political action in intergovernmental forums and resolution of disputes about power and authority through forms of judicial review.

The parallels are by no means complete, however. All arrangements above the level of the state involve a form of coming together: aggregation for particular purposes, rather than disaggregation. Participating states have a wider range of options in the face of dissatisfaction including withdrawal, non-compliance, and recourse to the uncertainty that such novel arrangements, without a single, final arbiter, necessarily entail. It is effectively impossible for levels of government above the state to become democratic in any presently received sense of the term. It follows that the body of regional or international law that applies is unlikely to be described in terms of constitutionalism, however it may otherwise be understood. In this respect at least, the position of states, at the lower level, is strengthened by their potentially democratic character, framed by the requirements of constitutionalism, whether adapted to multilevel constitutionalism or not.

Above the level of the state, the future of multilevel government faces somewhat different challenges. Multilevel constitutionalism may well be an answer, but it necessarily will take a different form, or forms, responding to the particular demands of regional and international action. Conceptualising these forms, designing the institutional frameworks through which they are best given effect, and resolving the practical difficulties that may arise is a project in its own right, albeit one that also is in need of attention.

18

A Hard Law Approach to States Systemic Violations of Article 2 of the Treaty of the European Union

Reasons and Means*

Miguel Poiares Maduro and Benedita Menezes Queiroz

I. Introduction

Paul Craig is one of Europe's leading public law scholars. Few, if any, have been able to merge the study of national and European public law as successfully as Paul Craig. A good part of the extraordinary quality of his scholarship is also linked to the way in which he has embedded the study of public law in democratic theory. This chapter pays tribute to his work by focusing on a matter that highlights the importance of both those facets for public law in Europe today.

When the European Communities were created, a mechanism of fundamental rights protection was absent from its legal order, as was any catalogue of fundamental rights. There are several reasons why the original Treaties did not contain a bill of rights or indeed any system of fundamental rights protection.[1] First, it must be recalled that when the original Treaties were drafted the founding Member States probably did not foresee either their transformation into a constitutional document or the extent of the powers to be assumed by the European Communities. The idea that the European Communities may come to threaten fundamental rights was very distant from the minds of the founding Member States. In this respect, the inclusion of a bill of rights in the Communities Treaties at this time would have given the Community legal order state-like characteristics that would have appeared more a threat than a guarantee.

Second, the original conception of the Treaties as international law instruments creating Communities of limited competences both reduced the scope of any

* This chapter is based on a policy paper originally written for the Friedrich Ebert Foundation by one of the authors (Miguel Poiares Maduro).

[1] For a more in-depth analysis see: JHH Weiler, 'Eurocracy and Distrust: Some Questions Concerning the Role of the European Court of Justice in the Protection of Fundamental Human Rights Within the Legal Order of the European Communities' (1986) 61 Washington L Rev 1103, 1110.

Miguel Poiares Maduro and Benedita Menezes Queiroz, *A Hard Law Approach to States Systemic Violations of Article 2 of the Treaty of the European Union* In: *The Foundations and Future of Public Law*. Edited by: Elizabeth Fisher, Jeff King, Alison L Young, Oxford University Press (2020).
DOI: 10.1093/oso/9780198845249.003.0018

possible threat that they could constitute fundamental rights at the national level and led Member States to assume that, if necessary, they could still control the acts of those Communities through national fundamental rights. On the one hand, the fact that Member States perceived Community competences to be clearly limited led them to assume that the scope of possible conflicts between Community acts and fundamental rights was to be closely circumscribed. It could be said that the expectation was that the compatibility of Community law with fundamental rights was addressed at the moment of delegating those competences. National constitutional review, when ratifying the Treaties, would be the appropriate instrument to guarantee the compatibility between the obligations assumed by the Member State under Community law and fundamental rights. On the other hand, if conflicts did arise, Member States probably expected their national constitutions to be the best guarantee for the protection of fundamental rights. Although it is a general principle of international law that no state can invoke domestic law to evade its international law obligations it is also well known that this has not always stopped virtually all national legal systems from determining the inapplicability of international law provisions when in conflict with certain national rules (in particular, national constitutions). The dualist conception of the relationship between domestic law and international law establishes that in such cases the state may be internationally liable for the violation of the international law provisions, but nevertheless continue to make national constitutions prevail over international norms. States could then assume that their national constitutions would continue to guarantee that no Community act would violate a fundamental right. Moreover, the degree and form of protection of fundamental rights would continue to be those established in the national constitution.

Third, it must also be remembered that judicial protection of fundamental rights was a relatively recent phenomenon in Europe. Although fundamental rights documents and bills of rights did exist for many years in European states, they were primarily understood as providing guidance to the political process but not to give legal grounds for judicial actions. They were expected to guide the drafting of laws by the legislator but did not serve to control the validity of such laws. The sovereignty of the legislator (either in the form of 'parliamentary sovereignty' or in the form of the 'volonté générale' expressed by the majority will) dominated the political organisation of European States for many years. The American tradition of constitutional judicial review was only introduced in Europe following the Second World War and the discovery of the risks that the majoritarian will may also entail. At the time the founding treaties of European integration were adopted, fundamental rights review was, therefore, a relatively recent concept in Europe. All this may have contributed to the absence of a system and catalogue of fundamental rights protection from the founding Treaties of the Communities.

These expectations were, however, overturned by the constitutional developments of the Community legal order and the scope of competences assumed by the Communities. On the one hand, the supremacy and direct effect attributed to Community acts meant that national constitutional provisions could no longer be used to guarantee the compatibility between those acts and fundamental rights. On the other hand, the increased perception of the wide scope of competences assumed by the Communities and of their open and undetermined character highlighted the risk of fundamental rights violations arising from the exercise of such Community powers.

The initial debate on fundamental rights in European integration was, therefore, about the risk that the new powers assumed at the European level might bring to the fundamental rights and rule of law usually guaranteed in its Member States. The initial cases brought to the Court of Justice concerned this matter. It is well known, and not necessary to develop here, how the Court of Justice 'introduced', in *Internationale Handelsgesellschaft*[2] such fundamental rights protection at EU level so as to prevent any challenge to EU law supremacy by national constitutional courts.

For years, the fundamental rights discourse on European integration therefore focused on the need for the Community legal order to take fundamental rights seriously in reviewing the powers of Community institutions rather than those of Member States. The protection of fundamental rights in the Member States was either to be addressed under national constitutions or under the European Convention of Human Rights (ECHR) and Fundamental Freedoms in the Treaties. Gradually, however, the focus has shifted to the need for the European Union also to guarantee fundamental rights and the rule of law at the Member-State level.

II. EU Protection of Fundamental Rights in its Member States: Reasons and Instruments

Increased European integration (bringing greater interdependence between its Member States, including in fundamental rights-sensitive issues), successive enlargements, and the incomplete nature of the ECHR system (limited in scope and with weak enforcement mechanisms) have driven the need to guarantee that Member States of the European Union comply with a basic set of fundamental values now defined in Article 2 Treaty on European Union (TEU). These comprise democracy, the rule of law, and fundamental rights. They are also accession criteria for any candidate Member State under Article 49 TEU.

It has become clear, however, that simply controlling compliance with such values at the moment of accession is not enough. It is in this context that Article

[2] Case 11/70, *Internationale Handelsgesellschaft mbH v Einfuhr- und Vorratsstelle für Getreide und Futtermittel* [1970] ECR 112.

7 TEU was inserted into the Treaties. Paragraphs 1 to 3 of Article 7 TEU state the following:

> 1. On a reasoned proposal by one third of the Member States, by the European Parliament or by the European Commission, the Council, acting by a majority of four fifths of its members after obtaining the consent of the European Parliament, may determine that there is a clear risk of a serious breach by a Member State of the values referred to in Article 2. Before making such a determination, the Council shall hear the Member State in question and may address recommendations to it, acting in accordance with the same procedure.
>
> The Council shall regularly verify that the grounds on which such a determination was made continue to apply.
>
> 2. The European Council, acting by unanimity on a proposal by one third of the Member States or by the Commission and after obtaining the consent of the European Parliament, may determine the existence of a serious and persistent breach by a Member State of the values referred to in Article 2, after inviting the Member State in question to submit its observations.
>
> 3. Where a determination under paragraph 2 has been made, the Council, acting by a qualified majority, may decide to suspend certain of the rights deriving from the application of the Treaties to the Member State in question, including the voting rights of the representative of the government of that Member State in the Council. In doing so, the Council shall take into account the possible consequences of such a suspension on the rights and obligations of natural and legal persons.
>
> The obligations of the Member State in question under the Treaties shall in any case continue to be binding on that State.

The problem with Article 7 TEU is that it depends on a political decision and not judicial enforcement, and the requirements triggering that political decision are extremely demanding. For instance, the unanimity, excluding the concerned Member State, necessary for applying sanctions in case of a serious and persistent violation of the values of Article 2 TEU is particularly hard to satisfy. This difficulty, together with the political character of the assessment, places a high political premium on triggering its application.[3] The Commission has recently, for the first time, initiated this procedure against Poland but even if it persuades four-fifths of the Member States to declare that there is clear risk of a serious breach, what if Poland continues to refuse to correct such a breach? Will it be possible to then

[3] Vaira Vike-Freiberga et al, 'A Free and Pluralistic Media to Sustain Democracy: The Report of the High Level Group on Media Freedom and Pluralism' (January 2013) https://ec.europa.eu/digital-single-market/en/news/public-consultation-independent-report-hlg-media-freedom-and-pluralism---read-contributions, accessed 7 July 2019, 18.

get the unanimous decision necessary to trigger sanctions? And what if a small number of Member States (or even a single other Member State under Article 7(2)) blocks the application of Article 7 TEU? The credibility of the European Union in terms of fundamental rights protection would be clearly threatened and Article 7 TEU perceived as totally ineffective. As a consequence, its deterrence value would be questioned.

The Commission has also tried to supplement some of the shortcomings of Article 7 TEU by introducing the rule of law dialogue procedure. This was initially thought to be a soft law mechanism alternative to Article 7 TEU whereby the Commission would engage in a constructive dialogue with the concerned Member State and, if necessary, issue recommendations in its regard. The expectation was that either the constructive approach might work by itself or that the name-and-shame phase of the procedure would eventually lead the Member State to correct the identified risks to the rule of law. So far, it has not worked that way. The instrument lacks the teeth necessary to drive Member States towards compliance, so much so that the Commission is now using the threat of triggering Article 7 TEU to try, so far unsuccessfully, to convince Member States to follow its recommendations. Naturally, the effectiveness of the threat is hindered by the difficulties in applying Article 7 TEU itself that I have mentioned.

In this context, the Commission has also tried, whenever possible, to link the fundamental rights or rule of law problem with another EU law issue. In other words, it has tried, whenever possible, to reframe fundamental rights and rule of law issues as questions involving other EU rules whose application to the actions of the Member States is incontestable. This was the case of the Hungarian law that instituted a retirement age of sixty-two years for judges, thereby allowing a massive replacement of judges in Hungary, arguably to give the ruling party the possibility to appoint judges more sympathetic to its views. The Commission used the Directive prohibiting age discrimination to start an infringement action against Hungary, which it subsequently won.[4] However, since the framing of the case was not the protection of judicial independence, it was possible for Hungary to remedy the situation by compensating the retired judges without reinstating most of them, thereby achieving the purported political intention of the Government contrary to the rule of law.

In any event, this approach has its limits on the number and scope of EU rules that directly address issues that can be related to specific aspects of the rule of law and fundamental rights. This would only change if EU fundamental rights would be directly applicable to the Member States, which is not the general principle so far. The extent to which EU fundamental rights can be used to review the acts of Member States can be referred to as the question of incorporation

[4] C-286/12, *Commission v Hungary* EU:C:2012:687 [2013] 1 CMLR 44.

of EU fundamental rights into national legal orders. This alludes to the process through which the American Supreme Court incorporated the Bill of Rights of the American Constitution[5] (which initially was only directed at the federal government) into the due process clause directed at the individual states. This, de facto, made the Bill of Rights applicable to states even within their purely domestic arenas. No such fully fledged incorporation has yet occurred in EU law. However, the European Court of Justice (CJEU) has extended the initial reach of EU fundamental rights to also cover Member State actions that fall within the scope of application of EU law, notably when they either implement EU law or derogate from it.[6] In this regard, Article 51(1) of the Charter of Fundamental Rights (Charter) could be argued even to restrict that scope since (at least in the English version)[7] it determines that the provisions of the Charter are only applicable to the Member States 'when they are implementing Union law'. This would appear indeed to limit the more extensive scope of application previously recognised in the case law of the CJEU. As mentioned earlier, it resulted from such case law that EU fundamental rights may also be applied to Member State acts that derogate from EU rules. If interpreted literally, Article 51(1) could instead lead to a more restrictive scope of application of EU fundamental rights. This has not, however, been the case and the CJEU has consistently decided that whether a Member State action is or is not reviewable under EU fundamental rights depends on whether that action falls within the scope of application of EU law. That can be the case, as in the Hungarian judges retirement law, because there is a dimension of a certain fundamental right (such as age discrimination) that is directly regulated by EU law or because the action of the Member State takes place in the context of implementing an EU act (eg transposing a Directive) or is an exception to another EU rule (eg a restriction to free movement). Outside this link to another EU provision, however, it has not been possible for EU law to be used to enforce fundamental rights and the rule of law in a Member State.

Arguments have been made in the past to extend the role of EU law and the Court in applying fundamental rights to Member actions. Famously, in his Opinion in *Konstantinidis*, Advocate General Jacobs expressed the view that any national of one Member State pursuing an economic activity in another Member State could invoke the protection of EU fundamental rights:

> In my opinion, a Community national who goes to another Member State as a worker or self-employed person … is entitled not just to pursue his trade or

[5] The Bill of Rights corresponds to the first ten amendments of the American Constitution.

[6] See Case 5/88 *Wachauf v Germany* [1989] ECR 2609; and Case C-260/89 *Elliniki Radiophonia Tileorassi AE v Domitiki Etairia Pliroforissis and Sotiris Kouvelas* [1991] ECR I-2925.

[7] Some of the other language versions of this provision are more open.

> profession and to enjoy the same living and working conditions as nationals of the host State; he is in addition entitled to assume that, wherever he goes to earn his living in the European Community, he will be treated in accordance with a common code of fundamental values, in particular those laid down in the European Convention of Human Rights. In other words, he is entitled to say '*civis europeus sum*' and to invoke that status in order to oppose any violation of his fundamental rights.[8]

The Court, however, had a different view and did not endorse the Advocate General's opinion that any violation, by the host State, of a fundamental right of a national from another Member State could hinder his or her right to free movement so long as that fundamental right could be said to be part of that '*civis europeus sum*'. The Court probably feared that it would be a step too far to introduce a general review of fundamental rights by EU law in Member States at that stage of European integration, taking into account the nature of the EU judicial system. Such a large expansion of the scope of EU fundamental rights review could also have as a consequence that a large array of national measures, otherwise not connected to EU law, could be challenged under EU law and, ultimately, brought to the CJEU (in the same way that fundamental rights give rise to a substantial body of litigation in most Member States' national judicial systems with centralised or decentralised review of fundamental rights). The consequences would be twofold: increased tension with national sovereignty on a large spectrum of issues; and a flood of cases to the Court that, without a *certiorari* mechanism that restricts the number of cases heard, would most likely have seen its workload become unmanageable.

In a later case,[9] one of the authors (then Advocate General at the CJEU) proposed a more nuanced approach that, while aiming to introduce some judicial oversight and enforcement of fundamental rights and the rule of law in Member States, would not raise the risks just mentioned since it would trigger EU law and the Court's intervention only on violations with systemic impact. The Court did not address this proposal in that judgment, having decided the case on a different basis. That proposal is, to a large extent, the basis for the position to be developed in this essay, also in light of more recent developments of EU law.[10]

[8] Case C-168/91, *Christos Konstantinidis v Stadt Altensteig—Standesamt and Landratsamt Calw—Ordnungsamt* [1993] ECR I-1191, para 46.

[9] Case C-380/05 *Centro Europa 7 Srl v Ministero delle Comunicazioni e Autorita per le Garanzie nelle Comunicazioni* [2008] ECR I-349.

[10] The theory advanced in that Opinion has been already been picked up and developed in the academic literature. The proposal made in here is, however, a further development and refinement of the approached put forward in that Opinion.

III. Reasons for the EU Role in Enforcing the Rule of Law at National Level

Before presenting the specifics of the proposal, it is important, however, summarily to articulate the possible reasons legitimating a role for EU law in this area. There are three possible justifications for a regional organisation or a supranational entity to intervene in the domestic sphere of Member States in protecting the rule of law, democracy, and fundamental rights. Depending on the reason or reasons that can be invoked, the scope and form of intervention might have to change. The stronger the political and/or normative authority claimed to legitimate such intervention, the stronger the authority to intervene and the scope and forms it can assume.

The first reason could be based on the moral and political externalities that violations of fundamental rights or the rule of law in a Member State may cause in another Member State. Of course, the concept of moral and political externalities is controversial. However, when Member States commit themselves to share a certain political and economic space it is legitimate to argue that they are entitled not to want to share the benefits and costs involved in that common endeavour with Member States that do not share a certain common set of fundamental values.

In some cases, the objective of cooperation between Member States may be precisely the promotion of such fundamental values, in which case the previous argument acquires additional strength. But this case can also be linked to a second reason: Member States may want to externally bind themselves to fundamental rights and the rule of law, creating a form of external constitutional discipline. This may be so because they do not have a domestic mechanism to guarantee such values and want to use the external mechanism to do it or because, in the face of past negative experiences, they want to add an external layer of constitutional discipline 'on top' of the domestic constitutions. In these instances, the authority to intervene of the international or supranational body results from a previous self-binding act and intent of the Member State: international or supranational law is, in these cases, a form of collective self-discipline that Member States have imposed upon themselves because past experience has showed that domestic mechanisms of countervailing powers and political and judicial control are not always effective in protecting fundamental rights and democracy. These two reasons certainly fit the case of the Council of Europe and the European Court of Human Rights, for example.

There is, however, a possible third reason in the case of the European Union. Member States have entered a form of integration generating such interdependence that violations of the rule of law, democracy, and fundamental rights by one Member State can directly impact on the other Member States, either because the latter are called in to give effect to decisions of the former Member State that may have been taken in violation of those values or because the violations of such values by that Member State puts into question the legitimacy and effectiveness of the decisions taken by all.

There is an important difference when invoking this third reason. The authority to intervene in protecting the rule of law, fundamental rights, or democracy results from the need to protect the legitimate and effective functioning of that zone of interdependence. This provides an additional authority to such intervention. The intervention is not only justified to protect the Member State from itself or because it is claimed that the actions of that Member State create a moral externality in violating a joint commitment to certain values. The intervention, in this case, also takes place to protect the other Member States from becoming unwilling participants in such violations either because they have to, directly or indirectly, enforce them or because they impact on the character of decisions taken by all; in other words, where problems with fundamental rights and the rule of law in a Member State become problems in complying with fundamental rights and the rule of law by the European Union itself.

IV. Correcting and Preventing Member States Systemic Rule of Law Problems Through Judicial Enforcement at EU Level

As stated in the *Centro Europa 7* Advocate-General opinion, while the provisions setting up the European Union and its Member States' commitment to the rule of law, fundamental rights, and democracy 'do not aim to extend the scope of application of fundamental rights, as a matter of EU law, to any Member State measure', they do

> give expression to the profound conviction that respect for fundamental rights is intrinsic in the EU legal order and that, without it, common action by and for the peoples of Europe would be unworthy and unfeasible. In that sense, the very existence of the European Union is predicated on respect for fundamental rights. Protection of the 'common code' of fundamental rights accordingly constitutes an existential requirement for the EU legal order.[11]

The opinion went on to say:

> In this respect, a distinction must be drawn between, on the one hand, jurisdiction to review any national measure in the light of fundamental rights and, on the other hand, jurisdiction to examine whether Member States provide the necessary level of protection in relation to fundamental rights in order to be able

[11] Case C-380/05 *Centro Europa 7 Srl* (n 9) para 19.

> adequately to fulfil their other obligations as members of the Union. The first type of review does not yet exist and is not within the Union's current competences. However, the second type of review flows logically from the nature of the process of European integration. It serves to guarantee that the basic conditions are in place for the proper functioning of the EU legal order and for the effective exercise of many of the rights granted to European citizens. Though the degree of protection of fundamental rights at national level does not have to be exactly the same as the degree of protection of fundamental rights at the level of the European Union, there must be some measure of equivalence in order to ensure that the law of the Union can operate effectively within the national legal order.[12]

In other words, certain systemic violations of fundamental rights and the rule of law can be of such nature and magnitude as to lead to the violation of certain fundamental principles or rules in law of the European Union.

A first example regards the principle of effectiveness of EU law. This principle is, notably, enshrined in Article 19 TEU that provides:

> The Court of Justice of the European Union shall include the Court of Justice, the General Court and specialised courts. It shall ensure that in the interpretation and application of the Treaties the law is observed.
>
> Member States shall provide remedies sufficient to ensure effective legal protection in the fields covered by Union law.

The CJEU has made clear that such principle requires the full implementation and enforcement of EU law and the protection of the rights granted by it to citizens.[13] Since EU law is usually applied via national courts and national procedural law, the principle of effectiveness has been used by the Court to review procedural and substantive aspects of national laws regulating the judiciary and judicial protection. This included considering that Member States were in violation of EU law because they did not provide for an adequate judicial remedy or its procedural requirements made it too difficult to protect an EU right or obtain redress for a past violation. In other words, through the principle of effectiveness the Court can review the extent to which a national judicial system (in its institutional, procedural, and substantive dimensions) is capable of guaranteeing the fair, impartial, and full application of EU law and protect the rights granted by it to citizens.

[12] Ibid para 20.

[13] Case 26/62 *Van Gend en Loos* [1963] Case C-213/89; *vs. Secretary of State for Transport, ex parte Factortame Ltd* [1990] ECR I- 2433; Joined Cases C-6/90 and C-9/90 *Francovich and Bonifaci v Italy* [1991] ECR I-5357; Case C–208/90 *Emmott v. Minister of Social Welfare* [1991] ECR I–4269; Case C-50/00P *Union de Pequeños Agricultores (UPA) v Council* [2002] ECR I-6677; Case C-432/05 *Unibet v Justitiekanslem* [2007] ECR I-2271; Case C-63/08 *Pontin v T-Comalux* [2009] ECR I-10467; Case C-583/11P *Inuit Tapiriit Kanatami I* EU:C:2013:625 [2014] 1 CMLR 54.

This has an immediate connection with a core aspect of the rule of law: judicial independence. National judges, when applying and interpreting EU law, are part of the EU judicial system. The preliminary ruling procedure in Article 267 Treaty on the Functioning of the European Union (TFEU) is the archetypal mechanism that ensures, through judicial dialogue,[14] the effective cooperation between national courts and the CJEU in the application of EU law.[15] Independence is one of the criteria that must be fulfilled for a public body to be considered a court or a tribunal of the Member State in accordance with Article 267 TFEU.[16] In addition to being independent, the public body has to be established by law, to be permanent, with compulsory jurisdiction, an *inter partes* procedure, and has to apply rules of law.[17] The respect for the principle of judicial independence is therefore an essential aspect for any national judicial system to be recognised as such under EU law and be entrusted its enforcement.

In this context, it is clear that a Member State with a systemic rule of law problem, notably due to a serious threat to the independence of its judiciary (as it is the current case with Poland), is not complying with the principle of effective judicial protection. It is this that the Court has made clear in a line of cases that concluded with the recent decision in the infringement action brought by the Commission against Poland.

In the first of these cases the Court established the principle, but without relevance to the specifics of the case. In *Associação Sindical dos Juízes Portugueses*,[18] the Court confirmed its role as 'the ultimate guarantor of the rule of law within the EU'.[19] It did so by widening the scope of the principle of effective judicial protection and affirming its competence to analyse the independence of Member States' judiciaries in 'the fields covered by EU law'. The judgment interpreted the meaning of judicial independence (in particular, the second subparagraph of Article 19(1) TEU, but also Article 47 of the Charter) in relation to general salary reduction measures introduced temporarily in 2014 to the Portuguese public sector (including judges) to eliminate an excessive budget deficit.[20]

[14] Allan Rosas, 'Methods of Interpretation: Judicial Dialogue' in Carl Baudenbacher and Erhard Busek (eds), *The Role of International Courts* (German Law Publishers 2008) 185–91.

[15] Case C- 221/88, *Busseni* [1990] ECR I-495, para 16.

[16] On the independence of national courts or tribunals of Member States, see for example Case C-54/96, *Dorsh Consult* EU:C:1997:413 [1997] ECR I-4961.

[17] For more on the set of criteria to a public body be considered a 'court or a tribunal of a Member State' (*Vaassen-Göbbels* criteria) see for example Case 61/65, *Vaassen-Göbbels* EU:C:1966:39 [1966] ECR 261 and Koen Lenaerts, Ignace Maselis, and Kathleen Gutman, *EU Procedural Law* (OUP 2014) 52–55 and Case C-503/15, *Margarit Panicello* EU:C:2017:16 [2017] 3 CMLR 7, para 27.

[18] Case C-64/16, *Associação Sindical dos Juízes Portugueses* EU:C:2018:117 [2018] 3 CMLR 16.

[19] Koen Lenaerts, 'The Court of Justice and National Courts: A Dialogue Based on Mutual Trust and Judicial Independence' (Speech at the Supreme Administrative Court of the Republic of Poland, 19 March 2018); available at: http://www.aca-europe.eu/index.php/en/114-library, accessed 7 July 2019.

[20] Case C-64/16, *Associação Sindical dos Juízes Portugueses* (n 18) para 27.

Members of the Tribunal de Contas (Court of Auditors), represented by Associação Sindical dos Juízes Portugueses, argued that these measures were an interference with the principle of judicial independence, which is guaranteed both by the Portuguese Constitution and EU law. Subsequently, the Supremo Tribunal Administrativo (Supreme Administrative Court) referred the issue to the CJEU. The Court considered that the salary reduction measures challenged in the proceedings did not violate the principle of judicial independence.[21] The Court concluded that those measures were not adopted specifically with regard to the members of the Tribunal de Contas, but instead were 'general measures seeking a contribution from all members of the national public administration to the austerity effort dictated by the mandatory requirements for reducing the Portuguese State's excessive budget deficit'.[22] Rather than in the outcome of these proceedings, the importance of this case, for the present issue, rests in the Court's reading of the principle of judicial independence and in its consequences.

In relation to the material scope of Article 19(1) TEU, the Court determined that it applied to 'the fields covered by Union law', independently of whether or not this equated to the implementation of EU law by a Member State in accordance with Article 51(1) of the Charter.[23] This means that the principle of judicial independence, given its wider material scope, would include situations where a Member State is not implementing EU law but which are covered by it.

In *Associação Sindical dos Juízes Portugueses* the Court opted to apply a treaty-based provision (Article 19(1) TEU) not limited by Article 51(1) of the Charter. The Court concluded that Article 19 TEU gives 'concrete expression to the value of the rule of law stated in Article 2 TEU', and ensures mutual trust between Member States, in particular with regard to the common values that founded the European Union.[24] Furthermore, the Court stated that 'the very existence of effective judicial review designed to ensure compliance with EU law is of the essence of the rule of law'.[25] The judgment highlights the importance of the cooperation and mutual trust between European courts. In particular, the decision focuses on the role of national judges guaranteeing the protection of the independence of the EU judicial system. In a timely interpretative exercise, the Court stated that 'national courts and tribunals, in collaboration of the Court of Justice, fulfil a duty entrusted to them jointly of ensuring that in the interpretation and application of the Treaties the law is observed'[26] and, as such, the principle of sincere cooperation Article 4(3)

[21] Ibid paras 44–52.
[22] Ibid para 49.
[23] Ibid para 29.
[24] Ibid paras 30 and 32.
[25] Ibid para 36 and Case C-72/15, *Rosneft* [2017] EU:C:2017:236 [2017] 3 CMLR 23, para 73.
[26] Case C-64/16, *Associação Sindical dos Juízes Portugueses* (n 18) para 33 and Opinion 1/09 (Agreement creating a Unified Litigation System) of 8 March 2011, EU:C:2011:123 and Case C-583/11P *Inuit Tapiriit Kanatami* (n 13) para 99.

TEU determines that Member States must provide remedies that ensure effective judicial protection for individual parties covered by EU law.[27]

Consequently, this cooperative relationship between EU courts, with the aim of ensuring the respect for the rule of law, prompts judicial dialogue at different levels and can itself be an instrument to protect the rule of law in all Member States. This also appears to be the understanding of the Court in *LM*,[28] delivered less than a month after *Associação Sindical dos Juízes Portugueses*. *LM* resulted from a request for a preliminary ruling submitted to the Court by the Irish Justice Aileen Donnelly in *Minister for Justice and Equality v Arthur Celmer*.[29]

In this case the Irish High Court questioned whether, in accordance with the European Arrest Warrant (EAW),[30] a national court should return a Polish national accused of a crime to their home country (the requesting Member State) when there is evidence that the rule of law is no longer respected. It was argued by the referring court that the recent changes to the judiciary in Poland damaged the rule of law and that its respect 'is also essential for mutual trust in the operation of the European arrest warrant'.[31] For the Irish court, returning this individual to Poland could expose him to the risk of unfair trial and could entail of violation of Articles 3 and 6 of the Charter and Articles 3 and 6 of the ECHR.

The Court's decision is a blend between *Aranyosi and Căldăraru*[32] and *Associação Sindical dos Juízes Portugueses*.[33] In *Aranyosi and Căldăraru* the CJEU held that where the national court makes an assessment that the surrender may result in the requested person being subject to inhuman or degrading treatment within the meaning of Article 4 of the Charter, the executing national court has the power to bring the surrender procedure established by the EAW to an end.[34] That decision focused on the individual circumstances of the person who is the subject of the EAW, in particular, in that case, with regard to the detention conditions in the prison system of the requesting Member State.[35] For the Court, the national court of the executing Member State 'when faced with evidence of the existence of such deficiencies that is objective, reliable, specific and properly updated' must determine whether there are substantial grounds to conclude that the individual would 'run a real risk of being subject in that Member State to inhuman or degrading treatment'.[36]

27 Case C-64/16, *Associação Sindical dos Juízes Portugueses* (n 18) paras 30 and 34.

28 C-216/18 *Minister for Justice and Equality v LM* EU:C:2018:586 [2019] 1 CMLR 18.

29 *Minister for Justice and Equality v. Artur Celmer*, 2013 295 EXT; 2014 8 EXT; 2017 291 EXT.

30 2002/584/JHA:Council Framework Decision of 13 June 2002 on the European arrest warrant and the surrender procedures between Member States [2002] OJ L190/1.

31 *LM* (n 28) paras 135 and 136.

32 Cases C-404/15, C-659/15, *Pál Aranyosi and Robert Căldăraru v Generalstaatsanwaltschaft Bremen* EU:C:2016:140 [2016] 3 CMLR 13.

33 Case C-64/16, *Associação Sindical dos Juízes Portugueses* (n 18).

34 N 30.

35 Cases C-404/15, C-659/15, *Pál Aranyosi* (n 32) para 94.

36 Ibid para 94.

In the *LM* decision the Court extends the possibility open in *Aranyosi and Căldăraru* to cases where judicial independence is in question. For the Court,

> the requirement of judicial independence forms part of the essence of the fundamental right to a fair trial, a right which is of cardinal importance as a guarantee that all the rights which individuals derive from EU law will be protected and that the values common to the Member States set out in Article 2 TEU, in particular the value of the rule of law, will be safeguarded.[37]

The Court went on to point out the necessary link between judicial independence and the effective enforcement of EU law by national courts required, *inter alia*, by Article 19 TEU. As a consequence, it follows, as already stated in *Associação Sindical dos Juízes Portugueses*, that 'every Member State must ensure that the bodies which, as "courts or tribunals" within the meaning of EU law, come within its judicial system in the fields covered by EU law meet the requirements of effective judicial protection'.[38]

The Court then states that, in the context of such challenge to the execution of a European Arrest Warrant, the first step of the executing authority must be to

> assess, on the basis of material that is objective, reliable, specific and properly updated concerning the operation of the system of justice in the issuing Member State (see, to that effect, judgment of 5 April 2016, *Aranyosi and Căldăraru*, C-404/15 and C-659/15 PPU, EU:C:2016:198, paragraph 89), whether there is a real risk, connected with a lack of independence of the courts of that Member State on account of systemic or generalised deficiencies there, of the fundamental right to a fair trial being breached.[39]

It is not irrelevant that the Court referred to the 'information in a reasoned proposal recently addressed by the Commission to the Council on the basis of Article 7(1) TEU is particularly relevant for the purposes of that assessment', and it went on to list a series of guarantees of judicial independence that, to a great extent, matched the infringement that had been brought against Poland.[40] Albeit the Court leaves the final assessment of the risk to fair trial, on account of generalised and systemic deficiencies concerning the judiciary of that country, to the Irish judge, it is rather clear that its own assessment highlights such a risk.

The Court, however, puts the brakes on the immediate consequences of such systemic assessment by returning to the second requirement of *Aranyosi and*

[37] C-216/18 PPU, *LM* (n 28) para 48.
[38] Ibid para 52.
[39] Ibid para 61.
[40] Ibid.

Căldăraru. The national court must also assess 'specifically and precisely whether, in the particular circumstances of the case, there are substantial grounds for believing that, following his surrender to the issuing Member State, the requested person will run that risk'.[41] This has been criticised as rendering the systemic assessment ineffective because of the burden imposed on the defendants and the dependency of national courts on information to be provided by a national court whose independence is, itself, in question. The systemic dimension would be consumed by the case by case assessment, rendering it both incapable of addressing the general problem in that Member State's judiciary and of providing an effective remedy in the specific cases.

This would not necessarily be the case. The Court's decision promotes a case-by-case assessment by national courts that could be understood as enlisting and empowering other national courts to protect the rule of law in Poland. In doing so it avoided an immediate and direct confrontation with Poland itself. The Court also perhaps trusted that the 'message' contained in the decision would be understood by the Polish authorities and possibly even prevent it from having to decide the infringement action that had been brought by the Commission against Poland. That was certainly not the case, since the Polish authorities did nothing to correct the deficiencies pointed out in the decision and the Court ended up having to engage directly itself with the issue. At the same time, *LM* remains important because it can be read as encouraging national courts to monitor each other's respect for the rule of law. It's the promotion of a 'bottom-up scrutiny of the rule of law across the EU'.[42]

In the wake of *Associação Sindical dos Juizes Portugueses* and *LM*, the decision of the Court in *Commission v Poland*[43] comes as no great surprise. In this case, the Commission brought long-awaited infringement proceedings against Poland, arguing that Poland's lowering of the mandatory retirement age for Supreme Court judges was a violation of Articles 19 TEU and 47 of the Charter. Nevertheless, *Commission v Poland* is a hugely important decision in its own right, being the first time a Member State has been found in violation of the rule of law in systemic terms.

The decision is based on Article 19(1) TEU, but it is also closely related to the values protected by Article 2 TEU. The Court starts by noting that the underlying assumption of the EU legal order is Member States' compliance with Article 2 TEU. That is crucial both for the mutual trust necessary between Member States and decentralised uniform enforcement of EU law by national courts across those Member States.[44] In this context, the Court conceives of Article 19(1) TEU as a

[41] Ibid para 68.

[42] Sergio Carrera and Valsamis Mitsilegas, *Upholding the Rule of Law by Scrutinising Judicial Independence—The Irish Court´s request for a preliminary ruling on the European Arrest Warrant* (CEPS Commentary, April 2018) https://www.ceps.eu/publications/upholding-rule-law-scrutinising-judicial-independence-irish-courts-request-preliminary, accessed 7 July 2019, 56.

[43] Case C-619/18 *Commission v Poland* EU:C:2019:531.

[44] Ibid paras 42–45.

particular expression of the rule of law affirmed in Article 2 TEU.[45] The Court then dismisses the arguments that such a control on the rule of law in Member States could only take place in the context of 'situations governed by EU law'.[46] For the Court, control of the rule of law and, in particular, of judicial independence of national courts can take place in systemic terms, under an infringement procedure, so long as the courts in question can be called on to apply EU law. The Court refers to the Charter to link judicial independence with the principle of effective judicial protection:

> To ensure that a body such as the Sąd Najwyższy (Supreme Court) is in a position to offer such protection, maintaining its independence is essential, as confirmed by the second paragraph of Article 47 of the Charter, which refers to access to an 'independent' tribunal as one of the requirements linked to the fundamental right to an effective remedy.[47]

It then concludes by stating:

> That requirement that courts be independent, which is inherent in the task of adjudication, forms part of the essence of the right to effective judicial protection and the fundamental right to a fair trial, which is of cardinal importance as a guarantee that all the rights which individuals derive from EU law will be protected and that the values common to the Member States set out in Article 2 TEU, in particular the value of the rule of law, will be safeguarded.[48]

Having established its power of judicial review over the rule of law in the Member States, the Court goes on to review the specific measures adopted by Poland and considers them contrary to EU law. This is a crucial example of the extent to which the level of interdependence between national legal orders and these legal orders and EU law requires EU law to play a role in safeguarding the rule of law in its Member States, as that is necessary to safeguard the rule of law in the EU legal order. What is important to stress is that EU law intervention is not legitimated by the aim of protecting the rule of law in its Member States but in EU law itself. The correction of such problems in the domestic sphere of the Member States is almost a side effect of the need to avoid the EU from being contaminated by them.

There is a second obvious example of how the degree of EU interdependence inevitably serves to transform national rule of law or democratic problems into EU problems. It is sufficient to consider the requirement that elections for the

[45] Ibid para 52.
[46] Ibid para 39.
[47] Ibid para. 57.
[48] Ibid para 58.

European Parliament must be free (Article 14 TEU) and comply with the EU commitment to democracy. The protection of free and fair elections and a democratically elected and functioning European Parliament requires certain minimum conditions to be guaranteed in all Member States. If in a certain Member State there is a serious threat to the freedom of expression or the freedom of the press, this might affect the elections for the European Parliament in that State, putting into question compliance with Articles 2 and 14 TEU by the European Parliament resulting from such elections. The same may be the case if elected Members of the European Parliament (MEPs) are not free in some Member States to exercise their functions because, for example, they are threatened, by (or with the complicity of) the authorities of the State, because of political positions they have taken while MEPs. If that is the case, then the freedom of MEPs is restricted, and it is the democratic functioning of the European Parliament and the European Union itself that is affected. This would again constitute a sufficient legal basis for an infringement action against the Member State where that situation occurred.[49]

This could be expanded to include the impact on the free movement of persons in cases where there is a systemic problem with fundamental rights in a Member State. That was the view argued in the Opinion in *Centro Europa 7*.[50] When the problem is of a systemic and grave nature then it is susceptible to amounting to a restriction on free movement itself.[51] In fact, the Court has already adopted a somewhat similar approach, focusing on systemic rule of law and fundamental rights challenges in the context of the area of freedom, security, and justice and the transfer of asylum seekers from one Member State to the other. The Court required a national court not to transfer an asylum seeker to another Member State if there is a serious risk of a fundamental rights violation of the asylum seeker in that latter state.[52] This risk is to be assessed in systemic terms. In other words, the problem needs to be of a systemic nature in order to trigger its relevance under EU law.

It is that same logic that is argued for here. When, in a Member State, there is a serious breach of the fundamental values of Article 2 TEU that has a systemic impact, this impact is not limited to the domestic sphere but necessarily affects the capacity of that Member State to comply with other obligations under EU law such as effective legal protection, free movement, or the free and democratic character of the European Parliament and the Union itself. When a breach of this kind is identified, it would therefore not only be possible but also desirable for the European

[49] Vike-Freiberga (n 3), 20.

[50] Case C-380/05 *Centro Europa 7 Srl* (n 9).

[51] As explained earlier, this is different from Case C-168/91 *Christos Konstantinidis* (n 8) and will not raise the same problems (also in terms of workload).

[52] Cases C-411/10 and C-493/10 *NS v Secretary of State for the Home Department* and *ME and Others v Refugee Applications Commissioner and Minister for Justice, Equality and Law Reform* [2011] ECR I-13905.

Commission to bring an infringement action under one or more of those legal bases against the Member State in question.

If anything, the way that systemic challenges to the rule of law and democracy in the Member States become rule of law and democracy challenges to the European Union itself renders visible how Paul Craig was right in anticipating the extent to which the borders between national and European public law would progressively fade away.

19

Brexit and the Challenges of a 'Post-Sovereign' Legal Landscape

Sionaidh Douglas Scott

Paul Craig's work was an important influence on me long before I worked in Oxford. I encountered Paul's work even before the magisterial Craig and de Búrca volume *EU Law* was published. My research into EU constitutional law was greatly enriched by reading Paul's scholarship on direct effect (eg an article with the snappy title of *Once Upon a Time in the West*) and supremacy, but also by his work on public law more generally, such as on the rule of law.[1] Wherever there was some new legal development within EU law, Paul had published an enlightening article. I also learned from his work, at an early stage in my career, that scholarship on EU law could go beyond competition or trade law (which tended to be the focus of nearly all UK interest in EU law until the early 1990s) and could ponder constitutional questions, and take it to yet a further level by relating it to matters of legal theory.

I. The Westphalian World, 'Post Sovereignty', and Legal Pluralism

In this contribution, I explore questions of law and governance as they occur at levels above and below, as well as at, state level. Such matters have, of course, been examined in Paul's work[2] as well as in that of the two other contributors to this section, Cheryl Saunders (Chapter 17) and Miguel Poiares Maduro and Benedita Menezes Queiroz (Chapter 18). Admittedly, mine is a limited exploration, confined to the UK–EU nexus, ignoring a larger, global canvas of transnational law, but I work within my own limits.

[1] Paul Craig, 'Once Upon a Time in the West: Direct Effect and the Federalization of EEC Law' (1992) 12 OJLS 453; Paul Craig, 'Formal and Substantive Conceptions of the Rule of Law: An Analytical Framework' [1997] PL 467.

[2] See eg Paul Craig, 'The United Kingdom, the European Union and Sovereignty' in Rick Rawlings, Peter Leyland, and Alison Young (eds), *Sovereignty and Law: Domestic, Regional and International Perspectives* (OUP 2013).

Sionaidh Douglas Scott, *Brexit and the Challenges of a 'Post-Sovereign' Legal Landscape* In: *The Foundations and Future of Public Law*. Edited by: Elizabeth Fisher, Jeff King, Alison L Young, Oxford University Press (2020).

DOI: 10.1093/oso/9780198845249.003.0019

I start by going back in time. For a relatively brief period—for about 300 years up to the mid-twentieth century—the 'Westphalian' order of sovereign states appeared to govern matters in western Europe. Prior to that, sovereignty was convoluted and fragmented, dispersed among, for example, feudalism, a shared Christianity under the ultimate Catholic ministration of the Pope, royal rulers of territories that looked different from today, and arcane entities such as the Holy Roman Empire. However, at least to some extent,[3] a new regime of sovereign states took over from this, and a new epoch ensued, from roughly the end of the Thirty Years War up until the end of the Second World War. To be sure, this was not an era of thoroughgoing peace and good relations, and disastrous wars occurred during this time. Consummate national sovereignty was not always a force for the good.

However, by the end of the Second World War, this post-Westphalian order was, in its turn, also under attack. In the year 2000, then German foreign minister, Joschka Fischer, suggested that, 'The core of the concept of Europe after 1945 was and still is a rejection of . . . hegemonic ambitions of individual states that had emerged following the Peace of Westphalia in 1648, a rejection which took the form of . . . the transfer of nation-state sovereign rights to supranational European institutions.'[4] The British diplomat, Robert Cooper, similarly saw 1945 as a crucial date. Cooper commented, 'What happened then was more far reaching than the events of 1789, 1815 or 1919 because it wrought a fundamental change in the European state system itself', continuing that, 'historically the best point of comparison is 1648', and that, '[i]n both cases, 1648 and 1945, the result was a recognition that there had been a radical failure and the system was changed', requiring a new vocabulary to describe it.[5]

In contrast to the earlier Westphalian world, a significant dimension of contemporary law has been its presence at a transnational level, above and beyond the state, whether promulgated by states, international bodies, or private parties. Philip Jessop, one of the first to pioneer the study of transnational law, defined it as 'all law which regulates actions or events that transcend national frontiers'.[6] From 1945, there was a shift to supra-, inter-, or transnational[7] institutions, such as the

[3] There were, of course, exceptions to this, most notably the British and Dutch East India companies, which were (nominally at least) private chartered companies, but controlled large areas of the globe. See eg Philip Stern, *The Company-State: Corporate Sovereignty and the Early Modern Foundations of the British Empire in India* (OUP 2011).

[4] In a now famous speech at Humboldt University Berlin, Joschka Fischer, 'From Confederacy to Federation—Thoughts on the Finality of European Integration' (Speech at Humboldt University Berlin, 12 May 2000); available at: http://ec.europa.eu/dorie/fileDownload.do?docId=192161&cardId=192161.

[5] Robert Cooper, *The Breaking of Nations* (Atlantic Books 2003) 2–3.

[6] Philip Jessup, *Transnational Law* (Yale UP 1956) 1.

[7] 'Supranational' is a little more specific than the term 'transnational'. In supranational law, nations explicitly submit specific of their sovereign rights to a set of common institutions; see eg Reuben Efron and Allan Nanes, 'The Common Market and Euratom Treaties: Supranationality and the Integration of Europe' (1957) ICLQ 670, 674.

United Nations, the European Union, and Council of Europe, and also a growth in the importance of international law. But this development also came in tandem with demands for self-government, or a downwards devolution, from sub-state nations, such as Scotland, Catalonia, or Quebec. Clearly, both (upward and downward) developments concern the nature and boundaries of political community and the location of ultimate authority. And for many legal scholars, the advent of a post-Westphalian order was taken to be a 'good thing'.

Either way, upward or downward, some writers, such as Neil MacCormick,[8] theorised such movements using the idea of 'post sovereignty'. This theory does not argue that the concept of sovereignty disappeared but instead that it had been transformed and was no longer the predominant mode of political organisation. MacCormick's view was that

> sovereignty and sovereign states, and the inexorable linkage of law with sovereignty and the state, have been but the passing phenomena of a few centuries, that their passing is by no means regrettable, and current developments in Europe exhibit the possibility of going beyond all that.[9]

This was echoed by William Twining, who suggested that the Westphalian state legal order should be viewed as the exception, existing for a mere two centuries or so in the North, an anomaly in a broader historical mass of legal experience of coexisting multiple legal orders.[10]

But 'post sovereignty' creates new problems of its own. Perhaps, within the European Union, the ultimate realisation of these problems has come with Brexit. The remainder of this chapter is concerned with this problem: how to resolve conflict between the European Union and its Member States in a post-sovereign world, when there (supposedly) is no ultimate sovereign.

A. EU law

EU law, the focus of much of Paul Craig's work, provides a very striking example of supranational law. On the one hand, EU law is a distinct legal order; it has self-referentiality (ie it sees no ultimate authority beyond itself). Indeed, the autonomy of EU law, and its specific, *sui generis* nature have been a running theme throughout its legal history. In *Costa v ENEL*,[11] the European Court of

[8] See eg Neil MacCormick, *Questioning Sovereignty* (OUP 1999) esp ch 8.

[9] Neil MacCormick, 'Beyond the Sovereign State' (1993) 56 MLR 1.

[10] William Twining, 'Normative and Legal Pluralism: A Global Perspective' (2010) 20 Duke J of Comp and Intl L 47.

[11] Case 6/64, *Costa v ENEL*. [1964] ECR 585. The French language version of this case describes the EEC treaty as '*une source autonome*'. The word is not used in the English version, which instead

Justice (CJEU) used the concept of autonomy to argue for the primacy of EU law over national law, stressing also the European Union as 'an independent source of law', which did not derive from national law. Moreover, in the external field, the CJEU has used autonomy to define the EU's relationship with international law.[12] Interestingly, the Court's insistence on autonomy has an air of a claim to sovereignty,[13] more traditionally associated with Westphalian concepts of the state (an interesting contrast to the CJEU's insistence in *Opinion 2/13* that the European Union is not a state). In *Miller*, in a comprehensive statement on the nature of EU law, the UK Supreme Court held that the European Communities Act 1972 'gives effect' to EU law, but that EU law itself is 'an independent and overriding source of domestic law'.[14]

Yet, in spite of these CJEU rulings and claims of autonomy, and in contrast, EU law also illustrates that legal systems are not necessarily impermeable, self-contained entities. The waning of the Westphalian era does not mean a centralised, dominant European Union at the apex of a new hierarchy. The CJEU might have stressed the autonomy of EU law, but it also introduced the doctrines of direct effect and supremacy of EU law, which, according to one academic, 'pierced the protective veil around national law'.[15] Direct effect means that EU law is part of national law, often without any national act of implementation, and the European Union relies on its Member States to enforce and apply most EU law—a point made to great effect by Paul Craig in *Once Upon a Time in the West*. Moreover, the bulk of EU law is litigated in national courts rather than the CJEU, a feature which is problematic for legal theories which identify 'norm applying' institutions (ie courts) as indicative of distinct legal systems.[16] This is because if Member State courts function as both national and EU courts, then which legal 'system' is at issue when a national court determines a point of EU law?[17] So, EU law blends and merges with national law in ways that defy easy categorisation.

In this way, EU law is neither a fully autonomous, separate legal system, nor yet fully integrated in its Member States' national law. It is not truly free-standing and could not exist without much supplementation by national law. But much of it has

reads: 'the law stemming from the treaty, an independent source of law, could not, because of its special and original nature, be overridden by domestic legal provisions' (*Costa*, 594).

[12] For example, Case C-402/05 P and C-415/05P *Kadi v. Council and Commission* [2008] ECR I-6351.

[13] See eg Opinion 2/13 *re ECHR Accession* EU:C:2014:2454

[14] *R (on the application of Miller and another) (Respondents) v Secretary of State for Exiting the EU* [2017] UKSC 5, [2018] AC 61.

[15] Direct effect was introduced in Case 26/62 *van Gend en Loos* [1963] ECR 1. The expression of piercing 'the protective veil' was used by Nico Krisch, *Beyond Constitutionalism: The Pluralist Structure of Postnational Law* (OUP 2010) 7.

[16] See eg Joseph Raz, *Practical Reason and Norms* (2nd edition, Princeton UP 1990) 129–31.

[17] See further on this Julie Dickson, 'Towards a Theory of European Union Legal Systems' in Julie Dickson and Pavlos Eleftheriadis (eds), *Philosophical Foundations of European Union Law* (OUP 2012) 25–53.

a force independent of national law and may supplant it. This suggests a complex European legal zone of overlapping jurisdictions, segmented authority, and possibly multiple loyalties.[18]

B. Legal pluralism

The European Union also provides a striking example of legal pluralism. Distinct legal orders in different Member States operate alongside EU law. Legal pluralism (by no means a new theory of law)[19] describes a state of affairs in which two or more legal orders occupy the same legal space, sometimes peacefully coexisting, but sometimes in direct competition with each other.

However, there are different ways of understanding what form legal pluralism takes within the European Union. Even if we accept a conception of EU law as an autonomous system of law running alongside national law, asserting priority over it, then how to theorise a resolution of the potential conflict between these two systems? EU law claims supremacy as a matter of EU law, and such supremacy has usually been observed. Yet the basis for acknowledging such supremacy is unclear. Is it because EU law tops the hierarchy of laws of its own accord (a view which posits an ultimate authority, but is unlikely to gain much acceptance outside EU institutions)?[20] Or, alternatively, is it because Member States have chosen, through their *constitutions*, to accord that supremacy, but the ultimate authority lies with their constitution, in which case there is a clash of two different constitutionalisms?[21]

This latter interpretation of the relationship between EU and national law, as an ultimate clash of constitutionalisms, fits with what Griffiths described as 'strong pluralism', where more than one law exists in one place and there is no clear overarching way of resolving conflicts (as opposed to 'weak pluralism', in which conflicts are resolved by a dominant law, as with the federal supremacy clause in the US Constitution).[22] In the absence of any EU state acknowledging the supremacy of EU law as justified *solely* by a matter of EU law, there is no conclusive way of resolving conflicts. Such an approach, of 'strong' or 'radical' pluralism, rejects claims for any dominant structure, or framework of ordering. Even if concepts such as

[18] For example, Bankowski and Scott characterised it as a legal space of interlocking normative spheres in which there are border points (eg supremacy of EC law, pre-emption) and bridging mechanisms (direct effect) rather than clear boundaries. Zenon Bankowski and Andrew Scott (eds), *The European Union and Its Order: The Legal Theory of European Integration* (Blackwell 2000).

[19] See eg John Griffiths, 'What is Legal Pluralism?' (1986) 24 J of Legal Pluralism, 2; see also Sally Engle Merry, 'Legal Pluralism' (1988) 22 Law & Society Review 869, for a full discussion of legal pluralism and its origins.

[20] And of course, there is no express mention of the supremacy of EU law in the treaties. It is a creation of the CJEU.

[21] See eg Pavlos Eleftheriadis, 'Begging the Constitutional Question' (1998) 36 JCMS 255.

[22] Per Griffiths (n 19) 5.

direct effect suggest a more interactive relationship, with an intermingling of state and EU law, this still does not resolve a collision whereby each institution of last resort (whether UK Parliament, national constitutional court, or CJEU) is likely to see itself as ultimate within that legal system.

So, a pluralistic landscape is not always a comfortable place. Pluralism can accentuate a lack of stability, certainty, and strong central authorities (which elements, of course, may not be perceived as desirable qualities by all). Hart warned of this instability when he characterised the possibility of multiple rules of recognition as a 'substandard, abnormal case, containing with it the threat that the legal system will dissolve'.[23] As a result, depictions of pluralism are not always flattering. William James wrote that 'the pluralistic empiricism which I profess offers but a sorry appearance. It is a turbid muddled gothic sort of affair, without a sweeping outline and with little pictorial nobility'.[24] My own contribution to this debate was to argue that this pluralistic legal landscape could be captured by the image of the Carina Nebula,[25] which is a vast complex of dust, stars, gas, forces, and energy situated 7,500 light years from Earth.

Much EU constitutional law scholarship in the early twenty-first century, before Brexit took over as an obsession (for those in the United Kingdom at least), seemed to concern a search for the 'right sort of pluralism' to solve some of the EU's problems of sovereignty and ultimate authority, a quest for a Holy Grail of structure that might somehow organise the EU's rather untidy legal arrangements and stabilise them by metaprinciples, or some sort of 'order of orders'.[26] Delmas-Marty proposed devices already familiar in European law: the margin of appreciation, subsidiarity, proportionality, as 'fuzzy' guiding principles, rather than precise codes. Her image of ordered pluralism was that of a land of 'organized clouds',[27] emphasising a need for sustainability and equilibrium rather than hegemonic processes. The notion of 'organized clouds' is intriguing, but ultimately perhaps vague and unsatisfying due to its extremely nebulous and ephemeral nature.

Other theorists espoused something more settled, looking to 'constitutionalism'[28] as an organisational schema to deal with conflicts between EU law and national law. Yet there is no EU *Grundnorm* of EU *Kompetenz-Kompetenz*. Nor is

[23] HLA Hart, *The Concept of Law*. (2nd edn, OUP 1994) 123.

[24] William James, *A Pluralistic Universe* (Longmans, Green, & Co. 1909).

[25] See eg Sionaidh Douglas-Scott, *Law After Modernity* (Hart 2013) for an image of the Carina Nebula.

[26] Per Neil Walker, 'Beyond Boundary Disputes and Basic Grids: Mapping the Global Disorder of Normative Orders' (2008) 6 Intl J of Constitutional L, 373–96.

[27] Mireille Delmas-Marty, *Ordering Pluralism* (Hart 2009) 12.

[28] See eg Mattias Kumm, 'The Jurisprudence of Constitutional Conflict: Constitutional Supremacy in Europe before and after the Constitutional Treaty' (2005) ELJ 262; Miguel Poiares Maduro, 'Contrapunctual Law: Europe's Constitutional Pluralism in Action' in Neil Walker (ed), *Sovereignty in Transition* (Hart 2003).

there a clear European *pouvoir constituent* to have the final say. In the European Union, constitutionalism has so far failed, resulting in the strong 'No' of the French and Dutch people in their national referendums on the draft European Constitution in 2005. Indeed, it might even be the *lack* of a clear hierarchy that appears to keep the system in motion. But is this a balanced, workable situation or an insecure instability? The point, however, to note is that this fragile equilibrium hardly evokes an overbearing, 'Hobbesian' sovereign as a replacement for national sovereignty. And for those unenamoured with the idea of restoring a seventeenth-century Leviathan, this is probably a good thing.

Nonetheless, both 'softer' and radical pluralism appear unsatisfactory.[29] They provide two ways of interpreting the European Union. Can it be both? Or neither? Soft pluralism rationalises an uncomfortable, unstable equilibrium. Radical pluralism creates rule of law issues, because conflicts between legal orders may dictate different legal rights and obligations within the same legal space, giving rise to conflicted loyalties.[30] Some national officials may not see their allegations as lying with national law. On the other hand, where national supremacy is preferred, one might argue the end point of such a conflict is Brexit.

II. Brexit: The Challenge to 'Post Sovereignty'

And so, we come to Brexit. For, although it might have seemed that the idea of the unitary state was on the retreat, Brexit challenges this vision of post-sovereignty. The European Union prompts animosity from many in the United Kingdom. To be sure, a lot of this is misplaced. As Paul Craig reminds us 'the UK has played a major role in shaping the EU as we know it today. Consider in this respect the fashioning of the single market project, which the UK pressed for so stridently in the 1980s; the many Area of Freedom Security and Justice initiatives that the UK supported; and the EU's eastward expansion that was backed by the UK under the banner of widening not deepening. The myth that the UK has been put upon as a member of the EU is just that, a myth.'[31]

However, the UK's economic prosperity as an EU member notwithstanding, further probing reveals Eurosceptic unease over the sovereignty question, and with the EU's *sui generis* approach, or its *Sonderweg*.[32] Brexiteers regret that a recently developed 'foreign' law such as EU law could override such an ancient,

29 However, for a different view, see Nico Krisch, 'Who's Afraid of Radical Pluralism? Legal Order and Political Stability in the Postnational Space' (2011) 24 Ratio Juris, 386–412.

30 For an interesting discussion of these issues see NW Barber, 'Legal Pluralism and the European Union' (2006) ELJ 306.

31 Paul Craig, 'Brexit: A Drama in Six Acts', 4 (2016) 41 European L Rev, 447.

32 Per JHH Weiler, 'Federalism without Constitutionalism: Europe's *Sonderweg*' in Kalypso Nicolaidis and Robert Howse (eds), *The Federal Vision* (OUP 2001).

organic system as the British Constitution.[33] The European Union cannot match such a constitutional pedigree, nor should it, in the view of many. In fact, even to mention that the European Union might have a 'Constitutional' identity is to provoke ire from some quarters. Yet a multilevel, fragmented authority may also create feelings of insecurity, and a yearning for old, simpler solutions. This partially explains, but does not necessarily justify, some of the animosity eurosceptics feel. Back in 2001, at a symposium at King's College London, entitled *Can Europe have a Constitution?*,[34] Miguel Poiares Maduro presented a paper with the title, 'Europe and the Constitution: what if this is as Good as it Gets?'[35] Many of us were urging for an EU Constitution, but Maduro's title was perhaps prescient, and at least for the United Kingdom and its relations with the European Union, that indeed was as good as it got.

Perhaps the most common constitutional idea to feature in Brexit debates has been sovereignty, often expressed as 'taking back control'.[36] So, for example, the Foreword to the Government 2017 White Paper on the 'Great Repeal Bill' stated: 'At the heart of that historic decision was sovereignty. A strong, independent country needs control of its own laws. That, more than anything else, was what drove the referendum result: a desire to take back control.'[37] This expressed an apparent yearning for a UK parliamentary sovereignty that could not be reconciled with continuing EU membership, along with a desire for a more clearly national constitutional architecture, one that 'repatriates' EU law, only retaining EU law as a matter of necessity, to avoid gaps, until something more national may take its place, and even then domesticating it, changing its name to 'retained EU law' in the EU (Withdrawal) Act 2018.

However, this nationalistic notion of sovereignty is confused and overly simplistic, as well as anachronistic. It fails to capture the way that pooling sovereignty in one area, for example by EU membership, may actually empower a state, which is one important reason why supranational approaches have been embraced. It is hard to put the 'post-sovereign' genie back in the bottle.

[33] For example, Charles Moore, 'Our Top Judges Have Become Too Powerful—We Need to Rein Them In' (23 October 2015, *Telegraph*); available at: https://www.telegraph.co.uk/news/politics/11951936/Our-top-judges-have-become-too-powerful-we-need-to-rein-them-in.html.

[34] An edition of the King's College Law Journal for 2001 was given over to this. Paul Craig also delivered a paper at this conference, as did Jürgen Habermas. I presented a paper arguing for an EU Constitution—Sionaidh Douglas-Scott 'Constituting Europe: In Defence of Public Reason' (2001) 12 King's LJ 75.

[35] Miguel Poiares Maduro, 'Europe and the Constitution: What if This is As Good as it Gets?' in JHH Weiler and Marlene Wind (eds), *European Constitutionalism Beyond The State* (CUP 2003).

[36] Of course, this might be a fig leaf, or displacement, masking perhaps a fear of immigration. Yet the sovereignty claim appears primary, because it asserts a national jurisdiction, including over immigration, that would not otherwise exist.

[37] department for Exiting the European Union, *Legislating for the United Kingdom's Withdrawal from the European Union* (Cm 9446, 2017) 7.

A. Three different conceptions of sovereignty

Although sovereignty has been frequently discussed in the Brexit context, there has been little clarity over what it actually means.[38] Indeed, no single standard exists for applying sovereignty,[39] and Harold Laski even suggested that '[i]t would be of lasting benefit if the whole concept of sovereignty were surrendered' on the grounds that 'it is at least possible that it has deleterious moral consequences',[40] and one is certainly tempted to agree with this statement as far as Brexit is concerned.

Confusion over sovereignty is exemplified by the UK Government Brexit White Paper which states: 'The sovereignty of Parliament is a fundamental principle of the UK constitution. Whilst Parliament has remained sovereign throughout our membership of the EU, it has not always felt like that.'[41] This admission, that Parliament has been sovereign during the UK's EU membership, is at odds with the Government's Foreword to the 'Great Repeal Bill' White Paper, cited above, where the Government argued regaining sovereignty was the motivation for Brexit. These two government statements illustrate the muddled and convoluted thinking at the heart of Brexit. Not only do they reveal confusion, but the reference to something as nebulous as feelings divulges the lack of solid ground on which the sovereignty claim rests.

Moreover, a brief examination reveals not one but at least three notions of sovereignty relevant to Brexit, which are too often confused. To start with there is *external sovereignty* (also often called 'national' sovereignty) whereby a state is acknowledged as independent, and hence sovereign, by the international community. The UK's external sovereignty was unaffected by its EU membership, and would be unchanged by EU withdrawal (although the UK's EU membership meant that the United Kingdom could comply with international obligations through its EU membership, which in fact often entailed more democratic input into treaty negotiations than from the United Kingdom acting alone).The remaining two varieties of sovereignty are *internal* in nature, relating to a state's domestic affairs. There is *parliamentary sovereignty*, which has a particular resonance in the United Kingdom where the Westminster Parliament has been characterised as a body with unlimited legislative power.[42] However, parliamentary sovereignty sometimes may appear inconsistent with *popular sovereignty* as

[38] A great deal has been written about sovereignty, most of which cannot be explored in this short chapter. Jean Bodin, writing in the sixteenth century, is often described as the 'father' of modern conceptions of sovereignty. But there has been a vast amount of scholarship since. For a useful, fairly recent collection see, Richard Rawlings, Peter Leyland, and Alison Young (eds), *Sovereignty and Law: Domestic, Regional and International Perspectives* (OUP 2013).

[39] Per Dieter Grimm, *Sovereignty: The Origin and Future of a Political and Legal Concept* (Columbia UP 2015) 101.

[40] Harold Laski, *A Grammar of Politics* (OUP 1941).

[41] HM Government, *The United Kingdom's Exit from and New Partnership with the European Union* (Cm 9417, 2017) ch 2 'Taking control of our own laws', 13.

[42] AV Dicey, *Introduction to the Study of the Law of the Constitution* (10th edn, Macmillan 1959).

exercised through a referendum. Popular sovereignty also has other implications, for example in Scotland, where an indigenous Scottish tradition claims that sovereignty resides in the Scottish people, in spite of alternative claims of Diceyan parliamentary sovereignty.

Confusion over these types of sovereignty has rendered Brexit debates incoherent just when clarity is crucial. I do not argue that there exists one correct, essential interpretation of sovereignty. My argument instead is that the weight of justification for Brexit cannot be borne by these incoherent and confused assertions of sovereignty. What this muddled assertion of retaking sovereignty and control ultimately appears to boil down to is an (unsubstantiated) claim for a unified English/Westminster/governmental sovereignty to the exclusion of other parties. These excluded parties include international organisations, courts, constituent nations and territories of the United Kingdom (eg Scotland, Gibraltar) and relevant persons (ie EU citizens denied a vote in the EU referendum, and UK nationals in the European Union). However, the exclusive, unified sovereignty claim is incoherent and not borne out by history, although history is often wrongly prayed in its aid. This claim is incoherent, because it conflates different conceptions of sovereignty, namely: Britain's external sovereignty (which was never threatened by EU membership), parliamentary sovereignty (a complex and contested notion, which the British government itself misrepresents and mangles), and popular sovereignty (which is insufficiently developed in UK constitutional law to ground an argument that it has replaced parliamentary sovereignty as a mandate for action).

Indeed, rather than 'taking back control', perhaps Brexit imperils national sovereignty. This is because, as well as threatening Britain's economic security (which itself impacts on Britain's sovereignty) it risks shattering the UK's balance and stability by threatening the peace settlement in Northern Ireland and possibly inciting another independence referendum in Scotland. In these circumstances, Brexit heralds potentially profound uncertainty and change, during which many foundations of the UK constitutional settlement will be tested.

B. Britain as 'unsettled state'

Indeed, the British Constitution is undergoing a 'profound moment of Constitutional fluidity'.[43] The standard account of the British Constitution characterises it as resting on the sovereignty of Parliament, and unwritten, flexible, uncodified in nature, with political conventions and ministerial accountability

[43] Evidence of Adam Tomkins, cited in House of Commons European Scrutiny Committee, *The EU Bill and Parliamentary Sovereignty* (HC 633-I, 2010–11) para 24.

often taking the place of hard law. In these circumstances, the British Constitution might be depicted as a thing of 'bits and pieces',[44] whose uncodified and sometimes implicit nature somehow gave rise to a holistic constitutional identity. However, this organic constitution has undergone a gradual reform process in recent decades. This has been provoked by developments affecting sovereignty and lines of authority, including EU membership; the 1998 Human Rights Act; devolution in Scotland, Wales, and Northern Ireland; removal of most hereditary peers in the House of Lords; and perhaps most dramatically, increasing use of referendums as instruments of constitutional change. All this has brought about a Constitution (and Britain) less unitary and more heterogeneous, more willing to recognise centres of power elsewhere, without however bringing any coherence or consolidation of constitutional form. Britain's EU membership has played a crucial role in this constitutional transformation. This constitutional fluidity has gone hand in hand with the development of multidimensionality and pluralism in law, undermining law's connection with the state.

Over the past twenty years of change there has been an increasing realisation that ad hoc Constitution making, in the traditional way of UK's evolutionary process, is unsatisfactory. As Sidney Low wrote over a century ago, 'we live under a system of tacit understandings. The understandings themselves are not always understood'.[45]

UK law is untidy. The European Union might furnish an example of pluralism, but there is also legal pluralism within the United Kingdom, and talk of a 'national' sovereignty rather begs the question of which nation is at issue—England, Scotland, Wales, or Northern Ireland? Devolution in the United Kingdom has not stabilised the structure of the British Constitution. Instead, UK devolution has had a symbiotic relationship with both the European Union and Brexit, adding to this constitutional instability. The devolved nations benefited from Britain's EU membership and (although not always acknowledged, and somewhat ironically) the European Union provided a framework for alleviating intra-UK sovereignty issues in practice, insulating devolved nations from a unitary UK-wide approach—by, for example, distributing EU funds on a basis more beneficial to some parts of the United Kingdom than others (eg agriculture). This approach is unlikely to continue post-Brexit, where a unified UK approach seems likely to predominate, however unfavourable to devolved interests. EU membership also facilitated conciliation between the United Kingdom and Ireland.

In the EU referendum, the United Kingdom as a whole voted to leave. However, 62 per cent of Scotland's voting electorate, and 56 per cent voting in Northern

[44] The use of this phrase above is deeply ironic, given Deirdre Curtin's highly critical use of it in the EU context in her famous article, 'The Constitutional System of the Union: A Europe of Bits and Pieces' (1993) 30 CML Rev, 17.

[45] Sidney Low, *The Governance of England* (TF Unwin 1904) 12.

Ireland, voted to remain. Yet the devolved nations played no formal role in Article 50 proceedings and had no means of ensuring their constitutional interests were protected. Brexit, whatever its final form, risks undermining the brittle devolution settlement and forcing it to change.[46] Indeed, the Scottish Parliament refused to grant its consent to section 12 European Union (Withdrawal) Act 2018, which was nonetheless adopted in Westminster, in spite of this. In addition, in March 2018, the Scottish Parliament adopted the *UK Withdrawal from the European Union (Legal Continuity) (Scotland) Act 2018* by ninety-five votes to thirty-two (which has not come into force, as the UK Supreme Court found its section 17 to be outside the Scottish Parliament's competence). [47]

The Union of Scotland and England was the founding act of the United Kingdom in 1707. Surprisingly, there has been little debate about what the 'Union' or 'Britain' is, or should be, even in the context of the first Scottish independence referendum. Indeed, an important question is whether it is correct to view the United Kingdom as a 'union state' rather than unitary in nature.[48] The term 'unitary state' suggests a constitutional order with a single, unrivalled, legal competence, from which may be derived a fundamental 'rule of recognition' which places a central agency (the Queen in Parliament) in a position of unequivocal authority. But many argue Britain now lacks an unequivocal, unitary sovereignty partly on account of devolution. For example, since 1998, Scotland has developed some progressive constitutional forms[49] as well as more pro-European inclinations that challenge the unitary constitutional approaches of London. The Scottish Parliament is to all intents and purposes permanent.[50] This raises questions about the relationship of

[46] As Cheryl Saunders argues, 'effective devolution to Scotland, Wales and Northern Ireland is compatible with parliamentary sovereignty only as long as constitutional convention restrains the UK government and Parliament from exceeding the bounds that have been agreed. If a greater measure of devolution is required, to respond to pressures for Scottish independence, enforceable legal constraints may be sought.' Cheryl Saunders, 'Parliamentary Sovereignty and Written Constitutions in Comparative Perspective' in Asanga Welikala (ed), *The Sri Lankan Republic at 40: Reflections on Constitutional History, Theory and Practice* (Centre for Policy Alternatives 2012).

[47] The legal competence of this Scottish legislation was challenged by the UK Government before the UK Supreme Court in *The UK Withdrawal from the European Union (Legal Continuity) (Scotland) Bill—A Reference by the Attorney General and the Advocate General for Scotland*, [2018] UKSC 64, [2019] 2 WLR 1. In a long and complex judgment, the Court found only s 17 of the Bill outside the Scottish Parliament's competence, due to enactments in the European Union (Withdrawal) Act 2018 (subsequent to the adoption of the Scottish Continuity legislation), which prohibited its own modification. However, this effectively killed off the Bill. It is hard not to conclude that the Continuity Bill was largely competent when adopted by the Scottish Parliament in March 2018.

[48] The term 'union state' was forged by Rokkan and Urwin to connote a polity distinct both from the unitary and the federal state. Stein Rokkan and Derek Urwin, *Economy, Territory, Identity: Politics of West European Territories* (Sage Publications 1983); see also Neil Walker, 'Beyond the Unitary Conception of the United Kingdom Constitution' [2000] PL 384. Also see further, <https://www.parliament.uk/business/committees/committees-a-z/lords-select/constitution-committee/inquiries/parliament-2015/the-union-and-devolution/publications/> accessed 1 July 2019.

[49] Such as proportional representation for elections to the Holyrood Parliament. The Scottish Parliament is also bounded—its legislation must comply with human rights and EU law.

[50] Section 1 Scotland Act 2016 states: 'The Scottish Parliament and the Scottish Government are a permanent part of the United Kingdom's constitutional arrangements.'

Britain's component parts to the centre, to each other, and to the European Union, and also implies a competing constitutional narrative more compatible with the rise of 'post-sovereignty' arguments referenced earlier.

It is unlikely that the 1688 constitutional settlement, which gave rise to parliamentary supremacy, can resolve the problems unleashed by Brexit, not least because devolved nations have already undergone some constitutional transformation, more accepting of qualified sovereignty than the rest of the United Kingdom. Britain is not a federal state. However, one might ponder whether a federal plan for a post-Brexit Britain could provide some solution to some of the conundrums outlined above? In 2016, the Constitution Reform Group argued for radical constitutional change to create a federal United Kingdom,[51] arguing that the existing UK union should be replaced with fully devolved government in each part of the United Kingdom, each with complete sovereignty over its own affairs.[52] There also exist alternatives. For example, Federacies,[53] such as the Åland Islands or Greenland, are instructive. Federacies share many features with traditional 'federal' systems, in that the sub-state unit and a larger state are linked in a federal relationship in which the sub-state unit has constitutionally guaranteed autonomy.

Yet, would supporters of Scottish independence, or a united Ireland, agree with an arrangement that would anchor them into the United Kingdom, even if it provided authoritative and legally enforceable constitutional procedures for protecting different national communities within the state? Moreover, those satisfied with the prospect of Brexit are unlikely to accept a written constitution or federal option, given that a desire for strong parliamentary sovereignty likely motivated their Euroscepticism in the first place. Such approaches, and distinct political identities, may militate against a comprehensive approach which would address the capacity of the British Constitution to deal with issues of disputed authority and challenges of Brexit.

And yet, the perils of persisting with a Diceyan conception of a unitary United Kingdom with ultimate Westminster parliamentary sovereignty, in the face of competing demands, may simply be too great. James Bryce, the nineteenth-century rival of Dicey, wrote of *centripetal* and *centrifugal* forces that work on Constitutions,[54] and the United Kingdom may exhibit its own fraught equilibrium. Centrifugal currents carry a risk of dissolution, whereby small sections of

[51] Martin Kettle, 'Brexit vote paves way for federal union to save UK, says all-party group' (10 July 2016, *Guardian*); available at: https://www.theguardian.com/politics/2016/jul/10/brexit-vote-paves-way-for-federal-union-says-all-party-group.

[52] The Group's proposals were drafted into an Act of Union bill promoted as a basis for discussion; available at: https://www.constitutionreformgroup.co.uk/publications-2/.

[53] See eg Eve Hepburn, 'Recrafting Sovereignty: Lessons from Small Island Autonomies?' in Alain Gagnon and Michael Keating (eds), *Political Autonomy and Divided Societies* (Palgrave Macmillan 2012).

[54] James Bryce, 'The Action of Centripetal and Centrifugal Forces on Political Constitutions' in James Bryce (ed), *Studies in History and Jurisprudence: Volume 1* (Clarendon Press 1901).

the population can determine futures. Brexit may operate centrifugally. It has been interpreted as requiring the United Kingdom to leave the European Union on the back of an 'advisory' referendum in which only 37 per cent of eligible UK voters voted to leave. Within the existing Westminster parliamentary framework, the (minority) government has appropriated a great deal of executive power to control the Brexit process. Indeed, it has often seemed as if a minority (the European Research Group) within an already minority government steered this process. Those excluded may seek a more complete detachment by way of independence. The interesting thing is that these centrifugal forces can be unleashed by an oppressive focus on the centripetal, by a demand for a post-Brexit national sovereignty that cannot function as its adherents might wish, or by a focus on a unitary constitutional identity at odds with Britain's constitutional developments over the past forty years.

III. Conclusion

What this brief survey of both EU law, and the UK's Brexit sojourn, reveal is something unresolved. Both EU and UK legal and constitutional orders are unstable, and to use Neil Walker's characterisation, 'unsettled'.[55]

EU law gives rise to competing hierarchies of state and national law but appears to leave open how there can be resolution in case of conflict. It is perceived by some as threatening national sovereignty and gives rise to rule-of-law problems of competing laws and legal loyalties. However, although it may seem possible to leave issues of finality unsettled, rather than opening an unpleasant can of worms (or sovereignty), these issues nevertheless bubble up, especially if fundamental constitutional laws are at stake. If national law is to be disapplied because of the supremacy of EU law, there had better be a good reason for asserting EU law's superior place in that hierarchy. But that good reason is sometimes wanting, or inexplicable.

On the other hand, what is the good reason for (re-) asserting national sovereignty when the benefits of cooperation in the single market, customs union, security cooperation and so on may be lost? Paul Craig's reminder of the myth of the UK's 'raw deal' from the European Union is salient, especially given that the national sovereignty asserted is obscure, contested, and multi-valenced. A retreat into (an unrealisable) national sovereignty solves nothing. What sense can be made of 'taking back control' when there are not, and cannot be, any completely sovereign states in today's world?

Neither a retreat into a nostalgic vision of sovereignty nor the EU's 'new legal order' can provide the conclusive sovereignty and constitutional arrangements

[55] Neil Walker, 'Our Constitutional Unsettlement' [2014] PL 529.

that might have existed in the Westphalian era. Neither system can successfully make its case, sovereignty or post-sovereignty, autonomy or cooperation, because both systems are 'unsettled'. Neither law, constitutional theory, nor legal theory has settled the issue of sovereignty. But the question is, should it attempt to do so? Law is a messy affair. EU law overlaps and intermingles with national law. The United Kingdom will lack constitutional stability, whether it remains in the European Union or not.

Both systems present a sense of being normatively adrift and lacking a coherent Constitutional vision. This does not mean we should never seek constitutional reform, nor a better constitutional architecture. But it does mean we should be clear-headed about the impossibility of asserting ultimate sovereignty and authority in a 'post-sovereign' world.

Paul Craig captured the dramatic tensions of our legal age when he described Brexit as a drama that could be broken down into six Acts, each foreshadowed by some select Shakespearian quotations that are pertinent to the discourse, adding that he hoped 'that it thereby enriches the analysis'.[56] It does indeed enrich the analysis and, ironically perhaps, the early modern language of Shakespearean theatre, both comedy and tragedy, may indeed be the best means we have of capturing the dramas of sovereignty in a post-sovereign era.

[56] Paul Craig, 'Brexit: A Drama in Six Acts' (n 31).

PART VII

CONCLUSION

20. Six Dimensions of Public Law: Pressure-Testing the UK and EU Systems
Paul Craig

20

Six Dimensions of Public Law

Pressure-Testing the UK and EU Systems

*Paul Craig**

This chapter draws on the six dimensions of public law covered in the book: theory, institutions and accountability, constitutions and rights, process and procedure, legislation, and case law. While there are perforce different ways to cut the public law cake, the six-part divide captures the principal dimensions of public law, irrespective of the particular polity in question. This chapter seeks to link these features, in order that the points can be connected. This in turn requires some foundational event that can be viewed through the preceding prism. The chosen event is Brexit, which, as my namesake, albeit unrelated, Robert Craig, states, is the constitutional gift that keeps on giving.[1]

This chapter is not, however, concerned with the contending arguments for leaving or remaining in the European Union. The focus is on the way in which Brexit has 'pressure-tested' the public law regime in the United Kingdom and the European Union. We are familiar with pressure-testing in a mechanical sense. We apply it to see how the system works when the strain on the system is ramped up, thereby determining strengths and weaknesses. The metaphor is apt in relation to Brexit, which has, in no small measure, pressure-tested the public law regime in the United Kingdom and the European Union. For the sake of clarity, it should be noted that what follows is based on the situation that prevailed in April 2019.

It has, moreover, done so in multiple ways that are thrown into sharp relief by the different dimensions of public law adumbrated above. It is axiomatic that these are not hermetically sealed, such that the same 'facts' may have implications for more than one facet of public law. All of which makes the inquiry more, not less, interesting. In keeping with the structure of this book, the different dimensions of public law will be considered in relation to both the United Kingdom and the European Union.

* I am very grateful to Liz Fisher, Jeff King, and Alison Young for organising the conference that gave rise to this book, and to all those who gave papers and attended the event. It was memorable on a personal level, and stimulating intellectually.

[1] Robert Craig, 'Could the Government Advise the Queen to Refuse Royal Assent to a Backbench Bill?', UK Const L Blog (22 January 2019).

Paul Craig, *Six Dimensions of Public Law* In: *The Foundations and Future of Public Law*. Edited by: Elizabeth Fisher, Jeff King, Alison L Young, Oxford University Press (2020). © Oxford University Press.
DOI: 10.1093/oso/9780198845249.003.0020

It might be argued that the 'test' for the UK and EU public law regimes is 'unfair', given the extraordinary nature of Brexit. It might, in this vein, be contended that any weaknesses revealed by the 'pressure-testing' will not have salience in more normal times. There is some truth in this, but less than might initially be thought.[2] This is in part because it is integral to the very idea of testing the strengths and weaknesses of a public law regime that the circumstances that precipitate the test will be unusual to some degree. It is in part because the fact that the circumstances are unusual does not mean that the lessons drawn therefrom are confined to such singular events. To the contrary, the flaws thus revealed may, as will be seen, have relevance in more normal circumstances.

I. Theory

A. UK: parliamentary and popular sovereignty

Brexit casts into sharp relief a number of theoretical issues, most notably the relationship, balance, or tension—choose the noun that you feel is most apposite—between parliamentary and popular sovereignty. If charitable donations were given every time that a politician or commentator opined that it would be undemocratic, or contrary to the expressed will of the people, to resile from the result of the referendum held on 23 June 2016, or even contemplate a second referendum, then charitable coffers would be considerably fuller than they are now. Asseveration is not, however, argumentation, and it is therefore important to press further to determine what lies beneath the veneer of this argument.[3] There is much to address in this chapter, so we should cut rapidly to the chase.

It might be argued, by way of initial response to the invocation of popular sovereignty that underpins fidelity to the result of the Brexit referendum, that the UK tradition is one of parliamentary sovereignty, and thus that the referendum result cannot formally bind the present or future parliaments. This is true in terms of constitutional tradition, but it is nonetheless doubly unsatisfying: in political terms, it will be regarded by pro-Brexiteers simply as a device whereby they can be 'robbed' of their victory; in normative terms, it obviates the need for more detailed inquiry concerning the status afforded to the initial popular vote. This is all the more salient given the concern with fundamentals that informs this book.

The more interesting line of inquiry is assuredly the contrast between the continuing nature of parliamentary sovereignty and the static conception of

[2] See also Mark Freedland (Chapter 16, this volume).
[3] See Albert Weale, *The Will of the People: A Modern Myth* (Polity Press 2018).

popular sovereignty that underpins this discourse. We regard it as constitutionally axiomatic that every parliament partakes of the same sovereignty, this being the normative foundation for the one limit to such sovereignty, this being that a parliament cannot bind its successors.[4] The contrast with the conception of popular sovereignty that buttressed Brexit is stark, since the discourse is markedly static, epitomised in the oft-repeated aphorism that the people have spoken, such that it would be democratic heresy to ignore this, or to put the same issue to them again.

The elision of these two scenarios, viz ignoring the will of the people, and putting the issue to them again, has been manifest in Brexit political speak. It makes perfect sense in terms of realpolitik, attesting to the cardinal lesson of political life, that when you have the answer you seek, you do not ask the same question again. We are, however, in an academic, not a political forum, and it is therefore fitting to press further and disaggregate these two scenarios that are normatively different.

Few, if any, would deny force to the result of the referendum. The people spoke and voted to leave. To ignore that result per se would be to denude the idea of popular sovereignty of all meaning, which would be unwarranted, notwithstanding our constitutional tradition of parliamentary sovereignty. There is, moreover, the fact that Parliament decided to put the question to the people in the EU Referendum Act 2015, which, although not binding as to result, was premised on a cross-party understanding evident in second reading speeches that the result would be respected.[5] So far so good, let us posit a general consensus about the first part of the proposition, to the effect that it would be undemocratic simply to resile from the result of the referendum.

This does not, however, sustain the second part of the inquiry, to the effect that a second referendum would itself be democratically misplaced or misguided. There is an inverse relationship between the force with which this is expressed and the strength of the rationale needed to support it. The rationale might be pragmatic or normative or some admixture of the two.

The pragmatic rationale might be that it would have been too difficult to frame the questions to be asked in a second referendum, that there was insufficient time to organise it, or that externalities in terms of the timing of elections to the European Parliament (EP) rendered it implausible. These considerations should not be belittled. They are important, but they are not insurmountable, and can be addressed.[6]

The normative rationale for the assertion that a second referendum would be undemocratic is predicated on the assumption that when the people have

[4] See, e.g, HWR Wade, 'The Basis of Legal Sovereignty' (1955) 13 CLJ 172.

[5] I am grateful to Jeff King for this point.

[6] Jess Sargeant, Alan Renwick, and Meg Russell, *The Mechanics of a Further Referendum on Brexit* (UCL Constitution Unit 2018).

spoken, it would be democratically dangerous and unwarranted to ask them the question again. This is the static dimension to popular sovereignty adverted to earlier. It is, however, far from self-evidently correct. People may change their minds for endogenous reasons, connoting in this respect a shift in moral values over time, exemplified by the likely different result, or balance of votes, in a referendum concerning LGBT rights twenty years ago and now. People may also change their minds for exogenous reasons, because circumstances have changed, or because they have a greater understanding of the consequences of their actions. The real issue is whether there are distinguishing features two years on from the first referendum which provide the requisite normative justification for the second referendum. The positive answer to this inquiry is grounded on two related arguments.

There is, on the one hand, the lack of consensus as to what type of Brexit the people really voted for, as attested to by the fact that this was the centre of vigorous political contestation in the two years following the initial vote. There is, on the other hand, the fact that two years on we knew a lot more about what the rival leave options might be, hard Brexit versus different forms of soft Brexit, and whether these would be preferable to staying in the European Union. People try to make decisions with the best possible information available, and commonly revise those decisions when more detailed data are obtainable. The normative foundation for a second referendum is an admixture of the preceding arguments.

There is, to address a likely counter-argument, nothing remotely elitist in this reasoning. It reflects how people make important decisions in their everyday life. To put the same point in a different way, try asking workers in Sunderland who voted to leave the European Union whether they might have liked a second vote when they became cognisant of Toyota's decision to invest elsewhere; try asking the same question of workers in Airbus and BMW who learned the lessons of diminished inward investment that will attend Brexit.[7]

The attention properly accorded to constitutional fundamentals does not mean that disagreement will magically disappear. This is manifestly not so since such disagreement is reflective of contestation as to the content of the relevant foundational proposition and the plurality of values that might inform it. The benefits of such discourse are, nonetheless, very real. The dialogue can clarify the nature of the differences between respective positions, and it can also reveal that certain precepts, such as a static conception of popular sovereignty, are not sustainable.

[7] Kana Inagaki, Sylvia Pfeifer, and Michael Pooler, 'Honda Says Up to 7,000 Jobs at Risk from Closure of UK' Plant (*Financial Times*, 19 Feburary 2019); available at: https://www.ft.com/content/77220374-3416-11e9-bd3a-8b2a211d90d5, accessed 2 July 2019.

B. EU: intergovernmentalism and supranationalism

Brexit has numerous implications for the theoretical dimensions of the European Union. The present focus will be on what Brexit tells us about a prominent aspect of this theoretical discourse, which is the tension between intergovernmentalism and supranationalism as explanations concerning the evolution of the European Union and its policy. This is not the place for detailed explication of these concepts.[8]

Suffice it to say for the present that liberal intergovernmentalism is rooted in a branch of international relations theory, which is premised on assumptions derived from economics, public choice, and the logic of collective action.[9] The central message is that states are the driving forces behind integration, that supranational actors are there largely at their behest, and that such actors have little independent impact on the pace of integration. The core of liberal intergovernmentalism is composed of three elements: 'the assumption of rational state behaviour, a liberal theory of national preference formation, and an intergovernmentalist analysis of interstate negotiation'.[10] The demand for integration is a function of domestic preference formation, which identifies the benefits of policy coordination at the European level. The supply of integration is a function of interstate bargaining and strategic interaction.

The liberal intergovernmentalist reading of EU integration was challenged by a more supranationalist account, 'wherein authority and policy-making were shared across multiple levels of government, subnational, national, and supranational'.[11] On this view, national governments are major players in this process, but they do not have a monopoly of control. Thus, while Member States may play the decisive role in the Treaty-making process, they do not exert a monopoly of influence. In relation to more day-to-day matters, the control exercised by the states collectively is less than that postulated by state-centric theorists since there is a multiplicity of factors that affect the ability of the 'Member State principals' to control the 'supranational agents', in particular the Commission and the Court of Justice of the European Union (CJEU). There is, therefore, a continuum between pure intergovernmental politics at one end of the spectrum, and supranational politics at the

[8] Paul Craig, 'Integration, Democracy and Legitimacy' in Paul Craig and Gráinne de Búrca (eds), *The Evolution of EU Law* (2nd edn, OUP 2011) ch 2.

[9] Andrew Moravcsik, 'Preferences and Power in the European Community: A Liberal Intergovernmentalist Approach' (1993) 31 JCMS 473; Andrew Moravcsik, *National Preference Formation and Interstate Bargaining in the European Community, 1955–86* (Harvard UP 1992); Andrew Moravcsik, 'Negotiating the Single European Act: National Interests and Conventional Statecraft in the European Community' (1991) 45 International Organization 19.

[10] Moravcsik, 'Preferences and Power' (n 9) 480.

[11] Gary Marks, Liesbet Hooghe, and Kermit Blank, 'European Integration from the 1980s: State-Centric v. Multiple-Level Governance' (1996) 34 JCMS 341, 342.

other, and different areas of EU policy could be located at different points along the spectrum.[12]

There has been further discourse concerning these rival theories, with refinement and modification in both camps.[13] The apposite issue for present purposes is the light that the EU's response to Brexit sheds on the theories of integration set out earlier. The answer is interesting and rational in equal measure.

An initial response might be that Member State power would predominate by way of analogy with moments of Treaty amendment, wherein it is national executives that exert dominant influence. Brexit, and the threat it entailed for the EU project, would, by any metric, be regarded as a major event, in which it might be expected that the Member States would wish to keep the reins of power firmly in their own hands. Intergovernmentalism, whether old or new, might then have been expected to be the order of the day, with the Member States controlling the supranational agents and directing them.

The reality was markedly different. To be sure, the European Council, as the highest embodiment of national power, set the general terms for negotiation at each stage of the Brexit process, albeit on the basis of drafts that had a large input from the Commission. The process thereafter was, however, very much in the hands of the EU institutions, as represented by Michel Barnier, Donald Tusk, and Jean-Claude Juncker. The reasons were not hard to divine. They were in part practical. The very complexity of the negotiations precluded meaningful national control over those representing the European Union, and this became ever more so as the degree of detail in those discussions became more specific. The reasons were, however, also conceptual. A centralised response from the European Union was regarded as rational from the perspective of the EU's own self-interest and survival. If the United Kingdom had its red lines in the protracted Brexit discourse, so too did the European Union, none more so than that the EU's survival was dependent on showing that a state really was better off staying in than being out.

This in turn had substantive and procedural second-order consequences. In substantive terms the exiting state could not be allowed to cherry-pick the best bits of EU membership; there had to be demonstrable differences between Member States and non-Member States. In procedural terms, while the Prime Minister might visit countries such as France and Germany, the United Kingdom was not allowed to engage in 'bilaterals' designed to undermine the centrally agreed position through side deals with other Member States. The EU negotiating position was centrally determined, albeit obviously with Member State input, and deviation from this was minimal.

[12] Alec Stone Sweet and Wayne Sandholtz, 'European Integration and Supranational Governance' (1997) 4 JEPP 297.

[13] See eg Andrew Moravcsik, *The Choice for Europe: Social Purpose and State Power from Messina to Maastricht* (Cornell UP 1998); Joseph Jupille, James Caporaso, and Jeffrey Checkel, 'Integrating Institutions: Rationalism, Constructivism, and the Study of the European Union' (2003) 36 Comparative Political Studies 7; Mark Pollack, *The Engines of European Integration: Delegation, Agency and Agenda Setting in the EU* (OUP 2003).

II. Institutions and Accountability

A. UK: Prime ministerial government, parliament, and the devolved regions

Brexit truly pressure-tested the UK institutional regime and the results were cause for some alarm. That statement is perforce tendentious, but so too in equal measure would be one which denied this conclusion. The argument thus stands or falls by its substance.

We are accustomed to thinking of relations at Westminster in terms of the executive dominating the legislature. It is the executive that sets the legislative agenda, and the Whips ensure passage of the legislation. Parliament, or more particularly the House of Commons, can seek amendments to draft legislation, and sometimes it secures them. The reality is nonetheless that the great majority of legislation is enacted as the executive would wish, which includes occasional amendments that it is willing to tolerate. There is academic discourse as to the degree of this domination,[14] and whether the House of Commons might have become more muscular in recent years, but the reality, as attested to by select committee reports over the years, is that the Government still holds most of the important cards.[15] The House of Commons' principal role is conceptualised in terms of scrutinising the Government via select committees and the like, rather than being the legislative engine room itself.

It would be over-simplistic to regard this picture as undemocratic, the argument being that the executive is delivering the wishes of the electorate, which entails the ability to manage the parliamentary machine, since otherwise business would not get done. It would, however, also be over-simplistic to invest too much weight in the previous sentiment, since it is often not clear what the electorate desires in terms of detailed legislative initiatives, and thus it is democratically legitimate for Parliament as a whole to have a real say in this. Brexit has had a threefold impact on this picture of our political ordering: institutional, normative, and territorial.

The institutional impact is manifest in the shift from executive to prime ministerial dominance. This topic is not new. The debate about the relative power of the Prime Minister versus the Cabinet has considerable lineage, with multiple factors playing into assessment of their respective power. Brexit nonetheless exemplified

[14] Meg Russell and Daniel Gover, *Legislation at Westminster* (OUP 2018); Meg Russell and Philip Cowley, 'The Policy Power of Westminster: The "Parliamentary State" and the Empirical Evidence' (2015) 29 Governance 121; Meg Russell, Daniel Gover, and Kristina Wollter, 'Does the Executive Dominate the Westminster Legislative Process? Six Reasons for Doubt' (2016) 69 Parliamentary Affairs 286.

[15] Hansard Society, *Making the Law, The Report of the Hansard Society Commission on the Legislative Process* (1992); Select Committee on Modernisation of the House of Commons, *First Report: The Legislative Process* (HC Paper No 190, 1997–98); Select Committee on Modernisation, *First Report: The Legislative Process* (HC Paper No 1097, 2005–06); L Thompson, 'More of the Same, or a Period of Change? The Impact of Public Bill Committees in the Twenty-First Century House of Commons' (2013) 66 Parliamentary Affairs 459.

prime ministerial power and control 'in spades'. A word of caution is warranted here lest this point should be misunderstood. It can be readily accepted that the Prime Minister's strategy was shaped by what she believed would be accepted by the different factions in the Cabinet. Thus was it ever so, and it could not readily be otherwise. This does not alter the fact that the UK's negotiating strategy was concentrated in the Prime Minister's hands throughout. It was apparent in that successive Brexit Secretaries of State bemoaned the fact that the real negotiations were being run by the Prime Minister's office, with the Department for Exiting the European Union being sidelined. It was evidenced by the fact that the Cabinet only had sight of the detailed 585-page draft Withdrawal Agreement a short time before discussing it.[16] It is attested to by the fact the Prime Minister resiled from the 11 December 2018 vote on that Agreement on the morning when it was scheduled to take place, when senior ministers had been on air earlier affirming that the vote would go ahead.[17] The trajectory has been for prime ministerial power to increase over time, ever more so as we drew closer to the business end of the two-year period. These examples could be multiplied many times over and will be developed further when considering process and procedure in section II.B.

The normative impact is equally dramatic. The Prime Minister accorded her vision of Brexit a normative status or weight such that attempts to question it were deemed to be illegitimate, that is, as preventing the will of the people as expressed in the referendum from being effectuated. The Prime Minister presented herself as the repository of understanding as to what the will of the people connoted when they voted to leave, even though there was in reality very considerable contestation on this issue. It is important once again to add a word of caution, lest this point be misunderstood. There were numerous backbench motions expressing disagreement with the substance of the Prime Minister's desired choice, as attested to most notably by the dramatic 230-vote defeat of the resolution concerning the Withdrawal Agreement on 15 January 2019. This does not, however, alter the fact that backbench efforts in this respect were routinely labelled as illegitimate being disruptive of an outcome, the content of which resided acutely in the personal vision of the Prime Minister. The institutional impact of Brexit, whereby power became ever more concentrated in the Prime Minister, fuelled a normative narrative wherein the PM's belief as to what the referendum 'meant' and how it could be 'honoured' assumed a disproportionate influence, manifest in the oft-repeated critique that those who had the temerity to differ were being disloyal to the people.

[16] BBC Business Matters, 'Cabinet Backs Brexit Withdrawal Agreement' (BBC Podcast 15 November 2018); available at: https://www.bbc.co.uk/programmes/w172w0q0lj03jn8, accessed 2 July 2019.

[17] News, 'Commons 'meaningful vote' on Brexit' (UK Parliament, 3 January 2019); available at: https://www.parliament.uk/business/news/2018/december/the-meaningful-vote/, accessed 2 July 2019.

The effect of Brexit on the UK's territorial constitution was also very significant.[18] The Government's Brexit strategy was, inevitably, crafted for the United Kingdom as a whole, since it was the United Kingdom that was a member of the European Union, and the Westminster Parliament retained competence over foreign policy. The flip side to this conception of indivisibility was that the strategy was meant to be beneficial to all parts of the United Kingdom, including Scotland, Wales, and Northern Ireland, and they were to be accorded voice in its shaping through the Joint Ministerial Committee. There was, however, a gap between rhetoric and reality. Truth to tell, the substantive fault lines between Westminster and the devolved assemblies were significant, and the procedural engagement a good deal less than the reader would divine from reading the official Westminster documentation, with the consequence that while the devolved bodies exercised their voice its impact at Westminster was muted.

This impact was further diminished because Scotland and Wales favoured soft rather than hard Brexit.[19] The tensions were evident from the very outset, when the Prime Minister gave her Lancaster House speech, in which she opted for hard Brexit, two days before a Joint Ministerial Committee meeting, without having discussed Scotland's policy document released a month earlier.[20] The strains were exacerbated over time, such that as the clock ticked down to the March 2019 deadline, the devolved institutions were ever more excluded from voice in the process.[21] These strains were, moreover, manifest in other ways, in the framing of the Brexit legislation, as we shall see shortly.

The preceding picture of the impact of Brexit on our political ordering is nonetheless incomplete in an important respect, which is that Parliament, for which read the House of Commons in this context, has been largely acquiescent in its domination by the Prime Minister and the executive during the Brexit process. There has, to be sure, been some rebellion, most notably in the record-breaking rejection of the Withdrawal Agreement by 230 votes. This must, nonetheless, be placed in broader perspective.

Sovereignty resides with Parliament and has done so for *circa* 400 years. It does not reside with the executive. Parliament could, therefore, at any time since 23 June 2016, have enacted a statute requiring the Government to seek its approval

[18] Sionaidh Douglas-Scott, 'Brexit and the Scottish Question' in Federico Fabbrini (ed), *The Law and Politics of Brexit* (OUP 2017) ch 6; Paul Craig, 'Brexit a Drama: The Interregnum' (2018) 36 Ybk European L 1, 16–20.

[19] Scottish Government, *Scotland's Place in Europe* (December 2016) and Welsh Government, *Securing Wales' Future, Transition from the European Union to a New Relationship with Europe* (January 2017).

[20] Scottish Government, 'JMC meeting on Brexit' (19 January 2017); available at :https://news.gov.scot/news/jmc-meeting-on-brexit, accessed 2 July 2019.

[21] See the letter sent to the UK Secretary of State for Exiting the European Union to the Scottish Minister for UK Negotiations on Scotland's Place in Europe on the 29 April 2017 and the reply on the 12 April 2017; available at: http://www.parliament.scot/S5_European/General%20Documents/CTEER_Minister_M.Russell_2017.04.27.pdf, accessed 2 July 2019.

before triggering Article 50 of the Treaty of the European Union (TEU); it could have attached conditions to the European Union (Notification of Withdrawal) Act 2017, which secured it more formal powers in relation to the Brexit negotiations and outcome thereof;[22] it could have forced amendments to the European Union (Withdrawal) Act 2018 (EUWA), to ensure that it had greater voice over the content of the final deal, and the possibility of no deal;[23] and it could have used its power to prevent the Prime Minister from gaming the House of Commons' procedural rules in the manner explained below.

It did none of these things, although it should, by way of balance, be acknowledged that section 13 of the EUWA, and the requirement of a resolution to approve the Withdrawal Agreement, provided the foundation for the parliamentary votes that led to historic defeats for the Prime Minister, when the House of Commons rejected that Agreement by margins of 230 and 149.

This still begs the question as to why Parliament was quiescent in this respect, to which the answer is eclectic. Some Members of Parliament (MPs) might genuinely have felt that the matter should, for reasons of principle, be left to the executive; others, particularly hard Brexiteers, were wary of anything on the floor of the House that might jeopardise their victory in the referendum; yet others were fearful of backlash from their constituents who had voted to leave, who would be angered if they felt that their victory was in danger of being undermined by subsequent development.

B. EU: two presidents, institutional decision-making, and liaison with Member States

The impact of Brexit on the European Union was indubitably dramatic, insofar as it embodied reversal of the pattern of integration since its inception. The very fact that a Member State sought to leave, for whatever concatenation of circumstance, shook the system to the core. It prompted alignment of intergovernmental and supranational modes of decision-making in the manner discussed in section I.

It also operated as a real-life test for EU institutional decision-making, more particularly the system of double-hatting that was institutionalised in the Lisbon Treaty. There was much debate prior to the Constitutional Treaty as to whether the European Union should have a single President, who would be the head of the Commission, or whether there should be separate Presidents of the Commission and the European Council. The Constitutional Treaty reflected the latter view,

[22] See Jeff King 'What Next? Legislative Authority for Triggering Article 50' UK Const L Blog (8 November 2016).

[23] There were amendments to the European Union (Withdrawal) Act 2018, s 13, but they fell short in terms of control by Parliament of the outcome of the negotiations from what had been proposed by the House of Lords.

known in the jargon of the trade as the 'separate hats' view, and it was taken over, largely unchanged, into the Lisbon Treaty. It was central to this view that the Presidency of the European Council would be strengthened and would no longer rotate between Member States on a six-monthly basis. It was felt that this would not work within an enlarged Union, and that greater continuity of policy would be required. This view was advocated by a number of the larger States, but was opposed by some of the smaller States.[24]

The opposition was in part institutional in the sense that it was felt that the longer-term Presidency of the European Council would be dominated by the larger Member States; it was also in part substantive, connoting the concern that exercise of executive power by both Presidents would be inefficient and could lead to conflicts between them. These concerns have not, in general, been borne out. In institutional terms, the two initial incumbents of the European Council Presidency have hailed from Belgium and Poland respectively, thereby belying fears that the post would be dominated by nationals from the larger Member States. In substantive terms, there has been little by way of serious tension between the two Presidents, even if there were instances where they might differ over detailed strategy.

It is, by definition, impossible to run a scientific controlled experiment to determine how the European Union would have operated if the opposite view had won out, such that there was only a single President of the European Union, this being vested in the Commission President. This would however have been doubly problematic: the heads of state in the European Council would never have accepted such accretion of power to the Commission President, and the Commission President would have been placed in an impossible position, trying to represent the interests of both the Commission and the Member States.

The double Presidency worked to good effect when pressure-tested in the context of the Brexit negotiations. The practical reality was that both Presidents participated in this discourse, and lent support to each other. Donald Tusk, the President of the European Council, commonly took the lead.[25] This was reflective of the centrality of that institution in Article 50 TEU since it was the European Council to which the Member State gave its notice to withdraw, and it was the European Council that issued the guidelines for the negotiations between the European

[24] Philip Norman, *The Accidental Constitution, The Making of Europe's Constitutional Treaty* (2nd edn, EuroComment 2005); Paul Craig, *The Lisbon Treaty, Law, Politics and Treaty Reform* (OUP 2010) ch 3.

[25] See, eg 'Remarks by President Donald Tusk on the Next Steps Following the UK Notification' (Council of the EU Press Release, 31 March 2017); available at: http://dsms.consilium.europa.eu/952/Actions/Newsletter.aspx?messageid=11790&customerid=16061&password=enc_3936444345424338_enc, accessed 2 July 2019; 'Invitation Letter by President Donald Tusk to the Members of the European Council (Art 50)', Council of the EU Press Release, 28 April 2017); available at: http://www.consilium.europa.eu/en/press/press-releases/2017/04/28-tusk-invitation-letter-euco-art50/, accessed 2 July 2019.

Union and the United Kingdom.[26] The very fact that the European Council had a long-term President gave it a natural authority, enabling it to operate as the voice of the twenty-seven heads of state. The difficulties of running Brexit negotiations over two years under the status quo ante, whereby the head of the European Council rotated every six months, would have been formidable, perhaps impossible.

There was, moreover, real interaction between the two Presidents. The reality was that the negotiating mandate adopted by the European Council had significant input from the Commission, and hence its President.[27] This was increasingly so as the talks became more advanced, since Commission papers would commonly flesh out the detail of, for example, the arrangements that should prevail for EU citizens living in the United Kingdom and vice-versa in a post-Brexit world, or the transitional arrangements that would have to be put in place to deal with the plethora of institutional changes attendant on the UK's exit from the European Union. The Commission President, Jean-Claude Juncker, was, moreover, vocal at various stages of the discourse, reaffirming Tusk's view as to what was and was not feasible, in the heated exchanges concerning the Northern Ireland backstop.

The EU institutional structure is *sui generis*, and the divide between legislative and executive power does not conform to that commonly found in nation states. The need for institutions that represent state interests and the people, and the need also for the Commission, which performs a plethora of different functions, resulted in the two Presidencies that were enshrined in the Lisbon Treaty. This institutional architecture worked well when tested in the difficult circumstances of Brexit, and the transparency in the EU negotiating position enhanced accountability.

III. Constitutions and Rights

A. UK and EU: constitutions

The impact of Brexit on the UK and EU constitutions is significant. There is commonality in so far as neither has a conventional written constitution of the kind that exists in nation states. There is also difference, in so far as the United Kingdom has no discrete written constitution while the European Union has a very lengthy written Treaty document, the entirety of which has constitutional status in the hierarchy of norms that prevails in the EU legal order.[28] The salient inquiry is,

[26] General Secretariat of the European Council, 'Special Meeting of the European Council (Art 50)—Guidelines (EUCO XT 20004/17, 29 April 2017); General Secretariat of the Council, 'Council Decision EU/Euratom authorising the opening of negotiations with the United Kingdom of Great Britain and Northern Ireland for an agreement setting out the arrangements for its withdrawal from the European Union, Annex, BXT 24' (XT 21016/17, 22 May 2017).

[27] Commission, 'Recommendation for a Council Decision Authorizing the Commission to Open Negotiations with the UK Setting out the Arrangements for its Withdrawal from the EU', COM(2017) 218 final.

[28] Dieter Grimm, 'The Democratic Costs of Constitutionalization: The European Case' (2015) 21 ELJ 460.

therefore, whether in terms of constitution, the United Kingdom has too little, and the European Union has too much: it prompts the question whether the United Kingdom should adopt a written constitution, and whether the European Union should amend the Treaties so as to limit the number of Treaty provisions that are invested with constitutional status. These issues will be considered in turn, and it will be seen that there is no certain answer.

This is not the place for general exegesis on whether the United Kingdom should have a written constitution. The relevant inquiry is what we think about this in the light of the experience with Brexit.[29] The answer will perforce be shaped by more general background beliefs about the desirability or not of a written constitution. The inquiry is, nonetheless, worth pursuing, precisely because Brexit provides concrete circumstances against which to test what difference, if any, the existence of a written constitution might have made.

There could be a long or a short answer to this question, but the latter is preferable in terms of exigencies of space and clarity of thought: whether a written constitution would have made a difference depends on identification of the infirmities of the Brexit process and conjecture as to whether these would have been avoided by the existence of a written constitution. This, therefore, requires identification of the alleged malaise and reasoned thought as to whether it might have been obviated by a written constitution. We cannot provide a definitive answer, since it will depend on the content of a written constitution if one were to exist, and whether the terms thereof would have alleviated the problems attendant on the Brexit process. The preceding strategy can, however, be exemplified and tested.

Take by way of example the way in which the devolved regions have been treated in the Brexit process. They were denied effective voice in the shaping of the Brexit process, ever more so the longer has the process gone on, and their substantive preferences received scant attention. Whether matters would have been different if we had a written constitution would depend very markedly on the terms thereof, which are not determined *a priori*. It is possible to imagine a UK written constitution that embodied the legal status quo, in which case the position of the devolved regions would be no better than at present, and might well be worse by reason of the fact that the status quo was invested with constitutional status. It is, by way of contrast, possible to imagine a very different form of constitutional ordering, which gave greater procedural protection to regional voice, invested the Sewel convention, namely that the Westminster Parliament cannot normally legislate on a matter within devolved competence without the consent of the devolved legislatures,[30] with binding constitutional force, and made constitutional provision for

[29] Vernon Bogdanor and Stefan Vogenauer, 'Enacting a British Constitution: Some Problems' [2008] PL 38; NW Barber, 'Against a Written Constitution' [2008] PL 11; House of Commons Political and Constitutional Reform Committee, *A New Magna Carta?* (HC 2014–15, 463); Vernon Bogdanor, *Beyond Brexit: Towards a British Constitution* (Hart 2019).

[30] Scotland Act 2016, s 2.

protection of the regions' substantive political preferences, within the areas that fell within their scope of authority.

Take by way of another example the balance between prime ministerial, executive, and legislative power revealed by Brexit. Concerns in this respect were set out in the previous section. Whether a written constitution would make any difference in this respect would depend on its terms. This is more especially so since constitutions do not have a good track record at identifying the nature of executive power and the boundaries thereof.[31] Nor are they particularly good at specifying the more granular detail of relations between the executive and the legislature.[32] There are, moreover, very real issues as to how far it is desirable to constitutionalise such issues, given the impediments to change that this might then entail.

There are, by way of balance, counter examples which are particularly relevant to the present discussion. Thus, if the United Kingdom had a written constitution then it is likely that our membership of the European Union would have been enshrined therein. It would have had constitutional status, the corollary being that it could only be changed by the process for constitutional amendment. Whatsoever such requirements for change might be, the reality is that a referendum, followed by an ordinary statute, would almost certainly not suffice to change the constitution.

The focus now shifts to the European Union and whether it is, in certain respects, over-constitutionalised in the manner described below. Constitutionalisation attaches to all Treaty provisions and operates both vertically and horizontally.

The vertical dimension captures the effect of such constitutionalisation on relations between the Member States and the European Union. Foundational EU constitutional doctrines such as supremacy and direct effect kick in to constrict Member State action that is contrary to any Treaty provision. Disquiet as to the limits thereby placed on Member State action is exacerbated by what is perceived to be the imbalance between the economic and the social within the European Union, with the consequence that constitutionalised EU law can place severe limits on this balance at Member State level.[33]

The horizontal dimension of constitutionalisation addresses the confines thereby placed on political choice at EU level. Constitutions restrict choices that can be made via every day politics. Constitutional pre-commitment thus confines choices that can be made thereafter, subject to constitutional amendment. The difference with respect to the European Union is one of degree, not of kind, but it is

[31] Paul Craig and Adam Tomkins (eds), *The Executive and Public Law: Power and Accountability in Comparative Perspective* (OUP 2005).

[32] Consider, for example, the US Constitution in this regard.

[33] Fritz Scharpf, 'Economic Integration, Democracy and the Welfare State' (1997) 4 JEPP 18; Fritz Scharpf, 'The European Social Model: Coping with the Challenges of Diversity' (2002) 40 JCMS 645; F Scharpf, 'Legitimate Diversity: The New Challenge of European Integration' in Tanja Borzel and Rachel Cichowski (eds), *The State of the European Union, Volume 6: Law, Politics and Society* (OUP 2003) 79–104.

significant nonetheless, since the constitutionalised EU Treaty is far more detailed than national constitutions. It leaves some room for choice as to the direction of EU policy. The EU Treaty, nonetheless, limits the range of such choice that rival political parties can place before the electorate. There is, therefore, much in the Treaty that constitutes substantive path dependency for the direction of EU policy, which limits the extent to which political choices can be expressed by the legislature that affect the direction of policy.

Concerns as to the preceding vertical and horizontal constraints have been voiced by scholars and jurists such as Grimm, who focused on what he termed the democratic costs of constitutionalisation.[34] His central thesis is that the EU Treaties are over-constitutionalised, with the consequence that issues are thereby taken off the agenda of normal politics, notwithstanding the fact that many would be regarded as within the province of ordinary law in Member States: 'in the EU the crucial difference between the rules for political decisions and the decisions themselves is to a large extent levelled'.[35] There may be too little constitutionalism, but there may also be too much, with the consequence that the democratic process is fettered.[36] These concerns were exacerbated by the implications of such constitutionalisation for the balance between legislative and judicial power. It led inexorably to an increase in the latter at the expense of the former. The EU courts routinely interpret EU legislative acts for compliance with the Treaty provisions. If they are felt to be wanting in this regard they are struck down. The only recourse for the EU institutions in the event of disagreement with the courts is for Treaty amendment, with all the consequential difficulty that this entails. For Grimm, the remedy was to limit the EU Treaties to their truly constitutional elements and downgrade other Treaty provisions that were not constitutional in nature to the status of secondary law.

The apposite inquiry for present purposes is whether Brexit sheds light on the issue of over-constitutionalisation. To put the point more specifically, the issue is whether Brexit might have unfolded differently if the Treaties had been less constitutionalised. There may well be differences of view in this respect. The real difficulty is, however, causation which can, for reasons that will become apparent, not be easily tested. The question is whether matters might have unfolded differently in relation to the UK's membership of the European Union if the Treaties had been less constitutionalised, more particularly if the four freedoms were reduced from their present status to that of secondary law in accord with Grimm's recommendation, with the consequence that the EU political institutions would have had greater choice as to, for example, their content and linked nature. If this had been so then the EU political institutions would have had greater choice with regard to

[34] Grimm (n 28).
[35] Ibid 470.
[36] Ibid 464.

the four freedoms than they currently possess, and as to the balance between the economic and the social within the overall EU project. This might then have led to modification of free movement rules so far as concerns workers, thereby taking out some of the 'heat' from UK opposition to the European Union. The problem is, however, as stated earlier, causality. The previous sentences contain many instances of the verb 'might'. Things might have unfolded in this way if the Treaties had been less constitutionalised, but they might not. We simply cannot know. The most that one can say with certitude is that the EU political institutions would have had greater choice on such matters.

There are, in any event, some significant difficulties with the idea that the rules on free movement and the like should be 'downgraded' to have the status of legislation. It is in part because attaining this is more difficult in technical legal terms than might appear at first sight. It is in part because if you did so, the greater latitude for political choice by EU institutions would mean, as a corollary, that the choices would have been removed from the Member States, or that Member States would have less control over the direction of policy in such areas, which may have created even more tension between the European Union and its Member States.[37]

B. UK and EU: rights

Brexit generates considerable uncertainty as to rights for both the United Kingdom and the European Union. This was most marked in the United Kingdom by the way in which the EU Charter of Rights was dealt with. The strategy of the EUWA of bringing the EU legal acquis into UK law was not applied to the EU Charter of Rights. The Charter is not part of domestic law on or after exit day,[38] but this exclusion is, however, said not to affect 'the retention in domestic law on or after exit day in accordance with this Act of any fundamental rights or principles which exist irrespective of the Charter'.[39] The difficulties for lawyers and citizens alike are exacerbated by the fact that the EUWA provides that general principles of EU law can be part of domestic law after exit day, provided that they were thus recognised by the CJEU before exit day.[40] There is, however, no right of action in domestic law, on or after exit day, based on a failure to comply with general principles of EU law,[41] and no court, tribunal, or other public authority may, on or after exit day, disapply or quash any enactment or other rule of law, or quash any conduct or otherwise

[37] I am grateful to Alison Young for this point.
[38] EUWA s 5(4).
[39] EUWA s 5(5).
[40] EUWA Sched 1, para 2.
[41] EUWA Sched 1, para 3(1).

decide that it is unlawful, because it is incompatible with any general principle of EU law.[42]

The treatment of the Charter is an unwarranted exception to the EUWA strategy of bringing the entire acquis of EU law into domestic law.[43] The official explanation for not retaining the Charter was that it did not create new rights but merely affirmed existing EU rights and principles, and therefore by converting the EU acquis into UK law, those underlying rights and principles would be converted into UK law, as provided for in the EUWA. There is, however, a marked difference between retention of particular rights singularly, in a disaggregated manner, as compared to their inclusion in a separate rights-based document. If the latter had been done in relation to the Charter, it would then have been for Parliament to decide whether it wished to retain, amend, or repeal it. There are, moreover, very considerable practical difficulties resulting from the EUWA provisions, more especially the exclusion of the Charter, the retention of fundamental rights that existed independently of the Charter, and the qualified retention of general principles of law.[44]

The difficulties concerning rights were not confined to the United Kingdom. There were also considerable problems for the European Union. These were most readily apparent in relation to the rights of EU citizens in the United Kingdom in a post-Brexit world, and the corresponding rights of UK citizens living in the European Union. The difficulty of securing agreement as to what these rights should be, of transforming the political agreement into legal language, and of then modifying the pre-existing EU legal rules so as to accommodate the new reality, was very considerable. This is readily apparent from a bare glance at the text of the Withdrawal Agreement dealing with these issues.[45] The Withdrawal Agreement attests more generally to the complexity of rights-based issues that required resolution, including, *inter alia*, rights that were in the process of resolution when Brexit occurred,[46] and the rights entailed by the Northern Ireland backstop.[47] The technical dimension of rights' protection that required resolution at EU level was itself reflective of the fact that the European Union was more substantively committed to the idea of rights as red lines, both in relation to EU citizens' rights and the rights of those in Northern Ireland.

42 EUWA Sched 1, para 3(2).

43 Nick Bamforth et al, The EU Charter after Brexit: Submission to Joint Committee on Human Rights (Oxford Human Rights Hub 2017); Arabella Lang, Vaughane Miller, and Jack Simson Caird, *EU (Withdrawal) Bill: The Charter, General Principles of EU law, and 'Francovich' Damages*, (House of Commons Briefing Paper Number 8140, 17 November 2017).

44 Catherine Barnard, 'So Long, Farewell, Auf Wiedersehen, Adieu: Brexit and the Charter of Fundamental Rights' (2019) 82 MLR 350; 'Paul Craig, 'Constitutional Principle, the Rule of Law and Political Reality: The European Union (Withdrawal) Act 2018' (2019) 82 MLR 319, 330–34.

45 Agreement on the Withdrawal of the United Kingdom of Great Britain and Northern Ireland from the European Union and the European Atomic Energy Community (25 November 2018) Articles 9–36.

46 Ibid Articles 39–125.

47 Ibid Protocol on Ireland/Northern Ireland.

IV. Process and Procedure

A. UK: two dimensions of process

Process is central to public law. There is process writ small, the paradigm being some form of hearing rights before a decision is made that affects an individual deleteriously; there is participatory process, as epitomised by procedures that facilitate citizen input to rule-making, or to planning-type decisions that impact on a wide group of people; and there is also process writ large, involving the electoral process and the fair representation of different parts of the electorate. Normative values underpin all types of process, with distinctive features that reflect differences in adjudicatory, participatory, and electoral process.

Brexit cast into sharp relief two features of process and procedure that have featured less prominently in academic discourse: parliamentary process, more especially that in the House of Commons; and a Brexit decision-making process that was premised on a distinction between the Withdrawal Agreement and the Political Declaration on the Framework for the Future Relationship Between the European Union and the United Kingdom. These two procedural dimensions are intimately connected and both raised issues of constitutional importance.

We can begin with House of Commons procedure. It is safe to say that UK public lawyers now know a very great deal more about this than they did hitherto. This is not saying much, given that the base line of knowledge hitherto was pretty low for most people, myself included.[48] Necessity is, however, not only the mother of invention but also the catalyst for acquisition of knowledge. It connoted, in this context, the need for an understanding of parliamentary procedure to grasp the machinations in the House of Commons associated with the vote on the Withdrawal Agreement, which was required by section 13 of the EUWA. This is not the place for detailed exegesis on the many and varied mysteries of such procedural rules. Suffice it to say that they include, *inter alia*, the rules that determine the priority of House of Commons business, the exceptions that can be made thereto, the way in which this can be done, which motions are amendable, and which amendable motions are binding on government, to name but a few. Jack Simson Caird has furnished much needed expertise and clarity on such issues.[49]

[48] This in turn raises interesting issues as to why this was so, and what it tells us more generally about how public lawyers think about process. Space precludes detailed inquiry, but two brief thoughts are that public lawyers have generally been more interested in adjudicative rather than legislative process, and they prefer the relevant norms to be laid down in case law, rather than complex written rules.

[49] Jack Simson Caird, 'The Commons' Verdict Delayed: A Decisive Shift in the Battle for Control of the Brexit Endgame?' (UK in a Changing Europe Blog, 19 December 2018); Jack Simson Caird, 'Brexit and the Speaker of the House of the Commons: Do the Ends Justify the Means?' (VerfBlog, 1 January 2019), Jack Simson Caird, 'What went wrong with the Meaningful Vote?' (*Huffington Post*, 7 February 2019).

The apposite issue for present purposes is the constitutional resonance of these procedural battles waged on the floor of the House, and the light that is thereby shed on the soundness of our constitutional arrangements. The cause for concern, or at least explication, is readily apparent. Whichever formulation is preferred it should not distract from the central issue: the pressure-testing of our constitutional system has thrown into sharp relief the power that the procedural rules afford to the Prime Minister, and these rules functioned as pillars to the substantive accretion of prime ministerial power considered earlier.

This naturally begs inquiry as to how we should regard this turn of events. The natural temptation is to resort to constitutional equanimity or outrage. Those who regard events in terms of constitutional equanimity would tell the following story: there is nothing unduly to concern us at the constitutional level by the Commons' machinations over procedure; truth to tell all the players were trying to game the system to gain maximum advantage from the existing rules, and the political marketplace would re-equilibrate in the same manner as economic markets. Those who view matters through the prism of constitutional outrage would tell a different tale: the procedural rules used by the Prime Minister to control events in the House of Commons were fundamentally misconceived; they enabled her to wield unprincipled power over the passage of events on the floor of the House, and used that power in circumstances where she could not command a majority in the House of Commons; and this constitutional infirmity demands constitutional reform.[50]

There is some merit in the respective stories, but both temptations should, nonetheless, be resisted. The reality is more nuanced. What we have is a classic legal conundrum. A rule is created for good purpose. The foundation of prime ministerial power is the procedural rule whereby government business can take priority over that of backbench MPs. The rule makes good sense in the ordinary course of events, since governments must be able to get business done without being unduly derailed. What we have witnessed is, however, the classic dilemma of a rule based on sound foundations used in a way that is far more contestable. Few can truly regard with constitutional equanimity the way in which the Prime Minister could play the House of Commons as master puppeteer, pulling the incidence of votes at the last moment, and delaying the vote as long as possible in order to gain maximum political advantage from the effluxion of time. Backbench MPs were complicit in their own fate, in so far as they refused to wrest control over the unfolding political saga, but this does not alter the fact that the default rules placed the Prime Minister in the driving seat in this respect. To put the same point in a different way, while all sides might be trying to game the system, the playing field on which they were doing so was not level. We should also recognise that there is no off-the-shelf,

50 See also Tony Wright and Henry Porter, 'The Hidden Battle for Parliament's Soul' (*Guardian*, 14 February 2010).

ready-made constitutional solution to this malaise. A solution would perforce have to be part of broader constitutional rethinking of the disposition of power between legislature and executive. It reveals once again the importance of thinking about constitutional fundamentals, and the way in which one's thoughts about constitutional detail reflect, at on stage removed, the more foundational principles on which the constitution rests.

The focus now turns to the second aspect of the process revealed by Brexit, which is the dichotomy between the decision concerning the Withdrawal Agreement and that concerning the Political Declaration on Future Trade. The connection between this and the first aspect of process is both stark and prosaic. The fierce battles over House of Commons' procedure were predicated on the assumption that the parliamentary vote on the Withdrawal Agreement would decide the principal issues concerning the relationship between the United Kingdom and the European Union. This was true in certain respects, none more so than whether we left with or without a deal. Many of the skirmishes in this battle were, however, also premised on the assumption that Parliament would thereby be deciding the nature of the trade relationship between the United Kingdom and European Union, hence the frequent discourse about variants of soft Brexit. Indeed, the backdrop to the fierceness of the procedural warfare was an assumption that what was at stake was the decision on the relative closeness or not of that future economic relationship.

Reality did not, however, accord with perception. The nature of the trade relationship between the United Kingdom and the European Union will only become clear post-Brexit, as negotiations proceed. The non-binding Political Declaration provides scant certitude in this respect, and the abstract principles contained therein could be taken in almost any conceivable direction. The decision-making process entailed, therefore, a largely blind Brexit, such that the parliamentary vote on whether to accept the Withdrawal Agreement was taken when Parliament had scant knowledge of the future relationship between the United Kingdom and the European Union.

This once again naturally begs inquiry as to how we should regard this turn of events, and it is, once again, natural to veer towards constitutional equanimity or outrage. The former view connotes argumentation to the effect that the executive has generally had a monopoly in the negotiation of trade agreements, and thus there is no cause for constitutional concern in so far as they would do so in a post-Brexit world. The latter view is predicated on the assumption that the dichotomy in Article 50 TEU between a withdrawal agreement and that on future trade relations was deeply flawed from the outset, a testimony to defective drafting of this new addition to the Lisbon Treaty.

There is some truth in both views, but the temptation to succumb to either should, nonetheless, be resisted. Constitutional equanimity can be taken too far. Thus, while it is perforce true that the executive paradigmatically negotiates trade agreements, the nature of the trade relationship between the United Kingdom and the European Union is, nonetheless, different in nature since the very choice as to the form of this economic ordering could have a significant impact on whether MPs and the people would choose to leave at all. It is, moreover, very difficult to contend that this choice should reside solely with the executive in a post-Brexit world given the seminal and contestable nature of the issues involved. By the same token, constitutional outrage must be leavened by acknowledgement of the dilemmas posed by exit from the European Union. It would, in practical terms, simply not be possible for a withdrawal agreement and that on future trade relations to proceed literally in tandem since the latter involves complex issues that may take years to resolve. It is, therefore, inevitable that the EU exit process will be blind, unless the departing state and the European Union have a very clear idea as to the nature of their future relationship.

There are then no ready-made or simple solutions to either procedural issue raised by Brexit. This does not, however, obviate the need for reasoned inquiry as to the constitutional implications of the procedural issues in the House of Commons, or of the dilemmas posed by the bifurcated nature of the procedure relating to the two agreements that are integral to Brexit. At the very least both inquiries share a commonality, in so far as they cast into stark relief claims that sovereignty entails a repatriation of sovereignty to the UK Parliament. They both, moreover, reveal the need to be mindful of the fundamental principles that do and should underpin our constitutional ordering.

B. EU: two dimensions of process

Brexit also raised two central issues from the EU perspective, which shed light on the process of decision-making on matters of constitutional significance in the European Union: executive domination of the procedure, and the role accorded to the European Parliament therein. They will be considered in turn.

The decision-making process under Article 50 TEU was explicitly grounded in the executive. This was readily apparent from the terms thereof, which placed the European Council in pole position through its setting of the negotiating guidelines. It was further attested to by the fact that Article 50 contained the direct link to the ordinary process for treaty negotiation in Article 218 TFEU. This process is premised on the centrality of the Council and the Commission in the negotiations, with the final agreement being signed off by the Council. The Brexit process was thus grounded on treaty foundations that accorded centre stage to executive institutions. This fitted naturally with the subject matter, since exit from the European Union necessarily raised issues of high politics that could only be resolved at the highest level, this being meetings of the heads of state. This explains why the European Council assumed a greater role in the talks than it might do in relation to other international agreements. The complexity of the issues raised by the Withdrawal Agreement also served to explain why the Commission was continuously involved in elaborating the detailed implications of the issues contained therein.

The role accorded to the European Parliament was also based on a combination of Article 50 TEU and Article 218 TFEU. The degree of parliamentary voice is *prima facie* determined by Article 218(6) TFEU, where either consent by the European Parliament is required, or consultation, depending on the subject matter of the particular international agreement. A withdrawal agreement made pursuant to Article 218 TFEU would not fall within the categories of agreement for which consent of the European Parliament was required under Article 218(6)(a) TFEU. Article 50(2) TEU nonetheless expressly provides that a withdrawal agreement can only be concluded by the Council by qualified majority after obtaining consent of the European Parliament. This addition was readily explicable. Thus, while power over negotiations was concentrated in EU executive institutions, the European Parliament had legitimate concerns as to the terms of withdrawal, given their importance for the overall EU project. The need to secure the European Parliament's consent had, in turn, implications for the conduct of the talks, since the European Council and Commission would be mindful as to what would be acceptable to the European Parliament.

These two process issues reflect foundational assumptions concerning the roles played by the respective EU institutions in the Article 50 process. The centrality accorded to the European Council is readily explicable for the reasons set out earlier, but it is instructive also the way in which the normal process of Treaty ratification in Article 218(6) TFEU was modified by Article 50 to accord the European Parliament a greater role than it would otherwise have had, thereby signifying the importance of a decision to leave the EU and the need for the European Parliament to be on board with the outcome.

V. Legislation

Discussion of legislation follows naturally from institutions and process. It is a little known, albeit incontrovertible fact that all lawyers, whether from the common law or civil law tradition, prefer case law to legislation. It is part of their DNA. Give them the choice of unravelling a complex case, or dissecting a difficult statute, and they will opt for the former pretty much every time. This may be inevitable, and indeed is undoubtedly so in so far as it is part of legal DNA, but it is nonetheless regrettable, given the importance of legislation and regulation for public law. Legislation and attendant regulatory instruments have an architecture, elegant or not as the case may be, the discernment of which is important in terms of positive law, and for appreciation of its normative underpinnings. Brexit has brought legislation very much to centre stage, for the reasons explicated below.

A. UK: two dimensions of legislative complexity

There are two dimensions to the legislative complexity resulting from Brexit, the macro and the micro. This complexity generates constitutional concerns as to the balance of legislative and executive power, and rule of law concerns as to the individual's ability to plan one's life cognisant of the legal consequences of one's action.

The *macro-level complexity* connotes the types of legislative response demanded by Brexit, which are of a kind never encountered hitherto.[51] The United Kingdom has been a member of the European Union since 1972, and many areas of life are regulated by EU law. Directives have already been transformed into UK law. There is, however, much EU law, such as regulations, that is directly applicable, taking effect in domestic law when enacted by the European Union, without the need for further national legislation. The European Communities Act 1972, section 2(1), furnished the legal foundation for direct applicability and direct effect within the UK constitutional order.

It would in theory be possible to consign this regulatory material to the legal dustbin in the event of Brexit. This would, however, lead to chaos. The existing EU rules regulate matters from product safety to creditworthiness of banks, from securities markets to intellectual property, and from the environment to consumer protection. There cannot simply be a legal void in these areas, and pre-existing UK law will often not exist. Consigning such legal rules to the legal scrap heap would also be irrational, since there is much that the United Kingdom helped to fashion.

This is the rationale for the EUWA. The foundational premise is that the entirety of the EU legal *acquis* is converted into UK law. Parliament can then decide, in two stages, which measures to retain, amend, or repeal. Stage one is to ensure that the EU rules retained as domestic law are fit for legal purpose when we leave the European Union, since there may be provisions that do not make sense in a post-Brexit world, such as reporting obligations to the Commission, which must be altered by exit day. Stage two is the period post-Brexit, when Parliament can decide at greater leisure whether it wishes to retain these rules.

The EUWA is, however, only part of the macro-level legislative response to Brexit. There will be separate statutes dealing with matters such as immigration, data protection, and customs. There will, moreover, be legislation designed to give effect to the Withdrawal Agreement, which is mandated by the EUWA.[52] It too

[51] Department for Exiting the European Union, *Legislating for the United Kingdom's Withdrawal from the European Union* (Cm 9446 2017) [1.13].
[52] EUWA s 13(1).

will be complex, since it will be bringing into UK law the 599 pages of dense legal provisions contained in the Withdrawal Agreement.[53] This legislation will amend the EUWA in certain respects. Thus, to take but one example, the EUWA is framed throughout in terms of 'exit day', which was initially defined in section 20(1) to be 29 March 2019 at 11 p.m. This can for, the purposes of UK law,[54] be altered by ministerial regulation to ensure that the date and time specified for exit cohere with the date and time when the Treaties cease to apply to the United Kingdom.[55] Such ministerial regulations may have to be issued because the Withdrawal Agreement provides for a transitional period that runs to 31 December 2020, with the possibility of one extension thereafter, during which the United Kingdom remains bound by EU law. The United Kingdom will also remain bound by some aspects of EU law if there is need to invoke the backstop in relation to Northern Ireland because a trade agreement that obviates the need for this has not yet been agreed. Section 20(1) of the EUWA has, moreover, already been altered, because of the extension accorded to the United Kingdom, so that the leaving date was stipulated to be 31 October 2019,[56] although this time line has now shifted again.

The *micro-level complexity* connotes the difficult and multifaceted legal issues that arise pursuant to the legislative initiatives adumbrated earlier. It is exemplified by many provisions of the EUWA. Thus, while the general aim of the legislation is clear, its detailed effectuation gives rise to a host of intricate legal issues, which can only be resolved by UK courts in a post-Brexit world. This is more especially so, given the fact that while the avowed aim is to bring the entire *acquis* of EU law into national law, this is subject to various qualifications, the meaning of which are often unclear.[57] The micro-level complexity is further evident in the complicated legal provisions for the enactment of statutory instruments contained in the EUWA. There are very real difficulties in securing their passage, with adequate scrutiny, given the temporal exigencies resulting from the Brexit deadlines. Numbers serve to put this issue into stark relief. Thus, it requires *circa* 1,000 statutory instruments to render the EU law brought into UK law fit for purpose by exit day. There was considerable disquiet during the passage of the EUWA as to the accretion of executive power flowing from this exercise, and the limited nature of parliamentary oversight provided in the EUWA. The House of Lords' Constitution Committee captured this powerfully, stating that the Act contained

[53] Agreement on the Withdrawal (n 45).

[54] From the perspective of EU law, Art 50(3) TEU requires unanimity from the other twenty-seven Member States before an extension can be granted.

[55] EUWA s 20(4).

[56] European Union (Withdrawal) Act 2018 (Exit Day) (Amendment) (No. 2) Regulations 2019/859, reg 2(2); European Union (Withdrawal) Act 2018 (Exit Day) (Amendment) Regulations 2019/718, reg 2(3).

[57] Mark Elliott and Stephen Tierney, 'Political Pragmatism and Constitutional Principle: the European Union (Withdrawal) Act 2018' [2019] PL 37; Craig, 'Constitutional Principle, the Rule of Law and Political Reality' (n 44).

> a tapestry of delegated powers that are breath-taking in terms of both their scope and potency . . . what is, in effect, an unprecedented and extraordinary portmanteau of effectively unlimited powers upon which the Government could draw.[58]

These general concerns have not been assuaged by the enactment of statutory instruments (SIs) prior to Brexit.[59]

B. EU: two dimensions of legislative complexity

The legislative complexity attendant on Brexit is not confined to the United Kingdom. It has also been manifest at the EU level, in both macro and micro terms.

The *macro-level complexity* connotes, as noted above, the types of legislative response demanded by Brexit. This has generated considerable legislative burdens for the European Union. The rationale is not difficult to divine: the EU legal services did the principal legal legwork to give shape to the provisions of the Withdrawal Agreement. The political players on both sides of the negotiations agree terms, which must then be turned into legal text. The EU legal services bore principal responsibility for this, because the law governing such matters was EU law, in which the EU legal services has expertise and authority. A mere glance at the 599-page Withdrawal Agreement confirms the difficulties that this entails. The very reason why the text is so legal and granular is because of the need for certainty, as to, for example, the rights of UK citizens living in the European Union and vice-versa in a post-Brexit world. This is equally true of the provisions dealing with the plethora of administrative and judicial issues that are ongoing at the date of departure, and other matters covered by the Withdrawal Agreement. The macro-level legislative complexity for the European Union was not, however, exhausted by the drafting of the provisions of the Withdrawal Agreement. Brexit also required other legislative responses to deal with matters such as the relocation of EU agencies, budgetary changes, customs, and regimes of equivalence.

The *micro-level complexity* captures the difficult and multifaceted legal issues that arise pursuant to the legislative initiatives adumbrated above. Some EU legislative acts required amendment. So too did delegated and implementing acts. Novel measures were required in certain areas. Concerns as to the rule of law, and being able to plan one's life cognisant of the legal consequences of one's action, are just as prevalent in the European Union as they are in the United Kingdom. The difficulties in this respect were further exacerbated by the fact that the European Union, like the United Kingdom, has had to make legislative provision for dealing with the many practical issues that would require legal resolution in the event of a no-deal Brexit. The European

[58] House of Lords Constitution Committee, *European Union (Withdrawal) Bill: Interim Report* (HL Paper 19, 2017) [2], [44].

[59] https://www.hansardsociety.org.uk/services/statutory-instrument-tracker, accessed 2 July 2019.

Union was ahead of the United Kingdom in this regard, with commensurate pressures on its legal services to draft the rules to cope with such an eventuality.

VI. Case Law and Doctrine

Courts commonly become involved when a constitutional system is pressure-tested. This proposition may be sustainable a priori, being an inevitable feature of high-profile constitutional moments. There is, however, no need for such intellectual inquiry at this juncture, since it suffices to note that such judicial engagement occurred as a matter of fact in both the United Kingdom and the European Union. There was, moreover, commonality in the nature of the involvement. The seminal judicial decisions entailed structural constitutional review, whereby the UK Supreme Court and the CJEU decided key issues concerning the relationship between institutions in the respective polities, which framed the subsequent political discourse, albeit not determining the outcome.

A. UK: framing the political discourse through structural constitutional review

Article 50(1) provides that a Member State may decide to leave the EU in accord with its own constitutional requirements. This is amplified by Article 50(2) TEU, which states, *inter alia*, that a Member State that decides whether to withdraw shall notify the European Council of its intentions. The referendum signalled that the United Kingdom would leave the European Union. However, the modality by which this was to be done gave rise to important constitutional issues as to whether Article 50 TEU could be triggered by the Government acting pursuant to the prerogative, or whether it required prior approval from Parliament.

There is prerogative power concerning the conduct of foreign relations, including the making of treaties. The Government believed that it could act pursuant to this power when notifying withdrawal from the European Union pursuant to Article 50. Gina Miller and Deir dos Santos, private citizens, believed that this could only be done after Parliament had given its approval through statute. This difference of view set the scene for litigation that gripped the legal and indeed national community as the case went through the courts.

The Supreme Court in *Miller*[60] upheld the judgment of the Divisional Court,[61] and decided that the Government could not trigger Article 50 TEU to

[60] *R (on the application of Miller) v Secretary of State for Exiting the European Union* [2017] UKSC 5, [2018] AC 61.

[61] *R (on the application of Miller) v The Secretary of State for Exiting the European Union* [2016] EWHC 2768 (Admin), [2017] 1 All ER 158.

begin withdrawing from the European Union without statutory authorisation from Parliament. The case concerned structural constitutional review, in which the Supreme Court demarcated the ambit of legislative and executive power, the latter being exercised through the prerogative.

The courts have long exercised control over whether the prerogative exists, and its extent, and more recently over manner of exercise.[62] *Miller* turned on contestation as to the second of these issues. The courts fashioned constraints that the prerogative cannot alter the law of the land or effect rights,[63] and that it cannot be used where it would place statute law in abeyance or frustrate statutory rules.[64]

The value that underlies these twin constraints on prerogative power is the sovereignty of Parliament. Parliament is the legitimate legislator within the United Kingdom and the limits protect that authority from being undermined. If the executive could change the law of its own volition, it could thereby bypass legislation without the need for amendment and repeal, hence the first constraint, which protects sovereignty directly. If the executive could use the prerogative where Parliament had already addressed the issue in a statute, it could then avoid the legislation crafted by Parliament, hence the second constraint, and its extension to cases where the prerogative would frustrate the legislation, which protects sovereignty indirectly, by precluding its use where the formal law is left intact, but the executive seeks to circumvent it by use of the prerogative.

The principal legal contestation in *Miller*, and subsequent academic commentary, concerned the application of these constraints to the giving of notice under Article 50, which inevitably led to contestation as to the ambit of the constraints themselves. Thus, the application of the first constraint in *Miller* raised difficult issues concerning the meaning of 'the law' that could not be changed through the prerogative, and the nature of the rights that could not be affected by use of the prerogative. This is not the place for detailed analysis of the contending arguments. Resolution of these intricate arguments is equally difficult, and cannot be undertaken here. Suffice it to say that I believe that the majority in *Miller* was correct, and my views in this regard can be found elsewhere.[65]

[62] Paul Craig, 'Prerogative, Precedent and Power' in Christopher Forsyth and Ivan Hare (eds), *The Golden Metwand and the Crooked Cord, Essays in Honour of Sir William Wade* (OUP 1998) 65–89; Sir Philip Sales, 'Crown Powers, the Royal Prerogative and Fundamental Rights' in Hanna Wilberg and Mark Elliott (eds), *The Scope and Intensity of Substantive Review, Traversing Taggart's Rainbow* (Hart 2017) ch 14.

[63] *Case of Proclamations* (1611) 12 Co Rep. 74, 75; Bill of Rights 1688, 1 Will and Mar.Sess 2, c 2, Articles 1–2; Sir Stephen Sedley, 'The Judges' Verdicts' (London Review of Books Online Extra, 30 January 2017).

[64] *Attorney General v De Keyser's Royal Hotel* [1920] AC 508.

[65] Paul Craig, '*Miller*, Structural Constitutional Review and the Limits of Prerogative Power' [2018] PL 48. See also, the articles in the Special Issue of Public Law devoted to the *Miller* decision, [2017] PL, Nov Supp (Brexit Special Extra Issue 2017). This chapter was completed in May 2019, and thus before *R (on the application of Miller) v Prime Minister, Cherry and others v Advocate General for Scotland* [2019] UKSC 41.

Courts can adjudicate the respective powers of the institutions that constitute the polity. It is then for those institutions to choose how to use them. The *Miller* decision demanded statutory approval before notification of withdrawal could be given under Article 50 TEU. It was then for Parliament to impose whatsoever controls or conditions it sought fit. The political reality was that Parliament was largely quiescent in this respect. Immediately after the *Miller* judgment, the Prime Minister introduced the European Union (Notification of Withdrawal) Bill 2017, which had undoubtedly been drafted earlier. The House of Commons duly passed the Bill by a large majority. There were attempts to impose substantive and procedural constraints on how the Government conducted the negotiations, but they were not successful, and the Bill secured its majority without amendment. There was stronger opposition in the House of Lords, but there was never any likelihood that it would block the legislation.

This begs the question as to why Parliament was quiescent in this respect, to which the answer is eclectic. Some MPs might genuinely have felt that the issue should, for reasons of principle, be left to the executive; others, particularly, hard Brexiteers, were committed functionally to the prerogative, since they were concerned in the aftermath of the referendum at attempts to undo their victory on the floor of the House. The principal explanation as to why most MPs did not, at that stage, seek to impose statutory conditions concerning conduct of the negotiations, or a requirement of statutory approval of the withdrawal agreement, was political. They were fearful of backlash from their constituents who had voted to leave, who would be angered if they felt that their victory was in danger of being undermined by demands for such a statute.

B. EU: framing the political discourse through structural constitutional review

The UK legal debate included discourse not only on who could trigger notification under Article 50, but also whether notification once given could be revoked, and if so on what conditions.[66]

[66] In favour of revocability: Charles Streeten, 'Putting the Toothpaste Back in the Tube: Can an Article 50 Notification Be Revoked?', UK Const L Blog (13 July 2016); Alan Dashwood, 'Invoking Article 50' (InFacts, 18 July 2016); House of Lords Select Committee on the Constitution, *The Process of Withdrawing from the European Union* (HL Paper 138, 2016), evidence of Derrick Wyatt and D Edward; Jean-Claude Piris, 'Article 50 is Not for Ever and the UK Could Change its Mind' (*Financial Times*, 1 September 2016); Aurel Sari, 'Biting the Bullet: Why the UK Is Free to Revoke Its Withdrawal Notification under Article 50 TEU', UK Const L Blog (17 October 2016); Paul Craig 'Brexit: Foundational Constitutional and Interpretive Principles: II' (OxHRH Blog, 28 October 2016); Takis Tridimas, 'Article 50: An Endgame without an End?' (2016) King's Law Journal 297; Aurel Sari, 'Reversing a Withdrawal Notification under Article 50 TEU: Can the Member States Change their Mind?' (Exeter Law School Working Paper Series, 19 November 2016); Piet Eeckhout and Eleni Frantziou, 'Brexit and Article 50 TEU: A Constitutionalist Reading' (UCL European Institute Working Paper, December 2016); Sir David

This issue was resolved in *Wightman*, where the CJEU,[67] in accord with the Opinion of the Advocate General,[68] held that Article 50 TEU could be revoked unilaterally by the United Kingdom. The Scottish Court of Session considered that it was neither academic nor premature to ask the CJEU whether it was legally possible for a Member State to revoke unilaterally the notification made under Article 50(2) TEU and to remain in the European Union.[69] The CJEU accepted that the answer could clarify the options open to MPs when they cast their votes on a Withdrawal Agreement between the United Kingdom and the European Union, since if the notification were to be revocable then MPs would have three options: withdrawal from the European Union without an agreement, withdrawal with the agreement laid before them, or revocation of the notification of the intention to withdraw and the United Kingdom's remaining in the European Union.

The CJEU, having decided that the case was admissible, then considered the contending arguments. The claimant argued that notification could be withdrawn unilaterally during the two-year period specified in Article 50(3) TEU. The Commission and the Council took the view that revocation during this period was only possible if the Member States were unanimously in favour. They were concerned that a unilateral right to revocation would be open to abuse: a Member State could in effect 'game the system' by using its right of revocation just before the end of the two-year period, and then notify a new intention to withdraw immediately after that period expired, thereby triggering a new two-year negotiation period. The Member State would thus gain, de facto, a right to negotiate its withdrawal without any time limit.

This is not the place for detailed exegesis as to the CJEU's reasoning, or the more detailed analysis of the Advocate General. Suffice it to say for the present that I agree with the reasoning and conclusion, which accord with views that I had expressed prior to the case.[70] The salient point for present purposes is the way in which the

Edward and others, 'In the Matter of Article 50 of the Treaty on European Union: Opinion' (Bindmans 2017); available at: https://www.bindmans.com/uploads/files/documents/Final_Article_50_Opinion_10.2.17.pdf, accessed 2 July 2019. See also, 'Speech by President Donald Tusk at the European Policy Centre conference' (Speech 575/16, 13 Oct 2016); available at: https://www.consilium.europa.eu/en/press/press-releases/2016/10/13/tusk-speech-epc/, accessed 2 July 2019; Jean-Claude Junker, Answer given by President Juncker on behalf of the Commission in response to European Parliamentary question p-008603/2016 (17 January 2017). Against revocability: NW Barber, Tom Hickman and Jeff King, 'Pulling the Article 50 'Trigger': Parliament's Indispensable Role', UK Const L Blog (27 June 2016); Joseph Weiler, 'A Second Referendum: What Makes You Think They Will Have You Back' (EJIL Talk, 26 November 2018); Jake Rylatt, 'The Irrevocability of an Article 50 Notification: Lex Specialis and the Irrelevance of the Purported Customary Right to Unilaterally Revoke' UK Const. L Blog (27 July 2016); Stijn Smismans, 'About the Revocability of Withdrawal: Why the EU (Law) Interpretation of Article 50 Matters' UK Const L Blog (29 November 2016).

[67] Case C-621/18 *Wightman v Secretary of State for Exiting the European Union*, EU:C:2018:999.
[68] Case C-621/18 *Wightman v Secretary of State for Exiting the European Union*, EU:C:2018:978.
[69] *Wightman v Secretary of State for Exiting the European Union* [2018] CSIH 22.
[70] Craig 'Brexit: Foundational Constitutional and Interpretive Principles: II' (n 66).

litigation required the CJEU to engage in structural constitutional review concerning the foundational relationships of the key players that constitute the EU polity. In *Miller* that contestation was, as we have seen, as to the respective powers of the executive and Parliament in relation to the notification of withdrawal. In *Wightman* it concerned the respective powers of the Member State seeking to leave and the other Member States within the Article 50 process.

The core normative assumption that underpinned the CJEU's judgment was the sovereignty of the state that had given notice of intent to withdraw. The CJEU acknowledged that Article 50 was silent as to whether the notification could be revoked, and if so on what terms. This silence could, said the CJEU, be interpreted either for or against revocation, but reached the former conclusion. This was in part because, in accord with the Advocate General, the CJEU emphasised the textual wording of Article 50(2), framed as it is in terms of intention to withdraw, concluding therefrom that such an intention was by its nature neither definitive nor irrevocable.[71] It was in part because of the wording of Article 50(1), which is framed in terms of a Member State deciding to withdraw from the EU in accordance with its own constitutional requirements, the CJEU concluding therefrom that the Member State was not required to take its decision in concert with the other Member States or with the EU institutions, and that the decision to withdraw 'depends solely on its sovereign choice'.[72] There was, said the CJEU, parity between accession and departure, in that a state 'cannot be forced to accede to the European Union against its will, neither can it be forced to withdraw from the European Union against its will'.[73]

It followed that a Member State could unilaterally revoke the notice of intent to withdraw prior to the conclusion of a withdrawal agreement, or prior to the end of the two-year period specified in Article 50(3). Any such revocation would have to be submitted in writing to the European Council and be unequivocal and unconditional, thereby confirming the EU membership of the Member State concerned under terms that are unchanged as regards its status as a Member State.[74]

The CJEU said little directly to address the concerns of the Commission and Council about possible abuse of the system, save for the fact that the CJEU made clear that revocation brought the withdrawal procedure to an end.[75] The issue was, however, addressed in the literature on revocation prior to *Wightman* and the reasoning was drawn on by the Advocate General.[76] Suffice it to say in the present context that the likelihood of any such potential abuse is low for a plethora of practical,

[71] Case C-621/18 *Wightman* (n 67) [49].
[72] Ibid [50].
[73] Ibid [65].
[74] Ibid [74].
[75] Ibid [74].
[76] Case C-621/18 *Wightman* (n 68) [152]–[153].

legal, and political reasons; and that if a Member State did attempt to do this there are well-tested legal tools to prevent its occurrence. There is, moreover, the fact that the dangers of gaming the system are in reality considerably greater if unanimity were to be required before a state could revoke notification of withdrawal, since it would give each Member State a veto on revocation, which they could deploy to gain other advantages in the EU political system as the price of their consent.

Courts can, as noted in the previous section, determine the respective powers of the institutions that constitute the polity, but it is then for those institutions to choose how to use them. This is equally true of EU jurisprudence as it is of case law at the national level. The obvious twist in this instance is that the institutions afforded the choice are largely the same as a result of *Wightman* as they were in the case of *Miller. Wightman* affords the United Kingdom the option to revoke the notice of withdrawal unilaterally if it so wishes to do so. If this were to be done, it would almost certainly require an Act of Parliament.[77] The power nonetheless resides with Parliament, but it would, in reality, not be used unless a second referendum produced a vote to remain in the EU. Legal discourse and rulings can, therefore, frame the political discourse, but in this context they are not determinative of the outcome.

VII. Conclusion

There will be no attempt to summarise the preceding arguments. Suffice it to say for the present that road-testing the approach taken to public law in this book, with the divide into the six dimensions, has revealed its methodological and substantive worth. These dimensions speak to different features of public law that are salient in most, if not all, legal systems, and the approach shines an arc light on the varied facets of public law that are implicated in any significant development. That is so irrespective of whether there is disagreement concerning the more particular content ascribed to one or more particular dimension of public law, when considered in the light of a particular set of facts. The approach serves, moreover, to take us out of our natural comfort zone, and to confront dimensions of public law other than the one that we might feel naturally most comfortable with. The interrelationship between the six dimensions is especially interesting, ever more so when the same foundational event, in this instance Brexit, impacts on more than one legal system. This can, in turn, facilitate an understanding of the fundamentals of public law, to which the chapters in this book have made such a valuable contribution.

[77] Gavin Phillipson and Alison L Young, '*Wightman*: What Would Be the UK's Constitutional Requirements to Revoke Article 50?' UK Const L Blog (10 December 2018).

Index

Note: *For the benefit of digital users, indexed terms that span two pages (e.g., 52–53) may, on occasion, appear on only one of those pages.*
Tables are indicated by *t* following the page number

abductive reasoning 95
the absent legislator 193, 199–205
abstraction, technique of 87–89, 137–39, 140–41
accountability
assembled accountability 255–56
automation 236, 242–43, 246–56, 291–92, 293–94, 297–98
Brexit 405–10
constitutionalism 345–46, 347, 350
democracy 346–47, 352, 359
disassembled accountability 250–54, 255–56
Europol 249–50, 255
formal accountability 233
information disconnect 250–51
institutions 233–34, 250–51, 405–10
interoperability 236, 243, 251–52
legal accountability 233
ministerial responsibility 216–17
multilevel government 345–47, 352, 353, 355, 360
Parliament 145–46, 163–69
political accountability 233, 254
Prime Minister 405–8
process and procedure 326–27
rationality 285
secrecy road-blocks 246–53
adjudication
adjudicative method 209, 217–18, 219–20, 224–26
legislation an adjudication, difference between 173, 189–91
non-adjudicative structures, debate on 211, 218
theory of adjudication 94–95
administrative law *see also* **public administration and administrative law**
definition 45
administrative material, engagement with 210–11, 227–28
adversarial procedure 128, 133, 279
Air Passengers Regulation 178–79, 180
algorithms 13
Alkali Inspectorate 212–13
Allan, Trevor 47, 78, 94–95
American Bar Association (ABA) 224
analogical reasoning 9–10, 13, 84, 89–90, 91–97, 104–5
abductive reasoning, as 95
abstraction, technique of 139
adjudication, theory of 94–95
Anisminic case 102–5
deductive reasoning 95–97, 104–5
definition 84, 85, 91–92
dialogue and reasoning by argument 95–96
dynamic process, as 95–96
heuristics 93–94, 95–96
inductive reasoning 95–97, 104–5
judicial activism 95
judicial review 103–4
life, right to 92–93
Northern Irish Abortion Case 92–95
ouster clauses 102–4
parliamentary sovereignty 104–5
precedents 94
Privacy International case 102–5
rule of law 103–5
separation of powers 104–5
taxonomies 95–97, 104–5
annulment actions 181–82
area of freedom, security and justice (AFSJ) 190, 233–34, 236, 255
Aristotle 53, 56, 133–34
Aronson, Mark 279
Article 2 TEU *see* **systemic violations by states of Article 2 TEU**
artificial intelligence (AI) 237–38, 278, 293–94, 295–96, 297–98
asylum seekers *see* **Dublin III Regulation; migrants and asylum seekers**
Atiyah, Patrick 197, 198
auditors, decision-making by 221
austerity measures 12–13
Australia, multilevel government in 346–47, 348–49, 355, 358–59

authority of the administration in UK 45–65
see also **office, concept of**
17th century, politics in the 7–8, 47–51, 64, 67
18th century, politics in the 46, 51–61, 64, 67
19th century, politics in the 46, 61, 65, 67
bases of authority claims 46
civic virtue, reinforcing 53–56
common law 45–46, 64–65
democracy 7–8, 61–64
historical context 46–64
independence, upholding 7–8, 56–57
judicial review 13, 45–46
legitimacy 7–8, 12–13, 46
point of the state 67–68, 72, 76–77
politics 7–8, 46–61, 64–65, 67
propriety and the official 51–61, 76–77
public trust 7–8
restoration of independence in property 57–61
ultra vires 13, 45, 64
automation *see also* **EU automated state**
accountability 293–94, 297–98
algorithms 13, 293–94
artificial intelligence 293–94, 295–96, 297–98
better government 291–92, 293–94
courts and tribunals 294–95
dehumanisation 295, 327
digitisation 278, 279, 295–96, 297–98
economy, efficiency, and effectiveness 291–92, 297–98
General Data Protection Regulation (GDPR) 293
Government Digital Service (GDS) 292–93
ICT 291–93, 297–98
individualisation 295–96
ineptitude of government 292–93
Internet 228, 291–92
modernisation 291–92
proceduralisation 327
proceduralism 12, 278, 291–96, 297–98
reasons, duty to give 323–24
technological revolution 291–96
transparency 291–92, 293–94, 297–98

Baker, Steven 166–67
Barber, Nick 198
Barnier, Michel 404
behavioural psychology 93
Belgium, plurinational federalism in 348
Benn, Ernest 218
Bentham, Jeremy 60–61
Bevan, Aneurin 271
bias 12, 279, 281, 297
Bingham, Lord (Bingham, Thomas) 330
biometric matching service 244
Blackstone, William 60–61
Blackwell, Joel 154, 158–60, 162
blocked progress, paradox of 42–43
Blom Cooper, Louis 169–70
Bodin, Jean 49–50
Bovens, Marc 250–51, 252
Brewer, John 95
Brexit 3, 10, 399–429 *see also* **EU (Withdrawal) Act 2018; notification of withdrawal from EU under Article 50; referendum on Brexit; Withdrawal Agreement**
accountability 405–10
Article 50, use of prerogative power to trigger 89
blind Brexit 418–19
Cabinet 405–6
Charter of Fundamental Rights of the EU 414–15
cherry-picking 404
CJEU 424, 427–29
Commission 408–10, 419–20, 427, 428–29
common law 87–89, 424–29
constitutions 88–89, 408–9, 410–14
cultural foundations of EU, effect on 43
delegated legislation 7, 202–5
absent legislator 193, 202–5
executive, transfer of powers to 13–14
Henry VIII powers 10–11, 145, 149–50, 151–52, 155, 157–60
democracy 400–2
Department for Exiting the EU 405–6
devolution 411–12
differentiation, paradox of 43
drafting primary legislation 202
elitism 402
enlargement 408–9
equality of treatment 43
EU (Notification of Withdrawal) Bill 2017 330, 426
European Communities Act 1972 421
European Council 408–10, 420, 427, 428–29
European Parliament 419–20
executive
accountability 405
delegated legislation 13–14
domination of EU executive 419–20
generality, idea of 43
legislature, balance with 405, 412, 417–18, 421, 422, 424–26, 427–28
monopoly on negotiation of trade agreements 418–19
negotiations 418–20
prerogative powers 424–26
Prime Minister 412, 417–18
exit day 421–22

general principles of EU law 414–15
Health and Social Care Act 2012 12–13
Henry VIII powers 10–11, 145, 149–50, 151–52, 155
  Cabinet Office. *Guide for Making Legislation* 155
  code of constitutional standards 157–58
  Delegated Powers Memorandum 158–60
  increase in use 155
institutions, accountability of 405–10
integration 6–7
intergovernmentalism 403–4
judicial review 87–89
Law Commission-sponsored legislation 202–3
legislation 202–3, 420–24
  accountability 405
  complexity 421–24
  direct applicability 421
  direct effect 421
  importance of legislation 420–21
Lisbon Treaty 408–9, 410
majority, lack of government 417
media 332
Miller I case 87–89, 331–32, 383–84, 424–26, 427–28, 429
multilevel government 346
negotiations
  accountability 409–10
  Commission 419–20
  European Council 419–20
  guidelines 419–20
  intergovernmentalism 404
  legislation 423
  transparency 410
no-deal Brexit 423–24
normative effect of Brexit 405, 406
Northern Ireland backstop 415, 421–22
Parliament 416–19
  accountability and institutions 405, 407–8
  sovereignty 400–2, 419
  time 202–3
Political Declaration 416, 418–19
popular sovereignty 400–2
preliminary rulings 11, 107, 108–9, 110–11, 124–25
prerogative powers 89, 424–26
presidents
  Commission 408–10
  Constitutional Treaty 408–9
  decision-making EU 408–10
  enlargement 408–9
  European Council 408–10
  liaison with member states EU 408–10
  Lisbon Treaty 408–9, 410
  negotiations 409–10
  opposition 408–9
  separate hats view 408–10
  single or separate presidents 408–10
pressure testing 10, 405
Prime Minister
  accountability 405–6
  Cabinet 405–6
  Department for Exiting the EU 405–6
  increase in power 416, 417–18
  legislature 412
  majority, lack of 417
  negotiations 405–6
  process and procedure 417–18
process and procedure 8–9, 323, 328–35, 416–20
public opinion 202
red lines 404, 415
rule of law 330–31, 421, 423–24
soft Brexit 418
sovereignty 427–28
structural constitutional review 424–29
supranationalism 334, 403–4, 408
Supreme Court 424
taxonomies 87
theory 400–4
transitional period 421–22
treaties
  constitutional status, with 410–11
  constitutions 412–14
truncated procedure, proposal for 202–3
two dimensions 416–21
Wightman case 87–88, 335, 427–29
will of the people 406
written constitutions 410–12
Brexit and post-sovereign legal landscape 11, 381–95
  autonomy 175–76
  conceptions of sovereignty 389–90
  Constitution of UK 390–92
  constitutional order, volatility of 394–95
  constitutionalism 385–87
  Costa v ENEL 175
  devolution 11–12, 393
  direct effect 384, 385–86
  European Communities Act 1972 175
  Euroscepticism 387–88, 393
  federacies 393
  legal pluralism 385–87, 390–91
    definition 385
    strong pluralism 385–86, 387
    weak pluralism 385–86, 387
  myth of a raw deal 387–88, 394
  national sovereignty 382, 386–87, 390, 393–95
  overlapping jurisdictions 175

Brexit and post-sovereign legal landscape (*Contd.*)
parliamentary sovereignty 393, 394
referendum 389–90, 391–94
retained EU law 388
rule of law 394
Scotland 389–90, 391–93
sovereignty 175, 382, 383, 387–90
national sovereignty 382, 386–87, 390, 393–95
parliamentary sovereignty 388, 389–90
popular sovereignty 389–90
supranationalism 388
'taking back control' 388, 390
UK, breaking up of 390
White Paper 389
supranationalism 175, 382–83
supremacy of EU law 175–384, 385–86, 394
unsettled state, Britain as a 390–94
Westphalian state 381–84, 394–95
Bridgeman, Viscount 223
Brouwer, Evelien 245
Brownlow Commission 224
Bryce, James 393–94

Cabinet
Cabinet Office. *Guide for Making Legislation* 155, 156
Prime Ministerial powers 405–6, 416, 417–18
Callanan, Lord (Callanan, Martin) 167
Canada 241–42
Cardozo, Benjamin 196
Carr, Cecil T 146–47, 148, 152, 200
Carrubba, Clifford 120
case law *see* **common law; judicial law-making**
centralisation
culture 356
decentralisation 214
delegated legislation 201
Germany 348
hierarchy 46, 61–62, 63, 65
multilevel government 340, 349, 353, 354–55, 359–60
office, concept of 46, 61–62, 63, 65
reasons, duty to give 299–300
certainty *see* **legal certainty**
Chalmers, James 160
Charles I, King of England 47, 50–51
Charter of Fundamental Rights of the EU
automation 241, 242–43
EU (Withdrawal) Act 2018 414–15
privacy 241, 242–43
proportionality 242–43
systemic violations by states of Article 2 TEU 367–68, 374–75, 377–78
values 281
citizenship
blocked progress, paradox of 42–43
consultation rights 79
moral equality of persons 78–79
multilevel government 351, 356–57
officials, independence of 56
point of public law 77–79
sovereignty 6–7, 351
the state and the EU 29–30
civic virtue 53–56, 60–61
civil service
18th century 56–57
centralisation 46
delegated legislation 147–48
delegation 64
democracy 46, 61–62
judiciary 62
professionalisation 282–83
reform 212–13
CJEU *see* **Court of Justice (CJEU)**
Clinical Commissioning Groups (CCGs) 260–71
codification 276, 277, 345–46
comitology 40
common law 83–105 *see also* **judicial law-making; precedent**
abstract review 87–89, 91, 99, 100–1, 104–5
accuracy 97–98, 99, 105
administrative law 209–10, 219
analogical reasoning 9–10, 13, 84, 89–90, 91–97
abductive reasoning, as 95
adjudication, theory of 94–95
deductive reasoning 95–97, 104–5
dialogue and reasoning by argument 95–96
heuristics 93–94, 95–96
inductive reasoning 95–97, 104–5
judicial review 103–4
Privacy International case 102–5
rule of law 103–5
taxonomies 95–97, 104–5
artificial reasoning, common law as 85, 95
authority of the administration 45–46, 64–65
autonomy 46
bottom-up reasoning 85, 87, 88–89, 96, 102
Brexit 424, 427–29
certainty 97–98, 99–100, 105
Competition and Markets Authority (CMA) 90–91, 100, 101–2
continuity of common law 85
deductive reasoning 9–10, 84, 90–92
analogical reasoning 95–97, 102, 104–5
inductive reasoning 97, 98
definition of common law reasoning 86
democracy 61, 62, 197–98
distillation (modification of common law) 85

evaluation of common law reasoning 91–97
evolution of common law reasoning 85
experimentation 85
foundations of public law 75
general principles 86–87, 88–89, 90–91, 94, 99
ideology 45
individual rights, protection of 45, 51–52, 65
inductive reasoning 9–10, 84, 91–92, 97–102
analogical reasoning 95–97, 104–5
deductive reasoning 97, 98, 102
inductive reasoning 97
public law/private law 97, 98–101, 102
rules and standards, difference between 97–102
standards 9–10, 97–100
taxonomies 97, 98, 100–2
interpretation 174
judicial review 83–85, 105
abstract review 87–88
heads 84, 90, 96
permission 87–88
taxonomies 84, 90–91
Wednesbury unreasonableness 90–91
legislation and case law, difference between 86
misconduct in public office 54
Northern Irish Abortion Case 88, 92–95, 100–2
office, concept of 48, 51–56
proceduralism 8, 280, 282–83, 286–88
suitability of common law reasoning for public law 83–91
taxonomies, development of 87, 90–91
analogical reasoning 95–97
inductive reasoning 97, 98, 100–2
top-down reasoning 85, 87, 88–89, 96, 100–1, 102
comparisons across legal cultures 195–98
competences 363–64
competition
abuse of a dominant position 260
anti-competitive agreements 260, 261, 262
Competition and Markets Authority (CMA) 90–91, 100, 101–2, 260
Health and Social Care Act 2012 260–62
conceptions of public law 25–28
culturalism 21, 26, 27–28, 36, 37–39, 40–41
idealism 26, 27
legitimacy 25–26
positivism 26, 27, 28, 37
pragmatism 26, 28
Constitution of UK 410–14
ad hoc constitution making 391
Brexit 410–14
impact on EU constitution 410–11, 412–14
impact on UK constitution 410–12
code of constitutional standards 157–58
conventions 390–91
devolution 390–92
flexibility 390–91
hereditary peers, removal of 390–91
ministerial responsibility 390–91
referendums, increase in use of 390–91
sovereignty 390–92
unwritten constitution 390–91
written constitution 410–12
Constitutional Treaty (EU) 386–87
constitutionalism 13, 43–44
accountability 345–46, 347, 350
automation 233
Brexit 385–87
codification 345–46
common law 45, 47, 51–52, 64
compound constitutionalism 11–12, 345, 359–60
Constitutional Treaty (EU) 43–44
contested concept, as 5
democracy 212–13, 340–41
Enlightenment 212–13
entrenchment 345–46
federalism 347–49
foundations 5
judicial review 345–46
multilevel 6–7, 11–12, 340–41, 345–61
principles 351–52
regionalism 347–48
rhetorical device, constitution as 43–44
sovereignty 6–7
transparency 350, 352
unitary 358
constitutions
Brexit 88–89, 410–14
impact on EU constitution 410–11, 412–14
impact on UK constitution 410–12
common constitutional traditions 37–38
common law 84
compliance 347
constitutional inflation 198
constitutional scale argument 88–89
Constitutional Treaty (EU) 43–44, 182, 408–9
constitutionalisation 412, 413–14
crisis, times of 328–35
federalism 351–52
interpretation 356–59
pluralism 116–17
principles, state as source of constitutional 13–14
reasons, duty to give 299–300, 304–8, 309–11, 315–17
review 357–58, 424–29
supremacy of EU 385
systemic violations by states of Article 2 TEU 363–64, 365

consultation rights 79, 282–83, 289–90
contextualism 14, 277, 286–87
Cooper, Robert 382
Cooper, Yvette 166–67
corruption 52–53, 58, 60–61
Court of Justice (CJEU) *see also* **Court of Justice (CJEU) in ruling on meaning of EU legislation, role of; preliminary ruling mechanism and relationship between UK courts and CJEU**
automation 236, 241
Brexit 424, 427–29
democracy 199
individual rights 367–68
judicial dialogue 373, 375
reasons, duty to give 8, 308–9
systemic violations by states of Article 2 TEU 367–68, 372–73, 374, 375
Court of Justice (CJEU) in ruling on meaning of EU legislation, role of 173–91
absent legislator, problem of the 193–94
adjudication and legislation, difference between 173, 189–91
area of freedom, security and justice (AFSJ) 190
bend a text, how far courts should 186–89
common law interpretive tradition 174
constructive re-interpretation, limit of 183–86
democracy 193–94
drafting legislation 13, 174
Amsterdam Treaty, Declaration 39 to 175
clarity 177
Commission 175, 176–77, 179–80
Council 175, 176–77
divergences between linguistic versions 177
English language 176–77, 178, 179–80
European Parliament 175, 176, 177
gap-filling 193–94
guidelines 175–76
Joint Practical Guide (JPG) of EP, Council and Commission 175
languages 174, 176–81
multinationalism 174, 176–77
red lines 176, 177
Dublin III Regulation 186–89
federalism 173
gap-filling 190, 193–94
interventionism 173
judicial activism 173, 193–94
judicial restraint 181–82
literal interpretation 173–74, 180, 190
not to take steps, court deciding 181–82
politics 175, 189, 193–94
purposive/teleological approach 180–81, 183–86, 190, 191, 193–94, 197, 199
separation of powers 173–74
standing 181–82
subsidiarity 193–94
travaux préparatoires 191
courts *see also* **Court of Justice of EU (CJEU)**
automation 294
Constitutional Courts 357–58
culture 356
delegated legislation 199
multilevel government 356–59
prerogative powers 48
Craig, Paul 2, 14–15, 20–21, 47
Administrative Law 2
all-rounder, as 22–25
Brexit 170–71, 334–35, 387
EU (Withdrawal Act) 2018 170–71
myth of a raw deal 387–88, 394, 395
unilateral revocation of notification of withdrawal 335
case law 83, 105
cause and effect 23
CJEU and national courts, relationship between 4, 107, 122
common law 75–76, 83–84
conceptual models of law 23
delegated legislation 170–71
democracy 363
development of administrative law 83
development of common law 4
direct effect 4, 381, 384
doctrinal lawyer, as 22–24, 25
EU 339, 380
Brexit 334–35
positivism and anti-positivism 25
preliminary references 107, 111–12
relevance of state paradigm 24–25
translatability of key principles 24–25
EU Administrative Law 2
EU Law: Text Cases and Materials. Craig, Paul and de Búrca, Gráinne 2, 381
explanandum rather than the *explanans*, law as the 22–23, 25
foundations of public law 2–3, 75
governance 381
Hamlyn lectures 2014 22, 339
historical, social, and political background 22, 23
holistic approach 22
institutions 4–5
judicial review 105

common law 83–84
heads 83
parliamentary intention 267–68
ultra vires 75–76, 83–84, 267–68
judiciary
justification of role 83
role 83, 320
justificatory ideas 23, 24–25
legality, principle of 267–68, 271
legislation 4
multilevel government 339
normative engagement 23–25
Once Upon a Time in the West article 381, 384
political regulation 326
political theory 3, 25
positivist/non-positivist distinction 25, 26
preliminary references 107, 111–12
process and procedure 5, 323–24, 326, 334–35
reputation and scholarship 2, 4, 22–25, 334–35
rule of law 257
six dimensions of public law 3
social science perspective 23
supranationalism 175
supremacy of EU law 381
textbooks 2, 22
theoretical foundations 22–25
translatability of key principles 24–25
ultra vires theory of judicial review 75–76, 83–84, 267–68
United States 339
criminal offences *see also* **Europol; police**
corruption 52–53, 58, 60–61
creation of offences 157–58, 160
European Arrest Warrant (EAW) 375, 376
European Criminal Records Information System (ECRIS) 244–45
European Criminal Records Information System for third country nationals (ECRIS-TCN) 244
maximum penalties 159–60
misconduct in public office 54–55
neglect of duty, offence of 54–55
office in politics of 18th century 52–55, 58, 60–61
terrorism 239, 242, 245, 248–49, 293
Croatia and migrant crisis 187, 188–89
crown *see* **the King**
Cuellár, Mariano-Florentino 253
culture
acquis communautaire 37–38
Brexit 43
common constitutional traditions 37–38
comparisons across legal cultures 195–98
courts 356
culturalism 21, 26, 27–28, 36, 37–39, 40–41
differentiation, paradox of 43
distinctiveness 38–39
elitism 37–39
enlargements 37–38
federalism 343
fundamental rights 37–38
general principles of EU law 37–38
German legal and political culture 196–97
imperialism 37–39
integration 40–41
judicial law-making 133
multilevel government 341, 352–53, 356, 359–60
politics 353, 359–60
pragmatism 42, 43–44
signifiers 40–41
socio-political and legal cultures 211–12
support, paradox of 42
universalism 37–39
custom or tradition 27–28

Daly, Paul 281–82
data mining 12, 240, 241–42
data protection 236–37, 238, 240–41, 253
Charter of Fundamental Rights of the EU 241, 242–43
General Data Protection Regulation (GDPR) 293
interoperability 243
privacy 240–41, 242–43
retention of data 238, 240, 242, 292–93
data sharing 12, 236–37, 240, 255
databases 233–37, 239, 254–55
accountability 251, 252
CJEU 114–15, 122–23
Europol 236, 245, 247–50
inflation 236–37
interoperability 243–46
joining up of European 236
law enforcement 236–37
Davis, KC 283
Davison, J 216
de Búrca, Gráinne 2, 381
de Hert, Paul 234–35
decentralisation 214
deductive reasoning 9–10, 84, 90–92
analogical reasoning 95–97, 102, 104–5
inductive reasoning 97, 98, 102
deformalisation, paradox of 42
Dehousse, Renaud 39–40

delegated legislation 145–71 *see also* **Donoughmore Committee; EU (Withdrawal Act) 2018 and delegated legislation**
absent legislator, problem of the 193, 199–205
abuses 145–46, 147–48
accountability of Parliament 145–46, 163–69
affirmative resolution procedure 162, 200
agency government 148–49
bills 152–54, 156, 157–60
Cabinet Office. *Guide for Making Legislation* 155, 156
centralisation 201
civil servants, attacks on 147–48
clarity 151
code of constitutional standards 157–58
committees 152–54, 162, 203–4
Deregulated Powers and Regulatory Reform Committee 152, 155, 156, 157–59, 161–62, 163
House of Lords Constitution Committee 145, 147, 155, 157–61
Joint Committee on Statutory Instruments 152, 161–62, 163
list of parliamentary 153*t*
policy scrutiny 152
proposals, scrutiny of 152
standing 151, 152
technical scrutiny 152
constitutional arrangements, alteration of 157–58
consultation 147
courts, control by 199
criminal offences
creation of 157–58, 160
maximum penalties 159–60
criteria for deciding between primary and secondary legislation 157–61
criticism 145–46, 147–48, 151, 154, 161
current practice 152–61
Delegated Legislation Committees, criticism of 162
democracy 13, 199–205
Deregulated Powers and Regulatory Reform Committee (DPRRC) 152, 155, 156, 157–59, 161–62, 163
deregulation programmes 149
Donoughmore Committee on Ministers' Powers 145–47, 148–52, 154, 155, 157–60
drafting 152–54, 202
emergency powers 146, 147
exceptional use of powers 149–51
expansion of delegated powers 154–55
expeditiousness 146, 200
experimentation 147
expertise 146, 200
absent legislator 200
administrative law 209–15, 216–18, 220–22, 224–26, 227, 228–29, 230
agency 209–10, 228
Attorney-General's Committee Report 1941 (US) 210–11, 224–26, 230
Donoughmore Committee 210–11, 230
forms 213–14
judicial law-making 131–34
New Deal 211–12
flexibility 146, 147, 156, 157, 200
grounds for quashing legislation 169–70
Henry VIII powers 10–11, 145, 149–50, 151–52, 155
Cabinet Office. *Guide for Making Legislation* 155
code of constitutional standards 157–58
Delegated Powers Memorandum 158–60
increase in use 155
House of Lords Constitution Committee 145, 147, 155, 157–61
interpretation 204–5
Joint Committee on Statutory Instruments 152, 161–62, 163
judiciary 145–46, 290
legitimacy 7, 146
levels of delegation 153*t*
negative resolution procedure 162, 200
normal use of powers 149–50
origin and rationale for delegated powers 146–49
ouster clauses 149–50, 151
Parliamentary and Legislative Business Committee (PBL Committee) 156
parliamentary oversight 7, 152–54, 200–1, 202
policy 146, 147, 149, 151, 152, 156
absent legislator 200, 201–2, 203–5
code of constitutional standards 157–58
scrutiny 152, 156–57
prayer motions 162
primary legislation 13–14, 200–1
amendments 157
criteria for distinguishing from secondary legislation 157–61
green papers 157
implementation 160–61
making 160–61
white papers 157
Public Law Project 169
public opinion 201–2
reasons for delegated powers 156–57, 200
regulatory state 148, 149

safeguards 145–46, 149–51
skeleton legislation 149–50, 152, 158–59
standing committees, role of 151, 152
sunset clauses 151
technical scrutiny 152
technicality of subject matter 147
time, limits on Parliamentary 146, 147, 148, 156
absent legislator 200, 201, 202–3
Brexit 202–3
time spent debating legislation 162–63, 163*t*
ultra vires 204–5
unforeseen contingencies, dealing with 147
United States, agency government in the 148–49
volume 146, 152, 161
voted down, number of SIs 161–62
welfare state, growth of 148, 149
wide delegation, problems of 149–50

Delmas-Marty, Mireille 386–87

democracy 193–206
19th century 46, 61–64
absent legislator 193–206
accountability 346–47, 352, 359
administrative law 212–13
application of law 197–98, 199
authority of the administration 7–8, 61–64
automation 254–55
Brexit, referendum on 400–2
CJEU 199
common law 61, 62, 197–98
comparisons across legal cultures 195–98
constitutionalism 212–13, 340–41
court's response to the absent legislator 195–99
deficits 63–64
delegated legislation 13, 199–205
delegation of authority 206
direct democracy 351–52
European Parliament, elections to 378–80
fairness 194
federalism 351–52, 359
German legal and political culture/UK 196–97
Health and Social Care Act 2012 8, 12–13, 271
inductive reasoning 97, 101, 102
institutions 79
interpretive role of courts 193–97, 198–200, 203–4, 205
judicial activism/creativity 195–96, 197
judicial law-making 193–206
judiciary and legislature, differences between law-making by 13–14
legitimacy 62–63, 101, 194, 195
literal interpretation 197
managerialism 197–98
multilevel government 344, 345–46, 347, 350, 359–61
accountability 346–47, 352, 359
constitutionalism 340–41
direct democracy 351–52
federation 351–52, 359
objects of public law in EU 20–21, 36, 37, 39–40, 42
office, concept of 46, 61–64
passenger name records (PNRs) 240
point of public law 77–78
post-democratic executive federalism 42
purposive/teleological interpretation 197, 199
rule of law 196–97
social expectations 196
sovereignty 7–8
support, paradox of 42
systemic violations by states of Article 2 TEU 11, 365, 370, 371, 378–80
temporal comparisons 195–96
United States/England 196, 197–98
utilitarianism 197–98
values 281

Denning, Lord (Denning, Alfred) 139–40, 141–42, 195

Department for Exiting the EU (DExEU) 405–6

devolution
Brexit 390–92, 393, 407, 411–12
Constitution of UK 390–92
federalism 343
indigenous people, self-government for 344
integration 6–7
multilevel government 277, 339–40
Westphalian state 382–83

Dicey, AV 147–48, 196–97, 216–18, 283, 389–90, 393–94

differentiation, paradox of 43

Diplock, Lord (Diplock, Kenneth) 280

direct and individual concern test 181–82, 305–6, 314

direct applicability 421

direct effect 384, 385–86, 412, 421

diverse objects of public law in EU 19–44
agency 39
conceptions of public law 25–28
constitutionalism 13, 43–44
culturalism 21, 26, 27–28, 36, 37–39, 40–41
democracy 20–21, 36, 37, 39–40, 42
foundations 11–12, 13, 19–44
integration 36, 39–41
legitimacy 21, 36–37, 43–44, 67
paradoxes 42–43
point of the state 67–68, 76–77
positivism 36, 39–40

diverse objects of public law in EU (*Contd.*)
pragmatism, limits of 42–44
special place of public law in EU 35–41
the state 19–21, 29–35
structural features 29–35, 39–40
supranationalism 20, 21, 29, 33, 36–37
theoretical foundations of EU 11–12, 19–44
Donaldson, Lord (Donaldson, John) 135
Donoughmore Committee
adjudication 226
administrative law 210–11
background 145–46, 222–23, 230
draft report 224
engaging with administrative material 210–11
expansion of powers 154, 155
expertise, fostering administrative 210–11, 230
final report, publication of 224
ideologies, reduction of legal reasoning to battle between 210–11
limits on public administration 223
origin and rationale for delegated legislation 146–47, 148–49
parliamentary sovereignty 222–23
primary and secondary legislation, criteria for deciding between 157–60
questionnaire 223–24, 227
recommendations 152
rule of law 224
safeguards 150–51
structural challenges 210–11, 227, 229, 231
terms of reference 222–25
wide delegation, problem of 149–50
dos Santos, Deir 424
drafting legislation
abstract drafting 174
Amsterdam Treaty, Declaration 39 to 175
better law-making 175
CJEU 13, 174–81, 193–94
clarity 177
Commission 175, 176–77, 179–80
Council 175, 176–77
delegated legislation 152–54
divergences between linguistic versions 177
English language 176–77, 178, 179–80
European Parliament 175, 176, 177
gap-filling 193–94
guidelines 175–76
Joint Practical Guide (JPG) of EP, Council and Commission 175
languages 174, 176–81
multinationalism 174, 176–77
Parliamentary Counsel 202
dualism 352, 354, 357, 363–64
Dublin III Regulation 186–89
burden sharing 186–89
criteria 186–89
Croatia 187, 188–89
Greece 189
Italy 189
migrant crisis 187, 188–89
time limits 187, 188
due process 234, 286–87, 297
Dworkin, Ronald 94–95, 139

ECSC *see* **European Coal and Steel Community (ECSC)**
Edward, David 109–11
efficiency and effectiveness
authority of the administration 7–8
automation 294, 297–98
Health and Social Care Act 2012 258, 265–66
judicial law-making 133
New Public Management (NPM) 283–84
office, concept of 63–64
preliminary rulings 113, 119
proceduralism 284, 285, 297
reasons, duty to give 300
systemic violations by states of Article 2 TEU 372–73, 374–75, 376–77
value for money (VFM) audits 284
elitism 37–39, 42, 346–47, 402
Elliott, Mark 75–76, 88–89
employment relationships, termination of 325–26
enlargement of EU 33, 37–38, 365–66
Entry/Exit System (EES) 244
environmental law 229
equality
Air Passengers Regulation 183–4
Brexit 43
common law 90–91, 97–98, 100, 102
Equality Act 2010 280–81
formal equality 97–98, 100, 102
public sector equality duty 280–81
substantive equality 97–98, 100, 102
Ericson, Richard 238
Ernst, Daniel 230–31
Erskine May: *Parliamentary Practice* 161
EU automated state 12, 233–56 *see also* **interoperability**
accountability 236, 242–43, 246–56
administrative decision-making 12
automation, definition of 233–34
bias in decision-making 12
blurring decision-making 237–38
Canada, agreement with 241–42

Charter of Fundamental Rights of the EU 241, 242–43
data assemblages 239–40, 255–56
data mining 12, 241–42
data protection 236–37, 238, 240–41, 242–26, 253
data sharing 12, 236–37, 240, 255
databases 233–37, 239, 251, 252, 254–55
deputisation of private actors 239–43
Eurodac 236–37, 244–45
Europol 236, 247–50, 253, 255
fragmentation 236
information
disconnect 250–51
power, centrality of information to 236
retention 238–39
sharing 238, 250–51, 252–53
institutions and officials 233–35, 236–39, 250–51
integration 238, 245, 255
legality challenges 240–43, 252–53, 254
opacity 250–51, 253–55
passenger name records (PNRs) 239–43
policing 236, 247–50, 251, 255–56
privacy 240–41, 242–43, 253
private actors
accountability and private and public actors 236
data assemblages 239–40
deputisation 239–43
proportionality 242–43
retention of data 238, 240, 242
secrecy 250, 251–53, 254
supranationalism 233, 234–35, 237–38
surveillance 237–38, 239, 242–43, 246
targeting methods 241

EU (Notification of Withdrawal) Bill 2017 330, 426

EU (Withdrawal) Act 2018 421–23 *see also* **EU (Withdrawal Act) 2018 and delegated legislation**
complexity 421–23
executive power, increase in 422
exit day, definition of 421–22
individual rights 414–15
multilevel government 346
process and procedure 330, 331–32
retention, amendment or repeal decisions 421
Scotland 391–92
Sewel Convention 346
Withdrawal Agreement 420, 421–22

EU (Withdrawal Act) 2018 and delegated legislation 7, 163–69
affirmative procedure 165, 166, 168–69
amend by regulation, power to 166
bill 145, 165–67
breadth of powers 164–65, 167, 170–71
committees 165–69
complexity 422–23
deficiencies, power to remedy 164
Delegated Legislation Committees 169
Delegated Powers and Regulatory Reform Committee (DPRRC) 145, 165, 166–67
deregulation by stealth 168–69
executive, transfer of powers to the 10–11, 145–46
Henry VIII powers 10–11, 145, 164–65
affirmative procedure 165
negative resolution procedure 165
volume of delegated legislation 168–69, 170–71
House of Lords
Constitution Committee 145, 165, 166–67
Secondary Legislation Scrutiny Committee (SLSC) 169
judiciary, role of 145–46, 170–71
negative resolution procedure 165, 166
policy decisions 167, 168–69
reaction 165–67
realisation 168–69
reassurances 167
remit 164–65
sifting mechanism 166, 168–69
sunset clause 165
technical changes 167
tertiary secondary legislation 164–65, 166
ultra vires 163–64, 166–67
vagueness 164–65
volume of delegated legislation 168–69, 170–71
White Paper 167

Eurodac 236–37, 244–45

European Arrest Warrant (EAW) 375, 376

European Coal and Steel Community (ECSC) 307–8, 313–14, 320–21
High Authority 300–1, 308–18
Treaty 300–1, 309–13, 314, 315–17

European Convention on Human Rights (ECHR) 365, 368–69, 370, 375

European Criminal Records Information System (ECRIS) 244–45

European Criminal Records Information System for third country nationals (ECRIS-TCN) 244

European Parliament, elections to 378–80

European Supervisory Authorities (ESAs) 299–300, 301–2
European Travel Information and Authorisation System (ETIAS) 244
European Union *see* **Brexit**
Europol 244, 245–50
accountability 249–50, 255
automation 236–37, 247–50, 253, 255
Convention 236–37, 247–48
databases 236, 245, 247–50
EU-LISA, memorandum of understanding with 245–46
Europol Information System (EIS) 247–49
Europol Regulation 247
intelligence sharing 247–49
interoperability 249–50
liaison officers 247–48
National Unit 249
Operational Centre 248–49
private parties, information sharing with 249
SIENA 247–49
SIS II 245–46
statistics 248–49
strategic partnerships 249
terrorism 248–49
United States 248–49
VIS 245–46
Euroscepticism 387–88, 393
Eurozone 42–43
ever closer union 33, 193–94
executive *see also* **civil service; multilevel government; Prime Minister**
accountability 13–14, 405, 407, 408
automation 233
Brexit 424–26, 427–28
accountability 405
domination of EU executive 419–20
EU (Withdrawal) Act 2018 10–11, 145–46, 422
legislature 421, 422
negotiations 418–20
process and procedure 417–20
Cabinet 405–6, 416, 417–18
Enlightenment 212–13
EU (Withdrawal) Act 2018 10–11, 145–46, 422
foundations of public law 5–6
gap-filling 193–94
legislature 424–26
accountability 407, 408
Brexit 417–18, 421, 422
multilevel government 357–58
ministerial responsibility 390–91
multilevel government 357–58
parliamentary or presidential systems 357–58
prerogative powers 424–26
process and procedure 325–26
reasons, duty to give 299–304, 307–8, 315, 316–21
sovereignty 7–8

fairness
democracy 194
fair trial, right to a 286, 375, 376
Health and Social Care Act 2012 258–59
judiciary 288, 289, 290–91
proceduralism 279, 280–81, 286, 297
process and procedure 326–27
values 288, 289, 290–91
farmers, deductions from aid under direct support schemes to 179–81
federalism
aggregation 342–43
autonomy 343–44
Bundestreue or federal loyalty 358–59
'coming together' 342–43
consent 343
constitutional amendment 342
constitutionalism 347–49
culture 343
definition 342, 343–44
democracy 351–52, 359
design 342–44, 352
devolution 343
disaggregation 342–43
federacies 393
'holding together' 342–43
integration 6–7, 354, 357
interdependence 347
multilevel government 339–40, 342–44, 358–59
constitutionalism 347–49
democracy 351–52, 359
design 342–44, 352
integrated federations 354, 357
interdependence 347
parliamentary sovereignty 348–49
plurinational federalism 349–50
rule of law 351–52
parliamentary sovereignty 348–49
plurinational federalism 348, 349–50
post-democratic executive federalism 42
regionalism 343–44
responsible government 348–49
rule of law 351–52
secession 342–43
separation of powers 342

shared rule 342
structure 342–43
financial markets
European Central Bank (ECB) 299–300, 301–2, 315, 316–17, 320
European Securities and Markets Authority (ESMA) 301–2
market intervention 301–3, 320
permanent reconciliation 318
regulation 299–300, 301–2, 315–18
short-selling 299–300, 301–2
Single Resolution Board (SRB) 299–300, 301–2, 315, 316–17, 320
Single Resolution Mechanism (SRM) 301–2, 316–17
threats to financial stability 301–3
Finnis, John 69–70, 71
Fischer, Joschka 382
fitness for human habitation 220–21
Fookes, Baroness (Fookes, Janet) 156
formalism 37, 197
foundations of public law 5–10
executive 5–6, 7–8
futures 1–2, 14–15
point of public law 75
process of law-making 5–6
rule of law 5–6
sovereignty and the state 5–7
trusts as foundational idea of public law 76–78
Fox, Ruth 154, 158–60, 162
France 347–48
Frank, Jerome 209–10, 216–17, 227, 230–31
Frankfurter, Felix 216, 217–18
free movement 379, 413–14
free riders 40
freedom of expression 378–79
freedom of information 228, 281–82, 325–26
freedom of the press 378–79
French Civil Code 174
Fry, Brian 213
Fuchs, Ralph 216–17
functionalism
office, concept of 62, 63–64
point of the state 68–69, 74
proceduralism 282–83
process and procedure 326–27, 328
values 282–83
fundamental rights *see* **individual rights**
futures of public law 1–2, 10–15

gap-filling 190, 193–94
Gardner, John 86
general principles of EU law 37–38, 308, 414–15
Germany
Bundesrat 354
centralisation 348
German Bürgerliches Gesetzbuch 174
Rechtsstaat 8, 196–97, 276
global financial crisis 42
globalisation 1, 13
centralisation 349
multilevel government 344, 349, 351, 360
sovereignty 351
state, beyond the 20
glocalisation 344
government *see* **executive**
Greece and migrant crisis 189
Griffith, JAG 282–83
Griffiths, John 385–86
Grimm, Dieter 340–41, 413–14
Gutwirth, Serge 234–35
Gwyer, Maurice 223, 224

habeas corpus 142
Habermas, Jürgen 36
Haggerty, Kevin 238
Haldane Committee 214
Haldane, Viscount (Haldane, Richard) 220–21
Harlow, Carol 209–10, 324, 326–28
Hart, HLA 386
Hayek, Friedrich 31–32
Hazell, Robert 157–58
Health and Social Care Act 2012 257–71
abuse of a dominant position 260
Accountable Care Organisations (ACOs) 263, 264–70
anti-competitive agreements 260, 261, 262
austerity measures 12–13
Brexit 12–13
Care Quality Commission (CQC) 259–60
changing agenda 262–70
Clinical Commissioning Groups (CCGs) 260–71
Accountable Care Organisations (ACOs) 263, 264–70
annual reports 261–62
performance assessments 261–62
Competition and Markets Authority (CMA) 260
competition law 260–62
consultation 263
context 258–62
democracy 8, 12–13, 271
discretion 269–70
efficiency 258, 265–66
equity 258–59
fairness 258–59
fundamentals of administrative law 267–70

Health and Social Care Act 2012 (*Contd.*)
GPs
Clinical Commissioning Groups (CCGs) 260–61
fundholders 259
Hutchinson case 257–58, 264–70
integrated care model 8, 257–58, 262–71
consultation 263
Integrated Care Partnership (ICP) model 263, 264–70
internal market, introduction of 8, 257–62
judicial review 257–58, 264–70
legality principle 267–70, 271
legitimacy 13–14
New Public Management (NPM) 258–59
NHS England 261–62, 263, 264, 271
NHS Forward View 262–63
NHS Foundation Trusts 259–60
NHS Improvement (Monitor) 259–60, 261, 262, 266, 271
NHS Long-Term Plan 271
NHS Trusts 259–60, 271
policy 12–13, 257–58, 262, 269–70
politics 258–59
Primary Care Trusts (PCTs) 259, 260–61
private providers 258–59
procurement 259, 261
providers 258–60
purchasers/commissioners 258–62, 264–67
quality of services 259–60
rule of law 12–13, 257
Shepherd case 257–58, 264–70
statutory interpretation 264–67, 268–70
Sustainability and Transformation Plans (STPs) 262–63
tariffs 259, 260, 264–70
ultra vires 8, 257–58, 264–70
Whole Population Annual Payment (WPAP) 264–70
Hen, Christian 314
Henderson, Edith 48
Henry VIII powers 10–11, 145, 149–50, 151–52
affirmative resolution procedure 165
Brexit 10–11, 145, 155, 164–65, 168–69, 170–71
Cabinet Office. *Guide for Making Legislation* 155
code of constitutional standards 157–58
Delegated Powers Memorandum 158–60
increase in use 155
negative resolution procedure 165
volume of delegated legislation 168–69, 170–71
heuristics 93–94, 95–96
Hewart, Lord (Hewart, Gordon) 61–62, 145–46, 147–48, 218, 223, 224
Hobbes, Thomas 206, 386–87
human rights *see* **individual rights**
Hume, David 60–61
Hungary 367

idealism 26, 27
identity
multilevel government 349–50, 359–60
national identity 349–50
political identity 29–30, 31
social institution constituted by rules, identity of state as a 68, 72–73
ideology 8, 45, 209–11, 229–30
impartiality 12, 279, 281, 297
imperialism 37–39
indigenous people, self-government for 344
individual rights 41, 414–15 *see also* **Charter of Fundamental Rights of the EU**
common law 45, 52, 65, 97, 100
culturalism 37–38
European Convention on Human Rights 365, 368–69, 370, 375
fair trial, right to a 375, 376
Human Rights Act 1998 279–80, 390–91
inhuman or degrading treatment 375
life, right to 92–93
office, concept of 63, 64
privacy 240–41, 242–43, 253
process and procedure 325–26
reasons, duty to give 365–69
systemic violations by states of Article 2 TEU 8–9, 11, 363, 365–69, 371–72
United States, civil rights in 349
inductive reasoning 9–10, 84, 91–92, 95–102, 104–5
information technology *see* **EU automated state**
inhuman or degrading treatment 375
institutions 3, 399, 405–10
19th century 211
accountability 233–34, 250–51, 405–10
administrative law 210, 212–13, 219–20, 227, 228–29, 230–31
automation 233–34, 236–39, 250–51
Brexit 405–10
creation of institutions 79
democracy 79
design 339–40
functionalism 68–69
independence 40
informal institutions 236–39

integration 238
Interinstitutional Agreement 1998 175
interoperability 234–35, 243–44
judicial law-making 133
judicial neutrality 41
law enforcement 239
reasons, duty to give 8, 299–321
risk regulation instruments 233
state as an institution 68–69, 72
supranationalism 237–38
integration 36, 39–41
agency 39–40
automation 238, 245, 255, 293
Brexit 6–7, 403–4, 408
culture 40–41
federalism 6–7
flexible integration 43
institutions 238
intergovernmentalism 403–4
multilevel government 354, 359
politics 39
positivism 39
reasons, duty to give 299–301, 311–13, 315, 316
the state 30–31
systemic violations by states of Article 2 TEU 365, 369, 370–71
universalism 40–41
intergovernmentalism 350–51, 353–57, 360, 403–4
internal market 36
international relations 349
Internet 228, 291–92
interoperability of public platforms 243–46, 254–55
accountability 236, 243, 251–52
common identity repository 244
definition 234–35
error 251–52
Eurodac 244–45
Europol 244, 245–46, 249–50
information sharing 243–44, 251–52
institutions 234–35, 243–44
legitimacy 234–35
migration control 245
multiple identity detector 244
passenger name records (PNRs) 244–45
police 243, 244, 245–46
private and public actors, joining up of 236
regulation 243–46
search portal 244
supranationalism 234–35, 243
Visa Information System (VIS) 244–46
Interpol's Stolen and Lost Travel Documents database 244
interpretation *see also* **Court of Justice (CJEU) in ruling on meaning of EU legislation, role of; purposive/teleological interpretation**
absent legislator 193–97, 198–200, 203–4, 205
constitutions 356–59
delegated legislation 204–5
democracy 193–97, 198–200, 203–4, 205
German legal and political culture/ UK 196–97
Health and Social Care Act 2012 264–67, 268–70
literal interpretation 173–74, 180, 190, 197
multilevel government 340
point of the state 68, 69–70, 74
preliminary rulings 108, 112–13, 116–22, 123, 124
reasons, duty to give 300
systematic interpretation 311
United States 197–98
Interstate Commerce Commission (ICC) 212–14, 215, 219–20

Jacobs, Francis 109, 118–19, 181–82, 368–69
Jaffe, Louis 197, 210
James VI and I, King of Scotland, England and Ireland 49
James VII and II, King of Scotland, England and Ireland 51
James, William 386
Jasanoff, Sheila 210–11
Jennings, Ivor 160
Jessop, Philip 382–83
Judge, Lord (Judge, Igor) 155
judgments
default judgments 128
execution 129
explanatory effect 131–33, 140
final, treating judgments as 130
legal effects 131–33, 140, 141
nature of judgments 127
norm, giving judgment is making a particular 129
ostensive effect 131–33, 140, 141
primary role of court as giving judgments 7, 128–29
reflexive, treating judgments as 130
valid, treating judgments as 130
judicial law-making 127–42 *see also* **precedent**
abstraction, technique of 137–39, 140–41
adversarial advocacy 128, 133
analogical reasoning 9–10, 13, 84, 89–90, 91–97, 104–5, 139

judicial law-making (*Contd.*)
appellate courts, promotions to get accomplished judges into 133
apply the law, duty to 134, 137
appointment and selection of judges 133
authority 131, 134–36
contextualised approach 14
coordination 132–34
cultural support 133
democracy 193–206
dissenting judgments 133
distinguishing 140
effectiveness 161
equity 133–34
execution of judgments 129
expertise 131–34
explanatory effect of judgments 131–33, 140
favourable statements of law 131
final, treating judgments as 130
flexibility 134
heroic law-making 136–37, 139, 141, 142
incidental jurisdiction to change the law 7, 9–10, 127, 134–36
innovation 127, 128, 135–36, 137–38, 139, 140, 141–42
institutional support 133
judgments, primary role of court as giving 7, 128–31
judicial activism 95, 173, 193–94, 195–96, 197, 280–81
judicial restraint 181–82
legal effects of judgments 140, 141
background and training of judges 133
explanatory effect 131–33, 140
ostensive effect 131–33, 136, 140, 141
legitimacy of the state 14
liability, rulings as to 129
nature of judgments 127
norm, giving judgment is making a particular 129
open-endedness of common law 137–41
ostensive effect of judgments 131–33, 140, 141
paradox of judicial law-making 7, 134–36, 141
prestige of courts 133
purposive law-making 127
reasons, giving 133
reflexive, treating judgments as 130
rule of law 128–29, 132, 134–35, 137, 141–42
source-based, case law is 127–28
standard case 136–37
statute law/legislation 127–28, 132, 134, 140–41
training of judges 133
judicial review
abductive reasoning 95
abstract review 87–89, 91, 99, 100–1, 104–5
adjudication, theory of 94–95
administrative law 219–22, 225–26
analogical reasoning 103–4
authority of the administration 13, 45–46
automation 12, 240, 295–96
centralisation 358
common law 13, 83–85, 87–88, 90–91, 96, 105
heads 84, 90, 96
permission 87–88
taxonomies 84, 90–91
Wednesbury unreasonableness 90–91
constitutionalism 345–46
delegation 295–96
development of principles 83–84
direct and individual concern 314
ECSC 313–14
expansion 325–26
fact/law distinction 219–20
fettering discretion 295–96
heads 90, 96
Health and Social Care Act 2012 257–58, 264–70
lower court/court of appeal analogy 219–20
multilevel government 358, 359–60
office, concept of 48, 62–64
ouster clauses 102–4, 149–50, 151
permission 87–88
point of public law 76–77, 78
pre-emptive judicial review 240
procedural review 287, 289, 290–91
proceduralism 277, 279, 280, 281, 286, 289–90
process and procedure 324, 325–26, 327
public understanding 313–14
reasons, duty to give 300–1, 302–4, 305–6, 309–10, 318
direct and individual concern 314
ECSC 313–14
High Authority 313
public understanding 313–14
transparency 313–14
relevant and irrelevant considerations 295–96
specificity, absence of 88
substantial evidence test 219–20
systemic violations by states of Article 2 TEU 369, 374–75, 378
taxonomies 84, 90–91
transparency 313–14
ultra vires 13, 45, 78
United States Supreme Court 219–20, 222
values 281, 327
Wednesbury unreasonableness 90–91, 295–96
judiciary *see also* **common law; judicial law-making**
asylum decisions, fast-tracking 290–91

authority of the administration 46
background of judges 133
centralised bureaucratic hierarchy 62
civil jurisdictions 37
civil service 62
consult, duty to 289–90
delegation 49–50
EU (Withdrawal Act) 2018 145–46, 170–71
German legal and political culture/ UK 196–97
independence 49–50, 58–59, 65, 373–78
Judge Over Your Shoulder (JOYS) 288–89
Judicial Appointments Commission 325–26
legal formalism 37
parliamentary sovereignty 62–63, 290
planning cases 288
proceduralism 286–91
process and procedure 325–26
property, office as 57–58
R (Osborn) v Parole Board 286–87
rationality 64
reasons, giving 287–89
retirement age 367
Ridge v Baldwin 286–87
rule of law 286, 291
tenure 49
training 133
values 286–87

Juncker, Jean-Claude 237–38, 404, 410
juridification 275–76, 286, 296

Kelsen, Hans 7, 129–31, 135, 136
the King
courts, passing of prerogatives to 48
delegation 49–50
forfeiture of kingship 51
independence of subordinate officials 46, 49–50
personal or direct rule 49, 51
power, limits of 46
prerogative powers 47, 48, 51
property in trust, kingship as 51
King, Jeff 193, 199–201, 203–5
Kingly power, limits of 46
Koops, Bert-Jaap 255

languages
interpretation 174, 176–81
official languages 7
preliminary rulings 108–9
Laski, Harold 389
law-making *see* **judicial law-making**
Laws, John 85
legal certainty
common law 97–98, 99–100, 105
deformalisation, paradox of 42
proceduralism 279–80
rules and standards, difference between 97–98, 99–100
legal pluralism 385–87, 390–91
legal realism 216, 227
legality, principle of
analogical reasoning 103–4
automation 240–43, 252–53, 254
delegated legislation 203, 204–5
foundational legality 270
Health and Social Care Act 2012 267–70, 271
passenger name records (PNRs) 240–43
policy 203, 204
reasons, duty to give 300–1, 303–6
legislation *see also* **delegated legislation; Court of Justice (CJEU) in ruling on meaning of EU legislation, role of; primary legislation**
the absent legislator 193, 199–205
accountability 405
adjudication and legislation, difference between 173, 189–91
agent, legislation as made by more than one 86
amendment by legislation 197–98
argumentation and discussion, doctrines in case law as arising from 86
Brexit 420–24
accountability 405
complexity of legislation 421–24
EU 423–24
macro-level 421–22, 423
micro-level 422–24
UK 421–23
case law distinguished 86
common law 52, 53
complexity of legislation 421–24
intentionally made, legislation as being 86
judicial law-making 127–28, 132, 134, 140–41
office in politics of 18th century 52, 59–60
open-endedness 140–41
parliamentary intention 86
point of public law 77–78
select committees 405
legislature *see* **parliament/legislature**
legitimacy 21, 43–44, 61–63, 67
authority of the administration 7–8, 12–13, 46
conceptions of public law 25–26
democracy 37, 62–63, 101, 194, 195
Health and Social Care Act 2012 13–14
input legitimacy 36–37
interoperability 234–35
judicial law-making 14
office, concept of 52–53, 61–63

legitimacy (*Contd.*)
- positivism 26, 37
- supranationalism 21
- United States 198

legitimate expectations 289, 325–26
Leijon, Karen 119
Lenin, Vladimir 73–74
life, right to 92–93
Lisvane, Lord (Rogers, Robert) 155, 165, 166–67
local administration *see also* **regionalism**
- 17th century 47–48
- 18th century 48, 52–53
- agencies 48
- arbitrary removal from office 48
- central government, relationship with 47
- Commonwealth 48
- democracy 61–62
- Independents of the Long Parliament 48
- Justices of Peace 47

Locke, John 47
locus standi 181–82, 305–6, 314
Loughlin, Martin 5–6, 8–9, 45, 78
Low, Sidney 391

Maastricht Treaty *see* **systemic violations by states of Article 2 TEU**
MacCormick, Neil 383
Mackenzie Stuart, Alexander 109
McLean, Janet 67–68, 71–72, 76–77, 78
maladministration 54
Malhotra, Seema 156–57
managerialism
- complaints-handling 279
- democracy 197–98
- New Public Management (NPM) 46, 258–59, 277, 283–85, 327
- proceduralism 278–79, 282–85, 296–97
- process and procedure 326–27
- values 327

Mashaw, Jerry 280–81, 287, 319
media 332, 378–79
Mendes, Joana 327–28
Micheler, Eva 293–94
migrants and asylum seekers
- crisis 187, 188–89
- Eurodac 236–37, 244–45
- fast-tracking asylum decisions 290–91
- terrorism 237–38, 245
- Visa Information System (VIS) 245

Miller, Gina 424
Milsom, SFC 197–98
ministerial responsibility 216–17
misconduct in public office 54–55
monarch *see* **the King**
monopoly of state of use of force 70
Montesquieu, Charles-Louis de 173–74
multilevel government 339–61, 381 *see also* **federalism**
- accountability 345–47, 352, 353, 355, 360
- Australia 346–47, 348–49, 355, 359
- balance between levels of government 345
- Brexit 346
- centralisation 340, 349, 353, 354–55, 358, 359–60
- citizenship 351, 356–57
- constitutionalism 11–12, 340–41, 345–61
- context 354, 356–58
- courts 356–59
- culture 341, 352–53, 356, 359–60
- democracy 344, 345–46, 347, 350, 359–61
  - accountability 346–47, 352, 359
  - constitutionalism 340–41
  - direct 351–52
  - federation 351–52, 359
- design 342–44, 352, 354, 355–56, 357–58
- devolution 277, 339–40
- dualism 352, 354, 357
- globalisation 344, 349, 351, 360
- identity 349–50, 359–60
- indigenous people, self-government for 344
- integration 354, 359
- intergovernmental relations 350–51, 353–58, 360
  - allocation of responsibilities 351
  - concurrency 357, 358
  - design 355–56, 357–58
  - mutual consideration 352
  - subsidiarity 358–59
- international relations 349
- judicial interpretation 340
- judicial review 358, 359–60
- justiciability of standards 358–59
- law 356–59
- localised decision-making 339–40, 344
- multilevel government 13, 339–40, 341–45
- nation, definition of 350
- national identity 349–50
- parliamentary sovereignty 348–49
- policy 346–47
- politics 341, 352, 353–56, 357–58, 359–60
- proceduralism 277
- public interest 352
- public understanding 346–47
- regionalism 343–44, 347–48, 360–61
- rule of law 346–47, 351–52
- secession 352
- separation of powers 342, 345, 348–49
- sovereignty 351
- subsidiarity 358–59

suprastate government 360
transparency 346–47, 352, 355
trust 352, 354
under-performance 340–41
unitary states 342–44, 347, 349–50, 353, 356, 358, 359–60
values 350, 351–52
vertical constraints 345, 353

multinationalism 174, 176–77
Munro, Horace 220

National Health Service *see* **Health and Social Care Act 2012**
nation state *see* **the state**
nationalism 11
natural law 27, 51, 79, 286–87, 325
neglect of duty, offence of 54–55
Neighbourhood Policy 37–38
Nepal 340
Neumann, Franz 196–97
New Approach to Harmonization 40
New Public Management (NPM) 46, 258–59, 277, 283–85, 327
NHS *see* **Health and Social Care Act 2012**
Nolan standards for conduct in public life 279–80
nomocracy and teleocracy, distinction between 31–32
Northern Ireland
backstop 415, 421–22
devolution 11–12
referendum on Brexit 391–92

notification of withdrawal from EU under Article 50 424–26
abuse of system 427, 428–29
Commission 427, 428–29
European Council 427, 428–29
executive and legislature, balance between 424–26, 427–28
Parliament, approval of 424–26
prerogative powers 424–26
revocation 426–29
abuse of system 427, 428–29
Commission 427, 428–29
conditions 426–27
European Council 427, 428–29
Scottish Court of Session 427
sovereignty 427–28
unilateral 427–28
veto, giving each member state a 428–29
Scottish Court of Session 427
sovereignty 427–28
triggering notification 424–26
unilateral revocation 427–28
veto, giving each member state a 428–29

nuisance legislation 215
Nyikos, Stacy 119

Oakeshott, Michael 31–32
oaths 53
obiter dicta 131
objects of public law in EU *see* **diverse objects of public law in EU**
Øe, Saugmandsgaard 240
office in politics of 17th century 46, 47–51
absolute sovereignty 49
arbitrary removal from office 48, 49
authority 46, 47–51
autonomy 48
common law 47, 48, 51
conferral of power 49–50
constitutional and administrative law, relationship between 51
constitutionalism 47, 51
delegation 49–50, 51
forfeiture of kingship 51
high politics 47
how authority was conferred 49–50
independence of subordinate officials 46, 49–50
judicial review, limited 48
judiciary, independence of the 49–50
jural status, office-holding as conferring a 49
King
courts, passing of prerogatives to 48
delegation 49–50
forfeiture of kingship 51
independence of subordinate officials 46, 49–50
personal or direct rule 49, 51
power, limits of 46
prerogative powers 47, 48, 51
property in trust, kingship as 51
local administration 47–48
Parliament, powers of 47
personal or direct rule 49, 51
profit, offices for 50
property, office as 48, 49, 50–51
sovereignty 48, 49, 50, 67–68
tenure 49

office in politics of 18th century 51–61
authority 46, 51–61, 64
bonds/sureties, payment of 53, 55
centralisation 52
civic virtue, reinforcement of 53–56, 60–61
civil service 56–57
common law 51–56
constitutionalism 51–52
corruption 60–61
delegation 58

office in politics of 18th century (*Contd.*)
individual rights, protection of 51–52
misconduct in public office 54
property, office as 57–58
public trust offences 54–55
statute 52, 53
virtue, enforcement of 53
conferral of duties 52
conflicts of interest 59
corruption 52–53, 58, 60–61
criminal law 52–55, 58, 60–61
delegation 52, 58–59
deputies, use of 58–59
disqualifications 56–57
enforcement of civic duties 53–55
Entick v Carrington 51
fines for refusal of office 53
House of Commons, service in the 56–57
independence
citizenship 56
House of Commons, service in the 56–57
patronage 56–57
restoration of independence on property 57–61
upholding 56–57
judicial review, limited 48
judiciary
independence 58–59
property, office as 57–58
legitimacy 52–53
local administration 48, 52–53
maladministration 54
misconduct in public office 54–55
neglect of duty, offence of 54–55
oaths 53
patronage 56–57
profits from office 53
property, office as 51, 57–61
propriety and the official 51–61
public trust 46, 54–55, 58
republicanism 52–53, 56
restoration of independence on property 57–61
sale of offices 58, 59–60
statutes 52, 59–60
Tories 52–53, 57
vicarious liability 55
virtue, enforcement of 53
Whigs 52–53, 57
official secrets 287
officials 46–64 *see also* **office in politics of 17th century; office in politics of 18th century**
19th century 46, 61–64, 65, 67
20th century 46, 61–64
agents, public servants as 61
authority 46, 61–64, 65
automation 233–34, 236–39, 250–51
centralised hierarchy 46, 61–62, 63, 65
civic virtue, reinforcing 53–56
common law 61, 62
concept of office 46–64
delegation 64
democracy 46, 61–64
discretion 62
efficiency 63–64
functionalism 62, 63–64
independence 56–62, 65
individual rights 63, 64
judges, independence of 65
judicial review 62–64
judiciary 62–63, 64
Kingly power, limits of 46
legitimacy 61–63
local administration 61–62
new bases of authority 63–64
ouster clauses, enforcement of 62–63
parliamentary sovereignty 62–63
privatised administration 63
propriety and the official 51–61, 76–78
public trust 46, 65
restoration of independence in property 57–61
social service state 61–62
technocratic administration 63–64
transnational administration 63
ultra vires 62, 63, 64
Oliver, Dawn 157–58
ombudspersons 277
Open Method of Coordination (OMC) 40, 284–85
Orwell, George 238
ouster clauses 62–63, 102–4

Page, Edward C 154
parking adjudication 295
parliament/legislature *see also* **parliamentary sovereignty**
accountability
Brexit 405, 407–8
delegated legislation 145–46, 163–69
administrative decision-making 220–22
authority claims 62–63
Brexit
accountability 405, 407–8
executive 417–18, 421, 422, 424–26
process and procedure 331–32, 416–19
centralised bureaucratic hierarchy 63
delegated legislation 199, 200–1, 202
Erskine May: *Parliamentary Practice* 161

executive 424–26
accountability 407, 408
Brexit 417–18, 421, 422
multilevel government 357–58
German legal and political culture/UK 196–97
hereditary peers, removal of 390–91
intention of Parliament 78, 86
judicial law-making 13–14
majority, lack of 417
notification of withdrawal 424–26
office in politics of 17th century 47
office in politics of 18th century 56–57
process and procedure 325–26
purposive interpretation 127
Scotland 392–93
Withdrawal Agreement 416–17, 418–19
parliamentary sovereignty
1688 constitutional settlement 393
analogical reasoning 104–5
bind its successors, parliament cannot 400–1
Brexit 388, 389–90, 393, 394, 400–2, 407–8
common law 89–90
Constitution of the UK 390–91
continuing nature 400–1
democracy 62–63
federalism 348–49
German legal and political culture/UK 196–97
House of Commons 419
judiciary 62–63, 290
multilevel government 348–49
popular sovereignty 400–2
prerogative powers 425
rule of law 89–90
passenger name records (PNRs) 239–43
algorithms 240
consent 240
data assemblages and private actors 239–40
directive 239
EU-US PNR agreement 239
interoperability 244–45
legality 240–43
privacy 240
terrorism 239
United States 239–40
patronage 56–57
personal or direct rule 49, 51
Pettit, Philip 68–69, 71
planning cases 288
Pocock, JGA 51–53
Poiares Maduro, Miguel 381, 387–88
point of public law 67, 74–79
citizenship 77–79
constraint, as a 76
democracy 77–78
fiduciary relationship between state and members 76–78
foundations of public law 75
institutions, creation of 79
judicial review 76–77, 78
justificatory practice, as 78
offices as property 76–78
property law analogy 76–78
rights focus 76
sources of law 76
trusts as foundational idea of public law 76–78
well-being 76
point of the state 67–79
actual purpose 71, 73–74
capacity of the state 68, 69–71, 72
community cohesion 71
constitutional principles, state as a source of 13–14
emergence of the state 68–69
empirical assessment 71
fiduciary relationship between state and members 76–78
functionalist claim 68–69, 74
institution, state as a 68–69, 72
interpretivist claim 68, 69–70, 74
judicial review 13
moral evaluation 68, 69–71
nature of the state 67
ostensible point 71, 73–74
persistence of the state 68–69
public law, point of 67, 74–79
social institution constituted by rules, identity of state as a 68, 72–73
structure of the state 70–71
well-being of members, advancement of 68, 69–70, 72–74, 76
Poland 11, 373, 375, 376–77
police *see also* **Europol**
automation 236, 238, 243–50, 251–52, 255–56
interoperability 243, 244, 245–46
personal records 234
police and security cooperation 236
secrecy 251–52
policy
amendments to primary legislation 200
automation 291–92
Brexit 167, 168–69, 202
delegated legislation 146, 147, 149, 151, 152, 156, 161
absent legislator 200, 201–2, 203–5
code of constitutional standards 157–58
EU (Withdrawal Act) 2018 167, 168–69
scrutiny 152, 156–57

policy (*Contd.*)
- EU (Withdrawal Act) 2018 167, 168–69
- Health and Social Care Act 2012 12–13, 257–58, 262, 269–70
- high policy 203–5
- legality, principle of 203, 204
- multilevel government 346–47
- Neighbourhood Policy 37–38
- partisan disagreement 203, 205
- primary legislation 200
- proceduralism 284, 291–77
- public opinion 201–2

Political Declaration (Brexit) 416, 418–19

politics 20–21 *see also* **office in politics of 17th century; office in politics of 18th century**
- 17th century 7–8, 47–51, 64, 67
- 18th century 46, 51–61, 64, 67
- 19th century 46, 61, 65, 67
- accountability 233, 254
- CJEU 175, 189, 193–94
- culture 353, 359–60
- delegated legislation 200–2, 203–4
- German legal and political culture 196–97
- Health and Social Care Act 2012 258–59
- identity 29–30, 31
- integration 39
- multilevel government 341, 352, 353–56, 357–58, 359–60
- reasons, duty to give 300, 311, 316–17
- sovereignty 8–9, 29–30, 48, 49, 50, 67–68
- supranationalism 36
- systemic violations by states of Article 2 TEU 366–67, 370
- unitary states 353

popular sovereignty 389–90, 400–2

populism 11

Port, Frederick 227

Portugal 373–75, 377

positivism 26, 27, 28, 37, 39, 196–97

Pound, Ezra 218

pragmatism 26, 28, 42–44

precedent 85–87, 135–36, 142
- abstraction, technique of 138, 139
- analogical reasoning 94
- definition 86
- distinguishing 140
- evolution of common law 85
- explanatory effect 131–33, 140
- justice 132
- ostensive aspect 131–33, 140, 141
- overruling 140
- preliminary rulings 109–10
- rule of law 132
- standards, precedents as 99–100
- *stare decisis* 131, 132

preliminary ruling mechanism and relationship between UK courts and CJEU 107–25
- academic literature 112–13, 114, 116–17, 123–24
- Advocates General, influence of British 108–9, 110–11, 121–22
- Brexit 11, 107, 108–9, 110–11, 124–25
- CJEU on UK courts, influence of 107, 112–15
- clear influence 121–22
- constitutional pluralism 116–17
- database of decisions following rulings 114–15, 122–23
- dialogue between national courts 116–17, 118–19, 123–24
- direct effect 112
- discrimination law 110–11
- drafting of judgments 109, 110–11
- English language 108–9, 110–11
- expedited or urgent procedure 117–18, 119
- French language 108–9
- government submissions, influence or impact of 116–17
- green light procedure 118–19
- guidance 113, 117–18
- influence of UK courts on CJEU 8–9, 107–8, 115–22, 123
  - Brexit 11
  - provisional views, encouragement to adopt 117–19
  - provisional views on UK courts, influence of 120–22
- informing CJEU of final decisions 114–15
- interpretation 108, 112–13, 116–22, 123, 124
- interventions to make observations 110–11, 120
- mandatory language 117–18
- mutual influence of UK courts and ECJ 111–22
- no attempted influence 121–22
- number of references 110–12, 115, 121–22
- oral hearings, asking questions during 109–10
- persuasive interpretations 116–17
- political sovereignty 8–9
- precedent, introduction of 109–10
- probable influence 121–22
- provisional opinions
  - clear influence 121–22
  - encouragement to adopt 117–19
  - no attempted influence 121–22
  - number 119, 122
  - probable influence 121–22
  - UK courts, influence of provisional views of 120–22, 123
  - unsuccessful attempted influence 121–22

purposive/teleological interpretation 112–13
reasons for references 117–18
received, stage at which rulings 113
return judgments 108, 113–15, 124
database of decisions 114–15, 122–23
implementation prejudice 114, 122–23
informing CJEU of final decisions 114–15
selection and appointment of judges 109
stage at which decisions to send are made 113
style of judgments 123
style of reasoning, changes in 109–10
supremacy of EU law 112, 116–17, 123–24
systemic violations by states of Article 2 TEU 373, 374
types of preliminary reference 110–11, 120–21
UK membership on CJEU, influence of 108–11
uniformity 123–24
unsuccessful attempted influence 121–22
voluntarism 117–18
willingness of UK court to send preliminary references to CJEU 110–12
prerogative powers 47, 48, 51, 424–26
primacy of EU law *see* **supremacy of EU law**
primary legislation
amendments 157
delegated legislation 13–14, 157–61, 200–1
drafting 202
green papers 157
policy 200
white papers 157
Prime Minister
accountability 405–8
Brexit 405–6, 417–18
Cabinet 405–6, 416, 417–18
Department for Exiting the EU 405–6
House of Commons 417–18
increase in power 407, 416, 417–18
legislature 412
majority, lack of 417
negotiations 405–6
process and procedure 417–18
privacy 240–41, 242–43, 253
private actors
automation 236, 239–43
Europol 249
Health and Social Care Act 2012 258–59
interoperability of public platforms 236
privatisation 63, 283–84
reasons, duty to give 301–3
private law/public law 97, 98–101, 102
proceduralism 13, 275–98, 324
automation 12, 278, 291–96, 297–98
bottom-up administrative justice 279
bureaucratic law-making 282–85
codification 276, 277
common law 8, 280, 282–83
consultation 282–83, 289
contextualisation 286–87
discretion 283
due process 297
economy, effectiveness and efficiency 284, 285, 297
equal treatment 280–81
fairness 279, 280–81, 286, 297
functionalism 282–83
governance 277–78, 285, 296–97
Human Rights Act 1998 279–80
impartiality 279, 281, 297
judicial engagement 286–91
judicial review 277, 279, 280, 281, 286, 289–90
juridification 275–76, 286, 296
legal certainty 279–80
managerialism 278–79, 282–85, 286–87, 296–97
multilevel governance 277
New Public Management (NPM) 277, 283–85
ombudspersons 277
policy 284, 291–77
prioritisation 280–81
proceduralisation 278, 282–83, 296, 326–27
definition of 275
drivers 286
internal drivers 277
judicial engagement 286, 287, 288, 289
juridification 286
New Public Management (NPM) 284
regulation 285
proceduralism, definition of 275–76
procedure, definition of 275
professionalisation of civil service 282–83
proportionality 279–80
rationality 280–81, 283, 285
regulation 277, 285, 296–97
rule of law 8, 286
soft law 276–77, 278
supranationalism 278
technological revolution 291–96
transparency 280–82, 283, 286
ultra vires 276
United States 282–83, 285
value for money (VFM) audits 284
values and tenets 276, 278–83, 286–87, 288, 289, 290–91, 297
procedure *see* **proceduralism; process and procedure**

process and procedure 5–6, 323–35 *see also* **proceduralism**
accountability 326–27
administrative state, processes and procedures in 323–28
austerity measures 12–13
automation 327
Brexit 8–9, 323, 328–35, 416–20
constitutional crisis, times of 328–35
EU (Notification of Withdrawal) Act 2017 330
EU Referendum Act 2015 330
EU (Withdrawal) Act 2018 330, 331–32
Withdrawal Agreement 416–17, 418–19
bureaucratisation 326–27
constitutional process in times of crisis 328–35
contextualism 326
crisis, times of 323, 328–35
disordered state, in a 323–35
due process 234
executive 325–26
functionalism 326–27, 328
judicial review 324, 325–26, 327
judiciary 325–26
legislature 325–26
managerialism 326–27
normal times and times of crisis 323, 329, 331–33
Ridge v Baldwin 325–26
rule of law 330
substantive and procedural disputes 333–34
sustainable governance 8–9
transparency 326–27
values 327
Withdrawal Agreement 416–17, 418–19
procurement 259, 261
Prüm 244–45
public administration and administrative law 209–31 *see also* **Donoughmore Committee**
19th century thought 211, 212–13, 219
20th century thought 8, 211, 213, 216, 226, 227
academic literature 213, 216–17, 228
adjudicative method 209, 217–18, 219–20, 224–26
administrative material, engagement with 210–11, 227–28
Attorney-General's Committee Report 1941 (US) 210–11
adjudication 225–26
administrative growth 224–25
Administrative Procedure Act 1946 226, 229
background 224
engaging with administrative material 210–11
expertise 210–11, 224–26, 230
ideologies, reduction of legal reasoning to battle between 210–11
judicial review 225–26
notice and comment rulemaking procedure 226
procedure and scope of review doctrine, relationship between 225–26
structural challenges 210–11, 227, 229, 231
terms of reference 224–25
auditors, decision-making by 221
binary nature between law and administration 13, 209–11, 216, 230
Chevron doctrine 209–10
common law 209–10, 219
constitutionalism 212–13
discipline, growth of administrative law as a 211, 216
emerging legal discourses 216–22
expansion of administration 222
expertise 210–15, 216–18, 220–22, 227, 228–29
agency 209–10, 228
Attorney-General's Committee Report 1941 (US) 210–11, 224–26, 230
forms 213–14
factual evaluation 212–15, 218, 226
First World War 214
fitness for human habitation 220–21
freedom of information 228
history, learning from 226–30
ideology 8, 209–11, 229–30
institutions 210, 212–13, 219–20, 227, 228–29, 230–31
Internet 228
judicial review 219–22, 225–26
law and administration, binary between 209–11, 216, 230
legal reasoning 209
legislative and administrative decision-making 220–22
New Deal 211–12, 224
non-adjudicative structures, debate on 211, 218
reasonableness 221–22
red light/green light models of administrative law 209–10
right-wing/left-wing lawyers 229
rule of law 218
sanitary and nuisance legislation 215
separation of powers 219
structural challenges 210–11, 227, 229, 231

systemised and informed decision-making 212–13
textbooks 213, 216, 222
tribunals 220
United States 8, 209–14, 216, 224, 228
expertise 213–14, 215, 216–17, 228
independent regulatory commissions 213–14
Interstate Commerce Commission (ICC) 212–14, 215, 219–20
judicial review by Supreme Court 219–20, 222
legal realism 216, 227
New Deal 211–12, 224
separation of powers 219
systemised and informed decision-making 212–13
tribunals 220
war pensions regime 212–13
Public Law Project 169
public opinion 201–2
public understanding 300–1, 313–15, 316–19
purposive/teleological interpretation
CJEU 180–81, 183–86, 190, 191, 193–94
democracy 197, 199
legislature 127
preliminary rulings 112–13
travaux préparatoires 191

Queiroz, Benedita Menezes 381

Raadschelders, Jos 213
Raine, John 294
ratio decidendi 131
rationality 64, 79, 280–81, 283, 305–6
Rawlings, Richard 209–10, 324, 326–28
reasons, duty to give 299–321, 324
automation 12
careful and impartial examination of cases 307
centralisation 299–300
CJEU, jurisprudence of 8, 308–9
conduct, norm of 304–8
constitutional foundations of duty 299–300, 309–11
constitutional function 304–8, 315–17
constitutive function of executive actors 8, 301–4, 312–13, 315, 320–21
control, norm of 304–9
Council of the EU 309–10
direct and individual concern 305–6, 314
discretion 303–4, 307
ECSC 307–8, 309–12, 313–14, 315–16, 320–21
High Authority 300–1, 308–18
Treaty 300–1, 309–13, 314, 315–17
efficiency 306
EU law 299–321, 324
European Supervisory Authorities (ESAs) 299–300, 301–2
executive 299–304, 307–8, 315, 316–21, 325–26
financial regulation 299–300, 301–2, 315–18
foundations of duty 299–300, 309–11
general principles of EU law 308
individual rights 365–69
institutions 8, 299–321
integration 299–301, 311–13, 315, 316
judicial review 300–1, 302–4, 305–6, 309–10, 318
direct and individual concern 314
ECSC 313–14
High Authority 313
public understanding 313–14
transparency 313–14
judiciary 133, 287–89
legal acts, reasons as category of 304–5, 308, 309–10, 316–17, 320–21, 328
legal implications 311
legality, principle of 300–1, 303–6
market intervention 301–3, 320
Member States' bodies, separation of tasks with 301–2
novel duty, as a 308–9, 320–21
origins of duty in EU law 308–15
planning cases 288
political significance 311, 316–17
private entities, effect of market intervention on rights and duties of 301–3
private sector measures 301–2
public action 300–1
public interest 300–1, 303–4, 307–8, 312–13, 315–19, 320–21
public understanding 300–1, 313–15, 316–19
rationality 305–6
reconstruction, from constitutional foundations to 315–19
self-regulation 300–1, 307–8, 318–19, 320–21, 327–28
separation of powers 306
short-selling 299–300, 301–2
systematic interpretation 311
threats to financial stability 301–3
transparency 328
Rechtsstaat 8, 196–97, 276
red light/green light models of administrative law 209–10
red lines 176, 177, 404, 415

referendum on Brexit
advisory, as 393–94
case law and doctrine 424, 426
change of mind 401–2
democracy 400–2
EU Referendum Act 2015 330
normative effect of Brexit 406
Northern Ireland 391–92
results 391–92
Scotland 389–90, 392–93
second referendum 400, 401–2
theory 400–2
referendums *see also* **referendum on Brexit**
increase in use 390–91
popular sovereignty 389–90
Scotland, independence referendum in 389–90, 392–93
regionalism 343–44, 347–48, 360–61 *see also* **local administration**
regulation
delegated legislation 148, 149
financial markets 299–300, 301–2, 315–18
independent regulatory commissions 213–14
interoperability 243–46
proceduralism 285, 296–97
risk regulation instruments 233
self-regulation 300–1, 307–8, 318–19, 320–21, 327–28
toolkits 285
republicanism 51, 52–53
Reuter, Paul 310–11, 315–16
Rippon, Lord (Rippon Geoffrey) 155
Robson, William 62, 147–48, 216–18
Roosevelt, FD 224
Root, Elihu 148–49
rule of law
administrative law 218
analogical reasoning 103–5
Brexit 330–31, 421, 423–24
correction and prevention of systemic problems 371–80
federalism 351–52
foundations 8–9
Health and Social Care Act 2012 12–13, 257
inductive reasoning 97, 102
judiciary 286, 291, 371–80
multilevel government 346–47, 351–52
parliamentary sovereignty 89–90
precedent 132
proceduralism 8, 286
process and procedure 330
systemic violations by states of Article 2 TEU 8–9, 11, 365, 367–68, 369–80
rules and standards, difference between 97–102
rules of recognition 386, 392–93

sanitary legislation 215
Sankey, Lord (Sankey, John) 217–18, 222
Saunders, Cheryl 381
Schauer, Frederick 93, 95–96
Schengen Agreement on open borders 33
Schengen Convention 236–37
Schengen Information System (SIS) 244, 245–46
Schengen Information System (SIS II) 244–45, 247–49
Schuster, Claud 222, 230
Schwarze, Jürgen 307
Scotland
Brexit
EU (Withdrawal) Act 2018 391–92
referendum 389–90, 392–93
territorial effect 407
devolution 11–12, 407
EU (Withdrawal) Act 2018 391–92
federacies 393
independence referendum 389–90, 392–93
popular sovereignty 389–90
referendum on Brexit 389–90, 392–93
revocation of notification of withdrawal 427–28
Scottish Parliament 392–93
Union of Scotland and England 1707 392–93
unitary state, UK as a 392–93
Scott, Leslie 224
Scottish Claim of Right 1689 51
secession 342–43, 352
secrecy 246–53, 254, 287
sedition 48
self-government *see* **devolution**
self-regulation 300–1, 307–8, 318–19, 320–21, 327–28
separation of powers
administrative law 219
analogical reasoning 104–5
CJEU 173–74
federation 342
multilevel government 342, 345, 348–49
reasons, duty to give 306
supranationalism 174
textbooks 216
unitary systems 174
values 281
Sewel Convention 346, 411–12
Shapiro, Sid 211–12
Sharpston, Eleanor 109, 193–94

short-selling 299–300, 301–2
SIENA 247–49
SIFT Project 168–69
Simon, Herbert 280
Simson Caird, Jack 157–58, 416
sincere cooperation, principle of 374–75
six dimensions of public law 3, 399–429
accountability and institutions 405–10
Brexit 3, 10, 399–429
accountability and institutions 405–10
case law and doctrine 424–29
constitutions 410–14
fundamental rights 414–15
legislation 420–24
pressure-testing public law, as 399, 417
process and procedure 416–20
theory 400–4
case law and doctrine 3, 399, 424–29
constitutions 3, 399, 410–14
individual rights 399, 414–15
institutions 3, 399, 405–10
intergovernmentalism and supranationalism 403–4
legislation 3, 399, 420–24
parliamentary and popular sovereignty in the UK 400–2
presidents, institutional decision-making, and liaison with member states in EU 408–10
prime ministerial government, parliament, and devolved regions in UK 405–8
process and procedure 3, 399, 416–20
supranationalism 403–4
theory 3–4, 399, 400–4
skeleton legislation 149–50, 152, 158–59
Slynn, Gordon 109
Smellie, KB 217–18
Smith, Adam 60–61
social service state 61–62
***societas* (civil association) and *universitas* (enterprise association), tension between** 31–32
soft law 276–77, 278, 325–26, 367
sovereignty 31 *see also* **Brexit and post-sovereign legal landscape; parliamentary sovereignty**
absolute sovereignty 49, 351
Brexit 175, 382, 383, 387–90, 427–28
citizenship 351
classical conception of the state 6–7
conceptions of sovereignty 389–90
constituent power 29–30
constitutionalism 6–7
definition 389
democracy 7–8
different conceptions 389–90
empowerment, pooling sovereignty as 388
executive 7–8
external sovereignty 351, 389–90
globalisation 351
internal sovereignty 389–90
legislative jurisdiction 37
multilevel government 351
national sovereignty 5–7, 382, 386–87, 390, 393–95
office in politics of 17th century 48, 49, 50, 67–68
parliamentary sovereignty 388, 389–90
politics 8–9, 29–30, 48, 49, 50, 67–68
popular sovereignty 6–7, 389–90
referenda 389–90
Scotland 389–90
the state 31
supranationalism 388
systemic violations by states of Article 2 TEU 364
'taking back control' 388, 390
terminology 351
UK, breaking up of 390
Westphalian state 175, 382, 383, 394–95
White Paper 389
Withdrawal Agreement 419
Spain, Catalan Statute of Autonomy in 347–48
Sri Lanka 340, 342–43
stability of law 1
standards and rules, difference between 97–102
standing (*locus standi*) 181–82, 305–6, 314
stare decisis 131, 132
the state *see also* **point of the state**
beyond the state 19–21
capacity 31
citizenship 29–30
collaborative and complementary polity 32–33
comprehensive and exclusive source of final authority 32–33
constituent power 29–30, 31
disordered state, process and procedure in a 323–35
EU 29–35
globalisation 20
inside-out perspective of EU polity 32–33
integration theory 30–31
international organisations 20
monopoly of state of use of force 70

the state (*Contd.*)
nomocracy and teleocracy, distinction between 31–32
originality of collective agency, EU as lacking 29–30
outside-in perspective of EU polity 33
political identity 29–30, 31
primacy of political identity, EU as lacking of 29–30
process and procedure 323–35
public goods 31–32
settled political form, state constitutional polity as a 34
singularity of normative design of state polity 33
social service state 61–62
societas (civil association) and *universitas* (enterprise association), tension between 31–32
sovereignty 31
spatiality 31, 32–33
structural features 29–35
supranationalism 20
temporality 31, 34
unlimited final authority, EU as lacking 29–30, 32–33
statute law *see* **legislation; primary legislation**
Stephens, Harold 217
Street, Harry 282–83
subsidiarity 193–94, 358–59
Summers, Robert 197, 198
sunset clauses 151, 165
support, paradox of 42
supranationalism 20, 21, 29, 33
automation 233, 234–35, 237–38
Brexit 175, 334, 382–83, 388, 403–4, 408
dual character 36
EMU 33
institutions 237–38
internal market 36
intergovernmentalism 403–4, 408
interoperability 234–35, 243
judiciary 37
legal supranationalism 36
legitimacy 21
political supranationalism 36
proceduralism 278
Schengen Agreement 33
separation of powers 174
the state 20
systemic violations by states of Article 2 TEU 11
Westphalian state 382–83
suprastate government 360
supremacy of EU law
Brexit 175–384, 385–86, 394
constitutions 385
preliminary rulings 112, 116–17, 123–24
surveillance 237–38, 239, 242–43, 246
Switzerland, multilevel constitutionalism in 349–50
systemic violations by states of Article 2 TEU 363–80, 381
Article 7 TEU 365–67
Charter of Fundamental Rights of the EU 367–68, 374–75, 377–78
CJEU 367–68, 372–73, 374, 375
Commission 366–67
Commission v Poland 11
competences 363–65
constitutions 363–64, 365
cooperation 370, 374–75
correction and prevention of systemic rule of law problems 371–80
democracy 11, 365, 370, 371, 378–80
deterrence 366–67
dualism 363–64
effectiveness 372–73, 374–75, 376–77
enforcement at national level, reasons for EU role in 370–71
enlargement, accession criteria for 365–66
European Arrest Warrant (EAW) 375, 376
European Convention on Human Rights 365, 368–69, 370, 375
fair trial, right to a 375, 376
free movement of persons 379
freedom of expression 378–79
freedom of the press 378–79
hard law approach 363–80
individual rights, protection of 8–9, 11, 363, 365–69, 375
inhuman or degrading treatment 375
initiation of proceedings 366–67
integration 365, 369, 370–71
interconnection between legal systems 11
intervene, authority to 370–71
judicial enforcement 371–80
judicial independence 373–78
judicial review 369, 374–75, 378
legislative sovereignty 364
Member actions 368–69
moral externalities 370
name-and-shame procedure 367
national level, enforcement at 370–71
nationalism 11
Poland 11, 373, 375, 376–77

politics
decisions, triggering 366–67
externalities 370
populism 11
Portugal 373–75, 377
reasons for EU role in enforcement at national level 370–71
recommendations 367
rule of law 8–9, 11, 365, 367–68, 369
correction and prevention of systemic problems 371–80
judicial enforcement 371–80
judicial independence 373–78
national level, reasons for EU role in enforcement at 370–71
other issues, links with 367
systemic problems, correction and prevention of 371–80
sanctions 366–67
serious and persistent violations 366–67
sincere cooperation, principle of 374–75
soft law 367
supranationalism 11
treaties 11, 363–80

Tamanaha, Brian 226
taxonomies 87, 90–91, 97, 98, 100–2, 104–5
technocratic administration 63–64
technology *see* **automation; EU automated state**
teleocracy and nomocracy, distinction between 31–32
teleological interpretation *see* **purposive/teleological interpretation**
terrorism 239, 242, 245, 248–49, 293
test cases 290–91
Teubner, Gunther 275–76, 296
textbooks 213, 216, 222
theory
Brexit 400–4
elitism 402
foundations of EU 11–12, 19–44
intergovernmentalism 403–4
parliamentary sovereignty 400–2
popular sovereignty 400–2
six dimensions of public law 3–4, 399, 400–4
supranationalism 403–4, 408
Thomas, Robert 295
Tierney, Stephen 349–50
Tomlinson, Joe 295
transnational law 6–7, 63, 382–83
transparency
automation 291–92, 293–94, 297–98
Brexit 410
constitutionalism 350, 352
freedom of information 281–82
good governance standards (OECD) 281–82
judiciary 288
multilevel government 346–47, 352, 355
proceduralism 280–82, 283, 286
process and procedure 326–27
rationality 285
reasons, duty to give 328
values 281–82
Treaty on European Union *see* **systemic violations by states of Article 2 TEU**
tribunals 220
trusts as foundational idea of public law 76–78
Tusk, Donald 404, 409–10
Twining, William 383

ultra vires
authority of the administration 13, 45, 64
delegated legislation 204–5
democracy 62, 63, 64
EU (Withdrawal Act) 2018 163–64, 166–67
Health and Social Care Act 2012 8, 257–58, 264–70
judicial review 13, 78
proceduralism 276
unitary states
constitutionalism 358
definition 392–93
multilevel government 342–44, 347, 349–50, 353, 356, 358, 359–60
politics 353
rule of recognition 392–93
separation of powers 174
UK, as 392–93
United States 8, 209–13
1930s, reports during 224
adjudication 224
administrative growth 213–14, 224
Administrative Procedure Act 283, 285
agency government 148–49
Bill of Rights 367–68
Brownlow Commission 224
civil rights 349
civil service reform 212–13
Clean Air Act 228
delegated legislation 148–49
Department of Homeland Security 239
discipline, growth of administrative law as a 216
England, comparison with 196, 197–98
expertise 213–14, 215, 216–17, 228
FBI Terrorist Screening Centre 248–49
federalism 349, 358–59
independent regulatory commissions 213–14

United States (*Contd.*)
Interstate Commerce Commission (ICC) 212–14, 215, 219–20
judicial review 219–20, 222, 364
legal realism 216, 227
New Deal 211–12, 224, 282–83
passenger name records (PNRs) 239–40
secession 342–43
separation of powers 219
slavery 349
Supreme Court 367–68
systemised and informed decision-making 212–13
tribunals 220
war pensions regime 212–13
Universal Credit 292
universalism 37–39, 40–41
***universitas* (enterprise association) and *societas* (civil association), tension between** 31–32
unsettled state, UK as a 390–94
utilitarianism 197–98

value for money (VFM) audits 284
values *see also* **systemic violations by states of Article 2 TEU**
Charter of Fundamental Rights of the EU 281
citizenship 78–79
common law 45
democracy 281
fairness 288, 289, 290–91
functionalism 282–83
good administration 281–82
judicial review 281, 327
judiciary 286–87
liberal values, protection of 45
managerialism 327
Nolan standards for conduct in public life 279–80
proceduralism 276, 278–83, 297
process and procedure 327
separation of powers 281
transparency 281–82
Vavoula, Niovi 242–43, 244
vicarious liability 55, 137–39
Visa Information System (VIS) 236–37, 244–46

Wade, John 60–61
Walker, Neil 67–68, 76–77, 78, 394
Warner, Jean-Pierre 109
Weber, Max 6–7, 70–71, 76, 78, 213, 228–29, 280
***Wednesbury* unreasonableness** 90–91, 295–96
Weiler, Joseph 36, 39
welfare state, growth of 148, 149
well-being 68, 69–70, 72–74, 76
Westphalian nation state 6–7
anomaly, as 383
Brexit 381–84, 394–95
post-sovereignty 383
post-Westphalian order 382–83
Second World War, end of 382
self-government/devolution 382–83
sovereignty 6–7, 175, 382, 383, 394–95
supranationalism 382–83
transnational law, rise of 6–7
Whaley, Anna 293–94
what works 26, 28
Wigmore, John 217
Wilberforce, Lord (Wilberforce, Richard) 141–42
Williams, David 154
Willis, John 282–83
Wilson of Dinton, Lord (Wilson, Richard) 165
Wilson, Woodrow 213, 230
Withdrawal Agreement
accountability 406, 407–8
Article 50, defective drafting of 418
Commission 419–20
complexity 423
delegated legislation 7, 10–11, 163–69
EU (Withdrawal) Act 2018 416
European Council 420
European Parliament, role of 420
House of Commons 416–17, 418–19
individual rights 415
legal certainty 423
legislation 421–22, 423
negotiations 423
normative effect of Brexit 406
Northern Ireland backstop 421–22
Political Declaration, distinction from 416, 418–19
Prime Minister 405–6
sovereignty 419
transitional period 421–22
unilateral revocation of notification 427, 428

The manufacturer's authorised representative in the EU for product safety is Oxford University Press España S.A. of el Parque Empresarial San Fernando de Henares, Avenida de Castilla, 2 – 28830 Madrid (www.oup.es/en or product.safety@oup.com). OUP España S.A. also acts as importer into Spain of products made by the manufacturer.

www.ingramcontent.com/pod-product-compliance
Lightning Source LLC
LaVergne TN
LVHW011900200926
848484LV00002B/491